Professional Review Guide for the RHIA and RHIT Examinations 2016 Edition

Professional Review Guide for the RHIA and RHIT Examinations 2016 Edition

Patricia J. Schnering, RHIA, CCS
Debra W. Cook, MAEd, RHIA
Lauralyn Kavanaugh-Burke, DrPH, RHIA, CHES, CHTS-IM
Marjorie H. McNeill, PhD, RHIA, CCS, FAHIMA
Lon'Tejuana S. Cooper, PhD, RHIA, CPM
Barbara W. Mosley, PhD, RHIA
Nanette B. Sayles, EdD, RHIA, CCS, CHPS, CPHIMS, FAHIMA
Kathy C. Trawick, EdD, RHIA, FAHIMA
Shelley C. Safian, PhD, CCS-P, CPC-H, CPC-I, CHA
Anita Hazelwood, MLS, RHIA, FAHIMA
Kristy Courville, MHA, RHIA
Sheila Carlon, PhD, RHIA, FAHIMA
Leslie Moore, RHIT, CCS
Marissa Lajaunie, MBA, RHIA

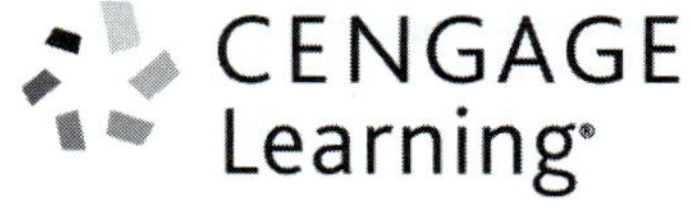

Australia • Brazil • Japan • Korea • Mexico • Singapore • Spain • United Kingdom • United States

Professional Review Guide for the RHIA and RHIT Examinations, 2016 Edition
Patricia J. Schnering, RHIA, CCS

SVP, GM Skills & Global Product Management: Dawn Gerrain

Product Director: Matthew Seeley

Product Manager: Jadin B. Kavanaugh

Senior Director, Development: Marah Bellegarde

Senior Product Development Manager: Juliet Steiner

Content Developer: Kaitlin Schlicht

Product Assistant: Mark Turner

Vice President, Marketing Services: Jennifer Ann Baker

Senior Production Director: Wendy Troeger

Production Director: Andrew Crouth

Content Project Manager: Andy Baker

Senior Art Director: Benjamin Gleeksman

Cover image(s): © Galyna Andrushko / Shutterstock

Library of Congress Control Number:

Book Only ISBN: 978-1-305-64864-7
Package ISBN: 978-1-305-64860-9

Cengage Learning
20 Channel Center Street
Boston, MA 02210
USA

Cengage Learning is a leading provider of customized learning solutions with employees residing in nearly 40 different countries and sales in more than 125 countries around the world. Find your local representative at **www.cengage.com.**

Cengage Learning products are represented in Canada by Nelson Education, Ltd.

To learn more about Cengage Learning, visit **www.cengage.com**

Purchase any of our products at your local college store or at our preferred online store **www.cengagebrain.com**

Printed in the United States of America
Print Number: 01 Print Year: 2016

ABOUT THE AUTHORS

Patricia J. Schnering, RHIA, CCS

Patricia J. Schnering founded PRG Publishing, Inc. and Professional Review Guides, Inc. Mrs. Schnering is a 1995 graduate of the Health Information Management program at St. Petersburg College in St. Petersburg, Florida. In 1998, she was certified as a CCS and in 1999 she received her RHIA certification. Her education includes a Baccalaureate degree from the University of South Florida in Tampa, Florida, with a major in Business Administration. Her HIM experience includes working as Health Information Services supervisor, as an HIM consultant, and as an adjunct HIM instructor at St. Petersburg College. Pat received the Florida Health Information Management Association (FHIMA) Literary Award in 2000 and 2005.

Debra W. Cook, MAEd, RHIA

Debra W. Cook is a graduate of the Medical Record Administration and the Adult Education programs at East Carolina University in Greenville, North Carolina. Her HIM experience includes 5 years in acute health care practice in a variety of positions, such as management, utilization management, coding, and consulting. She also has over 24 years' experience in HIM education at Alderson-Broaddus College and Marshall University in West Virginia, and Catawba Valley Community College in Hickory, North Carolina. Currently, she is the Department Head of Health Information Technology at CVCC and Director of the Workforce Development Program for Electronic Record Specialists. In addition to this, she serves on the Panel of Accreditation Reviewers for the Commission of Health Informatics and Information Management Education.

Nanette B. Sayles, EdD, RHIA, CCS, CHPS, CPHIMS, FAHIMA

Nanette Sayles is a 1985 graduate of the University of Alabama at Birmingham Medical Record Administration (now the Health Information Management) program. She earned her Master's of Science in Health Information Management (1995) and her Master's in Public Administration (1990) from the University of Alabama at Birmingham. She earned her doctorate in Adult Education from the University of Georgia (2003). She is currently Associate Professor for the Health Information Management program at East Central College in Union, Missouri. She has a wide range of health information management experience in hospitals, consulting, system development/implementation, and education. She also received the 2005 American Health Information Management Association Triumph Educator Award.

Anita Hazelwood, MLS, RHIA, FAHIMA

Anita Hazelwood is an Associate Professor in the Health Information Management Department at the University of Louisiana at Lafayette, located in Lafayette, Louisiana. She has a Bachelor's degree in Medical Record Science and a Master's degree in Library Science, and has been a credentialed Registered Health Information Administrator (RHIA) for 28 years.

Some of the courses she teaches include coding and classification systems such as ICD-10-CM/PCS and CPT coding; reimbursement methodologies such as DRGs and RBRVS; fraud and abuse; principles of health information management and alternative delivery systems. She is also the Clinical Experience Coordinator.

Anita has actively consulted in hospitals, nursing homes, clinics, facilities for the mentally retarded, and in other educational institutions. She has conducted numerous ICD-9-CM, ICD-10-CM/PCS, and CPT coding workshops throughout the state for hospitals and physicians' offices.

On a professional level, Anita has been a member of the American Health Information Management Association (AHIMA) for several years. She is also a member of the Society for Clinical Coding (SCC) and served on the SCC board as Secretary in 1998. Anita has been the Internet Task Force Chair for several years. She is a member of the AHIMA's Assembly on Education (AOE) and has served as Membership Chair, a member of the Nominating Committee, and on the Board of Directors.

Anita is a member of the Louisiana Health Information Management Association and was selected as its 1997 Distinguished Member.

Lon'Tejuana S. Cooper, PhD, RHIA, CPM

Lon'Tejuana S. Cooper is a 1998 graduate of the Health Informatics and Information Management (Formerly Health Information Management) program at Florida A&M University in Tallahassee, Florida. She completed the Certified Public Manager's program at Florida State University in 2002 and received her Master's of Science degree in Healthcare Administration in 2004. She also completed her doctorate degree in Educational Leadership and Human Services at Florida A&M University in 2014. Dr. Cooper has over 9 years of teaching experience in academia, teaching foundations in health information management, legal aspects of health care documentation, and professional development. She has more than 8 years of experience in managing PHI in electronic format, and has developed policies and procedures on implementing HIPAA requirements, developed training modules for staff training, and designed HIPAA assessment tools. For the past 9 years, Dr. Cooper has served as a faculty member in the Division of Health Informatics and Information Management at Florida A&M University.

Barbara W. Mosley, PhD, RHIA

Barbara W. Mosley is a 1976 graduate of the Health Information Management (formerly Medical Record Administration) program at the University of Tennessee Center for the Health Sciences in Memphis, Tennessee. She received her Master's degree in Public Administration with a concentration in Health Services Administration from the University of Memphis (formerly Memphis State University) in 1980. She earned her doctorate degree in Adult Education in 1990 from Florida State University. In 1996, Dr. Mosley was chosen Teacher of the Year at Florida A&M University. In 1998, she was chosen as the Advanced Teacher of the Year at Florida A&M University. Her experience in health information management includes:

- Twenty-six years as Health Information Management educator. Currently, she is a Professor in the Health Information Management Program and the Associate Dean for the School of Allied Health Sciences at Florida A&M University in Tallahassee, Florida.
- Nineteen years of consulting experience at several long-term care facilities in Tallahassee, Florida, and surrounding cities.
- Formerly, Assistant Director of Medical Record Department at the City of Memphis Hospital and the VA Medical Center in Birmingham, Alabama, and Director of Medical Records at the Southeast Memphis Mental Health Center.

Sheila A. Carlon, PhD, RHIA, FAHIMA

Dr. Carlon has a PhD in Organizational Development and Systems, a Master's degree in Health Services Administration, and Bachelor's degrees in Broadcast Journalism and Health Care Management. She is a Fellow of AHIMA and received the Educator of the Year Award in 2006 and Cypress College's Distinguished Alumni Award in 2008. Dr. Carlon has been a Program Director and Degree Chair in Regis University's College for Health Professions for the past 8 years, where she administers and teaches in four-degree programs. She also has extensive hospital and physician office management experience and has been a Health Care Consultant for Deloitte, Touche International. She is a frequent meeting facilitator and speaker both locally and nationally on such topics as technology, HIPAA, the Global EHR, E- HIM, leadership and management theory and development, HIM advocacy, education trends, and organizational assessment. Dr. Carlon volunteers as an Ombudsman for the Aging Services Division of the Denver Regional Council of Governments. She serves as a Board Member of the Golden Gate Fire Department in Golden, Colorado. She is a volunteer for the Ronald McDonald House, Project Homeless, Quarters for Kids, and Project Mercy in Yetebon, Ethiopia. She is currently helping to launch the field of HIM into the country of Ethiopia.

Marjorie H. McNeill, PhD, RHIA, CCS, FAHIMA

Dr. Marjorie McNeill is an Associate Professor and Director of the Division of Health Informatics and Information Management in the School of Allied Health Sciences at Florida A&M University, located in Tallahassee, Florida. She is a graduate of the Health Information Administration program at Georgia Regents University (formerly Medical College of Georgia). She received her MS degree in Health Education at Florida State University and her PhD in Educational Leadership at Florida A&M University.

Dr. McNeill is credentialed as a Registered Health Information Administrator (RHIA) and a Certified Coding Specialist (CCS). Her experience in health information management includes over 30 years as an HIM educator and 9 years of management and consulting experience in various health care facility practice settings (acute care hospital, ambulatory surgery, health maintenance organization, nursing home, mental retardation).

Dr. McNeill has several educational publications to her credit, including research articles in *Perspectives in Health Information Management*, *Journal of Allied Health*, and *Journal of the American Health Information Management Association*. She shares professional knowledge and experience through educational presentations to the AHIMA Assembly on Education, FHIMA, NWFHIMA, and National Society of Allied Health. She is the recipient of the 2015 American Health Information Management Association Educator Triumph Award, the 2015 Florida Health Information Management Association Educator Award, the 2010 Florida Health Information Management Association Literary Award, and the 2008 Florida Health Information Management Association Distinguished Service Award. Dr. McNeill is a Fellow of the American Health Information Management Association.

Kathy C. Trawick, EdD, RHIA, FAHIMA

Dr. Kathy Trawick is the Chairman and Associate Professor of the Health Information Management Department at the University of Arkansas for Medical Sciences in Little Rock, Arkansas. She is a 1985 graduate of the University of Alabama at Birmingham, Health Information Management (formerly Medical Record Administration) program. Dr. Trawick has expertise in Higher Education and in the Allied Health Sciences. Her basic research interests with keywords under the ERIC database include higher educational administration effectiveness, institutional effectiveness, and student satisfaction. Dr. Trawick has been a practitioner for 10 years in acute care facilities, as well as an HIM educator and program chairman since 1999. Topics of instruction include health care statistics, legal issues, HIM systems and the CPR, health administration, quality improvement, and cancer registry principles. She has coauthored a text (for AHIMA) on computer systems in HIT and has been a contributing author of texts on medical terminology and medical law and ethics. She has published articles in the *AHIMA Journal* and *Advance* magazine and written for Educational Perspectives in Health Information Management and the Mid-South Educational Research Association Proceedings. She is also a consultant to various types of health care facilities in Arkansas. In addition to holding offices at the state level in HIM and Cancer Registry associations, she currently serves on the CAHIIM Panel of Reviewers for HIT/HIA program accreditation.

Lauralyn Kavanaugh-Burke, DrPH, RHIA, CHES, CHTS-IM

After receiving a BS degree in Medical Record Administration with a minor in biology from York College of Pennsylvania, Dr. Burke worked in several hospitals in Virginia and Maryland in various management positions, including DRG Analyst, Assistant Director, and Director of the Medical Record / Health Information departments. During this time, her interest in pathophysiology intensified after working with several physicians in their research endeavors. She started teaching at an associate's degree Health Information Technology (HIT) program at Fairmont State College in West Virginia where she was able to strengthen her anatomy and pathophysiology skills, not only instructing HIT students, but also working with the medical laboratory and veterinary technology programs there. This position gave her the chance to complete her MS degree in Community Health Education from West Virginia University, which perfectly blended health information management and education. She achieved her Certified Health Education Specialist (CHES) credential shortly afterward. She then moved back to Pennsylvania and returned to the hospital arena as a DRG and coding consultant. Dr. Burke had the opportunity to teach at her alma mater and lay the foundation for an associate's degree program in HIT at a local community college.

Subsequent to relocating to Florida, she became a faculty member at Florida A&M University's BS degree program in Health Informatics & Information Management Division. She continued her pursuit of more training in pathophysiology, and soon after received her Doctor of Public Health (DrPH) with a concentration in epidemiology from Florida A&M University. Dr. Burke's main areas of interest are in disaster preparedness for hospitals, and bioterrorism and infectious diseases. She recently achieved certification as a Health Information Technology Implementation Manager (CHTS-IM) after completing her HITECH training through Santa Fe College.

Kristy Courville, MHA, RHIA

Kristy Courville is an Instructor in the Health Information Management Department at the University of Louisiana at Lafayette located in Lafayette, Louisiana. She has a Bachelor's degree in Health Information Management and a Master's degree in Health Services Administration. She teaches several courses including management, concepts of healthcare, and computers in healthcare organizations. Prior to teaching, she held a director of Health Information Management position within a system of healthcare facilities.

Mrs. Courville has been an active member of the American Health Information Management Association for 19 years. Additionally, she has been involved with committees and projects for the Louisiana Health Information Management Association and the Southwest District of the Louisiana Health Information Management Association.

Shelley C. Safian, PhD, CCS-P, CPC-H, CPC-I, CHA

Dr. Shelley C. Safian has been teaching Health Care Administration, Health Information Management, and Medical Billing and Coding, both onsite and online, for more than a decade.

She writes several articles each year on various aspects of coding both now and into the ICD-10 transition. In addition, she is the author of six textbooks, including "Essentials of Health Care Compliance" published by Cengage.

Dr. Safian is entering her third year as the Chair of the Continuing Education committee for FHIMA (Florida Health Information Management Association). In the past, she has served on several committees and practice councils on the national, state, and local levels of Health Information Management Associations.

Marissa Lajaunie, MBA, RHIA

Marissa Lajaunie is currently an Instructor in the Health Information Management Program at the University of Louisiana at Lafayette. She obtained a Bachelor of Science degree in Health Information Management and a Master of Business Administration. She has also been a Registered Health Information Administrator since 2009. Mrs. Lajaunie teaches several courses including Medical Terminology, Healthcare Statistics, Quality Improvement, Management Internship, and Concepts in Healthcare Delivery.

Prior to teaching, Mrs. Lajaunie held a management position at an inpatient psychiatric facility where she responsible for the overall leadership and operation of the facility's services, departments, and functions.

Mrs. Lajaunie is currently a member of the American Health Information Management Association, the Louisiana Health Information Management Association, as well as the President for the Southwest District of the Louisiana Health Information Management Association.

ACKNOWLEDGMENTS

First and foremost, I wish to express my gratitude to the contributing authors who created and revised the various chapters. They are wonderful people and have graciously provided whatever is needed at the right time while the work is in process. Each of the authors is a seasoned professional and an excellent educator. I can only say that they inspire me to work harder to produce a better product for each edition. With their contributions and assistance, we have been able to provide a broad overview of content from both the RHIA and RHIT programs. I am honored to call them my friends and associates.

I have enjoyed working with the staff at Cengage Learning. They have been quite accommodating and have taught me a lot about the process of publishing. Thank you, Jadin and the rest of the wonderful staff at Cengage Learning.

There have been very special people in my life who always knew I could do it when I was not sure I could. My late husband, Bob, always continued to keep me grounded while I would spin off in space working on the book. My mother, Emma Miller, has been my role model for perseverance leading to success. She embodied grace, courage, strength, and endurance. I will always be grateful for having had them in my life.

My thanks would not be complete without acknowledging all the HIM/HIT educators and students who support our efforts by using PRG products. I have been so fortunate in meeting such wonderful people in the HIM profession.

My reward is knowing that the materials you study here may assist you in preparing for the challenge of your examination. Thank you for the letters and words of encouragement.

Whichever credential you seek, I wish you the very best now and throughout your career.

Until we meet...

Patricia J. Schnering, RHIA, CCS

PJSPRG@AOL.COM

TABLE OF CONTENTS

Introduction

Patricia J. Schnering, RHIA, CCS

Introduction

Although we have no way of knowing what exactly will be on the examination, the authors tried to cover as many HIM concepts as possible. We have carefully selected questions that are generic enough to cover the broad topic categories. Researching the questions as you study should expand your knowledge such that, when you encounter similar questions, you can arrive at the correct answer. We believe this review material will jog your memory and serve to help you build on information you have already gained through your education.

With the collaboration of Health Information Administration and Technology educators, many questions have been updated and new questions added to enhance topic categories in this edition of the book. The more advanced questions for RHIA candidates are at the end of the chapters, where appropriate.

Professional Review Guide for the RHIA and RHIT Examinations by Content Areas

This review guide is arranged by content sections much as you studied in your classes. See Table I-1 for content areas and the number of questions in each content area. The number of questions does not indicate the importance of any one subject; it is merely an accounting of the questions in each section of this book. With the official implementation of ICD-10-CM in October 2015, both the RHIA and RHIT certification exams changed to tests on ICD-10-CM. Check the AHIMA Web site regularly for updates.

Table I-1 Professional Review Guide for the RHIA and RHIT Examinations, 2016 Edition Content Areas and Number of Questions

Professional Review Guide for the RHIA and RHIT Examinations, 2016 Edition Content Areas and Number of Questions	
Health Information Content Topic	Number of Questions
Health Data Content and Standards	98
Information Retention and Access	125
Classification Systems and Secondary Data Sources	87
Medical Billing and Reimbursement Systems	130
Medical Science	166
ICD-10-CM/PCS Coding	203
CPT Coding	217
Informatics and Information Systems	100
Health Information Privacy and Security	107
Health Statistics and Research	106
Health Law	100
Quality and Performance Improvement	115
Organization and Management	106
Human Resources	103
Mock Examination	180
Totals	1943

Examination Content and Insights

The test uses competency categories known as domains, subdomains, and tasks that have been shown to be essential entry-level competencies for HIM practice.

Before you begin your review for the examinations, we suggest that you obtain the latest AHIMA Examination Candidate Handbook. The handbook can be downloaded from AHIMA's Web site at www.ahima.org. Visit the Certification and Credentials section of the AHIMA Web site for the latest certification information.

The entry-level tasks are grouped into five domains for the RHIA and seven domains for the RHIT examination, as shown in Table I-2.

Table I-2 Entry-Level Domains for RHIA and RHIT

Entry-Level Domains for RHIA and RHIT Examinations	
RHIA	RHIT
1. Data Content, Structure, and Standards (Information Governance)	1. Data Analysis and Management
2. Information Protection: Access, Disclosure, Archival, Privacy, and Security	2. Coding
3. Informatics, Analytics, and Data Use	3. Compliance
4. Revenue Management	4. Information Technology
5. Leadership	5. Quality
	6. Legal
	7. Revenue Cycle

Reference: January 2015 AHIMA Candidate Guide

To determine the examination specifications as a whole, a job analysis is performed. The individual competencies are grouped into domains representing similar and specific content areas. These domains are divided further into subdomains that more clearly identify the content of each domain. Then, the weight for each domain is determined by considering each domain and the number and level of difficulty of the test items contained in each of the domains. Thus, each weight correlates to the degree of emphasis, or importance, and the level of difficulty given to each domain statement, as it relates to the HIM practice.

For both the RHIA and RHIT examinations, the cognitive levels are: 40% Recall/Understanding, 35% Application, and 25% Higher Thinking.

COMPETENCIES FOR THE RHIA EXAMINATION

The RHIA examination has 180 questions (160 questions scored and 20 that are not scored for the exam). The 160 scored questions are the basis for scoring your examination. The 20 unscored questions on the RHIA examination are to be used in obtaining statistical information to help in the construction of questions for future examinations. These 20 questions will not be identified in the exam, nor will they count toward the examination pass/fail score. Table I-3 presents the domains and equivalent weights for the RHIA examination. Review the current RHIA and RHIT Examination Candidate Handbook from AHIMA.

Table I-3 Domains and Equivalent Weights for the RHIA Certification Examination

Domains and Equivalent Weights for the RHIA Certification Examination		
Domain	Domain Name	Weight
1	Data Content, Structure, and Standards (Information Governance)	18-22%
2	Information Protection: Access, Disclosure, Archival, Privacy, and Security	23-27%
3	Informatics, Analytics, and Data Use	22-26%
4	Revenue Management	12-16%
5	Leadership Roles	12-16%

COMPETENCIES FOR THE RHIT EXAMINATION

The RHIT examination has 150 questions (130 questions scored and 20 that are not scored for the exam). The 130 scored questions are the basis for scoring the examination. The 20 unscored questions on the RHIT examination are to be used in obtaining statistical information to help in the construction of questions for future examinations. These 20 questions will not be identified in the exam, nor will they count toward the examination pass/fail score. Table I-4 presents the domains and equivalent weights for the RHIT examination. Review the current RHIA and RHIT Examination Candidate Handbook from AHIMA to verify the competencies.

Table I-4 Domains and Equivalent Weights for the RHIT Certification Examination

Domains and Equivalent Weights for the RHIT Certification Examination		
Domain	Domain Name	Weight
1	Data Analysis and Management	18-22%
2	Coding	16-20%
3	Compliance	14-18%
4	Information Technology	10-14%
5	Quality	10-14%
6	Legal	9-13%
7	Revenue Cycle	9-13%

In creating the review guide, we wanted to cover the competencies for both the RHIA and the RHIT. The questions in the chapters of this review guide relate to the competencies according to the breakdown of content for both the RHIA and RHIT exams.

Table I-5 provides a crosswalk between the RHIA competencies for and the number of questions in each competency by chapter.

Table I-6 provides a crosswalk of RHIT competencies by number of questions in each chapter.

Table I-7 shows the pass rates for the RHIA and RHIT examinations given in 2012, 2013, and 2014.

Table I-5 Crosswalk of RHIA Competencies by Chapter

Crosswalk of the RHIA Examination Competencies to Chapters						
	Domains					
Chapter	1	2	3	4	5	Total
Health Data Content and Standards	76	4	16	0	5	98
Information Retention and Access	40	7	57	0	21	125
Classification Systems and Secondary Data Sources	73	0	12	2	0	87
Medical Billing and Reimbursement Systems	0	0	0	130	0	130
Medical Science	166	0	0	0	0	166
ICD-10-CM/PCS Coding	203	0	0	0	0	203
CPT Coding	217	0	0	0	0	217
Informatics and Information Systems	0	0	100	0	0	100
Health Information Privacy and Security	0	107	0	0	0	107
Health Statistics and Research	0	0	106	0	0	106
Health Law	0	100	0	0	0	100
Quality and Performance Improvement	0	0	0	0	115	115
Organization and Management	0	0	0	106	0	106
Human Resources	0	0	0	103	0	103
Mock Examination	52	27	42	13	46	180
Totals	820	245	333	354	187	1943

Table I-6 RHIT Competencies by Chapter

Crosswalk of the RHIT Examination Competencies to Chapters								
	1	2	3	4	5	6	7	Total
Health Data Content and Standards	38	0	46	13	0	6	0	98
Information Retention and Retrieval	77	2	14	21	5	6	0	125
Classification Systems and Secondary Data Sources	42	44	1	0	0	0	0	87
Medical Billing and Reimbursement Systems	0	0	0	0	0	0	130	130
Medical Science	166	0	0	0	0	0	0	166
ICD-10-CM/PCS Coding	0	203	0	0	0	0	0	203
CPT Coding	0	217	0	0	0	0	0	217
Informatics and Information Systems	0	0	0	62	0	0	0	62
Health Information Privacy and Security	0	57	0	0	0	0	0	57
Health Statistics and Research	42	7	0	0	30	0	0	79
Health Law	0	0	0	0	0	100	0	100
Quality and Performance Improvement	0	0	0	0	115	0	0	115
Organization and Management	24	0	0	0	0	0	0	24
Human Resources	28	2	0	0	3	18	0	51
Mock Examination	31	34	19	19	24	15	8	150
Total RHIT Questions	448	566	80	115	177	145	138	1664

Table I-7 Passing Rates for the First-Time Test Taker for 2012, 2013, and 2014

Passing Rates for the First-Time Test Taker (2012–2014)			
*Pass Rates for First-Time Test Takers	2012	2013	2014
Registered Health Information Administrator (RHIA)	76.5%	76.0%	75.8%
Registered Health Information Technician (RHIT)	75.5%	76.0%	70.5%
*Exam pass rates are based on the calendar year. The current passing *scaled score* for the RHIA and RHIT examinations is 300 out of 400 points.			

Source: AHIMA (AHIMA.org).

ADDITIONAL INSIGHTS ABOUT EXAMINATIONS

1. **Computerized exam.** The test is taken electronically in an approved testing center. You will be able to return to previously answered questions to check your answers before you close the exam file on the computer. Visit AHIMA's Web site for examples of the screens you will be using.
2. **Statistical formulas** needed to complete the questions on health statistics will be available if needed in some form so that you can see it on the screen, thus eliminating the need to memorize all the formulas. You will be expected to know basic formulas like those for average, mean, and median. However, it is critical that you know how to apply the formulas accurately. We recommend that you spend time working through as many statistical problems as possible.
3. **Math throughout.** Be aware that mathematical calculations may also be required in other types of questions (for instance, calculating FTE requirements, budget questions, etc.), so basic math skills are a must! Become proficient in making mathematical calculations on the computer by practicing on the calculator provided in the accessories folder on your computer. If math is not a strong area for you, seek out assistance and practice, practice, practice. On the examination, you will need to use the calculator function on the computer.
4. **Informatics and information systems questions are interspersed throughout the other topics.** From the workplace setting you experienced during your professional practice experiences, you know that computers are involved in almost every aspect of HIM functions, for example, coding, record tracking, incomplete charts, release of information, etc. Therefore, it stands to reason that questions related to information systems could show up in many other categories.
5. **Legal questions are at the national level.** In reference to questions in the category of health care legal aspects, keep in mind that this is a national examination. Therefore, any state-specific laws would not be applicable. Concentrate on federal legislation, statutes, and legal issues that would be appropriate nationally in all 50 states. You can count on federal questions that relate to the HIPAA standards for privacy and security.
6. **Questions on the examinations are scrambled** and change topics from question to question. Therefore, you may have a legal question, followed by a management question, followed by a coding question, followed by a quality assurance question, etc. Be prepared to shift gears quickly throughout the exam.
7. **Quality and performance improvement focus.** Because the implementation of QA/PI is at the forefront of the health care industry, give special attention to Quality Assessment and Performance Improvement issues. Become familiar with the various QA/PI tools. Several resources for this subject are listed at the end of the Quality Assessment and Performance Improvement chapter of this book.
8. **Be sure to spend some time reviewing information governance and leadership principles, as well as organization and management** functions and techniques, especially those preparing for the RHIA examination.
9. **You will not need to bring your coding books to the test.** The questions are in a narrative form and any necessary codes and/or code narratives will be supplied on the computer screen for you to choose from. Study the guidelines for coding and reporting. Review reimbursement methodologies and compliance issues as they have become more and more important in the health care arena.
10. **Application and analysis emphasis.** The questions on both the RHIA and RHIT examinations have been increasingly skewed toward application and analysis rather than recall level of question difficulty. Questions on the examination may combine several concepts into one question, increasing the level of difficulty of the question. The cognitive levels for both the RHIA and RHIT examinations are as follows: 40% Recall/Understanding, 35% Application, and 25% Analysis and Higher Thinking. (Source: AHIMA.org.)

THE DAY BEFORE AND THE MORNING OF THE EXAM

1. Avoid studying the night before the exam. Last-minute studying tends to increase your anxiety level. However, you may want to spend a little time reviewing content you must memorize.
2. Organize in advance all the materials you need to take with you to the exam. Review the Candidate Handbook carefully and be sure to have all the items required, especially the admission card and appropriate proof of identity.
3. Get a good night's sleep and have a healthy meal before the exam.
4. Allow yourself plenty of time so that you arrive at the test site early. If necessary, spend the night before the examination in a hotel or motel near the exam test site.
5. Dress comfortably and plan for possible variations in room temperature. Dressing in layers may prove helpful.

TAKING THE EXAMINATION

You have stuck to your study schedule and have conditioned yourself to be in the best physical and mental shape possible. Now comes the moment of truth: the examination pops up on the screen before your eyes. Every paratrooper knows that, in addition to having a parachute, one must know how to open it. You have mastered the major topics; you have the parachute. Now you need to utilize good test-taking techniques to apply the knowledge you have gained; open the parachute!

1. Prior to starting the exam, you will be given a chance to practice taking an examination on the computer. Ten minutes will be allotted for this practice test; however, you may quit the practice test and begin the actual exam when you are comfortable with the computerized testing process.
2. Read all directions and questions carefully. Try to avoid reading too much into the questions. Be sensible and practical in your interpretation. Read ALL of the possible answers, because the first one that looks good may not be the best one.
3. Scan the computer screen quickly for the general format of the questions. Like the marathon runner, pace yourself for the distance. A good rule of thumb is 1–1.5 minutes per question. You may wish to keep the timer displayed on the computer to check your schedule throughout the exam. For example, at question 31, about one-half hour will have elapsed, etc.
4. Some people answer all questions that they are certain of first, and then go back through the exam a second time to answer any questions they were uncertain about. Others prefer not to skip questions but make their best choice on encountering each question and go on. Both can be good approaches; choose the one that works best for you. You can "mark" questions that you have left unanswered and/or those questions you may want to review. Before you sign off of the exam or run out of time, you have the ability to go back to those questions for a final review.
5. Answer all the questions. There are no penalties for guessing, but putting no answer is definitely a wrong answer.
6. Use deductive reasoning and the process of elimination to arrive at the most correct answer. Some questions will have more than one correct answer. You will be asked to select the "best" possible answer based on the information presented.
7. If the question is written in a scenario format, first identify the question being asked and then review the entire question for the information needed to determine the correct answer.
8. Use all the time available to recheck your answers. However, avoid changing your answers unless you are absolutely certain it is necessary. Second-guessing yourself often results in a wrong answer.

AFTER THE EXAM

Our advice is to reclaim your life and focus on your career. One good way to start is to plan a special reward for yourself at some point immediately following or shortly after the exam. Schedule a family vacation or a relaxing weekend get-away. Just find some way of being good to yourself. You certainly deserve it! You have worked hard, so relish your success.

Fully Revised Professional Review Guide Series Online Quizzing Software

Follow the instructions on the Printed Access Card bound into this text to access the online quizzing software for this title.

Features include:

- All of the quizzes and mock exams available in the text, customizable by subject area
- Immediate feedback options by subject area and competency for better self-assessment

For Instructors:

- Ability to track student and class progress by domain or subject area in real-time for better classroom focus
- Excel™ exporting feature for gradebooks

Go to www.cengagebrain.com to create a unique instructor user login. Contact your sales representative for more information.

I. Examination Study Strategies and Resources

Patricia J. Schnering, RHIA, CCS

FORMAT OF THE EXAMINATION

The questions developed for the examinations are based on specifications currently referred to as domains and subdomains. A complete copy of these entry-level specifications will be provided in the RHIA/RHIT Candidate Handbook provided by AHIMA.

The general format of the exams is primarily designed to engage your problem-solving and critical-thinking skills. These types of questions require that you translate what you have learned and apply it to a situation. To get a preview, you can access sample questions on AHIMA's Web site: www.ahima.org.

EXAMINATION STRATEGIES

Preparing for a major exam is similar to preparing for a marathon athletic event. The time allotted for the RHIA examination is 4 hours. The time allotted for the RHIT examination is 3½ hours. One suggestion is to use your study process to slowly build up your concentration time until you can focus your energy for the appropriate time. This is like the runner who begins jogging for 30 minutes and builds up to 1 hour, then 1½ hours, and so on, and gradually increases the endurance time to meet the demands of the race. Try this strategy; it could work for you!

Everyone has his or her own particular study style. Some people prefer to study alone and others work best in a group. Regardless of your preference, we strongly recommend that you take advantage of group study at least some of the time. Studying with others can prove very helpful when working through your weakest areas. Each member of the study team will bring strengths and weaknesses to the table, and all can benefit from the collaboration. So, even if you are a solitary learner, you may occasionally want to work with a group for those topics you find more challenging.

Theoretically, material known thoroughly after one's learning will fade predictably with time. After one day, the average person retains only 80% of what was learned; ultimately he or she will remember about 30% of it. That is why you are now relearning information you acquired over a period of years. Your aim is to achieve maximum recall through effective review.

Make your study process systematic. To facilitate this effort, we recommend that you design a 10-week study program. You should plan on spending an average of 10 to 12 hours per week studying. The idea is to study smart, not to bulldoze through tons of material in a haphazard way.

DEVELOPING YOUR STUDY HABITS

First, you must get organized. You have to be deliberate about making sure that you develop and stick to a regular study routine. Find a place where you can study, either at home or at the library.

How you schedule your study time during the week is an individual decision. However, we recommend that you avoid all-nighters and other unreasonably long study sessions. The last thing you want to do is burn yourself out by working too long and too hard at one time. Try to do a little bit at a time and maintain a steady pace that is manageable for you.

Develop your individual study program. Write the topics and subjects in a list. Outline the chapters in your HIM text. Pause at each chapter outline and recall basic points. Do you draw a blank, recall them more or less, or do you feel comfortable with your recall? Pinpoint your weakest subjects. By using this approach, you can see where you stand.

Weigh the importance of each subject. How the topics were emphasized in textbooks, in your class notes, and on previous exams (review the examination content information in the introduction of this book). Try to pick out concepts that would make good exam questions.

Avoid trying to make a head-on attack by giving equal time and attention to all topics. Use the outlines to identify your weakest topics. Determine which topics will require a significant amount of study time and which will only require a brief review. Make a list of the topics in the order that you plan to study them.

Your list will give you a clear mental picture of what you need to do and will keep you on track. There are three additional advantages to a list:

1. It builds your morale as you steadily cross off the items that you have completed, and you can monitor your progress.
2. Glancing back at the list from time to time serves to reassure you that you are on target.
3. You can readily see that you are applying your time and effort where they are most needed.

Keep the list conspicuously in view. Carefully plan your pre-exam study time and stick to your plan. Go to the exam like a trained and disciplined runner going to a marathon event!

A SUMMARY OF TIPS FOR ORGANIZING YOUR TIME AND MATERIALS

1. **Assess your strengths and weaknesses.** Review the major topic categories and the AHIMA competency listing to help in determining where your areas of strength are and what areas are in need of improvement.
2. **Set up a realistic study schedule.** Refer to the sample schedule provided in this book and customize it to meet your needs.
3. **Focus on your weaknesses.** Spend more time and energy studying your areas of weakness, especially if these categories had a significant percentage of questions associated with them on the AHIMA competency list. Remember, every question counts toward that passing score!
4. **Organize and review all of the following items:**
   - **a.** Course syllabi and outlines
   - **b.** Class notes
   - **c.** Tests and examinations
   - **d.** Textbooks
   - **e.** AHIMA test information and materials
5. **Take tests.** One of the best ways to study for a test is to take tests. Practice answering questions and working problems as much as possible. Work with your watch in front of you. Time yourself, so that you become accustomed to taking only 1 to 1½ minutes per question. Practice using the calculator on your computer to make mathematical calculations. When you take the practice tests presented online for this book, you can practice by choosing the section and then picking the competency you want to focus on.
6. **Read the AHIMA Candidate Handbook for the Certification Examinations.** If anything in the Candidate Handbook is unclear, seek assistance from your program director or call AHIMA. You are held accountable for the important information, deadlines, and instructions addressed in this material.

SAMPLE STUDY SCHEDULE

Week 1	Health Data Contents and Standards, and Information Retention and Access
Week 2	Legal and Ethical Aspects, and Health Information Privacy and Security
Week 3	Informatics and Information Systems
Week 4	Organization and Management and Human Resources
Week 5	Classification Systems and Secondary Data Sources
Week 6	Billing and Reimbursement and Medical Science
Week 7	Health Statistics and Research
Week 8	Quality and Performance Improvement
Week 9	CPT Coding
Week 10	ICD-10-CM/PCS Coding

STUDY RESOURCES

There are four basic sources of information: books, people, the Internet, and your educational program or college. If your studies become stagnant, do not sit and grind yourself down. If your text is not making the subject clear for you, don't spend time trying to memorize something you do not understand. The main issue is to understand the material, so you can use the knowledge in a practical way. Search for additional information that will help make the subject clear to you.

Books and other written resources may use another style of presentation that you are more receptive to. A different textbook may be all you need to gain better insight into the subject. It can offer a fresh point of view, provide relief from boredom, and encourage critical thinking in the process of comparing the texts.

Periodical literature in the health field provides well-written articles that may open up the subject to you and turn study into an adventure in learning. AHIMA publishes authoritative and insightful information on every aspect of HIM. Sometimes an article can help put the text material into practical perspective and pull it together, so that you gain a deeper understanding. With the rapidly changing health care world, HIM journals and magazines have the most current information and are frequently used as references for test questions. Review the AHIMA practice briefs.

Take advantage of the college library by using reserved materials set aside for your study purposes.

Professional contacts in your HIM community can also be helpful in your study effort. Most people in our field are eager to share their knowledge and are flattered by appeals for information.

Collaborating with classmates may reveal fresh viewpoints, stimulate thought by disagreement, or at least let you see that you are not alone in your quest. Organize study groups and set aside specific times to work together. This interaction can be truly beneficial in keeping you motivated and on task.

Classes, workshops, and seminars present opportunities to learn and review the subject matter in a new light. Take advantage of any examination review sessions available in your area. Talking to graduates who have recently taken the exam can also be of great assistance.

Don't overlook the power of The internet. In this dynamic, ever-changing environment, the most up-to-date materials may not be available in a book. There are myriad sites with updated information on any subject you choose to research. Just be aware, that the information is only as accurate as the website you are using is reliable. A few of my favorites are:

- American Health Information Management Association (AHIMA): *http://www.ahima.org/*
- Centers for Medicare and Medicaid Services: *cms.gov*
- CMS Medicare Learning Network: *https://www.cms.gov/Outreach-and-Education/Medicare-Learning-Network-MLN/MLNMattersArticles/*
- Center for Disease Control and Prevention: *http://www.cdc.gov/*
- Medline Plus: *http://www.nlm.nih.gov/medlineplus/druginformation.html*
- Labtestsonline: *http://labtestsonline.org/*
- FDA: *http://www.fda.gov/*
- National Library of Medicine: *http://www.nlm.nih.gov/*
- Office of the Federal Register: *https://www.federalregister.gov/*
- Health Resources and Services Administration: *http://www.hrsa.gov/quality/toolbox/methodology/qualityimprovement*

In summary, some of the study resources available to you include the following:

1. HIM textbooks and Class text books: There is a large variety of textbooks for HIM and coding available on the market. Both Cengage Learning (*www.cengage.com*) and AHIMA (*www.ahima.org*) have a variety of HIM products. For example, see the partial listing of books available through Cengage Learning.
2. Review books written for the RHIA and RHIT examinations.
3. Mock exam questions on the Cengage website are available for this book for practice taking computerized tests.
4. Class notes as well as the class tests and exams.
5. Examination review sessions.
6. On-the-job experience (be cautious because the exam tests theory and not each particular practice and the test uses national laws, rules, and regulations—not state and facility practice).
7. Study groups or partners.
8. Visit various Internet sites such as www.ahima.org and www.cms.gov for the latest information on the health care industry.

AHIMA has developed a series of HIM and coding resources.

To place an order, call (800) 335-5535.

Visit the AHIMA Web site at http://www.ahima.org for additional resources and information about the coding certification examinations.

Optum360 has an array of coding, reimbursement, and compliance products.

Contact them at 1-800-464-3649. (Choose option 1 for fastest service.)

Visit their Web site at https://www.optumcoding.com/.

Cengage Learning has a multitude of HIM products. In addition, they have partnered with Optum360, so that you can order your Optum360 coding resources through Cengage Learning.

For additional information on these Health Information resources, visit Cengage Learning at http//www.cengage.com.

The following is a partial listing of Cengage products for Health Information.

2015 Coding Workbook for the Physician's Office

Covell, Alice

3-2-1 Code It! (5th Edition)

Green, Michelle A.

A Guide to Health Insurance Billing (4th Edition)

Moisio, Marie A.

Basic Allied Health Statistics and Analysis (4th Edition)

Koch, G.

Case Studies for Health Information Management

McCuen, Charlotte; Sayles, Nanette; and Schnering, Patricia

Comparative Health Information Management
Peden, Ann
Essentials of Health Information Management Principles and Practices (3rd Edition)
Bowie, M. J. and Green, M. A.
Essentials of Healthcare Compliance
Safian, Shelly
Ethics Case Studies for Health Information Management
Grebner, Leah
Guide to Coding Compliance
Becker, Joanne M.
Health Services Research Methods
Shi, L.
Legal and Ethical Aspects of Health Information Management (4th Edition)
McWay, Dana C.
Medical Billing 101 (2nd Edition)
Clack, Crystal and Renfroe, Linda
Medical Terminology for Insurance and Coding
Moisio, Marie A.
Today's Health Information Management: An Integrated Approach (2nd Edition)
McWay, D. C.
Understanding Health Insurance: A Guide to Billing and Reimbursement (13th Edition)
Green, Michelle A. and Rowell, Jo Anne
Understanding Hospital Coding and Billing: A Worktext (3rd Edition)
Diamond, Marsha S.
Understanding ICD-10-CM and ICD-10-PCS: A Worktext (3rd Edition)
Bowie, Mary Jo and Schaffer, Regina M.
Understanding Medical Coding: A Comprehensive Guide (4th Edition)
Johnson, Sandra L. and Linker, R.
Understanding Procedural Coding: A Worktext (4th Edition)
Bowie, Mary Jo and Schaffer, Regina M.
Using the Electronic Health Record in the Healthcare Provider Practice
Eichenwald-Maki, Shirley and Petterson, Bonnie

For additional information on these Health Information resources, visit Cengage Learning at **www.cengage.com**

II. Test-Taking Skills

Patricia J. Schnering, RHIA, CCS

This section of the review book is designed to provide students with techniques that will help maximize their chances for success on the RHIA and RHIT national certification examinations. Five major areas are explored in this section:

1. Becoming "test wise"
2. The "truth" about test taking
3. Characteristics of successful test takers
4. Multiple-choice test question construction
5. Practical advice for exam preparation

Health Information Administration/Technology (HIA/HIT) students may view the test-taking experience as one that causes great anxiety and concern. Test-taking does not have to be a negative experience. Students can equip themselves with an array of techniques and practical strategies to master the test-taking situation. After all, the ultimate goal of taking the exam is to pass it and move forward with one's career aspirations.

BECOMING "TEST WISE"

This section will assist the student in becoming "test wise." Becoming test wise involves a set of skills that is acquired through practice and instruction. Being test wise does not mean that one will always achieve a very high score on the exam. What it does mean is that one will learn to overcome such factors as test anxiety, which often prevent students from passing examinations. The ultimate key to being test wise is knowledge of the subject matter that will be covered on the certification examination. No amount of tips or techniques can replace adequate preparation. A colleague I know in academia often states, "Adequate preparation prevents poor performance." If one does not have thorough knowledge of the subject, no amount of test-taking knowledge or skills will improve test performance. Now, let's turn our discussion to the first topic—the "truth" about test taking.

THE "TRUTH" ABOUT TEST TAKING

It is important to be realistic about what a test really is and what it is not. The exam is not a measure of your intelligence. It is not directly a measure of your knowledge of the course material. It is not a complete picture of what you know. It is certainly not a measure of your worth as a human being. Most importantly, failing to pass the certification examination does not imply that you are in the wrong profession. Many lawyers and certified public accountants require several attempts to obtain their credentials.

Now let's look at what a test is really all about. What does it measure? A test may measure your performance on a given day. It tells you how much you know about the questions you were asked, which represent a small sampling of the material you actually covered while studying to become a health information management professional. To some degree, a test measures your skills as a test taker, such as your ability to apply reasoning and logic, as well as your critical-thinking and problem-solving skills. The test also measures your ability to recall "correct answers."

It is important as you prepare for the certification examination that you maintain a realistic perspective. The certification examination is a professionally designed test that has been developed by educators and practitioners in health information management. It will measure your ability to answer questions in the major domains.

Knowing what is expected of you in order to pass the examination and improving your test-taking skills will provide you with valuable tools to apply in your study process. If you keep the examination in the proper perspective and prepare well, you will obtain the credentials that you so rightly deserve.

Learning how to take tests will usually help you overcome inappropriate test-taking habits and allow you to demonstrate what you know to the fullest degree in the testing situation. Here are 10 truths that you should know before attempting the certification examination.

10 TRUTHS

TRUTH 1: Test-taking skills can be learned.
Good test-taking skills make the most of what you know. That's just what this chapter is focused on.

TRUTH 2: Test-taking skills make a difference.
Two people can get scores that differ greatly on the test because one person has better test-taking skills.

TRUTH 3: Good preparation reduces anxiety.
Reducing anxiety by proper preparation improves test performance.

TRUTH 4: Attitude does make a difference.
A significant percentage of success on the test will depend on your attitude toward test-taking and your general attitude about yourself. Students should strive to feel good about the test-taking experience, knowing that they have done everything possible to prepare in advance for the examination.

TRUTH 5: Always answer the easy questions first.
Avoid attempting to answer the most difficult questions first, because they will interfere with your positive attitude and confidence. Agonizing over difficult questions will result in loss of time and points.

TRUTH 6: Failure to plan to pass the exam ensures planning to fail the exam.
This might sound a bit harsh and bitter to swallow, but it is indeed the truth. Do not let poor planning and a lack of preparation hinder you from peak performance on the examination. As the saying goes, "Plan your work and work your plan."

TRUTH 7: Usually your first hunch is your best.
Changing answers after you have selected what you believe or know to be the correct answer is not recommended. Usually, your first hunch is your best, unless of course you discover or uncover information in the examination that disqualifies or nullifies your first choice.

TRUTH 8: Educated guessing is better than guessing randomly.
It is appropriate to guess after you have narrowed down the four options to two possible answers.

TRUTH 9: The only thing that stands between you and passing the exam is ...
You guessed it: "YOU." If passing the exam is your number one goal at this point in your life, then your priorities should reflect this goal. Priority number one should be to find the time to plan to be successful on the exam.

TRUTH 10: No amount of "tips and tricks" replaces content knowledge.
As mentioned previously, strong content knowledge is essential. The suggestions in this chapter are meant to make the most of what you know, not to take the place of content preparation.

CHARACTERISTICS OF SUCCESSFUL TEST TAKERS

Have you ever wondered why it seems that some people pass the exam and others do not? What are the characteristics of successful test takers? If one looks at successful people in general, you will probably find that they demonstrate these traits and habits in different aspects of their personal and professional lives. Here are some of the characteristics of successful test takers in general.

1. **Good time management.** Time is looked upon by the successful test taker as something not to be feared, but rather a medium that must be mastered and controlled in order to complete the exam with confidence. Completion of the exam with confidence means that one will be able to manage his or her time effectively and have sufficient time to attempt to answer every question without heavily depending on guessing, whether educated guessing or guessing randomly. Ultimately, if your time is not managed well, the minutes will pass whether you have completed the exam or not. Remember to avoid spending excessive time on any one question.

2. **Read questions carefully.** Read the question twice, if necessary, to fully understand the directions or to fully comprehend what exactly is being asked. In lengthy scenario questions, it may be helpful to read the question portion of the statement first. Also, have a good understanding of key terms or phrases often used in health information management, such as "confidentiality" or "skilled nursing facility." Remember, there is no substitute for knowing the facts.

3. **Take the question at face value.** In other words, avoid reading something into the question that was not intended or explicitly stated. For example, consider the following question:

   In progressive counseling, the first step in disciplining for a first offense is
   A. termination.
   B. suspension.
   C. oral reprimand.
   D. written warning.

   The student who reads into the question may decide that in order to answer this question, he or she must know more about the specific offense. However, such details are not necessary. This question assumes that the offense is one that would not require immediate termination for the first offense. Therefore, in the process of applying progressive disciplinary action, an oral reprimand (answer C) is the correct answer.

4. **Read and consider all four options carefully.** One approach in answering multiple-choice questions is to read the answers first. In using this method, you will evaluate each answer separately and equally. Look for an answer that not only seems right on its own, but completes the question statement smoothly. Statistically, the least likely correct answer on a multiple-choice question is the first option.

   If you have narrowed the options down to two that seem correct, then you must study the options and compare them with each other to see what makes them different. Using deductive reasoning and the process of elimination, you should be able to arrive at the best answer.

5. **Approach questions systematically.** Break down each question into manageable parts and proceed systematically. Consider the following question:

   For a 2-week period, the HIM department had 1,200 worked hours and 1,280 total (or paid) hours on its payroll. During this same 2 weeks, there were 375 discharges. The department's standard is 3.3 worked hours per discharge. The number of worked hours per discharge for this 2-week period was
   A. 3.0.
   B. 3.2.
   C. 3.4.
   D. 3.8.

   Following the above principle of breaking down the question into component parts, what would you do to make this question more manageable? There are often several ways to arrive at the same answer. Some students may answer, "I would first pull out the number of discharges," or some may answer, "I would pull out the total hours worked." Whatever works for you to manage answering the question correctly is the right approach for you. The calculation for this question is 1,200 hours worked divided by 375 discharges equals 3.2 (answer B).

6. **Read carefully.** Reading directions thoroughly and identifying key words and phrases in the question are essential to test-taking success. For example, consider the following question:

   The health information manager exercises staff authority in the hospital when he or she
   A. abstracts a medical record.
   B. advises on a file system for the radiology department.
   C. teaches a file clerk a new procedure.
   D. writes a procedure for the correct filing of records.

   The stem states "exercises staff authority." If the student did not read the question carefully, he or she may have missed these key terms, which are critical to selecting the correct answer, which is B.

7. **Avoid applying preset solutions.** The successful test taker does not try to remember solutions to similar problems; rather, he or she solves each new problem independently.

WHEN AND HOW TO GUESS

There will be questions on the exam that will be totally unfamiliar to you. Choosing the correct answer may lie in the concept of "informed guessing." In applying this technique, the test taker eliminates the absurd options and guesses on the basis of familiarity.

It is helpful to relate possible answers to the question being asked. Read all the options before selecting the correct one. Usually, you can narrow the possible answers down to two by asking yourself:

- What is the question really asking?
- What is the main idea or point of this question?
- What answer would make the most sense?
- How can I rephrase or break down the question?

Sometimes the test taker can gain information about the correct answers from cues and information from other questions. Remember, however, this is when you are in the "informed guessing" mode. There will be information in a question that is irrelevant, and it is important for you to get to the heart of the question. Don't get too preoccupied with the content or meaning of a scenario before you know what the question is asking. Use logic and common sense whenever possible.

MULTIPLE-CHOICE TEST QUESTION CONSTRUCTION

The entire multiple-choice question is called an item. Each item consists of two main parts:

- **Stem:** The first part is known as the stem. The purpose of the stem is to present a problem in a clear and concise manner. The stem should contain all the details necessary to answer the question. The stem of an item can be a complete sentence that asks a question. It can also be presented as an incomplete sentence that becomes a complete sentence when it is combined with one of the options in the item.

- **Answer options:** The second part of the item is comprised of the options or possible answers. One of the options will answer the question posed in the stem correctly. The remaining options are called *distracters*. They are referred to as distracters because they are designed to distract you from the correct answer. Consider the following sample item.

	ITEM	
Stem	In quantitative research, the formulation of the hypothesis is an activity usually associated with	
Distracter	A.	data collection.
Correct	B.	identification of the problem.
Distracter	C.	analysis.
Distracter	D.	assembling the results.

COGNITIVE LEVELS

In addition to the stem and distracters, the item may also be measuring different cognitive levels. These levels are used to identify the candidates' knowledge of subject matter at different levels needed to perform on the job (see Table 2–1). An example of each of the three levels is shown after the table.

Table 2–1 Cognitive Levels

Cognitive Levels		
Cognitive Level	**Purpose**	**Performance Required**
Recall (RE)	Primarily, to measure memory.	Identify terms, specific facts, methods, procedures, basic concepts, basic theories, principles, and processes.
Application (AP)	To measure simple interpretation of limited data.	Apply concepts and principles to new situations, recognize relationships among data, apply laws and theories to practical situations, calculate solutions to mathematical problems, interpret charts and translate graphic data, classify items, interpret information.
Analysis (AN)	To measure the application of knowledge to solving a specific problem and the assembly of various elements into a meaningful whole.	Select an appropriate solution for responsive action; revise policy, procedure, or plan; evaluate a solution, case scenario, report, or plan; compare solutions, plans, ideas, or aspects of a problem; evaluate information or a situation; perform multiple calculations to arrive at one answer.

Recall: This question is at the "recall level." The student needs to be able to recall pertinent facts.

The medical record is the property of the

A. patient.
B. medical facility.
C. health information management department.
D. attending physician.

The answer is, of course, B. This question relied on your memory of this fact.

Application: Now let's look at the second-highest cognitive level, an application level question, which tests the student's ability to apply information.

The medical record is the property of the medical facility and can be removed in which of the following situations?

A. The patient is suing the hospital and wants the original record mailed to the attorney representing his case.
B. The attending physician wants to take the patient's original record to a professional conference for presentation.
C. The court issues a subpoena and needs the original record in court within 24 hours.
D. The attending physician is being sued and he wants to take the original patient record to court with him.

The correct answer in this case is C. The only instance when the original record should be removed from the hospital is in the case of the issuance of a subpoena *duces tecum*. This question requires the student to apply information about when a record can be removed from the health care facility. The application level goes beyond the student recalling the rule about who has legal ownership of the record.

Analysis (problem solving): The third and highest cognitive level utilized by test developers is the analysis level. At this level, the student will demonstrate the ability to analyze familiar information in new and different situations. This is often referred to as a problem-solving or critical-thinking question.

The information below is from a transcription service in your department.

Total average lines transcribed/month:	270,000
Standard per person:	1,200 lines in one day
21 workdays in a month	15% adjustment factor

The number of transcriptionists needed by this facility is

A. 10.7.
B. 11.7.
C. 12.3.
D. 16.0.

The correct answer for this question is C.

The mathematical calculation to achieve the answer is

270,000 × 0.15 adjustment factor = 40,500
270,000 + 40,500 = 310,500 potential lines of transcription per month
1,200 lines × 21 days = 25,200 lines one employee can produce in one month
310,500/25,200 = 12.3 transcriptionists

After reviewing the cognitive levels, it is clear that for both the RHIA and RHIT examinations the student must be prepared to answer questions from the lowest cognitive level (recall) to the highest cognitive level (analysis). Testing at all three levels will help ensure that students can apply their newly acquired knowledge and skills on the job.

As always, refer to the current copy of the AHIMA Candidate Handbook for a complete listing of the domains, subdomains, and task competencies.

PRACTICAL ADVICE FOR EXAM PREPARATION

As you become more proficient at applying effective test-taking techniques, you will truly understand the phrase that "knowledge is power." This is exactly what this information hopes to do, and that is to provide you with the knowledge and skills to empower you to achieve your ultimate goal—certification.

Research demonstrates that the test taker who approaches a test with physical, mental, and emotional authority is in a better position to master the testing situation and the outcome. Remember, failing to plan means planning to fail. Here are some recommendations for you to incorporate as part of your "success plan."

Recommendation 1: Follow your regular routine.
Follow your regular nightly routine the evening before and morning of the exam. Abruptly changing your schedule and habits for this testing event could throw your system off balance and negatively affect your performance.

Recommendation 2: Arrive early for the examination.
It is always better to have 15 to 30 minutes of extra time prior to the start of a major examination. By arriving early on test day, you will be able to visit the restroom, survey the situation, and collect your thoughts. Decide where you want to sit in the test area, if the seats are not assigned. By collecting your thoughts prior to the start of the exam, you can improve your mental attitude by knowing you are truly prepared for this time, this situation, and this test-taking process. Remember, you want to be in control of the test anxiety that is normal, despite all of your preparation. If you are unfamiliar with the test site, it is usually a good practice to travel to the test site in advance of the exam date. Becoming familiar with the test site will prevent you from getting lost on the exam day.

Recommendation 3: Maintain a positive mental attitude.
Perhaps you are sometimes plagued by a negative inner voice that says something like: "Well look at you… trying to pass the certification examination. Why don't you stop kidding yourself? You know you are not as smart as your classmates. They will probably all pass and you will probably fail!" Almost all of us have critical voices inside our heads. Sometimes the voice may tell us that we don't measure up to others in the class. At other times it tries to blame our performance on the test, the teacher, or some other convenient scapegoat. You can learn to replace your negative inner dialogue with positive self-talk.

Start by programming your inner voice to remind you of how long and hard you have prepared for this examination. Remind yourself that you deserve to pass because of the time and energy you have spent in school preparing for this examination. Repeat positive affirmation statements to yourself, such as "I am a wonderful, worthy person who is capable of achieving my goal of becoming an RHIA/RHIT."

Recommendation 4: Answer the questions you know first.
It is a good idea to begin the test by answering questions that build your confidence. Getting off to a good start allows you to establish a positive momentum, which will assist you when you encounter more difficult questions. Because time is critical, answering the easier questions first will assure you of getting credit for what you know.

Recommendation 5: Check your answers before exiting the computerized exam.
Make sure you have answered every question. Be careful about changing your answers. You may need to revisit any items in which you have made an educated guess or items you discovered answers to as you progressed through the questions. Submit your test knowing that you did your very best.

CONCLUSION

As you study for the exam, take a moment now and then to review the test-taking skills addressed in this section. Using these techniques will help you develop the characteristics of a successful test taker. Working through questions will help you become more and more comfortable with multiple-choice testing.

Knowing how questions are constructed and what to look for should greatly improve your correct answer ratio. A sense of the scheme of the test structure and cognitive levels will become second nature with practice.

During your exam preparation, you will find that you actually enjoy taking multiple-choice examinations as a study aid. Be sure to obtain any mock computerized test exams available online to gain experience taking the test on the computer.

This comfort zone will free you to apply your knowledge and skills effectively during the examination process. The real bonus is that you will be more focused on demonstrating your knowledge through the medium of testing than on the exam process itself.

III. Health Data Content and Standards

Debra W. Cook, MAEd, RHIA

1. In preparation for an EHR, you are conducting a total facility inventory of all forms currently used. You must name each form for bar coding and indexing into a document management system. The unnamed document in front of you includes a microscopic description of tissue excised during surgery. The document type you are most likely to give to this form is
   A. recovery room record.
   B. pathology report.
   C. operative report.
   D. discharge summary.

REFERENCE: Abdelhak, p 107
Bowie and Green, p 181
LaTour, Eichenwald-Maki, and Oachs, pp A32–A33
Sayles, p 88

2. Patient data collection requirements vary according to health care setting. A data element you would expect to be collected in the MDS, but NOT in the UHDDS would be
   A. personal identification.
   B. cognitive patterns.
   C. procedures and dates.
   D. principal diagnosis.

REFERENCE: Abdelhak, pp 135–137
LaTour, Eichenwald-Maki, and Oachs, p 30
Sayles, pp 147, 152

3. In the past, Joint Commission standards have focused on promoting the use of a facility-approved abbreviation list to be used by hospital care providers. With the advent of the Commission's national patient safety goals, the focus has shifted to the
   A. prohibited use of any abbreviations.
   B. flagrant use of specialty-specific abbreviations.
   C. use of prohibited or "dangerous" abbreviations.
   D. use of abbreviations in the final diagnosis.

REFERENCE: Abdelhak, p 111
LaTour, Eichenwald-Maki, and Oachs, pp 251, 264, 672

4. Engaging patients and their families in health care decisions is one of the core objectives for
   A. achieving meaningful use of EHRs.
   B. the Joint Commission's National Patient Safety goals.
   C. HIPAA 5010 regulations.
   D. establishing flexible clinical pathways.

REFERENCE: HealthIT.hhs.gov (1)
LaTour, Eichenwald-Maki, and Oachs, p 286

5. A risk manager needs to locate a full report of a patient's fall from his bed, including witness reports and probable reasons for the fall. She would most likely find this information in the
   A. doctors' progress notes.
   B. integrated progress notes.
   C. incident report.
   D. nurses' notes.

REFERENCE: Abdelhak, pp 465–466
Bowie and Green, p 97
Davis and LaCour, pp 378–380
LaTour and Eichenwald-Maki, p 861
McWay, p 132
Sayles, p 613

6. For continuity of care, ambulatory care providers are more likely than providers of acute care services to rely on the documentation found in the
   A. interdisciplinary patient care plan.
   B. discharge summary.
   C. transfer record.
   D. problem list.

REFERENCE: Abdelhak, p 113
Bowie and Green, p 207
Davis and LaCour, pp 10–11
Sayles, p 108

7. Joint Commission does not approve of auto authentication of entries in a health record. The primary objection to this practice is that
   A. it is too easy to delegate use of computer passwords.
   B. evidence cannot be provided that the physician actually reviewed and approved each report.
   C. electronic signatures are not acceptable in every state.
   D. tampering too often occurs with this method of authentication.

REFERENCE: Bowie and Green, p 85
LaTour, Eichenwald-Maki, and Oachs, pp 174, 897

8. As part of a quality improvement study, you have been asked to provide information on the menstrual history, number of pregnancies, and number of living children on each OB patient from a stack of old obstetrical records. The best place in the record to locate this information is the
   A. prenatal record.
   B. labor and delivery record.
   C. postpartum record.
   D. discharge summary.

REFERENCE: Abdelhak, p 108
Bowie and Green, p 191

9. As a concurrent record reviewer for an acute care facility, you have asked Dr. Crossman to provide an updated history and physical for one of her recent admissions. Dr. Crossman pages through the medical record to a copy of an H&P performed in her office a week before admission. You tell Dr. Crossman
   A. a new H&P is required for every inpatient admission.
   B. that you apologize for not noticing the H&P she provided.
   C. the H&P copy is acceptable as long as she documents any interval changes.
   D. Joint Commission standards do not allow copies of any kind in the original record.

REFERENCE: Abdelhak, p 103
Bowie and Green, p 158
LaTour and Eichenwald-Maki, p 196

10. You have been asked to identify every reportable case of cancer from the previous year. A key resource will be the facility's
   A. disease index.
   B. number control index.
   C. physicians' index.
   D. patient index.

REFERENCE: LaTour, Eichenwald-Maki, and Oachs, pp 245, 250–251
McWay, p 140
Sayles, p 437

11. Joint Commission requires the attending physician to countersign health record documentation that is entered by
    A. interns or medical students.
    B. business associates.
    C. consulting physicians.
    D. physician partners.

REFERENCE: Bowie and Green, p 86
Davis and LaCour, pp 105, 126–127

12. The minimum length of time for retaining original medical records is primarily governed by
    A. Joint Commission.
    B. medical staff.
    C. state law.
    D. readmission rates.

REFERENCE: Abdelhak, pp 164–168
Bowie and Green, p 102
Davis and LaCour, pp 283–284
LaTour, Eichenwald-Maki, and Oachs, pp 311–312
Sayles, p 995

13. Improving clinical outcomes and optimal continuity of care for patients are common goals of clinical documentation improvement programs in acute care hospitals. Additionally, CDI programs may work together with UM programs to
    A. reduce clinical denials for medical necessity.
    B. decrease medication errors through CPOE systems.
    C. increase patient engagement through patient portals.
    D. report sentinel events to the Joint Commission.

REFERENCE: AHIMA (1)

14. Discharge summary documentation must include
    A. a detailed history of the patient.
    B. a note from social services or discharge planning.
    C. significant findings during hospitalization.
    D. correct codes for significant procedures.

REFERENCE: Abdelhak, p 106
Bowie and Green, p 158
Davis and LaCour, pp 106–107
LaTour and Eichenwald-Maki, pp 200–201
Sayles, p 93

15. The performance of ongoing record reviews is an important tool in ensuring data quality. These reviews evaluate
    A. quality of care through the use of preestablished criteria.
    B. adverse effects and contraindications of drugs utilized during hospitalization.
    C. potentially compensable events.
    D. the overall quality of documentation in the record.

REFERENCE: Abdelhak, p 126
Davis and LaCour, pp 374–376
LaTour, Eichenwald-Maki, and Oachs, pp 250–251

16. Ultimate responsibility for the quality and completion of entries in patient health records belongs to the
    A. chief of staff.
    B. attending physician.
    C. HIM director.
    D. risk manager.

REFERENCE: LaTour, Eichenwald-Maki, and Oachs, p 242

17. The federally mandated resident assessment instrument used in long-term care facilities consists of three basic components, including the new care area assessment, utilization guidelines, and the
    A. UHDDS.
    B. MDS.
    C. OASIS.
    D. DEEDS.

REFERENCE: Sayles, p 111

18. The foundation for communicating all patient care goals in long-term care settings is the
    A. legal assessment.
    B. medical history.
    C. interdisciplinary plan of care.
    D. Uniform Hospital Discharge Data Set.

REFERENCE: Abdelhak, p 104
LaTour, Eichenwald-Maki, and Oachs, pp 31, 254
Sayles, p 83

19. As a working HIM professional, you are investigating the workforce development projections of electronic health record specialists as outlined by ARRA and HITECH. In order to keep abreast of changes in this program, you will need to regularly access the Web site of this governmental agency.
    A. ONC
    B. CMS
    C. OSHA
    D. CDC

REFERENCE: Sayles, pp 142, 162

20. As part of Joint Commission's National Patient Safety Goal initiative, acute care hospitals are now required to use a preoperative verification process to confirm the patient's true identity, and to confirm that necessary documents such as x-rays or medical records are available. They must also develop and use a process for
    A. including the primary caregiver in surgery consults.
    B. including the surgeon in the preanesthesia assessment.
    C. marking the surgical site.
    D. apprising the patient of all complications that might occur.

REFERENCE: Joint Commission
LaTour, Eichenwald-Maki, and Oachs, p 672

21. One of the patients at your physician group practice has asked for an electronic copy of her medical record. Your electronic computer system will not allow you to accommodate this request. Chances are, you are NOT in compliance with
    A. Joint Commission standards.
    B. the HIPAA privacy rule.
    C. Conditions of Coverage rules.
    D. meaningful use requirements.

REFERENCE: CMS (1)

22. One of the Joint Commission National Patient Safety Goals (NSPGs) requires that healthcare organizations eliminate wrong-site, wrong-patient, and wrong-procedure surgery. In order to accomplish this, which of the following would not be a considered part of a preoperative verification process?
    A. Confirm the patient's true identity.
    B. Mark the surgical site.
    C. Review the medical records and/or imaging studies.
    D. Follow the daily surgical patient listing for the surgery suite if the patient has been sedated.

REFERENCE: Joint Commission
LaTour, Eichenwald-Maki, and Oachs, p 672
Sayles, p 604

23. A qualitative review of a health record reveals that the history and physical for a patient admitted on June 26 was performed on June 30 and transcribed on July 1. Which of the following statements regarding the history and physical is true in this situation? Completion and charting of the H&P indicates
    A. noncompliance with Joint Commission standards.
    B. compliance with Joint Commission standards.
    C. compliance with Medicare regulations.
    D. compliance with Joint Commission standards for nonsurgical patients.

REFERENCE: Abdelhak, p 109
LaTour, Eichenwald-Maki, and Oachs, pp 245–246, 250–251

24. The final HITECH Omnibus Rule expanded some of HIPAA's original requirements, including changes in immunization disclosures. As a result, where states require immunization records of a minor prior to admitting a student to a school, a covered entity is permitted to
    A. require written authorization from a custodial parent before disclosing proof of the child's immunization to the school.
    B. allow the minor to authorize the disclosure of the proof of immunization to the school.
    C. simply document a written or oral agreement from a parent or guardian before releasing the immunization record to the school.
    D. allow school officials to authorize immunization disclosures on behalf of a child attending their school.

REFERENCE: AHIMA (2)

25. You have been asked by a peer review committee to print a list of the medical record numbers of all patients who had CABGs performed in the past year at your acute care hospital. Which secondary data source could be used to quickly gather this information?
    A. disease index
    B. physician index
    C. master patient index
    D. operation index

REFERENCE: LaTour, Eichenwald-Maki, and Oachs, p 369
Sayles, p 437

26. The best example of point-of-care service and documentation is
    A. using an automated tracking system to locate a record.
    B. using occurrence screens to identify adverse events.
    C. doctors using voice recognition systems to dictate radiology reports.
    D. nurses using bedside terminals to record vital signs.

REFERENCE: Abdelhak, pp 308–309
LaTour, Eichenwald-Maki, and Oachs, p 96

27. Many of the principles of forms design apply to both paper-based and computer-based systems. For example, the physical layout of the form and/or screen should be organized to match the way the information is requested. Facilities that are scanning and imaging paper records as part of a computer-based system must give careful consideration to
    A. placement of hospital logo.
    B. signature line for authentication.
    C. use of box design.
    D. bar code placement.

REFERENCE: Abdelhak, p 125
LaTour, Eichenwald-Maki, and Oachs, p 88

28. Which of the following is a form or view that is typically seen in the health record of a long-term care patient but is rarely seen in records of acute care patients?
    A. pharmacy consultation
    B. medical consultation
    C. physical exam
    D. emergency record

REFERENCE: Abdelhak, p 136

29. The health record states that the patient is a female, but the registration record has the patient listed as male. Which of the following characteristics of data quality has been compromised in this case?
    A. data comprehensiveness
    B. data granularity
    C. data precision
    D. data accuracy

REFERENCE: Abdelhak, p 128
Davis and LaCour, pp 356–358
Green, p 273
LaTour, Eichenwald-Maki, and Oachs, pp 175, 229

30. The first patient with cancer seen in your facility on January 1, 2015, was diagnosed with colon cancer with no known history of previous malignancies. The accession number assigned to this patient is
    A. 15-0000/00.
    B. 15-0000/01.
    C. 15-0001/00.
    D. 15-0001/01.

REFERENCE: LaTour, Eichenwald-Maki, and Oachs, p 371
Sayles, p 439

31. Setting up a drop-down menu to make sure that the registration clerk collects "gender" as "male, female, or unknown" is an example of ensuring data
    A. reliability.
    B. timeliness.
    C. precision.
    D. validity.

REFERENCE: Abdelhak, p 128
Bowie and Green, p 273
LaTour, Eichenwald-Maki, and Oachs, p 382

32. In determining your acute care facility's degree of compliance with prospective payment requirements for Medicare, the best resource to reference for recent certification standards is the
    A. CARF manual.
    B. hospital bylaws.
    C. Joint Commission accreditation manual.
    D. Federal Register.

REFERENCE: Abdelhak, p 448
Bowie and Green, p 34
LaTour, Eichenwald-Maki, and Oachs, pp 301–302, 453, 466, 915

33. In an acute care hospital, a complete history and physical may not be required for a new admission when
    A. the patient is readmitted for a similar problem within 1 year.
    B. the patient's stay is less than 24 hours.
    C. the patient has an uneventful course in the hospital.
    D. a legible copy of a current H&P performed in the attending physician's office is available.

REFERENCE: Abdelhak, p 103
Bowie and Green, p 158
LaTour, Eichenwald-Maki, and Oachs, pp 245, 252, 925

34. You are developing a complete data dictionary for your facility. Which of the following resources will be most helpful in providing standard definitions for data commonly collected in acute care hospitals?
    A. Minimum Data Set
    B. Uniform Hospital Discharge Data Set
    C. Conditions of Participation
    D. Federal Register

REFERENCE: Abdelhak, p 131
Bowie and Green, p 135
Davis and LaCour, pp 45, 61
LaTour, Eichenwald-Maki, and Oachs, pp 19, 213, 955
Sayles, p 146

35. Gerda Smith has presented to the ER in a coma with injuries sustained in a motor vehicle accident. According to her sister, Gerda has had a recent medical history taken at the public health department. The physician on call is grateful that she can access this patient information using the area's
    A. EDMS system.
    B. CPOE.
    C. expert system.
    D. RHIO.

REFERENCE: Bowie and Green, p 121
LaTour, Eichenwald-Maki, and Oachs, pp 221–222, 224, 230, 944
Sayles, p 326

36. When developing a data collection template, the most effective approach first considers
    A. the end user's needs.
    B. applicable accreditation standards.
    C. hardware requirements.
    D. facility preference.

REFERENCE: LaTour, Eichenwald-Maki, and Oachs, p 290
Sayles, pp 125, 354–355

37. A key data item you would expect to find recorded on an ER record but would probably NOT see in an acute care record is the
    A. physical findings.
    B. lab and diagnostic test results.
    C. time and means of arrival.
    D. instructions for follow-up care.

REFERENCE: Abdelhak, p 135
Davis and LaCour, pp 95, 221–222
LaTour, Eichenwald-Maki, and Oachs, p 255
Sayles, p 107

38. A data item to include on a qualitative review checklist of infant and children inpatient health records that need not be included on adult records would be
    A. chief complaint.
    B. condition on discharge.
    C. time and means of arrival.
    D. growth and development record.

REFERENCE: Sayles, p 110

39. You are the Director of Coding and Billing at a large group practice. The Practice Manager stops by your office on his way to a planning meeting to ask about the timeline for complying with HITECH requirements to adopt meaningful use EHR technology. You reply that the incentives began in 2011 and will end in 2014. You remind him that by 2015, sanctions for noncompliance will appear in the form of
    A. downward adjustments to Medicare reimbursement.
    B. the withdrawal of permission to treat Medicare and Medicaid patients.
    C. a mandatory action plan for implementing a meaningful use EHR.
    D. monetary fines up to $100,000.

REFERENCE: Davis and LaCour, pp 82–83
McWay, p 305
Sayles, pp 954, 987

40. In creating a new form or computer view, the designer should be most driven by
    A. QIO standards.
    B. medical staff bylaws.
    C. needs of the users.
    D. flow of data on the page or screen.

REFERENCE: Abdelhak, p 114
Bowie and Green, p 216
Davis and LaCour, pp 44, 49, 52
LaTour, Eichenwald-Maki, and Oachs, pp 103–105
Sayles, p 355

41. Under which of the following conditions can an original paper-based patient health record be physically removed from the hospital?
    A. when the patient is brought to the hospital emergency department following a motor vehicle accident and, after assessment, is transferred with his health record to a trauma designated emergency department at another hospital
    B. when the director of health records is acting in response to a subpoena *duces tecum* and takes the health record to court
    C. when the patient is discharged by the physician and at the time of discharge is transported to a long-term care facility with his health record
    D. when the record is taken to a physician's private office for a follow-up patient visit postdischarge

REFERENCE: Abdelhak, p 464
Sayles, p 776

42. According to the following table, the most serious record delinquency problem occurred in which of the following months?

Record Delinquency for Second Quarter	April	May	June
Percentage incomplete records	70%	88%	79%
Percentage delinquent records	51%	43%	61%
Percentage delinquent due to missing H&P	3%	1.4%	0.5%

A. April
B. May
C. June
D. cannot determine from these data

REFERENCE: Abdelhak, p 123
Bowie and Green, p 109

43. Using the SOAP style of documenting progress notes, choose the "subjective" statement from the following.
A. sciatica unimproved with hot pack therapy
B. patient moving about very cautiously, appears to be in pain
C. adjust pain medication; begin physical therapy tomorrow
D. patient states low back pain is as severe as it was on admission

REFERENCE: Abdelhak, p 113
Bowie and Green, p 99
Davis and LaCour, pp 41–43, 96–98, 516–520
LaTour and Eichenwald-Maki, p 91

44. In 1987, OBRA helped shift the focus in long-term care to patient outcomes. As a result, core assessment data elements are collected on each SNF resident as defined in the
A. UHDDS.
B. MDS.
C. Uniform Clinical Data Set.
D. Uniform Ambulatory Core Data.

REFERENCE: Abdelhak, p 97
Bowie and Green, p 269
Davis and LaCour, p 231
LaTour, Eichenwald-Maki, and Oachs, pp 199, 435, 931
Sayles, pp 150–152

45. As the Chair of a Forms Review Committee, you need to track the field name of a particular data field and the security levels applicable to that field. Your best source for this information would be the
A. facility's data dictionary.
B. MDS.
C. glossary of health care terms.
D. UHDDS.

REFERENCE: Abdelhak, pp 501–505
LaTour, Eichenwald-Maki, and Oachs, pp 202, 907, C7
Sayles, pp 882–883

46. You notice on the admission H&P that Mr. McKahan, a Medicare patient, was admitted for disc surgery, but the progress notes indicate that due to some heart irregularities, he may not be a good surgical risk. Because of your knowledge of COP regulations, you expect that a(n) __________ will be added to his health record.
    A. interval summary
    B. consultation report
    C. advance directive
    D. interdisciplinary care plan

REFERENCE: Abdelhak, p 106
Bowie and Green, p 165
Davis and LaCour, p 106
LaTour, Eichenwald-Maki, and Oachs, pp 249, 905

47. A major contribution to a successful CDI program is the ability to demonstrate the impact that documentation has on data reporting to a large percentage of the facility's staff. In this role, the Clinical Documentation specialist is acting as a(n)
    A. reviewer.
    B. analyst.
    C. educator.
    D. ambassador.

REFERENCE: AHIMA (1)

48. You have been appointed as Chair of the Health Record Committee at a new hospital. Your committee has been asked to recommend time-limited documentation standards for inclusion in the medical staff bylaws, rules, and regulations. The committee documentation standards must meet the standards of both the Joint Commission and the Medicare Conditions of Participation. The standards for the history and physical exam documentation are discussed first. You advise them that the time period for completion of this report should be set at
    A. 12 hours after admission.
    B. 24 hours after admission.
    C. 12 hours after admission or prior to surgery.
    D. 24 hours after admission or prior to surgery.

REFERENCE: Abdelhak, p 103
Bowie and Green, p 158
Davis and LaCour, p 100
LaTour, Eichenwald-Maki, and Oachs, p 245

49. Based on the following documentation in an acute care record, where would you expect this excerpt to appear?

    "With the patient in the supine position, the right side of the neck was appropriately prepped with betadine solution and draped. I was able to pass the central line, which was taped to skin and used for administration of drugs during resuscitation."

    A. physician progress notes
    B. operative record
    C. nursing progress notes
    D. physical examination

REFERENCE: Abdelhak, p 107
Davis and LaCour, p 110
LaTour, Eichenwald-Maki, and Oachs, p 250
Sayles, p 88

50. A Clinical Documentation Specialist performs many duties. These include reviewing the data, and looking for trends or patterns over time, as well as noting any variances that require further investigation. In this role, the CDS professional is acting as a(n)
   A. reviewer.
   B. analyst.
   C. educator.
   D. ambassador.

REFERENCE: AHIMA (1)

51. Joint Commission standards require that a complete history and physical be documented on the health records of operative patients. Does this report carry a time requirement?
   A. Yes, within 8 hours postsurgery
   B. No, as long as it is done ASAP
   C. Yes, prior to surgery
   D. Yes, within 24 hours postsurgery

REFERENCE: Abdelhak, p 103
Bowie and Green, p 178
Davis and LaCour, pp 100, 375
LaTour and Eichenwald-Maki, p 196

52. The old practices of flagging records for deficiencies and requiring retrospective documentation add little or no value to patient care. You try to convince the entire health care team to consistently enter data into the patient's record at the time and location of service instead of waiting for retrospective analysis to alert them to complete the record. You are proposing
   A. quantitative record review.
   B. clinical pertinence review.
   C. concurrent record analysis.
   D. point-of-care documentation.

REFERENCE: Abdelhak, p 309
LaTour, Eichenwald-Maki, and Oachs, pp 248, 254, 263, 285, 919

53. An example of a primary data source for health care statistics is the
   A. disease index.
   B. accession register.
   C. MPI.
   D. hospital census.

REFERENCE: Abdelhak, p 484
Horton, p 4
LaTour, Eichenwald-Maki, and Oachs, pp 289, 368

54. In the computerization of forms, good screen view design, along with the options of alerts and alarms, makes it easier to ensure that all essential data items have been captured. One essential item to be captured on the physical exam is the
   A. general appearance as assessed by the physician.
   B. chief complaint.
   C. family history as related by the patient.
   D. subjective review of systems.

REFERENCE: Abdelhak, p 105
Bowie and Green, p 162
Davis and LaCour, p 99
LaTour, Eichenwald-Maki, and Oachs, p 245
Sayles, p 80

55. During a retrospective review of Rose Hunter's inpatient health record, the health information clerk notes that on day 4 of hospitalization there was one missed dose of insulin. What type of review is this clerk performing?
    A. utilization review
    B. quantitative review
    C. legal review
    D. qualitative review

REFERENCE: Abdelhak, p 125
Bowie and Green, p 107
LaTour, Eichenwald-Maki, and Oachs, p 943
McWay, p 126

56. Which of the following is least likely to be identified by a deficiency analysis technician?
    A. missing discharge summary
    B. need for physician authentication of two verbal orders
    C. discrepancy between post-op diagnosis by the surgeon and pathology diagnosis by the pathologist
    D. x-ray report charted on the wrong record

REFERENCE: Abdelhak, p 125
Bowie and Green, p 107
McWay, p 126
Sayles, p 351

57. The Conditions of Participation requires that the medical staff bylaws, rules, and regulations address the status of consultants. Which of the following reports would normally be considered a consultation?
    A. tissue examination done by the pathologist
    B. impressions of a cardiologist asked to determine whether patient is a good surgical risk
    C. interpretation of a radiologic study
    D. technical interpretation of electrocardiogram

REFERENCE: Abdelhak, p 106
Bowie and Green, p 161
Davis and LaCour, p 106
LaTour, Eichenwald-Maki, and Oachs, p 115

58. The health care providers at your hospital do a very thorough job of periodic open record review to ensure the completeness of record documentation. A qualitative review of surgical records would likely include checking for documentation regarding
    A. the presence or absence of such items as preoperative and postoperative diagnosis, description of findings, and specimens removed.
    B. whether a postoperative infection occurred and how it was treated.
    C. the quality of follow-up care.
    D. whether the severity of illness and/or intensity of service warranted acute level care.

REFERENCE: Abdelhak, p 107
Bowie and Green, p 107
Davis and LaCour, p 374
LaTour, Eichenwald-Maki, and Oachs, pp 35, 655

59. In your facility it has become critical that information regarding patients who are transferred to the oncology unit be sent to an outpatient scheduling system to facilitate outpatient appointments. This information can be obtained most efficiently from
   A. generic screens used by record abstractors.
   B. disease index.
   C. R-ADT system.
   D. indicator monitoring program.

REFERENCE: Abdelhak, pp 305–306
LaTour, Eichenwald-Maki, and Oachs, p 944
Sayles, p 955

60. In your facility, the health care providers from every discipline document progress notes sequentially on the same form. Your facility is utilizing
   A. integrated progress notes.
   B. interdisciplinary treatment plans.
   C. source-oriented records.
   D. SOAP notes.

REFERENCE: Abdelhak, p 113
Bowie and Green, p 173
LaTour, Eichenwald-Maki, and Oachs, p 248

61. Which of the following services is LEAST likely to be provided by a facility accredited by CARF?
   A. chronic pain management
   B. palliative care
   C. brain injury management
   D. vocational evaluation

REFERENCE: Abdelhak, pp 136–137
Bowie and Green, p 65
LaTour, Eichenwald-Maki, and Oachs, p 254
Sayles, p 679

62. Which method of identification of authorship or authentication of entries would be inappropriate to use in a patient's health record?
   A. written signature of the provider of care
   B. identifiable initials of a nurse writing a nursing note
   C. a unique identification code entered by the person making the report
   D. delegated use of computer key by radiology secretary

REFERENCE: Bowie and Green, p 87
LaTour, Eichenwald-Maki, and Oachs, pp 258, 264, 897

63. Though you work in an integrated delivery network, not all systems in your network communicate with one another. As you meet with your partner organizations, you begin to sell them on the concept of an important development intended to support the exchange of health information across the continuum within a geographical community. You are promoting that your organization join a
   A. data warehouse.
   B. regional health information organization.
   C. continuum of care.
   D. data retrieval portal group.

REFERENCE: Abdelhak, p 92
LaTour and Eichenwald-Maki, p 51
McWay, p 273

64. As a trauma registrar working in an emergency department, you want to begin comparing your trauma care services to other hospital-based emergency departments. To ensure that your facility is collecting the same data as other facilities, you review elements from which data set?
    A. DEEDS
    B. UHDDS
    C. MDS
    D. ORYX

REFERENCE: Bowie and Green, p 266
LaTour, Eichenwald-Maki, and Oachs, p 211

65. As a new HIM manager of an acute care facility, you have been asked to update the facility's policy for a physician's verbal orders in accordance with Joint Commission standards and state law. Your first area of concern is the qualifications of those individuals in your facility who have been authorized to record verbal orders. For this information, you will consult the
    A. Consolidated Manual for Hospitals.
    B. Federal Register.
    C. Policy and Procedure Manual.
    D. Hospital Bylaws, Rules, and Regulations.

REFERENCE: Davis and LaCour, pp 102–104
Bowie and Green, p 168
LaTour, Eichenwald-Maki, and Oachs, pp 26, 239–240, 242, 265–267
Sayles, p 81

66. Reviewing a medical record to ensure that all diagnoses are justified by documentation throughout the chart is an example of
    A. peer review.
    B. quantitative review.
    C. qualitative review.
    D. legal analysis.

REFERENCE: Abdelhak, pp 125
Bowie and Green, p 107
Davis and LaCour, pp 374–376
LaTour, Eichenwald-Maki, and Oachs, pp 34–35
McWay, p 126

67. Accreditation by Joint Commission is a voluntary activity for a facility and it is
    A. considered unnecessary by most health care facilities.
    B. required for state licensure in all states.
    C. conducted in each facility annually.
    D. required for reimbursement of certain patient groups.

REFERENCE: Abdelhak, p 13
LaTour, Eichenwald-Maki, and Oachs, pp 37–38

68. The 2014 AHIMA Foundation's "Clinical Documentation Improvement Job Description Summative Report" identified that most Clinical Documentation Improvement Specialists report directly to the
    A. HIM Department.
    B. CEO.
    C. Quality Management Department.
    D. CFO.

REFERENCE: AHIMA (1)

69. Which of the four distinct components of the problem-oriented record serves to help index documentation throughout the record?
    A. database
    B. problem list
    C. initial plan
    D. progress notes

REFERENCE: Abdelhak, pp 112–113
Bowie and Green, p 97
Davis and LaCour, pp 55–56
LaTour, Eichenwald-Maki, and Oachs, pp 255–256
Sayles, p 126

70. As supervisor of the cancer registry, you report the registry's annual caseload to administration. The most efficient way to retrieve this information would be to use
    A. patient abstracts.
    B. patient index.
    C. accession register.
    D. follow-up files.

REFERENCE: LaTour, Eichenwald-Maki, and Oachs, p 371
Sayles, p 349

71. As the Compliance Officer for an acute care facility, you are interested in researching recent legislation designed to provide significant funding for health information technology for your next committee meeting. You begin by googling
    A. EMTALA.
    B. Health Care Quality Improvement Act.
    C. HIPAA.
    D. ARRA.

REFERENCE: LaTour, Eichenwald-Maki, and Oachs, p 17
McWay, pp 34–35
Sayles, pp 25, 162

72. Select the appropriate situation for which a final progress note may legitimately be substituted for a discharge summary in an inpatient medical record.
    A. Patient admitted with COPD 1/4/2016 and discharged 1/7/2016
    B. Baby Boy Hiltz, born 1/5/2016, maintained normal status, discharged 1/7/2016
    C. Baby Boy Hiltz's mother admitted 1/5/2016, C-section delivery, and discharged 1/7/2016
    D. Baby Boy Doe admitted 1/3/2016, died 1/4/2016

REFERENCE: Abdelhak, p 106
Bowie and Green, p 142
LaTour, Eichenwald-Maki, and Oachs, p 251

73. Based on the following documentation in an acute care record, where would you expect this excerpt to appear?

    "Initially the patient was admitted to the medical unit to evaluate the x-ray findings and the rub. He was started on Levaquin 500 mg initially and then 250 mg daily. The patient was hydrated with IV fluids and remained afebrile. Serial cardiac enzymes were done. The rub, chest pain, and shortness of breath resolved. EKGs remained unchanged. Patient will be discharged and followed as an outpatient."

    A. discharge summary
    B. physical exam
    C. admission note
    D. clinical laboratory report

REFERENCE: Abdelhak, p 107
Davis and LaCour, pp 106–107
LaTour, Eichenwald-Maki, and Oachs, p 251
Sayles, p 93

74. The information security officer is revising the policies at your rehabilitation facility for handling all patient clinical information. The best resource for checking out specific voluntary accreditation standards and guidelines is the
    A. Conditions of Participation for Rehabilitation Facilities.
    B. Medical Staff Bylaws, Rules, and Regulations.
    C. Joint Commission manual.
    D. CARF manual.

REFERENCE: Davis and LaCour, pp 26, 231, 351
LaTour, Eichenwald-Maki, and Oachs, p 903
Sayles, p 74

75. Stage I of meaningful use focused on data capture and sharing. Which of the following is included in the menu set of objectives for eligible hospitals in this stage?
    A. Use CPOE for medication orders
    B. Smoking cessation counseling for MI patients
    C. Appropriate use of HL-7 standards
    D. Establish critical pathways for complex, high-dollar cases

REFERENCE: HealthIT.hhs.gov
Davis and LaCour, pp 82–84

76. Which of the following is a secondary data source that would be used to quickly gather the health records of all juvenile patients treated for diabetes within the past 6 months?
    A. disease index
    B. patient register
    C. pediatric census sheet
    D. procedure index

REFERENCE: Bowie and Green, p 257
LaTour, Eichenwald-Maki, and Oachs, p 369
Sayles, p 436

77. As the Coding Supervisor, your job description includes working with agents who have been charged with detecting and correcting overpayments made to your hospital in the Medicare Fee for Service program. You will need to develop a professional relationship with
    A. the OIG.
    B. MEDPAR representatives.
    C. QIO physicians.
    D. recovery audit contractors.

REFERENCE: Bowie and Green, pp 129–130
LaTour, Eichenwald-Maki, and Oachs, pp 851, 944
Sayles, p 309

78. Using a template to collect data for key reports may help to prompt caregivers to document all required data elements in the patient record. This practice contributes to data
    A. timeliness.
    B. accuracy.
    C. comprehensiveness.
    D. security.

REFERENCE: Abdelhak, pp 129–130
Bowie and Green, p 258

79. In preparation for an upcoming site visit by Joint Commission, you discover that the number of delinquent records for the preceding month exceeded 50% of discharged patients. Even more alarming was the pattern you noticed in the type of delinquencies. Which of the following represents the most serious pattern of delinquencies? Fifteen percent of delinquent records show
    A. missing signatures on progress notes.
    B. missing discharge summaries.
    C. absence of SOAP format in progress notes.
    D. missing operative reports.

REFERENCE: Abdelhak, pp 122–123
Bowie and Green, pp 162–165
LaTour, Eichenwald-Maki, and Oachs, pp 266, 652–653

80. A primary focus of screen format design in a health record computer application should be to ensure that
    A. programmers develop standard screen formats for all hospitals.
    B. the user is capturing essential data elements.
    C. paper forms are easily converted to computer forms.
    D. data fields can be randomly accessed.

REFERENCE: Abdelhak, pp 114–118
LaTour, Eichenwald-Maki, and Oachs, p 51
McWay, pp 131–132
Sayles, pp 384–385

81. The new electronic system recently purchased at your physician practice allows for e-prescribing, exchange of data to a centralized immunization registry, and it allows your physicians to report on key clinical quality measures. In all likelihood, your practice has succeeded in choosing a (an)
    A. Joint Commission–approved system.
    B. Certified EHR.
    C. Functional EMR.
    D. AMA-approved product.

REFERENCE: CMS (1)
HealthIT.gov

82. Before making recommendations to the Executive Committee regarding new physicians who have applied for active membership, the Credentials Committee must query the
    A. peer review organization.
    B. National Practitioner Data Bank.
    C. risk manager.
    D. Health Plan Employer Data and Information Set.

REFERENCE: Abdelhak, pp 475–476
Bowie and Green, p 11
LaTour, Eichenwald-Maki, and Oachs, p 16

83. A qualitative analysis of OB records reveals a pattern of inconsistent data entries when comparing documentation of the same data elements captured on both the prenatal form and labor and delivery form. The characteristic of data quality that is being compromised in this case is data
   A. reliability.
   B. accessibility.
   C. legibility.
   D. completeness.

REFERENCE: Bowie and Green, p 273
LaTour, Eichenwald-Maki, and Oachs, pp 67, 383

84. Medicare rules state that the use of verbal orders should be infrequent and used only when the orders cannot be written or given electronically. In addition, verbal orders must be
   A. written within 24 hours of the patient's admission.
   B. accepted by charge nurses only.
   C. cosigned by the attending physician within 4 hours of giving the order.
   D. recorded by persons authorized by hospital regulations and procedures.

REFERENCES: LaTour, Eichenwald-Maki, and Oachs, pp 247–248
Davis and LaCour, pp 102–104

85. The lack of a discharge order may indicate that the patient left against medical advice. If this situation occurs, you would expect to see the circumstances of the leave
   A. documented in an incident report and filed in the patient's health record.
   B. reported as a potentially compensable event.
   C. reported to the Executive Committee.
   D. documented in both the progress notes and the discharge summary.

REFERENCE: LaTour, Eichenwald-Maki, and Oachs, pp 251, 910

86. Your committee is charged with developing procedures for the Health Information Services staff of a new home health agency. You recommend that the staff routinely check to verify that a summary on each patient is provided to the attending physician so that he or she can review, update, and recertify the patient as appropriate. The time frame for requiring this summary is at least every
   A. week.
   B. month.
   C. 60 days.
   D. 90 days.

REFERENCE: Abdelhak, p 138

87. You want to review one document in your facility that will spell out the documentation requirements for patient records, designate the time frame for completion by the active medical staff, and indicate the penalties for failure to comply with these record standards. Your best resource will be
   A. medical staff bylaws.
   B. quality management plan.
   C. Joint Commission accreditation manual.
   D. medical staff rules and regulations.

REFERENCE: Bowie and Green, p 21
LaTour, Eichenwald-Maki, and Oachs, p 26

88. A quarterly review reveals the following data for Springfield Hospital:

Springfield Hospital Quarterly Statistics	
Average monthly discharges	1,820
Average monthly operative procedures	458
Number of incomplete records	1,002
Number of delinquent records	590

What is the percentage of incomplete records during this quarter?

A. 55%
B. 54%
C. 33%
D. 32%

REFERENCE: Horton, p 19
Koch, p 108

89. Referring to the data in the previous question, determine the delinquent record rate for Springfield Hospital.

A. 55%
B. 32%
C. 33%
D. 54%

REFERENCE: Bowie and Green, p 84
Horton, p 108
Koch, p 108

90. Still referring to the information in the table in question 88 and the delinquent record rate shown in the answer for question 89, would the facility be out of compliance with Joint Commission standards?

A. Yes
B. No

REFERENCE: Abdelhak, p 122
Bowie and Green, p 84
Horton, p 19

91. In an acute care facility, the responsibility for educating physicians and other health care providers regarding proper documentation policies belongs to the

A. information security manager.
B. clinical data specialist.
C. health information manager.
D. risk manager.

REFERENCE: Bowie and Green, p 107
LaTour, Eichenwald-Maki, and Oachs, pp 353, 762

92. For inpatients, the first data item collected of a clinical nature is usually

A. principal diagnosis.
B. expected payer.
C. admitting diagnosis.
D. review of systems.

REFERENCE: Bowie and Green, p 135
Davis and LaCour, p 94

93. Documentation found in acute care health records should include core measure quality indicators required for compliance with Medicare's Health Care Quality Improvement Program (HCQIP). A typical indicator for patients with pneumonia is

A. beta blocker at discharge.
B. blood culture before first antibiotic received.
C. early administration of aspirin.
D. discharged on antithrombotic.

REFERENCE: CMS (2)

94. One record documentation requirement shared by BOTH acute care and emergency departments is
   A. patient's condition on discharge.
   B. time and means of arrival.
   C. advance directive.
   D. problem list.

REFERENCE: Abdelhak, pp 107, 135

95. In addition to diagnostic and therapeutic orders from the attending physician, you would expect every completed inpatient health record to contain
   A. standing orders.
   B. telephone orders.
   C. stop orders.
   D. discharge order.

REFERENCE: Abdelhak, p 105
Bowie and Green, p 167
LaTour, Eichenwald-Maki, and Oachs, p 248

96. As the Chair of the Forms Committee at your hospital, you are helping to design a template for house staff members to use while collecting information for the history and physical. When asked to explain how "review of systems" differs from "physical exam," you explain that the review of systems is used to document
   A. objective symptoms observed by the physician.
   B. past and current activities, such as smoking and drinking habits.
   C. a chronological description of patient's present condition from time of onset to present.
   D. subjective symptoms that the patient may have forgotten to mention or that may have seemed unimportant.

REFERENCE: Bowie and Green, pp 158–159

97. Skilled nursing facilities may choose to submit MDS data using RAVEN software, or software purchased commercially through a vendor, provided that the software meets
   A. Joint Commission standards.
   B. NHIN standards.
   C. HL-7 standards.
   D. CMS standards.

REFERENCE: Bowie and Green, p 269

98. Based on the following documentation in an acute care record, where would you expect this excerpt to appear?

   "The patient is alert and in no acute distress. Initial vital signs: T 98, P 102 and regular, R 20 and BP 120/69..."

   A. physical exam
   B. past medical history
   C. social history
   D. chief complaint

REFERENCE: Abdelhak, p 105
LaTour, Eichenwald-Maki, and Oachs, p 245

Answer Key for Health Data Content and Standards

ANSWER EXPLANATION

1. B Although a gross description of tissue removed may be mentioned on the operative note or discharge summary, only the pathology report will contain a microscopic description.
2. B The other answer choices represent items collected on Medicare inpatients according to UHDDS requirements. Only "cognitive patterns" represents a data item collected more typically in long-term care settings and required in the MDS.
3. C The Joint Commission requires hospitals to prohibit abbreviations that have caused confusion or problems in their handwritten form, such as "U" for unit, which can be mistaken for "O" or the number "4." Spelling out the unit is preferred.
4. A There are several core objectives for achieving meaningful use. Engaging patients and their families is one of these objectives.
5. C Factual summaries investigating unexpected facility events should not be treated as part of the patient's health information and therefore would not be recorded in the health record.
6. D Patient care plans, pharmacy consultations, and transfer summaries are likely to be found on the records of long-term care patients.
7. B Auto authentication is a policy adopted by some facilities that allow physicians to state in advance that transcribed reports should automatically be considered approved and signed (or authenticated) when the physician fails to make corrections within a preestablished time frame (e.g., "Consider it signed if I do not make changes within 7 days."). Another version of this practice is when physicians authorize the HIM department to send weekly lists of unsigned documents. The physician then signs the list in lieu of signing each individual report. Neither practice ensures that the physician has reviewed and approved each report individually.
8. A The antepartum record should include a comprehensive history and physical exam on each OB patient visit with particular attention to menstrual and reproductive history.
9. C Joint Commission and COP allow a legible copy of a recent H&P done in a doctor's office in lieu of an admission H&P as long as interval changes are documented in the record upon admission. In addition, when the patient is readmitted within 30 days for the same or a related problem, an interval history and physical exam may be completed if the original H&P is readily available.
10. A The major sources of case findings for cancer registry programs are the pathology department, the disease index, and the logs of patients treated in radiology and other outpatient departments. The number index identifies new health record numbers and the patients to whom they were assigned. The physicians' index identifies all patients treated by each doctor. The patient index links each patient treated in a facility with the health number under which the clinical information can be located.
11. A Those who make entries in the medical record are given that privilege by the medical staff. Only house staff members who are under the supervision of active staff members require countersignatures once the privilege has been granted.
12. C The statute of limitations for each state is information that is crucial in determining record retention schedules.
13. A "Decrease medication errors through CPOE systems" and "report sentinel events to the Joint Commission" are more closely associated with patient safety programs than CDI programs, and "increase patient engagement through patient portals" relates to HITECH goals for physician practices.

Answer Key for Health Data Content and Standards

ANSWER EXPLANATION

14. C "A detailed history of the patient": some reference to the patient's history may be found in the discharge summary but not a detailed history. "A note from social services or discharge planning": the attending physician records the discharge summary. "Correct codes for significant procedures": codes are usually recorded on a different form in the record.
15. D "Quality of care through the use of preestablished criteria" and "adverse effects and contraindications of drugs utilized during hospitalization" deal with issues directly linked to quality of care reviews. "Potentially compensable events" deals with risk management. Only "the overall quality of documentation in the record" points to a review aimed at evaluating the quality of documentation in the health record.
16. B Although the nursing staff, hospital administration, and the health information management professional play a role in ensuring an accurate and complete record, the major responsibility lies with the attending physician.
17. B The Minimum Data Set is a basic component of the long-term care RAI. UHDDS used in acute care; OASIS used in home health; DEEDS used in emergency departments.
18. C Unlike the acute care hospital, where most health care practitioners document separately, the patient care plan is the foundation around which patient care is organized in long-term care facilities because it contains the unique perspective of each discipline involved.
19. A Utilization review committees deal with the issues of the medical necessity of admissions and efficient utilization of facility resources. Risk management committees consider methods for reducing injury and financial loss. Joint conference committees act as a liaison between the governing body and the medical staff.
20. C The Joint Commission requires hospitals to mark the correct surgical site and to involve the patient in the marking process to help eliminate wrong site surgeries.
21. D Certified EHRs must have the functionality to allow the creation of an electronic copy of the patient's health record.
22. D The other answer choices are usually in the protocol to prevent wrong site, wrong patient, or wrong surgery. "Follow the daily surgical patient listing for the surgery suite if the patient has been sedated" would NOT be an appropriate step in making sure you have the correct identity of the patient, the correct site, or the correct surgery.
23. A Joint Commission specifies that H&Ps must be completed within 24 hours.
24. A "Require written authorization from a custodial parent before disclosing proof of the child's immunization to the school" is too stringent, while "simply document a written or oral agreement from a parent or guardian before releasing the immunization record to the school" and "allow school officials to authorize immunization disclosures on behalf of a child attending their school" are too lenient. The "Disclosure of Student Immunizations to Schools" provision of the final rule permits a covered entity to disclose proof of immunization to a school (where state law requires it prior to admitting a student) without written authorization of the parent. An agreement must still be obtained and documented, but no signature by the parent is required.
25. D The disease index is a listing in diagnostic code number order. The physician index is a listing of cases in order by physician name or number. The MPI cross-references the patient name and medical record number.
26. D The other answer choices all refer to a computer application of managing health information, but only "nurses using bedside terminals to record vital signs" deals with the clinical application of data entry into the patient's record at the time and location of service.
27. D Most facilities use bar-coded patient identification to ensure proper indexing into the imaging system.

Answer Key for Health Data Content and Standards

ANSWER EXPLANATION

28. A Pharmacy consults are required for elderly patients who typically take multiple medications. These consults review for potential drug interactions and/or discrepancies in medications given and those ordered.
29. D Data accuracy denotes that data are correct values. Data comprehensiveness denotes that all data items are included. Data granularity denotes that the attributes and values of data should be defined at the correct level of detail. Data precision denotes that data values should be just large enough to support the application of process.
30. C In accession number 13–0001/00, "13" represents the year that the patient first entered the database; "0001" indicates that this was the first case entered that year; "00" indicates that this patient has only one known neoplasm.
31. C Validity refers to the accuracy of data, while reliability refers to consistency of data. Timeliness refers to data being available within a time frame helpful to the user, and precision refers to data values that are just large enough to support the application of the process.
32. D CMS publishes both proposed and final rules for the Conditions of Participation for hospitals in the daily Federal Register.
33. D "The patient is readmitted for a similar problem within 1 year": an interval H&P can be used when a patient is readmitted for the same or related problem within 30 days. "The patient's stay is less than 24 hours" and "the patient has an uneventful course in the hospital": no matter how long the patient stays or how minor the condition, an H&P is required.
34 B The MDS is designed for use in long-term care facilities. The COP is the set of regulations that health care institutions must follow to receive Medicare reimbursement. The *Federal Register* is a daily government newspaper for publishing proposed and final rules of federal agencies.
35. D With the increasing number of health care entities implementing EHR systems, the networking of electronic information between facilities has become a reality in some areas due to the establishment of regional health information organizations. EDMS = electronic data management system. CPOE = computerized provider order entry system.
36. A The needs of the end user are always the primary concern when designing systems.
37. C The other answer choices are required items in BOTH acute and ER records.
38. D "Chief complaint" and "condition on discharge" are items that should be documented on any inpatient record. "Time and means of arrival" reflects a data item you would expect to find on ER records only.
39. A Government incentive funds for implementation of EHRs that meet meaningful use criteria expire in 2014 and the program is set to roll into sanctions on Medicare reimbursement in 2015.
40. C The needs of the user are the primary concern in forms design.
41. B In both of the following situations, a transfer summary or pertinent copies from the inpatient health record may accompany the patient, but the original record stays on the premises: "when the patient is brought to the hospital following a motor vehicle accident and, after assessment, is transferred with his health record to a trauma designated emergency department at another hospital" and "when the patient is discharged by the physician and at the time of discharge is transported to a long-term care facility with his health record".
42. A A recommendation for improvement from Joint Commission is indicated if the number of delinquent records is greater than 50% or if the percentage of records with delinquent records due to missing H&Ps exceeds 2% of the average monthly discharges. In the month of April, both of these delinquency problems are reflected. The percentage of incomplete records is not relevant.

Answer Key for Health Data Content and Standards

ANSWER EXPLANATION

43. D "Sciatica unimproved with hot pack therapy" represents the assessment statement. "Patient moving about very cautiously, appears to be in pain" represents the objective. "Adjust pain medication; begin physical therapy tomorrow" represents the plan. "Patient states low back pain is as severe as it was on admission" is the correct choice.
44. B OBRA mandates comprehensive functional assessments of long-term care residents using the Minimum Data Set for Long-Term Care.
45. A "MDS" and "UHDDS" are types of data sets for collecting data in long-term (MDS) and acute care (UHDDS) facilities. A data dictionary should include security levels for each field as well as definitions for all entities.
46. B COP requires a consultation report on patients who are not a good surgical risk as well as those with obscure diagnoses, patients whose physicians have doubts as to the best therapeutic measure to be taken, and patients for whom there is a question of criminal activity.
47. C The CDS professional may act as a reviewer and analyst, but the duties described are most representative of his/her role as an educator. The answer choice "ambassador" is a distractor.
48. D This meets both Joint Commission and COP standards.
49. B This entry is typical of a surgical procedure.
50. B The CDS professional may act as a reviewer and educator, but the duties described are most representative of his/her role as an analyst. The answer choice "ambassador" is a distractor.
51. C Joint Commission standards require the surgeon to document the history and physical examination prior to surgery.
52. D AHIMA's Position Statement supports that point-of-care documentation raises documentation standards and improves patient care. It is defined as data entry that occurs at the point and location of service.
53. D The other answer choices are examples of secondary data sources.
54. A The medical history (including chief complaint, history of present illness, past medical history, personal history, family history, and a review of systems) is provided by the patient or the most knowledgeable available source. The physical examination adds objective data to the subjective data provided by the patient. This exam begins with the physician's objective assessment of the patient's general condition.
55. D Quantitative analysis involves checking for the presence or absence of necessary reports and/or signatures, while qualitative analysis may involve checking documentation consistency, such as comparing a patient's pharmacy drug profile with the medication administration record.
56. C The other answer choices all represent common checks performed by a quantitative analysis clerk: missing reports, signatures, or patient identification. A "discrepancy between post-op diagnosis by the surgeon and pathology diagnosis by the pathologist" represents a more in-depth review dealing with the quality of the data documented.
57. B The other answer choices represent routine interpretations that are not normally considered to be consultations.
58. A "Whether a postoperative infection occurred and how it was treated" represents an appropriate job for the infection control officer. "The quality of follow-up care" represents the clinical care evaluation process, rather than the review of quality documentation. "Whether the severity of illness and/or intensity of service warranted acute level care" is a function of the utilization review program.
59. C For tracking in-house patients who have been transferred to a specialty unit, the best source of information is the registration-admission, discharge, and transfer system.
60. A Progress notes may be integrated or they may be separated, with nurses, physicians, and other health care providers writing on designated forms for each discipline.

Answer Key for Health Data Content and Standards

ANSWER EXPLANATION

61. B The Commission on Accreditation of Rehabilitation Facilities is an independent accrediting agency for rehabilitation facilities. Palliative care is most likely to be provided at a hospice.
62. D Written signatures, identifiable initials, unique computer codes, and rubber stamp signatures may all be allowed as legitimate means of authenticating an entry. However, the use of codes and stamped signatures MUST be confined to the owners and they are never to be used by anyone else.
63. B Regional health information organizations are intended to support health information exchange within a geographic region.
64. A Data Elements for Emergency Departments—recommended data set for hospital-based emergency departments; Uniform Hospital Data Set—required data set for acute care hospitals; Minimum Data Set—required data set for long-term care facilities; ORYX—an initiative of Joint Commission whereby five core measures are implemented to improve safety and quality of health care.
65. D Although Joint Commission, CMS, and state laws may include standards for verbal orders, the specific information regarding which employees have been given authority to transcribe verbal orders in your facility should be located in your hospital's bylaws, rules, and regulations.
66. C "Peer review" typically involves quality of care issues rather than quality of documentation issues. "Legal analysis" ensures that the record entries would be acceptable in a court of law.
67. D "Considered unnecessary by most health care facilities" is incorrect; advantages of accreditation are numerous and include financial and legal incentives. "Required for state licensure in all states" is incorrect because state licensure is required for accreditation but not the reverse. "Conducted in each facility annually" is incorrect because Joint Commission conducts unannounced on-site surveys approximately every 3 years.
68. A Although CDI programs differ in hierarchy, MOST CDS professionals report to the HIM Department, according to the Foundation report.
69. B In a POMR, the database contains the history and physical; the problem list includes titles, numbers, and dates of problems and serves as a table of contents of the record; the initial plan describes diagnostic, therapeutic, and patient education plans; and the progress notes document the progress of the patient throughout the episode of care, summarized in a discharge summary or transfer note at the end of the stay.
70. C The accession register is a permanent log of all the cases entered into the database. Each number assigned is preceded by the accession year, making it easy to assess annual workloads.
71. D The American Recovery and Reinvestment Act was signed into law in 2009, and included significant funding for health information technology.
72. B A final progress note may substitute for a discharge summary in the following cases: patients who are hospitalized less than 48 hours with problems of a minor nature, normal newborns, and uncomplicated obstetrical deliveries. The patient with COPD does not qualify because of the nature of the problem and the length of stay. The record for Baby Boy Hiltz's mother describes a complicated delivery, and the record for Baby Boy Doe cites a severely ill patient rather than one with a minor problem.
73. A The excerpt clearly indicates an overall summary of the patient's course in the hospital, which is a common element of the discharge summary.
74. D The manual published by the Commission on Accreditation of Rehabilitation Facilities will have the most specific and comprehensive standards for a rehabilitation facility.
75. A See all objectives for Stage I of meaningful use on the HealthIT.hhs.gov website.

Answer Key for Health Data Content and Standards

ANSWER EXPLANATION

76. A The disease index is compiled as a result of abstracting patient code numbers into a computer database, allowing a variety of reports to be generated.
77. D The RAC program is mandated to find and correct improper Medicare payments paid to health care providers participating in the Medicare reimbursement program. OIG (Office of Inspector General); MEDPAR (Medicare Provider Analysis and Review); QIO (Quality Improvement Organization).
78. C Data comprehensiveness refers specifically to the presence of all required data elements.
79. D "Missing signatures on progress notes" and "missing discharge summaries": both signature omissions and discharge summary reports can be captured after discharge, but history and physicals should be on the chart within 24 hours of the patient's admission. "Absence of SOAP format in progress notes": the SOAP format is not a requirement of Joint Commission. "Missing operative reports": institutions are given a Type I recommendation when 2% of delinquent records are due to missing history and physicals or operative reports.
80. B Both paper-based and computer-based records share similar forms and view design considerations. Among these are the selection and sequencing of essential data items.
81. B The system functionality outlined demonstrates meaningful use standards required for certified EHRs.
82. B With the passage of the Health Care Quality Improvement Act of 1986, the NPDB was established. Hospitals are required to query the data bank before granting clinical privileges to physicians.
83. A Data reliability implies that data are consistent no matter how many times the same data are collected and entered into the system. Accessibility implies that data are available to authorized people when and where needed. Legibility implies data that are readable. Completeness implies that all required data are present in the information system.
84. D Only persons designated by hospital policies and procedures and state and federal law are to accept verbal orders.
85. D Incident reports are written accounts of unusual events that have an adverse effect on a patient, employee, or facility visitor and should never be filed with the patient's record. PCEs are occurrences that could result in financial liability at some future time. A patient leaving AMA does not in itself suggest a PCE. It is not typical to report AMAs to the Executive Committee. Documenting the event is crucial in protecting the legal interests of the health care team and facility.
86. C This 60-day time frame is often referred to as the patient's certification period. Recertification can continue every 62 days until the patient is discharged from home health services.
87. D Although the medical staff bylaws reflect general principles and policies of the medical staff, the rules and regulations outline the details for implementing these principles, including the process and time frames for completing records, and the penalties for failure to comply.
88. A Using the basic rate formula, calculate as follows:
Incomplete records × 100 divided by average monthly discharges, or
$$\frac{1{,}002 \times 100}{1820} = 55.1\%$$
89. B Using the basic rate formula, calculate as follows:
Delinquent records × 100 divided by average monthly discharges, or
$$\frac{590 \times 100}{1820} = 32.4\%$$

Answer Key for Health Data Content and Standards

ANSWER EXPLANATION

90. B Using the basic rate formula, the delinquent record rate is 32%. Even though the delinquent record rate is 32%, this does not exceed the Joint Commission requirement to keep this statistic below 50%.
91. C Although all of the positions listed have an interest in proper documentation in an acute care facility, the health information manager is in the best position to keep abreast of documentation standards and advocate change where poor documentation patterns exist.
92. C Clinical data include all health care information collected during a patient's episode of care. During the registration or intake process, the admitting diagnosis, provided by the attending physician, is entered on the face sheet. If the patient is admitted through the ED, the chief complaint listed on the ED record is usually the first clinical data collected. The principal diagnosis is often not known until after diagnostic tests are conducted. Demographic data are not clinical in nature. The review of systems is collected during the history and physical, which is typically done after admission to the hospital.
93 B "Beta blocker at discharge" and "early administration of aspirin" represent quality indicators for patients with acute myocardial infarction; "discharged on antithrombotic" represents a quality indicator for stroke patients.
94. A Time and means of arrival is required on ED records only. Evidence of known advance directive is required on inpatient records only. Problem list is required on ambulatory records by the third visit.
95. D Although many patient health records may feasibly contain all of the orders listed, only the discharge order is required to document the formal release of a patient from the facility. Absence of a discharge order would indicate that the patient left against medical advice and this event should be thoroughly documented as well.
96. D "Objective symptoms observed by the physician" refers to the Physical Exam. "Past and current activities" refers to the Social History. "A chronological description of patient's present condition from time of onset to present" refers to the History of Present Illness.
97. D MDS data are reported directly to the Centers for Medicare and Medicaid Services and must conform to agency standards.
98. A The other answer choices represent components of the medical history as supplied by the patient, while the physical exam is an entry obtained through objective observation and measurement made by the provider.

REFERENCES

AHIMA (1) "Best Practices in the Art and Science of Clinical Documentation Improvement," *Journal of AHIMA* 86, no. 7 (July 2015): 46–50. Chicago: American Health Information Management Association (AHIMA).

AHIMA (2) "HITECH Frequently Asked Privacy, Security Questions: Part 3," Rose, Angela Dinh; Greene, Adam H., *Journal of AHIMA* 88, no. 3 (March 2014): 42–44.

Abdelhak, M. & Hanken, M.A., (2016). *Health information: Management of a strategic resource* (5th ed.). Philadelphia: Saunders, an imprint of Elsevier.

Bowie, M. J. and Green, M. A. (2016). *Essentials of health information management: Principles and practices* (3rd ed.). Clifton Park, NY: Cengage Learning.

CMS (1) Meaningful use references from CMS https://www.cms.gov/Regulations-and-Guidance/Legislation/EHRIncentivePrograms/downloads/MU_Stage1_ReqOverview.pdf

CMS (2). Fiscal Year 2009 Quality Measure Reporting for 2010 Payment Update https://www.cms.gov/HospitalQualityInits/downloads/HospitalRHQDAPU200808.pdf

http://www.cms.gov/Regulations-and-Guidance/Legislation/EHRIncentivePrograms/Meaningful_Use.html

http://www.cms.gov/eHealth/ListServ_Stage2_EngagingPatients.html

Davis and LaCour. (2014). *Health information technology* (3rd ed.). Maryland, MO: Elsevier (Saunders).

Health IT.gov

http://www.healthit.gov/policy-researchers-implementers/meaningful-use-regulations

Horton, L. (2011) *Calculating and reporting healthcare statistics* (4th ed.) Chicago: American Health Information Management Association (AHIMA).

Joint Commission. National Patient Safety Goals www.jointcommission.org

http://www.jointcommission.org/assets/1/6/2015_HAP_NPSG_ER.pdf

Koch, G. (2015). *Basic allied health statistics and analysis* (4th ed.). Clifton Park, NY: Cengage Learning.

LaTour, Eichenwald-Maki (2013). *Health information management: Concepts, principles and practice* (4th ed.). Chicago: American Health Information Management Association (AHIMA).

McWay, D. C. (2014). *Today's health information management, an integrated approach* (2nd ed.). Clifton Park, NY: Cengage Learning.

Sayles, N. (2013). *Health information management technology: An applied approach* (4th ed.). Chicago: American Health Information Management Association (AHIMA).

RHIA AND RHIT COMPETENCIES BY QUESTION FOR HEALTH DATA													
Question	RHIA Domain Competencies						RHIT Domain Competencies						
	1	2	3	4	5		1	2	3	4	5	6	7
1	X						X						
2	X						X						
3	X								X				
4			X							X			
5		X										X	
6	X						X						
7			X						X				
8	X						X						
9	X								X				
10	X						X						
11		X										X	
12	X											X	
13	X								X				
14	X						X						
15	X						X						
16	X								X				
17	X						X						
18	X						X						
19			X						X				
20	X								X				
21			X						X				
22	X								X				
23	X						X						
24		X										X	
25	X						X						
26			X							X			
27			X							X			
28	X						X						
29			X						X				
30	X						X						
31			X							X			
32	X								X				
33	X								X				
34	X									X			
35			X							X			
36	X								X				
37	X						X						
38	X						X						
39	X								X				
40	X								X				
41		X										X	
42	X								X				
43	X						X						
44	X								X				
45	X									X			
46	X								X				
47	X								X				
48	X								X				
49	X						X						
50	X								X				

RHIA AND RHIT COMPETENCIES BY QUESTION FOR HEALTH DATA												
Question	RHIA Domain Competencies					RHIT Domain Competencies						
	1	2	3	4	5	1	2	3	4	5	6	7
51	X							X				
52	X							X				
53	X					X						
54			X						X			
55	X							X				
56	X							X				
57	X							X				
58	X							X				
59			X						X			
60	X					X						
61	X					X						
62	X							X				
63			X						X			
64	X					X						
65	X					X						
66	X					X						
67	X					X						
68					X						X	
69	X					X						
70	X					X						
71					X			X				
72	X					X		X				
73	X					X						
74	X							X				
75			X					X				
76	X					X						
77	X							X				
78	X					X		X				
79	X							X				
80	X		X						X			
81			X					X	X			
82					X			X				
83	X							X				
84	X							X				
85	X					X		X				
86	X							X				
87	X				X	X						
88	X							X				
89	X							X				
90	X							X				
91	X				X	X						
92	X					X						
93	X							X				
94	X					X						
95	X					X						
96	X					X						
97			X					X	X			
98	X					X						

IV. Information Retention and Access

Marjorie H. McNeill, PhD, RHIA, CCS, FAHIMA

1. Which one of the following actions would NOT be included in the professional obligations of the health information practitioner that lead to responsible handling of patient health information?
   A. Educate consumers about their rights and responsibilities regarding the use of their personal health information.
   B. Extend privacy and security principles into all aspects of the data use, access, and control program adopted in the organization.
   C. Honor the patient-centric direction of the national agenda.
   D. Take a compromising position toward optimal interpretation of nonspecific regulations and laws.

REFERENCE: LaTour, Eichenwald-Maki, and Oachs, pp 346–350

2. If there is more than one patient with the identical last name, first name, and middle initial, the master patient index entries are then arranged according to the
   A. date of birth.
   B. date of admission.
   C. social security number.
   D. mother's maiden name.

REFERENCE: Sayles, p 332

3. Which one of the following is NOT a step in developing a health record retention schedule?
   A. conducting an inventory of the facility's records
   B. determining the format and location of storage
   C. assigning all records the same retention period
   D. destroying records that are no longer needed

REFERENCE: Abdelhak, pp 164–167, 225
Bowie and Green, pp 102–106
LaTour, Eichenwald-Maki, and Oachs, pp 274–279
McWay, pp 136–139
Sayles, pp 345–346, 364, 788–789

4. What type of filing system is being used if records are filed in the following order: 12-23-75, 12-34-29, 12-35-71, 13-42-14, and 14-32-79?
   A. terminal digit
   B. straight numeric
   C. social security number
   D. middle digit

REFERENCE: Bowie and Green, pp 222–225, 228–230
LaTour, Eichenwald-Maki, and Oachs, pp 270–271
Sayles, p 333

5. If there are 150,000 records and the HIM Department receives 3,545 requests for records within a given period of time, what is the request rate?
   A. 2.4%
   B. 3.5%
   C. 4.6%
   D. 5.1%

REFERENCE: LaTour, Eichenwald-Maki, and Oachs, p 484
Math Calculation
McWay, p 204

6. Which of the following is NOT an advantage of a centralized filing system?
   A. There is less transportation time and effort when a facility operates from several sites.
   B. There is less duplication of effort to create, maintain, and store records.
   C. Record control and security are easier to maintain.
   D. There is decreased cost in space and equipment.

REFERENCE: Bowie and Green, pp 230–232
Sayles, p 334

7. In a terminal digit filing system, what would be the record number immediately in front of record number 01-06-26?
   A. 00-06-26
   B. 02-06-26
   C. 03-06-26
   D. 99-99-25

REFERENCE: Abdelhak, p 152
Bowie and Green, pp 228–230
LaTour, Eichenwald-Maki, and Oachs, pp 270–271
Sayles, p 333

8. The HIM Department at General Hospital has been experiencing an average 30-minute delay in the retrieval of records requested by the Emergency Department. Which of the following corrective actions would be most effective in reducing the delay in retrieval of requested records?
   A. Offer a prize to the employee who locates the requested records first.
   B. Review and possibly reengineer the retrieval process to decrease retrieval time.
   C. Allow the requesters to retrieve the record themselves.
   D. Increase file area staff to include one additional file clerk devoted to pulling records for the emergency room.

REFERENCE: LaTour, Eichenwald-Maki, and Oachs, pp 273–274
Sayles and Trawick, pp 90, 147

9. Which one of the following is NOT an advantage of a computerized master patient index?
   A. It allows access to data alphabetically, phonetically, or by date of birth, social security number, medical record, or billing number.
   B. It solves most space and retrieval problems.
   C. It provides other departments with immediate access to the information maintained in the master patient index.
   D. Duplication of patient registration can never occur.

REFERENCE: Bowie and Green, pp 255–256
LaTour, Eichenwald-Maki, and Oachs, pp 271–272
Sayles, pp 324–326

10. Color coding of record folders is used to assist in the control of
   A. record tracking.
   B. loose reports.
   C. record completion.
   D. misfiles.

REFERENCE: Bowie and Green, pp 236–238
LaTour, Eichenwald-Maki, and Oachs, p 274
Sayles, p 340

11. Information found in which of the following would not be considered secondary data?
    A. disease index
    B. implant registry
    C. health record
    D. National Practitioner Data

REFERENCE: Bowie and Green, pp 96–97
LaTour, Eichenwald-Maki, and Oachs, p 368
McWay, p 139
Sayles, p 433

12. Under the Patient Self-Determination Act of 1990, evidence of advance directives
    A. are required to be documented in the health record.
    B. are not required to be documented in the health record.
    C. require a doctor's approval.
    D. must be prepared by an attorney.

REFERENCE: Abdelhak, p 12
Bowie and Green, p 139
LaTour, Eichenwald-Maki, and Oachs, p 244
McWay, p 77
Sayles, p 104

13. A new Health Information Department has purchased 200 units of 6-shelf files and plans to implement a terminal digit filing system. How many shelves should be allocated to each primary number?
    A. 6
    B. 8
    C. 10
    D. 12

REFERENCE: LaTour, Eichenwald-Maki, and Oachs, p 274
Math Calculation

14. A 200-bed acute care hospital currently has 15 years of paper health records and filing space is limited. What action should be taken?
    A. Return inactive records to each individual patient.
    B. Destroy records of all deceased patients.
    C. Destroy inactive records that exceed the statute of limitations.
    D. Maintain the records indefinitely in hard copy.

REFERENCE: Abdelhak, p 165
Bowie and Green, p 101
LaTour, Eichenwald-Maki, and Oachs, p 276
McWay, pp 136–139

15. Which filing system would provide the most convenient method for the record retrieval of 200 patients consecutively admitted to the hospital?
    A. terminal digit
    B. unit
    C. straight numeric
    D. serial unit

REFERENCE: Bowie and Green, p 228
LaTour, Eichenwald-Maki, and Oachs, p 270

16. What is the chief criterion for determining record inactivity?
    A. Medicare's definition of inactivity
    B. amount of space available for storage of newer records
    C. efficiency of microfilming
    D. preference of the medical staff

REFERENCE: Bowie and Green, pp 101–102
LaTour, Eichenwald-Maki, and Oachs, p 273

17. Out of 2,543 records requested from the HIM Department, 2,375 were located. What is the filing accuracy rate?
    A. 6.61%
    B. 75.33%
    C. 89.01%
    D. 93.39%

REFERENCE: McWay, p 204
Math Calculation
Sayles, pp 358–359

18. Which set of records filed consecutively on a shelf displays terminal digit filing order?
    A. 00-79-99, 00-79-01, 99-78-99
    B. 57-78-00, 57-78-01, 56-78-99
    C. 99-05-26, 01-06-26, 49-04-02
    D. 55-55-55, 33-33-33, 44-44-44

REFERENCE: Bowie and Green, pp 228–229
LaTour, Eichenwald-Maki, and Oachs, pp 270–271
Sayles, p 333

19. In the master patient index, which is filed by last name, Jill Thomas-Jones would be
    A. J-I-L-L-T-H-O-M-A-S-J-O-N-E-S
    B. T-H-O-M-A-S-J-O-N-E-S, J-I-L-L
    C. T-H-O-M-A-S, J-I-L-L-J-O-N-E-S
    D. J-O-N-E-S, J-I-L-L-T-H-O-M-A-S

REFERENCE: Bowie and Green, pp 226–227
Sayles, p 329

20. According to terminal digit filing, what would be the number of the record immediately after record number 99-99-30?
    A. 99-98-30
    B. 00-00-31
    C. 01-00-31
    D. 99-99-31

REFERENCE: Bowie and Green, pp 228–229
LaTour, Eichenwald-Maki, and Oachs, pp 270–271
Sayles, p 333

21. How many years does the CMS regulations require that health records be maintained? Medicare's Conditions of Participation for Hospitals requires that patient health records be retained for at least _______ years unless a longer period is required by state or local laws.
    A. 3
    B. 5
    C. 7
    D. 10

REFERENCE: Bowie and Green, p 102
LaTour, Eichenwald-Maki, and Oachs, p 275

22. Your state regulations require health records to be kept for a statute of limitations period of 7 years. Federal law requires records to be retained for 5 years. The minimum retention period for health records in your facility should be
    A. 5 years.
    B. 7 years.
    C. 10 years.
    D. either 5 or 7 years, as determined by the facility.

REFERENCE: Abdelhak, p 164
LaTour, Eichenwald-Maki, and Oachs, p 275
McWay, p 136
Sayles, p 345

23. Which of the following technologies works best with automated record-tracking systems to speed the data entry process?
    A. discharge lists
    B. bar codes
    C. compressible filing units
    D. computerized chart-out slips

REFERENCE: Abdelhak, pp 309–310
Bowie and Green, p 242
LaTour, Eichenwald-Maki, and Oachs, p 88
Sayles, p 874

24. A HIM Department, currently using 2,540 linear filing inches to store records, plans to purchase new open-shelf filing units. Each of the shelves in a new 6-shelf unit measures 36 linear filing inches. It is estimated that an additional 400 filing inches should be planned for to allow for 5-year expansion needs. How many new file shelving units should be purchased?
    A. 11
    B. 12
    C. 13
    D. 14

REFERENCE: Bowie and Green, p 235
LaTour, Eichenwald-Maki, and Oachs, p 274
McWay, p 135
Sayles, pp 337–339

25. Microfilmed records are considered
    A. inadmissible evidence.
    B. never admissible as hearsay evidence.
    C. acceptable as courtroom evidence.
    D. not admissible as secondary evidence.

REFERENCE: Sayles, p 341

26. A research request has been received by the HIM Department from the Quality Improvement Committee. The Committee plans to review the records of all patients who were admitted with CHF in the month of January 2016. Which of the following indices would be the best source in locating the needed records?
    A. master patient index
    B. physician index
    C. disease index
    D. operation index

REFERENCE: Bowie and Green, p 257
LaTour, Eichenwald-Maki, and Oachs, p 370
McWay, p 140
Sayles, pp 436–337

27. How many inches are recommended for aisles between file units when using stationary open-shelf files?
    A. 24
    B. 36
    C. 60
    D. 72

REFERENCE: LaTour, Eichenwald-Maki, and Oachs, p 274

28. Which of the following is NOT a mandatory disclosure according to the HIPAA Privacy Rule?
    A. emergencies concerning public health
    B. quality assurance reviews by authorized authorities
    C. instances concerning victims of domestic violence
    D. reporting of traffic fatalities

REFERENCE: McWay, p 74

29. Which of the following should NOT be included in the documentation of record destruction?
    A. statement that records were destroyed in the normal course of business
    B. method of destruction
    C. signature of the individuals supervising and witnessing the destruction
    D. dates not covered in destruction

REFERENCE: AHIMA Practice Brief (1)
Bowie and Green, pp 204–205
LaTour, Eichenwald-Maki, and Oachs, p 279
McWay, p 139
Sayles, p 347

30. If the HIM Department has purchased 100 units of 8-shelf files and plans to use the terminal digit filing system, how many shelves should be allocated to each primary number?
    A. 8
    B. 10
    C. 12
    D. 100

REFERENCE: Math Calculation

31. Which of the following is NOT a consideration when implementing a disaster plan?
    A. Include disaster training in staff orientation.
    B. Establish a plan for conducting drills.
    C. Provide staff with tools needed to implement the plan.
    D. Test the disaster plan only once.

REFERENCE: LaTour, Eichenwald-Maki, and Oachs, p 292
McWay, pp 326–328

32. Which of the following lists is in correct alphabetical order?
    A. Ferlazzo, Joshua; Ferlazzo, Joshua P.; Ferlazzo, Joshua Philip; Ferlazzo, J.
    B. Ferlazzo, J.; Ferlazzo, Joshua; Ferlazzo, Joshua P.; Ferlazzo, Joshua Philip
    C. Ferlazzo, Joshua; Ferlazzo, Joshua P.; Ferlazzo, J.; Ferlazzo, Joshua Philip
    D. Ferlazzo, Joshua A.; Ferlazzo, B.; Ferlazzo, Joshua; Ferlazzo, Joshua Phillip

REFERENCE: Bowie and Green, p 226
Sayles, p 332

33. Mary Schnering was admitted to Community Hospital on 10/3/15 and assigned a record number of 54-47-53. The patient was later admitted on 1/14/16 and assigned the number 54-88-42. Both records were eventually filed under 54-88-42. What type of numbering/filing system is being used at Community Hospital?
    A. serial-unit
    B. serial
    C. unit
    D. terminal digit

REFERENCE: Bowie and Green, p 225
LaTour, Eichenwald-Maki, and Oachs, p 270
McWay, p 135
Sayles, p 328

34. Capital Health Center is moving to a new facility in December 2016. The CEO is projecting a conversion to an electronic health record system by then. This new facility will not include space for filing of paper-based health records. Which of the following items would not be considered when planning this conversion?
    A. changing role of department functions and work flow
    B. challenges of maintaining records that are partially paper and partially electronic
    C. whether to scan older paper records
    D. relationship with the microfilm vendor

REFERENCE: LaTour, Eichenwald-Maki, and Oachs, pp 289–290

35. What microform should the HIM practitioner select if the records must be unitized and color-coded for filing purposes?
    A. roll microfilm
    B. cartridge
    C. jacket microfilm
    D. cassette

REFERENCE: LaTour, Eichenwald-Maki, and Oachs, pp 276–277

36. What is the business of buying and selling information as a commodity?
    A. information brokering
    B. e-health consumerism
    C. telehealth
    D. competitive data

REFERENCE: McWay, p 311

37. At Community Hospital the average admission will create a file that will take up 0.25 inch of file space. Each new ER record requires 0.125 inch of file space. Approximately 25,000 new patients are admitted per year and 15,000 ER patients are treated per year. The shelving cost is $1.05 per filing inch. How much money should be allocated for storage space in next year's budget?
    A. $8,531.25
    B. $8,125.00
    C. $853.25
    D. $1,875.00

REFERENCE: LaTour, Eichenwald-Maki, and Oachs, p 274
Math Calculation
Sayles, pp 337–339

38. On his 12/23/15 admission to Metropolitan Hospital, David Robinson was assigned the medical record number 07-23-38. The previous record number assigned to Mr. Robinson during a 9/1/15 admission was 07-10-47. In a serial numbering/filing system, how would these records be filed?
   A. Both records are combined under 07-10-47.
   B. Both records are combined under 07-23-38.
   C. Each admission is filed under its own number.
   D. Previous records are brought forward and filed under the latest number issued.

REFERENCE: Bowie and Green, p 223
LaTour, Eichenwald-Maki, and Oachs, p 270
McWay, p 135
Sayles, pp 327–328

39. The same patient was admitted on three different occasions and assigned a new medical record number each time. In order to correct this situation in a unit numbering system, which medical record number should be used given the following information?

Admitted 5/04/15	Patty Miller	23-33-56
Admitted 6/05/15	P. J. Miller	25-56-88
Admitted 9/27/15	Patricia Miller	27-12-12

   A. Void the first and last numbers and file all admissions under 25-56-88.
   B. Delete all previous numbers and assign a completely new number.
   C. Void the first two numbers and file all admissions under 27-12-12.
   D. Void the last two numbers and file all admissions under 23-33-56.

REFERENCE: Bowie and Green, p 224
LaTour, Eichenwald-Maki, and Oachs, p 270
McWay, p 135
Sayles, p 328

40. The health care providers in an acute care hospital require access to paper health records 24 hours a day, 7 days a week. To secure the area and continue to maintain accessibility, the Director of the HIM Department should
   A. staff the department with personnel 24 hours a day.
   B. be on call every evening and weekends for emergency requests.
   C. train security guards to retrieve records after the department closes.
   D. arrange for records to be retrieved at 7:00 AM every morning.

REFERENCE: Bowie and Green, p 244
LaTour, Eichenwald-Maki, and Oachs, p 723

41. As a prerequisite in the implementation of an electronic health record, what process would facilitate automatic indexing?
   A. redesigning forms to include bar codes
   B. removing portions of the patient record that will not be scanned
   C. converting all microfilm to optical disk format
   D. scanning only emergency room records initially

REFERENCE: LaTour, Eichenwald-Maki, and Oachs, p 268
McWay, p 313
Sayles, p 874

42. Which of the following is NOT a safety hazard in the HIM Department?
    A. tightly packed open-shelf files
    B. heavy objects placed in top file drawers
    C. stepladders that are fully open and locked in place
    D. plastic wastebasket for trash

REFERENCE: Abdelhak, p 670
McWay, p 373

43. A HIM Department wants to buy new open-shelf filing units for its file expansion. Each of the shelves in a new 6-shelf unit measures 33 linear filing inches. There will be an estimated 1,000 records to file. The average record is 1-inch thick. How many filing units should be purchased?
    A. 2
    B. 4
    C. 6
    D. 8

REFERENCE: Bowie and Green, p 235
LaTour, Eichenwald-Maki, and Oachs, p 274
Sayles, pp 337–339

44. Which of the following microform types is the least expensive to prepare and results in the greatest storage density?
    A. microfilm jackets
    B. roll microfilm
    C. microfiche
    D. ultrafiche

REFERENCE: Bowie and Green, pp 103–104
LaTour, Eichenwald-Maki, and Oachs, pp 276–277
Sayles, pp 340–341

45. Brian Hills was discharged from the hospital after a 3-day hospitalization and instructed to return to the outpatient department for follow-up care. On his first visit as an outpatient, a new record was created and he was assigned a new record number. Following completion of the outpatient appointment, his outpatient record is filed permanently in the outpatient department. What is the filing system used in this situation?
    A. decentralized
    B. unit record
    C. centralized
    D. terminal digit

REFERENCE: Bowie and Green, pp 230–232
LaTour, Eichenwald-Maki, and Oachs, p 221

46. The master patient index must, at a minimum, include sufficient information to
    A. summarize the patient's medical history.
    B. list all physicians who have ever treated the patient.
    C. uniquely identify the patient.
    D. justify the patient's hospital bill.

REFERENCE: Abdelhak, p 153
Bowie and Green, pp 252–253
LaTour, Eichenwald-Maki, and Oachs, pp 271–272
McWay, pp 139–140
Sayles, pp 322, 436

47. Dr. Gray has applied for medical staff privileges at your hospital. What database would you research to determine if he has been denied medical staff privileges at another hospital?
    A. National Practitioner Data Bank
    B. Healthcare Integrity and Protection Data Bank
    C. MEDPAR file
    D. State Administrative Data Bank

REFERENCE: Abdelhak, p 476
Bowie and Green, p 11
LaTour, Eichenwald-Maki, and Oachs, p 330
Sayles, p 657

48. It is recommended that all but which of the following information should be permanently retained in some format, even when the remainder of the health record is destroyed?
    A. discharge summaries
    B. physician names
    C. nursing notes
    D. dates of admission, discharge, and encounters

REFERENCE: Abdelhak, p 165

49. A health information manager develops a formal plan or record retention schedule for the automatic transfer of records to inactive storage and potential destruction based on all but which one of the following factors?
    A. statute of limitations
    B. volume of research
    C. readmission rate
    D. department staffing

REFERENCE: Bowie and Green, pp 101–102
LaTour, Eichenwald-Maki, and Oachs, pp 276–279
McWay, pp 136–139
Sayles, p 364

50. Which of the following is NOT a benefit of the electronic document management system in the HIM Department?
    A. online availability of information
    B. multiuser simultaneous access
    C. decreased use of computer technology
    D. system security and confidentiality

REFERENCE: Bowie and Green, pp 117–118
McWay, p 312
Sayles, pp 361–364

51. Which one of the following is an advantage of straight numeric filing over terminal digit filing?
    A. All sections of the file expand uniformly.
    B. The training period is short.
    C. Work can be evenly distributed, causing accountability for accuracy in each of the 100 sections.
    D. Inactive records can be purged evenly.

REFERENCE: Bowie and Green, p 228
LaTour, Eichenwald-Maki, and Oachs, p 270
Sayles, p 333

52. Which one of the following is NOT an electronic document management system component?
    A. scanner
    B. file server
    C. laser printer
    D. reader-printer

REFERENCE: Sayles and Trawick, pp 145–147

53. Which of the following items is the Health Information Manager primarily concerned with when purchasing file guides?
    A. cost and color
    B. durability and visibility
    C. cost and visibility
    D. color and durability

REFERENCE: Bowie and Green, pp 235–236

54. Palm Beach Healthcare Center has been in operation for 13 years. It has 6,000 admissions per year. The facility has expanded and will allow for 200 more admissions per year from now on. There are 2,500 linear feet of filing space available and half is being used. The facility expects a 30% readmission rate. If a unit numbering/filing system is used, how many file folders will be needed for the next year?
    A. 1,800
    B. 1,860
    C. 4,340
    D. 6,200

REFERENCE: Math Calculation

55. As Director of the HIM Department you have become aware of instances of unauthorized access to the record file area. After considering several options to limit or restrict access to the area, you decide to
    A. install a computerized access control panel.
    B. hire a security guard to monitor entrance to the file area.
    C. convert from a terminal digit filing system to serial unit filing.
    D. utilize a sign-in and sign-out log for admittance to the file area.

REFERENCE: Abdelhak, p 160
LaTour, Eichenwald-Maki, and Oachs, p 133
McWay, p 265
Sayles and Trawick, p 218

56. Which one of the following is NOT a technical security control employed by electronic health record systems?
    A. audit trails
    B. data encryption protocols
    C. user-based access controls
    D. automatic logon

REFERENCE: Sayles, pp 1056–1058
Sayles and Trawick, pp 214–217

57. The Chief of the Medical Staff requests a report on the number of coronary artery bypass grafts performed by a particular physician in April of the previous year. Where would the health information manager look for this information?
    A. patient register
    B. disease index
    C. operation index
    D. birth defects register

REFERENCE: Bowie and Green, p 257
LaTour, Eichenwald-Maki, and Oachs, p 369
McWay, p 140
Sayles, p 437

58. A major consideration in a hospital or facility closure is to
    A. notify all patients to pick up their original records by the date of closure.
    B. seek approval for destruction of all records with a last date of treatment over 3 years ago.
    C. ensure that authorized parties have access to the information as provided by law.
    D. arrange for donating the records to an HIA/HIT education program for student use.

REFERENCE: Bowie and Green, pp 105–106
LaTour, Eichenwald-Maki, and Oachs, p 276
McWay, p 138

59. What follow-up rate does the American College of Surgeons mandate for all cancer cases to meet approval requirements as a cancer program?
    A. 70%
    B. 80%
    C. 90%
    D. 100%

REFERENCE: American College of Surgeons' Cancer Program Manual

60. In negotiating a contract with a commercial storage company for storage of inactive records, what would be the most important issue to clarify in writing?
    A. who completes the list of what records are to be stored
    B. what are the billing terms
    C. who will purge inactive files for transfer
    D. confidentiality policies and liability concerns

REFERENCE: Bowie and Green, p 103
Sayles and Trawick, pp 82–85

61. Which index is used by the HIM department to link the patient's name and number in relation to access and retention of the patient record?
    A. physician index
    B. disease index
    C. master patient index
    D. operation index

REFERENCE: Abdelhak, p 153
LaTour, Eichenwald-Maki, and Oachs, pp 271–272
McWay, p 139
Sayles, p 436

62. Unless state or federal laws require longer time periods, AHIMA recommends that patient health information for minors be retained for at least how long?
    A. age of majority plus statute of limitation
    B. 10 years after the most recent encounter
    C. 10 years after the age of majority
    D. permanently

REFERENCE: AHIMA Practice Brief (1) "Retention and Destruction of Health Information"
Bowie and Green, p 102
LaTour, Eichenwald-Maki, and Oachs, pp 278, 285
McWay, p 136
Sayles, pp 346, 789

63. A health care facility has made a decision to destroy computerized data. AHIMA recommends which one of the following as the preferred method of destruction for computerized data?
    A. overwriting data with a series of characters
    B. disk reformatting
    C. magnetic degaussing
    D. overwriting the backup tapes

REFERENCE: AHIMA Practice Brief (1)
Sayles, pp 346–347, 1060

64. Which of the following statements would be found in the laboratory report section of the health record?
    A. BUN reported as 20 mg
    B. Morphine sulfate gr. 1/4 q.4h. for pain
    C. IV sodium Pentothal 1% started at 9:05 AM
    D. TPR recorded q.h. for 12 hours

REFERENCE: Abdelhak, p 109
Bowie and Green, pp 186–187
LaTour, Eichenwald-Maki, and Oachs, p 250
Sayles, pp 85–86

65. Which of the following is a disadvantage of terminal digit filing as compared to straight numeric filing?
    A. File personnel are crowded in the highest numbers.
    B. Inactive records are pulled from one common area.
    C. The training period is slightly longer.
    D. Files expand at the end of the number series, requiring back shifting.

REFERENCE: Bowie and Green, pp 229–230
Sayles, p 333

66. What component of the history and physical examination includes an inventory designed to uncover current or past subjective symptoms?
    A. past medical history
    B. social and personal history
    C. chief complaint
    D. review of systems

REFERENCE: LaTour, Eichenwald-Maki, and Oachs, p 246

67. Electronic health record built-in tools that can make data capture easier include all but which one of the following?
    A. data dictionaries
    B. flow process charts
    C. automated quality measures
    D. clinical decision support systems

REFERENCE: LaTour, Eichenwald-Maki, and Oachs, p 172

68. If the department staff are having trouble locating the terminal digit sections quickly, the supervisor could add more
    A. outguides.
    B. file guides.
    C. requisitions.
    D. staff.

REFERENCE: Bowie and Green, p 240

69. The HIM Department receives a request for a certified copy of a birth certificate on a patient born in the hospital 30 years ago. The Department should
    A. issue a copy of the birth certificate from the patient's record.
    B. direct the request to the state's office of vital records.
    C. direct the request to the attending physician.
    D. issue a copy of the newborn's record.

REFERENCE: Bowie and Green, p 247
Sayles, p 455

70. A surgeon requests the name of a patient he admitted on January 11, 2013. Which of the following would be used to retrieve this information?
    A. master patient index
    B. number index
    C. admission register
    D. operation index

REFERENCE: Bowie and Green, p 253
McWay, p 142

71. Which of the following is NOT a consideration in file folder size and design?
    A. reinforced top and side panels
    B. scoring on folder bottoms
    C. vendor location
    D. weight of folder

REFERENCE: Bowie and Green, p 236
Sayles, pp 339–340

72. Where in the health record would the following statement be located?
    "Microscopic Diagnosis: Liver (needle biopsy), metastatic adenocarcinoma"?
    A. operative report
    B. pathology report
    C. anesthesia report
    D. radiology report

REFERENCE: Abdelhak, p 107
Bowie and Green, pp 181, 183–184
LaTour, Eichenwald-Maki, and Oachs, p 250
Sayles, pp 85, 92

73. What term involves moving a document from one episode of care to a different episode of care within the same patient record?
    A. correction
    B. reassignment
    C. resequencing

REFERENCE: Sayles, p 365

74. A file area has limited space, medium file activity, and two file clerks. The HIM department would benefit from choosing which type of storage equipment?
   A. compressible filing units
   B. lateral filing cabinets
   C. open shelf files
   D. motorized revolving units

REFERENCE: LaTour, Eichenwald-Maki, and Oachs, p 274
Sayles, p 336

75. When evaluating an outside contract microfilm company, all but which of the following are important factors to rate?
   A. cost
   B. emergency returns
   C. storage after filming
   D. cache memory

REFERENCE: LaTour, Eichenwald-Maki, and Oachs, p 227
Sayles, pp 340–341

76. Under the HIPAA Privacy Rule, when destruction services are outsourced to a business associate, the contract must provide that the business associate will establish the permitted and required uses and disclosures and include all but which of the following elements?
   A. method of destruction or disposal
   B. time that will elapse between acquisition and destruction or disposal
   C. safeguards against breaches
   D. the hospital's liability insurance in specified amounts

REFERENCE: AHIMA Practice Brief (1)
Sayles, pp 794–796

77. The clinical laboratory department staff can use a database that allows them to see what laboratory tests were conducted and the results of those tests. By contrast, the billing department staff can only see that portion of the database that lists the laboratory tests that generate a charge, but they cannot see the test results. What kind of control is this an example of?
   A. concurrency
   B. access
   C. integrity
   D. cost

REFERENCE: McWay, p 265
Sayles, pp 381–382
Sayles and Trawick, p 218

78. When operating under the Health Insurance Portability and Accountability Act of 1996, what is a basic tenet in information security for health care professionals to follow?
   A. Security training is provided to all levels of staff.
   B. Patients are not educated about their right to confidentiality of health information.
   C. The information system encourages mass copying, printing, and downloading of patient records.
   D. When paper-based records are no longer needed, they are bundled and sent to a recycling center.

REFERENCE: AHIMA Practice Brief (2)
McWay, p 292
Sayles, pp 1040, 1053

79. Which of the following features should NOT be considered when designing screens to capture quality health data?
    A. a prompt for more information
    B. built-in alerts to notify users of possible errors
    C. the use of abbreviations on data fields
    D. left to right and bottom to top formatting

REFERENCE: Sayles, pp 385–386
Sayles and Trawick, p 88

80. When health care facilities close or medical practices dissolve, procedures for disposition of patient records should take into consideration all of the following EXCEPT
    A. state laws and licensing standards.
    B. Communities of Practice requirements.
    C. needs of patients.
    D. Medicare requirements.

REFERENCE: AHIMA Practice Brief (3)
Bowie and Green, pp 105–106
McWay, p 138

81. Case finding methods for patients with diabetes include a review of all but which one of the following?
    A. health plans
    B. CPT diagnostic codes
    C. billing data
    D. medication lists

REFERENCE: LaTour, Eichenwald-Maki, and Oachs, p 373
Sayles, pp 437, 443–444

82. What type of plan is a Joint Commission–accredited facility required to maintain to protect health information from catastrophes such as fire, flooding, bomb threats, and theft?
    A. budget
    B. disaster
    C. case management
    D. patient care

REFERENCE: AHIMA Practice Brief, (3)
McWay, p 326

83. Which of the following is NOT an alternative storage method for paper-based records?
    A. microfilm
    B. optical imaging
    C. computer
    D. outguide

REFERENCE: Bowie and Green, pp 103–104
LaTour, Eichenwald-Maki, and Oachs, pp 273–274

84. Which of the following issues would be of LEAST concern when storing health records in off-site storage?
    A. operating hours of the storage facility
    B. safety and confidentiality procedures
    C. filing order of the records
    D. procedure for request of a record in an emergency

REFERENCE: Bowie and Green, p 103
LaTour, Eichenwald-Maki, and Oachs, p 278
Sayles, pp 1027–1028

85. The HIM Department maintains 500,000 records and responds to 5,000 requests for records in a given period of time. What is the record usage rate?
    A. 0.01%
    B. 1%
    C. 5%
    D. 10%

REFERENCE: LaTour, Eichenwald-Maki, and Oachs, p 274
McWay, p 204
Math Calculation

86. Which one of the following is NOT a data retrieval tool?
    A. color
    B. sound
    C. point-and-click fields
    D. icons

REFERENCE: Sayles and Trawick, p 177

87. When engaging the services of a microfilm vendor, all but which one of the following factors should be included in the contract?
    A. who performs record preparation
    B. provision for destruction of original records
    C. type of reader or printer needed to view the microfilm
    D. confidentiality of information being filmed

REFERENCE: LaTour, Eichenwald-Maki, and Oachs, p 277

88. What would be the most cost-effective and prudent course of action for the storage or disposition of 250,000 records at a large teaching and research hospital?
    A. storing the records off-site at a cost of $25,000 per year
    B. scanning all 250,000 records for a cost of $195,000
    C. purging and storing all death records off-site at a cost of $20,000 per year
    D. destroying all records older than 3 years for a cost of $50,000

REFERENCE: Abdelhak, p 160
LaTour, Eichenwald-Maki, and Oachs, pp 276–279
McWay, pp 136–139

89. The total number of records filed during the month is 2,500 and, upon completion of a filing accuracy study, 90 records were not found. What is the accuracy rate for filing?
    A. 1%
    B. 4%
    C. 28%
    D. 96%

REFERENCE: McWay, p 204
Math Calculation

90. A quality control measure that should be established for the filing, storage, and retrieval of health records includes criteria for the
    A. accuracy of analyzing records.
    B. number of incomplete records.
    C. inclusion of late reports.
    D. tracking of release of information requests.

REFERENCE: LaTour, Eichenwald-Maki, and Oachs, pp 273–274
Sayles, p 358

91. According to AHIMA's recommended retention standards, which of the following types of health information does NOT need to be retained permanently?
   A. physician index
   B. register of births
   C. register of surgical procedures
   D. register of deaths

REFERENCE: AHIMA Practice Brief (1)
McWay, p 136
Sayles, p 346

92. For a health care facility to meet its document destruction needs, the certificate of destruction should include all but which of the following elements?
   A. unique and serialized transaction number
   B. location of destruction
   C. patient notification
   D. acceptance of fiduciary responsibility

REFERENCE: LaTour, Eichenwald-Maki, and Oachs, p 279
McWay, p 139
Sayles, p 348

93. The steps in developing a record retention program include all but which of the following?
   A. determining the storage format and location
   B. notifying the courts of the destruction
   C. assigning each record a retention period
   D. destroying records that are no longer needed

REFERENCE: LaTour, Eichenwald-Maki, and Oachs, pp 276–279
McWay, pp 136–139
Sayles, pp 343–347, 364

94. A health care facility has received a request to participate in a statewide study on cleft lip and cleft palate. This study would include data from the past year and subsequent years. Given that each of the data sources cited below contains the necessary information, the initial data would be most easily collected from the
   A. newborn records.
   B. state bureau of vital statistics.
   C. maternal records.
   D. birth defects registry.

REFERENCE: Abdelhak, pp 492–494
LaTour, Eichenwald-Maki, and Oachs, p 373
Sayles, pp 442–443

95. An example of a primary data source is the
   A. physician index.
   B. health record.
   C. cancer registry.
   D. hospital statistical report.

REFERENCE: Abdelhak, p 484
LaTour, Eichenwald-Maki, and Oachs, p 368
McWay, p 139
Sayles, p 433

96. Which of the following is NOT considered a challenge in the adoption of an electronic health record system?
    A. design of the work flow and processes
    B. physician willingness to adopt
    C. contribution to the quality of patient care
    D. individual state legal and regulatory issues

REFERENCE: LaTour, Eichenwald-Maki, and Oachs, p 119
Sayles and Trawick, pp 159–160

97. Fetal monitoring strips are part of the _______ record and should be maintained_______.
    A. newborn's; 10 years past the age of majority
    B. mother's; according to the length of time required for a minor's records
    C. newborn's; according to the time period specified in the state's statute of limitations
    D. mother's; 10 years

REFERENCE: Abdelhak, p 108
LaTour, Eichenwald-Maki, and Oachs, p 275

98. Which one of the following would NOT be a strategy when purchasing an electronic health record system?
    A. Recognize stakeholders from different organizational levels and engage them appropriately.
    B. Determine return on investment or cost-benefit analysis.
    C. Identify system requirements.
    D. Broaden the vendor field and select several vendors of choice.

REFERENCE: AHIMA Practice Brief (4) "Purchasing Strategies for EHR Systems"
LaTour, Eichenwald-Maki, and Oachs, pp 145–146
Sayles, p 862

99. How many years does the Food and Drug Administration require research records pertaining to cancer patients be maintained?
    A. 5
    B. 7
    C. 30
    D. permanently

REFERENCE: AHIMA Practice Brief "Retention and Destruction of Health Information"

100. What data cannot be retrieved from the MEDPAR?
    A. ICD-10-CM diagnosis codes
    B. Charges broken down by specific types of services
    C. Non-Medicare patient data
    D. Data on the provider

REFERENCE: LaTour, Eichenwald-Maki, and Oachs, p 377
McWay, p 187
Sayles, pp 145, 450–451

101. As the record retention supervisor, you are evaluating storage devices for a new health information management system. Which of the following would you NOT consider as an option for storing health information?
    A. light pen
    B. optical disc drive
    C. microfilm
    D. magnetic tape

REFERENCE: Sayles, p 874
Sayles and Trawick, p 6

102. General Hospital utilizes various related files that include clinical and financial data to generate reports such as MS-DRG case mix reports. What application would be MOST effective for this activity?
   A. desktop publishing
   B. word processing
   C. database management system
   D. command interpreter

REFERENCE: Abdelhak, p 298
LaTour, Eichenwald-Maki, and Oachs, pp 185–186
Sayles, pp 879–880

103. The Director of Health Information Management has been asked by the Board of Trustees to justify support for the use of handheld devices by the medical staff for point-of-service input. Which one of the following reasons would NOT be included in the Director's response?
   A. decreased clinical documentation errors
   B. increased work efficiency
   C. faster access to health data
   D. elimination of the need for expensive desktop computers

REFERENCE: Abdelhak, pp 308–309
LaTour, Eichenwald-Maki, and Oachs, p 96

104. The Assistant Director of Record Processing is evaluating software packages for a chart tracking system in the HIM Department. What is the BEST method to verify that the software will work as marketed?
   A. Visit corporate headquarters of the vendor.
   B. Perform a vendor reference check.
   C. Read consumer reports before buying.
   D. Test the software prior to purchase.

REFERENCE: Abdelhak, pp 163–164
LaTour, Eichenwald-Maki, and Oachs, pp 146–148
Sayles, p 862

105. Concern for health data loss and misuse within the HIM department requires that the health information practitioner evaluate all but which of the following?
   A. security controls and access privileges of staff
   B. policies and procedures developed to safeguard privacy and security
   C. use of a back-up system
   D. salary for the database administrator

REFERENCE: LaTour, Eichenwald-Maki, and Oachs, pp 187–188
McWay, pp 290–292
Sayles, pp 1065–1066

106. Lewis-Beck Medical Center has been collecting data on patient satisfaction for six months. It is ready to start retrieving data from the database to improve clinical services. Which tool should be used?
   A. HTML
   B. SQL
   C. XML
   D. data dictionary

REFERENCE: Sayles, p 876
Sayles and Trawick, p 107

107. The Assistant Director of HIM is evaluating software that would use electronic logging of the location of incomplete and delinquent records as they move through the completion process. What departmental function is this most useful for?
A. release of information
B. coding
C. chart tracking
D. transcription

REFERENCE: Bowie and Green, pp 240–242
LaTour, Eichenwald-Maki, and Oachs, p 266
Sayles, p 959

108. The hospital administrator is making a strategic decision by querying various institutional databases for information. What type of system is the hospital administrator using?
A. electronic health record system
B. results reporting system
C. financial information system
D. executive information system

REFERENCE: LaTour, Eichenwald-Maki, and Oachs, p 95
Sayles, pp 914, 924
Sayles and Trawick, p 131

109. University Hospital has the messaging technology to securely route an alert for a patient's possible drug interaction or abnormal lab result to the appropriate physician's pager number. Which one of the following is the medical staff using?
A. intranet
B. extranet
C. Internet
D. clinical information system

REFERENCE: LaTour, Eichenwald-Maki, and Oachs, p 90
Sayles, p 914
Sayles and Trawick, pp 139–141

110. The HIM practitioner's duty to retain health information via the archiving and storage of health data includes all but which of the following?
A. strategies that consider accessibility, natural disasters, and innovations in storage technology
B. strategies ensuring that inactive records are as secure as active records
C. a retention plan for multiple volumes of records
D. a retention plan for financial data

REFERENCE: Abdelhak, pp 196–197
McWay, pp 132–139
Sayles, pp 788–789

111. As HIM director, you must ensure a means to regulate access and ensure preservation of data in the health care facility's computer system. Which of the following is NOT a security measure that can be implemented to prevent privacy violations in this computer system?
A. authentication
B. encryption
C. disaster recovery plan
D. stonewall

REFERENCE: LaTour, Eichenwald-Maki, and Oachs, p 133
McWay, p 290
Sayles, pp 1037–1039
Sayles and Trawick, pp 218–220

112. Health Informatics, Inc. is a vendor with a large collection of clinical information systems and hospital information systems that are designed to share data without human or technical intervention. This is a(an)

   A. interfaced system.
   B. integrated system.
   C. OLAP.
   D. standard.

REFERENCE: LaTour, Eichenwald-Maki, and Oachs, pp 132–133
Sayles and Trawick, p 68

113. The function of a(an) _______ is limited to data retrieval.

   A. electronic health record
   B. executive information system
   C. database management system
   D. clinical data repository

REFERENCE: Abdelhak, p 112
LaTour, Eichenwald-Maki, and Oachs, p 84
Sayles, p 994
Sayles and Trawick, pp 34, 59

114. The Director of the HIM Department is explaining incentives to physicians for entering their clinical documentation in the electronic health record. Which of the following would be the key advantage in using this type of data entry?

   A. Enhanced databases will provide information for improved clinical care.
   B. Training will be offered by the hospital.
   C. Those physicians not in compliance will be denied admitting privileges.
   D. Multiple users will not have access to the same information simultaneously.

REFERENCE: LaTour, Eichenwald-Maki, and Oachs, pp 140–142

115. University Hospital, a 900-bed tertiary health care organization, is undergoing an information systems development. What system would best meet its needs?

   A. application service provider model
   B. clinical workstation
   C. IBM Medical Information Systems Program
   D. legacy system

REFERENCE: Abdelhak, p 320
LaTour, Eichenwald-Maki, and Oachs, p 140
Sayles, pp 863, 1183

116. A 16-year-old female delivers a stillborn infant in Mercy Hospital. The clinical documentation on the stillborn infant would

   A. be filed in a health record created for the infant.
   B. be filed in the mother's record.
   C. be retained in a separate file in the administrative offices.
   D. not be retained in hospital records.

REFERENCE: LaTour, Eichenwald-Maki, and Oachs, p 252
Sayles, pp 95–98

117. Which of the following is a NOT major management challenge in the storage and retention of electronic health record systems?
   A. Following state and federal laws and accreditation requirements when developing retention and destruction policies.
   B. Keeping technology updated in order to retrieve data.
   C. Ensuring that health information can be retrieved in a timely manner.
   D. Maintaining the paper-based storage system.

REFERENCE: Abdelhak, p 225
LaTour, Eichenwald-Maki, and Oachs, pp 138–145

118. When implementing the electronic health record, what is the technical security standard that requires unique user identification, emergency access procedures, automatic log-off, and encryption and decryption of data?
   A. audit control
   B. person or entity authentication
   C. transmission security
   D. access control

REFERENCE: LaTour, Eichenwald-Maki, and Oachs, p 133
Sayles, p 1056
Sayles and Trawick, p 218

119. Which of the following is NOT a factor to consider when developing a record retention program?
   A. legal requirements as determined by statute of limitations
   B. record usage in the facility determined by health care provider activity
   C. reimbursement guidelines
   D. cost of space to maintain paper records

REFERENCE: LaTour, Eichenwald-Maki, and Oachs, pp 276–279
Bowie and Green, p 102
Sayles, pp 788–789

120. Of 750 records filed during the week, 75 were not located. What is the filing error rate?
   A. 10%
   B. 90%
   C. 0.1%
   D. 0.9%

REFERENCE: McWay, p 204
Math Calculation

121. Which of the following is NOT a document input device in the electronic document management system?
   A. scanner
   B. bar codes
   C. printer
   D touch screen

REFERENCE: Sayles and Trawick, pp 6–7

122. Which of the following statements is FALSE when addressing characteristics of the legal health record in an electronic document management system?
   A. The storage media used and the format of the scanned documents must protect data from loss and damage.
   B. The storage format must be efficient, manageable, and in compliance with laws and regulations.
   C. The backup and disaster recovery process is certified to ensure that all data can be recovered.
   D. Direct electronic interfaces from ancillary department systems to the document imaging system will not eliminate the need to scan documents and integrate the data from these ancillary systems.

REFERENCE: Abdelhak, pp 190–191
LaTour, Eichenwald-Maki, and Oachs, pp 332–335

123. Which of the following is NOT a data retrieval tool?
   A. light pen
   B. SQL
   C. color, animation, sound, icons
   D. screen design

REFERENCE: Sayles and Trawick, pp 106–107

124. Messenger, pneumatic tube, dumbwaiter, and conveyor belt are all examples of
   A. record security systems.
   B. record circulation systems.
   C. loose filing.
   D. filing controls.

REFERENCE: Bowie and Green, p 244

125. Which item is collected and maintained in the organ transplant registry?
   A. vaccine manufacturer
   B. histocompatibility information
   C. cytogenetic results
   D. stage at the time of diagnosis

REFERENCE: Abdelhak, p 496
LaTour, Eichenwald-Maki, and Oachs, p 375
Sayles, pp 446–447

Answer Key for Information Retention and Access

NOTE: *Explanations are provided for those questions that require mathematical calculations and questions that are not clearly explained in the references that are cited.*

	ANSWER	EXPLANATION
1.	D	
2.	A	
3.	C	
4.	B	
5.	A	(3,545 × 100) divided by 15,000 = 2.36% = 2.4%
6.	A	
7.	A	
8.	B	
9.	D	
10.	D	
11.	C	
12.	A	
13.	D	200 units × 6 shelves per unit = 1,200 shelves total 1,200 shelves divided by 100 primary numbers (00–99) = 12 shelves per primary number
14.	C	
15.	C	
16.	B	
17.	D	(2,375 records retrieved from proper locations × 100) divided by 2,543 records requested = 93.39% filing accuracy
18.	B	
19.	B	
20.	B	
21.	B	
22.	B	
23.	B	
24.	D	2,540 + 400 = 2,940 inches needed 36 × 6 = 216 inches per unit 2,940 (inches needed) divided by 216 (inches per unit) = 13.61 shelves You must buy 14 units because you cannot purchase a 0.14 filing shelf.
25.	C	
26.	C	
27.	B	
28.	D	
29.	D	
30.	A	8 shelves per unit × 100 units = 800 total shelves 800 shelves divided by 100 primary digits (00–99) = 8 shelves per primary digit
31.	D	
32.	B	
33.	A	
34.	D	
35.	C	
36.	A	

Answer Key for Information Retention and Access

ANSWER	EXPLANATION
37. A	25,000 inpatients × 0.25 inch/record = 6,250 inches 15,000 ER patients × 0.125 inch/record = 1,875 inches 6,250 inches + 1,875 inches = 8,125 total inches of filing space/year 8,125 total inches × $1.05/filing inch = $8,531.25 budget allocation for storage space
38. C	
39. D	
40. A	
41. A	
42. C	
43. C	33 inches per shelf × 6 shelves per unit = 198 linear filing inches per unit 1,000 records × 1 inch per record = 1,000 inches of records to be filed 1,000 (inches of records needed) divided by 198 inches per unit = 5.05 filing units In order to provide for the total expansion, 6 filing units need to be purchased.
44. B	
45. A	
46. C	
47. A	
48. D	
49. D	
50. C	
51. B	
52. D	
53. B	
54. C	6,000 admissions (year currently) + 200 additional admissions/year 6,200 total admissions next year 6,200 total admissions × 30% readmission rate 1,860 readmissions next year 6,200 total admissions −1,860 readmissions 4,340 new file folders needed for next year
55. A	
56. D	
57. C	
58. C	
59. C	
60. D	
61. C	
62. A	
63. C	
64. A	
65. C	

Answer Key for Information Retention and Access

	ANSWER	EXPLANATION
66.	D	
67.	B	
68.	B	
69.	B	
70.	C	
71.	C	
72.	B	
73.	B	
74.	A	
75	D	
76	D	
77.	B	
78.	A	
79.	D	
80.	B	
81.	B	
82.	B	
83.	D	
84.	C	
85.	B	(5,000 × 100) divided by 500,000 = 1%
86.	C	
87.	C	
88.	B	
89.	D	2,500 − 90 = 2,410 (2,410 × 100) divided by 2,500 = 96.4% filing accuracy
90.	C	
91.	A	
92.	C	
93.	B	
94.	D	
95.	B	
96.	C	
97.	B	
98.	D	
99.	C	
100.	C	
101.	A	
102.	C	
103.	D	
104.	D	
105	D	
106.	B	
107.	C	

Answer Key for Information Retention and Access

ANSWER	EXPLANATION
108. D	
109. D	
110. D	
111. D	
112. A	
113. D	
114. A	
115. A	
116. B	
117. D	
118. D	
119. C	
120. A	
121. C	
122. D	
123. A	
124. B	
125. B	

REFERENCES

Abdelhak, M. and Hanken, M. (2016). *Health information: Management of a strategic resource* (5th ed.). St. Louis: Elsevier.

AHIMA Practice Briefs. All are published by the American Health Information Management Association, Chicago.

1. AHIMA Practice Brief (1): "Retention and Destruction of Health Information" (10/15/2013)
2. AHIMA Practice Brief (2): "Information Security: An Overview" (1/2/2014)
3. AHIMA Practice Brief (3): "Disaster Planning and Recovery Toolkit" (7/31/2013)
4. AHIMA Practice Brief (4): "Purchasing Strategies for EHR Systems" (5/2/2006)
5. AHIMA Practice Brief (5): "Protecting Patient Information After a Facility Closure" (8/15/2011)

American College of Surgeons. (2012). *Cancer program standards 2012: Ensuring patient-centered care.* Chicago: American College of Surgeons Commission on Cancer. https://www.facs.org/quality-programs/cancer

Bowie, M. J. and Green, M. A. (2015). *Essentials of health information management: Principles and practices* (3rd ed.). Clifton Park, NY: Cengage Learning.

LaTour, K., Eichenwald-Maki, S., and Oachs, P. (2013). *Health information management: Concepts, principles and practice* (4th ed.). Chicago: American Health Information Management Association.

McWay, D. C. (2014). *Today's health information management: An integrated approach* (2nd ed.). Clifton Park, NY: Cengage Learning.

Sayles, N. (2013). *Health information management technology: An applied approach* (4th ed.). Chicago: American Health Information Management Association.

Sayles, N. and Trawick, K. (2014). *Introduction to computer systems for health information technology* (2nd ed.). Chicago: American Health Information Management Association.

RHIA AND RHIT COMPETENCIES BY QUESTION FOR INFORMATION RETENTION AND ACCESS													
Question	RHIA Domain Competencies						RHIT Domain Competencies						
	1	2	3	4	5		1	2	3	4	5	6	7
1		X									X		
2			X				X						
3	X										X		
4			X				X						
5					X		X						
6			X				X						
7			X				X						
8					X		X						
9			X							X			
10			X				X						
11	X						X						
12	X											X	
13			X				X						
14	X						X						
15			X				X						
16	X						X						
17					X		X						
18			X				X						
19			X				X						
20			X				X						
21	X								X				
22	X								X				
23			X							X			
24			X									X	
25		X					X						
26	X						X						
27			X				X						
28			X						X				
29	X						X						
30			X				X						
31	X						X						
32			X				X						
33			X				X						
34			X				X						
35			X							X			
36			X							X			
37					X		X						
38			X				X						
39			X				X						
40					X		X						
41			X				X						
42					X		X						
43					X		X						
44			X				X						
45			X				X						
46			X				X						
47	X									X			
48			X							X			
49	X											X	
50			X								X		
51			X				X						
52			X								X		
53			X				X						

RHIA AND RHIT COMPETENCIES BY QUESTION FOR INFORMATION RETENTION AND ACCESS													
Question	RHIA Domain Competencies						RHIT Domain Competencies						
	1	2	3	4	5		1	2	3	4	5	6	7
54					X		X						
55		X					X						
56			X				X						
57	X						X						
58		X										X	
59	X								X				
60					X		X						
61			X						X				
62	X								X				
63	X											X	
64	X						X						
65			X				X						
66			X				X						
67			X							X			
68					X		X						
69	X						X						
70	X						X						
71			X				X						
72	X						X						
73					X		X						
74			X				X						
75					X		X						
76					X			X					
77	X									X			
78		X							X				
79			X							X			
80	X								X				
81	X						X						
82	X								X				
83			X				X						
84			X				X						
85					X		X						
86			X				X						
87					X		X						
88	X						X						
89					X		X						
90					X		X						
91	X								X				
92	X								X				
93	X								X				
94	X						X						
95	X						X						
96			X							X			
97	X						X						
98					X					X			
99	X						X						
100	X							X					
101			X				X						
102			X				X						
103					X					X			

RHIA AND RHIT COMPETENCIES BY QUESTION FOR INFORMATION RETENTION AND ACCESS														
Question	RHIA Domain Competencies							RHIT Domain Competencies						
	1	2	3	4	5			1	2	3	4	5	6	7
104					X						X			
105		X						X						
106			X					X						
107			X					X						
108			X								X			
109			X								X			
110	X							X						
111		X									X			
112			X								X			
113	X										X			
114	X										X			
115			X								X			
116	X							X						
117	X							X						
118			X							X				
119	X									X				
120					X			X						
121			X								X			
122			X										X	
123			X									X		
124			X					X						
125	X							X						

V. Classification Systems and Secondary Data Sources

Marissa Lajaunie, MBA, RHIA

1. Which system is a classification of health and health-related domains that describe body functions and structures, domains of activities and participation, and environmental factors that interact with all of these components?
   A. International Classification of Primary Care (ICPC-2)
   B. International Classification on Functioning, Disability, and Health (ICF)
   C. National Drug Codes
   D. Clinical Care Classification (CCC)

REFERENCE: Latour, Eichenwald-Maki, and Oachs, p 393
Sayles, pp 196–197

2. A physician performed an outpatient surgical procedure on the eye orbit of a patient with Medicare. Upon searching the CPT codes and consulting with the physician, the coder is unable to find a code for the procedure. The coder should assign
   A. an unlisted Evaluation and Management code from the E/M section.
   B. an unlisted procedure code located in the eye and ocular adnexa section.
   C. a HCPCS Level Two (alphanumeric) code.
   D. an ophthalmologic treatment service code.

REFERENCE: AMA (2015), pp 67–68
Green, p 515
Smith, p 24

3. A system of preferred terminology for naming disease processes is known as a
   A. set of categories.
   B. classification system.
   C. medical nomenclature.
   D. diagnosis listing.

REFERENCE: Abdelhak, p 256
Bowie and Green, p 318
Green, p 9
LaTour, Eichenwald-Maki, and Oachs, pp 207–208, 348, 388–389
McWay, pp 149–150
Sayles, p 180

4. Which of the following is NOT included as a part of the minimum data maintained in the MPI?
   A. principal diagnosis
   B. patient medical record number
   C. full name (last, first, and middle)
   D. date of birth

REFERENCE: Abdelhak, p 130
Bowie and Green, pp 252–255
LaTour, Eichenwald-Maki, and Oachs, pp 170, 271–272
McWay, pp 139–140
Sayles, pp 322–323

5. The Health Information Department receives research requests from various committees in the hospital. The Medicine Committee wishes to review all patients having a diagnosis of anterolateral myocardial infarction within the past 6 months. Which of the following would be the best source to identify the necessary charts?
   A. operation index
   B. consultation index
   C. disease index
   D. physician's index

REFERENCE: Bowie and Green, p 257
LaTour, Eichenwald-Maki, and Oachs, pp 369–370
McWay, p 140
Sayles, pp 436–437

6. One of the major functions of the cancer registry is to ensure that patients receive regular and continued observation and management. How long should patient follow-up be continued?
   A. until remission occurs
   B. 10 years
   C. for the life of the patient
   D. 1 year

REFERENCE: Abdelhak, pp 490–491
LaTour, Eichenwald-Maki, and Oachs, pp 370–372
McWay, pp 142–143
Sayles, pp 438–440

7. In reviewing the medical record of a patient admitted for a left herniorrhaphy, the coder discovers an extremely low potassium level on the laboratory report. In examining the physician's orders, the coder notices that intravenous potassium was ordered. The physician has not listed any indication of an abnormal potassium level or any related condition on the discharge summary. The best course of action for the coder to take is to
   A. confer with the physician and ask him or her to list the condition as a final diagnosis if he or she considers the abnormal potassium level to be clinically significant.
   B. code the record as is.
   C. code the condition as abnormal blood chemistry.
   D. code the abnormal potassium level as a complication following surgery.

REFERENCE: Green, pp 15–16
LaTour, Eichenwald-Maki, and Oachs, pp 441–442

8. DSM-IV-TR is used most frequently in what type of healthcare setting?
   A. behavioral health centers
   B. ambulatory surgery centers
   C. home health agencies
   D. nursing homes

REFERENCE: Green, pp 950–952
LaTour, Eichenwald-Maki, and Oachs, pp 394–395
McWay, p 152
Sayles, pp 208–210

9. A coder notes that a patient is taking prescription Pilocarpine. The final diagnoses on the discharge summary are congestive heart failure and diabetes mellitus. The coder should query the physician about adding a diagnosis of
   A. arthritis.
   B. glaucoma.
   C. bronchitis.
   D. laryngitis.

REFERENCE: Green, pp 15–16, 176–178
Woodrow, p 345

10. The patient is diagnosed with congestive heart failure. A drug of choice is
   A. ibuprofen.
   B. oxytocin.
   C. haloperidol.
   D. digoxin.

REFERENCE: Woodrow, p 503

11. ICD-10-CM utilizes a placeholder character. This is used as a 5th character placeholder at certain 6 character codes to allow for future expansion. The placeholder character is
   A. "Z."
   B. "O."
   C. "1."
   D. "x."

REFERENCE: Bowie, p 30
Green, p 74

12. The local safety council requests statistics on the number of head injuries occurring as a result of skateboarding accidents during the last year. To retrieve this data, you will need to have the correct
    A. CPT code.
    B. Standard Nomenclature of Injuries codes.
    C. ICD-10-CM codes.
    D. HCPCS Level II codes.

REFERENCE: Green, pp 207–208, 211–212
McWay, pp 154–155
Schraffenberger, p 469

13. All children will be entered into which of the following registries at birth, and thus will continue to be monitored by the registry in their geographic area?
    A. Birth defects registry
    B. Trauma registry
    C. Cancer registry
    D. Immunization registry

REFERENCE: Latour, Eichenwald-Maki, and Oachs, p 375
McWay, p 141
Sayles, pp 447–449

14. In general, all three key components (history, physical examination, and medical decision making) for the E/M codes in CPT should be met or exceeded when
    A. the patient is established.
    B. a new patient is seen in the office.
    C. the patient is given subsequent care in the hospital.
    D. the patient is seen for a follow-up inpatient consultation.

REFERENCE: AMA (2015), pp 11–12
Bowie, p 63
Green, pp 541–542, 546

15. This registry collects data on recipients of heart valves and pacemakers.
    A. Transplant registry
    B. Implant registry
    C. Cancer registry
    D. Hypertension registry

REFERENCE: LaTour, Eichenwald-Maki, and Oachs, p 374
McWay, p 141
Sayles, pp 445–446

16. Which classification system was developed to standardize terminology and codes for use in clinical laboratories?
    A. Systematized Nomenclature of Human and Veterinary Medicine International (SNOMED)
    B. Systematized Nomenclature of Pathology (SNOP)
    C. Read Codes
    D. Logical Observation Identifiers, Names and Codes (LOINC)

REFERENCE: Abdelhak, p 200
Latour, Eichenwald-Maki, and Oachs, pp 399–400
McWay, p 151

17. Which classification system is used to classify neoplasms according to site, morphology, and behavior?
   A. International Classification of Diseases for Oncology (ICD-O)
   B. Systematized Nomenclature of Human and Veterinary Medicine International (SNOMED)
   C. Diagnostic and Statistical Manual of Mental Disorders (DSM)
   D. Current Procedural Terminology (CPT)

REFERENCE: Abdelhak, p 282
Latour, Eichenwald-Maki, and Oachs, pp 392–393

18. According to the UHDDS, a procedure that is surgical in nature, carries a procedural or anesthetic risk, or requires special training is defined as a
   A. principal procedure.
   B. significant procedure.
   C. operating room procedure.
   D. therapeutic procedure.

REFERENCE: Green, pp 356, 383
Latour, Eichenwald-Maki, and Oachs, p 197
Schraffenberger, p 91

19. You need to analyze data on the types of care provided to Medicare patients in your geographic area by DRG. Which of the following would be most helpful?
   A. National Practitioner Data Bank
   B. MEDPAR
   C. Vital Statistics
   D. RxNorm

REFERENCE: LaTour, Eichenwald-Maki, and Oachs, p 377
McWay, p 187
Sayles, pp 450–451

20. An encoder that prompts the coder to answer a series of questions and choices based on the documentation in the medical record is called a(n)
   A. logic-based encoder.
   B. automated codebook.
   C. grouper.
   D. automatic code assignment.

REFERENCE: LaTour, Eichenwald-Maki, and Oachs, p 444

21. Which of the following classification systems was designed with electronic systems in mind and is currently being used for problem lists, ICU unit monitoring, patient care assessments, data collection, medical research studies, clinical trials, disease surveillance, and images?
   A. SNOMED CT
   B. SNDO
   C. ICDPC-2
   D. GEM

REFERENCE: Abdelhak, pp 266–268
LaTour, Eichenwald-Maki, and Oachs, pp 398–399
McWay, pp 150–151

22. The Unified Medical Language System (UMLS) is a project sponsored by the
   A. National Library of Medicine.
   B. CMS.
   C. World Health Organization.
   D. Office of Inspector General.

REFERENCE: LaTour, Eichenwald-Maki, and Oachs, pp 405–406
McWay, p 151
Sayles, p 458

23. You have recently been hired as the Medical Staff Coordinator at your local hospital. Which database/registry will you utilize most often?
    A. Trauma Registry
    B. MEDPAR
    C. LOINC
    D. National Practitioner Data Bank (NPDB)

REFERENCE: LaTour, Eichenwald-Maki, and Oachs, p 377
McWay, p 270
Sayles, p 451

24. You need to retrieve information on a particular physician in your facility. Specifically, you need to know how many cases he saw during the month of May. What would be your best source of information?
    A. Healthcare Integrity and Protection Data Banks (HIPDB)
    B. Physician Index
    C. MEDLINE database
    D. National Practitioner Data Bank (NPDB)

REFERENCE: LaTour, Eichenwald-Maki, and Oachs, pp 369–370
McWay, p 140
Sayles, p 437

25. You just completed a process through which you reviewed a patient record and entered the required elements into a database. What is this process called?
    A. Case finding
    B. Staging
    C. Abstracting
    D. Nomenclature

REFERENCE: LaTour, Eichenwald-Maki, and Oachs, p 382
McWay, p 140
Sayles, p 394

26. Which system is used primarily to report services and supplies for reimbursement purposes?
    A. LOINC
    B. HCPCS
    C. NLM
    D. ASTM

REFERENCE: Green, pp 471–473
LaTour, Eichenwald-Maki, and Oachs, p 394
McWay, p 164
Sayles, p 182

27. You are looking at statistics for your facility that include average length of stay (ALOS) and discharge data by DRG. What type of data are you reviewing?
    A. Aggregate data
    B. Patient-identifiable data
    C. MPI data
    D. Protocol data

REFERENCE: LaTour, Eichenwald-Maki, and Oachs, p 368
McWay, p 208
Sayles, p 41

28. In which registry would you expect to find an Injury Severity Score (ISS)?
    A. Cancer Registry
    B. Birth Defects Registry
    C. Trauma Registry
    D. Transplant Registry

REFERENCE: LaTour, Eichenwald-Maki, and Oachs, p 372
Sayles, pp 441–442

29. A service provided by a physician whose opinion or advice regarding evaluation and/or management of a specific problem is requested by another physician is referred to as
    A. a referral.
    B. a consultation.
    C. risk factor intervention.
    D. concurrent care.

REFERENCE: AMA (2015), pp 19–20
Bowie, pp 61–63
Green, pp 568–570
Smith, pp 205–206

30. Which of the following groups maintain healthcare databases in the public and private sectors?
    A. Healthcare provider organizations
    B. Healthcare data organizations
    C. Healthcare payor organizations
    D. Healthcare supplier organizations

REFERENCE: LaTour, Eichenwald-Maki, and Oachs, p 59

31. The most widely discussed and debated unique patient identifier is the
    A. patient's date of birth.
    B. patient's first and last names.
    C. patient's social security number.
    D. Unique Physician Identification Number (UPIN).

REFERENCE: LaTour, Eichenwald-Maki, and Oachs, pp 243–244

32. A nomenclature of codes and medical terms that provides standard terminology for reporting physicians' services for third-party reimbursement is
    A. Current Medical Information and Terminology (CMIT).
    B. Current Procedural Terminology (CPT).
    C. Systematized Nomenclature of Pathology (SNOP).
    D. Diagnostic and Statistical Manual of Mental Disorders (DSM).

REFERENCE: Bowie, p 8
Green, p 10
Schraffenberger and Kuehn, p 10

33. A cancer program is surveyed for approval by the
    A. American Cancer Society.
    B. Commission on Cancer of the American College of Surgeons.
    C. State Department of Health.
    D. Joint Commission on Accreditation of Healthcare Organizations.

REFERENCE: Abdelhak, p 491
LaTour, Eichenwald-Maki, and Oachs, pp 371–372
Sayles, p 440

34. The nursing staff would most likely use which of the following to facilitate aggregation of data for comparison at local, regional, national, and international levels?
    A. READ codes
    B. ABC codes
    C. SPECIALIST Lexicon
    D. LOINC

REFERENCE: Bowie and Green, p 323
McWay, p 164

35. The Level II (national) codes of the HCPCS coding system are maintained by the
    A. American Medical Association.
    B. CPT Editorial Panel.
    C. local fiscal intermediary.
    D. Centers for Medicare and Medicaid Services.

REFERENCE: Bowie, p 9
Bowie and Green, p 30

36. A patient is admitted with pneumonia. Cultures are requested to determine the infecting organism. Which of the following, if present, would alert the coder to ask the physician whether or not this should be coded as gram-negative pneumonia?
    A. pseudomonas
    B. clostridium
    C. staphylococcus
    D. listeria

REFERENCE: Green, pp 15–17

37. The Level I (CPT) codes of the HCPCS coding system are maintained by the
    A. American Medical Association.
    B. American Hospital Association.
    C. local fiscal intermediary.
    D. Centers for Medicare and Medicaid Services.

REFERENCE: Bowie, pp 2, 9
Bowie and Green, p 30
Green, p 471
McWay, p 416

38. A physician excises a 3.1 cm malignant lesion of the scalp that requires full-thickness graft from the thigh to the scalp. In CPT, which of the following procedures should be coded?
    A. full-thickness skin graft to scalp only
    B. excision of lesion; full-thickness skin graft to scalp
    C. excision of lesion; full-thickness skin graft to scalp; excision of skin from thigh
    D. code 15004 for surgical preparation of recipient site; full-thickness skin graft to scalp

REFERENCE: Green, pp 651–654, 661–663
Smith, pp 60–62, 72–75

39. A patient is seen by a surgeon who determines that an emergency procedure is necessary. Identify the modifier that may be reported to indicate that the decision to do surgery was made on this office visit.
    A. -25 B. -55 C. -57 D. -58

REFERENCE: AMA (2015), p 710
Bowie, p 21
Green, pp 519, 521, 571
Smith, p 202

40. A patient develops difficulty during surgery and the physician discontinues the procedure. Identify the modifier that may be reported by the physician to indicate that the procedure was discontinued.
    A. -52 B. -53 C. -73 D. -74

REFERENCE: AMA (2015), p 710
Bowie, pp 20, 23
Green, pp 519, 521
Smith, p 46

41. A barrier to widespread use of automated code assignment is
    A. inadequate technology.
    B. poor quality of documentation.
    C. resistance by physicians.
    D. resistance by HIM professionals.

REFERENCE: LaTour, Eichenwald-Maki, and Oachs, pp 444–445

42. In assigning E/M codes, three key components are used. These are
    A. history, examination, counseling.
    B. history, examination, time.
    C. history, nature of presenting problem, time.
    D. history, examination, medical decision making.

REFERENCE: AMA (2015), pp 9–10
Bowie, pp 42–43
Green, p 546
Smith, p 187

43. Mrs. Jones had an appendectomy on November 1. She was taken back to surgery on November 2 for evacuation of a hematoma of the wound site. Identify the modifier that may be reported for the November 2 visit.
    A. -58 B. -76 C. -78 D. -79

REFERENCE: AMA (2015), p 711
Bowie, p 24
Green, pp 520, 524
Smith, p 49

44. The primary goal of a hospital-based cancer registry is to
    A. improve patient care.
    B. allocate hospital resources appropriately.
    C. determine the need for professional and public education programs.
    D. monitor cancer incidence.

REFERENCE: Abdelhak, p 491
McWay, pp 142–143

45. A secondary data source that houses and aggregates extensive data about patients with a certain diagnosis is a(n)
    A. disease index.
    B. master patient index.
    C. disease registry.
    D. admissions register.

REFERENCE: Bowie and Green, p 257
LaTour, Eichenwald-Maki, and Oachs, p 370

46. After reviewing the following excerpt from CPT, code 27646 would be interpreted as

27645	Radical resection of tumor; tibia
27646	Fibula
27647	Talus or calcaneus

    A. 27646 radical resection of tumor; tibia and fibula.
    B. 27646 radical resection of tumor; fibula.
    C. 27646 radical resection of tumor; fibula or tibia.
    D. 27646 radical resection of tumor; fibula, talus, or calcaneus.

REFERENCE: Bowie, pp 5–6
Green, p 701
Smith, p 20

47. A population-based cancer registry that is designed to determine rates and trends in a defined population is a(n)
    A. incidence-only population-based registry.
    B. cancer control population-based registry.
    C. research-oriented population-based registry.
    D. patient care population-based registry.

REFERENCE: Abdelhak, p 491
LaTour, Eichenwald-Maki, and Oachs, p 370
Sayles, pp 438–440

48. Given the diagnosis "carcinoma of axillary lymph nodes and lungs, metastatic from breast," what is the primary cancer site(s)?
    A. axillary lymph nodes
    B. lungs
    C. breast
    D. A and B

REFERENCE: Green, pp 168–172
Schraffenberger, pp 140–141

49. According to CPT, in which of the following cases would an established E/M code be used?
    A. A home visit with a 45-year-old male with a long history of drug abuse and alcoholism. The man is seen at the request of Adult Protective Services for an assessment of his mental capabilities.
    B. John and his family have just moved to town. John has asthma and requires medication to control the problem. He has an appointment with Dr. You and will bring his records from his previous physician.
    C. Tom is seen by Dr. X for a sore throat. Dr. X is on call for Tom's regular physician, Dr. Y. The last time that Tom saw Dr. Y was a couple of years ago.
    D. A 78-year-old female with weight loss and progressive agitation over the past 2 months is seen by her primary care physician for drug therapy. She has not seen her primary care physician in 4 years.

REFERENCE: AMA (2015), pp 4–5
Bowie, pp 38–42
Green, pp 542–543
Smith, p 186

50. In order to use the inpatient CPT consultation codes, the consulting physician must
    A. order diagnostic tests.
    B. document his findings in the patient's medical record.
    C. communicate orally his opinion to the attending physician.
    D. use the term "referral" in his report.

REFERENCE: AMA (2015), pp 19–22
Bowie, pp 61–63
Smith, pp 205–206

51. The attending physician requests a consultation from a cardiologist. The cardiologist takes a detailed history, performs a detailed examination, and utilizes moderate medical decision making. The cardiologist orders diagnostic tests and prescribes medication. He documents his findings in the patient's medical record and communicates in writing with the attending physician. The following day the consultant visits the patient to evaluate the patient's response to the medication, to review results from the diagnostic tests, and to discuss treatment options. What codes should the consultant report for the two visits?
    A. an initial inpatient consult and a follow-up consult
    B. an initial inpatient consult for both visits
    C. an initial inpatient consult and a subsequent hospital visit
    D. an initial inpatient consult and initial hospital care

REFERENCE: AMA (2015), pp 19–22
Bowie, pp 61–63
Green, pp 569–572
Smith, pp 205–206

52. According to the American Medical Association, medical decision making is measured by all of the following except the
    A. number of diagnoses or management options.
    B. amount and complexity of data reviewed.
    C. risk of complications.
    D. specialty of the treating physician.

REFERENCE: AMA (2015), p 10
Bowie, pp 53–54
Green, p 548
Smith, p 195

53. CPT provides Level I modifiers to explain all of the following situations EXCEPT
    A. when a service or procedure is partially reduced or eliminated at the physician's discretion.
    B. when one surgeon provides only postoperative services.
    C. when a patient sees a surgeon for follow-up care after surgery.
    D. when the same laboratory test is repeated multiple times on the same day.

REFERENCE: AMA (2015), pp 709–714
Bowie, pp 16–26
Green, pp 519–527

54. The best place to ascertain the size of an excised lesion for accurate CPT coding is the
    A. discharge summary.
    B. pathology report.
    C. operative report.
    D. anesthesia record.

REFERENCE: Green, pp 651–654
Smith, pp 61–62

55. Which of the following is expected to enable hospitals to collect more specific information for use in patient care, benchmarking, quality assessment, research, public health reporting, strategic planning, and reimbursement?
    A. LOINC
    B. ICD-10-CM
    C. NDC
    D. NANDA

REFERENCE: Abdelhak, p 255

56. Case definition is important for all types of registries. Age will certainly be an important criterion for accessing a case in a(n) ____________ registry.
    A. implant
    B. trauma
    C. HIV/AIDS
    D. birth defects

REFERENCE: LaTour, Eichenwald-Maki, and Oachs, p 373

57. To gather statistics for surgical services provided on an outpatient basis, which of the following codes are needed?
    A. ICD-10-CM codes
    B. evaluation and management codes
    C. HCPCS Level II codes
    D. CPT codes

REFERENCE: Bowie and Green, p 257
McWay, p 164
Schraffenberger and Kuehn, p 10

58. The Cancer Committee at your hospital requests a list of all patients entered into your cancer registry in the last year. This information would be obtained by checking the
    A. disease index.
    B. tickler file.
    C. suspense file.
    D. accession register.

REFERENCE: LaTour, Eichenwald-Maki, and Oachs, p 371
Sayles, p 439

59. The reference date for a cancer registry is
    A. January 1 of the year in which the registry was established.
    B. the date when data collection began.
    C. the date that the Cancer Committee is established.
    D. the date that the cancer program applies for approval by the American College of Surgeons.

REFERENCE: Abdelhak, p 491

60. The abstract completed on the patients in your hospital contains the following items: patient demographics; prehospital interventions; vital signs on admission; procedures and treatment prior to hospitalization; transport modality; and injury severity score. The hospital uses these data for its
    A. AIDS registry.
    B. diabetes registry.
    C. implant registry.
    D. trauma registry.

REFERENCE: Abdelhak, p 497
LaTour, Eichenwald-Maki, and Oachs, pp 372–373
Sayles, pp 441–442

61. In relation to birth defects registries, active surveillance systems
    A. use trained staff to identify cases in all hospitals, clinics, and other facilities through review of patient records, indexes, vital records, and hospital logs.
    B. are commonly used in all 50 states.
    C. miss 10% to 30% of all cases.
    D. rely on reports submitted by hospitals, clinics, or other sources.

REFERENCE: Abdelhak, p 492

62. In regard to quality of coding, the degree to which the same results (same codes) are obtained by different coders or on multiple attempts by the same coder refers to
    A. reliability.
    B. validity.
    C. completeness.
    D. timeliness.

REFERENCE: LaTour, Eichenwald-Maki, and Oachs, pp 442–443

63. The Healthcare Cost and Utilization Project (HCUP) consists of a set of databases that include data on inpatients whose care is paid for by third-party payers. HCUP is an initiative of the
   A. Agency for Healthcare Research and Quality.
   B. Centers for Medicare and Medicaid Services.
   C. National Library of Medicine.
   D. World Health Organization.

REFERENCE: LaTour, Eichenwald-Maki, and Oachs, pp 381, 631
McWay, p 175

64. The coding supervisor notices that the coders are routinely failing to code all possible diagnoses and procedures for a patient encounter. This indicates to the supervisor that there is a problem with
   A. completeness.
   B. validity.
   C. reliability.
   D. timeliness.

REFERENCE: LaTour, Eichenwald-Maki, and Oachs, pp 442–443

65. When coding free skin grafts, which of the following is NOT an essential item of data needed for accurate coding?
   A. recipient site
   B. donor site
   C. size of defect
   D. type of repair

REFERENCE: Bowie, p 122
Green, pp 661–663
Smith, pp 72–76

66. In CPT, Category III codes include codes
   A. to describe emerging technologies.
   B. to measure performance.
   C. for use by nonphysician practitioners.
   D. for supplies, drugs, and durable medical equipment.

REFERENCE: AMA (2015), p 687
Bowie, p 9
Smith, p 4

67. The information collected for your registry includes patient demographic information, diagnosis codes, functional status, and histocompatibility information. This type of registry is a
   A. birth defects registry.
   B. diabetes registry.
   C. transplant registry.
   D. trauma registry.

REFERENCE: LaTour, Eichenwald-Maki, and Oachs, pp 374–375

68. Patient Jamey Smith has been seen at Oceanside Hospital three times prior to this current encounter. Unfortunately, because of clerical errors, Jamey's information was entered into the MPI incorrectly on the three previous admissions and consequently has three different medical record numbers. The unit numbering system is used at Oceanside Hospital. Jamey's previous entries into the MPI are as follows:

09/03/12	Jamey Smith	MR# 10361
03/10/13	Jamey Smith Doe	MR# 33998
07/23/14	Jamie Smith Doe	MR# 36723

The next available number to be assigned at Oceanside Hospital is 41369. Duplicate entries in the MPI should be scrubbed and all of Jamey's medical records should be filed under medical record number

A. 10361.
B. 33998.
C. 36723.
D. 41369.

REFERENCE: Bowie and Green, pp 252–256
McWay, pp 139–140

69. The method of calculating errors in a coding audit that allows for benchmarking with other hospitals, and permits the reviewer to track errors by case type, is the

A. record-over-record method.
B. benchmarking method.
C. code method.
D. focused review method.

REFERENCE: Schraffenberger and Kuehn, p 319

70. The most common type of registry located in hospitals of all sizes and in every region of the country is the

A. trauma registry.
B. cancer registry.
C. AIDS registry.
D. birth defects registry.

REFERENCE: Bowie and Green, p 262
McWay, p 142

71. A radiologist is asked to review a patient's CT scan that was taken at another facility. The modifier –26 attached to the code indicates that the physician is billing for what component of the procedure?

A. professional
B. technical
C. global
D. confirmatory

REFERENCE: Bowie, p 18
Green, p 519

72. The committee that is responsible for establishing the quality improvement priorities of the cancer program and for monitoring the effectiveness of quality improvement activities is the

A. Medical Staff Committee.
B. Cancer Committee.
C. Governing Board Committee.
D. Quality Improvement Committee.

REFERENCE: Abdelhak, p 492

73. According to CPT, antepartum care includes all of the following EXCEPT
   A. initial and subsequent history.
   B. physical examination.
   C. monthly visits up to 36 weeks.
   D. routine chemical urinalysis.

REFERENCE: Bowie, pp 331–332
Green, pp 831–832
Smith, p 140

74. The Cancer Committee at Wharton General Hospital wants to compare long-term survival rates for pancreatic cancer by evaluating medical versus surgical treatment of the cancer. The best source of these data is the
   A. disease index.
   B. operation index.
   C. master patient index.
   D. cancer registry abstracts.

REFERENCE: Abdelhak, pp 490–492
LaTour, Eichenwald-Maki, and Oachs, pp 370–371
McWay, pp 142–143

75. A list or collection of clinical words or phrases with their meanings is a
   A. data dictionary.
   B. language.
   C. medical nomenclature.
   D. clinical vocabulary.

REFERENCE: LaTour, Eichenwald-Maki, and Oachs, p 389

76. The main difference between concurrent and retrospective coding is
   A. when the coding is done.
   B. what classification system is used.
   C. the credentials of the coder.
   D. the involvement of the physician.

REFERENCE: Sayles, p 396
Schraffenberger and Kuehn, p 30

77. A PEG procedure would most likely be done to facilitate
   A. breathing.
   B. eating.
   C. urination.
   D. None of these answers apply.

REFERENCE: Schraffenberger, p 294

78. CMS published a final rule indicating a compliance date to implement ICD-10-CM and ICD-10-PCS. The use of these two code sets will be effective on
   A. January 1, 2014.
   B. October 1, 2014.
   C. January 1, 2015.
   D. October 1, 2015.

REFERENCE: Schraffenberger, pp viii–ix

79. Mappings between ICD-9-CM and ICD-10-CM were developed and released by the National Center for Health Statistics (NCHS) to facilitate the transition from one code set to another. They are called
   A. GEMS (General Equivalency Mappings).
   B. Medical Mappings.
   C. Code Maps.
   D. ICD Code Maps.

REFERENCE: Green, pp 86–87
LaTour, Eichenwald-Maki, and Oachs, p 392

80. The code structure for ICD-10-CM differs from the code structure of ICD-9-CM. An ICD-10-CM code consists of
   A. five alphanumeric characters.
   B. 10 characters.
   C. three to seven characters.
   D. seven digits.

REFERENCE: Bowie, p 566
Green, pp 72–74

81. The first character for all of the codes assigned in ICD-10-CM is
   A. an alphabet.
   B. a number.
   C. an alphabet or a number.
   D. a digit.

REFERENCE: Green, pp 72–74

82. ICD-10-PCS will be implemented in the United States to code
   A. hospital inpatient procedures.
   B. physician office procedures.
   C. hospital inpatient diagnoses.
   D. hospital outpatient diagnoses.

REFERENCE: Green, p 79

83. ICD-10-PCS codes have a unique structure. An example of a valid code in the ICD-10-PCS system is
   A. L03.311.
   B. 013.2.
   C. B2151.
   D. 2W3FX1Z.

REFERENCE: Green, pp 80–81
Schraffenberger, pp 66–67

84. ICD-10-PCS utilizes the third character in the Medical and Surgical section to identify the "root operation." The name of the root operation that describes "cutting out or off, without replacing a portion of a body part" is
   A. destruction.
   B. extirpation.
   C. excision.
   D. removal.

REFERENCE: Green, p 392
Schraffenberger, pp 70–72

85. In ICD-10-PCS, to code "removal of a thumbnail," the root operation would be
   A. removal.
   B. extraction.
   C. fragmentation.
   D. extirpation.

REFERENCE: Green, p 392
Schraffenberger, pp 70–72

86. In ICD-10-CM, the final character of the code indicates laterality. An unspecified side code is also provided should the site not be identified in the medical record. If no bilateral code is provided and the condition is bilateral, the ICD-10-CM Official Coding Guidelines direct the coder to
   A. assign the unspecified side code.
   B. assign separate codes for both the left and right side.
   C. not assign a code.
   D. query the physician.

REFERENCE: Green, p 250

87. An example of a valid code in ICD-10-CM is
   A. 576.212D.
   B. Z3A.34
   C. 329.6677.
   D. BJRT23x.

REFERENCE: Green, p 73

Answer Key for Classification Systems and Secondary Data Sources

NOTE: *Explanations are provided for those questions that require mathematical calculations and questions that are not clearly explained in the references that are cited.*

	ANSWER	EXPLANATION
1.	B	
2.	B	
3.	C	
4.	A	
5.	C	
6.	C	
7.	A	A coder should never assign a code on the basis of laboratory results alone. If findings are clearly outside the normal range and the physician has ordered additional testing or treatment, it is appropriate to consult with the physician as to whether a diagnosis should be added or whether the abnormal finding should be listed.
8.	A	
9.	B	Pilocarpine is used to treat open-angle and angle-closure glaucoma to reduce intraocular pressure.
10.	D	Digoxin is used for maintenance therapy in congestive heart failure, atrial fibrillation, atrial flutter, and paroxysmal atrial tachycardia. Ibuprofen is an anti-inflammatory drug. Oxytocin is used to initiate or improve uterine contractions at term, and haloperidol is used to manage psychotic disorders.
11.	D	
12.	C	HCPCS codes (Levels I and II) would only give the code for any procedures that were performed and would not identify the diagnosis code or cause of the accident. The correct name of the nomenclature for athletic injuries is the Standard Nomenclature of Athletic Injuries and is used to identify sports injuries. It has not been revised since 1976.
13.	D	
14.	B	All three key components (history, physical examination, and medical decision making) are required for new patients and initial visits. At least two of the three key components are required for established patients and subsequent visits.
15.	B	
16.	D	
17.	A	
18.	B	
19.	B	
20.	A	
21.	A	
22.	A	
23.	D	

Answer Key for Classification Systems and Secondary Data Sources

	ANSWER	EXPLANATION
24.	B	
25.	C	
26.	B	
27.	A	
28.	C	
29.	B	
30.	B	
31.	C	
32.	B	
33.	B	
34.	B	
35.	D	
36.	A	
37.	A	
38.	B	
39.	C	
40.	B	
41.	B	
42.	D	
43.	C	
44.	A	
45.	C	
46.	B	
47.	A	
48.	C	
49.	C	
50.	B	
51.	C	
52.	D	
53.	C	
54.	C	
55.	B	
56.	D	
57.	D	
58.	D	
59.	B	
60.	D	
61.	A	
62.	A	
63.	A	
64.	A	
65.	B	
66	A	
67.	C	
68.	A	
69.	A	
70.	B	

Answer Key for Classification Systems and Secondary Data Sources

	ANSWER	EXPLANATION
71.	A	With CPT radiology codes, there are three components that have to be considered. These are the professional, technical, and global components. The professional component describes the services of a physician who supervises the taking of an x-ray film and the interpretation with report of the results. The technical component describes the services of the person who uses the equipment, the film, and other supplies. The global component describes the combination of both professional and technical components. If the billing radiologist's services include only the supervision and interpretation component, the radiologist bills the procedure code and adds the modifier –26 to indicate that he or she did only the professional component of the procedure.
72.	B	
73.	C	
74.	D	
75.	D	
76.	A	
77.	B	
78.	D	
79.	A	
80.	C	
81.	A	
82.	A	
83.	D	Immobilization of Left Hand Using Splint 2W3FX1Z is a billable ICD-10-PCS procedure code that can be used to specify a medical procedure.
84.	C	
85.	B	
86.	B	
87.	B	ICD-10-CM codes begin with an alphabetical letter. There is a decimal after the third character. Codes can consist of three to seven characters.

ICD-10-CM Official Guidelines for Coding and Reporting FY 2015
Section 15: Pregnancy, Childbirth, and the Puerperium
(15.b.1) Selection of OB Principal or First-listed Diagnosis
Routine outpatient prenatal visits
For routine outpatient prenatal visits when no complications are present, a code from category Z34, Encounter for supervision of normal pregnancy, should be used as the first-listed diagnosis. These codes should not be used in conjunction with chapter 15 codes.
Section 21: Factors influencing health status and contact with health services (Z00-Z99)
(21.c.11) Encounters for Obstetrical and Reproductive Services
See Section I.C.15. Pregnancy, Childbirth, and the Puerperium, for further instruction on the use of these codes.
Codes in category Z3A, Weeks of gestation, may be assigned to provide additional information about the pregnancy. The date of the admission should be used to determine weeks of gestation for inpatient admissions that encompass more than one gestational week.

REFERENCES

Abdelhak, M. and Hanken, M.A. (2016). *Health information: Management of a strategic resource* (5th ed.). St. Louis, MO: Saunders Elsevier.

AHIMA. *ICD-10-CM coder training manual, 2015 edition.*

American Medical Association (AMA). (2015). *Current procedural terminology (CPT) 2015 professional edition.* Chicago: Author.

Bowie, M. J. (2014). *Understanding ICD-10-CM and ICD-10-PCS: A worktext* (2nd ed.). Clifton Park, NY: Cengage Learning.

Bowie, M. J. (2015). *Understanding procedural coding: A worktext* (4th ed.). Clifton Park, NY: Cengage Learning.

Bowie, M. J. and Green, M. A. (2016). *Essentials of health information management: Principles and practices* (3rd ed.). Clifton Park, NY: Cengage Learning.

Green, M. (2016). *3-2-1 Code it* (5th ed.). Clifton Park, NY: Cengage Learning.

LaTour, K., Eichenwald-Maki, S., and Oachs, P. (2013). *Health information management: Concepts, principles and practice* (4th ed.). Chicago: American Health Information Management Association (AHIMA).

McWay, D. C. (2014). *Today's health information management: An integrated approach* (2nd ed.). Clifton Park, NY: Cengage Learning.

Sayles, N. (2013). *Health information management technology: An applied approach* (4th ed.). Chicago: American Health Information Management Association (AHIMA).

Schraffenberger, L. A. (2015). *Basic ICD-10-CM/PCS and ICD-9-CM coding*. Chicago: American Health Information Management Association (AHIMA).

Schraffenberger, L. A., & Kuehn, L. (2011). *Effective management of coding services* (4th ed.). Chicago: American Health Information Management Association (AHIMA).

Smith, G. (2015). *Basic current procedural terminology and HCPCS coding 2015.* Chicago: American Health Information Management Association (AHIMA).

Woodrow, R., Colbert, B. J., and Smith, D. M. (2015). Essentials of pharmacology for health professions (7th ed.). Clifton Park, NY: Cengage Learning.

RHIA AND RHIT COMPETENCIES BY QUESTION FOR CLASSIFICATION SYSTEMS AND SECONDARY DATA SOURCES													
Question	RHIA Domain Competencies						RHIT Domain Competencies						
	1	2	3	4	5		1	2	3	4	5	6	7
1	X						X						
2	X							X					
3	X						X						
4			X				X						
5			X				X						
6	X						X						
7	X							X					
8	X						X						
9	X							X					
10	X						X						
11	X						X						
12			X				X						
13	X							X					
14	X						X						
15	X						X						
16	X						X						
17	X						X						
18	X							X					
19			X					X					
20			X					X					
21	X						X						
22	X						X						
23	X						X						
24			X				X						
25	X						X						
26	X							X					
27			X				X						
28	X								X				
29	X							X					
30			X				X						
31	X							X					
32	X							X					
33	X						X						
34	X						X						
35	X						X						
36	X						X						
37	X						X						
38	X						X						
39	X							X					
40	X							X					
41	X						X						
42	X							X					
43	X							X					
44	X							X					
45			X					X					
46	X							X					
47	X							X					
48	X						X						
49	X							X					
50	X						X						
51	X							X					
52	X							X					
53	X							X					

RHIA AND RHIT COMPETENCIES BY QUESTION FOR CLASSIFICATION SYSTEMS AND SECONDARY DATA SOURCES												
Question	RHIA Domain Competencies					RHIT Domain Competencies						
	1	2	3	4	5	1	2	3	4	5	6	7
54	X						X					
55	X					X						
56	X						X					
57	X						X					
58			X				X					
59	X						X					
60	X						X					
61	X						X					
62				X			X					
63	X						X					
64				X		X						
65	X					X						
66	X					X						
67	X					X						
68			X			X						
69	X					X						
70	X					X						
71	X						X					
72	X					X						
73	X						X					
74			X				X					
75	X						X					
76	X					X						
77	X						X					
78	X						X					
79	X						X					
80	X						X					
81	X						X					
82	X						X					
83	X						X					
84	X						X					
85	X					X						
86	X					X						
87	X					X						

VI. Medical Billing and Reimbursement Systems

Shelley C. Safian, PhD, CCS-P, CPC-H, CPC-I, CHA

AHIMA-Approved ICD-10-CM/PCS Trainer

1. The case-mix management system that utilizes information from the Minimum Data Set (MDS) in long-term care settings is called
   A. Medicare Severity Diagnosis Related Groups (MS-DRGs).
   B. Resource Based Relative Value System (RBRVS).
   C. Resource Utilization Groups (RUGs).
   D. Ambulatory Patient Classifications (APCs).

REFERENCE: Green, p 344

2. The prospective payment system used to reimburse home health agencies for patients with Medicare utilizes data from the:
   A. MDS (Minimum Data Set).
   B. OASIS (Outcome and Assessment Information Set).
   C. UHDDS (Uniform Hospital Discharge Data Set).
   D. UACDS (Uniform Ambulatory Core Data Set).

REFERENCE: Green, p 423
LaTour, Eichenwald-Maki, and Oachs, p 438

3. Under APCs, the payment status indicator "N" means that the payment
   A. is for ancillary services.
   B. is for a clinic or an emergency visit.
   C. is discounted at 50%.
   D. is packaged into the payment for other services.

REFERENCE: LaTour, Eichenwald-Maki, and Oachs, p 435

4. All of the following items are "packaged" under the Medicare outpatient prospective payment system, EXCEPT for
   A. recovery room.
   B. medical supplies.
   C. anesthesia.
   D. medical visits.

REFERENCE: Green, pp 640–644
LaTour, Eichenwald-Maki, and Oachs, pp 431, 435
Sayles, p 330

5. Under the RBRVS, each HCPCS/CPT code contains three components, each having assigned relative value units. These three components are
   A. geographic index, wage index, and cost of living index.
   B. fee-for-service, per diem payment, and capitation.
   C. conversion factor, CMS weight, and hospital-specific rate.
   D. physician work, practice expense, and malpractice insurance expense.

REFERENCE: Green, p 1011

6. The prospective payment system used to reimburse hospitals for Medicare hospital outpatients is called
   A. APGs.
   B. RBRVS.
   C. APCs.
   D. MS-DRGs.

REFERENCE: Bowie and Green, p 328
Green, pp 1002, 1007–1008

7. A Medicare patient was seen by Dr. Zachary, who is a nonparticipating physician. The charge for the office visit was $125. The Medicare beneficiary had already met his deductible. The Medicare Fee Schedule amount is $100. Dr. Zachary does not accept assignment. The office manager will apply a practice termed as "balance billing," which means that the patient is
   A. financially liable for the Medicare Fee Schedule amount.
   B. financially liable for charges in excess of the Medicare Fee Schedule, up to a limit.
   C. not financially liable for any amount.
   D. financially liable for only the deductible.

REFERENCE: LaTour, Eichenwald-Maki, and Oachs, p 449
Sayles, pp 295–297

8. The prospective payment system based on resource utilization groups (RUGs) is used for reimbursement to ____________________ for patients with Medicare.
   A. freestanding ambulatory surgery centers
   B. hospital-based outpatients
   C. intermediate care facilities
   D. skilled nursing facilities

REFERENCE: Green, pp 1006–1007
Schraffenberger, p 544

9. The _______________ is a statement sent to the provider to explain payments made by third-party payers.
   A. remittance advice
   B. advance beneficiary notice
   C. attestation statement
   D. acknowledgment notice

REFERENCE: Green, p 1030
Green and Rowell, p 89

10. HIPAA administrative simplification provisions require all of the following code sets to be used EXCEPT
   A. ICD-10-CM
   B. CDT
   C. DSM
   D. CPT

REFERENCE: Green, p 1034

11. The computer-to-computer transfer of data between providers and third-party payers in a data format agreed upon by both parties is called
   A. HIPAA (Health Insurance Portability and Accountability Act).
   B. electronic data interchange (EDI).
   C. health information exchange (HIE).
   D. health data exchange (HDE).

REFERENCE: Green, p 1030

12. A computer software program that assigns appropriate MS-DRGs according to the information provided for each episode of care is called a(n)
   A. encoder.
   B. case-mix analyzer.
   C. grouper.
   D. scrubber.

REFERENCE: LaTour, Eichenwald-Maki, and Oachs, p 432

13. The standard claim form used by hospitals to request reimbursement for inpatient and outpatient procedures performed or services provided is called the
    A. UB-04.
    B. CMS-1500.
    C. CMS-1491.
    D. CMS-1600.

REFERENCE: Green and Rowell, p 741
LaTour, Eichenwald-Maki, and Oachs, p 445

14. Under ASC PPS, when multiple procedures are performed during the same surgical session, a payment reduction is applied. The procedure in the highest level group is reimbursed at _____ and all remaining procedures are reimbursed at ______.
    A. 50%, 25%
    B. 100%, 50%
    C. 100%, 25%
    D. 100%, 75%

REFERENCE: LaTour, Eichenwald-Maki, and Oachs, p 437

15. The ________________________ refers to a statement sent to the patient to show how much the provider billed, how much Medicare reimbursed the provider, and what the patient must pay the provider.
    A. Medicare summary notice
    B. remittance advice
    C. advance beneficiary notice
    D. coordination of benefits

REFERENCE: Green and Rowell, p 731
LaTour, Eichenwald-Maki, and Oachs, p 445
Sayles, pp 289–290

16. Currently, which prospective payment system is used to determine the payment to the "physician" for physician services covered under Medicare Part B, such as outpatient surgery performed on a Medicare patient?
    A. MS-DRGs
    B. APCs
    C. RBRVS
    D. ASCs

REFERENCE: Green, pp 1007–1008, 1011
Schraffenberger and Kuehn, p 210

17. Which of the following best describes the situation of a provider who agrees to accept assignment for Medicare Part B services?
    A. The provider is reimbursed at 15% above the allowed charge.
    B. The provider is paid according to the Medicare Physician Fee Schedule (MPFS) plus 10%.
    C. The provider cannot bill the patients for the balance between the MPFS amount and the total charges.
    D. The provider is a nonparticipating provider.

REFERENCE: Green, p 1011

18. When the MS-DRG payment received by the hospital is lower than the actual charges for providing the inpatient services for a patient with Medicare, then the hospital
    A. makes a profit.
    B. can bill the patient for the difference.
    C. absorbs the loss.
    D. can bill Medicare for the difference.

REFERENCE: LaTour, Eichenwald-Maki, and Oachs, p 432

29. ____ are errors in medical care that are clearly identifiable, preventable, and serious in their consequences for patients.
   A. Misadventures
   B. Adverse preventable events
   C. Never events or Sentinel events
   D. Potential compensable events

REFERENCE: Bowie and Green, p 326
LaTour, Eichenwald-Maki, and Oachs, pp 672–673

30. When a provider, knowingly or unknowingly, uses practices that are inconsistent with accepted medical practice and that directly or indirectly result in unnecessary costs to the Medicare program, this is called
   A. fraud.
   B. abuse.
   C. unbundling.
   D. hypercoding.

REFERENCE: Abdelhak, Gostick, and Hanken, p 672
Green, pp 12, 529–530
Kuen, pp 351, 376
LaTour, Eichenwald-Maki, and Oachs, p 452

31. What prospective payment system reimburses the provider according to prospectively determined rates for a 60-day episode of care?
   A. home health resource groups
   B. inpatient rehabilitation facility
   C. long-term care Medicare severity diagnosis-related groups
   D. the skilled nursing facility prospective payment system

REFERENCE: Bowie and Green, p 313
LaTour, Eichenwald-Maki, and Oachs, p 438

32. If the Medicare non-PAR approved payment amount is $128.00 for a proctoscopy, what is the total Medicare approved payment amount for a doctor who does not accept assignment, applying the limiting charge for this procedure?
   A. $140.80
   B. $143.00
   C. $192.00
   D. $147.20

REFERENCE: Green and Rowell, p 66

33. Under the inpatient prospective payment system (IPPS), there is a 3-day payment window (formerly referred to as the 72-hour rule). This rule requires that outpatient preadmission services that are provided by a hospital up to three calendar days prior to a patient's inpatient admission be covered by the IPPS MS-DRG payment for
   A. diagnostic services.
   B. therapeutic (or nondiagnostic) services whereby the inpatient principal diagnosis code (ICD-10-CM) exactly matches the code used for preadmission services.
   C. therapeutic (or nondiagnostic) services whereby the inpatient principal diagnosis code (ICD-10-CM) does not match the code used for preadmission services.
   D. diganostic services *and* therapeutic (or nondiagnostic) services whereby the inpatient principal diagnosis code (ICD-10-CM) exactly matches the code used for preadmission services.

REFERENCE: Green, p 1002
Bowie and Green, p 313
Green and Rowell, p 325

34. This initiative was instituted by the government to eliminate fraud and abuse and recover overpayments, and involves the use of ______________. Charts are audited to identify Medicare overpayments and underpayments. These entities are paid based on a percentage of money they identify and collect on behalf of the government.
    A. Clinical Data Abstraction Centers (CDAC)
    B. Quality Improvement Organizations (QIO)
    C. Medicare Code Editors (MCE)
    D. Recovery Audit Contractors (RAC)

REFERENCE: LaTour, Eichenwald-Maki, and Oachs, p 856

35. When a patient is discharged from the inpatient rehabilitation facility and returns within three calendar days (prior to midnight on the third day) this is called a(n)
    A. interrupted stay.
    B. transfer.
    C. per diem.
    D. qualified discharge.

REFERENCE: LaTour, Eichenwald-Maki, and Oachs, p 440

36. In a global payment methodology, which is sometimes applied to radiological and similar types of procedures that involve professional and technical components, all of the following are part of the "technical" components EXCEPT
    A. radiological equipment.
    B. physician services.
    C. radiological supplies.
    D. radiologic technicians.

REFERENCE: Green and Rowell, pp 275–276
LaTour, Eichenwald-Maki, and Oachs, p 430
Sayles, pp 263–264

37. Changes in case-mix index (CMI) may be attributed to all of the following factors EXCEPT
    A. changes in medical staff composition.
    B. changes in coding rules.
    C. changes in services offered.
    D. changes in coding productivity.

REFERENCE: LaTour, Eichenwald-Maki, and Oachs, pp 496–497

38. This prospective payment system replaced the Medicare physician payment system of "customary, prevailing, and reasonable (CPR)" charges whereby physicians were reimbursed according to their historical record of the charge for the provision of each service.
    A. Medicare Physician Fee Schedule (MPFS)
    B. Medicare Severity-Diagnosis Related Groups (MS-DRGs)
    C. Global payment
    D. Capitation

REFERENCE: Green, p 1011
Green and Rowell, pp 379–380

39. CMS-identified "Hospital-Acquired Conditions" mean that when a particular diagnosis is not "present on admission," CMS determines it to be
    A. medically necessary.
    B. reasonably preventable.
    C. a valid comorbidity.
    D. the principal diagnosis.

REFERENCE: LaTour, Eichenwald-Maki, and Oachs, pp 433–434

40. This process involves the gathering of charge documents from all departments within the facility that have provided services to patients. The purpose is to make certain that all charges are coded and entered into the billing system.
    A. precertification
    B. insurance verification
    C. charge capturing
    D. revenue cycle

REFERENCE: Diamond, p 10
LaTour, Eichenwald-Maki, and Oachs, p 465

41. The Correct Coding Initiative (CCI) edits contain a listing of codes under two columns titled "comprehensive codes" and "component codes." According to the CCI edits, when a provider bills Medicare for a procedure that appears in both columns for the same beneficiary on the same date of service
    A. code only the component code.
    B. do not code either one.
    C. code only the comprehensive code.
    D. code both the comprehensive code and the component code.

REFERENCE: Green, p 1024
Green and Rowell, pp 283–288

42. The following type of hospital is considered excluded when it applies for and receives a waiver from CMS. This means that the hospital does not participate in the inpatient prospective payment system (IPPS)
    A. rehabilitation hospital
    B. long-term care hospital
    C. psychiatric hospital
    D. cancer hospital

REFERENCE: Green, p 1001

43. These are financial protections to ensure that certain types of facilities (e.g., children's hospitals) recoup all of their losses due to the differences in their APC payments and the pre-APC payments.
    A. limiting charge
    B. indemnity insurance
    C. hold harmless
    D. pass through

REFERENCE: Green, p 989

44. LCDs and NCDs are review policies that describe the circumstances of coverage for various types of medical treatment. They advise physicians which services Medicare considers reasonable and necessary and may indicate the need for an advance beneficiary notice. They are developed by the Centers for Medicare and Medicaid Services (CMS) and Medicare Administrative Contractors. LCD and NCD are acronyms that stand for
    A. local covered determinations and noncovered determinations.
    B. local coverage determinations and national coverage determinations.
    C. list of covered decisions and noncovered decisions.
    D. local contractor's decisions and national contractor's decisions.

REFERENCE: Green, pp 488, 920
Green and Rowell, pp 305–307

Use the following table to answer questions 45 through 50.

EXAMPLE OF A CHARGE DESCRIPTION MASTER (CDM) FILE LAYOUT

Charge Service Code	Item Service Description	General Ledger Key	HCPCS Code		Charge	Revenue Code	Activity Date
			Medicare	Medicaid			
49683105	CT scan; head; w/out contrast	3	70450	70450	500.00	0351	1/1/2013
49683106	CT scan; head; with contrast	3	70460	70460	675.00	0351	1/1/2013

45. This information is printed on the UB-04 claim form to represent the cost center (e.g., lab, radiology, cardiology, respiratory, etc.) for the department in which the item is provided. It is used for Medicare billing.
    A. HCPCS
    B. revenue code
    C. charge/service code
    D. general ledger key

REFERENCE: Green, pp 1014–1015
Green and Rowell, p 342
LaTour, Eichenwald-Maki, and Oachs, pp 449–451

46. This information is used because it provides a uniform system of identifying procedures, services, or supplies. Multiple columns can be available for various financial classes.
    A. HCPCS code
    B. revenue code
    C. general ledger key
    D. charge/service code

REFERENCE: Green, p 471
Green and Rowell, p 295

47. This information provides a narrative name of the services provided. This information should be presented in a clear and concise manner. When possible, the narratives from the HCPCS/CPT book should be utilized.
    A. general ledger key
    B. HCPCS
    C. item/service description
    D. revenue code

REFERENCE: Green, p 474
Green and Rowell, pp 340–342

48. This information is the numerical identification of the service or supply. Each item has a unique number with a prefix that indicates the department number (the number assigned to a specific ancillary department) and an item number (the number assigned by the accounting department or the business office) for a specific procedure or service represented on the chargemaster.
    A. charge/service code
    B. HCPCS code
    C. revenue code
    D. general ledger key

REFERENCE: Green, p 471
Green and Rowell, pp 340–342

49. This information is used to assign each item to a particular section of the general ledger in a particular facility's accounting section. Reports can be generated from this information to include statistics related to volume in terms of numbers, dollars, and payer types.
   A. general ledger key
   B. charge/service code
   C. revenue code
   D. HCPCS code

REFERENCE: LaTour, Eichenwald-Maki, and Oachs, p 449

50. Under ASC-PPS the patient is responsible for paying the coinsurance amount based upon ____ of the national median charge for the services rendered.
   A. 50%
   B. 15%
   C. 20%
   D. 80%

REFERENCE: Green, p 1009
Bowie and Green, p 314
LaTour, Eichenwald-Maki, and Oachs, p 437

51. ____ is a joint federal and state program that provides health care coverage to low-income populations and certain aged and disabled individuals.
   A. TRICARE
   B. Medicare Part A
   C. Medicaid
   D. Medicare Part B

REFERENCE: Green, p 995

52. The DNFB report includes all patients who have been discharged from the facility but for whom, for one reason or another, the billing process is not complete. DNFB is an acronym for ____________.
   A. diagnosis not finally balanced
   B. days not fiscally balanced
   C. dollars not fully billed
   D. discharged no final bill

REFERENCE: LaTour, Eichenwald-Maki, and Oachs, p 470

53. The limiting charge is a percentage limit on fees specified by legislation that the nonparticipating physician may bill Medicare beneficiaries above the non-PAR fee schedule amount. The limiting charge is
   A. 10%.
   B. 15%.
   C. 20%.
   D. 50%.

REFERENCE: Green and Rowell, p 498

Use the following case scenario to answer questions 54 through 58.

> A patient with Medicare is seen in the physician's office.
> The total charge for this office visit is $250.00.
> The patient has previously paid his deductible under Medicare Part B.
> The PAR Medicare Fee Schedule amount for this service is $200.00.
> The non-PAR Medicare Fee Schedule amount for this service is $190.00.

54. The patient is financially liable for the coinsurance amount, which is
   A. 80%.
   B. 100%.
   C. 20%.
   D. 15%.

REFERENCE: Green and Rowell, p 498

55. If this physician is a participating physician who accepts assignment for this claim, the total amount the physician will receive is
    A. $200.00.
    B. $250.00.
    C. $218.50.
    D. $190.00.

REFERENCE: Green and Rowell, p 498

56. If this physician is a nonparticipating physician who does NOT accept assignment for this claim, the total amount the physician will receive is
    A. $250.00.
    B. $200.00.
    C. $218.50.
    D. $190.00.

REFERENCE: Green and Rowell, p 498

57. If this physician is a participating physician who accepts assignment for this claim, the total amount of the patient's financial liability (out-of-pocket expense) is
    A. $200.00.
    B. $40.00.
    C. $160.00.
    D. $30.00.

REFERENCE: Green and Rowell, p 498

58. If this physician is a nonparticipating physician who does NOT accept assignment for this claim, the total amount of the patient's financial liability (out-of-pocket expense) is
    A. $66.50.
    B. $38.00.
    C. $190.00.
    D. $152.00.

REFERENCE: Green and Rowell, p 498

59. A Medicare Summary Notice (MSN) is sent to ________ as their EOB.
    A. physicians
    B. patients (beneficiaries)
    C. hospitals
    D. skilled nursing facilities

Reference: Clack and Renfroe, p 98
Green, p 1031

60. There are times when documentation is incomplete or insufficient to support the diagnoses found in the chart. The most common way of communicating with the physician for answers is by
    A. e-mailing physicians.
    B. using physician query forms.
    C. calling the physician's office.
    D. leaving notes in the chart.

REFERENCE: Green, pp 15–18

61. Under APCs, payment status indicator "X" means
    A. ancillary services.
    B. clinic or emergency department visit (medical visits).
    C. significant procedure, multiple procedure reduction applies.
    D. significant procedure, not discounted when multiple.

REFERENCE: Diamond, pp 278–279
LaTour, Eichenwald-Maki, and Oachs, p 436

62. Under APCs, payment status indicator "V" means
    A. ancillary services.
    B. clinic or emergency department visit (medical visits).
    C. inpatient procedure.
    D. significant procedure, not discounted when multiple.

REFERENCE: Diamond, p 279
LaTour, Eichenwald-Maki, and Oachs, p 436

63. Under APCs, payment status indicator "S" means
    A. ancillary services.
    B. clinic or emergency department visit (medical visits).
    C. significant procedure, multiple procedure reduction applies.
    D. significant procedure, multiple procedure reduction does not apply.

REFERENCE: Diamond, p 279
Green, p 1007
Green and Rowell, p 279
LaTour, Eichenwald-Maki, and Oachs, p 436

64. Under APCs, payment status indicator "T" means
    A. ancillary services.
    B. clinic or emergency department visit (medical visits).
    C. significant procedure, multiple procedure reduction applies.
    D. significant procedure, not discounted when multiple.

REFERENCE: Diamond, p 279
Green, p 1007
LaTour, Eichenwald-Maki, and Oachs, p 436

65. Under APCs, payment status indicator "C" means
    A. ancillary services.
    B. inpatient procedures/services.
    C. significant procedure, multiple procedure reduction applies.
    D. significant procedure, not discounted when multiple.

REFERENCE: Diamond, p 278
LaTour, Eichenwald-Maki, and Oachs, p 436

66. This is a 10-digit, intelligence-free, numeric identifier designed to replace all previous provider legacy numbers. This number identifies the physician universally to all payers. This number is issued to all HIPAA-covered entities. It is mandatory on the CMS-1500 and UB-04 claim forms.
    A. National Practitioner Databank (NPD)
    B. Universal Physician Number (UPN)
    C. Master Patient Index (MPI)
    D. National Provider Identifier (NPI)

REFERENCE: Green and Rowell, p 886
LaTour, Eichenwald-Maki, and Oachs, p 205

67. In the managed care industry, there are specific reimbursement concepts, such as "capitation." All of the following statements are true in regard to the concept of "capitation," EXCEPT
   A. each service is paid based on the actual charges.
   B. the volume of services and their expense do not affect reimbursement.
   C. capitation means paying a fixed amount per member per month.
   D. capitation involves a group of physicians or an individual physician.

REFERENCE: Green, p 996
Green and Rowell, p 45

68. Which of the following statements is FALSE regarding the use of modifiers with the CPT codes?
   A. All modifiers will alter (increase or decrease) the reimbursement of the procedure.
   B. Some procedures may require more than one modifier.
   C. Modifiers are appended to the end of the CPT code.
   D. Not all procedures need a modifier.

REFERENCE: Clack, Renfroe, and Rimmer, pp 25–26
Green, p 517

69. This document is published by the Office of Inspector General (OIG) every year. It details the OIG's focus for Medicare fraud and abuse for that year. It gives health care providers an indication of general and specific areas that are targeted for review. It can be found on the Internet on CMS' Web site.
   A. the OIG's Evaluation and Management Documentation Guidelines
   B. the OIG's Model Compliance Plan
   C. the Federal Register
   D. the OIG's Workplan

REFERENCE: LaTour, Eichenwald-Maki, and Oachs, p 454
Sayles, p 305

70. Accounts Receivable (A/R) refers to
   A. cases that have not yet been paid.
   B. the amount the hospital was paid.
   C. cases that have been paid.
   D. denials that have been returned to the hospital.

REFERENCE: LaTour, Eichenwald-Maki, and Oachs, p 770

71. The following coding system(s) is/are utilized in the MS-DRG prospective payment methodology for assignment and proper reimbursement.
   A. HCPCS/CPT codes
   B. ICD-10-CM/ICD-10-PCS codes
   C. both HCPCS/CPT codes and ICD-10-CM/ICD-10-PCS codes
   D. NPI codes

REFERENCE: Green, pp 1002–1004
Sayles, p 267

72. The following coding system(s) is/are utilized in the Inpatient Psychiatric Facilities (IPFs) prospective payment methodology for assignment and proper reimbursement.
   A. HCPCS/CPT codes
   B. ICD-10-CM/ICD-10-PCS codes
   C. both HCPCS/CPT codes and ICD-10-CM/ICD-10-PCS codes
   D. Revenue codes

REFERENCE: Green, p 1009
Sayles, p 285

73. An Advance Beneficiary Notice (ABN) is a document signed by the
    A. utilization review coordinator indicating that the patient stay is not medically necessary.
    B. physician advisor indicating that the patient's stay is denied.
    C. patient indicating whether he/she wants to receive services that Medicare probably will not pay for.
    D. provider indicating that Medicare will not pay for certain services.

REFERENCE: Green, p 488
LaTour, Eichenwald-Maki, and Oachs, pp 449–450

74. CMS identified Hospital-Acquired Conditions (HACs). Some of these HACs include foreign objects retained after surgery, blood incompatibility, and catheter-associated urinary tract infection. The importance of the HAC payment provision is that the hospital
    A. will receive additional payment for these conditions when they are not present on admission.
    B. will not receive additional payment for these conditions when they are not present on admission.
    C. will receive additional payment for these conditions whether they are present on admission or not.
    D. will not receive additional payment for these conditions when they are present on admission.

REFERENCE: LaTour, Eichenwald-Maki, and Oachs, pp 433–434

75. Under Medicare Part B, all of the following statements are true and are applicable to nonparticipating physician providers, EXCEPT
    A. providers must file all Medicare claims.
    B. nonparticipating providers have a higher fee schedule than that for participating providers.
    C. fees are restricted to charging no more than the "limiting charge" on nonassigned claims.
    D. collections are restricted to only the deductible and coinsurance due at the time of service on an assigned claim.

REFERENCE: Green and Rowell, pp 380–383

76. Under Medicare, a beneficiary has lifetime reserve days. All of the following statements are true, EXCEPT
    A. the patient has a total of 60 lifetime reserve days.
    B. lifetime reserve days are usually reserved for use during the patient's final (terminal) hospital stay.
    C. lifetime reserve days are paid under Medicare Part B.
    D. lifetime reserve days are not renewable, meaning once a patient uses all of their lifetime reserve days, the patient is responsible for the total charges.

REFERENCE: Green and Rowell, pp 528–529

77. When a provider bills separately for procedures that are a part of the major procedure, this is called
    A. fraud.
    B. packaging.
    C. unbundling.
    D. discounting.

REFERENCE:

78. Health care claims transactions use one of three electronic formats, excluding which one of those listed below?
    A. CMS-1500 flat-file format.
    B. National Claim Format.
    C. ANSI ASC X12N 837 format.
    D. Medicare Summary Notice format.

REFERENCE: Green, pp 1032–1033

79. The process by which health care facilities and providers ensure their financial viability by increasing revenue, improving cash flow and enhancing the patient's experience is called
    A. patient orientation.
    B. revenue cycle management.
    C. accounts receivable.
    D. auditing.

REFERENCE: Green, pp 1017–1018

80. Under the APC methodology, discounted payments occur when
    A. there are two or more (multiple) procedures that are assigned to status indicator "T."
    B. there are two or more (multiple) procedures that are assigned to status indicator "S."
    C. modifier-78 is used to indicate a procedure is terminated after the patient is prepared but before anesthesia is started.
    D. pass-through drugs are assigned to status indicator "K."

REFERENCE: Green, pp 1007–1008
Green and Rowell, pp 373–374
LaTour, Eichenwald-Maki, and Oachs, p 436

81. This prospective payment system is for ________________ and utilizes a Patient Assessment Instrument (PAI) to classify patients into case-mix groups (CMGs).
    A. skilled nursing facilities
    B. inpatient rehabilitation facilities
    C. home health agencies
    D. long-term acute care hospitals

REFERENCE: Green and Rowell, p 331
LaTour, Eichenwald-Maki, and Oachs, p 439

82. Home Health Agencies (HHAs) utilize a data entry software system developed by the Centers for Medicare and Medicaid Services (CMS). This software is available to HHAs at no cost through the CMS Web site or on a CD-ROM.
    A. PACE (Patient Assessment and Comprehensive Evaluation)
    B. HAVEN (Home Assessment Validation and Entry)
    C. HHASS (Home Health Agency Software System)
    D. PEPP (Payment Error Prevention Program)

REFERENCE: Green and Rowell, p 321
LaTour, Eichenwald-Maki, and Oachs, p 438
Sayles, p 278

83. This information is published by the Medicare Administrative Contractors (MACs) to describe when and under what circumstances Medicare will cover a service. The ICD-10-CM, ICD-10-PCS, and CPT/HCPCS codes are listed in the memoranda.
    A. LCD (Local Coverage Determinations)
    B. SI/IS (Severity of llness/Intensity of Service Criteria)
    C. OSHA (Occupational Safety and Health Administration)
    D. PEPP (Payment Error Prevention Program)

REFERENCE: Green and Rowell, p 377
LaTour, Eichenwald-Maki, and Oachs, p 462

84. The term "hard coding" refers to
   A. HCPCS/CPT codes that are coded by the coders.
   B. HCPCS/CPT codes that appear in the hospital's chargemaster and will be included automatically on the patient's bill.
   C. ICD-10-CM/ICD-10-PCS codes that are coded by the coders.
   D. ICD-10-CM/ICD-10-PCS codes that appear in the hospital's chargemaster and that are automatically included on the patient's bill.

REFERENCE: LaTour, Eichenwald-Maki, and Oachs, p 451

85. This is the amount collected by the facility for the services it bills.
   A. costs
   B. charges
   C. reimbursement
   D. contractual allowance

REFERENCE: Kuehn, p 311

86. Assume the patient has already met his or her deductible and that the physician is a Medicare participating (PAR) provider. The physician's standard fee for the services provided is $120.00. Medicare's PAR fee is $60.00. How much reimbursement will the physician receive from Medicare?
   A. $120.00
   B. $ 60.00
   C. $ 48.00
   D. $ 96.00

REFERENCE: Green and Rowell, p 498

87. This accounting method attributes a dollar figure to every input required to provide a service.
   A. cost accounting
   B. charge accounting
   C. reimbursement
   D. contractual allowance

REFERENCE: Kuehn, p 316

88. This is the amount the facility actually bills for the services it provides.
   A. costs
   B. charges
   C. reimbursement
   D. contractual allowance

REFERENCE: Kuehn, p 312

89. This is the difference between what is charged and what is paid.
   A. costs
   B. customary
   C. reimbursement
   D. contractual allowance

REFERENCE: Kuehn, pp 312–316

90. When appropriate, under the outpatient PPS, a hospital can use this CPT code in place of, but not in addition to, a code for a medical visit or emergency department service.
   A. CPT Code 99291 (critical care)
   B. CPT Code 99358 (prolonged evaluation and management service)
   C. CPT Code 35001 (direct repair of aneurysm)
   D. CPT Code 50300 (donor nephrectomy)

REFERENCE: Green, pp 575, 580
Kuehn, pp 64–65

91. To monitor timely claims processing in a hospital, a summary report of "patient receivables" is generated frequently. Aged receivables can negatively affect a facility's cash flow; therefore, to maintain the facility's fiscal integrity, the HIM manager must routinely analyze this report. Though this report has no standard title, it is often called the
    A. remittance advice.
    B. periodic interim payments.
    C. DNFB (discharged, no final bill).
    D. chargemaster.

REFERENCE: LaTour, Eichenwald-Maki, and Oachs, p 470

92. Assume the patient has already met his or her deductible and that the physician is a nonparticipating Medicare provider but does accept assignment. The standard fee for the services provided is $120.00. Medicare's PAR fee is $60.00 and Medicare's non-PAR fee is $57.00. How much reimbursement will the physician receive from Medicare?
    A. $120.00
    B. $60.00
    C. $57.00
    D. $45.60

REFERENCE: Green and Rowell, p 498

93. CMS assigns one _______________ to each APC and each _______________ code.
    A. payment status indicator, HCPCS
    B. CPT code, HCPCS
    C. MS-DRG, CPT
    D. payment status indicator, ICD-10-CM and ICD-10-PCS

REFERENCE: Green, pp 1007–1008

94. All of the following statements are true of MS-DRGs, EXCEPT
    A. a patient claim may have multiple MS-DRGs.
    B. the MS-DRG payment received by the hospital may be lower than the actual cost of providing the services.
    C. special circumstances can result in a cost outlier payment to the hospital.
    D. there are several types of hospitals that are excluded from the Medicare inpatient PPS.

REFERENCE: Green and Rowell, pp 367–370
LaTour, Eichenwald-Maki, and Oachs, pp 431–433
Sayles, pp 266–270

95. This program, formerly called CHAMPUS (Civilian Health and Medical Program—Uniformed Services), is a health care program for active members of the military and other qualified family members.
    A. TRICARE
    B. CHAMPVA
    C. Indian Health Service
    D. workers' compensation

REFERENCE: Clack, Renfroe and RImmer, pp 15–16
Green and Rowell, p 573
LaTour, Eichenwald-Maki, and Oachs, p 424
Sayles, p 251

96. When health care providers are found guilty under any of the civil false claims statutes, the Office of Inspector General is responsible for negotiating these settlements and the provider is placed under a
   A. Fraud Prevention Memorandum of Understanding.
   B. Noncompliance Agreement.
   C. Corporate Integrity Agreement.
   D. Recovery Audit Contract.

REFERENCE: LaTour, Eichenwald-Maki, and Oachs, p 857

97. Regarding hospital emergency department and hospital outpatient evaluation and management CPT code assignment, which statement is true?
   A. Each facility is accountable for developing and implementing its own methodology.
   B. The level of service codes reported by the facility must match those reported by the physician.
   C. Each facility must use the same methodology used by physician coders based on the history, examination, and medical decision-making components.
   D. Each facility must use acuity sheets with acuity levels and assign points for each service performed.

REFERENCE: Green, p 538

98. CMS adjusts the Medicare Severity DRGs and the reimbursement rates every
   A. calendar year beginning January 1.
   B. quarter.
   C. month.
   D. fiscal year beginning October 1.

REFERENCE: LaTour, Eichenwald-Maki, and Oachs, p 431
Sayles, p 268

99. In calculating the fee for a physician's reimbursement, the three relative value units are each multiplied by the
   A. geographic practice cost indices.
   B. national conversion factor.
   C. usual and customary fees for the service.
   D. cost of living index for the particular region.

REFERENCE: Green, p 1011
Green and Rowell, pp 333–334

100. If a participating provider's usual fee for a service is $700.00 and Medicare's allowed amount is $450.00, what amount is written off by the physician?
   A. none of it is written off
   B. $250.00
   C. $340.00
   D. $391.00

REFERENCE: Green and Rowell, pp 380–383

101. Health plans that use ___________ reimbursement methods issue lump-sum payments to providers to compensate them for all the health care services delivered to a patient for a specific illness and/or over a specific period of time.
   A. episode-of-care (EOC)
   B. capitation
   C. fee-for-service
   D. bundled

REFERENCE: Sayles, p 262

102. ______________________ offers voluntary, supplemental medical insurance to help pay for physician's services, outpatient hospital services, medical services, and medical-surgical supplies not covered by the hospitalization plan.
   A. Medicare Part A
   B. Medicare Part B
   C. Medicare Part C
   D. Medicare Part D

REFERENCE: Abdelhak, p 34

103. Commercial insurance plans usually reimburse health care providers under some type of __________ payment system, whereas the federal Medicare program uses some type of _________ payment system.
   A. prospective, retrospective
   B. retrospective, concurrent
   C. retrospective, prospective
   D. prospective, concurrent

REFERENCE: Green and Rowell, p 51
LaTour, Eichenwald-Maki, and Oachs, p 429
Sayles, pp 260–261

104. When the third-party payer refuses to grant payment to the provider, this is called a
   A. denied claim.
   B. clean claim.
   C. rejected claim.
   D. unprocessed claim.

REFERENCE: Green, p 29
LaTour, Eichenwald-Maki, and Oachs, p 471

105. Some services are performed by a nonphysician practitioner (such as a Physician Assistant). These services are an integral yet incidental component of a physician's treatment. A physician must have personally performed an initial visit and must remain actively involved in the continuing care. Medicare requires direct supervision for these services to be billed. This is called
   A. "Technical component" billing.
   B. "Assignment" billing.
   C. "Incident to" billing.
   D. "Assistant" billing.

REFERENCE: Green and Rowell, pp 339, 417

106. When payments can be made to the provider by EFT, this means that the reimbursement is
   A. sent to the provider by check.
   B. sent to the patient, who then pays the provider.
   C. combined with all other payments from the third party payer.
   D. directly deposited into the provider's bank account.

REFERENCE: Clack, Renfroe, and Rimmer, 98

107. The following services are excluded under the Hospital Outpatient Prospective Payment System (OPPS) Ambulatory Payment Classification (APC) methodology.
   A. surgical procedures
   B. clinical lab services
   C. clinic/emergency visits
   D. radiology/radiation therapy

REFERENCE: Green, pp 1007–1008, 1010

108. A HIPPS (Health Insurance Prospective Payment System) code is a five-character alphanumeric code. A HIPPS code is used by home health agencies (HHA) and ____
   A. ambulatory surgery centers (ASC).
   B. physical therapy (PT) centers.
   C. inpatient rehabilitation facilities (IRF).
   D. skilled nursing facilities (SNF).

REFERENCE: cms.gov

109. The Centers for Medicare and Medicaid Services (CMS) will make an adjustment to the MS-DRG payment for certain conditions that the patient was not admitted with, but were acquired during the hospital stay. Therefore, hospitals are required to report an indicator for each diagnosis. This indicator is referred to as
   A. a sentinel event.
   B. a payment status indicator.
   C. a hospital acquired condition.
   D. present on admission.

REFERENCE: Abdelhak, p 284
Bowie, p 342
Green, p 1005
LaTour, Eichenwald-Maki, and Oachs, pp 433–434
Rizzo and Fields, p 174

110. A patient is admitted for a diagnostic workup for cachexia. The final diagnosis is malignant neoplasm of lung with metastasis. The present on admission (POA) indicator is
   A. Y = Present at the time of inpatient admission.
   B. N = Not present at the time of inpatient admission.
   C. U = Documentation is insufficient to determine if condition was present at the time of admission.
   D. W = Provider is unable to clinically determine if condition was present at the time of admission.

REFERENCE: Green, p 1005
LaTour, Eichenwald-Maki, and Oachs, pp 433–434

111. A patient undergoes outpatient surgery. During the recovery period, the patient develops atrial fibrillation and is subsequently admitted to the hospital as an inpatient. The present on admission (POA) indicator is
   A. Y = Present at the time of inpatient admission.
   B. N = Not present at the time of inpatient admission.
   C. U = Documentation is insufficient to determine if condition was present at the time of admission.
   D. W = Provider is unable to clinically determine if condition was present at the time of admission.

REFERENCE: Green, p 1005
LaTour, Eichenwald-Maki, and Oachs, pp 433–434

112. A patient is admitted to the hospital for a coronary artery bypass surgery. Postoperatively, he develops a pulmonary embolism. The present on admission (POA) indicator is
   A. Y = Present at the time of inpatient admission.
   B. N = Not present at the time of inpatient admission.
   C. U = Documentation is insufficient to determine if condition was present at the time of admission.
   D. W = Provider is unable to clinically determine if condition was present at the time of admission.

REFERENCE: Green, p 1005
LaTour, Eichenwald-Maki, and Oachs, pp 433–434

113. The nursing initial assessment upon admission documents the presence of a decubitus ulcer. There is no mention of the decubitus ulcer in the physician documentation until several days after admission. The present on admission (POA) indicator is
   A. Y = Present at the time of inpatient admission.
   B. N = Not present at the time of inpatient admission.
   C. U = Documentation is insufficient to determine if condition was present at the time of admission.
   D. W = Provider is unable to clinically determine if condition was present at the time of admission.

REFERENCE: Green, p 1005
LaTour, Eichenwald-Maki, and Oachs, pp 433–434

114. The present on admission (POA) indicator is required to be assigned to the __________ diagnosis(es) for _________________claims on _________________admissions.
   A. principal and secondary, Medicare, inpatient
   B. principal, all, inpatient
   C. principal and secondary, all, inpatient and outpatient
   D. principal, Medicare, inpatient and outpatient

REFERENCE: Green, p 1005
LaTour, Eichenwald-Maki, and Oachs, pp 433–434

115. The first prospective payment system (PPS) for inpatient care was developed in 1983. The newest PPS is used to manage the costs for
   A. home health care.
   B. medical homes.
   C. inpatient psychiatric facilities.
   D. assisted living facilities.

REFERENCE: LaTour, Eichenwald-Maki, and Oachs, p 414

116. Coinsurance payments are paid by the _______ and determined by a specified ratio.
   A. physician
   B. third-party payer
   C. facility
   D. patient (insured)

REFERENCE: LaTour, Eichenwald-Maki, and Oachs, p 415

117. Terminally ill patients with life expectancies of ______ may opt to receive hospice services.
   A. 6 months or less
   B. 6 months to a year
   C. one year or more
   D. one year or less

REFERENCE: LaTour, Eichenwald Maki, and Oachs, p 419

118. State Medicaid programs are required to offer medical assistance for
   A. all individuals age 65 and over.
   B. individuals with qualified financial need.
   C. patients with end stage renal disease.
   D. patients receiving dialysis for permanent kidney failure.

REFERENCE: LaTour, Eichenwald Maki, and Oachs, pp 422–423

119. A lump-sum payment distributed among the physicians who performed the procedure or interpreted its results and the health care facility that provided equipment, supplies, and technical support is known as
   A. capitation.
   B. fee-for-service.
   C. a prospective payment system.
   D. a global payment.

REFERENCE: LaTour, Eichenwald Maki, and Oachs, p 430

120. Of the following, which is a hospital-acquired condition (HAC)?
   A. air embolism
   B. Stage I pressure ulcer
   C. traumatic wound infection
   D. breach birth

REFERENCE: Green, p 1005
LaTour, Eichenwald Maki, and Oachs, p 434

121. APCs are groups of services that the OPPS will reimburse. Which one of the following services is not included in APCs?
   A. radiation therapy
   B. preventive services
   C. screening exams
   D. organ transplantation

REFERENCE: LaTour, Eichenwald Maki, and Oachs, p 435

122. A patient is being cared for in her home by a qualified agency participating in Medicare. The data-entry software used to conduct all patient assessments is known as
   A. HHRG.
   B. RBRVS.
   C. HAVEN.
   D. IRVEN.

REFERENCE: Green, pp 442, 1007
LaTour, Eichenwald Maki, and Oachs, p 438

123. There are seven criteria for high-quality clinical documentation. All of these elements are included EXCEPT
   A. precise.
   B. complete.
   C. consistent.
   D. covered (by third-party payer).

REFERENCE: LaTour, Eichenwald Maki, and Oachs, p 443

124. A three-digit code that describes a classification of a product or service provided to a patient is a
   A. ICD-10-CM code.
   B. CPT code.
   C. HCPCS Level II code.
   D. Revenue code.

REFERENCE: LaTour, Eichenwald Maki, and Oachs, p 449

125. The category "Commercial payers" includes private health information and
   A. Medicare/Medicaid.
   B. employer-based group health insurers.
   C. TriCare.
   D. Blue Cross Blue Shield.

REFERENCE: Green, p 993

126. ICD-10-PCS procedure codes are used on which of the following forms to report services provided to a patient?
   A. UB-04
   B. CMS-1500
   C. CMS-1491
   D. MDC 02

REFERENCE: Green, p 993

127. ______ classify inpatient hospital cases into groups that are expected to consume similar hospital resources.
   A. IPPS
   B. CMS
   C. DRG
   D. MAC

REFERENCE: Green, p 1002

128. Based on CMS's DRG system, other systems have been developed for payment purposes. The one that classifies the non-Medicare population, such as HIV patients, neonates, and pediatric patients, is known as
   A. AP-DRGs.
   B. RDRGs.
   C. IR-DRGs.
   D. APR-DRGs.

REFERENCE: Green, p 1004

129. For those qualified, the ____ rule states that hospitals are paid a graduated per diem rate for each day of the patient's stay, not to exceed the prospective payment DRG rate.
   A. POA Indicator
   B. MS-DRG
   C. IPPS Transfer
   D. OASIS

REFERENCE: Green, p 1005

130. In a hospital, a document that contains a computer-generated list of procedures, services, and supplies, along with their revenue codes and charges for each item, is known as a(n)
   A. Encounter form.
   B. Superbill.
   C. Revenue master.
   D. Chargemaster.

REFERENCE: Green, p 1014

Answer Key for Medical Billing and Reimbursement Systems

	ANSWER	EXPLANATION
1.	C	
2.	B	
3.	D	
4.	D	
5.	D	
6.	C	
7.	B	
8.	D	
9.	A	
10.	C	
11.	B	
12.	C	
13.	A	The UB-04 is used by hospitals. The CMS-1500 is used by physicians and other noninstitutional providers and suppliers. The CMS-1491 is used by ambulance services.
14.	B	
15.	A	
16.	D	
17.	C	Since the provider accepts assignment, he will accept the Medicare Physician Fee Schedule (MPFS) payment as payment in full.
18.	C	
19.	D	
20.	B	12781.730/10,000 = 1.278

MS-DRG	Description	Number of Patients	CMS Relative Weight	Total CMS Relative Weight
470	Major joint replacement or reattachment of lower extremity w/o MCC	2,750	1.9871	5464.525
392	Esophagitis, gastroent & misc. digestive disorders w/o MCC	2,200	0.7121	1566.620
194	Simple pneumonia & pleurisy w CC	1,150	1.0235	1177.025
247	Perc cardiovasc proc 2 drug-eluting stent w/o MCC	900	2.1255	1912.950
293	Heart failure & shock w/o CC/MCC	850	0.8765	745.025
313	Chest pain	650	0.5489	356.785
292	Heart failure & shock w CC	550	1.0134	557.350
690	Kidney & urinary tract infections w/o MCC	400	0.8000	320.000
192	Chronic obstructive pulmonary disease w/o CC/MCC	300	0.8145	244.350
871	Septicemia w/o MV 96+ hours w MCC	250	1.7484	437.100
	Total	10,000		12781.730
	Case-Mix Index Total CMS Relative Weights (12781.730) divided by (10,000) patients			1.278

Answer Key for Medical Billing and Reimbursement Systems

	ANSWER	EXPLANATION
21.	A	(See table on answer key under question 20.)
22.	A	(See table on answer key under question 20.)
23.	D	Total profit cannot be determined from this information alone. A comparison of the total charges on the bills and the PPS amount (reimbursement amount) that the hospital would receive for each MS-DRG could identify the total profit.
24.	A	
25.	A	
26.	D	
27.	D	
28.	D	
29.	C	
30.	B	
31.	A	
32.	D	The limiting charge is 15% above Medicare's approved payment amount for doctors who do NOT accept assignment ($128.00 × 1.15 = $147.20).
33.	D	
34.	D	
35.	A	
36.	B	
37.	D	Coding productivity will not directly affect CMI. Inaccuracy or poor coding quality can affect CMI.
38.	A	The Medicare Physician Fee Schedule (MPFS) reimburses providers according to predetermined rates assigned to services.
39.	B	
40.	C	
41.	C	
42.	D	Cancer hospitals can apply for and receive waivers from the Centers for Medicare and Medicaid Services (CMS) and are therefore excluded from the inpatient prospective payment system (MS-DRGs). Rehabilitation hospitals are reimbursed under the Inpatient Rehabilitation Prospective Payment System (IRF PPS). Long-term care hospitals are reimbursed under the Long-Term Care Hospital Prospective Payment System (LTCH PPS). Skilled nursing facilities are reimbursed under the Skilled Nursing Facility Prospective Payment System (SNF PPS).
43.	C	
44.	B	
45.	B	
46.	A	
47.	C	
48.	A	
49.	A	
50.	C	
51.	C	
52.	D	
53.	B	
54.	C	

Answer Key for Medical Billing and Reimbursement Systems

	ANSWER	EXPLANATION
55.	A	If a physician is a participating physician who accepts assignment, he will receive the lesser of "the total charges" or "the PAR Medicare Fee Schedule amount." In this case, the Medicare Fee Schedule amount is less; therefore, the total received by the physician is $200.00.
56.	C	If a physician is a nonparticipating physician who does not accept assignment, he can collect a maximum of 15% (the limiting charge) over the non-PAR Medicare Fee Schedule amount. In this case, the non-PAR Medicare Fee Schedule amount is $190.00 and 15% over this amount is $28.50; therefore, the total that he can collect is $218.50.
57.	B	The PAR Medicare Fee Schedule amount is $200.00. The patient has already met the deductible. Of the $200.00, the patient is responsible for 20% ($40.00). Medicare will pay 80% ($160.00). Therefore, the total financial liability for the patient is $40.00.
58.	A	If a physician is a nonparticipating physician who does not accept assignment, he may collect a maximum of 15% (the limiting charge) over the non-PAR Medicare Fee Schedule amount. $190.00 = non-PAR Medicare Fee Schedule amount $190.00 × 0.20 = <u>$38.00</u> = patient liable for 20% coinsurance (patient previously met the deductible) $190.00 × 0.80 = $<u>152.00</u> = Medicare pays 80% $190.00 × 0.15 = <u>$28.50</u> = 15% (limiting charge) over non-PAR Medicare Fee Schedule amount Physician can balance bill and collect from the patient the difference between the non-PAR Medicare Fee Schedule amount and the total charge amount. Therefore, the patient's financial liability is $38.00 (coinsurance) + 28.50 (limiting charge) = $66.50.
59.	B	
60.	B	
61.	A	Under the APC system, there exists a list of status indicators (also called service indicators, payment status indicators, or payment indicators). This indicator is provided for every HCPCS/CPT code and identifies how the service or procedure would be paid (if covered) by Medicare for hospital outpatient visits.
62.	B	Under the APC system, there exists a list of status indicators (also called service indicators, payment status indicators, or payment indicators). This indicator is provided for every HCPCS/CPT code and identifies how the service or procedure would be paid (if covered) by Medicare for hospital outpatient visits.
63.	D	Under the APC system, there exists a list of status indicators (also called service indicators, payment status indicators, or payment indicators). This indicator is provided for every HCPCS/CPT code and identifies how the service or procedure would be paid (if covered) by Medicare for hospital outpatient visits. Payment Status Indicator (PSI) "S" means that if a patient has more than one CPT code with this PSI, none of the procedures will be discounted or reduced. They will all be paid at 100%.
64.	C	Under the APC system, there exists a list of status indicators (also called service indicators, payment status indicators, or payment indicators). This indicator is provided for every HCPCS/CPT code and identifies how the service or procedure would be paid (if covered) by Medicare for hospital outpatient visits. Payment Status Indicator (PSI) "T" means that if a patient has more than one CPT code with this PSI, the procedure with the highest weight will be paid at 100% and all others will be reduced or discounted and paid at 50%.

Answer Key for Medical Billing and Reimbursement Systems

	ANSWER	EXPLANATION
65.	B	Under the APC system, there exists a list of status indicators (also called service indicators, payment status indicators, or payment indicators). This indicator is provided for every HCPCS/CPT code and identifies how the service or procedure would be paid (if covered) by Medicare for hospital outpatient visits.
66.	D	
67.	A	
68.	A	
69.	D	
70.	A	
71.	B	
72.	B	
73.	C	
74.	B	When these conditions are not present on admission, it is assumed that it was hospital acquired and therefore, the hospital may not receive additional payment.
75.	B	Under Medicare Part B, Congress has mandated special incentives to increase the number of health care providers signing PAR (participating) agreements with Medicare. One of those incentives includes a 5% higher fee schedule for PAR providers than for non-PAR (nonparticipating) providers.
76.	C	Lifetime reserve days are applicable for hospital inpatient stays that are payable under Medicare Part A, not Medicare Part B.
77.	C	
78.	C	
79.	B	
80.	A	Discounts are applied to those multiple procedures identified by CPT codes with status indicator "T."
81.	B	
82.	B	
83.	A	Local Coverage Determinations (LCDs) were formerly called local medical review policies (LMRPs).
84.	B	
85.	C	
86	C	If the physician is a participating physician (PAR) who accepts the assignment, he will receive the lesser of the "total charges" or the "PAR amount" (on the Medicare Physician Fee Schedule). Since the PAR amount is lower, the physician collects 80% of the PAR amount ($60.00) x .80 =$48.00, from Medicare. The remaining 20% ($60.00 x .20 = $12.00) of the PAR amount is paid by the patient to the physician. Therefore, the physician will receive $48.00 directly from Medicare.
87	A	
88.	B	
89	D	
90.	A	When a patient meets the definition of critical care, the hospital must use CPT Code 99291 to bill for outpatient encounters in which critical care services are furnished. This code is used instead of another E&M code.

Answer Key for Medical Billing and Reimbursement Systems

	ANSWER	EXPLANATION
91.	C	DNFB stands for "Discharged, No Final Bill"
92.	D	Since the physician is a nonparticipating physician, he will receive the non-PAR fee. The Medicare non-PAR fee is $57.00. Medicare will pay 80% of the non-PAR fee ($57.00 x 0.80 = $45.60). The patient will pay 20% of the non-PAR fee ($57.00 x 0.20 = $11.40). Since the physician is accepting assignment on this claim, he cannot charge the patient any more than the 20% copayment. Therefore, the physician will receive $45.60 directly from Medicare.
93.	A	
94.	A	Only one MS-DRG is assigned per inpatient hospitalization.
95.	A	
96.	C	
97.	B	
98.	D	
99.	A	The three relative value units are physician work, practice expense, and malpractice expense. These are adjusted by multiplying them by the geographical practice cost indices. Then, this total is multiplied by the national conversion factor.
100	B	The participating physician agrees to accept Medicare's fee as payment in full; therefore, the physician would write off the difference between $700.00 and $450.00, which is 250.00.
101	A	
102	B	
103.	C	
104.	A	
105.	C	
106.	D	
107.	B	
108.	C	Inpatient Rehabilitation Facilities (IRF) reports the HIPPS (Health Insurance Prospective Payment System) code on the claim. The HIPPS code is a five-digit CMG (Case Mix Group). Therefore, the HIPPS code for a patient with tier 1 comorbidity and a CMG of 0109 is B0109. Home Health Agencies (HHA) report the HIPPS code on the claim. The HIPPS code is a five-character alphanumeric code. The first character is the letter "H." The second, third, and fourth characters represent the HHRG (Home Health Resource Group). The fifth character represents what elements are computed or derived. Therefore, the HIPPS code for the HHRG C0F0S0 would be HAEJ1.
109.	D	
110.	A	The malignant neoplasm was clearly present on admission, although it was not diagnosed until after the admission occurred.
111.	A	The atrial fibrillation developed prior to a written order for inpatient admission; therefore, it was present at the time of inpatient admission.
112.	B	The pulmonary embolism is an acute condition that was not present on admission because it developed after the patient was admitted and after the patient had surgery.
113.	C	Query the physician as to whether the decubitus ulcer was present on admission or developed after admission.
114.	A	

Answer Key for Medical Billing and Reimbursement Systems

	ANSWER	EXPLANATION
115.	C	
116.	D	
117.	A	
118.	B	
119.	D	
120.	A	
121.	D	
122.	C	
123.	D	
124.	D	
125.	B	
126.	A	
127.	C	
128.	D	
129.	C	
130.	D	

REFERENCES

Abdelhak, M., and Hanken, M. (2016). *Health information management: Management of a strategic resource* (5th ed.). St. Louis, MO: Elsevier Saunders.

Bowie, M. J., and Green, M. A. (2016). *Essentials of health information management: Principles and practices* (3rd ed.). Clifton Park, NY: Cengage Learning.

Clack, C., Renfroe, L., and Rimmer, M. M. (2016). *Medical billing* 101 (2nd ed.). Clifton Park, NY: Cengage Learning.

cms.gov

The following websites provide links to pages containing official informational materials on the Medicare Fee-For-Service Payment:

CMS website: http://www.cms.hhs.gov/home/Medicare.asp

https://www.cms.gov/Regulations-and-Guidance/Regulations-and-Guidance.html

https://www.cms.gov/Outreach-and-Education/Medicare-Learning-Network-MLN/MLNProducts/downloads/MLNCatalog.pdf

https://www.cms.gov/Medicare/Coding/NationalCorrectCodInitEd/index.html

https://www.cms.gov/Medicare/Medicare-Fee-for-Service-Payment/ProspMedicareFeeSvcPmtGen/HIPPSCodes.html

Diamond, M. S. (2016). *Understanding hospital coding and billing: A worktext* (3rd ed.). Clifton Park, NY: Cengage Learning.

Green, M. A. (2016). *3-2-1-Code It!* (5th ed.). Clifton Park, NY: Cengage Learning.

Green, M. A., and Rowell, J. C. (2015). *Understanding health insurance: A guide to billing and reimbursement* (12th ed.). Clifton Park, NY: Cengage Learning.

Kuehn, L. (2015) *Procedural coding and reimbursement for physician services: Applying current procedural terminology and HCPCS 2015 Edition*. Chicago: American Health Information Association (AHIMA).

LaTour, K., Eichenwald-Maki, S., and Oachs, P. (2013). *Health information management: Concepts, principles, and practice* (4th ed.). Chicago: American Health Information Management Association (AHIMA).

Sayles, N. (2013). *Health information management technology: An applied approach* (4th ed.). Chicago: American Health Information Management Association (AHIMA).

Schraffenberger, L. A. (2015). *Basic ICD-10-CM and ICD-10-CM coding*. Chicago: American Health Information Management Association (AHIMA).

Medical Billing and Reimbursement Systems Competencies

Question	RHIA Domain	RHIT Domain
1–130	4	7

VII. Medical Science

Lauralyn Kavanaugh-Burke, DrPH, RHIA, CHES, CHTS-IM

Infectious and Parasitic Diseases

1. The prevention of illness through vaccination occurs due to the formation of
   A. helper B cells.
   B. immunosurveillance.
   C. mast cells.
   D. memory cells.

REFERENCE: Jones, pp 350–351
Scott and Fong, p 307

2. Many bacterial diseases are transmitted directly from person to person. Which of the diseases listed next is a bacterial disease transmitted by way of a tick vector?
   A. Legionnaires' disease
   B. Lyme disease
   C. tetanus
   D. tuberculosis

REFERENCE: Jones, pp 228–229
Moisio, p 434
Neighbors and Tannehill-Jones, pp 345, 441
Scott and Fong, p 329

3. All of the following are examples of direct transmission of a disease EXCEPT
   A. contaminated foods.
   B. coughing or sneezing.
   C. droplet spread.
   D. physical contact.

REFERENCE: Scott and Fong, pp 328–329

4. The most common rickettsial disease in the United States is
   A. hantavirus.
   B. Lyme disease.
   C. Rocky Mountain spotted fever.
   D. syphilis.

REFERENCE: Moisio, pp 434–435
Neighbors and Tannehill-Jones, p 64
Scott and Fong, p 326

5. The most common bloodborne infection in the United States is
   A. *Helicobacter pylori*.
   B. hepatitis A.
   C. hepatitis C.
   D. hemophilia.

REFERENCE: Scott and Fong, p 389

6. The causative organism for severe acute respiratory syndrome (SARS) is a
   A. bacterium.
   B. coronavirus.
   C. fungus.
   D. retrovirus.

REFERENCE: Mayo Clinic (3)
Moisio, p 241
NLM (5)
Scott and Fong, p 360

7. The childhood viral disease that unvaccinated pregnant women should be prevented from contracting because it may be passed to the fetus, thus causing congenital anomalies such as mental retardation, blindness, and deafness, is
   A. rickets.
   B. rubeola.
   C. rubella.
   D. tetanus.

REFERENCE: Moisio, p 435
Neighbors and Tannehill-Jones, p 505

8. United States healthcare providers are concerned about a possible pandemic of avian flu because
   A. there is no vaccine currently available.
   B. it is caused by a group of viruses that mutate very easily.
   C. the causative virus is being spread around the world by migratory birds.
   D. All answers apply.

REFERENCE: CDC (2)

9. Ingrid Anderson presents with a skin infection that began as a raised, itchy bump, resembling an insect bite. Within 1 to 2 days, it developed into a vesicle. Now it is a painless ulcer, about 2 cm in diameter, with a black necrotic area in the center. During the history, her doctor learns that she has recently returned from an overseas vacation and becomes concerned that she may have become infected with anthrax. He will prescribe an
   A. antibiotic.
   B. antineoplastic.
   C. antiparasitic.
   D. antiviral.

REFERENCE: Scott and Fong, p 360

10. The organism transmitted by a mosquito bite that causes malaria is a
    A. bacteria.
    B. prion.
    C. protozoa.
    D. virus.

REFERENCE: Moisio, p 432
Neighbors and Tannehill-Jones, p 61
Rizzo, p 309
Scott and Fong, p 326

11. A pharyngeal culture is taken from a 13-year-old male patient presenting to the ER with fever, painful cervical lymph nodes, purulent tonsillar exudate, and difficulty swallowing. A blood agar culture plate shows complete hemolysis around *Streptococcus pyogenes* bacterial colonies. The patient is given a prescription for erythromycin. The diagnosis in this case is
    A. a group A beta-hemolytic streptococcal throat infection.
    B. a methicillin-resistant *Staphylococcus aureus* skin infection.
    C. tuberculosis with drug-resistant *Mycobacterium tuberculosis*-positive sputum.
    D. meningitis due to *Neisseria meningitidis*-positive cerebrospinal fluid.

REFERENCE: Estridge and Reynolds, pp 739–742
Labtestsonline (7)

12. A 19-year-old college student, who lives on campus in a dormitory, is brought to the ER by his roommates, complaining of a severe headache, nuchal rigidity, fever, and photophobia. The ER physician performs an LP and orders a CSF analysis with a bacterial culture and sensitivity. The young man is admitted to the ICU with a provisional diagnosis of
    A. a group A beta-hemolytic streptococcal throat infection.
    B. a methicillin-resistant *Staphylococcus aureus* skin infection.
    C. tuberculosis with drug-resistant *Mycobacterium tuberculosis*-positive sputum.
    D. meningitis due to *Neisseria meningitidis*-positive cerebrospinal fluid.

REFERENCE: CDC (12)
Labtestsonline (10)

13. There has been a significant increase in the number of cases and deaths from pertussis. Health care professionals attribute this disease trend to which of the following?
    A. A decrease in the number of people immunized with TDaP
    B. An increase in the virulence of the bacteria
    C. Drug-resistant strains of the bacteria
    D. All answers apply.

REFERENCE: CDC (5)

14. A new strain of influenza, H1N1, is a highly virulent strain that spread all over the world. This type of epidemiological disease pattern is referred to as a(n)
    A. cluster.
    B. outbreak.
    C. epidemic.
    D. pandemic.

REFERENCE: CDC (7)

Neoplasia

15. Dr. Zambrano ordered a CEA test for Mr. Logan, a 67-year-old African American male patient. Dr. Zambrano may be considering a diagnosis of
    A. cancer.
    B. carpal tunnel syndrome.
    C. cardiomyopathy.
    D. congestive heart failure.

REFERENCE: NLM (4)

16. Which disease is a malignancy of the lymphatic system?
    A. cystic fibrosis
    B. Hodgkin's disease
    C. neutropenia
    D. Von Willebrand's disease

REFERENCE: Jones, p 355
Moisio, p 216
Neighbors and Tannehill-Jones, p 142
Rizzo, p 354
Scott and Fong, p 305

17. ____________ is the most common type of skin cancer and _________ is the most deadly type of skin cancer.
    A. Malignant melanoma, basal cell carcinoma
    B. Basal cell carcinoma, malignant melanoma
    C. Oat cell carcinoma, squamous cell carcinoma
    D. Squamous cell carcinoma, oat cell carcinoma

REFERENCE: Jones, pp 117, 122–123, 934–935, 939–940
Neighbors and Tannehill-Jones, pp 455–456
Rizzo, p 132
Scott and Fong, p 75
Sormunen, pp 114, 115

18. Cancer derived from epithelial tissue is classified as a(n)
    A. adenoma.
    B. carcinoma.
    C. lipoma.
    D. sarcoma.

REFERENCE: Jones, p 931
Neighbors and Tannehill-Jones, pp 30–31
Rizzo, p 90
Sormunen, p 302

19. The most fatal type of lung cancer is
    A. adenocarcinoma.
    B. large cell cancer.
    C. small cell cancer.
    D. squamous cell cancer.

REFERENCE: Scott and Fong, p 362

20. A pathological diagnosis of transitional cell carcinoma is made. The examined tissue was removed from the
    A. bladder.
    B. esophagus.
    C. oral cavity.
    D. pleura.

REFERENCE: Neighbors and Tannehill-Jones, p 294
Rizzo, pp 102–103

21. The patient's pathology report revealed the presence of Reed–Sternberg cells. This is indicative of
    A. Hodgkin's disease.
    B. leukemia.
    C. non-Hodgkin's lymphoma.
    D. sarcoma.

REFERENCE: Neighbors and Tannehill-Jones, p 142

22. Which of the following BEST summarizes the current treatment of cervical cancer?
    A. A new three-shot vaccination series protects against the types of HPV that cause most cervical cancer cases.
    B. All stages have extremely high cure rates.
    C. Early detection and treatment of cervical cancer does not improve patient survival rates.
    D. Over 99% of cases are linked to long-term HPV infections.

REFERENCE: CDC (1)

23. A 63-year-old patient with terminal pancreatic cancer has started palliative chemotherapy. Palliative means
    A. alleviating or eliminating distressing symptoms of the disease.
    B. increasing the immune response to fight infections.
    C. quick destruction of cancerous cells.
    D. the combining of several medications to cure the cancer.

REFERENCE: ACS (3)
Woodrow, p 229

24. Mary Smith, a 48-year-old patient, is receiving an IV mixture of four different medications to treat stage 2 invasive ductal breast carcinoma. Each of the medications acts upon a different aspect of the cancer cells. This mixture is typically termed a(n)
    A. amalgamation.
    B. cocktail.
    C. blend.
    D. mash-up.

REFERENCE: CDC (8)

Endocrine, Nutritional, and Metabolic Disorders

25. Mary Mulholland has diabetes. Her physician has told her about some factors that put her more at risk for infections. Which of the following factors would probably NOT be applicable?
    A. hypoxia
    B. increased glucose in body fluids
    C. increased blood supply
    D. both hypoxia and increased blood supply

REFERENCE: Neighbors and Tannehill-Jones, pp 253–257

26. Which of the organs listed below has endocrine and exocrine functions?
    A. kidney
    B. liver
    C. lung
    D. pancreas

REFERENCE: Moisio, p 266
Neighbors and Tannehill-Jones, p 259
Rizzo, pp 282–283, 274
Scott and Fong, p 212

27. Which of the following is an effect of insulin?
    A. decreases glycogen concentration in liver
    B. increases blood glucose
    C. increases the breakdown of fats
    D. increases glucose metabolism

REFERENCE: Moisio, pp 301–302, 304
Neighbors and Tannehill-Jones, pp 315–318
Rizzo, pp 274–276, 282, 284–285
Scott and Fong, pp 222–223
Sormunen, p 554

28. Diabetic microvascular disease occurs
    A. as a direct result of elevated serum glucose.
    B. as a result of elevated fat in blood.
    C. due to damage to nerve cells.
    D. only in patients with type 1 diabetes.

REFERENCE: Neighbors and Tannehill-Jones, p 371
Rizzo, pp 284–285
Scott and Fong, pp 227–229

29. Old age, obesity, and a family history of diabetes are all characteristics of
    A. type 1 diabetes.
    B. type 2 diabetes.
    C. juvenile diabetes.
    D. IDDM.

REFERENCE: Rizzo, pp 284–285
Scott and Fong, p 228

30. Clinical manifestations of this disease include polydipsia, polyuria, polyphagia, weight loss, and hyperglycemia. Which of the following tests would be ordered to confirm the disease?
    A. fasting blood sugar
    B. glucagon
    C. glucose tolerance test
    D. postprandial blood sugar

REFERENCE: Neighbors and Tannehill-Jones, pp 315–318
Rizzo, pp 84–85
Scott and Fong, pp 229–230

31. Which of the following is characteristic of Graves' disease?
    A. It is an autoimmune disease.
    B. It most commonly affects males.
    C. It usually cannot be treated.
    D. It usually affects the elderly.

REFERENCE: Jones, p 560
Neighbors and Tannehill-Jones, p 309
Rizzo, pp 280, 285
Scott and Fong, p 310

32. A toxic goiter has what distinguishing characteristic?
    A. iodine deficiency
    B. parathyroid involvement
    C. presence of muscle spasm
    D. thyroid hyperfunction

REFERENCE: Moisio, p 304
Neighbors and Tannehill-Jones, pp 308–310
Rizzo, p 280
Sormunen, p 567

33. How can Graves' disease be treated?
    A. antithyroid drugs
    B. radioactive iodine therapy
    C. surgery
    D. All answers apply.

REFERENCE: Jones, pp 560–561
Neighbors and Tannehill-Jones, p 309
Rizzo, p 285
Sormunen, p 567

Blood and Blood-Forming Conditions

34. The etiology of aplastic anemia is
    A. acute blood loss.
    B. bone marrow failure.
    C. chronic blood loss.
    D. inadequate iron intake.

REFERENCE: Jones, pp 331, 337, 340
Moisio, p 213
Neighbors and Tannehill-Jones, pp 139–140
Scott and Fong, p 246

35. A 75-year-old patient has a sore tongue with tingling and numbness of the hands and feet. She has headaches and is fatigued. Following diagnostic workup, the doctor orders monthly injections of vitamin B_{12}. This patient most likely has which of the following conditions?
    A. aplastic anemia
    B. autoimmune hemolytic anemia
    C. pernicious anemia
    D. sickle cell anemia

REFERENCE: Jones, p 332
Moisio, p 213
Neighbors and Tannehill-Jones, pp 137–138
Scott and Fong, p 245

36. Which one of the following is NOT a pathophysiological factor in anemia?
    A. excessive RBC breakdown
    B. lack of RBC maturation
    C. loss of bone marrow function
    D. loss of spleen function

REFERENCE: Jones, pp 331–333, 338–341
Neighbors and Tannehill-Jones, pp 136–137
Rizzo, p 308
Scott and Fong, pp 245–246

37. In systemic circulation, which of the following vessels carries oxygenated blood?
    A. right vena cava
    B. renal arteries
    C. pulmonary veins
    D. left ventricle

REFERENCE: Jones, pp 380–382
Moisio, pp 176–178
Rizzo, pp 322, 335
Scott and Fong, pp 277-279
Sormunen, p 206

38. O_2 is carried in the blood
    A. bound to hemoglobin.
    B. in the form of carbonic acid.
    C. plasma.
    D. serum.

REFERENCE: Moisio, p 208
Neighbors and Tannehill-Jones, pp 133–134
Rizzo, pp 408, 413
Sormunen, p 247

39. In general, excessive RBC breakdown could result in
    A. Crohn's disease.
    B. elevated BUN.
    C. high bilirubin levels.
    D. peptic ulcers.

REFERENCE: Labtestsonline (1)
Neighbors and Tannehill-Jones, p 259
NLM (1)

40. In ______________ anemia, the red blood cells become shaped like elongated crescents in the presence of low oxygen concentration.
    A. aplastic
    B. folic acid
    C. sickle cell
    D. vitamin B_{12}

REFERENCE: Jones, p 333
Moisio, p 213
Rizzo, p 308
Scott and Fong, p 246

41. A 72-year-old white male patient is on Coumadin therapy. Which of the following tests is commonly ordered to monitor the patient's Coumadin levels?
    A. bleeding time
    B. blood smear
    C. partial thromboplastin time
    D. prothrombin time

REFERENCE: Jones, p 339
Labtestsonline (3)
Moisio, p 219
NLM (2)

42. An African American couple are undergoing genetic counseling to determine the likelihood of producing children with a recessively genetic blood condition. The genetic tests reveal that the father carries the trait to produce abnormal hemoglobin, HbS, which causes crystallization in RBCs and deforms their shape when O_2 is low. This condition causes painful crises and multiple infarcts and is termed
   A. hemophilia.
   B. thalassemia.
   C. sickle cell anemia.
   D. iron-deficiency anemia.

REFERENCE: Estridge and Reynolds, pp 328–330
Labtestsonline (4)

Mental Disorders

43. The most common etiology of dementia in the United States is
   A. autism.
   B. Alzheimer's disease.
   C. alcohol abuse.
   D. anxiety disorder.

REFERENCE: Jones, p 1084
Neighbors and Tannehill-Jones, pp 343–344

44. Contributing factors of mental disorders include
   A. heredity.
   B. stress.
   C. trauma.
   D. All answers apply.

REFERENCE: Jones, pp 1008, 1010
Neighbors and Tannehill-Jones, p 532

45. Why are there "black box warnings" on antidepressant medications regarding children and adolescents?
   A. Antidepressants increase the risk of suicidal thinking and behavior in some children and adolescents.
   B. Dosage requirements must be significantly higher in children and adolescents compared to adults.
   C. There is no established medical need for treatment of depression in children and adolescents.
   D. Antidepressants interfere with physiological growth patterns in children and adolescents.

REFERENCE: FDA (2)
Woodrow, p 379

Nervous System/Sense Organ Disorders

46. The leading cause of blindness in the United States is a vision-related pathology caused by diabetes. It is called
   A. retinal detachment.
   B. retinoblastoma.
   C. retinopathy.
   D. rhabdomyosarcoma.

REFERENCE: Jones, pp 569, 606–607, 1075–1077
Moisio, p 403
Neighbors and Tannehill-Jones, pp 318, 371–372
Scott and Fong, p 192

47. Which of the following is a hereditary disease of the cerebral cortex that includes progressive muscle spasticity and mental impairment leading to dementia?
    A. Huntington's disease
    B. Lou Gehrig's disease
    C. Bell's palsy
    D. Guillain–Barré syndrome

REFERENCE: Jones, pp 277–278
Moisio, p 294
Neighbors and Tannehill-Jones, pp 484–485
Scott and Fong, p 473

48. A disease of the inner ear with fluid disruption in the semicircular canal that causes vertigo is
    A. labyrinthitis.
    B. mastoiditis.
    C. Meniere's disease.
    D. both labyrinthitis and Meniere's disease.

REFERENCE: Moisio, pp 411–412
Neighbors and Tannehill-Jones, p 381
Scott and Fong, pp 198-199

49. A treatment for sensorineural hearing loss is
    A. cochlear implants.
    B. myringotomy.
    C. removal of impacted cerumen.
    D. stapedectomy.

REFERENCE: Jones, p 628
Scott and Fong, p 199

50. A condition that involves the fifth cranial nerve, also known as "tic douloureux," causes intense pain in the eye and forehead; lower lip, the section of the cheek closest to the ear and the outer segment of the tongue; or the upper lip, nose, and cheek.
    A. Bell's palsy
    B. thrush
    C. trigeminal neuralgia
    D. Tourette's disorder

REFERENCE: Jones, pp 283, 288
Moisio, p 396
Scott and Fong, p 178

51. The hypothalamus, thalamus, and pituitary gland are all parts of the
    A. brainstem.
    B. cerebellum.
    C. exocrine system.
    D. limbic system.

REFERENCE: Rizzo, pp 157–158

52. Photophobia or visual aura preceding a severe headache is characteristic of
    A. malnutrition.
    B. mastitis.
    C. migraines.
    D. myasthenia gravis.

REFERENCE: Jones, pp 275–276
Neighbors and Tannehill-Jones, p 340
Scott and Fong, p 160

53. A "pill-rolling" tremor of the hand is a characteristic symptom of
    A. epilepsy.
    B. Guillain–Barré syndrome.
    C. myasthenia gravis.
    D. Parkinson disease.

REFERENCE: Jones, pp 282–283, 1066–1067
Neighbors and Tannehill-Jones, pp 342–343
Scott and Fong, p 159

54. Etiologies of dementia include
   A. brain tumors.
   B. ischemia.
   C. trauma.
   D. All answers apply.

REFERENCE: Neighbors and Tannehill-Jones, pp 343–345
Rizzo, pp 937, 946
Sormunen, p 597

55. Which of the following pieces of equipment records the electrical activity of the brain?
   A. EEG
   B. EMG
   C. ECG
   D. EKG

REFERENCE: Jones, p 290
Moisio, p 397
NLM (5)

Cardiac Disorders

56. Which of the following conditions is NOT a predisposing risk associated with essential hypertension?
   A. age
   B. cigarette smoking
   C. low dietary sodium intake
   D. obesity

REFERENCE: Jones, p 404
Neighbors and Tannehill-Jones, p 160
Scott and Fong, pp 289–290

57. Which of the following is a lethal arrhythmia?
   A. atrial fibrillation
   B. atrial tachycardia
   C. bradycardia
   D. ventricular fibrillation

REFERENCE: Jones, p 411
Neighbors and Tannehill-Jones, p 174

58. Diastole occurs when
   A. cardiac insufficiency is present.
   B. the atria contracts.
   C. the ventricles contract.
   D. the ventricles fill.

REFERENCE: Jones, pp 384, 387
Neighbors and Tannehill-Jones, p 154
Rizzo, p 333
Scott and Fong, pp 285–286
Sormunen, p 207

59. Henry experienced sudden sharp chest pain that he described as heavy and crushing. His pain and past medical history caused Dr. James to suspect that Henry was having an acute myocardial infarction (AMI). Which of the following tests is a more specific marker for an AMI?
   A. AST
   B. CK-MB
   C. LDH1
   D. Troponin I

REFERENCE: Labtestsonline (2)

60. Margaret Vargas needs to have her mitral valve replaced. Her surgeon will discuss which of the following issues with her before the surgery?
   A. A mechanical valve will require that she take a "blood thinner" for the rest of her life.
   B. A biological valve (usually porcine) will last 10 to 15 years.
   C. A mechanical valve increases the risk of blood clots that can cause stroke.
   D. All answers apply.

REFERENCE: NHLBI

61. A common cardiac glycoside medication that increases the force of the cardiac contraction without increasing the oxygen consumption, thereby increasing the cardiac output is typically given to patients with heart failure. However, a very narrow therapeutic window between effectiveness and toxicity and the patient must be monitored closely. This common cardiac medication is
   A. COX-2 inhibitor.
   B. nitroglycerin.
   C. digoxin.
   D. acetylsalicylic acid.

REFERENCE: NLM (9)
Woodrow, pp 31, 503–504

Respiratory Disorders

62. Each of the following conditions fall under the category of COPD EXCEPT
   A. chronic bronchitis.
   B. emphysema.
   C. pneumonia.
   D. smoking.

REFERENCE: Moisio, pp 238, 240
Neighbors and Tannehill-Jones, pp 194–196
Rizzo, p 407
Scott and Fong, pp 361–362

63. Which of the following sequences correctly depicts the flow of blood through the heart to the lungs in order for gas exchange to occur?
   A. right atrium, right ventricle, lungs, pulmonary artery
   B. right atrium, right ventricle, pulmonary artery, lungs
   C. right ventricle, right atrium, lungs, pulmonary artery
   D. right ventricle, right atrium, pulmonary artery, lungs

REFERENCE: Jones, pp 380–382
Moisio, pp 176–177
Rizzo, pp 322, 325
Scott and Fong, pp 277–279
Sormunen, p 206

64. Gas exchange in the lungs takes place at the
   A. alveoli.
   B. bronchi.
   C. bronchioles.
   D. trachea.

REFERENCE: Neighbors and Tannehill-Jones, p 187
Rizzo, pp 402–404
Scott and Fong, p 277
Sormunen, p 345

65. Most carbon dioxide is carried in the
    A. blood as CO_2 gas.
    B. blood bound to hemoglobin.
    C. blood plasma in the form of carbonic acid.
    D. red blood cells.

REFERENCE: Rizzo, pp 408, 413
Scott and Fong, p 239
Sormunen, p 247

66. The presence of fluid in the alveoli of the lungs is characteristic of
    A. COPD.
    B. Crohn's disease.
    C. pneumonia.
    D. tuberculosis.

REFERENCE: Neighbors and Tannehill-Jones, pp 197–198
Rizzo, p 407

67. Which of the following BEST describes tuberculosis?
    A. a chronic, systemic disease whose initial infection is in the lungs
    B. an acute bacterial infection of the lung
    C. an ordinary lung infection
    D. a viral infection of the lungs

REFERENCE: Neighbors and Tannehill-Jones, pp 199–201
Scott and Fong, pp 359–360
Sormunen, p 272

68. A sweat test was done on a patient with the following symptoms: frequent respiratory infections, chronic cough, and foul-smelling bloody stools. Which of the following diseases is probably suspected?
    A. cystic breast disease
    B. cystic fibrosis
    C. cystic lung disease
    D. cystic pancreas

REFERENCE: Neighbors and Tannehill-Jones, p 494

69. *Mycobacterium tuberculosis* is the organism that causes tuberculosis (TB), typically a respiratory disorder. It is currently experiencing resurgence in the United States and many other countries. What is the average timeframe in which all patients with new, previously untreated TB must have daily antibiotic therapy?
    A. 4–7 days
    B. 6–9 months
    C. 6–9 weeks
    D. 4–7 years

REFERENCE: CDC (4)
Labtestsonline (13)

70. Which of the following is a severe, chronic, two-phased, bacterial respiratory infection that has become increasingly difficult to treat because many antibiotics are no longer effective against it?
    A. SARS
    B. MDR-TB
    C. MRSA
    D. H1N1

REFERENCE: CDC (6)

Digestive System Disorders

71. Which of the following anatomical parts is involved in both the respiratory and digestive systems?
    A. larynx
    B. nasal cavity
    C. pharynx
    D. trachea

REFERENCE: Moisio, p 233
Rizzo, p 371
Scott and Fong, pp 348–349
Sormunen, pp 344, 383

72. Most of the digestion of food and absorption of nutrients occur in the
    A. ascending colon.
    B. esophagus.
    C. small intestine.
    D. stomach.

REFERENCE: Neighbors and Tannehill-Jones, p 185
Rizzo, pp 377–378
Scott and Fong, pp 383–384
Sormunen, p 374

73. A chronic inflammatory bowel disease where affected segments of the bowel may be separated by normal bowel tissue is characteristic of
    A. appendicitis.
    B. Crohn's disease.
    C. diverticulitis.
    D. Graves' disease.

REFERENCE: Moisio, p 270
Neighbors and Tannehill-Jones, pp 239–240
Rizzo, p 381
Sormunen, p 392

74. Early detection programs apply screening guidelines to detect cancers at an early stage, which provides the likelihood of increased survival and decreased morbidity. Which of the following would NOT be a diagnostic or screening test for colorectal cancer?
    A. double contrast barium enema
    B. sigmoidoscopy
    C. fecal occult blood test
    D. upper GI x-ray

REFERENCE: ACS (1)
Scott and Fong, p 392

75. Prevention programs identify risk factors and use strategies to modify attitudes and behaviors to reduce the chance of developing cancers. Which of the following would NOT be an identified risk factor for colorectal cancer?
    A. alcohol use
    B. physical inactivity
    C. a high-fiber diet
    D. obesity

REFERENCE: ACS (2)

76. The first stage of alcoholic liver disease is
    A. alcoholic hepatitis.
    B. cirrhosis.
    C. fatty liver.
    D. jaundice.

REFERENCE: Neighbors and Tannehill-Jones, p 262

77. Portal hypertension can contribute to all of the following EXCEPT
   A. ascites.
   B. dilation of the blood vessels lining the intestinal tract.
   C. esophageal varices.
   D. kidney failure.

REFERENCE: Mayo Clinic (1)
Neighbors and Tannehill-Jones, pp 263–264

78. Which of the following is a risk factor involved in the etiology of gallstones?
   A. being overweight
   B. being an adolescent
   C. low-fat diets
   D. the presence of a peptic ulcer

REFERENCE: Rizzo, p 215

79. Increasing peristalsis of the intestines, increasing salivation, and a slowing heart rate are examples of
   A. automatic nervous system responses.
   B. higher brain functions.
   C. parasympathetic nervous system responses.
   D. sympathetic nervous system responses.

REFERENCE: Jones, p 263
Rizzo, pp 227, 251
Scott and Fong, pp 176–177
Sormunen, p 585

80. One of the most common causes of peptic ulcer disease is the consumption of aspirin and NSAIDs. Another common cause is infection by *Helicobacter pylori,* and the usual treatment for this condition is use of
   A. antivirals.
   B. antibiotics.
   C. antifungals.
   D. antiemetics.

REFERENCE: NLM (10)
Woodrow, p 300

Genitourinary Conditions

81. Genital warts are caused by
   A. HAV.
   B. HIV.
   C. HPV.
   D. VZV.

REFERENCE: Jones, p 716
Moisio, p 436
Scott and Fong, p 460

82. A physician prescribes a diuretic for his patient. He could be treating any of the following disorders EXCEPT
   A. congestive heart failure.
   B. mitral stenosis.
   C. pneumonia.
   D. pulmonary edema.

REFERENCE: Neighbors and Tannehill-Jones, p 172

83. Common kidney stone treatments that allow small particles to be flushed out of the body through the urinary system include all of the following EXCEPT
   A. extracorporeal shock wave lithotripsy.
   B. fluid hydration.
   C. ureteroscopy and stone basketing.
   D. using medication to dissolve the stone(s).

REFERENCE: Neighbors and Tannehill-Jones, pp 286–287

84. Which of the following tubes conveys sperm from the seminal vesicle to the urethra?
   A. ejaculatory duct
   B. epididymis
   C. oviduct
   D. vas deferens

REFERENCE: Moisio, p 332
Rizzo, p 444

85. The most common type of vaginitis is
   A. yeast.
   B. protozoan.
   C. viral.
   D. both yeast and protozoan.

REFERENCE: Neighbors and Tannehill-Jones, pp 397–398

86. ______________ is usually the first symptom of benign prostate hyperplasia.
   A. Abdominal pain
   B. Burning pain during urination
   C. Difficulty in urinating
   D. Pelvic pain

REFERENCE: Neighbors and Tannehill-Jones, pp 142, 397–398
Rizzo, p 444
Scott and Fong, pp 457–458

87. A 37-year-old female goes to her family physician complaining of dysuria, urgency, fever, and malaise. A UA is performed and upon gross examination is found to be turbid and has an unusual odor. Microscopic examination reveals a rod-shaped microorganism. A 24-hour culture produces a colony count greater than 100,000/mL of *Escherichia coli*. This would indicate a diagnosis of
   A. UTI.
   B. FUO.
   C. PID.
   D. KUB.

REFERENCE: Estridge and Reynolds, pp 751–753
Labtestsonline (5)

88. Microbiological lab culture and sensitivity tests were performed on the skin scrapings of a groin lesion on a 27-year-old male patient who presented to a local health department clinic. The results confirm infection with *Treponema pallidum*. He was given a prescription for penicillin and told to return for a follow-up visit in 2 weeks. His diagnosis is
   A. syphilis.
   B. HIV.
   C. herpes.
   D. HPV.

REFERENCE: CDC (13)
Labtestsonline (11)

89. A common contraceptive that is implanted in the uterus induces slight endometrial inflammation, which attracts neutrophils to the uterus. These neutrophils are toxic to sperm and prevent the fertilization of the ovum. This contraception is termed
   A. oral contraceptives.
   B. progestin injections.
   C. spermicides.
   D. an IUD.

REFERENCE: Jones, pp 755–756

Pregnancy, Childbirth, Perperium Conditions

90. Cervical cerclage is a procedure used to help prevent
    A. breathing restrictions.
    B. miscarriage.
    C. torsion.
    D. torticollis.

REFERENCE: Jones, pp 802, 817

91. A 28-year-old female presents to her general practitioner with morning nausea and vomiting, weight gain, and two missed menstrual cycles. The physician orders a pregnancy test. What chemical in the urine does this lab test detect?
    A. alpha-fetoprotein
    B. creatine phosphokinase
    C. carcinoembryonic antigen
    D. human chorionic gonadotropin

REFERENCE: Estridge and Reynolds, pp 471–472
Labtestsonline (9)

92. What common vitamin should be taken by pregnant women to substantially reduce the occurrence of neural tube defects, such as spina bifida, in a developing fetus?
    A. folic acid
    B. calcium
    C. B_{12}
    D. E

REFERENCE: CDC (10)

Skin/Subcutaneous Tissue Disorders

93. Impetigo can be
    A. spread through autoinoculation.
    B. caused by *Streptococcus pyogenes.*
    C. caused by *Staphylococcus aureus.*
    D. either spread through autoinoculation or caused by *Streptococcus pyogenes.*

REFERENCE: Jones, pp 121, 855
Neighbors and Tannehill-Jones, pp 438, 510
Scott and Fong, pp 72

94. Pain is a symptom of which of the following conditions?
    A. first-degree burn (superficial)
    B. second-degree burn (partial thickness)
    C. third-degree burn (full thickness)
    D. both first-degree burn (superficial) and second-degree burn (partial thickness)

REFERENCE: Jones, pp 116–117
Neighbors and Tannehill-Jones, p 356
Scott and Fong, pp 76–77

95. Necrosis extending down to the underlying fascia is characteristic of a decubitus ulcer in stage
    A. one.
    B. two.
    C. three.
    D. four.

REFERENCE: Scott and Fong, pp 77, 79

96. Scabies, a highly contagious condition that produces intense pruritus and a rash, is caused by
    A. pediculosis capitis.
    B. itch mites.
    C. candidiasis.
    D. ringworm.

REFERENCE: Jones, pp 124–125
Moisio, p 108
Neighbors and Tannehill-Jones, p 446

97. When a decubitus ulcer has progressed to a stage in which osteomyelitis is present, the ulcer has extended to the
    A. bone.
    B. fascia.
    C. muscle.
    D. subcutaneous tissue.

REFERENCE: Neighbors and Tannehill-Jones, p 764
Scott and Fong, p 79

Musculoskeletal and Connective Tissue Disorders

98. Softening of the bone in children is termed ________.
    A. Raynaud's disease
    B. Reye's syndrome
    C. rickets
    D. rubella

REFERENCE: Rizzo, p 147
Scott and Fong, p 110

99. The Phalen's wrist flexor test is a noninvasive method for diagnosing
    A. carpal tunnel syndrome.
    B. Down syndrome.
    C. severe acute respiratory syndrome.
    D. Tourette's syndrome.

REFERENCE: NINDS

100. Rheumatoid arthritis typically affects the
    A. intervertebral disks.
    B. hips and shoulders.
    C. knees and small joints of the hands and feet.
    D. large, weight-bearing joints.

REFERENCE: Jones, p 230
Moisio, p 149
Neighbors and Tannehill-Jones, pp 82–83, 109–111
Rizzo, p 183
Scott and Fong, pp 106–107

101. Fractures occur in patients with osteoporosis due to
    A. falling from loss of balance.
    B. fibrous joint adhesions tearing apart small bones.
    C. loss of bone mass.
    D. a tendency to fall from a lack of joint mobility.

REFERENCE: Jones, pp 174–175
Moisio, p 149
Neighbors and Tannehill-Jones, pp 105–107
Scott and Fong, p 109

102. Henrietta Dawson presents with a chief complaint of pain and weakness in her arms and neck. After an H and P and a review of diagnostic tests that include a myelogram, her doctor diagnoses a herniated nucleus pulposus at the _________ level of her spine.
   A. cervical
   B. lumbar
   C. sacral
   D. thoracic

REFERENCE: Jones, pp 160, 228, 277
Moisio, p 147
Rizzo, pp 157, 170
Sormunen, pp 158, 161

103. Carpal tunnel syndrome is caused by entrapment of the
   A. medial nerve.
   B. radial nerve.
   C. tibial nerve.
   D. ulnar nerve.

REFERENCE: Jones, p 270
Moisio, p 142
Neighbors and Tannehill-Jones, pp 122–123
NINDS
Rizzo, p 182
Sormunen, p 158

Congenital Disorders

104. Sex-linked genetic diseases
   A. are transmitted during sexual activity.
   B. involve a defect on a chromosome.
   C. occur equally between males and females.
   D. occur only in males.

REFERENCE: Neighbors and Tannehill-Jones, pp 478–479
Rizzo, p 457
Scott and Fong, pp 470–471

105. Before leaving the hospital, all newborns are screened for an autosomal recessive genetic disorder of defective enzymatic conversion in protein metabolism. With early detection and a protein-restricted diet, brain damage is prevented. This disease is
   A. cystic fibrosis.
   B. hereditary hemochromatosis.
   C. phenylketonuria.
   D. Tay–Sachs disease.

REFERENCE: Neighbors and Tannehill-Jones, p 491
Scott and Fong, p 472

106. Which of the following is a congenital condition that is the most severe neural tube defect?
   A. meningocele
   B. myelomeningocele
   C. severe combined immunodeficiency
   D. spina bifida occulta

REFERENCE: Neighbors and Tannehill-Jones, p 484

Perinatal Conditions

107. Children at higher risk for sudden infant death syndrome (SIDS) include those
   A. with sleep apnea.
   B. with respiratory problems.
   C. who are premature infants.
   D. All answers apply.

REFERENCE: Jones, pp 455, 867–868
Neighbors and Tannehill-Jones, p 515
Scott and Fong, p 362

Injuries and Poisonings

108. Sam Spade has been severely injured in an MVA because he was not wearing a seat belt. The organ in his body, situated at the upper left of his abdominal cavity, under the ribs, that is part of his lymphatic system has been ruptured, and he is bleeding internally. Sam needs a surgical procedure known as
   A. sequestrectomy.
   B. sialoadenectomy.
   C. sigmoidoscopy.
   D. splenectomy.

REFERENCE: Jones, p 345
Moisio, p 219
Rizzo, p 346
Sormunen, pp 275, 399

109. John Palmer was in a car accident and sustained severe chest trauma resulting in a tension pneumothorax. Manifestations of this disorder include all of the following EXCEPT
   A. severe chest pain.
   B. dyspnea.
   C. shock.
   D. clubbing.

REFERENCE: Jones, p 454
Neighbors and Tannehill-Jones, pp 204–207

Immune System Conditions

110. A bee stung little Bobby. He experiences itching, erythema, and respiratory distress caused by laryngeal edema and vascular collapse. In the emergency room where he is given an epinephrine injection, Bobby is diagnosed with
   A. allergic rhinitis.
   B. allergic sinusitis.
   C. anaphylactic shock.
   D. asthma.

REFERENCE: Jones, pp 965, 974
Neighbors and Tannehill-Jones, p 178

111. Which of the following cells produce histamine in a type I hypersensitivity reaction?
   A. lymphocyte
   B. macrophages
   C. mast cells
   D. neutrophils

REFERENCE: Jones, p 106
Neighbors and Tannehill-Jones, p 76
Rizzo, p 104

112. Which one of the following cells produces antibodies?
   A. A cells
   B. cytotoxic T cells
   C. helper T cells
   D. plasma cells

REFERENCE: Neighbors and Tannehill-Jones, pp 21, 52, 74
Rizzo, pp 349, 350, 352

113. A patient, who is HIV positive, has raised red or purple lesions that appear on his skin, in his mouth, and most anywhere on his body. What is the stage of his disease process in today's medical terminology?
   A. ARC
   B. AIDS
   C. AZT
   D. HIV positive

REFERENCE: Jones, pp 714–715
Neighbors and Tannehill-Jones, pp 91–93

114. Which of the following autoimmune diseases affects tissues of the nervous system?
   A. Goodpasture's syndrome
   B. Hashimoto's disease
   C. myasthenia gravis
   D. rheumatoid arthritis

REFERENCE: Jones, pp 281–282, 356
Neighbors and Tannehill-Jones, pp 83–85
Scott and Fong, pp 136, 310

115. Full-blown AIDS sets in as
   A. CD4 receptors increase.
   B. helper T-cell concentrations decrease.
   C. HIV virus concentrations decrease.
   D. immunity to HIV increases.

REFERENCE: Scott and Fong, pp 316–319
Sormunen, p 271

116. The HPV vaccine, Gardasil, is recommended for all children/young adults between the ages of 9 and 26 years. It is a quadrivalent vaccine. What is the definition of quadrivalent?
   A. It must be administered every 4 years to be effective.
   B. It is administered in a series of four shots over a 6-month period.
   C. It prevents infection from the four most prevalent types of HPV that cause cervical cancer.
   D. It reduces the risk of infection by four times.

REFERENCE: CDC (3)
FDA (1)
Labtestsonline (12)

117. Some immunizations, such as tetanus, require a second application, to strengthen or "remind" the immune system in response to antigens. The subsequent injections are termed
   A. alerting shots.
   B. warning shots.
   C. booster shots.
   D. unnecessary shots.

REFERENCE: CDC (9)

118. Why must influenza immunizations be developed and administered on an annual basis?
   A. The virus mutates significantly each year.
   B. People develop resistance to the vaccine.
   C. The immunization is only strong enough for one year.
   D. The pharmaceutical companies produce the lowest dosage possible.

REFERENCE: CDC (11)

Pharmacology

119. The drug commonly used to treat bipolar mood swings is
    A. Lanoxin.
    B. Lasix.
    C. lithium carbonate.
    D. lorazepam.

REFERENCE: Woodrow, p 385

120. Penicillin is effective in the treatment of all of the following diseases EXCEPT
    A. influenza.
    B. Lyme disease.
    C. strep throat.
    D. syphilis.

REFERENCE: Jones, pp 453, 1070
Neighbors and Tannehill-Jones, p 62
Rizzo, p 459

121. The positive belief in a drug and its ability to cure a patient's illness, even if this drug is an inactive or inert substance, typically positively influences a patient's perception of their outcome. This effect is termed a
    A. synergistic effect.
    B. potentiation effect.
    C. placebo effect.
    D. antagonistic effect.

REFERENCE: Sormunen, pp 79, 92
Woodrow, pp 32, 352

122. The interaction of two drugs working together to where each simultaneously helps the other achieve an effect that neither could produce alone is termed a
    A. placebo effect.
    B. synergistic effect.
    C. potentiation effect.
    D. antagonistic effect.

REFERENCE: Woodrow, p 33

123. The opposing interaction of two drugs in which one decreases or cancels out the effects of the other is termed a
    A. placebo effect.
    B. potentiation effect.
    C. synergistic effect.
    D. antagonistic effect.

REFERENCE: Woodrow, p 33

Surgical and Medical Procedures

124. A stapedectomy is a common treatment for
    A. atherosclerosis.
    B. multiple sclerosis.
    C. otosclerosis.
    D. scoliosis.

REFERENCE: Jones, p 630
Moisio, pp 412–413
Neighbors and Tannehill-Jones, pp 377–378
Scott and Fong, p 198

125. A procedure performed with an instrument that freezes and destroys abnormal tissues (including seborrheic keratoses, basal cell carcinomas, and squamous cell carcinomas) is
    A. cryosurgery.
    B. electrodesiccation.
    C. phacoemulsification.
    D. photocautery.

REFERENCE: Moisio, p 110
Rizzo, pp 81, 469

126. Maria Giovanni is in the hospital recovering from colon resection surgery. Based on her symptoms, her doctors are concerned about the possibility that she has developed a pulmonary embolism. Which of the following procedures will provide the definitive diagnosis?
A. chest x-ray
B. lung scan
C. pulmonary angiography
D. none of the above

REFERENCE: Neighbors and Tannehill-Jones, p 206
Scott and Fong, p 362

127. A surgical procedure that cuts into the skull to drain blood from a subdural hematoma in order to decrease the intracranial pressure is termed a(n)
A. craniectomy.
B. craniotomy.
C. angioplasty.
D. hemispherectomy.

REFERENCE: NLM (6)

128. A surgical procedure that is performed to realign and stabilize a fractured femur with a rod and screws is referred to as a(n)
A. closed reduction with external fixation.
B. closed reduction with internal fixation.
C. osteotomy.
D. open reduction with internal fixation.

REFERENCE: Jones, pp 180–181
Moisio, p 152

129. Which of the following procedures is typically performed on children to facilitate the drainage of serous exudate behind the tympanic membrane in chronic otitis media?
A. cochlear implants
B. stapedectomy
C. myringotomy with tympanostomy tubes
D. cerumen evacuation

REFERENCE: Jones, p 624
Moisio, p 413

130. Coronary arteries may become blocked, either partially or totally, due to athereosclerosis and lead to an AMI. Which of the following procedures would be used to improve the coronary blood flow by building an alternate route for the blood to bypass the blockage by inserting a portion of another blood vessel, typically the saphenous vein?
A. PTCA
B. CABG
C. carotid endarterectomy
D. cardiac catheterization

REFERENCE: Jones, p 1086
Moisio, pp 185–186

131. A standard surgical procedure used for the treatment of early-stage breast cancer involves the removal of the cancerous tumor, skin, breast tissue, areola, nipple, and most of the axillary lymph nodes, but leaves the underlying chest muscles intact. This procedure is termed a(n)
A. modified radical mastectomy.
B. partial mastectomy.
C. lumpectomy.
D. incisional breast biopsy.

REFERENCE: Jones, pp 760, 936
Moisio, p 361
WebMD.com (1)

132. The least invasive restrictive gastric surgery used to reduce the size of the stomach to facilitate weight loss in obese patients is
    A. a gastric bypass.
    B. Roux-en-Y gastric surgery.
    C. laparoscopic gastric banding.
    D. a biliopancreatic diversion.

REFERENCE: WebMD.com (2)

133. Which of the following procedures would be performed for the removal of the gall bladder due to excessive gallstone formation?
    A. ERCP
    B. cholangiography
    C. hemicolectomy
    D. cholecystectomy

REFERENCE: WebMD.com (3)
NLM (7)

Laboratory Tests

134. A patient's history includes the following documentation:
    - Small ulcers (chancres) appeared on the genitalia and resolved after 4 to 6 weeks
    - Elevated temperature, skin rash, and enlarged lymph nodes

    Which procedure will be used to initially diagnose the patient?
    A. bone marrow test
    B. chest x-ray
    C. serology test
    D. thyroid scan

REFERENCE: Jones, p 328
Moisio, p 437
Neighbors and Tannehill-Jones, pp 417–420

135. Diagnostic testing for meningitis usually involves
    A. blood cultures.
    B. cerebrospinal fluid analysis.
    C. stool C and S.
    D. testing urine.

REFERENCE: Jones, p 292
Neighbors and Tannehill-Jones, p 333

136. Which of the following is a liver function test?
    A. AST (SGOT)
    B. BUN
    C. ECG
    D. TSH

REFERENCE: Neighbors and Tannehill-Jones, p 259
Sormunen, p 389

137. A serum potassium level of 2.8 would indicate
    A. Addison's disease.
    B. anemia.
    C. diabetic ketoacidosis.
    D. hypokalemia.

REFERENCE: Mayo Clinic (2)
NLM (3)

138. An elevated serum amylase would be characteristic of
   A. acute pancreatitis.
   B. gallbladder disease.
   C. postrenal failure.
   D. prerenal failure.

REFERENCE: Neighbors and Tannehill-Jones, pp 269–270

139. A 68-year-old female patient has no visible bleeding, but remains anemic. Her physician is concerned about possible gastrointestinal bleeding. Which of the following tests might be ordered?
   A. DEXA scan
   B. guaiac smear test
   C. Pap smear test
   D. prostatic-specific antigen test

REFERENCE: Estridge and Reynolds, pp 680–681
Sormunen, p 388

140. When a physician orders a liver panel, which of the following tests are NOT included?
   A. albumin
   B. alkaline phosphatase
   C. bilirubin
   D. creatinine

REFERENCE: Estridge and Reynolds, pp 608–609

141. A 13-year-old patient is brought to her pediatrician with a 2-week history of fatigue, an occasional low-grade fever, and malaise. The pediatrician indicates it is a possible infection but needs to know what type of infection. She orders a hematology laboratory test to determine the relative number and percentage of each type of leukocytes. This test is referred to as a
   A. hematocrit.
   B. CBC.
   C. WBC diff.
   D. hemoglobin determination.

REFERENCE: Estridge and Reynolds, p 198

142. A 62-year-old female presents to her family doctor complaining of fatigue; constantly feeling cold, especially in her hands and feet; weakness; and pallor. O_2 must be transported to the cells and exchanged with CO_2, which is then transported back to the lungs to be expelled. A hematology laboratory test that evaluates the oxygen-carrying capacity of blood is referred to as a
   A. hematocrit.
   B. CBC.
   C. WBC diff.
   D. hemoglobin determination.

REFERENCE: Estridge and Reynolds, pp 206–207
Labtestsonline (15)

143. A 57-year-old male patient is having his annual physical. Due to a family history of coronary artery disease and his sedentary lifestyle, his doctor orders a total blood cholesterol panel. What is the optimal level of total cholesterol in the blood for adults?
   A. <200 mg/dL
   B. 200–239 mg/dL
   C. 300–339 mg/dL
   D. >500 mg/dL

REFERENCE: Estridge and Reynolds, pp 662–667
Labtestsonline (6)

144. An 81-year-old male with arteriosclerosis and a long-standing history of taking Coumadin presents to his physician's office for his biweekly prothrombin time (PT) test. The PT test is one of the most common hemostasis tests used as a presurgery screening and monitoring Coumadin (warfarin) therapy. This test evaluates
   A. coagulation of the blood.
   B. the iron-binding capacity of RBCs.
   C. the oxygen-carrying capacity of RBCs.
   D. the type and cross-match of blood.

REFERENCE: Estridge and Reynolds, p 394
Labtestsonline (8)

Radiological Tests and Procedures

145. The key diagnostic finding for typical pneumonia is
   A. abnormal chemical electrolytes.
   B. elevated WBC.
   C. lung consolidation on CXR.
   D. a positive sputum culture.

REFERENCE: Neighbors and Tannehill-Jones, pp 197–198

146. A radiological test for bone mineral density (BMD) is a useful diagnostic tool for diagnosing
   A. osteoarthritis.
   B. osteomyelitis.
   C. osteoporosis.
   D. rheumatoid arthritis.

REFERENCE: Jones, p 184
Neighbors and Tannehill-Jones, pp 105–107

Anatomy and Physiology

147. The state of balance or normality that the human body continuously tries to attain is referred to as
   A. pathogenesis.
   B. iatrogenic.
   C. etiology.
   D. homeostasis.

REFERENCE: Neighbors and Tannehill-Jones, p 4

148. The progress of a disease, including initiating factors, signs and symptoms, physical manifestations, residual sequela, prognosis, and finally, the end result, is termed
   A. pathogenesis.
   B. iatrogenic.
   C. etiology.
   D. homeostasis.

REFERENCE: Neighbors and Tannehill-Jones, p 4

149. When the body's immune system reverses itself and attacks the organs and tissues, this process is called
   A. allergy.
   B. autoimmunity.
   C. immunodeficiency.
   D. immunosuppression.

REFERENCE: Neighbors and Tannehill-Jones, p 21

150. The process of cancer development, from exposure through the cellular changes of hyperplasia to neoplasia, is termed
   A. pathogenesis.
   B. metastasis.
   C. carcinogenesis.
   D. staging.

REFERENCE: Neighbors and Tannehill-Jones, p 36

151. Which type of joint, such as the sutures of the skull, has no movement?
   A. synarthrosis
   B. amphiarthrosis
   C. diarthrosis
   D. arthritis

REFERENCE: Neighbors and Tannehill-Jones, p 100

152. Which type of diagnostic test involves the use of electromagnetic waves to produce very detailed images of soft tissue structures of the body?
   A. MRI
   B. CAT or CT scan
   C. x-ray
   D. electrophoresis

REFERENCE: Neighbors and Tannehill-Jones, p 102

153. Which valve is between the left atrium and left ventricle?
   A. tricuspid
   B. mitral
   C. pulmonary
   D. aortic

REFERENCE: Neighbors and Tannehill-Jones, p 152

154. On an EKG, what signifies the electronic stimulation of the ventricles?
   A. the spacing of the waves
   B. the QRS wave
   C. the P wave
   D. the height of the waves

REFERENCE: Neighbors and Tannehill-Jones, p 153

155. The nose, mouth, sinuses, pharynx, and larynx make up the
   A. upper gastrointestinal tract.
   B. lower gastrointestinal tract.
   C. the upper respiratory tract.
   D. the lower respiratory tract.

REFERENCE: Neighbors and Tannehill-Jones, p 186

156. What is the large serous membrane that covers the abdominal organs and lines the abdominal wall?
   A. perineum
   B. pleural membrane
   C. pericardial membrane
   D. peritoneum

REFERENCE: Neighbors and Tannehill-Jones, p 226

157. The muscular contractions that move food through the alimentary canal from the mouth to the anus is referred to as
   A. paralysis.
   B. peritonitis.
   C. pleural effusion.
   D. peristalsis.

REFERENCE: Neighbors and Tannehill-Jones, p 227

158. The _____ is the largest solid organ of the body, but the ____ is the largest organ overall.
   A. skin, brain
   B. intestine, liver
   C. brain, latissimus dorsi
   D. liver, skin

REFERENCE: Neighbors and Tannehill-Jones, p 258

159. Which structure transports urine from the kidneys to the bladder?
   A. urethra
   B. meatus
   C. ureter
   D. vas deferens

REFERENCE: Neighbors and Tannehill-Jones, p 278

160. In which gender is the urethra significantly longer?
   A. males
   B. females
   C. It is the same length regardless of gender.
   D. It depends upon the height of the individual.

REFERENCE: Neighbors and Tannehill-Jones, p 278

161. Which endocrine gland secretes melatonin, which controls the circadian rhythm of an individual?
A. pineal
B. adrenal medulla
C. beta cells of the pancreas
D. alpha cells of the pancreas

REFERENCE: Neighbors and Tannehill-Jones, p 303

162. Which endocrine gland secretes epinephrine, which activates the "fight or flight" response and increases blood pressure and metabolism?
A. pineal
B. adrenal medulla
C. beta cells of the pancreas
D. alpha cells of the pancreas

REFERENCE: Neighbors and Tannehill-Jones, p 303

163. In which brain lobe is the processing of smell and hearing stimuli performed?
A. occipital
B. frontal
C. parietal
D. temporal

REFERENCE: Neighbors and Tannehill-Jones, p 328

164. In which brain lobe is the processing of emotions, intellect, and personality performed?
A. occipital
B. frontal
C. parietal
D. temporal

REFERENCE: Neighbors and Tannehill-Jones, p 328

165. Which set of muscles controls the movement of the eye up and down?
A. superior and inferior rectus
B. medial and lateral rectus
C. superior and inferior oblique
D. medial and lateral oblique

REFERENCE: Neighbors and Tannehill-Jones, p 360

166. Which of the following is not one of the five layers of the epidermis?
A. stratum corneum
B. stratum spinosum
C. stratum fascia
D. stratum lucidum

REFERENCE: Neighbors and Tannehill-Jones, p 432

Answer Key for Medical Science

1. D
2. B
3. A
4. C
5. C
6. B
7. C
8. D
9. A
10. C
11. A
12. D
13. A
14. D
15. A
16. B
17. B
18. B
19. C
20. A
21. A
22. A
23. A
24. B
25. C
26. D
27. D
28. A
29. B
30. C
31. A
32. D
33. D
34. B
35. C
36. D
37. D
38. A
39. C
40. C
41. D
42. C
43. B
44. D
45. A
46. C
47. A
48. D
49. A
50. C
51. D
52. C
53. D
54. D
55. A
56. C
57. D
58. D
59. B
60. D
61. C
62. C
63. B
64. A
65. D
66. C
67. A
68. B
69. B
70. B
71. C
72. C
73. B
74. D
75. C
76. C
77. D
78. A
79. C
80. B
81. C
82. C
83. C
84. A
85. D
86. C
87. A
88. A
89. D
90. B
91. D
92. A
93. D
94. D
95. C
96. B
97. A
98. C
99. A
100. C
101. C
102. A
103. A
104. B
105. C
106. B
107. D
108. D
109. D
110. C
111. C
112. D
113. B
114. C
115. B
116. C
117. C
118. A
119. C
120. A
121. C
122. B
123. D
124. C
125. A
126. C
127. B
128. D
129. C
130. B
131. A
132. C
133. D
134. C
135. B
136. A
137. C
138. A
139. B
140. D
141. C
142. D
143. A
144. A
145. C
146. C
147. D
148. A
149. B
150. C
151. A
152. A
153. B
154. B
155. C
156. C
157. D
158. D
159. D
160. C
161. A
162. A
163. B
164. D
165. A
166. C

REFERENCES

American Cancer Society (ACS). http://www.cancer.org

ACS (1)

http://www.cancer.org/healthy/findcancerearly/index

http://www.cancer.org/healthy/findcancerearly

ACS (2)

http://www.cancer.org/acs/groups/cid/documents/webcontent/003096-pdf.pdf

http://www.cancer.org/acs/groups/cid/documents/webcontent/003096-pdf.pdf

ACS (3)

http://www.cancer.org/acs/groups/cid/documents/webcontent/003092-pdf.pdf

Centers for Disease Control and Prevention (CDC). http://www.cdc.gov/index.htm

CDC (1)

http://www.cdc.gov/std/Hpv/STDFact-HPV-vaccine-young-women.htm#why

CDC (2)

http://www.cdc.gov/flu/avian/gen-info/pdf/avian_facts.pdf

CDC (3)

http://www.cdc.gov/Features/HPVvaccine/

CDC (4)

http://www.cdc.gov/tb/topic/treatment/default.htm

CDC (5)

http://www.cdc.gov/pertussis/outbreaks-faqs.html

CDC (6)

http://www.cdc.gov/tb/topic/treatment/default.htm

CDC (7)

http://www.cdc.gov/flu/spotlights/pandemic-global-estimates.htm

CDC (8)

http://www.cdc.gov/cancer/breast/basic_info/

CDC (9)

http://www.cdc.gov/vaccines/vac-gen/default.htm

CDC (10)

http://www.cdc.gov/NCBDDD/folicacid/about.html

CDC (11)

http://www.cdc.gov/vaccines/vac-gen/default.htm

Estridge, B. H., & Reynolds, A. P. (2012). *Basic clinical laboratory techniques* (6th ed.). Clifton Park, NY: Cengage Learning.

Food and Drug Administration (FDA). http://www.fda.gov/default.htm

http://www.fda.gov/BiologicsBloodVaccines/Vaccines/ApprovedProducts/ucm094042.htm

Jones, B. D. (2016). *Comprehensive medical terminology* (5th ed.). Clifton Park, NY: Cengage Learning.

Labtestsonline. http://www.labtestsonline.org

Labtestsonline (1)

http://www.labtestsonline.org/understanding/analytes/bilirubin/glance.html

Labtestsonline (2)

http://www.labtestsonline.org/understanding/analytes/troponin/related.html

Labtestsonline (3)

http://www.labtestsonline.org/understanding/analytes/pt/test.html

REFERENCES (continued)

Labtestsonline (4)
http://labtestsonline.org/understanding/conditions/sickle
Labtestsonline (5)
http://labtestsonline.org/understanding/analytes/urinalysis/tab/test
Labtestsonline (6)
http://labtestsonline.org/understanding/analytes/cholesterol/tab/test
Labtestsonline (7)
http://labtestsonline.org/understanding/analytes/strep/tab/sample
Labtestsonline (8)
http://labtestsonline.org/understanding/analytes/pt/tab/sample
Labtestsonline (9)
https://labtestsonline.org/understanding/wellness/pregnancy/first-trimester/hcg
Labtestsonline (10)
http://labtestsonline.org/understanding/conditions/meningitis?start=3
Labtestsonline (11)
http://labtestsonline.org/understanding/analytes/syphilis/tab/glance
Labtestsonline (12)
http://www.cdc.gov/vaccines/vpd-vac/hpv/default.htm
Labtestsonline (13)
http://labtestsonline.org/understanding/conditions/tuberculosis/?start=4

Mayo Clinic. http://www.mayoclinic.com
Mayo Clinic (1)
http://www.mayoclinic.com/print/esophageal-varices/DS00820/
Mayo Clinic (2)
http://www.mayoclinic.com/health/diabetic-ketoacidosis/DS00674
Mayo Clinic (3)
http://www.mayoclinic.org/diseases-conditions/sars/basics/causes/con-20024278

Moisio, M. A. (2010). *Medical terminology for insurance and coding*. Clifton Park, NY: Cengage Learning.

National Library of Medicine. http://www.nlm.nih.gov/medlineplus/
NLM (1)
http://www.nhlbi.nih.gov/health/dci/Diseases/ha/ha_diagnosis.html
http://www.nlm.nih.gov/medlineplus/ency/article/003479.htm
NLM (2)
http://www.nlm.nih.gov/medlineplus/ency/article/003652.htm
NLM (3)
http://www.nlm.nih.gov/medlineplus/ency/article/003498.htm
NLM (4)
http://www.nlm.nih.gov/medlineplus/ency/article/003574.htm
NLM (5)
http://www.nlm.nih.gov/medlineplus/ency/article/007192.htm

NHLBI—National Heart Lung and Blood Institute. http://www.nhlbi.nih.gov
http://www.nhlbi.nih.gov/health/dci/Diseases/hvd/hvd_treatments.html

NINDS—National Institute of Neurological Disorders and Stroke.
http://www.ninds.nih.gov/disorders/carpal_tunnel/detail_carpal_tunnel.htm

Neighbors, M., & Tannehill-Jones, R. (2015). *Human diseases* (4th ed.). Clifton Park, NY: Cengage Learning.

REFERENCES (continued)

Rizzo, D. C. (2006). *Fundamentals of anatomy and physiology* (2006). (2nd ed.) . Clifton Park, NY: Cengage Learning.

Scott, A. S., & Fong, P. E. (2014). *Body structures and functions* (12th ed.). Clifton Park, NY: Cengage Learning.

Sormunen, C. (2010). *Terminology for allied health professionals* (6th ed.). Clifton Park, NY: Cengage Learning.

Woodrow, R. (2015). *Essentials of pharmacology for health occupations* (7th ed.). Clifton Park, NY: Cengage Learning.

Medical Sciences Competencies

Questions	RHIA Domain	RHIT Domain
1–166	Domain 1	Domain 1

VIII. ICD-10-CM/PCS Coding

Leslie Moore, RHIT, CCS

ICD-10-CM PREFACE 2016

This 2016 update of the International Statistical Classification of Diseases and Related Health Problems, 10th revision, Clinical Modification (ICD-10-CM) is being published by the United States Government in recognition of its responsibility to promulgate this classification throughout the United States for morbidity coding. The International Statistical Classification of Diseases and Related Health Problems, 10th Revision (ICD-10), published by the World Health Organization (WHO), is the foundation of ICD-10-CM. ICD-10 continues to be the classification used in cause-of-death coding in the United States. The ICD-10-CM is comparable with the ICD-10. The WHO Collaborating Center for the Family of International Classifications in North America, housed at the Centers for Disease Control and Prevention's National Center for Health Statistics (NCHS), has responsibility for the implementation of ICD and other WHO-FIC classifications and serves as a liaison with the WHO, fulfilling international obligations for comparable classifications and the national health data needs of the United States. The historical background of ICD and ICD-10 can be found in the Introduction to the International Classification of Diseases and Related Health Problems (ICD-10), 2008, World Health Organization, Geneva, Switzerland.

ICD-10-CM is the United States' clinical modification of the World Health Organization's ICD-10. The term "clinical" is used to emphasize the modification's intent: to serve as a useful tool in the area of classification of morbidity data for indexing of health records, medical care review, and ambulatory and other health care programs, as well as for basic health statistics. To describe the clinical picture of the patient, the codes must be more precise than those needed only for statistical groupings and trend analysis.

Characteristics of ICD-10-CM

ICD-10-CM far exceeds its predecessors in the number of concepts and codes provided. The disease classification has been expanded to include health-related conditions and to provide greater specificity at the sixth and seventh character level. The sixth and seventh characters are not optional and are intended for use in recording the information documented in the clinical record.

ICD-10-CM extensions, interpretations, modifications, addenda, or errata other than those approved by the Centers for Disease Control and Prevention are not to be considered official and should not be utilized. Continuous maintenance of the ICD-10-CM is the responsibility of the aforementioned agencies. However, because the ICD-10-CM represents the best in contemporary thinking of clinicians, nosologists, epidemiologists, and statisticians from both public and private sectors, when future modifications are considered, advice will be sought from all stakeholders.

All official authorized addenda through October 1, 2015, have been included in this revision. The complete official authorized addenda to ICD-10-CM, including the "ICD-10-CM Official Guidelines for Coding and Reporting," can be accessed at the following website:
http://www.cdc.gov/nchs/icd/icd10cm.htm#10update
A description of the ICD-10-CM updating and maintenance process can be found at the following website:
http://www.cdc.gov/nchs/icd/icd9cm_maintenance.htm

Reference: http://www.cdc.gov/nchs/data/icd/2015_icd10cm_preface.pdf

ICD-10-CM and ICD-10-PCS

The compliance date for implementation of ICD-10-CM/PCS is October 1, 2015, for all Health Insurance Portability and Accountability Act (HIPAA)-covered entities.

ICD-10-CM, including the "ICD-10-CM Official Guidelines for Coding and Reporting," will replace ICD-9-CM Diagnosis Codes in all health care settings for diagnosis reporting with dates of service, or dates of discharge for inpatients, that occur on or after October 1, 2015.

ICD-10-PCS, including the "ICD-10-PCS Official Guidelines for Coding and Reporting," will replace ICD-9-CM Procedure Codes.

BENEFITS OF ICD-10-CM

ICD-10-CM incorporates much greater clinical detail and specificity than ICD-9-CM. Terminology and disease classification are updated to be consistent with current clinical practice. The modern classification system will provide much better data needed for:

- Measuring the quality, safety, and efficacy of care;
- Reducing the need for attachments to explain the patient's condition;
- Designing payment systems and processing claims for reimbursement;
- Conducting research, epidemiological studies, and clinical trials;
- Setting health policy;
- Operational and strategic planning;
- Designing health care delivery systems;
- Monitoring resource use;
- Improving clinical, financial, and administrative performance;
- Preventing and detecting health care fraud and abuse; and
- Tracking public health and risks.

Non-specific codes are still available for use when medical record documentation does not support a more specific code.

ICD-10-CM Diagnosis Codes:

There are 3–7 digits;

Digit 1 is alpha;

Digit 2 is numeric;

Digits 3–7 are alpha or numeric (alpha characters are not case sensitive); and a decimal is used after the third character.

Examples:

A78–Q	Fever;
A69.21	Meningitis due to Lyme disease; and
S52.131A	Displaced fracture of neck of right radius, initial encounter for closed fracture.

NEW FEATURES IN ICD-10-CM

The following new features can be found in ICD-10-CM:

1) Laterality (Left, Right, Bilateral)

Examples:

C50.511 – Malignant neoplasm of lower-outer quadrant of right female breast;
H16.013 – Central corneal ulcer, bilateral; and
L89.012 – Pressure ulcer of right elbow, stage II.

2) Combination Codes for Certain Conditions and Common Associated Symptoms and Manifestations

Examples:

K57.21 – Diverticulitis of large intestine with perforation and abscess with bleeding;
E11.341 – Type 2 diabetes mellitus with severe nonproliferative diabetic retinopathy with macular edema; and
I25.110 – Atherosclerotic heart disease of native coronary artery with unstable angina pectoris.

3) Combination Codes for Poisonings and Their Associated External Cause

Example:

T42.3x2S – Poisoning by barbiturates, intentional self-harm, sequela.

4) Obstetric Codes Identify Trimester Instead of Episode of Care

Example:

O26.02 – Excessive weight gain in pregnancy, second trimester.

5) Character "x" Is Used as a 5th Character Placeholder in Certain 6 Character Codes to Allow for Future Expansion and to Fill in Other Empty Characters (For Example, Character 5 and/or 6) When a Code that Is Less than 6 Characters in Length Requires a 7th Character

Examples:

T46.1x5A – Adverse effect of calcium-channel blockers, initial encounter; and
T15.02xD – Foreign body in cornea, left eye, subsequent encounter.

6) Two Types of Excludes Notes

Excludes 1 Indicates that the code excluded should never be used with the code where the note is located (do not report both codes).

Example:

Q03 – Congenital hydrocephalus.
Excludes 1: Acquired hydrocephalus (**G91.-**).

Excludes 2 Indicates that the condition excluded is not part of the condition represented by the code, but a patient may have both conditions at the same time, in which case both codes may be assigned together (both codes can be reported to capture both conditions).

Example:

L27.2 – Dermatitis due to ingested food.
Excludes 2: Dermatitis due to food in contact with skin (L23.6, L24.6, L25.4).

7) *Inclusion of Clinical Concepts that Do Not Exist in ICD-9-CM (For Example, Underdosing, Blood Type, Blood Alcohol Level)*

Examples:

T45.526D – Underdosing of antithrombotic drugs, subsequent encounter;
Z67.40 – Type O blood, Rh positive; and
Y90.6 – Blood alcohol level of 120–199 mg/100 ml.

8) *A Number of Codes Are Significantly Expanded (For Example, Injuries, Diabetes, Substance Abuse, Postoperative Complications)*

Examples:

E10.610 – Type 1 diabetes mellitus with diabetic neuropathic arthropathy;
F10.182 – Alcohol abuse with alcohol-induced sleep disorder; and
T82.02xA – Displacement of heart valve prosthesis, initial encounter.

9) *Codes for Postoperative Complications Are Expanded and a Distinction Is Made Between Intraoperative Complications and Postprocedural Disorders*

Examples:

D78.01 – Intraoperative hemorrhage and hematoma of spleen complicating a procedure on the spleen; and
D78.21 – Postprocedural hemorrhage and hematoma of spleen following a procedure on the spleen.

ADDITIONAL CHANGES IN ICD-10-CM

The additional changes that can be found in ICD-10-CM are as follows:

- Injuries are grouped by anatomical site rather than by type of injury;
- Category restructuring and code reorganization occur in a number of ICD-10-CM chapters, resulting in the classification of certain diseases and disorders that are different from ICD-9-CM;
- Certain diseases are reclassified to different chapters or sections to reflect current medical knowledge;
- New code definitions (for example, definition of acute myocardial infarction is now 4 weeks rather than 8 weeks); and
- The codes corresponding to ICD-9-CM V codes (Factors Influencing Health Status and Contact with Health Services) and E codes (External Causes of Injury and Poisoning) are incorporated into the main classification (in ICD-9-CM, they were separated into supplementary classifications).

USE OF EXTERNAL CAUSE AND UNSPECIFIED CODES IN ICD-10-CM

Similar to ICD-9-CM, there is no national requirement for mandatory ICD-10-CM external cause code reporting. Unless you are subject to a State-based external cause code reporting mandate or these codes are required by a particular payer, you are not required to report ICD-10-CM codes found in Chapter 20, External Causes of Morbidity.

If you have not been reporting ICD-9-CM external cause codes, you will not be required to report ICD-10-CM codes found in Chapter 20 unless a new State or payer-based requirement about the reporting of these codes is instituted. If such a requirement is instituted, it would be independent of ICD-10-CM implementation.

In the absence of a mandatory reporting requirement, you are encouraged to voluntarily report external cause codes, as they provide valuable data for injury research and evaluation of injury prevention strategies.

In both ICD-9-CM and ICD-10-CM, sign/symptom and unspecified codes have acceptable, even necessary, uses. While specific diagnosis codes should be reported when they are supported by the available medical record documentation and clinical knowledge of the patient's health condition, in some instances signs/symptoms or unspecified codes are the best choice to accurately reflect the health care encounter.

Each health care encounter should be coded to the level of certainty known for that encounter. If a definitive diagnosis has not been established by the end of the encounter, it is appropriate to report codes for sign(s) and/or symptom(s) in lieu of a definitive diagnosis. When sufficient clinical information is not known or available about a particular health condition to assign a more specific code, it is acceptable to report the appropriate unspecified code (for example, a diagnosis of pneumonia has been determined, but the specific type has not been determined). In fact, unspecified codes should be reported when they are the codes that most accurately reflect what is known about the patient's condition at the time of that particular encounter. It is inappropriate to select a specific code that is not supported by the medical record documentation or conduct medically unnecessary diagnostic testing to determine a more specific code. Reference: MLM Matters CMS Website

2015 release of ICD-10-CM

These files have been created by the National Center for Health Statistics (NCHS), under authorization by the World Health Organization.

These files linked below are the 2015 update of the ICD-10-CM. Content changes to the full ICD-10-CM files are described in the respective addenda files. This year, in addition to PDF (Adobe) files, the XML format is also being made available. Most files are provided in a compressed zip format for ease in downloading. These files have been created by the National Center for Health Statistics (NCHS), under authorization by the World Health Organization.

As noted earlier, the effective implementation date for ICD-10-CM (and ICD-10-PCS) is October 1, 2015. Updates to this version of ICD-10-CM are anticipated prior to its implementation.

- Preface
- ICD-10-CM Guidelines [PDF - 926 KB]
- ICD-10-CM PDF Format Zip Archive file
- ICD-10-CM XML Format Zip Archive File
- ICD-10-CM List of Codes and Descriptions Zip Archive File
- General Equivalence Mapping Files [ZIP - 1 MB]
- Present on Admission (POA) Exempt Codes [ZIP - 1 MB]
- Interim advice on excludes 1 note on conditions unrelated [PDF - 92 KB]

To download these files, go to: http://www.cdc.gov/nchs/icd/icd10cm.htm#10update

Content source: CDC/National Center for Health Statistics
Page maintained by: Office of Information Services
http://www.cdc.gov/nchs/icd/icd10cm.htm

Development of the ICD-10 Procedure Coding System (ICD-10-PCS)

Richard F. Averill, M.S., Robert L. Mullin, M.D., Barbara A. Steinbeck, RHIT, Norbert I. Goldfield, M.D., Thelma M. Grant, RHIA, Rhonda R. Butler, CCS, CCS-P

The International Classification of Diseases 10th Revision Procedure Coding System (ICD-10-PCS) has been developed as a replacement for Volume 3 of the International Classification of Diseases 9th Revision (ICD-9-CM). The development of ICD-10-PCS was funded by the U.S. Centers for Medicare and Medicaid Services (CMS). ICD-10-PCS has a multiaxial, seven-character, alphanumeric code structure that provides a unique code for all substantially different procedures, and allows new procedures to be easily incorporated as new codes. ICD-10-PCS was under development for over 5 years. The initial draft was formally tested and evaluated by an independent contractor; the final version was released in the Spring of 1998, with annual updates since the final release. The design, development, and testing of ICD-10-PCS are discussed.

Introduction

Volume 3 of the International Classification of Diseases 9th Revision Clinical Modification (ICD-9-CM) has been used in the United States for the reporting of inpatient procedures since 1979. The structure of Volume 3 of ICD-9-CM has not allowed new procedures associated with rapidly changing technology to be effectively incorporated as new codes. As a result, in 1992 the U.S. Centers for Medicare and Medicaid Services (CMS) funded a project to design a replacement for Volume 3 of ICD-9-CM. After a review of the preliminary design, CMS in 1995 awarded 3M Health Information Systems a 3-year contract to complete development of the replacement system. The new system is the ICD-10 Procedure Coding System (ICD-10-PCS).

Attributes Used in Development

The development of ICD-10-PCS had as its goal the incorporation of four major attributes:

- Completeness

There should be a unique code for all substantially different procedures. In Volume 3 of ICD-9-CM, procedures on different body parts, with different approaches, or of different types are sometimes assigned to the same code.

- Expandability

As new procedures are developed, the structure of ICD-10-PCS should allow them to be easily incorporated as unique codes.

- Multiaxial

ICD-10-PCS codes should consist of independent characters, with each individual axis retaining its meaning across broad ranges of codes to the extent possible.

- Standardized Terminology

ICD-10-PCS should include definitions of the terminology used. While the meaning of specific words varies in common usage, ICD-10-PCS should not include multiple meanings for the same term, and each term must be assigned a specific meaning.

If these four objectives are met, then ICD-10-PCS should enhance the ability of health information coders to construct accurate codes with minimal effort.

General Development Principles

In the development of ICD-10-PCS, several general principles were followed:

• *Diagnostic Information Is Not Included in Procedure Description*

When procedures are performed for specific diseases or disorders, the disease or disorder is not contained in the procedure code. There are no codes for procedures exclusive to aneurysms, cleft lip, strictures, neoplasms, hernias, etc. The diagnosis codes, not the procedure codes, specify the disease or disorder.

• *Not Otherwise Specified (NOS) Options Are Restricted*

ICD-9-CM often provides a "not otherwise specified" code option. Certain NOS options made available in ICD-10-PCS are restricted to the uses laid out in the ICD-10-PCS official guidelines. A minimal level of specificity is required for each component of the procedure.

• *Limited Use of Not Elsewhere Classified (NEC) Option*

ICD-9-CM often provides a "not elsewhere classified" code option.

Because all significant components of a procedure are specified in ICD-10-PCS, there is generally no need for an NEC code option. However, limited NEC options are incorporated into ICD-10-PCS where necessary. For example, new devices are frequently developed, and therefore it is necessary to provide an "Other Device" option for use until the new device can be explicitly added to the coding system. Additional NEC options are discussed later, in the sections of the system where they occur.

• *Level of Specificity*

All procedures currently performed can be specified in ICD-10-PCS. The frequency with which a procedure is performed was not a consideration in the development of the system. Rather, a unique code is available for variations of a procedure that can be performed.

ICD-10-PCS has a seven-character, alphanumeric code structure. Each character contains up to 34 possible values. Each value represents a specific option for the general character definition (e.g., stomach is one of the values for the body part character). The 10 digits 0–9 and the 24 letters A–H, J–N, and P–Z may be used in each character. The letters O and I are not used in order to avoid confusion with the digits 0 and 1.

Procedures are divided into sections that identify the general type of procedure (e.g., medical and surgical, obstetrics, imaging). The first character of the procedure code always specifies the section. The sections are shown in Table 1.

Table 1: ICD-10-PCS Sections

0	Medical and Surgical
1	Obstetrics
2	Placement
3	Administration
4	Measurement and Monitoring
5	Extracorporeal Assistance and Performance
6	Extracorporeal Therapies
7	Osteopathic
8	Other Procedures
9	Chiropractic
B	Imaging
C	Nuclear Medicine
D	Radiation Oncology
F	Physical Rehabilitation and Diagnostic Audiology
G	Mental Health
H	Substance Abuse Treatment

The second through seventh characters mean the same thing within each section, but may mean different things in other sections. In all sections, the third character specifies the general type of procedure performed (e.g., resection, transfusion, fluoroscopy), while the other characters give additional information such as the body part and approach. In ICD-10-PCS, the term "procedure" refers to the complete specification of the seven characters.

HEALTH RECORD CODING REVIEW

CODING PROCESS

Fine-tune your coding skills by seeking complete documentation and selecting the most detailed codes.

1. Assess the case by performing a quick review of the record's demographic information and the first few lines of the History and Physical.
2. Get an overview of key reports because they contain valuable detailed information.
   A. The discharge summary sums up the patient's hospital course and confirms conditions or complications. In ambulatory records, look at the final progress note and/or discharge instructions.
   B. Review the physician orders for treatment protocols. The orders may indicate chronic or acute conditions for which the patient is receiving treatment.
   C. Review the history and physical to complete the clinical picture. Social and family history, as well as past and present illnesses, may have clinical implications.
   D. Read the progress notes to track the course of hospitalization or outpatient treatment. These provide information concerning daily status, reactions, or postoperative complications.
   E. Study the operative reports. Additional procedures may be identified in the body of the operative report.
3. Check all data from clinical reports.
   A. Laboratory reports may show evidence of conditions such as anemia, renal failure, infections, and metabolic imbalances.
   B. Radiology reports may confirm diagnosis of pneumonia, COPD, CHF, degenerative joint diseases, and traumatic injuries.
   C. Medication Administration Reports (MARs) indicate all drugs that were administered to the patient. Look for documentation of diagnoses elsewhere in the medical record to correlate with each drug. If uncertain why a medication was administered, query the physician.
   D. Respiratory therapy notes document the use of mechanical ventilation and describe severity of respiratory disorders.
   E. Physical therapy reports detail useful information for coding musculoskeletal dysfunctions.
   F. Dietary reports describe nutritional deficiencies (e.g., malnutrition).
   G. Speech pathology reports give information on dysphasia, aphasia, and other speech-related conditions.
   H. Pathology reports are essential for accurate coding of conditions where excised tissue has been submitted for interpretation.
4. Perform a coding evaluation.
   A. Establish the principal diagnosis and formulate secondary diagnoses codes.
   B. Exclude all conditions not relevant to the case. Abnormal lab and X-ray findings and previous conditions having no effect on current management of the patient are not coded.

5. Take time to review and refine your coding.
   A. Review all diagnoses and procedures to confirm the selections of appropriate principal and secondary diagnoses and all procedure codes.
   B. For inpatient records, determine if each diagnosis was present on admission (POA) to adequately identify the POA indicator.
   C. Refine code assignments, where necessary, to make changes to more accurately classify the diagnoses and procedure codes selected.

Sample 10-Step Inpatient ICD-10-CM Coding Process
1. Locate Patient's Gender, Age, and Discharge Date.
2. Locate Discharge Status (Disposition). Some examples include: **01:** Home **02:** Short-term hospital **03:** Skilled nursing facility **04:** Facility providing custodial or supportive care **05:** Cancer or child hospital **06:** Home health services **07:** Against medical advice **20:** Expired **30:** Still a patient **61:** Swing bed **62:** Inpatient rehab facility or distinct rehab unit **63:** Long-term care hospital **65:** Psychiatric hospital or distinct psych unit **66:** Critical access hospital
3. List consultants as you go through the consults. **Write down pertinent diagnoses** (histories and present illnesses).
4. Locate and list all procedures. Review description of each procedure performed.
5. Go through the physician orders and medication administration orders. This is where you will find drugs ordered and administered. Make sure that you look for the diagnosis that corresponds with each medication. If not, query the physician.
6. Read the H&P, ER record, and progress notes. **Write down all diagnoses that meet criteria for principal and secondary diagnosis:** If a diagnosis is ruled out, just cross it off the list.
7. Select the Principal Diagnosis. UHDDS Definition: The condition established *after study* to be chiefly responsible for occasioning the admission of the patient to the hospital for care.

Sample 10-Step Inpatient ICD-10-CM Coding Process (continued)

<table>
<tr><td>

8. Select Other Diagnoses and indicate whether each was present on admission (POA) or not.

UHDDS Definition: All conditions that coexist at the time of admission, develop subsequently, or affect the treatment received and/or the length of stay. Diagnoses that relate to an earlier episode of care that have no bearing on the current hospital stay are to be excluded.

Complication UHDDS Definition: A condition arising during hospitalization, which increases the patient's length of stay by 1 day in 75% of cases.

Comorbidity UHDDS Definition: Condition present at admission, in addition to the principal diagnosis, which increases the patient's length of stay by 1 day in 75% of cases.

For reporting purposes, the definition of "other diagnoses" is interpreted as additional conditions that affect patient care in terms of requiring:

- clinical evaluation
- therapeutic treatment
- diagnostic procedures
- extended length of hospital stay
- increased nursing care and/or monitoring

</td></tr>
<tr><td>

9. Principal Procedure.

UHDDS Definition: One performed for definitive treatment (rather than performed for diagnostic or exploratory purposes) or one that was necessary to care for a complication. If two or more procedures appear to meet the definition, then the one most closely related to the principal diagnosis should be selected as the principal procedure.

</td></tr>
<tr><td>

10. Other Procedures

UHDDS Definition for significant procedures: One that meets any of the following conditions: is surgical in nature, carries an anesthetic risk, carries a procedural risk, or requires specialized training.

</td></tr>
</table>

Some Additional Tips for Coding

1. When a patient is admitted with or develops a condition during his or her stay, look to see if there is documentation to differentiate if the complication is acute, chronic, or both acute and chronic.
2. When a patient presents with or develops infectious conditions, seek documentation of any positive cultures (urine, wound, sputum, blood) pertaining to that condition. If the positive cultures are available for that condition (e.g., sepsis due to Pseudomonas), it will help in being more specific in coding the diagnoses and may increase reimbursement in some cases. For example, in a case of pneumonia due to Pseudomonas, the MS-DRG may increase considerably. According to coding guidelines, if the culture is not documented, even though present in laboratory reports, the condition is to be coded as unspecified, which can affect reimbursement. Examples: sepsis, cellulitis, UTI, pneumonia, etc.
3. If a condition is due to surgery, ask the physician to verify and document that it is due to the procedure. If the patient has been discharged, and you are not sure but believe it was due to the procedure, seek verification that it is possibly due to the procedure by querying the physician.
4. If the patient had outpatient surgery for removal of a lesion, look for documentation of the size of the lesion that may have been removed. It should be documented in the operative report.
   The American Medical Association's publication, *CPT Assistant* (issues from Fall 1995 and August 2000) states, "Since the physician can make an accurate measurement of the lesion(s) at the time of the excision, the size of the lesion should be documented in the OP (operative) report. A pathology report is likely to contain a less accurate measurement due to the shrinking of the specimen or the fact that the specimen may be fragmented."

   Reimbursement is based on the diameter of the lesion(s). Even 1 millimeter (mm) off in the diameter calculation can mean fewer dollars for the hospital and the physician. The documentation in the record ensures appropriate reimbursement.
5. Look for documentation in the final diagnoses in the discharge summary for clarification or to differentiate whether specific conditions are currently present, or if the patient only has a history of the condition.

   Examples:
   1. Acute CVA versus history of CVA
   2. Current drug or alcohol abuse versus history of drug or alcohol abuse
   3. Current neoplasm being treated versus history of malignancy
6. Verify if a condition is a manifestation of an existing condition.
   Example: CRF secondary to DM or CRF due to HTN
7. Look for documentation of conditions that are secondary to previous conditions.
   Examples:
   1. Quadriplegia due to fall
   2. Dysphagia due to previous CVA

ICD-10-CM Outpatient/Ambulatory Coding Guidelines

Note: This is a brief overview. ICD-10-CM codes are used for diagnoses. CPT codes are used for procedures for billing purposes.

1. Documentation should include specific diagnoses as well as symptoms, problems, and reasons for visits.

2. First-listed diagnosis is listed first with other codes following.

3. Chronic diseases may be coded as long as the patient receives treatment.

4. Code all documented conditions that coexist at the time of the visit and are treated or affect treatment. History codes may be used if they impact treatment.

5. Diagnosis coding for Diagnostic Services: Code the diagnosis chiefly responsible for the service. Secondary codes may follow.

   Instructions to Determine the Reason for the Test: The referring physicians are required to provide diagnostic information to the testing entity at the time the test is ordered. All diagnostic tests "must be ordered by the physician who is treating the beneficiary." An order by the physician may include the following forms of communication:
   1. A written document signed by the treating physician/practitioner, which is hand delivered, mailed, or faxed to the testing facility.
   2. A telephone call by the treating physician/practitioner or his or her office to the testing facility.
   3. An electronic mail by the treating physician or practitioner or his or her office to the testing facility.

   Note: Telephone orders must be documented by both the treating physician or practitioner office and the testing facility.

   If the interpreting physician does not have diagnostic information as to the reason for the test, and the referring physician is unavailable, it is appropriate to obtain the information directly from the patient or patient's medical record. Attempt to confirm any information obtained from the patient by contacting the referring physician.

6. Diagnosis coding for Therapeutic Services: Code the diagnosis chiefly responsible for the service. Secondary codes may follow.

7. Diagnosis coding for Ambulatory Surgery: Code the diagnosis for which surgery was done. Use the postoperative diagnosis if it is available and more specific.

Commonly Missed Complications and Comorbidities (CCs)

Depending on the patient's principal diagnosis, this list of commonly missed complications and comorbidities (CCs) and major complications and comorbidities (MCCs) may or may not help the MS-DRG when documented and coded. If any of these conditions are being managed while the patient is being hospitalized, it may change the MS-DRG to a higher paying one. Some MS-DRGs will not change even if these are present. The MS-DRG may or may not change if the patient has a major procedure performed. Some of these conditions may be considered CCs, while others may be considered Major CCs.

- Acidosis
- Alcoholism acute/chronic
- Alkalosis
- Anemia due to blood loss, acute/chronic (e.g., from GI bleed, or surgery)
- Angina pectoris (stable or unstable angina)
- Atrial fibrillation/flutter
- Atelectasis
- Cachexia
- Cardiogenic shock
- Cardiomyopathy
- Cellulitis
- CHF
- Combination of both acidosis/alkalosis
- COPD
- Decubitus ulcer
- Dehydration (volume depletion)
- Diabetes: If DM is uncontrolled (type 1 or 2)
- Electrolyte imbalance
- Hematuria
- Hematemesis
- Hypertension (HTN) accelerated or malignant HTN only qualifies (not uncontrolled, hypertensive urgency or hypertensive crisis)
- Hypertensive heart disease with CHF
- Hyponatremia (↓ Na)
- Hypernatremia (↑ Na)
- Hypochloremia (↓ Cl)
- Hyperchloremia (↑ Cl)
- Hyperpotassemia (↑ K)
- Malnutrition
- Melena
- Pleural effusion (especially if it has to be treated by a procedure, e.g., thoracentesis)
- Pneumonia
- Pneumothorax
- Postoperative complications
- Renal failure, acute or chronic (not renal insufficiency)
- Respiratory failure
- Septicemia
- Urinary retention
- UTI (e.g., urosepsis): If urosepsis is documented, it will be coded as a UTI unless otherwise specified.

Note: This is not an all-inclusive listing of possible complications and comorbidities.

SOME AREAS OF SPECIAL INTEREST

Adhesions

- When minor adhesions are present, but do not cause symptoms or increase the difficulty of an operative procedure, coding a diagnosis of adhesions and a lysis procedure is inappropriate.
- When adhesions are dense or strong or create problems during a surgical procedure, it is appropriate to code both the diagnosis of adhesions and the operative procedure to lyse the adhesions.

Anemia

- The coder must distinguish between chronic blood loss anemia and acute blood loss anemia because the two conditions are assigned to different category codes.
- Acute blood loss anemia occurring after surgery may or may not be a complication of surgery.
- The physician must clearly identify postoperative anemia as a complication of the surgery in order to use the complication code.
- Depending on the primary reason for admission, anemia of chronic disease can be used as the principal diagnosis (if the reason for admit is to treat the anemia) or as the secondary diagnosis.
- When assigning code D63.1 (anemia in chronic kidney disease), also assign a code from category N18.3 (chronic kidney disease) to identify the stage of chronic kidney disease.

Asthma

- Acute exacerbation of asthma is increased severity of asthma symptoms, such as wheezing and shortness of breath.
- Terms suggesting status asthmaticus include intractable asthma, refractory asthma, severe intractable wheezing, and airway obstruction not relieved by medication. It is a life-threatening complication that requires emergency care.
- The coder must not assume status asthmaticus is present. The physician must document the condition in order to code it.

Body Mass Index (BMI)

- The code(s) for body mass index should only be reported as secondary diagnoses and must meet the definition of a reportable additional diagnosis.
- Documentation from clinicians (such as dieticians) may be used for code assignment as long as the physician has documented the diagnosis of obesity.
- If there is conflicting documentation, query the attending physician.

Burns

- When coding multiple burns, assign separate codes for each site and sequence the burn with the highest degree first.
- When coding burns of the same site with varying degrees, code only the highest degree. Necrosis of burned skin is coded as a nonhealing burn. Nonhealing burns are coded as acute burns.

Cellulitis

- Coders must not assume that documentation of redness at the edges of a wound represents cellulitis. Rely on physician documentation of cellulitis.
- Coding of cellulitis with an injury or burn requires one code for the injury and one for the cellulitis. Sequencing will depend on the circumstances of admission.
- When the patient is seen primarily for treating the original injury, sequence that code first. When the patient is seen primarily for treatment of the cellulitis, the code for cellulitis is the principal diagnosis.

Complications

- When coding complications of surgical and medical care, if the code fully describes the condition, no additional code is necessary. If it does not fully describe the condition, an additional code should be assigned. Codes for medical and surgical care are found within the body system chapters.

Congenital Anomalies

- Congenital anomaly codes have been assigned to categories Q00–Q99 and may be used for a principal or secondary diagnosis.
- When there is a code that identifies the congenital anomaly, do not assign additional codes for the inherent manifestations. Do assign additional codes for manifestations that are not an inherent component.
- For the birth admission, category Z38 is still the principal diagnosis followed by any congenital anomaly code (Q00–Q99).
- Codes from Chapter 17, Congenital Anomalies, can be reported for patients of any age. Many congenital anomalies do not manifest any symptoms until much later in life.

Diabetes Mellitus

- When the type of diabetes mellitus is not documented, code it as type 2.
- Diabetes with a manifestation or complication requires documentation of a causal relationship to be coded. Assign as many codes from the diabetes category as needed to identify all associated conditions.
- Even if the patient is using insulin, it does not necessarily mean that the patient is type 1.
- Most patients with type 1 diabetes develop the condition before reaching puberty. That is why type 1 diabetes mellitus is also referred to as juvenile diabetes.
- For type 2 patients who routinely use insulin, code (long-term, current use of insulin) should also be assigned. Do not use this code if the patient receives insulin to temporarily bring a type 2 patient's blood sugar under control.
- An underdose of insulin due to an insulin pump failure should be assigned T85.6- (mechanical complications due to insulin pump) as the principal diagnosis code, followed by a code from categories E08–E13.
- When the patient has an insulin pump malfunction resulting in an overdose of insulin, assign a code from the T85.6- category as the principal diagnosis code with an additional code of T38.3- (poisoning by insulin and antidiabetic agents). Also code the appropriate diabetes mellitus code from E08–E13.
- Use codes from category E08.9- (secondary diabetes mellitus) to identify diabetes caused by another condition or event. Category code E08.9- is listed first followed by the code for the associated condition.

- The patient may be admitted for treatment of the secondary diabetes or one of its associated conditions OR for treatment of the condition causing the secondary diabetes. Code the primary reason for the encounter as the principal diagnosis, which will be a code from category E08.9 followed by the code for the associated condition or a code for the cause of the secondary diabetes.
- Assign code E89.1 for post-pancreatectomy diabetes mellitus. Assign a category code from E08.9 for secondary diabetes mellitus. Also assign Z90.410 for acquired absence of the pancreas. Also code any diabetes manifestations.

Dysplasia of the Vulva and Cervix

- A diagnosis of cervical intraepithelial neoplasia (CIN) III or vulvar intraepithelial neoplasia
- VIN) III is classified as carcinoma in situ of the site.
- A diagnosis of CIN III or VIN III is made only on the basis of pathological evaluation of tissue.

Elevated Blood Pressure vs. Hypertension

- A diagnosis of high or elevated blood pressure without a firm diagnosis of hypertension is reported using code R03.0.
- This code is never assigned on the basis of a review of blood pressure readings; the physician must document elevated blood pressure/hypertension.

Fracture

- Traumatic fractures are coded as long as the patient is receiving active treatment.
- Subsequent care of traumatic fractures are coded to the acute fracture code with the appropriate seventh character. Aftercare Z-codes should not be reported for aftercare of traumatic fractures.
- An open fracture is one in which there is communication with the bone. The following terms indicate open fracture: compound, infected, missile, puncture, and with foreign body.
- A closed fracture does not produce an open wound. Some types of closed fractures are impacted, comminuted, depressed, elevated, greenstick, spiral, and simple.
- When a fracture is not identified as open or closed, the code for a closed fracture is used.
- Internal fixation devices include screws, pins, rods, staples, and plates.
- External fixation devices include casts, splints, and traction device (Kirschner wire) (Steinman pin).

Gastrointestinal Hemorrhage

- Patients may be admitted for an endoscopy after a history of GI bleeding. It is acceptable to use a code for GI hemorrhage even if there is no hemorrhage noted on the current encounter.

Hematuria

- Blood in the urine discovered on a urinalysis is not coded as hematuria but as R82.3, Hemoglobinuria.
- Hematuria following a urinary procedure is not considered a postoperative complication.

Human Immunodeficiency Virus (HIV)

- Documentation of HIV infection as "suspected," "possible," "likely," or "questionable": physician must be queried for clarification. Code only confirmed cases of HIV infection. Confirmation does not require documentation of positive test results for HIV. A physician's documentation is sufficient.
- B20: Patients with symptomatic HIV disease or AIDS. If HIV test results are positive and the patient has symptoms. Patients with known diagnosis of HIV-related illness should be coded to B20 on every subsequent admission.
- Z21: Patients with physician-documented asymptomatic HIV infection who have never had an HIV-related illness. If HIV results are positive and the patient is without symptoms. Do not use this code if the term "AIDS" is used or if the patient is being treated for HIV-related conditions. In these cases, use code B20.
- Patients previously diagnosed with HIV-related illness (B20) should never be assigned Z21
- Z11.4: Patient seen to determine his or her HIV status (screening).
- Patients admitted with an HIV-related condition are assigned code B20 as the principal diagnosis followed by additional diagnosis codes for all reported HIV-related conditions.
- Patients admitted for a condition unrelated to the HIV (such as traumatic injury) are assigned the code for the unrelated condition as the principal diagnosis, then code B20.
- When an obstetric patient has the HIV infection, a code from subcategory O98.7 is sequenced first with either code B20 (symptomatic) or V08 (asymptomatic) used as an additional code.

Hypertension

- Hypertensive heart disease I11. Physician must document causal relationship between hypertension and heart disease that is stated as "due to hypertension" or implied by documenting "hypertensive." Use an additional code from category I50 to identify the type of heart failure, if present. If the heart disease is stated as occurring "with hypertension," do not assume a cause-and-effect relationship and code it separately.
- Hypertensive chronic kidney disease I12-. ICD-10-CM assumes a causal relationship between hypertension and chronic kidney disease. There is no causal relationship with acute renal failure. Use an additional code from category N18 to identify the stage of CKD.
- Hypertensive heart and chronic kidney disease I13.0-. Physician must document causal relationship with the heart disease, but you may assume a causal relationship with chronic kidney disease. Assign an additional code for category I50 to identify the type of heart failure, if present. More than one code for category I50 may be assigned if the patient has systolic or diastolic failure and congestive heart failure. Use an additional code from category N18 to identify the stage of CKD.

Injuries

- Superficial injuries (e.g., abrasions, contusions) are not coded when there are more severe injuries of the same site.

Mechanical Ventilation

- Codes for intubation or tracheostomy should also be assigned.
- It is possible for a patient to be placed back on mechanical ventilation, thus necessitating two codes for mechanical ventilation on the same admission.

Methicillin-Resistant **Staphylococcus aureus** *(MRSA)*

- To code a current infection due to MRSA when that infection does not have a combination code that includes MRSA, code the infection first, and then add code A49.02; B95.62 (MRSA).
- Use code Z22.321 for MSSA (Methicillin-Susceptible Staphylococcus aureus) colonization.
- Use code Z22.322 for MRSA (Methicillin-Resistant Staphylococcus aureus) colonization.
- Use code Z22.31; Z22.39 for other types of *Staphylococcus* colonization.

Myocardial Infarction (MI)

- An MI that is documented as acute or with a duration of 4 weeks or less is coded to category I21, Acute MI.
- When a patient has a subsequent infarction at the time of the encounter for the original infarction, both the initial and the subsequent AMI should be reported with codes from categories I21.- and I22.-
- Subcategory codes I21.0–I21.2 are used for "ST elevation MI" (STEMI).
- Subcategory I21.4 is used for "non-ST elevation MI" (NSTEMI) and nontransmural MI.
- If only STEMI or transmural MI without the documentation of the site, query the physician.
- If an AMI is documented as transmural or subendocardial, but the site is provided, it is still coded as subendocardial AMI.
- If STEMI converts to an NSTEMI due to thrombolytic therapy, it is still coded as STEMI.

Neoplasms

- Neoplasms are listed in the Alphabetic Index in two ways:
  - The Table of Neoplasms provides code numbers for neoplasms by anatomic site. For each site, there are six possible code numbers according to whether the behavior of the neoplasm is malignant primary, malignant secondary, malignant in situ, benign, of uncertain behavior, or of unspecified nature.
  - Histological terms for neoplasms (e.g., adenoma, adenocarcinoma, and sarcoma) are listed as main terms in the appropriate alphabetic sequence and are usually followed by a cross reference to the neoplasm table.
- In sequencing neoplasms, when the treatment is directed toward the malignancy, then the malignancy of that site is designated as the principal diagnosis, unless the patient is admitted for one of the reasons listed next.
- When the patient has a primary neoplasm with metastasis and the treatment is directed toward the secondary site only, the secondary site is sequenced as the principal diagnosis.
- When a patient is admitted solely for chemotherapy, immunotherapy, or radiation therapy, a code from category V58 (V58.11, V58.12, or V58.0) is assigned as the principal diagnosis with the malignant neoplasm coded as an additional diagnosis.
- Codes from category Z85.00–Z85.89 are used when the primary neoplasm is totally eradicated and the patient is no longer having treatment and there is no evidence of any existing primary malignancy. Codes from category Z85 can be listed only as an additional code, not as a principal diagnosis. If extension, invasion, or metastasis is mentioned, code secondary malignant neoplasm to that site as the principal diagnosis.
- When a patient is admitted for pain management associated with the malignancy, code G89.3 as the principal diagnosis followed by the appropriate code for the malignancy. When a patient is admitted for management of the malignancy, code the malignancy as the principal diagnosis with code G89.3 as an additional code.

- When a patient is admitted for management of an anemia associated with the malignancy, and the treatment is only for anemia, code the anemia code D63.0 as the principal diagnosis followed by the appropriate code for the malignancy. Code D63.0 can be used as a secondary code if the patient has anemia and is being treated for the malignancy.
- When a patient is admitted for management of dehydration associated with the malignancy or the therapy, or both, and only the dehydration is being treated (intravenous rehydration), the dehydration is sequenced first, followed by the code(s) for the malignancy.
- If the patient is admitted for surgical removal of a neoplasm followed by chemotherapy or radiation therapy, code the neoplasm (primary or secondary) as the principal diagnosis.
- If the patient has anemia associated with chemotherapy, immunotherapy, or radiotherapy and the only treatment is for the anemia, code anemia due to antineoplastic chemotherapy, and then code the neoplasm as an additional code.
- If the patient is admitted for chemotherapy, immunotherapy, or radiation therapy and then complications occur (such as uncontrolled nausea and vomiting or dehydration); assign the appropriate code for chemotherapy, immunotherapy, or radiation therapy as the principal diagnosis followed by any codes for the complications.
- If the primary reason for admission is to determine the context of the malignancy or for a procedure, even though chemotherapy or radiotherapy is administered, code the malignancy (primary and secondary site) as the principal diagnosis.
- When a malignant neoplasm is associated with a transplanted organ, assign a code from category T86 (complications of transplanted organ), followed by code C80.2 (malignant neoplasm associated with transplanted organ) followed by a code for the specific malignancy.

Newborn

- Newborn (perinatal) codes P00–P96 are never used on the maternal record.
- The perinatal period is defined as before birth through the 28th day following birth.
- A code from category Z38.0 is assigned as the principal diagnosis for any live birth.
- Other diagnoses may be coded for significant conditions noted after birth as secondary diagnoses.
- Insignificant or transient conditions that resolve without treatment are not coded.
- Assign codes from subcategories P00–P04 for evaluation of newborns and infants for suspected condition not found, is used when a healthy baby is evaluated for a suspected condition that proves to not exist. These codes are used when the baby exhibits no signs or symptoms.

Obstetrics

- Chapter 15 codes take sequencing precedence over other chapter codes, which may be assigned to provide further specificity as needed.
- The postpartum period begins immediately after delivery and continues for 6 weeks after delivery.
- The peripartum period is defined as the last month of pregnancy to 5 months.
- Codes from Chapter 15 can continue to be used after the 6-week period if the doctor documents that it is pregnancy related.
- When the mother delivers outside the hospital prior to admission and no complications are documented, code Z39.0 (postpartum care and examination immediately after delivery) as the principal diagnosis. If there are complications, the complications would be coded instead. Do not code a delivery diagnosis code because she delivered prior to admission.
- Principal diagnosis is determined by the circumstances of the encounter or admission.

- Complications: Any condition that occurs during pregnancy, childbirth, or the puerperium is considered to be a complication unless the physician specifically documents otherwise.
- A code from category Z37 is assigned as an additional code to indicate the outcome of delivery on the maternal chart. Z38 codes are not to be used on subsequent records or on the newborn record.
- Code O80, normal delivery, is used only when a delivery is perfectly normal and results in a single live birth. No abnormalities of labor or delivery or postpartum conditions can be present; therefore, there can be no additional code from Chapter 16. Z38.0-, single liveborn, is the only outcome of delivery code appropriate for use with O80.
- Z-codes from category Z34 are used when no obstetric complications are present and should not be used with any codes from Chapter 16.
- When the fetal condition is responsible for modifying the management of the mother (requires diagnostic studies or additional observation, special care, or termination of pregnancy), use codes from categories O35 and O36. The mere fact that the condition exists does not justify assigning a code from categories O35 and O36.
- When in utero surgery is performed on the fetus, assign codes from category O35. No code from Chapter 16 (the perinatal codes) should be used on the mother's record to identify fetal conditions.
- Patients with an HIV-related illness during pregnancy, childbirth, or the puerperium should have codes O98.7- and B20.
- Patients with asymptomatic HIV infection status during pregnancy, childbirth, or the puerperium should have codes O98.7- and V08.
- Patients with diabetes during pregnancy, childbirth, or puerperium should have codes O24 and categories E08–E13. Also code Z79.4 (long-term, current use of insulin), if the diabetes is being treated with insulin.

Pain

- Use a code from category G89 in addition to other codes to provide more detail about whether the pain is acute, chronic, or neoplasm-related.
- If pain is not specified as acute or chronic, do not assign a code from category G89 except for postthoracotomy pain, postoperative pain, neoplasm-related pain, or central pain syndrome.
- A code from subcategories G89.1 and G89.2 should not be used if the underlying diagnosis is known unless the primary reason for admission is pain control.
- A code from category G89 can be the principal or first-listed diagnosis code when pain control or management is the reason for the admission or encounter. Code the underlying cause of the pain as an additional diagnosis.
- When a patient is admitted for a procedure for purposes of treating the underlying condition (e.g., spinal fusion), code the underlying condition (e.g., spinal stenosis) as the principal diagnosis. Do not code the pain from category G89.
- When a patient is admitted for the insertion of a neurostimulator for pain control, assign the code for pain as the principal diagnosis.
- If the patient is admitted primarily for a procedure to treat the underlying condition and a neurostimulator is inserted for pain, code the underlying condition as the principal diagnosis, followed by a code for the pain.
- If a code describes the site of the pain, but does not indicate whether the type of pain is acute or chronic (category G89), use two codes (one for the site and one for the type). If the admission is for pain control, assign category code G89 (acute or chronic) as the principal diagnosis. If the admission is not for pain control and a related definitive diagnosis is not documented, assign the code for the specific site of the pain as the principal diagnosis.

- Routine or expected postoperative pain immediately after surgery should not be coded.
- Postoperative pain not associated with a specific postoperative complication is coded using the appropriate code in category G89.
- Postoperative pain can be listed as the principal diagnosis when the reason for admission is pain control.

Pleural Effusion

- Pleural effusion is almost always integral to the underlying condition and therefore is usually not coded.
- When the effusion is addressed and treated separately, it can be coded.
- Pleural effusion noted only on an X-ray is not coded.

Pneumonia

- There are many combination codes that describe the pneumonia and the infecting organism.
- In some situations, the pneumonia is a manifestation of an underlying condition. In this situation, two codes are needed—one for the underlying condition and the other for the pneumonia.
- Lobar pneumonia does not refer to the lobe of the lung that is affected. It is a particular type of pneumonia.
- Gram-negative pneumonias are much more difficult to treat than gram-positive pneumonias. If the findings suggest a gram-negative pneumonia, and it is not documented as such, query the physician.
- Signs of gram-negative pneumonia include: worsening of cough, dyspnea, fever, purulent sputum, elevated leukocyte count, and patchy infiltrate on chest X-ray.
- When the physician has documented Ventilator Associated Pneumonia (VAP), use code J95.851.
- Add an additional code to identify the organism. Do not assign an additional code from categories J12–J18 to identify the type of pneumonia. Do not use code J95.851 just because the patient is on a ventilator and has pneumonia. The physician must document that the pneumonia is attributed to the ventilator.

Postoperative Complications

- Physician must document that a condition is a complication of the procedure before assigning a complication code.
- "Expected" conditions occur in the immediate post-op period. These are not reported unless they exceed the usual post-op period and meet the criteria for reporting as an additional diagnosis.

Pressure Ulcers

- When the patient has multiple pressure ulcers at different sites and each is at different stages, code each of the sites and each of the different stages.
- When the patient has pressure ulcers documented as "healed," no code is assigned.
- When the patient has pressure ulcers documented as "healing," code the site(s) and the stage(s).
- When the patient has a pressure ulcer at one stage at the time of admission, but then it progresses to a higher stage, assign the code for the highest stage.

Pulmonary Edema

- Pulmonary edema can be cardiogenic or noncardiogenic.
- Pulmonary edema is a manifestation of heart failure and, as such, is included in heart failure, hypertension, or rheumatic heart disease. Therefore, it is not coded separately.
- Noncardiogenic acute pulmonary edema occurs in the absence of heart failure or other heart disease.

Respiratory Failure (Acute)

- Careful review of the medical record is required for the coding and sequencing of acute respiratory failure. If it meets the definition of principal diagnosis, it is coded as such. If it does not, it is coded as a secondary diagnosis.
- When a patient is admitted with acute respiratory failure and another acute condition, the principal diagnosis will depend on the individual patient's condition and the chief (main) reason that caused the admission of the patient to the hospital.

Septicemia

- A diagnosis of bacteremia R78.81 refers to the presence of bacteria in the bloodstream following a relatively minor injury or infection.
- Septicemia and sepsis are often used to mean the same thing, but they have two distinct and separate meanings.
- Septicemia is a systemic condition associated with pathogenic microorganisms or toxins in the blood (such as bacteria, viruses, fungi, or other organisms). Most septicemias are classified to category A41.-. Additional codes are assigned for any manifestations, if present.
- Negative blood cultures do not preclude a diagnosis of septicemia or sepsis. Query the physician.
- A code for septicemia is used only when the physician documents a diagnosis of septicemia.
- Urosepsis is not a condition that is classified in ICD-10-CM. A physician query should be initiated for clarification of the condition under treatment.
- Systemic Inflammatory Response Syndrome (SIRS) refers to the systemic response to infection, trauma, burns, or other insult (such as cancer) with symptoms (such as fever, tachycardia, tachypnea, and leukocytosis).
- When a patient has SIRS with no subsequent infection, and is a result of a noninfectious disease (such as trauma, cancer, or pancreatitis), code the noninfectious disease first, and then code R65.10 or R65.11. If an acute organ dysfunction is documented, code that also.
- Sepsis generally refers to SIRS due to infection.
- Severe sepsis generally refers to sepsis with associated acute organ dysfunction.
- If sepsis or severe sepsis is present on admission and meets the definition of principal diagnosis, the systemic infection code should be coded first, followed by the appropriate code from subcategory R65.2-. Codes from subcategory R65.2- can never be assigned as a principal diagnosis. An additional code should be added for any localized infection, if present.
- If sepsis or severe sepsis develops during admission, assign the code for the systemic infection and a code from subcategory R65.2- as a secondary code.
- Septic shock is defined as sepsis with hypotension, which is a failure of the cardiovascular system. Septic shock is used as an additional code when the underlying infection is present.
- For all cases of septic shock, code the systemic infection first (such as A40.-; A41.-; B37.7) followed by code R65.21. Any additional codes for other acute organ dysfunction should also be assigned.

Substance Abuse

- Substance abuse and dependence are classified as mental disorders in ICD-10-CM.
- Alcohol dependence is classified to category F10.2, and nondependent alcohol use is coded to category F10.1.
- The physician documentation must indicate the pattern of use.
- There are codes for alcohol withdrawal and drug withdrawal symptoms. These codes are used in conjunction with the dependence codes.
- When a patient is admitted in withdrawal or when withdrawal develops after admission, the withdrawal code is principal.
- There are procedure codes for rehabilitation, detoxification, and combination rehabilitation and detoxification for both alcohol and drug dependence.

Z-Codes

Z-codes (Z00–Z99) characterize the purpose for an encounter when a disease or injury is not the reason a patient is seeking healthcare services. Z-codes can be used in any healthcare setting. Certain Z-codes can be assigned as the principal or first listed diagnosis.

- Special main terms for Z-codes in the Alphabetic Index of Diseases include:

Abnormal
Admission
Aftercare Anomaly
Attention to
(personal) Boarder
Care of
Carrier
Checking
Complication
Contraception
Counseling
Delivery
Dialysis
Donor
Examination
Exposure to
Fitting of
Follow-up
Foreign Body
Healthy
History (family)
History
Maintenance
Maladjustment
Observation
Problem with
Procedure (surgical)
Prophylactic
Replacement
Screening
Status
Supervision (of)
Test
Transplant
Unavailability of medical facilities
Vaccination

ICD-10-CM CODING SECTION

Infectious and Parasitic Diseases

1. The patient was admitted with AIDS-related Kaposi's sarcoma of the skin.
   A. B20, C46.1
   B. C46.0, B20
   C. B20, C46.7
   D. B20, C46.0

REFERENCE: AHA I-10 Coding Handbook, p 157
Bowie, pp 79–80

2. A patient was admitted with severe sepsis due to MRSA with septic shock and acute respiratory failure with hypoxia.
   A. R65.21, A41.02, J96.02
   B. A41.02, R65.21, J96.01
   C. A49.01, R65.21, J96.01
   D. J96.01, R65.21, A41.02

REFERENCE: AHA I-10 Coding Handbook, p 151
Bowie, pp 73, 83

3. Patient was initially admitted and treated for an amebic abscess of the liver. During the stay the patient developed a "hospital acquired bacterial pneumonia."
   A. A06.4, J15.9, Y95
   B. A06.4, J15.8; Y95
   C. A06.4, J18.9, Y95
   D. A06.4, J95.89, Y95

REFERENCE: AHA I-10 Coding Handbook, pp 153–154

4. A patient is admitted with fever and severe headache. The physician's diagnostic statement at discharge is: Fever and severe headache probably due to viral meningitis.
   A. A87.9, R50.9, R51
   B. A87.8, R50.9, R51
   C. A87.9
   D. A87.8

REFERENCE: AHA I-10 Coding Handbook, p 57
Bowie, pp 48, 55

5. Positive HIV test in a patient who is asymptomatic and has a high-risk lifestyle for HIV infection.
   A. B20, Z20.6, Z72.89
   B. B20, Z21, Z72.89
   C. B20, Z20.6, Z72.89
   D. Z21, Z72.89

REFERENCE: AHA I-10 Coding Handbook, p 157
Bowie, pp 79–80

6. A 32-year-old female patient presents with right arm (dominant) paralysis due to childhood poliomyelitis.
   A. A80.39
   B. A80.39, G83.21
   C. B91, G83.21
   D. A80.39, G83.3

REFERENCE: AHA I-10 Coding Handbook, pp 60–149
Bowie, p 50

Neoplasms

7. A patient is admitted for chemotherapy for treatment of breast cancer with liver metastasis. She had a mastectomy 4 months ago. Chemotherapy is given today. (Do not assign a procedure code for the chemotherapy.)
   A. C78.7, C85.3, Z51.11
   B. C85.3, C78.7, Z51.11
   C. C78.7, C85.3
   D. Z51.11, C78.7, Z85.3

REFERENCE: AHA I-10 Coding Handbook, pp 458–460

8. A patient with a history of malignant neoplasm of the lung status post lobectomy was admitted after experiencing a violent seizure lasting more than several minutes. During the course of the hospitalization the patient has continued to have seizures. Workup revealed metastatic lesions to the brain. The patient's seizures were treated with IV Dilantin.
   A. C79.3, Z85.118, F56.9
   B. C79.31, F56.9
   C. C79.31, R56.9, Z85.118
   D. F56.9 C79.32, Z85.118

REFERENCE: AHA I-10 Coding Handbook, pp 449–451

9. A patient is admitted to the hospital for treatment of dehydration following chemotherapy as treatment for right ovarian cancer.
   A. E86.0, C56.1
   B. E86.9, C56.1
   C. C56.1, 86.9
   D. C56.1, E86.0

REFERENCE: AHA I-10 Coding Handbook, p 460
Bowie, p 107

10. A patient has malignant melanoma of the skin of the back, nose, and scalp. The patient will be scheduled to undergo a radical excision of the melanoma
    A. 173.59, 86.4, 86.63
    B. C43.59, C43.31, C43.4
    C. 173.59, 86.3, 86.63
    D. 172.5, 86.3, 86.63

REFERENCE: AHA I-10 Coding Handbook, pp 443, 456, 460
Bowie, p 101

11. A patient is admitted with abdominal pain. A CT and MRI of the abdomen reveal a malignant neoplasm to the head of the pancreas with metastatic disease to the peritoneal cavity.
    A. C25.1, C78.6
    B. C78.89, C78.89
    C. C25.0, C78.6
    D. D01.7, C78.6

REFERENCE: AHA I-10 Coding Handbook, pp 446–450
Bowie, pp 101–102

12. A patient to an OP Clinic with a large growth on the left side of the neck. An MRI is performed and demonstrates metastatic disease to the lymph nodes.
    A. C77.2, C80.0
    B. C77.0, C80.1
    C. C77.2, R22.1, C81.1
    D. C77.8, C80.0

REFERENCE: AHA I-10 Coding Handbook, pp 446–450, 454
Bowie, pp 101–102

Endocrine, Nutritional, and Metabolic Diseases and Immunity Disorders

13. A female, 68 years old, was admitted with type 2 diabetes mellitus with a diabetic ulcer of the left heel involving the subcutaneous layer of the skin. The patient will be scheduled for wound care with whirlpool treatments.
    A. E11.621, L97.421   C. E11.621
    B. E11.620, I97.421   D. L97.421, E11.621

REFERENCE: AHA I-10 Coding Handbook, pp 160–161, 164
Bowie, pp 149–151

14. A 67-year-old man is admitted with acute dehydration secondary to nausea and vomiting that is due to acute gastroenteritis. He is treated with IV fluids for the dehydration.
    A. K52.9, E86.0   C. 86.0, E11.2, K52.9
    B. E11.2, 52.9, E86.0   D. E86.0, K52.9

REFERENCE: AHA I-10 Coding Handbook, pp 30–33
Bowie, p 260

15. A patient was found at home in a hypoglycemic coma. This patient had never been diagnosed as being diabetic.
    A. E16.2   C. E16.1
    B. E15   D. E16.9

REFERENCE: AHA I-10 Coding Handbook, p 167
Bowie, p 144

16. A patient is admitted with aplastic anemia secondary to chemotherapy administered for multiple myeloma initial encounter.
    A. D61.1, T45.1x5A, C90.00   C. C90.00, T45.1x5A, D61.1
    B. T45.1x5A, C90.00, D61.3   D. D61.1, T45.1x5A, D61.3

REFERENCE: AHA I-10 Coding Handbook, p 460
Bowie, pp 106–107

17. A male patient is admitted with gastrointestinal hemorrhage resulting in acute blood-loss anemia. A bleeding scan fails to reveal the source of the bleed.
    A. K92, D63.8   C. K92.2, D62
    B. K92.1, D62   D. K92.2, D63.8

REFERENCE: AHA I-10 Coding Handbook, p 193
Bowie, pp 126, 263

18. A patient is admitted with severe protein calorie malnutrition.
    A. E42   C. E46
    B. E43   D. E40

REFERENCE: AHA I-10 Coding Handbook, p 168
Bowie, p 153

Diseases of the Blood and Blood-Forming Organs

19. A patient is admitted with idiopathic thrombocytopenia and purpura.
    A. D61
    B. D69.3, D61
    C. D69.49
    D. D69.3

REFERENCE: AHA I-10 Coding Handbook, p 199
Bowie, pp 127–129

20. A patient is admitted with sickle cell anemia with crisis.
    A. D57.00, D57.3
    B. D57.00
    C. D57.1
    D. D57.819

REFERENCE: AHA I-10 Coding Handbook, pp 191, 196

21. A patient is admitted with sickle cell pain crisis.
    A. D57.00
    B. D57.00, D57.3
    C. D57.819
    D. D57.1

REFERENCE: AHA I-10 Coding Handbook, pp 191, 196
Bowie, p 125

22. A patient is readmitted for post-op anemia due to acute blood loss. Patient is 5 days status post-cholecystectomy.
    A. D62, R58
    B. K91.840, D62
    C. K91.89, D62
    D. D62

REFERENCE: AHA I-10 Coding Handbook, pp 193, 528
Bowie, p 126

23. A patient is admitted with anemia due to end-stage renal disease. The patient is treated for anemia.
    A. N18.6, D63.8
    B. D63.1, N18.6
    C. D63.1, N18.5
    D. D63.1

REFERENCE: AHA I-10 Coding Handbook, p 194
Bowie, pp 263, 307

24. A patient is admitted for treatment of anemia, neutropenia, and thrombocytopenia.
    A. D70.8, D69.59, D59.2
    B. D61.810
    C. D70.8, D69.59, D59.2, D61.810
    D. D61.818

REFERENCE: AHA I-10 Coding Handbook, pp 195, 199
Bowie, p 126

Mental Disorders

25. A patient is admitted with severe recurrent major depression without psychotic features.
    A. F33.0
    B. F33.3
    C. F32.2
    D. F33.2

REFERENCE: AHA I-10 Coding Handbook, p 175
Bowie, pp 166–167

26. A patient is admitted with acute alcohol intoxication with a blood alcohol level of 113 mg/100 ml.
    A. Y90.5, F10.129
    B. F10.129, Y90.5
    C. F10.129, Y90.6
    D. F10.129, Y90.4

REFERENCE: AHA I-10 Coding Handbook, p 181
Bowie, pp 164, 418

27. A patient is admitted with delirium tremens with alcohol dependence.
    A. F10.221
    B. F10.222
    C. F10.121
    D. F10.231

REFERENCE: AHA I-10 Coding Handbook, p 181
Bowie, pp 164, 418

28. A patient is admitted with catatonic schizophrenia.
    A. F20
    B. F14.221
    C. F20.2
    D. F14.29

REFERENCE: AHA I-10 Coding Handbook, p 174
Bowie, p 166

29. A patient with chronic paranoia due to cocaine dependence with intoxication and drug delirium.
    A. F14.129
    B. F14.221
    C. F14.159
    D. F14.19, F22

REFERENCE: AHA I-10 Coding Handbook, pp 181–182
Bowie, p 165

30. A patient is diagnosed with psychogenic paroxysmal tachycardia.
    A. I47.9
    B. F54
    C. I47.8, F54
    D. I47.9, F54

REFERENCE: AHA I-10 Coding Handbook, p 177
Bowie, pp 168, 229

Diseases of the Nervous System and Sense Organs

31. A patient is admitted with sensorineural deafness of the left ear. The patient was fitted for a hearing aid.
    A. H90.71
    B. H90.72
    C. H90.42
    D. H90.41

REFERENCE: AHA I-10 Coding Handbook, p 220
Bowie, p 210

32. A patient is a type 2 diabetic with chronic kidney disease requiring dialysis.
    A. E09.29, N18.6, Z99.2
    B. E11.22, N18.6, Z99.2
    C. E11.21, N18.6, Z99.2
    D. E13.21, N18.6, Z99.2

REFERENCE: AHA I-10 Coding Handbook, pp 265–266
Bowie, pp 144, 307

33. A patient has intractable status epilepticus.
   A. G40.311
   B. G40.301
   C. G40.31
   D. G40.201

REFERENCE: AHA I-10 Coding Handbook, p 206
Bowie, p 184

34. A patient is diagnosed with Alzheimer's disease and early onset dementia, and frequently wanders away from home.
   A. G30.8, F02.81, Z91.83
   B. F02.81, G30.0, Z91.73
   C. G30.0, F02.81, Z91.83
   D. G30.0, Z91.73

REFERENCE: AHA I-10 Coding Handbook, pp 173, 206
Bowie, pp 162–163, 182, 438

35. A patient is admitted with poliovirus meningitis.
   A. G02, A80.9
   B. A80.9, G02
   C. A80.3, G02
   D. A80.0, G02

REFERENCE: AHA I-10 Coding Handbook, p 205
Bowie, pp 76, 180–181

36. A patient is admitted for pain control secondary to metastatic carcinoma of the spinal cord.
   A. G89.3, C79.49
   B. C79.51, C80.1, G89.3
   C. C79.49, C80.1 , G89.3
   D. G89.3, C79.49, C80.1

REFERENCE: AHA I-10 Coding Handbook, p 210
Bowie, p 108

Diseases of the Circulatory System

37. A patient is admitted with a thrombosis of the right middle cerebral artery, with hemiplegia affecting the right dominant side.
   A. I66.01, I69.351
   B. I63.311, I69.353
   C. I63.311
   D. I63.311, I69.351

REFERENCE: AHA I-10 Coding Handbook, p 209
Bowie, pp 230–231

38. A patient is admitted with multiple problems. He has hypertensive kidney disease, CKD stage III, and acute systolic congestive heart failure.
   A. N18.3, I12.9, I50.21
   B. I50.21, I12.9, N18.3
   C. I12.9, N18.3, I50.21
   D. I12.9

REFERENCE: AHA I-10 Coding Handbook, pp 394–395, 404–405
Bowie, pp 222, 227, 307–308

39. A patient is admitted with acute ST Inferolateral wall myocardial infarction. Several days later during the same episode of care, the patient sustained a subsequent non-ST subendocardial myocardial infarction.
   A. I21.09, I22.8
   B. I21.02, I22.8
   C. I22.2, I21.02
   D. I21.19, I22.2

REFERENCE: AHA I-10 Coding Handbook, pp 389–391
Bowie, pp 226–227

40. A patient with a diagnosis of coronary artery disease with ischemic chest pain. No history of CABG.
    A. I25.119 C. I25.9
    B. I25.119, I20.9 D. I25.10, I20.9

REFERENCE: AHA I-10 Coding Handbook, pp 392–393
Bowie, p 227

41. A patient with atherosclerotic peripheral vascular disease of the left lower leg with intermittent claudication. Past surgical history is negative.
    A. I70.219 C. I70.298
    B. I70.212 D. I70.208

REFERENCE: AHA I-10 Coding Handbook, p 407
Bowie, p 231

Diseases of the Respiratory System

42. A patient presents to the outpatient department for a chest x-ray. The physician's order lists the following reasons for the chest x-ray: fever and cough, rule out pneumonia. The radiologist reports that the chest x-ray is positive for double pneumonia.
    A. J18.9 C. J18.1
    B. J18.8 D. J12.9

REFERENCE: AHA I-10 Coding Handbook, pp 140–141
Bowie, pp 243–244

43. A patient has aspiration pneumonia with pneumonia due to *Staphylococcus aureus*.
    A. J15.211 C. J69.0, J15
    B. J69.0 D. J69.0, J15.211

REFERENCE: AHA I-10 Coding Handbook, pp 224, 227, 229
Bowie, pp 243–244, 246

44. A patient is admitted with acute respiratory failure with hypercapnia due to acute asthmatic bronchitis with status asthmaticus. Treatment consisted of IV steroids.
    A. J45.902, J96.02 C. J45.901, J96.02
    B. J96.02, J45.902 D. J45.52, J96.02

REFERENCE: AHA I-10 Coding Handbook, pp 231, 233, 235
Bowie, pp 246–248

45. A patient is admitted for treatment of influenza and pneumonia.
    A. J11.1, J18.9 C. J11.08, J11.1
    B. J11.00 D. J11.1

REFERENCE: AHA I-10 Coding Handbook, p 228
Bowie, pp 243–244

46. A patient is admitted with acute exacerbation chronic obstructive pulmonary disease with a history of tobacco dependence.
    A. J44.1, Z87.891 C. J44.0, Z87.891
    B. J44.9, Z72.0 D. J44.1, Z72.0

REFERENCE: AHA I-10 Coding Handbook, p 230
Bowie, pp 245, 438–439

47. A patient is admitted with extrinsic asthma with status asthmaticus with bronchospasm.
   A. J45.901 C. J45.902
   B. J45.32 D. J45.902

REFERENCE: AHA I-10 Coding Handbook, pp 230– 231
Bowie, p 245

48. A patient is admitted for infection of the tracheostomy stoma secondary to cellulitis of the neck.
   A. L03.221, J95.02 C. J95.03, L03.221
   B. J95.02, L03.221 D. J95.09, L03.221

REFERENCE: AHA I-10 Coding Handbook, pp 224, 288–289
Bowie, pp 247, 273

Diseases of the Digestive System

49. A patient is admitted to the hospital for repair of a recurrent incarcerated ventral hernia. The surgery is canceled after the chest x-ray revealed lower lobe pneumonia. The patient is placed on antibiotics for treatment of the pneumonia.
   A. K43.0, J18.9, Z53.09 C. K43.6, J18.9
   B. J18.9, K43.0, Z53.09 D. J18.9, J43.6

REFERENCE: AHA I-10 Coding Handbook, p 253
Bowie, pp 243–244, 259–260, 436

50. A patient is admitted with acute gastric ulcer with hemorrhage and perforation.
   A. K25.0, K25.1 C. K25.4, K25.6
   B. K25.6 D. K25.2

REFERENCE: AHA I-10 Coding Handbook, p 246
Bowie, p 258

51. A patient has diverticulitis of the large bowel with abscess. Patient was treated with IV antibiotics.
   A. K57.92 C. K57.20
   B. K57.12 D. K57.52

REFERENCE: AHA I-10 Coding Handbook, p 247
Bowie, pp 260–261

52. A patient is admitted with acute gangrenous cholecystitis with cholelithiasis.
   A. K80.00 C. K81.0, K80.80
   B. K80.12 D. K80.32

REFERENCE: AHA I-10 Coding Handbook, p 249
Bowie, p 262

53. A patient is admitted with bleeding esophageal varices with alcoholic liver cirrhosis and portal hypertension. The patient is alcohol dependent.
   A. K76.6, I85.11, K70.30 C. K70.30, I85.11, K76.6
   B. I85.11, K76.6, K70.30 D. K70.0. I85.11, K76.6

REFERENCE: AHA I-10 Coding Handbook, p 246
Bowie, pp 231–232, 261

54. A patient is admitted for rectal bleeding. The laboratory results reveal chronic blood-loss anemia. The CT and the Bleeding Scan results of the abdomen revealed that the rectal bleeding is due to Crohn's disease of the descending colon.
A. K50.118, D50.0
B. K50.111, D50.0
C. K50.011, D50.0
D. K50.911, D50.0

REFERENCE: AHA I-10 Coding Handbook, p 248
Bowie, pp 260–261

Diseases of the Genitourinary System

55. A patient is admitted with acute urinary tract infection due to *E. coli*.
A. N39.0, B96.20
B. N11.9, B96.20
C. N30.90, B96.20
D. N10, B96.20

REFERENCE: AHA I-10 Coding Handbook, pp 260– 261
Bowie, pp 67, 309

56. A patient admitted with gross hematuria and benign prostatic hypertrophy.
A. R31.0, N40.0
B. R31.0, N40.1
C. N40.0, R31.0
D. N40.1, R31.0

REFERENCE: AHA I-10 Coding Handbook, pp 262, 270
Bowie, pp 272–273, 311

57. A male patient presents to the ED with acute renal failure. He is also being treated for hypertension.
A. I12.9, N17.9
B. N17.9, I15.9
C. N17.9, I12.9
D. N17.9, I10

REFERENCE: AHA I-10 Coding Handbook, p 264
Bowie, pp 222, 307–308

58. A patient is admitted with acute hemorrhagic cystitis. The patient was treated with IV antibiotics.
A. N30.00
B. N30.91
C. N30.01
D. N30.81

REFERENCE: AHA I-10 Coding Handbook, pp 260– 261
Bowie, p 309

59. A patient is admitted with chronic kidney disease stage III due to hypertension and type 1 diabetes mellitus.
A. E11.22, I12.0, N18.3
B. E10.22, I12.0, N18.3
C. I12.0, E11.22, N18.3
D. E08.22, I12.0, N18.3

REFERENCE: AHA I-10 Coding Handbook, p 265
Bowie, pp 222, 307–308

60. A patient has end-stage kidney disease, which resulted from malignant hypertension.
A. I12.0, N18.6
B. I10, N18.6
C. I13.11, N18.6
D. I15.1, N18.6

REFERENCE: AHA I-10 Coding Handbook, pp 263–264
Bowie, pp 221–222, 307–308

Complications of Pregnancy, Childbirth, and the Puerperium

61. A woman has a vaginal delivery of a full-term liveborn infant after 38 weeks gestation.
    A. O80, Z37.0, Z3A.38
    B. O80, Z37.0
    C. Z3A.38, O80, Z37.0
    D. Z37.0, Z3A.38, O80

REFERENCE: AHA I-10 Coding Handbook, pp 316, 319
Bowie, pp 331–332

62. A patient is admitted with pregnancy-induced hypertension with severe edema and 24 weeks gestation.
    A. O14.12
    B. I10, Z33.1
    C. O14.12, Z3A24
    D. O14.00, 23A24

REFERENCE: AHA I-10 Coding Handbook, p 325
Bowie, pp 235–236

63. A patient is admitted with obstructed labor due to breech presentation. A single liveborn infant was delivered via Cesarean section. Do not assign the code for the procedure.
    A. O32.1xx0
    B. O32.1xx0, Z37.0
    C. 032.8xx0, Z37.0
    D. O32.6xx0, Z37.0

REFERENCE: AHA I-10 Coding Handbook, p 327
Bowie, pp 327, 332

64. A patient is admitted for gestation diabetes insulin controlled 28 weeks gestation.
    A. O24.414
    B. E11.69, O09.892
    C. O24.419, Z3A28
    D. O24.414, Z3A28

REFERENCE: AHA I-10 Coding Handbook, p 325
Bowie, pp 326–327

65. A patient is seen in the ED at 22 weeks gestation who is HIV positive.
    A. B20, O98.712, Z3A.22
    B. O98.712, Z21, Z3A.22
    C. Z21, O98.712
    D. P98.712, B20

REFERENCE: AHA I-10 Coding Handbook, p 326
Bowie, pp 333, 433

66. A patient is admitted who is 39 weeks gestation normal delivery single full-term newborn. During the same episode of care, patient experiences a 36-hour delayed hemorrhage following the delivery.
    A. O80, O72.2, Z37.0
    B. O72.2, Z37.0
    C. Z3A.39, O72.2, Z37.0
    D. O72.2, Z3A.39, Z37.0

REFERENCE: AHA I-10 Coding Handbook, p 319
Bowie, pp 330, 433

Diseases of the Skin and Subcutaneous Tissue

67. A patient had a cholecystectomy 3 days ago and is now readmitted with cellulitis at the site of the operative incision.
    A. T81.4, K68.11, 95.61
    B. T81.4xxA, L03.311
    C. K68.11, B95.61
    D. L03.31, T81.4xxA

REFERENCE: AHA I-10 Coding Handbook, p 288
Bowie, pp 273, 398–399

68. A patient is admitted with a wound open to the left finger with cellulitis due to a dog bite initial encounter. The patient is given IV antibiotics for treatment of the infection.
   A. L03.012 C. S61.201A
   B. L03.011 D. L03.012, S61.201A

REFERENCE: AHA I-10 Coding Handbook, p 288
Bowie, pp 373, 384

69. A patient is admitted with Diabetes Mellitus Type II; diabetic heel ulcer with necrosis of the muscle.
   A. E11.621, L97.403 C. E11.622, L97.403
   B. E10.622, L97.403 D. E10.628, L97.403

REFERENCE: AHA I-10 Coding Handbook, pp 286–287
Bowie, pp 144, 277–279

70. A patient is admitted with dermatitis due to prescription topical antibiotic cream used as directed by a physician, initial encounter.
   A. L08.89, T49.0x5 C. L02.91, T49.0x5
   B. L25.1, T49.0x5A D. T49.0x5, L25.1

REFERENCE: AHA I-10 Coding Handbook, p 284
Bowie, pp 274, 395–396

71. A patient is admitted with a pressure ulcer left buttock stage 2.
   A. L89.322 C. L89.152
   B. L98.411 D. L03.317

REFERENCE: AHA I-10 Coding Handbook, p 287
Bowie, pp 277–279

72. A patient is admitted with a stage 1 pressure ulcer of the sacrum. During the hospitalization, the ulcer progressed to a stage 2
   A. L89.125 C. L89.152
   B. L89.151, L89.152 D. L89.153

REFERENCE: AHA I-10 Coding Handbook, p 287
Bowie, pp 277–279

Diseases of the Musculoskeletal System and Connective Tissue

73. A patient has a pathological fracture of the left femur due to metastatic bone cancer. The past medical history is significant for lung cancer.
   A. C79.51, S72.92xG, Z85.118 C. C79.51, S72.92xS, Z85.118
   B. M84.552, C79.51, Z85.118 D. C79.51, M84.552, Z85.118

REFERENCE: AHA I-10 Coding Handbook, pp 299–300, 460, 489
Bowie, pp 97, 295, 439

74. A patient is admitted with a back pain. A myelogram demonstrated the reason for the back pain is a herniated lumbar intervertebral disc with radiculopathy.
   A. M51.26, M54.16 C. M51.26
   B. M84.552, C79.51, Z85.118 D. M51.16

REFERENCE: AHA I-10 Coding Handbook, p 296
Bowie, p 291

75. A patient is admitted with pyogenic arthritis of the right hip due to Group A *Streptococcus*. Treatment consisted of IV antibiotics.
   A. M16.11, A49.1
   B. M16.7, A49.1
   C. M00.251
   D. M00.851

REFERENCE: AHA I-10 Coding Handbook, p 298
Bowie, p 288

76. A patient is admitted with a fracture to the L1 vertebrae secondary to postmenopausal senile osteoporosis, initial encounter.
   A. M80.08
   B. M80.88
   C. M80.88xA
   D. M80.08xA

REFERENCE: AHA I-10 Coding Handbook, p 300
Bowie, p 288

77. A patient developed a malunion of the medical condyle humeral fracture. The original injury occurred 4 months ago.
   A. S42.462K
   B. S42.462G
   C. S42.462P
   D. S42.462D

REFERENCE: AHA I-10 Coding Handbook, p 486
Bowie, pp 50, 390

78. A patient was admitted for removal of internal pins from the left ankle. One month ago the patient sustained a displaced bimalleolar fracture to the left ankle.
   A. S82.842K
   B. S82.842D
   C. S82.842S
   D. S84.842G

REFERENCE: AHA I-10 Coding Handbook, p 286
Bowie, p 390

Congenital Anomalies

79. A Newborn infant is born in the hospital vaginal delivery with a unilateral hard cleft palate and cleft lip.
   A. O37.1, Z38.00
   B. O37.2, Z38.00
   C. Z38.00, O37.1
   D. Z38.00, O37.2

REFERENCE: AHA I-10 Coding Handbook, p 360
Bowie, pp 320, 333–334

80. A newborn is born in the hospital vaginal delivery. Physical examination demonstrates molding of the baby's scalp, which resolved prior to discharge without treatment.
   A. Z38.00, Q82.9
   B. Z38.00, Q82.8
   C. Z38.00, L98.8
   D. Z38.00

REFERENCE: AHA I-10 Coding Handbook, p 367
Bowie, pp 333–334

81. A newborn infant is transferred to Community General Hospital for treatment of an esophageal atresia. What codes should be reported for Community General Hospital?
   A. Z38.00, Q39.0
   B. Q39.0
   C. Z38.00, Q39.1
   D. Q39.1

REFERENCE: AHA I-10 Coding Handbook, p 367
Bowie, p 356

82. A patient is admitted with cervical spina bifida with hydrocephalus.
   A. Q76.0
   B. Q05
   C. Q05.0
   D. Q05.5

REFERENCE: AHA I-10 Coding Handbook, p 359
Bowie, p 363

83. A newborn infant is born in the hospital, delivered vaginally, and sustained a fracture of the clavicle due to birth trauma.
   A. Z38.00, P13.4
   B. Z38.00, S42.009A
   C. P13.4
   D. Z38.00, P13.4, S42.009A

REFERENCE: AHA I-10 Coding Handbook, p 367
Bowie, pp 343–344, 434–444

84. A full-term infant born in hospital vaginal delivery was diagnosed with polycystic kidneys.
   A. Z38.00, Q61.11
   B. Z38.00, Q61.19
   C. Z38.00, Q61.3
   D. Z38.00, Q61.8

REFERENCE: AHA I-10 Coding Handbook, p 361
Bowie, pp 387–388, 434–444

Certain Conditions Originating in the Perinatal Period

85. A full-term newborn vaginal delivery was born in the hospital to a mother who is addicted to cocaine; however, the infant tested negative.
   A. Z38.00, F14.10
   B. Z38.00, F14.129
   C. Z38.00, F14.20
   D. Z38.00, Z03.79

REFERENCE: AHA I-10 Coding Handbook, p 373
Bowie, pp 428, 433–444

86. A preterm infant 34 weeks gestation is born via Cesarean section and has severe birth asphyxia.
   A. Z38.01, P84, P07.37
   B. Z38.01, P84, R09.01
   C. Z38.01, P84, R09.02
   D. Z38.01, P84, R09.2, P07.37

REFERENCE: AHA I-10 Coding Handbook, pp 368–369

87. A preterm infant born in the hospital vaginal delivery 36 weeks gestation is treated for neonatal jaundice.
   A. Z38.00, P59.9, P07.39
   B. Z38.00, P59.8, P07.39
   C. Z38.00, P59.29, P07.39
   D. Z38.00, P59.3, P07.39

REFERENCE: AHA I-10 Coding Handbook, pp 367, 368
Bowie, pp 342, 345, 433–434

88. A 1-week-old infant is admitted to the hospital with a diagnosis of urinary tract infection contracted prior to birth. The urine culture is positive for *E. coli*.
   A. P39.3
   B. P39.3, N39.0, A49.8
   C. P39.3, N30.90, A49.8
   D. P39.3, A49.8

REFERENCE: AHA I-10 Coding Handbook, p 366
Bowie, pp 66–67, 344

89. An infant has hypoglycemia and a mother with diabetes.
   A. P70.0 C. P70.1
   B. P70.2 D. P70.4

REFERENCE: AHA I-10 Coding Handbook, p 373
Bowie, pp 345–346

90. A full-term newborn vaginal delivery born in the hospital. The birth is complicated by cord compression, which affected the newborn.
   A. Z38.00, P02.5 C. Z38.00, P02.4
   B. P02.5 D. Z38.00, P02.69

REFERENCE: AHA I-10 Coding Handbook, p 367
Bowie, pp 341–342

Symptoms, Signs, and Ill-Defined Conditions

91. A patient is admitted with right lower quadrant abdominal pain. The discharge diagnosis is listed as abdominal pain due to gastroenteritis or diverticulosis.
   A. K52.9, K57.90 C. R10.31, K52.9, K57.90
   B. K57.90, K52.9 D. K52.9, K57.90, R10.31

REFERENCE: AHA I-10 Coding Handbook, p 140
Bowie, pp 360–361, 366, 368

92. A patient was admitted with hemoptysis; a CT of the chest revealed a lung mass.
   A. R91.8 C. R04.2
   B. R91.8, R04.2 D. R91.8, F04.1

REFERENCE: AHA I-10 Coding Handbook, pp 140–142

93. A woman has a Pap smear that detected cervical high-risk human papillomavirus (HPV). The DNA test was positive.
   A. R87.810 C. R87.820
   B. R87.811 D. R87.811

REFERENCE: AHA I-10 Coding Handbook, pp 140–141
Bowie, p 376

94. A patient is admitted with malignant ascites with widespread metastatic peritoneal lesions, primary site sigmoid colon; sigmoid colon resection 6 months ago.
   A. R18.8, C78.6, Z85.038 C. R18.0, C78.6, Z85.038
   B. R18.8, C78.6, C18.9 D. R18.0, C78.6, C18.9

REFERENCE: AHA I-10 Coding Handbook, pp 460–461
Bowie, pp 348–349, 371

95. A patient is admitted with fever due to bacteremia.
   A. R78.81 C. R78.81, F50.81
   B. R50.9 D. R78.81, R50.9

REFERENCE: AHA I-10 Coding Handbook, pp 147, 150, 153
Bowie, p 368

96. A patient is admitted that has urinary retention secondary to benign prostatic hypertrophy.
    A. N40.0, R33.8
    B. N40.1, R39.11, R33.9
    C. N40.1, R33.8
    D. N40.3, R33.8

REFERENCE: AHA I-10 Coding Handbook, p 270
Bowie, pp 311, 369

Injury and Poisoning

97. A patient is admitted with a nondisplaced fracture of the left medial malleolus, initial encounter. The fracture was treated with a cast.
    A. S82.52xB
    B. S82.52xA
    C. S82.62xA
    D. S82.63xA

REFERENCE: AHA I-10 Coding Handbook, p 486
Bowie, p 390

98. A patient is admitted with an anaphylactic reaction due to eating strawberries, initial encounter.
    A. T78.04xA
    B. T78.49
    C. T78.2
    D. T78.04

REFERENCE: AHA I-10 Coding Handbook, p 500
Bowie, pp 397–398

99. A patient is admitted with a gunshot wound to the right upper quadrant of the abdomen, which involves a moderate laceration to the liver, initial encounter.
    A. S36.118A
    B. S36.115A, S31.101A
    C. S36.115A
    D. S36.115A, S31.600A

REFERENCE: AHA I-10 Coding Handbook, p 496
Bowie, p 390

100. A woman experienced third-degree burns to her thigh and second-degree burns to her right and left foot, initial encounter. She stated that the burns were from hot liquid.
    A. T24.319A, T25.229A
    B. T24.31xA, T24.331A, T24.332A
    C. T24.319A, T25.222A, T25.221A
    D. T24.719A, T25.222A, T25.221A

REFERENCE: AHA I-10 Coding Handbook, pp 506–509
Bowie, pp 392–395

101. A patient is seen for a cast removal. Six weeks ago, the patient underwent open reduction internal fixation for a displaced fracture left radial styloid process.
    A. S52.512D
    B. Z47.89
    C. S52.515A
    D. Z47.2

REFERENCE: AHA I-10 Coding Handbook, p 486
Bowie, p 690

102. A patient is admitted with a left wrist laceration, with embedded glass that involved the radical nerve, initial encounter.
    A. S64.22xA
    B. S62.522A
    C. S61.512, S64.22xA
    D. S61.522A, S64.22xA

REFERENCE: AHA I-10 Coding Handbook, p 496
Bowie, p 390

103. A patient is admitted with a left nondisplaced comminuted patella fracture, a displaced left spiral fracture of the shaft of the fibula, and a displaced comminuted fracture of the shaft of the left tibia, initial encounter.
   A. S82.045A, S82.442A
   B. S82.045, S82.252A
   C. S82.045A, S82.442A, S82.252A
   D. S82.045A, S82.442A, S82.255A

REFERENCE: AHA I-10 Coding Handbook, p 489
Bowie, p 390

104. A patient is admitted with dizziness as a result of taking phenobarbital as prescribed, initial encounter.
   A. R42, T42.4x1A
   B. R42, T42.3x5A
   C. T42.4x2A, R42
   D. T42.4x1A, R42

REFERENCE: AHA I-10 Coding Handbook, p 518
Bowie, pp 373, 395–396

105. A patient is admitted for control of exacerbation of chronic obstructive lung disease. The patient had stopped taking the prednisone as prescribed due to gaining weight, a known side effect for this drug.
   A. J44.1, T38.0x6A, Z91.14
   B. T38.0x6A, J44.1, Z91.14
   C. J44.0, T38.0x6A, Z91.14
   D. T38.0x6A, Z91.14, J44.0

REFERENCE: AHA I-10 Coding Handbook, pp 516–518
Bowie, pp 247, 395–396, 438–439

106. A patient is admitted for intentional overdose of valium and acute respiratory failure with hypoxia.
   A. J96.01, T42.4x2A
   B. J96.01, T42.4x2A, R09.02
   C. T42.4x2A, J96.01
   D. T42.4x2A, J96.00, R09.02

REFERENCE: AHA I-10 Coding Handbook, p 516
Bowie, pp 297, 373

Z-Codes

107. A patient is being admitted for chemotherapy for primary lung cancer, left lower lobe.
   A. Z51.11
   B. Z51.11, Z85.118
   C. C34.32, Z51.11
   D. Z51.11, C34.32

REFERENCE: AHA I-10 Coding Handbook, p 461
Bowie, pp 106, 436

108. The patient presents for a screening examination for lung cancer.
   A. Z03.89
   B. C78.00
   C. Z12.2
   D. C34.90

REFERENCE: AHA I-10 Coding Handbook, p 132
Bowie, pp 429–431

109. A patient is admitted for observation for a head injury. The patient was struck while playing football. The patient also suffered a minor laceration to the forehead. Head injury was ruled out.
   A. Z71.4
   B. S01.81xA, Z71.4
   C. S01.81xA
   D. Z04.3, S01.81xA

REFERENCE: AHA I-10 Coding Handbook, pp 129–131
Bowie, pp 384, 427

ICD-10-PCS Coding

Identify the correct root operation for the following:

110. Excision gallbladder
   A. Resection
   B. Excision
   C. Incision
   D. Removal

   REFERENCE: AHA I-10 Coding Handbook, p 93
   Kuehn, pp 9, 41–45, 71–76, 135

111. Excision descending colon
   A. Resection
   B. Excision
   C. Incision
   D. Bypass

   REFERENCE: AHA I-10 Coding Handbook, p 93
   Kuehn, pp 9, 41–45, 71–76, 135

112. Removal FB right external auditory cancel
   A. Removal
   B. Extirpation
   C. Inspection
   D. Excision

   REFERENCE: AHA I-10 Coding Handbook, p 95
   Kuehn, p 84

113. Amputation first left toe
   A. Excision
   B. Amputation
   C. Resection
   D. Detachment

   REFERENCE: AHA I-10 Coding Handbook, p 93
   Kuehn, pp 76–79, 149, 150, 154

114. Reduction fracture right femoral shaft
   A. Transfer
   B. Reduction
   C. Reposition
   D. Reattachment

   REFERENCE: AHA I-10 Coding Handbook, p 96
   Kuehn, pp 45, 797, 360, 460

115. Colon polyp fulguration
   A. Excision
   B. Destruction
   C. Extraction
   D. Detachment

   REFERENCE: AHA I-10 Coding Handbook, p 93
   Kuehn, pp 8, 79

116. Reattachment fourth finger
   A. Reattachment
   B. Reposition
   C. Transfer
   D. Repair

   REFERENCE: AHA I-10 Coding Handbook, p 96
   Kuehn, pp 9, 95, 154, 312, 332

117. Cystoscopy
   A. Inspection
   B. Endoscopy
   C. Insertion
   D. Drainage

   REFERENCE: AHA I-10 Coding Handbook, p 101
   Kuehn, pp 9, 43–44, 125–128, 148–388

118. Removal deep left vein thrombosis
   A. Excision
   B. Removal
   C. Resection
   D. Extirpation

   REFERENCE: AHA I-10 Coding Handbook, p 95
   Kuehn, pp 9, 36, 84, 243

119. Total left knee replacement
   A. Insertion
   B. Resection
   C. Excision
   D. Replacement

   REFERENCE: AHA I-10 Coding Handbook, p 99
   Kuehn, pp 9, 359

120. Lysis of abdominal adhesions
   A. Excision
   B. Division
   C. Incision
   D. Release

   REFERENCE: AHA I-10 Coding Handbook, p 96
   Kuehn, pp 9, 45, 92, 271

121. Percutaneous angioplasty right coronary artery
   A. Dilation
   B. Restriction
   C. Insertion
   D. Excision

   REFERENCE: AHA I-10 Coding Handbook, p 98
   Kuehn, pp 9, 112, 242

122. Ligation right fallopian tube
   A. Restriction
   B. Occlusion
   C. Dilation
   D. Bypass

   REFERENCE: AHA I-10 Coding Handbook, p 98
   Kuehn, pp 9, 23, 420–421

123. Removal cardiac pacemaker
   A. Change
   B. Excision
   C. Revision
   D. Removal

   REFERENCE: AHA I-10 Coding Handbook, p 99
   Kuehn, pp 115, 462

124. Creation of arteriovenous graft brachial artery left arm for hemodialysis
   A. Bypass
   B. Creation
   C. Alteration
   D. Insertion

   REFERENCE: AHA I-10 Coding Handbook, p 98
   Kuehn, pp 40–41, 109–110

125. Lithotripsy left ureter with removal of fragment
   A. Drainage
   B. Fragmentation
   C. Removal
   D. Extirpation

   REFERENCE: AHA I-10 Coding Handbook, p 95
   Kuehn, pp 9, 36, 85, 388

126. Endometrial ablation of cervical polyps
   A. Destruction
   B. Excision
   C. Removal
   D. Extraction

   REFERENCE: AHA I-10 Coding Handbook, p 93
   Kuehn, pp 8, 421–422

127. Angioplasty abdominal iliac artery
   A. Dilation
   B. Repair
   C. Angioplasty
   D. Insertion

   REFERENCE: AHA I-10 Coding Handbook, p 98
   Kuehn, pp 9, 242

128. Radiofrequency ablation right kidney
   A. Excision
   B. Removal
   C. Destruction
   D. Ablation

   REFERENCE: AHA I-10 Coding Handbook, p 93
   Kuehn, pp 8, 79

129. Cryoablation external genital warts
   A. Destruction
   B. Cryoablation
   C. Excision
   D. Resection

   REFERENCE: AHA I-10 Coding Handbook, p 93
   Kuehn, pp 8, 79, 220, 404

130. Gastric lap band for treatment of morbid obesity
   A. Dilation
   B. Occlusion
   C. Restriction
   D. Bypass

   REFERENCE: AHA I-10 Coding Handbook, p 98
   Kuehn, pp 9, 105–106, 243

131. Excisional debridement of a chronic skin ulcer
   A. Debridement
   B. Excision
   C. Incision
   D. Resection

   REFERENCE: AHA I-10 Coding Handbook, p 93
   Kuehn, pp 9, 105–106, 243

132. Application of skin graft to the nose status post excision malignant neoplasm
   A. Transfer
   B. Creation
   C. Replacement
   D. Alteration

   REFERENCE: AHA I-10 Coding Handbook, p 99
   Kuehn, pp 9, 95, 317

133. Spinal fusion cervical C1–C2
   A. Arthrodesis
   B. Repair
   C. Creation
   D. Fusion

   REFERENCE: AHA I-10 Coding Handbook, p 103
   Kuehn, pp 9, 43, 369

134. Tracheostomy
   A. Bypass
   B. Creation
   C. Reposition
   D. Insertion

   REFERENCE: AHA I-10 Coding Handbook, p 98
   Kuehn pp 8, 40–41, 109, 241

135. Percutaneous needle biopsy left lung
   A. Incision
   B. Excision
   C. Drainage
   D. Resection

   REFERENCE: AHA I-10 Coding Handbook, pp 92–93
   Kuehn, pp 71–74

136. Extraction left intraocular lens, open
   A. Extirpation
   B. Fragmentation
   C. Extraction
   D. Excision

   REFERENCE: AHA I-10 Coding Handbook, p 93
   Kuehn, pp 9, 80, 194–195, 197

137. Uterine dilation and curettage
   A. Extraction
   B. Dilation
   C. Excision
   D. Destruction

   REFERENCE: AHA I-10 Coding Handbook, p 94
   Kuehn, p 422

138. Excision right popliteal artery with graft replacement, open
   A. Excision
   B. Resection
   C. Replacement
   D. Repair

   REFERENCE: AHA I-10 Coding Handbook, p 99
   Kuehn, pp 9, 118

139. Mitral valve annuloplasty using ring, open
   A. Supplement
   B. Replacement
   C. Resection
   D. Repair

   REFERENCE: AHA I-10 Coding Handbook, p 99
   Kuehn, pp 9, 119, 243

140. Left common carotid endarterectomy, open
   A. Excision
   B. Resection
   C. Extirpation
   D. Release

   REFERENCE: AHA I-10 Coding Handbook, p 95
   Kuehn, pp 9, 36, 84

141. Excision malignant lesion skin of left ear
   A. 0HB3XZZ
   B. 0HC3XZZ
   C. 0H53XZZ
   D. 0HD3XZZ

   REFERENCE: AHA I-10 Coding Handbook, pp 92, 93, 289
   Kuehn, pp 9, 57

142. Left below the knee amputation, proximal tibia/fibula
   A. 0YBJ0ZZ
   B. 0Y6H0ZZ
   C. 0Y6J0Z1
   D. 0Y6J0Z3

   REFERENCE: AHA I-10 Coding Handbook, pp 86, 495, 496
   Kuehn, pp 8, 149, 154

143. Thoracoscopic pleurodesis right side
   A. 0BBN4ZZ
   B. 0BPQ40Z
   C. 0B5N4ZZ
   D. 0BCN4ZZ

   REFERENCE: AHA I-10 Coding Handbook, pp 94, 236
   Kuehn, pp 8, 220

144. Extraction left intraocular lens without replacement, percutaneous
   A. 08DK3ZZ
   B. 08PK3JZ
   C. 08QK3ZZ
   D. 08BK3ZZ

   REFERENCE: AHA I-10 Coding Handbook, p 94
   Kuehn, pp 9, 197

145. Routine insertion of indwelling Foley catheter
   A. 0T9B7ZZ
   B. 0T9B70Z
   C. 0T9C80Z
   D. 0T9C8ZZ

   REFERENCE: AHA I-10 Coding Handbook, p 99
   Kuehn, pp 9, 144, 388

146. EGD with removal FB from duodenum
   A. 0DC98ZZ
   B. 0DF98ZZ
   C. 0D898ZZ
   D. 0D798ZZ

   REFERENCE: AHA I-10 Coding Handbook, p 95
   Kuehn, pp 9, 36

147. Facelift, open
   A. 0WQ20ZZ
   B. 0WU20KZ
   C. 0WB20ZZ
   D. 0W020ZZ

   REFERENCE: AHA I-10 Coding Handbook, pp 8, 102, 135, 197

148. Normal delivery with episiotomy
   A. 0W8NXZZ
   B. 0WQNXZZ
   C. 0WBNXZZ
   D. 0WMN0ZZ

   REFERENCE: AHA I-10 Coding Handbook, pp 149, 336, 444

149. Percutaneous endoscopic clipping cerebral aneurysm
   A. 03VG4CZ
   B. 03LG0DZ
   C. 03BG0ZZ
   D. 03CG0ZZ

   REFERENCE: AHA I-10 Coding Handbook, pp 98, 436
   Kuehn, pp 9, 44, 105–106

150. Left knee arthroscopy with reposition of the anterior horn medial meniscus
   A. 0MQP4ZZ
   B. 0MQP3ZZ
   C. 0MSP0ZZ
   D. 0MSP4ZZ

   REFERENCE: AHA I-10 Coding Handbook, pp 96, 97
   Kuehn, pp 9, 97

151. Heart transplant using porcine heart, open
   A. 02YA0Z2
   B. 02QA0ZZ
   C. 02YA0Z0
   D. 02Y0Z1

   REFERENCE: AHA I-10 Coding Handbook, p 435
   Kuehn, pp 9, 94

152. ESWL left ureter
   A. 0TF7XZZ
   B. 0TP930Z
   C. 0TB63ZZ
   D. 0TC63ZZ

   REFERENCE: AHA I-10 Coding Handbook, p 269

153. Reattachment severed left ear
   A. 09WJXZZ
   B. 09Q1XZZ
   C. 09M1XZZ
   D. 09S1XZZ

   REFERENCE: AHA I-10 Coding Handbook, pp 96, 97
   Kuehn, pp 9, 95

154. Transuretheral cystoscopy with removal of right ureteral calculus
   A. 0TB68ZZ
   B. 0TJ98ZZ
   C. 0T68ZZ
   D. 0TC68ZZ

   REFERENCE: AHA I-10 Coding Handbook, p 269
   Kuehn, pp 9, 36, 388

155. Open reduction fracture left tibia
   A. 0QSH0ZZ
   B. 0QSH04Z
   C. 0QWH04Z
   D. 0QQH0ZZ

   REFERENCE: AHA I-10 Coding Handbook, pp 96, 97, 489, 490
   Kuehn, pp 4, 9, 97, 360

156. Percutaneous insertion Greenfield IVC filer
   A. 06H03DZ
   B. 06L03DZ
   C. 06Q03ZZ
   D. 06V03DZ

   REFERENCE: AHA I-10 Coding Handbook, p 99
   Kuehn, pp 9, 114, 388

157. Incision and drainage external perianal abscess
   A. 0D9Q30Z
   B. 0D9RX0Z
   C. 0D9QXZZ
   D. 0D9QX0Z

   REFERENCE: AHA I-10 Coding Handbook, p 95
   Kuehn, pp 9, 51, 81–83, 502

158. Removal FB left cornea
   A. 08B8XZZ
   B. 0858XZZ
   C. 08D8XZZ
   D. 08C9XZZ

   REFERENCE: AHA I-10 Coding Handbook, p 95
   Kuehn, p 84

159. Percutaneous transposition left radial nerve
   A. 01X40ZZ
   B. 01S63ZZ
   C. 01Q63ZZ
   D. 01860ZZ

   REFERENCE: AHA I-10 Coding Handbook, pp 96, 97
   Kuehn, pp 9, 97

160. Right TRAM pedicle flap reconstruction status post mastectomy, muscle only open
   A. 0KXK0Z
   B. 0KXF0ZZ
   C. 0KXK0Z6
   D. 0KXK0ZZ

   REFERENCE: AHA I-10 Coding Handbook, pp 276, 277
   Kuehn, p 312

161. Laparotomy with exploration and adhesiolysis of the left ureter
   A. 0TN74ZZ
   B. 0TN70ZZ
   C. 0TN70ZZ
   D. 0T8N0ZZ

   REFERENCE: AHA I-10 Coding Handbook, p 96
   Kuehn, pp 9, 45, 92, 271

162. Thoracentesis right pleural effusion
   A. 0W930ZZ
   B. 0W9C3ZZ
   C. 0W993ZZ
   D. 0W9C30Z

   REFERENCE: AHA I-10 Coding Handbook, p 236
   Kuehn p 9, 51, 81–83

163. Percutaneous radiofrequency ablation of the left vocal cord
   A. 0CBV3ZZ
   B. 0CPS30Z
   C. 0C5V3ZZ
   D. 0CYV0ZZ

   REFERENCE: AHA I-10 Coding Handbook, p 94
   Kuehn, pp 8, 79

164. Excision malignant lesion upper lip
   A. 0CC00ZZ
   B. 0CQ00ZZ
   C. 0CT00ZZ
   D. 0CB0XZZ

   REFERENCE: AHA I-10 Coding Handbook, p 289
   Kuehn, pp 9, 41–42, 57, 71–73, 135

165. Laparoscopic appendectomy
   A. 0DBJ4ZZ
   B. 0DTJ4ZZ
   C. 0DNJ4ZZ
   D. 0DT8ZZ

   REFERENCE: AHA I-10 Coding Handbook, p 93
   Kuehn, pp 9, 41, 76, 197, 294

166. Nonexcisional debridement left heel ulcer
   A. 0HDNXZZ
   B. 0HBNXZZ
   C. 0HQNXZZ
   D. 0H5LXZZ

   REFERENCE: AHA I-10 Coding Handbook, p 94
   Kuehn, pp 9, 80

167. Transurethral cystoscopy with fragmentation of bladder neck stones
   A. 0TBC8ZZ
   B. 0TFC8ZZ
   C. 0TFC8ZZ
   D. 0TPB8ZZ

   REFERENCE: AHA I-10 Coding Handbook, pp 95, 268
   Kuehn, pp 9, 85

168. Laparoscopy with bilateral occlusion fallopian tubes using external clips
    A. 0UH843Z
    B. 0U774DZ
    C. 0UL74CZ
    D. 0UW84DZ

    REFERENCE: AHA I-10 Coding Handbook, pp 98, 436
    Kuehn, pp 9, 45, 92, 271

169. Incision scar contracture right knee
    A. 0H8KXZZ
    B. 0HBKXZZ
    C. 0HNKXZZ
    D. 0HQKXZZ

    REFERENCE: AHA I-10 Coding Handbook, p 96
    Kuehn, pp 9, 45, 92, 197

170. Colonoscopy with sigmoid colon polypectomy
    A. 0DFN8ZZ
    B. 0DBN8ZZ
    C. 0DCM8ZZ
    D. 0D5N8ZZ

    REFERENCE: AHA I-10 Coding Handbook, pp 92, 93
    Kuehn, pp 127–128, 197

171. A percutaneous fascia transfer to cover defect of the anterior neck
    A. 0JX53ZZ
    B. 0JX43ZZ
    C. 0JR43ZZ
    D. 0JQ43ZZ

    REFERENCE: AHA I-10 Coding Handbook, pp 96, 97
    Kuehn, pp 9, 95, 317

172. Percutaneous embolization left uterine artery using coils
    A. 04VF3DZ
    B. 04QF3ZZ
    C. 04LF3DU
    D. 04LF3CZ

    REFERENCE: AHA I-10 Coding Handbook, pp 98, 436
    Kuehn, pp 9, 243, 420–421

173. Endoscopic retrograde cholangiopancreatography with lithotripsy of the pancreas
    A. 0FCD8ZZ
    B. 0FJD8ZZ
    C. 0FFD8ZZ
    D. 0FJD8ZZ

    REFERENCE: AHA I-10 Coding Handbook, pp 250, 251
    Kuehn, pp 9, 36

174. Open left neck total lymphadenectomy
   A. 07T20ZZ
   B. 07B20ZZ
   C. 07520ZZ
   D. 07C20ZZ

   REFERENCE: AHA I-10 Coding Handbook, p 93
   Kuehn, pp 71, 292–296

175. Percutaneous chest tube placement left pneumothorax
   A. 0W9B30Z
   B. 0W9D30Z
   C. 0W9B3ZZ
   D. 0W9D3ZZ

   REFERENCE: AHA I-10 Coding Handbook, p 95
   Kuehn, pp 9, 222

176. Laparoscopy with excision old sutures from the peritoneum
   A. 0DBW4ZZ
   B. 0DNW4ZZ
   C. 0DCW4ZZ
   D. 0DPW4ZZ

   REFERENCE: AHA I-10 Coding Handbook, p 95
   Kuehn, pp 9, 36, 84

177. Closed reduction with percutaneous internal fixation left femoral neck fracture
   A. 0QSC34Z
   B. 0QS734Z
   C. 0QS934Z
   D. 0QS7X4Z

   REFERENCE: AHA I-10 Coding Handbook, pp 96, 97
   Kuehn, p 460

178. Laparotomy and drain placement left lobe liver abscess
   A. 0F900ZZ
   B. 0F900ZZ
   C. 0F9030Z
   D. 0F9200Z

   REFERENCE: AHA I-10 Coding Handbook, p 95
   Kuehn, pp 9, 388

179. Hysteroscopy with D&C, diagnostic
   A. 0UDB82X
   B. 0UDN82X
   C. 0U898ZZ
   D. 0U798ZZ

   REFERENCE: AHA I-10 Coding Handbook, p 94
   Kuehn, pp 9, 80, 422

180. Laparoscopy with destruction of endometriosis left ovary
 A. 0UB14ZZ
 B. 0UT14ZZ
 C. 0UP340Z
 D. 0U514ZZ

 REFERENCE: AHA I-10 Coding Handbook, p 94
 Kuehn, pp 8, 79, 412, 422

181. DIP joint amputation left thumb
 A. 0X6M0Z3
 B. 0XGM022
 C. 0XGM021
 D. 0XGM020

 REFERENCE: AHA I-10 Coding Handbook, pp 86, 495
 Kuehn, pp 76–79, 149–150, 154

182. Removal right index fingernail
 A. 0HDQXZZ
 B. 0HPRXZZ
 C. 0HNQXZZ
 D. 0HTQXZZ

 REFERENCE: AHA I-10 Coding Handbook, p 94
 Kuehn, pp 9, 80

183. Percutaneous drainage abdominal ascites
 A. 0W9G3ZZ
 B. 0W9G3ZZ
 C. 0W930Z
 D. 0W9H3ZZ

 REFERENCE: AHA I-10 Coding Handbook, p 95
 Kuehn, pp 9, 51, 81–83, 502

184. Transurethral endoscopic ablation right hepatic duct
 A. 0F558ZZ
 B. 0FB58ZZ
 C. 0FT04ZZ
 D. 0FP040Z

 REFERENCE: AHA I-10 Coding Handbook, p 94
 Kuehn, pp 9, 107

185. ERCP with balloon dilation cystic duct
 A. 0F784DZ
 B. 0F788ZZ
 C. 0F783DZ
 D. 0FT83ZZ

 REFERENCE: AHA I-10 Coding Handbook, p 98
 Kuehn, pp 9, 107

186. Control of postoperative tonsillectomy is coded to which root operation?
A. Revision
B. Repair
C. Control
D. Change

REFERENCE: AHA I-10 Coding Handbook, p 102
Kuehn, pp 8, 41, 130–131, 148

187. In the Medical Surgical Section, the third character position represents?
A. Body System
B. Approach
C. Root Operation
D. Qualifier

REFERENCE: AHA I-10 Coding Handbook, p 72
Kuehn, p 8

188. In the Medical Surgical Section, the second character position represents?
A. Body System
B. Body Part
C. Qualifier
D. Approach

REFERENCE: AHA I-10 Coding Handbook, p 70
Kuehn, pp 6–7

189. In the Medical Surgical Section, the seventh character position represents?
A. Qualifier
B. Device
C. Body System
D. Approach

REFERENCE: AHA I-10 Coding Handbook, p 80
Kuehn, p 20

190 In the Medical Surgical Section, the fourth character position represents?
A. Section
B. Body Part
C. Body System
D. Approach

REFERENCE: AHA I-10 Coding Handbook, p 73
Kuehn, pp 11–12

191. A complete redo of a knee replacement requiring a new prosthesis is coded to which root operation?
A. Revision
B. Replacement
C. Change
D. Insertion

REFERENCE: AHA I-10 Coding Handbook, pp 99–100, 301
Kuehn, pp 9, 118, 359

192. Reposition of a malfunctioning pacemaker lead is coded to which root operation?
A. Change
B. Revision
C. Replacement
D. Reposition

REFERENCE: AHA I-10 Coding Handbook, pp 99–100, 416
Kuehn, pp 9, 117, 462

193. Dilation of the ureter with insertion of a stent is coded to which root operation?
A. Insertion
B. Dilation
C. Supplemental
D. Inspection

REFERENCE: AHA I-10 Coding Handbook, p 98
Kuehn, pp 9, 387

194. ERCP with biopsy of the common bile duct. Identify the approach.
   A. External
   B. Percutaneous Endoscopic Open
   C. Percutaneous
   D. Open

   REFERENCE: AHA I-10 Coding Handbook, p 75
   Kuehn, pp 12–13

195. Percutaneous insertion nephrostomy tube. Identify the approach.
   A. External
   B. Open
   C. Percutaneous
   D. Percutaneous Endoscopic

   REFERENCE: AHA I-10 Coding Handbook, p 75
   Kuehn, pp 12–13

196. Fulguration of anal warts. Identify the approach.
   A. Percutaneous
   B. External Endoscopic
   C. Percutaneous
   D. Open

   REFERENCE: AHA I-10 Coding Handbook, p 75
   Kuehn, pp 12–13

197. Percutaneous placement of pacemaker lead. Identify the approach.
   A. External
   B. Via natural or Artificial opening
   C. Percutaneous Endoscopic
   D. Percutaneous

   REFERENCE: AHA I-10 Coding Handbook, p 75
   Kuehn, pp 12–13

198. ESWL left ureter. Identify the approach.
   A. Percutaneous
   B. Via natural or Artificial opening
   C. External
   D. Open

   REFERENCE: AHA I-10 Coding Handbook, p 75
   Kuehn, pp 12–13

199. Laparoscopy with destruction of endometriosis. Identify the approach.
   A. Percutaneous
   B. Via natural/artificial opening
   C. Percutaneous Endoscopic
   D. External

   REFERENCE: AHA I-10 Coding Handbook, p 75
   Kuehn, pp 12–13

200. Colonoscopy. Identify the approach.
   A. Percutaneous
   B. Via natural or Artificial opening
   C. Percutaneous Endoscopic
   D. External

   REFERENCE: AHA I-10 Coding Handbook, p 75
   Kuehn, pp 12–13

Use this information to answer questions, pp 201–203.
Present on admission (POA) guidelines were established to identify and report diagnoses that are present at the time of a patient's admission. The reporting options for each ICD-9-CM code are

A. Y = Yes
B. N = No
C. U = Unknown
D. W = clinically undetermined
E. Unreported/Not Used (Exempt from POA) reporting

201. The physician explicitly documents that a condition is not present at the time of admission.
A. Y = Yes
B. N = No
C. U = Unknown
D. W = clinically undetermined
E. Unreported/Not Used (Exempt from POA) reporting

REFERENCE: AHA I-10 Coding Handbook, pp 571–574

202. The physician documents that the patient has diabetes that was diagnosed prior to admission.
A. Y = Yes
B. N = No
C. U = Unknown
D. W = clinically undetermined
E. Unreported/Not Used (Exempt from POA) reporting

REFERENCE: AHA I-10 Coding Handbook, pp 571–574

203. The medical record documentation is unclear as to whether the condition was present on admission.
A. Y = Yes
B. N = No
C. U = Unknown
D. W = clinically undetermined
E. Unreported/Not Used (Exempt from POA) reporting

REFERENCE: AHA I-10 Coding Handbook, pp 571–574

Answer Key for ICD-10-CM Coding

1. D
2. B
3. A
4. C
5. D
6. C
7. D
8. C
9. A
10. B
11. C
12. B
13. A
14. D
15. B
16. A
17. C
18. B
19. D
20. B
21. A
22. D
23. B
24. D
25. D
26. B
27. A
28. C
29. B
30. D
31. C
32. B
33. A
34. C
35. B
36. D
37. D
38. C
39. D
40. A
41. B
42. A
43. D
44. A
45. B
46. A
47. C
48. B
49. A
50. D
51. C
52. A
53. C
54. B
55. A
56. C
57. D
58. A
59. C
60. A
61. A
62. C
63. B
64. D
65. B
66. D
67. B
68. D
69. A
70. B
71. A
72. C
73. B
74. D
75. C
76. D
77. C
78. B
79. C
80. D
81. B
82. C
83. A
84. B
85. D
86. A
87. A
88. D
89. C
90. A
91. C
92. B
93. A
94. C
95. D
96. C
97. B
98. A
99. D
100. C
101. A
102. D
103. C
104. B
105. A
106. C
107. D
108. C
109. D
110. A
111. A
112. B
113. D
114. C
115. B
116. A
117. A
118. D
119. D
120. D
121. A
122. B
123. D
124. D
125. D
126. A
127. A
128. C
129. A
130. C
131. B
132. C
133. D
134. A
135. B
136. C
137. A
138. C
139. A
140. C
141. A
142. C
143. A
144. A
145. B
146. A
147. D
148. A
149. A
150. D
151. A
152. A
153. C
154. D
155. A
156. A
157. C
158. D
159. B
160. A
161. B
162. C
163. C
164. D
165 B
166. A
167. C
168. C
169. C
170. B
171. B
172. C
173. C
174. A
175. A
176. C
177. A
178. D
179. A
180. D
181. A
182. A
183. A
184. A
185. B
186. C
187. C
188. A
189. A
190. B
191. A
192. B
193. B
194. B
195. C
196. B
197. D
198. C
199. C
200. B
201. B
202. A
203. C

REFERENCES

Leon-Chisen, N. (2016). *AHA ICD-10-CM and ICD-10-PCS coding handbook 2016*. Chicago: American Hospital Association (AHA).

Bowie, M. J. (2014). *Understanding ICD-10-CM and ICD-10-PCS: A worktext* (2nd ed.). Clifton Park, NY: Cengage Learning.

Kuehn, L. M. and Jorwic, T. M. (2014). *ICD-10-PCS: An applied approach* (2015 ed.). Chicago: American Health Information Management Association (AHIMA).

ICD-10-CM/PCS Chapter Competencies

Question	RHIA Domain	RHIT Domain
1–203	1	2

IX. CPT Coding

Marissa Lajaunie, MBA, RHIA

Evaluation and Management

1. Patient is admitted to the hospital with acute abdominal pain. The attending medical physician requests a surgical consult. The consultant agrees to see the patient and conducts a comprehensive history and physical examination. To rule out pancreatitis, the physician orders lab work, along with an ultrasound of the gallbladder and an abdominal x-ray. Due to the various diagnosis possibilities and the tests reviewed, a moderate medical decision was made.
   A. 99244 C. 99254
   B. 99222 D. 99204

REFERENCE: AMA, 2016
Bowie, p 63
Green, pp 548–554
Johnson and Linker, pp 153–154
Kuehn, pp 68–69
Smith, pp 205–206

2. An established patient returns to the physician's office for follow-up on his hypertension and diabetes. The physician takes the blood pressure and references the patient's last three glucose tests. The patient is still running above-normal glucose levels, so the physician decides to adjust the patient's insulin. An expanded history was taken and a physical examination was performed.
   A. 99213 C. 99202
   B. 99232 D. 99214

REFERENCE: AMA, 2016
Bowie, pp 42, 65
Green, pp 541–543
Johnson and Linker, p 149
Kuehn, pp 64–65
Smith, p 204

3. Patient arrives in the emergency room via a medical helicopter. The patient has sustained multiple life-threatening injuries due to a multiple car accident. The patient goes into cardiac arrest 10 minutes after arrival. An hour and 30 minutes of critical care time is spent trying to stabilize the patient.
   A. 99285, 99288, 99291 C. 99291, 99292, 99285
   B. 99291, 99292 D. 99282

REFERENCE: AMA, 2016
Bowie, p 65
Green, pp 573–576
Johnson and Linker, pp 155–157
Kuehn, p 57
Smith, p 207

4. The physician provided services to a new patient who was in a rest home for an ulcerative sore on the hip. A problem-focused history and physical examination were performed and a straightforward medical decision was made.
   A. 99304
   B. 99325
   C. 99324
   D. 99334

REFERENCE: AMA, 2016
Bowie, pp 70–71
Green, pp 577–578
Johnson and Linker, pp 158–159
Kuehn, p 67
Smith, p 208

5. A doctor provides critical care services in the emergency department for a patient in respiratory failure. He initiates ventilator management and spends an hour and 10 minutes providing critical care for this patient.
   A. 99281, 99291, 99292, 94002
   B. 99291, 99292, 94002
   C. 99291, 94002
   D. 99291

REFERENCE: AMA, 2016
Bowie, p 65
Green, pp 573–576
Johnson and Linker, pp 155–157
Kuehn, pp 64–65
Smith, p 207

6. Services were provided to a patient in the emergency room after the patient twisted her ankle stepping down from a curb. The emergency room physician ordered x-rays of the ankle, which came back negative for a fracture. A problem-focused history and physical examination were performed and ankle strapping was applied. A prescription for pain was given to the patient. Code the emergency room visit only.
   A. 99201
   B. 99282
   C. 99281
   D. 99211

REFERENCE: AMA, 2016
Bowie, p 64
Green, pp 572–573
Johnson and Linker, pp 155–157
Kuehn, p 64
Smith, p 206

7. An established patient was seen in her primary physician's office. The patient fell at home and came to the physician's office for an examination. Due to a possible concussion, the patient was sent to the hospital to be admitted as an observation patient. A detailed history and physical examination were performed and the medical decision was low complexity. The patient stayed overnight and was discharged the next afternoon.
   A. 99214, 99234
   B. 99214, 99218, 99217
   C. 99218
   D. 99218, 99217

REFERENCE: AMA, 2016
Bowie, p 58
Green, pp 563–564
Johnson and Linker, p 155
Kuehn, pp 58–59
Smith, p 205

8. An out-of-town patient presents to a walk-in clinic to have a prescription refilled for a nonsteroidal anti-inflammatory drug. The physician performs a problem-focused history and physical examination with a straightforward decision.
   A. 99211 C. 99212
   B. 99201 D. 99202

REFERENCE: AMA, 2016
Bowie, p 58
Green, pp 541–551
Johnson and Linker, p 149
Keuhn, pp 56–57
Smith, p 204

9. An office consultation is performed for a postmenopausal woman who is complaining of spotting in the past 6 months with right lower-quadrant tenderness. A detailed history and physical examination were performed with a low-complexity medical decision.
   A. 99242 C. 99253
   B. 99243 D. 99254

REFERENCE: AMA, 2016
Bowie, pp 60–61
Green, pp 541–551
Johnson and Linker, pp 153–154
Kuehn, pp 62–63
Smith, pp 205–206

Anesthesia

10. Code anesthesia for upper abdominal ventral hernia repair.
    A. 00832 C. 00752
    B. 00750 D. 00830

REFERENCE: AMA, 2016
Bowie, p 91
Green, pp 596–604, 619
Johnson and Linker, p 175
Kuehn, p 88
Smith, pp 239–242

11. Code anesthesia for total hip replacement.
    A. 01210 C. 01230
    B. 01402 D. 01214

REFERENCE: AMA, 2016
Bowie, p 91
Green, pp 596–604, 619
Kuehn, p 88
Smith, pp 239–242

12. Code anesthesia for vaginal hysterectomy.
    A. 00846
    B. 00944
    C. 00840
    D. 01963

REFERENCE: AMA, 2016
Green, pp 596–604, 619
Kuehn, p 88
Smith, pp 239–242

13. Code anesthesia for placement of vascular shunt in forearm.
    A. 01844
    B. 01850
    C. 00532
    D. 01840

REFERENCE: AMA, 2016
Bowie, p 91
Green, pp 596–604, 621
Smith, pp 239–242

14. Code anesthesia for decortication of left lung.
    A. 01638
    B. 00542
    C. 00546
    D. 00500

REFERENCE: AMA, 2016
Bowie, p 91
Green, pp 596–604, 617
Kuehn, p 88
Smith, pp 239–242

15. Code anesthesia for total shoulder replacement.
    A. 01760
    B. 01630
    C. 01402
    D. 01638

REFERENCE: AMA, 2016
Bowie, p 91
Green, pp 596–604, 621
Kuehn, p 88
Smith, pp 239–242

16. Code anesthesia for cesarean section.
    A. 00840
    B. 01961
    C. 00940
    D. 01960

REFERENCE: AMA, 2016
Bowie, p 91
Green, pp 596–604, 623
Kuehn, p 88
Smith, pp 239–242

17. Code anesthesia for procedures on bony pelvis.
    A. 00400 C. 01120
    B. 01170 D. 01190

REFERENCE: AMA, 2016
Bowie, p 91
Green, pp 596–604, 620
Kuehn, p 88
Smith, pp 239–242

18. Code anesthesia for corneal transplant.
    A. 00144 C. 00147
    B. 00140 D. 00190

REFERENCE: AMA, 2016
Bowie, p 91
Green, pp 596–604, 620
Kuehn, p 88
Smith, pp 239–242

Surgery—Integumentary System

19. Patient presents to the hospital for skin grafts due to previous third-degree burns. The burn eschar of the back was removed. Once the eschar was removed, the defect size measured 10 cm x 10 cm. A skin graft from a donor bank was placed onto the defect and sewn into place as a temporary wound closure.
    A. 15002, 15130 C. 15002, 15200
    B. 15002, 15271, 15272, 15272, 15272 D. 15002, 15273

REFERENCE: AMA, 2016
Bowie, pp 123, 126
Green, pp 662–663
Keuhn, pp 115–117

20. Patient presents to the operating room for excision of a 4.5-cm malignant melanoma of the left forearm. A 6 cm x 6 cm rotation flap was created for closure.
    A. 14021 C. 14301
    B. 11606, 14020 D. 11606, 15100

REFERENCE: AMA, 2016
Bowie, pp 16–17
Green, pp 651–654, 661
Kuehn, pp 112–113
Smith, pp 61–62, 72–73
Smith (2), pp 26–27

21. Female patient has a percutaneous needle biopsy of the left breast lesion in the lower outer quadrant. Following the biopsy frozen section results, the physician followed this with an excisional removal of the same lesion.
    A. 19100, 19125
    B. 19100, 19120-LT
    C. 19120-LT
    D. 19100, 19120, 19120

REFERENCE: AMA, 2016
Bowie, pp 132–133
Green, pp 651–654, 669–672
Smith, pp 78–79
Smith (2), p 30

22. Patient presents to the emergency room with lacerations of right lower leg that involved the fascia. Lacerations measured 5 cm and 2.7 cm.
    A. 11406, 11403
    B. 12034
    C. 12032, 12031
    D. 12032

REFERENCE: AMA, 2016
Bowie, pp 119–120
Green, pp 658–660
Smith, pp 66–68
Smith (2), p 21

23. A 10-square-centimeter epidermal autograft to the face from the back.
    A. 15110
    B. 15115
    C. 15110, 15115
    D. 15120

REFERENCE: AMA, 2016
Bowie, pp 23–24
Green, p 661
Smith (2), p 27

24. Nonhuman graft for temporary wound closure. Patient has a 5-cm defect on the scalp.
    A. 15275, 15276
    B. 15271
    C. 15275
    D. 15271, 15272

REFERENCE: AMA, 2016
Green, p 661

25. Patient is admitted for a blepharoplasty of the left lower eyelid and a repair for a tarsal strip of the left upper lid.
    A. 67917-E1, 15822-E2
    B. 67917-E1, 15820-E2
    C. 67917-E1
    D. 67917-E1, 15823-E2

REFERENCE: AMA, 2016
Bowie, pp 129, 378
Green, p 665
Smith (2), p 165

26. Patient presents to the emergency room with lacerations sustained in an automobile accident. Repairs of the 3.3-cm skin laceration of the left leg that involved the fascia, 2.5-cm and 3-cm lacerations of the left arm involving the fascia, and 2.7 cm of the left foot, which required simple sutures, were performed. Sterile dressings were applied.
    A. 12032, 12032-59, 12031-59, 12002-59
    B. 12002, 12002-59
    C. 12034, 12002-59
    D. 13151, 12032-59, 12032-59, 12001-59

REFERENCE: AMA, 2016
Bowie, pp 119–120
Green, pp 658–660
Smith, pp 66–68
Smith (2), p 24

27. Patient presents to the operating room for excision of three lesions. The 1.5-cm and 2-cm lesions of the back were excised with one excision. The 0.5-cm lesion of the hand was excised. The pathology report identified both back lesions as squamous cell carcinoma. The hand lesion was identified as seborrheic keratosis.
    A. 11604, 11420
    B. 11402, 11420, 11403
    C. 11403, 11642, 11642
    D. 11602, 11402

REFERENCE: AMA, 2016
Bowie, p 120
Green, pp 651–654
Smith, pp 61–62
Smith (2), pp 21–22

28. Patient presents to the radiology department where a fine-needle aspiration of the breast is performed utilizing computed tomography.
    A. 19085, 77012
    B. 19100
    C. 19125
    D. 10022, 77012

REFERENCE: AMA, 2016
Bowie, pp 11–12, 407
Green, pp 669, 887–888
Smith (2), p 29

29. Patient presents to the operating room where a 3.2-cm malignant lesion of the shoulder was excised and repaired with simple sutures. A 2-cm benign lesion of the cheek was excised and was repaired with a rotation skin graft.
    A. 11604, 11442, 14040, 12001
    B. 14040, 11604
    C. 15002, 15120
    D. 17264, 17000, 12001

REFERENCE: AMA, 2016
Bowie, pp 113, 122
Green, pp 651–654, 660–661
Smith, pp 61–62, 72–75
Smith (2), pp 26–27

30. Patient was admitted to the hospital for removal of excessive tissue due to massive weight loss. Liposuction of the abdomen and bilateral thighs was performed.
    A. 15830
    B. 15830, 15833, 15833
    C. 15877, 15879-50
    D. 15839

REFERENCE: AMA, 2016
Bowie, p 129

Surgery—Musculoskeletal

31. Patient presents to the hospital with ulcer of the right foot. Patient is taken to the operating room where a revision of the right metatarsal head is performed.
    A. 28104-RT
    B. 28111-RT
    C. 28288-RT
    D. 28899-RT

REFERENCE: AMA, 2016
Green, pp 680–690, 701

32. Patient presents to the emergency room following a fall. X-rays were ordered for the lower leg and results showed a fracture of the proximal left tibia. The emergency room physician performed a closed manipulation of the fracture with skeletal traction.
    A. 27532-LT
    B. 27536-LT
    C. 27530-LT
    D. 27524-LT

REFERENCE: AMA, 2016
Green, pp 680–689, 701
Smith, pp 84–85
Smith (2), pp 42–44

33. Trauma patient was rushed to the operating room with multiple injuries. Open reduction with internal fixation of intertrochanteric femoral fracture, and open reduction of the tibial and fibula shaft with internal fixation was performed.
    A. 27245, 27759
    B. 20690
    C. 27248, 27756
    D. 27244, 27758

REFERENCE: AMA, 2016
Green, pp 680–689, 699–701
Smith, pp 84–85
Smith (2), pp 42–44

34. Open I&D of a deep abscess of the cervical spine.
    A. 22010
    B. 22015
    C. 10060
    D. 10140

REFERENCE: AMA, 2016
Green, pp 692–694

35. Patient presents to the emergency room following an assault. Examination of the patient reveals blunt trauma to the face. Radiology reports that the patient suffers from a fracture to the frontal skull and a blow-out fracture of the orbital floor. Patient is admitted and taken to the operating room where a periorbital approach to the orbital fracture is employed and an implant is inserted.
    A. 21407, 21275
    B. 21387, 61330
    C. 21390
    D. 61340, 21401

REFERENCE: AMA, 2016
Green, pp 689–690
Smith, pp 84–85
Smith (2), pp 42–44

36. Patient presents with a traumatic partial amputation of the second, third, and fourth fingers on the right hand. Patient was taken to the operating room where completion of the amputation of three fingers was performed with direct closure.
    A. 26910-F6, 26910-F7, 26910-F8
    B. 26843-RT
    C. 26951-F6, 26951-F7, 26951-F8
    D. 26550-RT

REFERENCE: AMA, 2016
Green, p 698

37. Patient is brought to the emergency room following a shark attack. The paramedics have the patient's amputated foot. The patient is taken directly to the operating room to reattach the patient's foot.
    A. 28800
    B. 28200, 28208
    C. 28110
    D. 20838

REFERENCE: AMA, 2016
Green, p 701

38. Patient presents to the hospital with a right index trigger finger. Release of the trigger finger was performed.
    A. 26060-F7
    B. 26055-F6
    C. 26170-F6
    D. 26110

REFERENCE: AMA, 2016
Green, p 698

39. Patient had been diagnosed with a bunion. Patient was taken to the operating room where a simple resection of the base of the proximal phalanx along with the medial eminence was performed. Kirschner wire was placed to hold the joint in place.
    A. 28292
    B. 28290
    C. 28293
    D. 28294

REFERENCE: AMA, 2016
Bowie, pp 50–51
Green, p 701
Smith (2), pp 47–49

Surgery—Respiratory

40. Patient has a bronchoscopy with endobronchial biopsies of three sites.
    A. 31625, 31625, 31625
    B. 31625
    C. 31622, 31625
    D. 31622, 31625, 31625, 31625

REFERENCE: AMA, 2016
Bowie, pp 183–184
Green, pp 713–714
Smith, pp 96–97
Smith (2), p 61

41. Patient presents to the surgical unit and undergoes unilateral nasal endoscopy, partial ethmoidectomy, and maxillary antrostomy.
    A. 31254, 31256-51
    B. 31201, 31225-51
    C. 31290, 31267-51
    D. 31233, 31231-51

REFERENCE: AMA, 2016
Bowie, pp 177–178
Green, pp 706–710
Smith, pp 91–92
Smith (2), p 59

42. Patient has been diagnosed with metastatic laryngeal carcinoma. Patient underwent subtotal supraglottic laryngectomy with radical neck dissection.
    A. 31540
    B. 31367
    C. 31365
    D. 31368

REFERENCE: AMA, 2016
Green, pp 711–712

43. Patient was involved in an accident and has been sent to the hospital. During transport the patient develops breathing problems and, upon arrival at the hospital, an emergency transtracheal tracheostomy was performed. Following various x-rays, the patient was diagnosed with traumatic pneumothorax. A thoracentesis with insertion of tube was performed.
    A. 31603, 31612
    B. 31610, 32555
    C. 31603, 23554
    D. 31603, 32555

REFERENCE: AMA, 2016
Green, pp 713–714

44. Patient with laryngeal cancer has a tracheoesophageal fistula created and has a voicebox inserted.
    A. 31611
    B. 31580
    C. 31395
    D. 31502

REFERENCE: AMA, 2016
Green, pp 713–714

45. Upper lobectomy of the right lung with repair of the bronchus.
A. 32480
B. 32486
C. 32320
D. 32480, 32501

REFERENCE: AMA, 2016
Bowie, pp 185–186
Green, pp 715–718
Smith (2), pp 61–62

46. Patient with a deviated nasal septum that was repaired by septoplasty.
A. 30400
B. 30620
C. 30520
D. 30630

REFERENCE: AMA, 2016
Green, pp 706–708

47. Lye burn of the larynx repaired by laryngoplasty.
A. 31588
B. 16020
C. 31360
D. 31540

REFERENCE: AMA, 2016
Green, pp 711–712

48. Bronchoscopy with multiple transbronchial right upper and right lower lobe lung biopsy with fluoroscopic guidance.
A. 31628-RT, 76000-RT
B. 31717-RT, 31632-RT
C. 32405-RT
D. 31628-RT, 31632-RT

REFERENCE: AMA, 2016
Bowie, pp 83–84
Green, pp 713–716
Smith, pp 96–97
Smith (2), p 61

49. Patient has recurrent spontaneous pneumothorax, which has resulted in a chemical pleurodesis by thoracoscopy.
A. 32650
B. 32310, 32601
C. 32601
D. 32960

REFERENCE: AMA, 2016
Green, pp 716–717

50. Laryngoscopic stripping of vocal cords for leukoplakia of the vocal cords.
A. 31535
B. 31540
C. 31541
D. 31570

REFERENCE: AMA, 2016
Bowie, p 181
Green, pp 711–712
Smith, pp 94–95

Surgery—Cardiovascular System

51. Patient returns to the operating room following open-heart bypass for exploration of blood vessel to control postoperative bleeding in the chest.
    A. 35820
    B. 20101
    C. 35761
    D. 35905

REFERENCE: AMA, 2016
Green, p 752

52. Patient undergoes construction of apical aortic conduit with an insertion of a single-ventricle ventricular assist device.
    A. 33404
    B. 33975
    C. 33977
    D. 33975, 33404

REFERENCE: AMA, 2016
Green, p 744

53. Patient presents to the operating room where a CABG x 3 is performed using the mammary artery and two sections of the saphenous vein.
    A. 33534, 33511
    B. 33534, 33518, 33511
    C. 33535
    D. 33533, 33518

REFERENCE: AMA, 2016
Bowie, pp 207–208
Green, p 739
Smith, pp 104–105
Smith (2), pp 74–75

54. Patient complains of recurrent syncope following carotid thromboendarterectomy. Patient returns 2 weeks after initial surgery and undergoes repeat carotid thromboendarterectomy.
    A. 33510
    B. 35301
    C. 35201
    D. 35301, 35390

REFERENCE: AMA, 2016
Green, p 749
Smith (2), pp 78–79

55. Patient is admitted with alcohol cirrhosis and has a TIPS procedure performed.
    A. 35476, 36011, 36481
    B. 37183
    C. 37182
    D. 37140

REFERENCE: AMA, 2016
Green, pp 757–758

56. Eighty-year-old patient has carcinoma and presents to the operating room for placement of a tunneled implantable centrally inserted venous access port.
    A. 36558
    B. 36571
    C. 36561
    D. 36481

REFERENCE: AMA, 2016
Green, pp 755–757
Smith, pp 109–111
Smith (2), pp 79–80

57. Patient presents to the operating room and undergoes an endovascular repair of an infrarenal abdominal aortic aneurysm utilizing a unibody bifurcated prosthesis.
    A. 34800, 34813
    B. 34802
    C. 34804
    D. 35081

REFERENCE: AMA, 2016
Bowie, p 119
Green, p 738
Smith (2), pp 76–77

58. The physician punctures the left common femoral to examine the right common iliac.
    A. 36245
    B. 36246
    C. 36247
    D. 36140

REFERENCE: AMA, 2016
Bowie, pp 218–219
Green, p 754

59. Patient has a history of PVD for many years and experiences chest pains. The patient underwent Doppler evaluation, which showed a common femoral DVT. Patient is now admitted for thromboendarterectomy.
    A. 35371
    B. 35372
    C. 37224
    D. 35256

REFERENCE: AMA, 2016
Smith (2), pp 78–79

60. Patient undergoes percutaneous transluminal iliac artery balloon angioplasty.
    A. 37228
    B. 37220
    C. 37222
    D. 37224

REFERENCE: AMA, 2016
Green, p 750
Smith, pp 111–112

Surgery—Hemic and Lymphatic Systems, Mediastinum, and Diaphragm

61. Patient has breast carcinoma and is now undergoing sentinel node biopsy. Patient was injected for sentinel node identification and two deep axillary lymph nodes showed up intensely. These two lymph nodes were completely excised. Path report was positive for metastatic carcinoma.
    A. 38525, 38790
    B. 38589
    C. 38308, 38790
    D. 38525, 38792

REFERENCE: AMA, 2016
Green, pp 761–764

62. Patient has a history of hiatal hernia for many years, which has progressively gotten worse. The decision to repair the hernia was made and the patient was sent to the operating room where the repair took place via the thorax and abdomen.
    A. 39545
    B. 43336
    C. 43332
    D. 39503

REFERENCE: AMA, 2016
Green, pp 772–773

63. Patient has a bone marrow aspiration of the iliac crest and of the tibia.
 A. 38220, 38220-59
 B. 38221
 C. 38230
 D. 38220

REFERENCE: AMA, 2016
Bowie, p 130
Green, p 763

64. Trauma patient is rushed to the operating room with multiple injuries. The patient had his spleen removed due to a massive rupture, with repair of the lacerated diaphragm.
 A. 38115, 39501
 B. 38120, 39599
 C. 38102, 39540
 D. 38100, 39501

REFERENCE: AMA, 2016
Green, pp 762, 772–773

65. Laparoscopic retroperitoneal lymph node biopsy.
 A. 38570
 B. 38780
 C. 49323
 D. 38589

REFERENCE: AMA, 2016
Green, pp 761–764

66. Excision of mediastinal cyst.
 A. 11400
 B. 39200
 C. 17000
 D. 39400

REFERENCE: AMA, 2016
Bowie, pp 240–241

67. Patient diagnosed with cystic hygroma of the axilla, which was excised.
 A. 38555
 B. 11400
 C. 38550
 D. 38300

REFERENCE: AMA, 2016
Bowie, p 116

68. Laparoscopy with multiple biopsies of retroperitoneal lymph nodes.
 A. 38570
 B. 38571
 C. 38570-22
 D. 38572

REFERENCE: AMA, 2016
Green, pp 761–764

69. Cannulation of the thoracic duct.
 A. 38794
 B. 36810
 C. 36260
 D. 38999

REFERENCE: AMA, 2016
Bowie, pp 223–234

70. Patient has been on the bone marrow transplant recipient list for 3 months. A perfect match was made and the patient came in and received a peripheral stem cell transplant.
    A. 38242
    B. 38230
    C. 38241
    D. 38240

REFERENCE: AMA, 2016
Green, p 763

Surgery—Digestive System

71. Laparoscopic gastric banding.
    A. 43842
    B. 43843
    C. 43770
    D. 43771

REFERENCE: AMA, 2016
Green, pp 785–786

72. Patient presents with a history of upper abdominal pain. Cholangiogram was negative and patient was sent to the hospital for ERCP. During the procedure the sphincter was incised and a stent was placed for drainage.
    A. 43260, 43262, 43264
    B. 43262
    C. 43275
    D. 43274

REFERENCE: AMA, 2016
Smith (2), pp 92–93

73. Patient presents to the emergency room with right lower abdominal pains. Emergency room physician suspects possible appendicitis. Patient was taken to the operating room where a laparoscopic appendectomy was performed. Pathology report was negative for appendicitis.
    A. 44950
    B. 44950, 49320
    C. 44970
    D. 44979

REFERENCE: AMA, 2016
Bowie, p 126
Green, p 790
Smith (2), p 97

74. Morbidly obese patient comes in for vertical banding of the stomach.
    A. 43848
    B. 43659
    C. 43842
    D. 43999

REFERENCE: AMA, 2016
Green, pp 785–786

75. Patient underwent anoscopy followed by colonoscopy. The physician examined the colon to 60 cm.
    A. 46600, 45378
    B. 46600, 45378-59
    C. 45378
    D. 45999

REFERENCE: AMA, 2016
Green, pp 791–792
Smith, pp 118–119
Smith (2), p 93

76. Injection snoreplasty for treatment of palatal snoring.
    A. 42299
    B. 42145
    C. 42999
    D. 40899

REFERENCE: AMA, 2016
Green, pp 778–779

77. Patient arrives to the hospital and has a Nissen fundoplasty done laparoscopically.
    A. 43410
    B. 43415
    C. 43502
    D. 43280

REFERENCE: AMA, 2016
Green, pp 785–786
Smith (2), p 97

78. Young child presents with cleft lip and cleft palate. This is the first attempt of repair, which includes major revision of the cleft palate and unilateral cleft lip repair.
    A. 42200, 40701
    B. 42225, 40700
    C. 42220, 40720
    D. 42215, 40700

REFERENCE: AMA, 2016
Green, pp 779–778

79. Patient has a history of chronic alcohol abuse with portal hypertension. Patient has been vomiting blood for the past 3 days and presented to his physician's office. Patient was sent to the hospital for evaluation and an EGD was performed. Biopsy findings showed gastritis, esophagitis, and bleeding esophageal varices, which were injected with sclerosing solution.
    A. 43235, 43244, 43204
    B. 43239, 43244
    C. 43239, 43243
    D. 43239, 43243, 43204

REFERENCE: AMA, 2016
Bowie, p 256
Green, pp 782–784
Smith, pp 115–117
Smith (2), p 92

Surgery—Urinary System

80. Patient is admitted for contact laser vaporization of the prostate. The physician performed a TURP and transurethral resection of the bladder neck at the same time.
    A. 52648
    B. 52648, 52450, 52500
    C. 52450, 53500
    D. 52648, 52450

REFERENCE: AMA, 2016
Bowie, p 294
Green, pp 807–808
Smith (2), p 122

81. Patient comes to the hospital with a history of right flank pain. Urine tests are negative. Radiology examination reveals that the patient has renal cysts. Patient is now admitted for laparoscopic ablation of the cysts.
A. 50541
B. 50390
C. 50280
D. 50920

REFERENCE: AMA, 2016
Bowie, p 288
Green, pp 800–802

82. Patient has extensive bladder cancer. She underwent a complete cystectomy with bilateral pelvic lymphadenectomy and creation of ureteroileal conduit.
A. 51575, 50820
B. 50825, 51570, 38770
C. 51595
D. 51550, 38770

REFERENCE: AMA, 2016
Bowie, p 291

83. Patient presents to the hospital with right ureteral calculus. Patient is taken to the operating room where a cystoscopy with ureteroscopy is performed to remove the calculus.
A. 52353
B. 52310
C. 51065
D. 52352

REFERENCE: AMA, 2016
Green, pp 803–806
Smith, p 130
Smith (2), pp 111–112

84. Female with 6 months of stress incontinence. Outpatient therapies are not working and the patient decides to have the problem fixed. Laparoscopic urethral suspension was completed.
A. 51992
B. 51990
C. 51840
D. 51845

REFERENCE: AMA, 2016
Green, p 803

85. Patient has ovarian vein syndrome and has ureterolysis performed.
A. 58679
B. 58660
C. 52351
D. 50722

REFERENCE: AMA, 2016
Green, p 803

86. Male patient has been diagnosed with benign prostatic hypertrophy and undergoes a transurethral destruction of the prostate by radiofrequency thermotherapy.
A. 52648
B. 53852
C. 52601
D. 53850

REFERENCE: AMA, 2016
Bowie, p 295

87. Nephrectomy with resection of half of the ureter.
    A. 50220
    B. 50234
    C. 50230, 50650
    D. 50546

REFERENCE: AMA, 2016
Green, pp 801–803

88. Male with urinary incontinence. Sling procedure was performed 6 months ago and now the patient has returned for a revision of the sling procedure.
    A. 53449
    B. 53442
    C. 53440
    D. 53431

REFERENCE: AMA, 2016
Bowie, p 291

89. Excision of 2.5-cm bladder tumor with cystoscopy.
    A. 51550
    B. 51530
    C. 52235
    D. 51060

REFERENCE: AMA, 2016
Bowie, p 294
Green, pp 804–806
Smith, p 130

90. Closure of ureterocutaneous fistula.
    A. 50930
    B. 50920
    C. 57310
    D. 50520

REFERENCE: AMA, 2016
Green, p 803

Surgery—Male Genital System

91. Removal of nephrostomy tube with fluoroscopic guidance.
    A. 50387
    B. 50389
    C. 99212
    D. 99213

REFERENCE: AMA, 2016
Bowie, p 305

92. Patient has been diagnosed with prostate cancer. Patient arrived in the operating room where a therapeutic orchiectomy is performed.
    A. 54560
    B. 54530
    C. 55899
    D. 54520

REFERENCE: AMA, 2016
Green, pp 819–820
Smith (2), p 122

93. Patient undergoes laparoscopic orchiopexy for intra-abdominal testes.
   A. 54650 C. 54692
   B. 54699 D. 55899

REFERENCE: AMA, 2016
Green, pp 819–820
Smith (2), p 122

94. Scrotal wall abscess drainage.
   A. 55100 C. 54700
   B. 55150 D. 55110

REFERENCE: AMA, 2016
Bowie, p 305

95. Hydrocelectomy of spermatic cord.
   A. 55500 C. 55041
   B. 55000 D. 55520

REFERENCE: AMA, 2016
Bowie, p 305

96. Patient has been followed by his primary care physician for elevated PSA. Patient underwent prostate needle biopsy in the physician's office 2 weeks ago and the final pathology was positive for carcinoma. Patient is admitted for prostatectomy. The frozen section of the prostate and one lymph node is positive for prostate cancer with metastatic disease to the lymph node. Prostatectomy became a radical perineal with bilateral pelvic lymphadenectomy.
   A. 55845 C. 55815, 38562
   B. 55815 D. 38770

REFERENCE: AMA, 2016
Green, pp 821–822
Smith (2), p 122

97. Male presented to operating room for sterilization by bilateral vasectomy.
   A. 55200 C. 55250
   B. 55400 D. 55450

REFERENCE: AMA, 2016
Green, pp 820–821

98. Laser destruction of penile condylomas.
   A. 54057 C. 17270
   B. 17106 D. 54055

REFERENCE: AMA, 2016
Smith, p 134

99. First-stage repair for hypospadias with skin flaps.
   A. 54300 C. 54322
   B. 54308, 14040 D. 54304

REFERENCE: AMA, 2016
Bowie, pp 304–305

100. Priapism operation with spongiosum shunt.
   A. 54450
   B. 54352
   C. 54430
   D. 55899

REFERENCE: AMA, 2016
Bowie, pp 304–305

Surgery—Female Genital System

101. Patient was admitted to the hospital with sharp pelvic pains. A pelvic ultrasound was ordered and the results showed a possible ovarian cyst. The patient was taken to the operating room where a laparoscopic destruction of two corpus luteum cysts was performed.
   A. 49321
   B. 58925
   C. 58561
   D. 58662

REFERENCE: AMA, 2016
Smith (2), p 534

102. Patient was admitted with a cystocele and rectocele. An anterior colporrhaphy was performed.
   A. 57250
   B. 57260
   C. 57240
   D. 57110

REFERENCE: AMA, 2016
Bowie, pp 319–320

103. Patient has a Bartholin's gland cyst that was marsupialized.
   A. 54640
   B. 10060
   C. 58999
   D. 56440

REFERENCE: AMA, 2016
Bowie, pp 316–314

104. Patient is at a fertility clinic and undergoes intrauterine embryo transplant.
   A. 58679
   B. 58322
   C. 58323
   D. 58974

REFERENCE: AMA, 2016
Bowie, p 324

105. Patient has been diagnosed with carcinoma of the vagina, and she has a radical vaginectomy with complete removal of the vaginal wall.
   A. 57107
   B. 57110
   C. 58150
   D. 57111

REFERENCE: AMA, 2016
Smith (2), p 133

106. Patient has been diagnosed with uterine fibroids and undergoes a total abdominal hysterectomy with bilateral salpingo-oophorectomy.
   A. 58200
   B. 58150
   C. 58262
   D. 58150, 58720

REFERENCE: AMA, 2016
Bowie, p 322
Green, p 829
Johnson and Linker, p 380
Smith, pp 139–410
Smith (2), p 133

107. Hysteroscopy with D&C and polypectomy.
   A. 58563
   B. 58558
   C. 58120, 58100, 58555
   D. 58558, 58120

REFERENCE: AMA, 2016
Bowie, p 323
Green, pp 827–829
Smith, p 139
Smith (2), p 132

108. Laparoscopic tubal ligation utilizing Endoloop.
   A. 58670
   B. 58615
   C. 58671
   D. 58611

REFERENCE: AMA, 2016
Bowie, p 323
Green, pp 828–829

109. Laser destruction of extensive herpetic lesions of the vulva.
   A. 17106
   B. 17004
   C. 56515
   D. 56501

REFERENCE: AMA, 2016
Smith (2), p 131

110. Patient undergoes hysteroscopy with excision uterine fibroids.
   A. 58545
   B. 58140
   C. 58561
   D. 58140, 49320

REFERENCE: AMA, 2016
Bowie, p 323
Green, pp 827–829
Smith, p 139
Smith (2), p 132

Surgery—Maternity Care and Delivery

111. Attempted vaginal delivery in a previous cesarean section patient, which resulted in a repeat cesarean section.
   A. 59409
   B. 59612
   C. 59620
   D. 59514

REFERENCE: AMA, 2016
Bowie, p 336
Green, pp 830–834
Smith, p 140

112. Patient is admitted to the hospital following an ultrasound at 25 weeks, which revealed fetal pleural effusion. A fetal thoracentesis was performed.
   A. 59074
   B. 32554
   C. 32555
   D. 76815

REFERENCE: AMA, 2016
Bowie, pp 334–335

113. Patient in late stages of labor arrives at the hospital. Her OB physician is not able to make the delivery and the house physician delivers the baby vaginally. Primary care physician resumes care after delivery. Code the delivery.
   A. 59409
   B. 59612
   C. 59620
   D. 59400

REFERENCE: AMA, 2016
Bowie, pp 334–335
Green, pp 830–834
Smith, p 140

114. Patient is 24 weeks pregnant and arrives in the emergency room following an automobile accident. No fetal movement or heartbeat noted. Patient is taken to the OB ward where prostaglandin is given to induce abortion.
   A. 59200
   B. 59855
   C. 59821
   D. 59410

REFERENCE: AMA, 2016
Green, pp 830–834

115. Patient is 6 weeks pregnant and complains of left-sided abdominal pains. Patient is suspected of having an ectopic pregnancy. Patient has a laparoscopic salpingectomy with removal of the ectopic tubal pregnancy.
   A. 59120
   B. 59200
   C. 59121
   D. 59151

REFERENCE: AMA, 2016
Bowie, pp 334–335
Green, pp 830–834

116. Cesarean delivery with antepartum and postpartum care.
A. 59610
B. 59514
C. 59400
D. 59510

REFERENCE: AMA, 2016
Bowie, pp 334–335
Green, pp 830–834
Smith, p 140

117. A pregnant patient has an incompetent cervix, which was repaired using a vaginal cerclage.
A. 57700
B. 57531
C. 59320
D. 59325

REFERENCE: AMA, 2016
Bowie, p 333

118. A D&C is performed for postpartum hemorrhage.
A. 59160
B. 58120
C. 58558
D. 58578

REFERENCE: AMA, 2016
Bowie, p 333

119. Hysterotomy for hydatidifom mole and tubal ligation.
A. 58285, 58600
B. 58150, 58605
C. 51900, 58605
D. 59100, 58611

REFERENCE: AMA, 2016
Bowie, pp 323–324

120. D&C performed for patient with a diagnosis of incomplete abortion at 8 weeks.
A. 59812
B. 59820
C. 58120
D. 59160

REFERENCE: AMA, 2016
Green, pp 830–834

Surgery—Endocrine System

121. Patient comes in for a percutaneous needle biopsy of the thyroid gland.
A. 60000
B. 60270
C. 60699
D. 60100

REFERENCE: AMA, 2016
Green, p 835

122. Laparoscopic adrenalectomy, complete.
A. 60650
B. 60650-50
C. 60659
D. 60540

REFERENCE: AMA, 2016
Green, p 836

123. Left carotid artery excision for tumor of carotid body.
  A. 60650
  B. 60600
  C. 60605
  D. 60699

REFERENCE: AMA, 2016
Green, p 836

124. Patient undergoes total thyroidectomy with parathyroid autotransplantation.
  A. 60240, 60512
  B. 60520, 60500
  C. 60260, 60512
  D. 60650, 60500

REFERENCE: AMA, 2016
Green, p 835

125. Unilateral partial thyroidectomy.
  A. 60252
  B. 60210
  C. 60220
  D. 60520

REFERENCE: AMA, 2016
Green, p 835

Surgery—Nervous System

126. Patient comes in through the emergency room with a wound that was caused by an electric saw. Patient is taken to the operating room where two ulna nerves are sutured.
  A. 64837
  B. 64892, 69990
  C. 64836, 64837
  D. 64856, 64859

REFERENCE: AMA, 2016
Smith (2), p 153

127. Laminectomy and excision of intradural lumbar lesion.
  A. 63272
  B. 63267
  C. 63282
  D. 63252

REFERENCE: AMA, 2016
Green, pp 843, 845–846
Smith (2), p 149

128. Patient comes in for steroid injection for lumbar herniated disk. Marcaine and Aristocort were injected into the L2-L3 space.
  A. 64520
  B. 64483
  C. 62311
  D. 64714

REFERENCE: AMA, 2016
Smith, p 146
Smith (2), p 148

129. Patient with Parkinson's disease is admitted for insertion of a brain neurostimulator pulse generator with one electrode array.
   A. 61885
   B. 61850, 61863
   C. 61888
   D. 61867, 61870

REFERENCE: AMA, 2016
Bowie, p 361
Green, p 841
Smith (2), p 145

130. Patient has rhinorrhea, which requires repair of the CSF leak with craniotomy.
   A. 63707
   B. 63709
   C. 62100
   D. 62010

REFERENCE: AMA, 2016
Green, pp 838–840
Smith (2), pp 143–144

131. Patient has metastatic brain lesions. Patient undergoes stereotactic radiosurgery gamma knife of two lesions.
   A. 61533
   B. 61500
   C. 61796, 61797
   D. 61796

REFERENCE: AMA, 2016
Bowie, p 264

132. Patient has right sacroiliac joint dysfunction and requires a right S2-S3 paravertebral facet joint anesthetic nerve block with image guidance.
   A. 62311
   B. 64493
   C. 64490
   D. 64520

REFERENCE: AMA, 2016
Green, p 847
Smith (2), pp 152–153

133. Patient requires repair of a 6-cm meningocele.
   A. 63700
   B. 63709
   C. 63180
   D. 63702

REFERENCE: AMA, 2016
Smith (2), pp 151–152

134. Patient comes in through the emergency room with a laceration of the posterior tibial nerve. Patient is taken to the operating room where the nerve requires transposition and suture.
   A. 64856
   B. 64831, 64832, 64876
   C. 64840, 64874
   D. 64834, 64859, 64872

REFERENCE: AMA, 2016
Green, p 849
Smith (2), p 153

Surgery—Eye and Ocular Adnexa

135. Patient returns to the physician's office complaining of obscured vision. Patient has had cataract surgery 6 months prior. Patient requires laser discission of secondary cataract.
    A. 66821
    B. 66940
    C. 67835
    D. 66830

REFERENCE: AMA, 2016
Bowie, pp 373–374
Green, pp 852–853
Smith, pp 149–150
Smith (2), pp 162–163

136. Patient undergoes enucleation of left eye, and muscles were reattached to an implant.
    A. 65135-LT
    B. 65105-LT
    C. 65730-LT
    D. 65103-LT

REFERENCE: AMA, 2016
Smith (2), p 161

137. Patient suffers from strabismus and requires surgery. Recession of the lateral rectus (horizontal) muscle with adjustable sutures was performed.
    A. 67340, 67500
    B. 67314, 67320
    C. 67332, 67334
    D. 67311, 67335

REFERENCE: AMA, 2016
Bowie, pp 377–379
Green, pp 853–854
Smith, p 152
Smith (2), p 165

138. Radial keratotomy.
    A. 92071
    B. 65855
    C. 65767
    D. 65771

REFERENCE: AMA, 2016
Green, pp 852–853
Smith (2), pp 162–163

139. Correction of trichiasis by incision of lid margin.
    A. 67840
    B. 67830
    C. 67835
    D. 67850

REFERENCE: AMA, 2016
Smith (2), p 165

140. Patient undergoes ocular resurfacing construction utilizing stem cell allograft from a cadaver.
    A. 67320
    B. 66999
    C. 68371
    D. 65781

REFERENCE: AMA, 2016
Green, pp 853–854
Smith (2), pp 162–163

141. Patient presents for procedure for aphakia penetrating corneal transplant.
    A. 65755
    B. 65730
    C. 65750
    D. 65765

REFERENCE: AMA, 2016
Bowie, pp 373–374
Green, p 852
Smith (2), pp 162–163

142. Lagophthalmos correction with implantation using gold weight.
    A. 67912
    B. 67911
    C. 67901
    D. 67121

REFERENCE: AMA, 2016
Smith (2), p 165

143. Lacrimal fistula closure.
    A. 68760
    B. 68761
    C. 68700
    D. 68770

REFERENCE: AMA, 2016
Bowie, pp 379–380
Green, pp 854–855
Smith (2), pp 165–166

Surgery—Auditory

144. Patient comes into the office for removal of impacted earwax.
    A. 69210
    B. 69200
    C. 69222
    D. 69000

REFERENCE: AMA, 2016
Bowie, p 389
Green, pp 856–857
Smith (2), p 120

145. Patient with a traumatic rupture of the eardrum. Repaired with tympanoplasty with incision of the mastoid. Repair of ossicular chain not required.
    A. 69641
    B. 69646
    C. 69642
    D. 69635

REFERENCE: AMA, 2016
Bowie, p 389
Green, pp 857–858
Smith (2), p 173

146. Patient came in for excision of a middle ear lesion.
    A. 11440
    B. 69540
    C. 69552
    D. 69535

REFERENCE: AMA, 2016
Green, pp 857–858
Smith (2), p 173

147. Patient with chronic otitis media requiring eustachian tube catheterization.
   A. 69420
   B. 69424
   C. 69421
   D. 69799

REFERENCE: AMA, 2016
Bowie, p 391
Green, pp 857–858
Smith (2), p 173

148. Modified radical mastoidectomy.
   A. 69511
   B. 69505
   C. 69635
   D. 69641

REFERENCE: AMA, 2016
Green, pp 857–858
Smith (2), p 173

149. Decompression internal auditory canal.
   A. 69979
   B. 69915
   C. 69970
   D. 69960

REFERENCE: AMA, 2016
Green, p 858
Smith (2), pp 172–173

150. Myringoplasty.
   A. 69620
   B. 69635
   C. 69610
   D. 69420

REFERENCE: AMA, 2016
Bowie, p 391
Green, pp 857–858

151. Insertion of cochlear device inner ear.
   A. 69711
   B. 69949
   C. 69930
   D. 69960, 69990

REFERENCE: AMA, 2016
Bowie, p 392
Green, p 858
Smith (2), p 173

152. Patient with Bell's palsy requiring a total facial nerve decompression.
   A. 64742
   B. 64771
   C. 69955
   D. 64864

REFERENCE: AMA, 2016
Green, p 858
Smith (2), p 173

153. Drainage of simple external ear abscess.
    A. 69000 C. 10060
    B. 69100 D. 69020

REFERENCE: AMA, 2016
Green, pp 856–857
Smith (2), p 173

Radiology

154. Administration of initial oral radionuclide therapy for hyperthyroidism.
    A. 78015 C. 78099
    B. 77402 D. 79005

REFERENCE: AMA, 2016
Green, p 908

155. Patient comes into the outpatient department at the local hospital for an MRI of the cervical spine with contrast. Patient status post automobile accident.
    A. 72156 C. 72149
    B. 72142 D. 72126

REFERENCE: AMA, 2016
Green, pp 881, 889
Smith, pp 165–166

156. Obstetric patient comes in for a pelvimetry with placental placement.
    A. 74710 C. 76805
    B. 76946 D. 76825

REFERENCE: AMA, 2016
Bowie, pp 402–403

157. Patient comes into his physician's office complaining of wrist pain. Physician gives the patient an injection and sends the patient to the hospital for an arthrography. Code the complete procedure.
    A. 73115 C. 73110
    B. 73100 D. 25246, 73115

REFERENCE: AMA, 2016
Bowie, pp 151, 402–403

158. Patient has carcinoma of the breast and undergoes proton beam delivery of radiation to the breast with a single port.
    A. 77523 C. 77520
    B. 77432 D. 77402

REFERENCE: AMA, 2016
Bowie, p 410
Green, p 903
Smith, p 170

159. CT scan of the head with contrast.
   A. 70460
   B. 70542
   C. 70551
   D. 70470

REFERENCE: AMA, 2016
Bowie, p 403
Green, pp 887–888
Smith, pp 165–166

160. Patient undergoes x-ray of the foot with three views.
   A. 73620
   B. 3610
   C. 73630
   D. 27648, 73615

REFERENCE: AMA, 2016
Green, pp 884–885
Smith, pp 165–166

161. Unilateral mammogram with computer-aided detection with further physician review and interpretation.
   A. 77055, 77022
   B. 77055-22
   C. 77056-52, 77051
   D. 77055, 77051

REFERENCE: AMA, 2016
Bowie, pp 402–403
Green, pp 895–896

162. Pregnant female comes in for a complete fetal and maternal evaluation via ultrasound.
   A. 76856
   B. 76805
   C. 76811
   D. 76810

REFERENCE: AMA, 2016
Bowie, pp 406–407
Green, p 894

163. Ultrasonic guidance for the needle biopsy of the liver. Code the complete procedure.
   A. 47000, 76942
   B. 47000, 76937
   C. 47000, 76999
   D. 47000, 77002

REFERENCE: AMA, 2016
Bowie, pp 269, 406–407
Green, p 894

Pathology and Laboratory

164. What code is used for a culture of embryos less than 4 days old?
   A. 89251
   B. 89272
   C. 89268
   D. 89250

REFERENCE: AMA, 2016
Bowie, p 424
Green, pp 936–937

165. Basic metabolic panel (calcium, total) and total bilirubin.
   A. 80048, 82247
   B. 80053
   C. 80053
   D. 82239, 80400, 80051

REFERENCE: AMA, 2016
Bowie, pp 422–423
Green, pp 923–924, 927–928
Smith, pp 176–180

166. Huhner test and semen analysis.
   A. 89325
   B. 89258
   C. 89310
   D. 89300

REFERENCE: AMA, 2016
Green, pp 931–932

167. Chlamydia culture.
   A. 87110
   B. 87106
   C. 87118
   D. 87109, 87168

REFERENCE: AMA, 2016
Green, pp 785–786

168. Partial thromboplastin time utilizing whole blood.
   A. 85732
   B. 85730
   C. 85245
   D. 85246

REFERENCE: AMA, 2016
Smith, p 180

169. Pathologist bills for gross and microscopic examination of medial meniscus.
   A. 88300
   B. 88302, 88311
   C. 88325
   D. 88304

REFERENCE: AMA, 2016
Bowie, p 423
Green, pp 934–936
Smith, p 180

170. Cytopathology of cervical Pap smear with automated thin-layer preparation utilizing computer screening and manual rescreening under physician supervision.
   A. 88175
   B. 88148
   C. 88160, 88141
   D. 88161

REFERENCE: AMA, 2016
Bowie, p 423
Green, pp 932–933

171. Pathologist performs a postmortem examination, including the brain, of an adult. Tissue is sent to the lab for microscopic examination.
   A. 88309
   B. 88025
   C. 88099
   D. 88028

REFERENCE: AMA, 2016
Green, p 932
Smith, p 180

172. Clotting factor VII.
A. 85220
B. 85240
C. 85362
D. 85230

REFERENCE: AMA, 2016
Green, pp 928–929
Smith, p 180

Medicine Section

173. IV push of one antineoplastic drug.
A. 96401
B. 96409
C. 96411
D. 96413

REFERENCE: AMA, 2016
Bowie, pp 438–439
Green, pp 972–973
Smith, p 232

174. One-half hour of IV chemotherapy by infusion followed by IV push of a different drug.
A. 96413
B. 96413, 96411
C. 96413, 96409
D. 96409, 96411

REFERENCE: AMA, 2016
Bowie, p 438
Green, pp 972–973
Smith, p 232

175. Caloric vestibular test using air.
A. 92543, 92700
B. 92543, 92543
C. 92700
D. 92543

REFERENCE: AMA, 2016
Bowie, p 435

176. Patient presents to the emergency room with chest pains. The patient is admitted as a 23-hour observation. The cardiologist orders cardiac workup and the patient undergoes left heart catheterization via the left femoral artery with visualization of the coronary arteries and left ventriculography. The physician interprets the report. Code the heart catheterization.
A. 93452, 93455
B. 93452, 93458
C. 93458
D. 93459

REFERENCE: AMA, 2016

177. Patient with hematochromatosis had a therapeutic phlebotomy performed on an outpatient basis.
A. 99195
B. 36522
C. 36514
D. 99199

REFERENCE: AMA, 2016
Bowie, p 439

178. A physician performs a PTCA with drug-eluting stent placement in the left anterior descending artery and angioplasty only in the right coronary artery.
    A. 92928-LD, 92929-RC
    B. 92928-LD, 92920-RC
    C. 92928-LD, 92920-RC
    D. 92920-RC, 92929-LD

REFERENCE: AMA, 2016
Bowie, pp 435–436
Smith, pp 221–223

179. Transesophageal echocardiography (TEE) with probe placement, image, and interpretation and report.
    A. 93307
    B. 93303, 93325
    C. 93312, 93313, 93314
    D. 93312

REFERENCE: AMA, 2016
Bowie, pp 435–436

180. Which code listed below would be used to report an esophageal electrogram during an EPS?
    A. 93600
    B. 93615
    C. 93612
    D. 93616

REFERENCE: AMA, 2016
Smith, p 227

181. Cardioversion of cardiac arrhythmia by external forces.
    A. 92961
    B. 92950
    C. 92960
    D. 92970

REFERENCE: AMA, 2016
Bowie, pp 435–436

182. Osteopathic manipulative treatment to three body regions.
    A. 98926
    B. 98941
    C. 97110
    D. 97012

REFERENCE: AMA, 2016
Green, p 975

183. Patient presents to the Respiratory Therapy Department and undergoes a pulmonary stress test. CO_2 production with O_2 uptake with recordings was also performed.
    A. 94450
    B. 94620
    C. 94002
    D. 94621

REFERENCE: AMA, 2016
Bowie, p 436

For the following questions, you will be utilizing the codes provided for the scenarios. You will need to code appropriate CPT-4 codes only.

184. Patient presents to the hospital for debridement of a diabetic ulcer of the left ankle. The patient has a history of recurrent ulcers. Medication taken by the patient includes Diabeta and the patient was covered in the hospital with insulin sliding scales. The decubitus ulcer was debrided down to the bone.

11043	Debridement, muscle and/or fascia (includes epidermis, dermis, and subcutaneous tissue, if performed); first 20 cm^2 or less
11044	Debridement, bone (includes epidermis, dermis, subcutaneous tissue, muscle and/or fascia, if performed); first 20 cm^2 or less
+11046	Each additional 20 cm^2 thereof (List separately in addition to code for primary procedure.) (Use 11046 in conjunction with 11043.)
+11047	Each additional 20 cm^2, or part thereof (List separately in addition to code for primary procedure.) (Use 11047 in conjunction with 11047.)

A. 11043, +11047
B. 11043, +11046
C. 11044
D. 11044, +11047

REFERENCE: AMA, 2016
Bowie, pp 112–114

185. Patient presents to the emergency room following a fall from a tree. X-rays were ordered for the left upper arm, which showed a fracture of the humerus shaft. The emergency room physician performed a closed reduction of the fracture and placed the patient in a long arm spica cast. Code the diagnoses and procedures, excluding the x-ray.

24500	Closed treatment of humeral shaft fracture; without manipulation
24505	Closed treatment of humeral shaft fracture; with manipulation, with or without skeletal traction
24515	Open treatment of humeral shaft fracture with plate/screws, with or without cerclage
29065	Application, cast; shoulder to hand (long arm) LT Left side

A. 24505-LT
B. 24515-LT
C. 24505-LT, 29065
D. 24500-LT

REFERENCE: AMA, 2016
Bowie, p 157
Green, pp 697–698
Smith, pp 84–85

186. Patient was admitted with hemoptysis and underwent a bronchoscopy with transbronchial lung biopsy. Following the bronchoscopy, the patient was taken to the operating room where a left lower lobe lobectomy was performed without complications. Pathology reported large cell carcinoma of the left lower lobe.

31625	Bronchoscopy with bronchial or endobronchial biopsy, with or without fluoroscopic guidance
31628	Bronchoscopy with transbronchial lung biopsy, with or without fluoroscopic guidance
32405	Biopsy, lung or mediastinum, percutaneous needle
32440	Removal of lung, total pneumonectomy
32480	Removal of lung, other than total pneumonectomy, single lobe (lobectomy)
32484	Removal of lung, other than total pneumonectomy, single segment (segmentectomy)

A. 31625
B. 31628, 32480
C. 32405, 32484
D. 32440

REFERENCE: AMA, 2016
Bowie, pp 177–178
Green, pp 713–716
Smith, pp 96–98

187. Patient was admitted for right upper quadrant pain. Workup included various x-rays that showed cholelithiasis. Patient was taken to the operating room where a laparoscopic cholecystectomy was performed. During the procedure, the physician was unable to visualize through the ports and an open cholecystectomy was elected to be performed. An intraoperative cholangiogram was performed. Pathology report states acute and chronic cholecystitis with cholelithiasis.

47605	Cholecystectomy with cholangiography
47563	Laparoscopy, surgical; cholecystectomy with cholangiography

A. 47563
B. 47563, 47605
C. 47605

REFERENCE: AMA, 2016
Bowie, pp 267–268, 264
Green, p 796

188. Patient presents to the emergency room complaining of right forearm/elbow pain after racquetball last night. Patient states that he did not fall, but overworked his arm. Past medical history is negative and the physical examination reveals the patient is unable to supinate. A four-view x-ray of the right elbow is performed and is negative. The physician signs the patient out with right elbow sprain. Prescription of Motrin is given to the patient.

73040	X-ray of shoulder, arthrography radiological supervision and interpretation
73070	X-ray of elbow, two views
73080	X-ray of elbow, complete, minimum of three views
99281	E/M visit to emergency room—problem-focused history, problem-focused exam, straightforward medical decision
99282	E/M visit to emergency room—expanded problem-focused history, expanded problem-focused exam, and medical decision of low complexity
-25	Significant, separately identifiable evaluation and management service by the same physician on the same day of the procedure or other service

A. 73080
B. 99281, 73070
C. 73080, 99282, 73040
D. 99281-25, 73080

REFERENCE: AMA, 2016
Bowie, pp 64, 402–403
Smith, pp 165, 206

189. A physician orders a lipid panel on a 54-year-old male with hypercholesterolemia, hypertension, and a family history of heart disease. The lab employee in his office performs and reports the total cholesterol and HDL cholesterol only.

80061	Lipid panel; this panel must include the following: Cholesterol, serum, total (82465); Lipoprotein, direct measurement, high density cholesterol (HDL cholesterol) (83718); Triglycerides (84478)
82465	Cholesterol, serum or whole blood, total
83718	Lipoprotein, direct measurement; high density cholesterol (HDL cholesterol)
84478	Triglycerides
-52	Reduced services

A. 80061
B. 80061-52
C. 82465, 83718
D. 82465, 84478

REFERENCE: AMA, 2016
Bowie, p 423
Green, pp 927–928
Smith, pp 176–180

190. Chronic nontraumatic rotator cuff tear. Arthroscopic subacromial decompression with coracoacromial ligament release, and open rotator cuff repair.

23410	Repair of ruptured musculotendinous cuff (e.g., rotator cuff); open, acute
23412	Repair of ruptured musculotendinous cuff (e.g., rotator cuff) open; chronic
29821	Arthroscopy, shoulder, surgical; synovectomy, complete
29823	Arthroscopy, shoulder, surgical; debridement, extensive
+29826	Arthroscopy, shoulder, surgical; decompression of subacromial space with partial acromioplasty, with coracoacromial ligament release (List separately in addition to code from primary procedure.)
29827	Arthroscopy, shoulder, surgical; with rotator cuff repair
-59	Distinct procedural service

A. 29823
B. 23412, 29826-59
C. 29826, 29821
D. 23410

REFERENCE: AMA, 2016
Bowie, pp 161–162
Smith, pp 83–85, 88

191. The patient is on vacation and presents to a physician's office with a lacerated finger. The physician repairs the laceration and gives a prescription for pain control and has the patient follow up with his primary physician when he returns home. The physician fills out the superbill as a problem-focused history and physical examination with straightforward medical decision making. Also checked is a laceration repair for a 1.5-cm finger wound.

99201	New patient office visit with a problem-focused history, problem-focused examination and straightforward medical decision making
99212	Established patient office visit with a problem-focused history, problem-focused examination and straightforward medical decision making
12001	Simple repair of superficial wounds of scalp, neck, axillae, external genitalia, trunk, and/or extremities (including hands and feet); 2.5 cm or less
13131	Repair, complex, forehead, cheeks, chin, mouth, neck, axillae, genitalia, hands, and/or feet; 1.1 cm to 2.5 cm

A. 99212, 13131
B. 12001
C. 99212, 12001
D. 99201, 12001

REFERENCE: AMA, 2016
Bowie, pp 38–39, 115–116
Green, 542–543, 658–660
Smith, pp 66–68, 204

192. A 69-year-old established female patient presents to the office with chronic obstructive lung disease, congestive heart failure, and hypertension. The physician conducts a comprehensive history and physical examination and makes a medical decision of moderate complexity. Physician admits the patient from the office to the hospital for acute exacerbation of CHF.

99212	Established office visit for problem-focused history and exam, straightforward medical decision making
99214	Established office visit for a detailed history and physical exam, moderate medical decision making
99222	Initial hospital care for comprehensive history and physical exam, moderate medical decision making
99223	Initial hospital care for comprehensive history and physical exam, high medical decision making

A. 99214
B. 99223
C. 99222
D. 99212

REFERENCE: AMA, 2016
Bowie, p 58
Green, pp 566–567
Smith, pp 204–205

193. Established 42-year-old patient comes into your office to obtain vaccines required for his trip to Sri Lanka. The nurse injects intramuscularly the following vaccines: hepatitis A and B vaccines, cholera vaccine, and yellow fever vaccine. As the coding specialist, what would you report on the CMS 1500 form?
A. office visit, hepatitis A and B vaccine, cholera vaccine, and yellow fever vaccine
B. office visit, intramuscular injection; HCPCS Level II codes
C. office visit; administration of two or more single vaccines; vaccine products for hepatitis A and B, cholera, and yellow fever
D. administration of two or more single vaccines; vaccine products for hepatitis A and B, cholera, and yellow fever

REFERENCE: AMA, 2016
Green, pp 948–949
Smith, p 216

194. Patient presents to the operating room where the physician performed, using imaging guidance, a percutaneous breast biopsy utilizing a rotating biopsy device.

19000	Puncture aspiration of cyst of breast
19081	Biopsy, breast, with imaging of the biopsy specimen, percutaneous; first lesion, including stereotactic guidance
19120	Excision of cyst, fibroadenoma, or other benign or malignant tumor, aberrant breast tissue, duct lesion, nipple or areolar lesion (except 19300), open, male or female, one or more lesions
19125	Excision of breast lesion identified by preoperative placement of radiological marker, open; single lesion
19283	Placement of breast localization device(s) (ed clip, metallic pellet, wire/needle, radioactive seeds), percutaneous; first lesion, including stereotactic guidance

A. 19081
B. 19125, 19283
C. 19120
D. 19000

REFERENCE: AMA, 2016
Bowie, p 132
Green, pp 669–670
Smith, pp 78–79

195. Facelift utilizing the superficial musculoaponeurotic system (SMAS) flap technique.

15788	Chemical peel, facial; epidermal
15825	Rhytidectomy; neck with platysmal tightening (platysmal flap, P-flap)
15828	Rhytidectomy; cheek, chin, and neck
15829	Rhytidectomy; SMAS flap

A. 15825
B. 15788
C. 15829
D. 15828

REFERENCE: AMA, 2016
Green, pp 661–665

196. Tracheostoma revision with flap rotation.

31613	Tracheostoma revision; simple, without flap rotation
31614	Tracheostoma revision; complex, with flap rotation
31750	Tracheoplasty; cervical
31830	Revision of tracheostomy scar

A. 31830
B. 31750
C. 31614
D. 31613

REFERENCE: AMA, 2016
Bowie, pp 182–184

197. Blood transfusion of three units of packed red blood cells.

36430	Transfusion, blood or blood components
36455	Exchange transfusion; blood, other than newborn
36460	Transfusion, intrauterine, fetal

A. 36430
B. 36430, 36430, 36430
C. 36460
D. 36455

REFERENCE: AMA, 2016
Bowie, pp 218–219

198. Two-year-old patient returns to the hospital for cleft palate repair where a secondary lengthening procedure takes place.

40720	Plastic repair of cleft lip/nasal deformity; secondary, by re-creation of defect and reclosure
42145	Palatopharyngoplasty
42220	Palatoplasty for cleft palate; secondary lengthening procedure
42226	Lengthening of palate and pharyngeal flap

A. 40720
B. 42220
C. 42226
D. 42145

REFERENCE: AMA, 2016

199. Tonsillectomy on a 14-year-old.

42820	Tonsillectomy and adenoidectomy; under age 12
42821	Tonsillectomy and adenoidectomy; age 12 or over
42825	Tonsillectomy, primary or secondary; under age 12
42826	Tonsillectomy, primary or secondary; age 12 or over

A. 42820
B. 42821
C. 42825
D. 42826

REFERENCE: AMA, 2016
Green, p 780

200. Laparoscopic repair of umbilical hernia.

49580	Repair umbilical hernia, under age 5 years, reducible
49585	Repair umbilical hernia, age 5 years or over, reducible
49652	Laparoscopy, surgical, repair, ventral, umbilical, spigelian, or epigastric hernia (includes mesh insertion when performed); reducible
49654	Laparoscopy, surgical, repair, incisional hernia (includes mesh insertion when performed); reducible

A. 49580
B. 49654
C. 49585
D. 49652

REFERENCE: AMA, 2016
Bowie, p 272

201. Ureterolithotomy completed laparoscopically.

50600	Ureterotomy with exploration or drainage (separate procedure)
50945	Laparoscopy, surgical ureterolithotomy
52325	Cystourethroscopy; with fragmentation of ureteral calculus
52352	Cystourethroscopy, with urethroscopy and/or pyeloscopy; with removal or manipulation of calculus (ureteral catheterization is included)

A. 52352
B. 52325
C. 50600
D. 50945

REFERENCE: AMA, 2016
Bowie, p 290

202. Patient undergoes partial nephrectomy for carcinoma of the kidney.

50220	Nephrectomy, including partial ureterectomy, any open approach including rib resection
50234	Nephrectomy with total ureterectomy and bladder cuff; through same incision
50240	Nephrectomy, partial
50340	Recipient nephrectomy (separate procedure)

A. 50234
B. 50220
C. 50340
D. 50240

REFERENCE: AMA, 2016
Bowie, p 285
Green, pp 800–802

203. Patient presents to the operating room for fulguration of bladder tumors. The cystoscope was inserted and entered the urethra, which was normal. Bladder tumors measuring approximately 1.5 cm were removed.

50957	Ureteral endoscopy through established ureterostomy, with or without irrigation, instillation, or ureteropyelography, exclusive of radiologic service; with fulguration and/or incision, with or without biopsy
51530	Cystotomy; for excision of bladder tumor
52214	Cystourethroscopy, with fulguration of trigone, bladder neck, prostatic fossa, urethra, or periurethral glands
52234	Cystourethroscopy, with fulguration (including cryosurgery or laser surgery) and/or resection of small bladder tumor(s) (0.5 up to 2.0 cm)

A. 52234
B. 50957
C. 52214
D. 51530

REFERENCE: AMA, 2016
Bowie, p 295
Green, pp 806–807
Smith, pp 129–130

204. Excision of Cowper's gland.

53220	Excision or fulguration of carcinoma of urethra
53250	Excision of bulbourethral gland (Cowper's gland)
53260	Excision or fulguration; urethral polyp(s), distal urethra
53450	Urethromeatoplasty, with mucosal advancement

A. 53250
B. 53450
C. 53260
D. 53220

REFERENCE: AMA, 2016
Bowie, p 295

205. Placement of double-J stent.

52320	Cystourethroscopy (including ureteral catheterization); with removal of ureteral calculus
52330	Cystourethroscopy; with manipulation, without removal of ureteral calculus
52332	Cystourethroscopy with insertion of indwelling ureteral stent (e.g., Gibbons or double-J type)
52341	Cystourethroscopy, with treatment of ureteral stricture (e.g., balloon dilation, laser electrocautery, and incision)

A. 52341
B. 52320
C. 52330, 52332
D. 52332

REFERENCE: AMA, 2016
Bowie, p 294
Green, pp 806–807
Smith, pp 129–130

206. Litholapaxy, 3 cm calculus.

50590	Lithotripsy, extracorporeal shock wave
52317	Litholapaxy, simple or small (< 2.5 cm)
52318	Litholapaxy, complicated or large (over 2.5 cm)
52353	Cystourethroscopy, with ureteroscopy and/or pyeloscopy; with lithotripsy

A. 52353
B. 50590
C. 52318
D. 52317

REFERENCE: AMA, 2016
Bowie, pp 304–305

207. Patient presented to the operating room where an incision was made in the epigastric region for a repair of ureterovisceral fistula.

50520	Closure of nephrocutaneous or pyelocutaneous fistula
50525	Closure of nephrovisceral fistula, including visceral repair; abdominal approach
50526	Closure of nephrovisceral fistula, including visceral repair; thoracic approach
50930	Closure of ureterovisceral fistula (including visceral repair)

A. 50526
B. 50930
C. 50520
D. 50525

REFERENCE: AMA, 2016
Bowie, p 287

208. Amniocentesis.

57530	Trachelectomy, amputation of cervix (separate procedure)
57550	Excision of cervical stump, vaginal approach
59000	Amniocentesis, diagnostic
59200	Insertion of cervical dilator (separate procedure)

A. 59000
B. 59200
C. 57550
D. 57530

REFERENCE: AMA, 2016
Bowie, p 332

209. Patient is admitted to the hospital with facial droop and left-sided paralysis. CT scan of the brain shows subdural hematoma. Burr holes were performed to evacuate the hematoma.

61150	Burr hole(s) or trephine; with drainage of brain abscess or cyst
61154	Burr hole(s) with evacuation and/or drainage of hematoma, extradural or subdural
61156	Burr hole(s); with aspiration of hematoma or cyst, intracerebral
61314	Craniectomy or craniotomy for evacuation of hematoma, infratentorial; extradural or subdural

A. 61156
B. 61314
C. 61154
D. 61150

REFERENCE: AMA, 2016
Green, pp 838–840

210. Spinal tap.

62268	Percutaneous aspiration, spinal cord cyst or syrinx
62270	Spinal puncture, lumbar diagnostic
62272	Spinal puncture, therapeutic, for drainage of cerebrospinal fluid (by needle or catheter)
64999	Unlisted procedure, nervous system

A. 62272
B. 64999
C. 62268
D. 62270

REFERENCE: AMA, 2016
Bowie, p 363

211. Injection of anesthesia for nerve block of the brachial plexus.

64413	Injection, anesthetic agent; cervical plexus
64415	Injection, anesthetic agent; brachial plexus, single
64510	Injection, anesthetic agent; stellate ganglion (cervical sympathetic)
64530	Injection, anesthetic agent; celiac plexus, with or without radiologic monitoring

A. 64415
B. 64413
C. 64530
D. 64510

REFERENCE: AMA, 2016
Bowie, p 364
Green, pp 596–598

212. SPECT bone imaging.

77080	Dual energy x-ray absorptiometry (DXA), bone density study, one or more sites; axial skeleton (e.g., hips, pelvis, spine)
76977	Ultrasound bone density measurement and interpretation, peripheral site(s), any method
78300	Bone and/or joint imaging; limited area
78320	Bone and/or joint imaging; tomographic (SPECT)

A. 76977
B. 78320
C. 77080
D. 76977

REFERENCE: AMA, 2016
Bowie, pp 410–411

213. Vitamin B_{12}

82180	Ascorbic acid (vitamin C), blood
82607	Cyanocobalamin (vitamin B_{12})
84590	Vitamin A
84591	Vitamin, not otherwise specified

A. 84590
B. 82180
C. 84591
D. 82607

REFERENCE: AMA, 2016
Green, pp 927–928
Smith, p 180

214. Hepatitis C antibody.

86803	Hepatitis C antibody
86804	Hepatitis C antibody; confirmatory test (e.g., immunoblot)
87520	Infectious agent detection by nucleic acid (DNA or RNA); hepatitis C, direct probe technique
87522	Infectious agent detection by nucleic acid (DNA or RNA); hepatitis C, quantification

A. 86804
B. 86803
C. 87522
D. 87520

REFERENCE: AMA, 2016
Green, p 930

215. Creatinine clearance.

82550	Creatine kinase (CK), (CPK); total
82565	Creatinine; blood
82575	Creatinine; clearance
82585	Cryofibrinogen

A. 82550
B. 82565
C. 82575
D. 82585

REFERENCE: AMA, 2016
Green, pp 927–928
Smith, pp 178–180

216. Comprehensive electrophysiologic evaluation (EPS) with induction of arrhythmia.

93618	Induction of arrhythmia by electrical pacing
93619	Comprehensive electrophysiologic evaluation with right atrial pacing and recording, right ventricular pacing and recording, His bundle recording, including insertion and repositioning of multiple electrode catheters, without induction or attempted induction of arrhythmia
93620	Comprehensive electrophysiologic evaluation including insertion and repositioning of multiple electrode catheters with induction or attempted induction of arrhythmia; with right atrial pacing and recording, right ventricular pacing and recording, His bundle recording
+93623	Programmed stimulation and pacing after intravenous drug infusion (list separately in addition to code for primary procedure)
93640	Electrophysiologic evaluation of single- or dual-chamber pacing cardioverter-defibrillator leads including defibrillation threshold evaluation (induction of arrhythmia, evaluation of sensing and pacing for arrhythmia termination) at time of initial implantation or replacement

A. 93618, 93620
B. 93620
C. 93640, 93623
D. 93619, 93620

REFERENCE: AMA, 2016
Bowie, pp 435–436

217. Patient presents to the hospital for a two-view chest x-ray for a cough. The radiology report comes back negative. What would be the correct codes to report to the insurance company?

71010 Radiologic examination, chest; single view, frontal
71020 Radiologic examination, chest, two views, frontal and lateral
71035 Radiologic examination, chest, special views

A. 71010
B. 71020
C. 71035

REFERENCE: AMA, 2016
Bowie, pp 402–403

Answer Key for CPT-4 Coding

1. C
2. A
3. B
4. C
5. D
6. C
7. D
8. B
9. B
10. C
11. D
12. B
13. A
14. B
15. D
16. B
17. C
18. A
19. D The supply of skin substitutes graft(s) should be reported separately.
20. C
21. C
22. B
23. B
24. C The supply of skin substitutes graft(s) should be reported separately.
25. B
26. C
27. A If two lesions are removed with one excision, only one excision code would be reported.
28. D
29. B
30. C
31. D
32. A
33. D
34. A Codes 10060 and 10140 are used for I&Ds of superficial abscesses.
35. C
36. C
37. D
38. B
39. A
40. B
41. A
42. D
43. C
44. A
45. D
46. C
47. A
48. D
49. A
50. B
51. A
52. B
53. D
54. B
55. C
56. C
57. C
58. A
59. A
60. B
61. D
62. B
63. A
64. D
65. A
66. B
67. C
68. A
69. A
70. D
71. C
72. D Radiology codes would be used for the supervision and interpretation.
73. C
74. C
75. C
76. A
77. D
78. D
79. C
80. A
81. A
82. C
83. D
84. B
85. D
86. B
87. A
88. B
89. C
90. B
91. B

Answer Key for CPT-4 Coding

92. D
93. C
94. A
95. A
96. B
97. C
98. A
99. D
100. C
101. D
102. C
103. D
104. D
105. D
106. B
107. B
108. C
109. C
110. C
111. C
112. A
113. A
114. B
115. D
116. D
117. C
118. A
119. D When tubal ligation is performed at the same time as hysterotomy, use 58611 in addition to 59100.
120. A
121. D
122. A
123. C
124. A
125. B
126. C
127. A
128. C
129. A
130. C
131. C
132. B
133. D
134. C
135. A
136. B
137. D
138. D
139. B
140. D
141. C
142. A
143. D
144. A
145. D
146. B
147. D
148. B
149. D
150. A
151. C
152. C
153. A
154. D
155. B
156. A
157. D
158. C
159. A
160. C
161. D
162. C
163. A
164. D
165. A
166. D
167. A
168. B
169. D
170. A
171. B
172. D
173. B
174. B
175. C Use code 92543 when an irrigation substance is used.
176. C
177. A
178. B
179. D
180. B
181. C
182 A

Answer Key for CPT-4 Coding

183. D
184. C
185. A Casting is included in the surgical procedure.
186. B
187. C
188. D
189. C In order to use the code for the panel, every test must have been performed.
190. B Code both the arthroscopic procedure and the open procedure. Both need to be reported because there were two separate procedures. Modifier -59 must be added to code 29826 because it is a component of the comprehensive procedure 23412. That is allowed if an appropriate modifier is used per NCCI edits.
191. D
192. C According to CPT guidelines, when a patient is admitted to the hospital on the same day as an office visit, the office visit is not billable.
193. D According to the CPT coding and guidelines for vaccines, only a separate identifiable Evaluation Management code may be billed in addition to the vaccine. In this scenario, the patient was seen only for his vaccines. This guideline immediately eliminates all the other answers.
194. A
195. C
196. C
197. A Report this code only once no matter how many units were given.
198. B
199. D
200. D
201. D
202. D
203. A
204. A
205. D
206. C
207. B
208. A
209. C
210. D
211. A
212. B
213. D
214. B
215. C
216. B
217. B

REFERENCES

American Medical Association (AMA). (2015). *Physician's current procedural terminology (CPT) 2016 professional edition.* Chicago: Author.

Bowie, M. J. (2015). *Understanding procedural coding: A worktext.* Clifton Park, NY: Cengage Learning.

Green, M. (2016). *3-2-1 Code It!* (5th ed.). Clifton Park, NY: Cengage Learning.

Johnson, S. L. & Linker, R. (2013). *Understanding medical coding: A comprehensive guide* (3rd ed.). Clifton Park, NY: Cengage Learning.

Smith, G. (2015). *Basic current procedural terminology and HCPCS coding, 2015 edition.* Chicago: American Health Information Management Association (AHIMA).

Smith, G. (2) (2011). *Coding surgical procedures: Beyond the basics.* Clifton Park, NY: Cengage Learning.

CPT Coding Competencies

Questions	RHIA Domain	RHIT Domain
1–217	1	2

X. Informatics and Information Systems

Nanette B. Sayles, EdD, RHIA, CCS, CHPS, CPHIMS, FAHIMA

Special Note

The Information Technology and Systems domains are very different for the RHIA and RHIT Examinations. Questions with only an RHIA competency begin at question 56. We advise that RHIT students should also study these questions. It is always better to know more than less.

1. You use the Internet to log in to a system and from there you are able to access several systems. This technology is known a(n):
   A. authentication
   B. application
   C. link
   D. portal

REFERENCE: Sayles, p 289

2. Your release of information system has part of the computing on the workstation and part on the file server. What type of technology is being used?
   A. Internet
   B. client server
   C. LAN
   D. operating system

REFERENCE: Eichenwald-Maki and Petterson, pp 29–30, 288
Sayles, p 999

3. Dr. Smith is entering a medication order in a CPOE. A window pops up with the following message:

   Patient is on beta-blocker, which is a contraindication for this medication. Do you want to order this medication? Yes or No.

   This is an example of a(n)
   A. reminder.
   B. alert.
   C. allergy.
   D. structured entry.

REFERENCE: Eichenwald-Maki and Petterson, pp 128, 130, 131–133, 287

4. Barbara is being seen at a physician's office that she has never been to before. This physician practice is independently owned and is not associated with a hospital or other physician practice. She did not have to request copies of her medical records, but the physician has everything that she needs. The physician must be part of a(n)
   A. integrated health network.
   B. corporation.
   C. health information exchange.
   D. electronic health record.

REFERENCE: McWay, pp 272–273
Sayles, pp 983–984

5. What types of software provide a front-end structure/interface that presents information in a familiar format leading to a natural style of interaction through the use of icons and a mouse?
   A. graphical user interface
   B. fiber optics
   C. assembly level language
   D. machine language

REFERENCE: Abdelhak, p 119
Sayles, p 877

6. With data exchange standards, the ability to transfer data from one system to another system is called
   A. data sets.
   B. messaging standards.
   C. interfaces.
   D. interoperability.

REFERENCE: Eichenwald-Maki and Petterson, p 3
LaTour, Eichenwald-Maki, and Oachs, p 116
Sayles, p 919

7. Which of the following would be a foreign key in the patient table?
   A. last name
   B. address
   C. medical record number
   D. billing number

REFERENCE: Sayles and Trawick, p 91

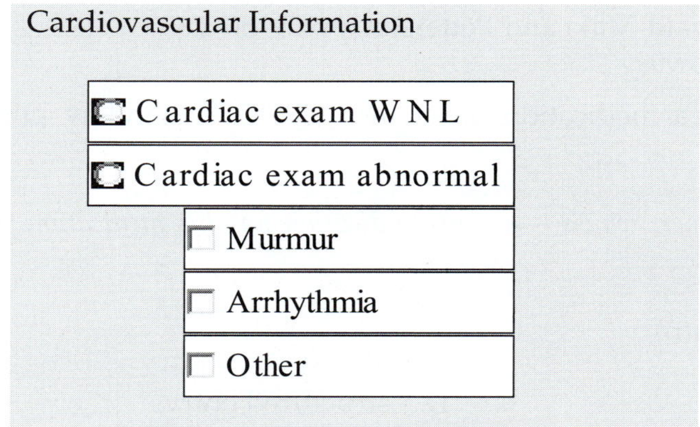

8. Review the simplistic screen above. This is an example of how ___________ data can be entered.
   A. unstructured
   B. structured
   C. nomenclature
   D. template

REFERENCE: Amatayakul, p 248
Eichenwald-Maki and Petterson, pp 35–37, 108

9. You use an information system to create a letter notifying a requester that your facility does not have any records on file for the individual's records requested. What system are you using?
   A. chart deficiency
   B. chart locator
   C. release of information
   D. cancer registry

REFERENCE: Sayles and Trawick, p 114

10. The information systems are testing whether or not the system works for lab equipment and printers. This type of testing is called
   A. volume testing.
   B. acceptance testing.
   C. integration testing.
   D. application testing.

REFERENCE: Sayles and Trawick (2014)

11. You need to identify some patterns in our database. What technology should you use?
   A. reminders
   B. alerts
   C. data mining
   D. clinical guidelines

REFERENCE: Amatayakul, p 30
Bowie and Green, p 273
LaTour, Eichenwald-Maki, and Oachs, p 86
McWay, p 268

12. The vendor has provided an update to their software. With this update, the system has new functions. This is known as a
   A. fix.
   B. version.
   C. release.
   D. link.

REFERENCE: McWay, p 287

13. Your role is to help patients determine where to store their personal health record. What area do you specialize in?
   A. privacy
   B. HIM management
   C. standards development
   D. consumer health informatics

REFERENCE: Abdelhak, p 195

14. Mary is designing a computer screen that will be used to collect patient demographic information. What input design should be utilized for the state field?
   A. an icon
   B. a dialog box
   C. the drop-down menu
   D. free form text

REFERENCE: Abdelhak, p 126
Eichenwald-Maki and Petterson, pp 33–35

15. Auburn Medical Center is implementing a new EHR. They are developing a training plan. Which of the following should be included?
   A. functions
   B. policies
   C. settings
   D. agenda

REFERENCE: Sayles, p 92

16. Which of the following tests determines how well new systems being implemented work with existing systems?
   A. volume test
   B. system test
   C. unit test
   D. integration test

REFERENCE: Abdelhak, p 363

17. Data from the laboratory information system, radiology information system, and many other systems are all stored real-time in a single database. This database is known as a(n)
   A. electronic health record.
   B. personal health record.
   C. clinical data repository.
   D. health information exchange.

REFERENCE: Bowie and Green, p 119
McWay, p 267

18. Administration has asked your team to investigate the possibility of purchasing a decision support system. Which of the following would you conduct?
    A. risk assessment
    B. feasibility study
    C. request for proposal
    D. request for information

REFERENCE: Sayles and Trawick, p 66

19. The decision on which system to purchase should be:
    A. quantifiable
    B. qualitative
    C. negotiated
    D. audited

REFERENCE: Sayles and Trawick, p 81

20. In selecting a messaging standard for use in a picture archival communication system, the BEST choice would be
    A. Consolidated Health Informatics Initiatives.
    B. National Drug Code.
    C. HL7.
    D. DICOM.

REFERENCE: LaTour, Eichenwald-Maki, and Oachs, p 132

21. Sandusky Hospital is adding a new service. They need to update the information system to reflect the new service. Where should they make the change?
    A. data model
    B. data standard
    C. settings
    D. data dictionary

REFERENCE: Sayles and Trawick, pp 53–54

22. What Medicare program requires the use of a certified electronic health record?
    A. meaningful use
    B. prospective payment
    C. health information exchange
    D. data standards

REFERENCE: McWay, p 305

23. The electronic health record that we are implementing in your multi-disciplinary medical practice will be implemented for your family practice physicians. Future projects will expand this to other specialties. What is this description of the project called?
    A. vision
    B. critical success factors
    C. project scope
    D. scope creep

REFERENCE: Wager, p 245

24. In the RFP, you have asked for information regarding the amount of time that a vendor has been in business and the number of installations of the product under consideration. If you want to review this information, you would go to the ________________ section.
    A. functional specifications
    B. organizational profile
    C. vendor profile
    D. licensing and contractual details

REFERENCE: Abdelhak, p 375
Amatayakul, p 385
McWay, p 401

25. There is a problem with the software. The drop-down fields do not have all of the options that are needed. This type of field is known as a:
    A. structured data entry
    B. unstructured data entry
    C. direct data capture
    D. patient data entry

REFERENCE: Sayles, p 1000

26. One of the ways that an EHR is distinguished from a clinical data repository is that the EHR
    A. has clinical decision support capabilities.
    B. has data from multiple information systems.
    C. can have digital images.
    D. aggregates data.

REFERENCE: McWay, p 126

27. You have been asked to give an example of a clinical information system. Which one of the following would you cite?
    A. laboratory information system
    B. financial information system
    C. billing system
    D. Admission, Discharge, Transfer

REFERENCE: McWay, pp 302–303

28. Which of the following systems would provide a snapshot of information about the patient's condition?
    A. EHR
    B. continuity of care record
    C. personal health record
    D. SMART card

REFERENCE: Sayles and Trawick, p 243

29. You are entering orders into an information system. This system prevented you from ordering a duplicate radiology test and prevented you from ordering a medication that the patient was allergic to. What system are you using?
    A. order entry/results reporting
    B. electronic health record
    C. clinical provider order entry
    D. decision support system

REFERENCE: Sayles, p 961

30. The EHR software is not working correctly. The link between the fetal monitoring system and the EHR is down. When you call the information system department, what should you tell them has failed?
    A. source code
    B. setting configuration
    C. interface
    D. network

REFERENCE: Sayles and Trawick, p 89

31. You are developing a list of functions needed by users of a release of information system. You are also evaluating the current system to see what opportunities there are to improve the system. Which stage of the system developmental life cycle stages are you in?
    A. analysis
    B. implementation
    C. design
    D. obsolescence

REFERENCE: LaTour, Eichenwald-Maki, and Oachs, pp 105–106
McWay, pp 286–287

32. Which of the following technologies can be used to check on a patient who is homebound?
    A. interactive voice recognition
    B. digital imaging
    C. radio frequency identification
    D. natural language processing

REFERENCE: McWay, p 312

33. In performing a "what if" query to determine whether the facility should expand the emergency department, which of the following systems would be used?
    A. decision support system
    B. financial information system
    C. clinical decision support system
    D. knowledge-based system

REFERENCE: Abdelhak, p 307
Sayles, p 854

34. What type of system would be purchased to provide information on the census, update the master patient index, and distribute demographic data?
    A. Admission, Discharge, Transfer
    B. executive information system
    C. clinical information system
    D. financial information system

REFERENCE: McWay, p 313

35. As HIM Department Director, you are on the implementation team for the new MPI. You have been assigned the responsibility of looking at every data element stored in the system and establishing criteria for the use of each. An example of what you are doing is shown below.

Name	Last name
Description	This field is for the patient's last name
Number of characters	30
Alphanumeric	Alpha
Acceptable characters	a–z
Responsible person	HIM Director
Used in reports	Admissions list, discharge list, transfer list, health record number list, UB-92, CMS-1500

You are responsible for the
    A. data flow diagram.
    B. decision tree.
    C. data dictionary.
    D. rules based algorithms.

REFERENCE: Amatayakul, p 270
Eichenwald-Maki and Petterson, p 27
Bowie and Green, p 266
McWay, p 262
Sayles, pp 882–884

36. A milestone is
    A. the distance between the users and the data center.
    B. a step in the path to the implementation of a system such as the EHR.
    C. a project plan.
    D. a module of an information system such as the EHR.

REFERENCE: Amatayakul, p 120

37. A common language used in data definition and data manipulation is
    A. unified modeling language.
    B. metadata.
    C. HTML.
    D. SQL.

REFERENCE: McWay, p 171
Sayles and Trawick, p 177

38. You are trying to ensure a patient's name, but the entire name will not fit in the field. Only the first eight characters will fit. This is a problem with which of the following?
    A. the data model
    B. policy and procedure
    C. the data dictionary
    D. data mapping

REFERENCE: Sayles and Trawick, p 94

39. Differentiate between the physical and logical data models.
    A. The physical data model shows how the logical model will be created, and the logical data model shows the technology plan to be used.
    B. The logical data model shows what the system should do, and the physical data model shows how the logical data model will be created.
    C. The logical data model uses DFDs, and the physical data model uses entity relationship models.
    D. The physical data model uses DFDs, and the logical uses entity relationship model.

REFERENCE: Sayles and Trawick, p 196

40. The administrator has asked us to develop a patient satisfaction database internally. This database will be used to collect data that can be used to improve our services. He does not want this to be a long, drawn-out process. Which of the following could speed up this process?
    A. RFI
    B. RFP
    C. prototyping
    D. functional requirements

REFERENCE: Sayles and Trawick, p 130

41. You need to know the structures in the database, the types of records stored, and the fields used. In which component of database design will you find this information?
    A. data dictionary
    B. data model
    C. database design specification
    D. database management

REFERENCE: McWay, p 263

42. The medical staff wants a speech recognition system where the staff dictates and then the editing of the dictation is done by editors. What type of speech recognition is this?
    A. key-word spotting
    B. hidden Markov model
    C. back-end speech recognition
    D. front-end speech recognition

REFERENCE: Sayles and Trawick, p 284

43. The EHR system implementation team is using simulated patients and simulated patient information to add progress notes, nurses' notes, and so on, to the EHR prior to implementation. Which system development life cycle phase is the team involved in?
    A. conversion
    B. testing
    C. analysis
    D. site preparation

REFERENCE: Abdelhak, p 339
LaTour, Eichenwald-Maki, and Oachs, p 107
Sayles, p 886

44. You are interested in performing some data analysis on patients with cardiac problems. You have downloaded the data that you need on the cardiology patients from the data warehouse into a smaller database that you can work with. You are using a
    A. data mart.
    B. clinical data repository.
    C. specialized data warehouse.
    D. executive information system.

REFERENCE: Abdelhak, p 322
Amatayakul, p 274
LaTour, Eichenwald-Maki, and Oachs, p 94
McWay, p 268
Sayles, p 925

45. The laboratory system was installed 3 years ago. It is running well and meeting the needs of the department. In which stage of the IS life cycle is the lab system?
    A. initiation
    B. development
    C. implementation
    D. operations

REFERENCE: Abdelhak, p 340
LaTour, Eichenwald-Maki, and Oachs, p 107
McWay, p 287

46. The type of documentation that uses drop boxes, radio buttons, and pick lists is called
    A. structured data entry.
    B. free text.
    C. natural language processing.
    D. unstructured data entry.

REFERENCE: Amatayakul, p 321

47. The facility Hospital Information System team has been researching network topologies and has decided on one that combines the attributes of bus, ring, and star topologies. What topology has the team chosen?
    A. hybrid network
    B. network protocol
    C. physical topology
    D. TCP/IP

REFERENCE: Sayles and Trawick, p 28

48. Your facility has created a list of systems that need to be implemented between now and the implementation of the EHR. This list is in the order that they should be implemented. This document is known as the
    A. migration path
    B. implementation strategy
    C. dependencies
    D. decision support

REFERENCE: Sayles and Trawick, p 265

49. You are given the task of choosing the type of database that your facility will use. You choose one that stores the data in tables. What model did you choose?
    A. relational
    B. object-oriented
    C. hierarchical
    D. structured

REFERENCE: McWay, p 262

System Evaluation: Chart Location System							
Requirement	Priority	System A	System B	System C	System A Weighted	System B Weighted	System C Weighted
Ad hoc reporting	2	1	3	2	2	6	4
Check-out chart	3	3	3	3	9	9	9
Mass check out of chart	3	3	3	3	9	9	9
Unlimited locations	1	2	2	1	2	2	1
Password security	2	2	3	2	4	6	4
User-friendly	3	3	2	3	9	6	9
Check-in chart	3	1	3	3	3	9	9
Total					38	47	45

50. The EHR system selection committee evaluated three systems on a scale of 1 to 3 with a score of 3 being the best. The priority is ranked on a scale of 1 to 3 with 3 being the highest. Based on the evaluation above, which of the following systems should be purchased?
    A. System A
    B. System B
    C. System C
    D. neither System A, System B, nor System C

REFERENCE: Sayles and Trawick, pp 126–127

51. Upon final review of the RFP that is to be sent out to prospective vendors, you notice that there is content that should not be included in the operational requirement section of the document. Which of the following information should be deleted from this section?
    A. response time
    B. data architecture
    C. data conversion
    D. data analysis tools

REFERENCE: Amatayakul, p 386
McWay, p 401

52. You need a system that will work with your existing system but not necessarily from the same vendor. What type of system are you looking for?
    A. commercial
    B. interfaced
    C. integrated
    D. cloud computing

REFERENCE: Sayles and Trawick, p 68

53. Maria has received a request to update a patient's address. What system should she use?
    A. executive information system
    B. clinical decision support system
    C. admission–discharge–transfer system
    D. laboratory information system

REFERENCE: Abdelhak, p 293
Bowie and Green, p 253
Sayles, pp 912–913

54. The database being implemented must be able to store video, images, and audio. Which of the following database models should be considered?
    A. relational
    B. object oriented
    C. network
    D. hierarchical

REFERENCE: LaTour, Eichenwald-Maki, and Oachs, p 172
McWay, p 263

55. To enter the results of a urinalysis into the computer system, you would use a(n)
    A. laboratory system.
    B. radiology system.
    C. pharmacy system.
    D. order entry/results reporting system.

REFERENCE: Sayles and Trawick, p 99

56. Which of these functions is found in an ambulatory EHR but not in an acute care EHR?
    A. results review
    B. online documentation
    C. eMAR
    D. registration

REFERENCE: Amatayakul, p 511

57. Mountaintop Hospital has decided to use the "best of breed" philosophy. Because of this, they need a(n) __________ to manage the sharing of data.
    A. DBMS
    B. RFP
    C. consultant
    D. interface engine

REFERENCE: Amatayakul, p 375

58. The HIM supervisor is evaluating software that would utilize electronic logging and monitoring of requests for copies of patient information and develop an accounting of disclosure. What department function is this most useful for?
    A. release of information/disclosure management
    B. record completion
    C. record location/tracking
    D. transcription

REFERENCE: Bowie and Green, p 310
Sayles and Trawick, p 182

59. The patient's blood pressure is automatically being recorded. This is an example of what type of clinical information system?
    A. patient monitoring system
    B. medical documentation
    C. nursing applications
    D. patient registration

REFERENCE: Bowie and Green, p 124

60. You have been asked to establish guidelines on screen design that will be used in all of your information system projects. Which of the following standards would be included in your guidelines?
    A. The screen should read right to left.
    B. Eliminate all hyperlinks.
    C. Provide instructions on how to complete the screen.
    D. Use red and green to flag key data.

REFERENCE: Abdelhak, p 121

61. The patient has been on medication X for several years. A physician ordered medication Y. The information system immediately sends the physician a message that says that medication Y is contraindicated due to medication X. What technology is being used?
    A. point-of-care system
    B. clinical decision support systems
    C. EHR
    D. order entry results reporting

REFERENCE: Abdelhak, p 344
Sayles and Trawick, p 249

62. The new computer hardware arrived and the technical staff was not able to install it because there was not enough space in the computer room. Which of the following implementation steps was not properly executed?
    A. system evaluation
    B. conversion
    C. site preparation
    D. user preparation

REFERENCE: Abdelhak, p 363
Sayles and Trawick, p 132

The following questions represent advanced competencies.

63. In developing your Information Systems Strategic Plan, which of the following should be the basis for the plan?
    A. organization business plan
    B. previous IS strategic plan
    C. consultant's recommendations
    D. previous IS budgets

REFERENCE: Sayles, p 857

64. The vendor that you work for has decided to get into the EHR market. What standard should you suggest using in developing the functions performed by the EHR?
    A. DICOM
    B. LOINC
    C. HL7 EHR functional model
    D. IEEE 1073

REFERENCE: Sayles, p 953

65. When negotiating an information system contract, which of the following would be an example of a performance warranty specified in the contract?
    A. remedies
    B. operational practices
    C. insurances
    D. uptime

REFERENCE: Amatayakul, p 420

66. Critique the following statement:

    The EHR utilizes existing source systems to supply data.

    A. This is true because the EHR uses many source systems to populate the data.
    B. This is false because the EHR is a stand-alone system.
    C. This is false because the EHR requires the latest and greatest system, thus eliminating legacy systems.
    D. This is true because the EHR obtains information SOLELY from the source documents.

REFERENCE: Amatayakul, p 417

67. You have been asked how to handle versioning of documents in the EDMS. Which of the following should be your response?
    A. Delete the first version and retain the second.
    B. Display the second version but identify that a previous version exists.
    C. Do not allow edits to the system.
    D. Display both versions side by side.

REFERENCE: Abdelhak, p 376

68. You need to document the major tasks and milestones for the system that is being implemented. What document do you include this information in?
    A. contract
    B. strategic plan
    C. vision
    D. project plan

REFERENCE: Wager, p 247

69. The chief financial officer has decided that he wants to drop bills 36 hours after patient discharge. What would have to be updated?
    A. prototype
    B. interface
    C. code
    D. setting configuration

REFERENCE: Sayles and Trawick, p 132

70. Dr. Smith accesses the EHR in his office to see what patients are ready to be seen and what calls he needs to make. This functionality is called
    A. checkout
    B. the in-basket function
    C. registration
    D. the patient summary

REFERENCE: Amatayakul, p 515

71. Which one of the following is necessary during the strategic planning process for the EHR?
    A. gauging the user's readiness for the EHR
    B. writing the request for proposal to be used in selecting the EHR
    C. selecting the EHR to be used
    D. creating a newsletter to keep users informed of the status of EHR

REFERENCE: Amatayakul, p 77

72. The hospital is undergoing the development of an information system strategic plan. The part of the process where changes in the community, legislation, and other factors are monitored is called
    A. health information exchange.
    B. alerts.
    C. environmental scanning.
    D. critical path analysis.

REFERENCE: McWay, p 325

73. Which of the following data field types is best used for the health record number?
    A. alphanumeric
    B. auto-numbering
    C. numeric
    D. time and date

REFERENCE: Sayles and Trawick, p 51

Patient
Last name
First name
Middle initial
Street address
City
State
Zip
Medical record number
Date of birth

74. You are developing an entity relationship diagram. In the entity of the patient shown above, which of the attributes is the primary key?
    A. last name
    B. combination of last and first names
    C. street address
    D. medical record number

REFERENCE: McWay, pp 263–264
Sayles and Trawick, p 96

75. A preliminary step prior to issuing a formal RFP, which allows the facility to narrow down the field of potential vendors for procurement of a new hospital-wide computer system, would be to
    A. select the system to be purchased.
    B. create a Gantt chart to monitor project progress.
    C. issue a request for information (RFI) to potential vendors.
    D. initiate contract negotiations.

REFERENCE: LaTour, Eichenwald-Maki, and Oachs, p 106
McWay, p 401

76. Administration has asked the clinical provider order-entry task force to select the method of implementation that will reduce risk to the hospital. What method should they choose?
    A. Implement all modules across the entire organization.
    B. Implement one module in one unit while running the current system in parallel.
    C. Implement all modules across the entire organization while running the current system in parallel.
    D. Implement one module in one unit while shutting down the existing system.

REFERENCE: Sayles, p 867

77. A survey of your patients has found that they want access to test results and the ability to schedule appointments online. What technology should be used to provide these services?
    A. personal health record
    B. single sign-on
    C. intranet
    D. portal

REFERENCE: McWay, p 289

78. You recently installed a new computer system and you just learned that the vendor does not have the right to use one portion of the system. Another company owns the rights to the information contained in this portion of the system. What clause in your contract would you review to see if you are protected from being sued by the other company?
   A. warranties
   B. indemnification
   C. support
   D. force majeure

REFERENCE: Abdelhak, p 573

79. Your facility has implemented the clinical systems needed to support the EHR. The knowledge-based and decision support systems will be installed next. Your team has a firm plan to indicate the direction you should take and the expected timeframe. This is called a
   A. cost-benefit analysis.
   B. migration path.
   C. critical path.
   D. value realization.

REFERENCE: Amatayakul, p 162

80. As Director of Health Information Services, you are negotiating a contract to purchase a new computerized dictation system that will be used across three satellite ambulatory clinics. What element is most critical in the contract negotiation to ensure use of the software in multiple environments?
   A. delivery terms
   B. scope and term of warranties
   C. price and payment terms
   D. license grant

REFERENCE: Abdelhak, p 380

81. The most secure model of signatures used in information systems is
   A. digital signature.
   B. electronic signature.
   C. digitized signature.
   D. there is no difference in the level of security between these models.

REFERENCE: Sayles and Trawick, p 253

82. Which of the following situations would be an appropriate use of a DSS?
   A. determining the number of staff needed on the nursing unit
   B. establishing the productivity standard for the organization
   C. generating a report that aggregates data from multiple information system, including both clinical and financial data
   D. determining whether or not to purchase a new MRI machine so that there are two instead of just one

REFERENCE: LaTour, Eichenwald-Maki, and Oachs, p 194

83. You need a report that includes only Medicare patients. What operation enables you to generate this report?
   A. filtering
   B. sorting
   C. grouping
   D. calculations

REFERENCE: Sayles and Trawick, p 174

84. Which of the following is a risky practice in the EHR?
   A. copy and paste
   B. data reuse
   C. free text
   D. graphical user interface

REFERENCE: Amatayakul, p 321

85. Patients at your facility wear a bracelet with a small chip embedded in it. It is scanned to retrieve data. What is this technology?
    A. radio frequency identification device
    B. barcode
    C. encryption
    D. linkage

REFERENCE: McWay, p 313

86. The facility is implementing a new PACS. They know that the volume of data that will be passing over the Internet will significantly increase. As a result, they have updated their network. They want to determine whether the updated network can handle the amount of data that is expected to be sent across the system. Which type of testing would they use?
    A. conversion
    B. functionality
    C. interface
    D. load or volume

REFERENCE: Abdelhak, p 363
Amatayakul, p 419

87. Which of the following relationships does the diagram above demonstrate?
    A. one to one
    B. many to many
    C. one to many
    D. one and only one

REFERENCE: Abdelhak, p 360

88. There was an unexpected hardware failure for our EHR. It is expected to be up and operational in 3 hours. Until then, which of the following plans would you need to initiate?
    A. information system strategic plan
    B. implementation plan
    C. business continuity plan
    D. project planning

REFERENCE: Sayles and Trawick, pp 173–174

89. You have been asked to develop scenarios that will be used to design and program a new release of information system. These scenarios will include the processes to be used in detail. What are you designing?
    A. strategic plan
    B. functional requirements
    C. use cases
    D. request for proposal

REFERENCE: Abdelhak, p 348
Sayles and Trawick, p 258

90. You have been asked to identify and display the existing record processing workflow with the paper record. After you finish this, you will redesign the process and display the new process. What tool should you use?
    A. policy and procedure
    B. data dictionary
    C. data flow diagram
    D data mapping

REFERENCE: Abdelhak, p 352
Sayles and Trawick, p 97

91. Installation of a new electronic document management system is scheduled for the HIM department. The department director calls a meeting of the HIM supervisors to coordinate plans for training the HIM staff. What key factors must be taken into consideration as part of the training preparation process?
    A. the total storage capacity and price of the new system
    B. collecting the results of the RFP responses and vendor selection process used during the selection process
    C. presentation content and scheduling to accommodate all employee shifts
    D. scheduling training times and locations for all physicians and hospital personnel who will use the system

REFERENCE: Abdelhak, p 339

LaTour, Eichenwald-Maki, and Oachs, p 107

92. You are entering the valid choices for each of the data elements, defining each data element and more. You must be managing the
    A. functional requirement.
    B. data dictionary.
    C. system analysis.
    D. data flow diagram.

REFERENCE: Abdelhak, p 354
LaTour, Eichenwald-Maki, and Oachs, p 172
McWay, p 262
Sayles, p 884

93. When calling the HIM Department, you say the word "two" to reach the release of information system. What technology is this?
    A. artificial neural network
    B. gesture recognition technology
    C. interactive voice recognition
    D. voice over Internet protocol

REFERENCE: McWay, p 312

94. What Web 2.0 technology would you recommend for someone who wants to share their battle with cancer?
    A. a blog
    B. a chat room
    C. web pages
    D. an extranet

REFERENCE: LaTour, Eichenwald-Maki, and Oachs, p 99
Wager, p 300

95. Your facility has decided to implement the new laboratory information system on one unit and then add more units as your confidence in the system grows. What go-live model are you using?
    A. phased
    B. pilot
    C. big bang
    D. straight turnover

REFERENCE: Sayles and Trawick, p 97

96. You have had a problem with duplicate medical record numbers in your facility's MPI. Now you are joining a health information exchange, so you will need to clean up your database and prevent the duplicates from happening again. If you want to find near matches as well as identical matches in your MPI, you should implement a _________ algorithm.
    A. probabilistic
    B. deterministic
    C. fuzzy
    D. neither probabilistic, deterministic, nor fuzzy

REFERENCE: Sayles and Trawick, p 217

97. The radiology information system was recently implemented. During the system evaluation, what do you need to learn?
   A. the employee who worked the hardest
   B. the user's favorite new function
   C. how you can improve the next implementation
   D. the effectiveness of the testing environment

REFERENCE: Sayles and Trawick, pp 145-146

98. You have been asked to make a recommendation about the framework for the state's health information exchange. The committee wants a system that does not require the health information exchange to store the patient information. What model should you recommend?
   A. linkage
   B. centralized
   C. hybrid
   D. federated

REFERENCE: Wager, p 196

99. Dr. Smith has a practice in Macon, Georgia. He is treating a patient who is physically located in Soperton, Georgia, which is about 70 miles away. Dr. Smith, however, treats the patient while remaining in his Macon office. What technology is required for Dr. Smith to treat the patient?
   A. EHR
   B. clinical data repository
   C. telehealth
   D. cloud computing

REFERENCE: LaTour, Eichenwald-Maki, and Oachs, p 97

100. You are considering three vendors for your new encoder. Your facility wants to purchase the system from a stable company. After reviewing the vendor profile information below, which of the vendors would you eliminate from consideration?

Topic	Vendor A	Vendor B	Vendor C
Number of years in business	2	10	3
Number of installations	72	135	5
Number of installation staff	3	4	1
Age of product	2	6	3
Financial standing	Good	Excellent	Fair

   A. Vendor A
   B. Vendor B
   C. Vendor C
   D. You cannot eliminate any of the vendors.

REFERENCE: Sayles and Trawick, p 126

Answer Key for Informatics and Information Systems

1. D
2. B
3. B
4. C
5. A
6. D
7. D
8. B
9. C
10. C
11. C
12. B
13. A
14. C
15. D
16. D
17. C
18. B
19. A
20. D
21. D
22. A
23. C
24. C
25. A
26. A
27. A
28. B
29. C
30. C
31. A
32. C
33. A
34. B
35. C
36. B
37. D
38. D
39. B
40. C
41. B
42. C
43. C
44. A
45. D
46. A
47. A
48. A
49. A
50. B
51. C
52. B
53. C
54. A
55. A
56. D
57. A Although the facility may benefit from the services of a consultant and they will need a DBMS to manage the database for the new systems, it is the interface engine that will be needed to manage communication between the various systems.
58. A
59. A
60. A
61. B
62. C
63. A
64. A
65. C
66. D
67. B
68. D
69. D
70. A
71. C
72. B
73. D
74. C
75. B
76. D
77. B
78. B
79. D
80. A
81. D
82. A
83. D
84. A

Answer Key for Informatics and Information Systems

85. A
86. D
87. A
88. C
89. C
90. C
91. C
92. B
93. C
94. A
95. B
96. A
97. C
98. D
99. C
100. C

REFERENCES

Abdelhak, M., and Hanken, M. A. (2016). *Health information: Management of a strategic resource* (5th ed.). Philadelphia: W. B. Saunders.

Amatayakul, M. K. (2012). *Electronic health records: A practical guide for professionals and organizations* (5th ed.). Chicago: American Health Information Management Association.

Bowie, M. J., and Green, M. A. (2016). *Essentials of health information management* (3rd ed.). Clifton Park, NY: Cengage Learning.

Eichenwald-Maki, S., and Petterson, B. (2014). *Using the electronic health record* (2nd ed.). Clifton Park, NY: Cengage Learning.

LaTour, K., Eichenwald-Maki, S., and Oachs, P. (2013). *Health information management: Concepts, principles, and practice* (3rd ed.). Chicago: American Health Information Management Association (AHIMA).

McWay, D. (2014). *Today's health information management: An integrated approach* (2nd ed.). Chicago: Cengage Learning.

Sayles, N. B. (2013). *Health information management technology: An applied approach* (4th ed.). Chicago: AHIMA Press.

Sayles N. B., and Trawick, K. (2010). *Introduction to computer systems for health information technology.* Chicago: American Health Information Management Association.

Wager, K. A., Lee, F. W., and Glaser, J. P. (2013). *Health care information systems: A practical approach for health care management* (3rd ed.). San Francisco: Josey Bass.

Informatics and Information Systems Chapter Domains

Question	RHIA Domain	RHIT Domain
1–100	3	
1–62		4

XI. Health Information Privacy and Security

Nanette B. Sayles, EdD, RHIA, CCS, CHPS, CPHIMS, FAHIMA

1. As Chief Privacy Officer for Premier Medical Center, you are responsible for which of the following?
   A. backing up data
   B. developing a plan for reporting privacy complaints
   C. writing policies on protecting hardware
   D. writing policies on encryption standards

REFERENCE: Bowie and Green, p 51
McWay (2014), p 39
Sayles, p 829

2. Which of the following situations violates a patient's privacy?
   A. The hospital sends patients who are scheduled for deliveries information on free childbirth classes.
   B. The physician on the quality improvement committee reviews medical records for potential quality problems.
   C. The hospital provides patient names and addresses to a pharmaceutical company to be used in a mass mailing of free drug samples.
   D. The hospital uses aggregate data to determine whether or not to add a new operating room suite.

REFERENCE: Bowie and Green, p 307
Sayles, p 827

3. The patient has the right to control access to his or her health information. This is known as
   A. security.
   B. confidentiality.
   C. privacy.
   D. disclosure.

REFERENCE: McWay (2016), p 214

4. Mary processed a request for information and mailed it out last week. Today, the requestor, an attorney, called and said that all of the requested information was not provided. Mary pulls the documentation, including the authorization and what was sent. She believes that she sent everything that was required based on what was requested. She confirms this with her supervisor. The requestor still believes that some extra documentation is required. Given the above information, which of the following statements is true?
   A. Mary is not required to release the extra documentation because the facility has the right to interpret a request and apply the minimum standard rule.
   B. Mary is required to release the extra documentation because the requestor knows what is needed.
   C. Mary is required to release the extra documentation because, in the customer service program for the facility, the customer is always right.
   D. Mary is not required to release the additional information because her administrator agrees with her.

REFERENCE: McWay (2016), p 214
McWay (2014), pp 73–74
Sayles, p 799

5. Mountain Hospital has discovered a security breach. Someone hacked into the system and viewed 50 medical records. According to ARRA, what is the responsibility of the covered entity?
   A. ARRA does not address this issue.
   B. All individuals must be notified within 30 days.
   C. All individuals must be notified within 60 days.
   D. ARRA requires oral notification.

REFERENCE: Sayles, pp 826–827

6. Physical safeguards include

   1. tools to monitor access
   2. tools to control access to computer systems
   3. fire protection
   4. tools preventing unauthorized access to data

   A. 1 and 2 only
   B. 1 and 3 only
   C. 2 and 3 only
   D. 2 and 4 only

REFERENCE: Bowie and Green, pp 294–295
McWay (2016), p 305
Sayles, p 1055

7. You are reviewing your privacy and security policies, procedures, training program, and so on, and comparing them to the HIPAA and ARRA regulations. You are conducting a
   A. policy assessment.
   B. risk assessment.
   C. compliance audit.
   D. risk management.

REFERENCE: McWay (2016), p 312

8. Which of the following can be released without consent or authorization?
   A. summary of patient care
   B. de-identified health information
   C. personal health information
   D. protected health information

REFERENCE: McWay (2014), p 72

9. Kyle, the HIM Director, has received a request to amend a patient's medical record. The appropriate action for him to take is
   A. make the modification because you have received the request.
   B. file the request in the chart to document the disagreement with the information contained in the medical record.
   C. route the request to the physician who wrote the note in question to determine appropriateness of the amendment.
   D. return the notice to the patient because amendments are not allowed.

REFERENCE: Bowie and Green, pp 92–93
McWay (2014), p 104
Sayles, p 803

10. An employee in the admission department took the patient's name, Social Security number, and other information and used it to get a charge card in the patient's name. This is an example of
    A. identity theft.
    B. mitigation.
    C. disclosure.
    D. release of information.

REFERENCE: McWay (2016), p 231

11. A patient has submitted an authorization to release information to a physician office for continued care. The release of information clerk wants to limit the information provided because of the minimum necessary rule. What should the supervisor tell the clerk?
    A. Good call.
    B. The patient is an exception to the minimum necessary rule, so process the request as written.
    C. The minimum necessary rule was eliminated with ARRA.
    D. The minimum necessary rule only applies to attorneys.

REFERENCE: McWay (2014), p 73
McWay (2016), p 214

12. Patricia is processing a request for medical records. The record contains an operative note and a discharge summary from another hospital. The records are going to another physician for patient care. What should Patricia do?
    A. Notify the requestor that redisclosure is illegal and so he must get the operative and discharge summary records from the original source hospital.
    B. Include the documents from the other hospital.
    C. Redisclose when necessary for patient care.
    D. Redisclose when allowed by law.

REFERENCE: Bowie and Green, pp 209–210
Sayles, p 799

13. Before a user is allowed to access protected health information, the system confirms that the patient is who he or she says they are. This is known as
    A. access control.
    B. notification.
    C. authorization.
    D. authentication.

REFERENCE: McWay (2014), p 290

14. Contingency planning includes which of the following processes?
    A. data quality
    B. systems analysis
    C. disaster planning
    D. hiring practices

REFERENCE: McWay (2014), p 290

15. Which of the following disclosures would require patient authorization?
    A. law enforcement activities
    B. workers' compensation
    C. release to patient's family
    D. public health activities

REFERENCE: Bowie and Green, p 306
LaTour, Eichenwald-Maki, and Oachs, p 316

16. Your department was unable to provide a patient with a copy of his record within the 30-day limitation. What should you do?
    A. Call the patient and apologize.
    B. Call the patient and let him know that you will need a 30-day extension.
    C. Write the patient and tell him that you will need a 30-day extension.
    D. Both write and call the patient to tell him you need a 30-day extension.

REFERENCE: Bowie and Green, p 309

17. I have been asked if I want to be in the directory. The admission clerk explains that if I am in the directory,
    A. my friends and family can find out my room number.
    B. my condition can be discussed with any caller in detail.
    C. my condition can be released to the news media.
    D. my condition can be released to hospital staff only.

REFERENCE: Sayles, p 907

18. Which of the following techniques would a facility employ for access control?

    1. automatic logoff
    2. authentication
    3. integrity controls
    4. unique user identification

    A. 1 and 4 only
    B. 1 and 2 only
    C. 2 and 4 only
    D. 3 and 4 only

REFERENCE: Bowie and Green, p 295
Sayles, p 1037

19. Which of the following statements is true about the Privacy Act of 1974?
    A. It applies to all organizations that maintain health care data in any form.
    B. It applies to all health care organizations.
    C. It applies to the federal government.
    D. It applies to federal government except for the Veterans Health Administration.

REFERENCE: LaTour, Eichenwald-Maki, and Oachs, p 310

20. Which of the following statements is true about a requested restriction?
    A. ARRA mandates that a CE must comply with a requested restriction.
    B. ARRA states that a CE does not have to agree to a requested restriction.
    C. ARRA mandates that a CE must comply with a requested restriction unless it meets one of the exceptions.
    D. ARRA does not address restrictions to PHI.

REFERENCE: Sayles, p 807

21. Which of the following is an example of administrative safeguards under the security rule?
    A. encryption
    B. monitoring the computer access activity of the user
    C. assigning unique identifiers
    D. monitoring traffic on the network

REFERENCE: McWay (2014), p 291

22. Someone accessed the covered entity's electronic health record and sold the information that was accessed. This person is known as which of the following?
    A. malware
    B. a virus
    C. a hacker
    D. a cracker

REFERENCE: McWay (2014), p 290

23. Intentional threats to security could include
    A. a natural disaster (flood).
    B. equipment failure (software failure).
    C. human error (data entry error).
    D. data theft (unauthorized downloading of files).

REFERENCE: Sayles, pp 1029–1030

24. Which of the following would be a business associate?
    A. release of information company
    B. bulk food service provider
    C. childbirth class instructor
    D. security guards

REFERENCE: McWay (2010), p 226
McWay (2014), p 68

25. Which of the following statements demonstrates a violation of protected health information?
    A. "Can you help me find Mary Smith's record?"
    B. A member of the physician's office staff calls centralized scheduling and says, "Dr. Smith wants to perform a bunionectomy on Mary Jones next Tuesday."
    C. "Mary, at work yesterday I saw that Susan had a hysterectomy."
    D. Dr. Jones tells a nurse on the floor to give Ms. Brown Demerol for her pain.

REFERENCE: McWay (2014), p 72
Sayles, p 799

26. You are a nurse who works on 3West during the day shift. One day, you had to work the night shift because they were shorthanded. However, you were unable to access the EHR. What type of access control(s) are being used?
    A. user-based
    B. context-based
    C. role-based
    D. either user- or role-based

REFERENCE: Rinehart-Thompson, p 86

27. In case your system crashes, your facility has defined the policies and procedures necessary to keep your business going. This is known as:
    A. core operations
    B. business continuity plan
    C. data recovery
    D. data backup

REFERENCE: Rinehart-Thompson, p 128

28. You are defining the designated record set for South Beach Healthcare Center. Which of the following would be included?
    A. quality reports
    B. psychotherapy notes
    C. discharge summary
    D. information compiled for use in civil hearing

REFERENCE: LaTour, Eichenwald-Maki, and Oachs, p 314
Sayles, pp 798–799

29. You have been asked to provide examples of technical security measures. Which of the following would you include in your list of examples?
    A. locked doors
    B. automatic logout
    C. minimum necessary
    D. training

REFERENCE: Bowie and Green, p 295
McWay (2014), p 292

30. Which security measure utilizes fingerprints or retina scans?
    A. audit trail
    B. biometrics
    C. authentication
    D. encryption

REFERENCE: Sayles, p 1038

31. Ms. Thomas was a patient at your facility. She has been told that there are some records that she cannot have access to. These records are most likely
    A. psychotherapy notes.
    B. alcohol and drug records.
    C. AIDS records.
    D. mental health assessment.

REFERENCE: Bowie and Green, p 291
Sayles, p 800

32. Your organization is sending confidential patient information across the Internet using technology that will transform the original data into unintelligible code that can be re-created by authorized users. This technique is called
    A. a firewall.
    B. validity processing.
    C. a call-back process.
    D. data encryption.

REFERENCE: Abdelhak, p 320
McWay (2014), p 290
Sayles, p 1042

33. When patients are able to obtain a copy of their health record, this is an example of which of the following?
    A. a required standard
    B. an addressable requirement
    C. a patient right
    D. a preemption

REFERENCE: McWay (2014), p 69

34. Which of the following should the record destruction program include?
    A. the method of destruction
    B. the name of the supervisor of the person destroying the records
    C. citing the laws followed
    D. requirement of daily destruction

REFERENCE: Bowie and Green, p 104
LaTour, Eichenwald-Maki, and Oachs, p 279
McWay (2014), p 136
Sayles, pp 346–347

35. You are looking for potential problems and violations of the privacy rule. What is this security management process called?
    A. risk management
    B. risk assessment
    C. risk aversion
    D. business continuity planning

REFERENCE: Bowie and Green, p 293

36. The administrator states that he should not have to participate in privacy and security training as he does not use PHI. How should you respond?
    A. "All employees are required to participate in the training, including top administration."
    B. "I will record that in my files."
    C. "Did you read the privacy rules?"
    D. "You are correct. There is no reason for you to participate in the training."

REFERENCE: Sayles, p 829

37. The surgeon comes out to speak to a patient's family. He tells them that the patient came through the surgery fine. The mass was benign and they could see the patient in an hour. He talks low so that the other people in the waiting room will not hear but someone walked by and heard. This is called a(n)
    A. privacy breach.
    B. violation of policy.
    C. incidental disclosure.
    D. privacy incident.

REFERENCE: Sayles, p 819

38. A patient signed an authorization to release information to a physician but decided not to go see that physician. Can he stop the release?
    A. No, once the release is signed, it cannot be reversed
    B. Yes – in all circumstances
    C. Yes, as long has it has not been released already
    D. Yes, as long as the physician agrees

REFERENCE: Bowie and Green, p 287

39. A mechanism to ensure that PHI has not been altered or destroyed inappropriately has been established. This process is called
    A. entity authentication.
    B. audit controls.
    C. access control.
    D. integrity.

REFERENCE: Bowie and Green, p 295

40. Which of the following documents is subject to the HIPAA security rule?
    A. document faxed to the facility
    B. copy of discharge summary
    C. paper medical record
    D. scanned operative report stored on CD

REFERENCE: McWay (2014), p 291
Roach, p 459

41. The hospital has received a request for an amendment. How long does the facility have in order to accept or deny the request?
    A. 30 days
    B. 60 days
    C. 14 days
    D. 10 days

REFERENCE: Bowie and Green, p 287
Sayles (2013), p 804

42. You work for a 60-bed hospital in a rural community. You are conducting research on what you need to do to comply with HIPAA. You are afraid that you will have to implement all of the steps that your friend at a 900-bed teaching hospital is implementing at his facility. You continue reading and learn that you only have to implement what is prudent and reasonable for your facility. This is called
    A. scalable.
    B. risk assessment.
    C. technology neutral.
    D. access control.

REFERENCE: McWay (2014), p 291

43. Barbara, a nurse, has been flagged for review because she logged in to the EHR in the evening when she usually works the day shift. Why should this conduct be reviewed?
    A. This is a privacy violation.
    B. This needs to be investigated before a decision is made because there may be a legitimate reason why she logged in at this time.
    C. This is not a violation since Barbara, as a nurse, has full access to data in the EHR.
    D. No action is required.

REFERENCE: Sayles and Trawick, p 324

44. Alisa has trouble remembering her password. She is trying to come up with a solution that will help her remember. Which one of the following would be the BEST practice?
    A. using the word "password" for her password
    B. using her daughter's name for her password
    C. writing the complex password on the last page of her calendar
    D. creating a password that utilizes a combination of letters and numbers

REFERENCE: Sayles, p 1038

45. Which statement is true about when a family member can be provided with PHI?
    A. The patient's mother can always receive PHI on their child.
    B. The family member lives out of town and cannot come to the facility to check on the patient.
    C. The family member is a health care professional.
    D. The family member is directly involved in the patient's care.

REFERENCE: Green & Bowie, p 287

46. A covered entity
    A. is exempt from the HIPAA privacy and security rules.
    B. includes all health care providers.
    C. includes health care providers who perform specified actions electronically.
    D. must utilize business associates.

REFERENCE: McWay (2014), p 68
Sayles, p 794

47. Protected health information includes
    A. only electronic individually identifiable health information.
    B. only paper individually identifiable health information.
    C. individually identifiable health information in any format stored by a health care provider.
    D. individually identifiable health information in any format stored by a health care provider or business associate.

REFERENCE: Bowie and Green, p 286
LaTour, Eichenwald-Maki, and Oachs, p 313
McWay (2014), p 69
Sayles, p 797

48. Mabel is a volunteer at a hospital. She works at the information desk. A visitor comes to the desk and says that he wants to know what room John Brown is in. What should Mabel do?
    A. Look the patient up and give the room number to the visitor.
    B. Look the patient up to see if John has agreed to be in the directory. If he has, then give the room number to the visitor.
    C. Look the patient up to see if the patient signed a notice of privacy practice. If so, then give the visitor the room number.
    D. Look the patient up in the system to determine if he has agreed to TPO usage. If the patient has done so, then give the room number to the visitor.

REFERENCE: LaTour, Eichenwald-Maki, and Oachs, p 316
Sayles, p 815

49. To prevent their network from going down, a company has duplicated much of its hardware and cables. This duplication is called
    A. an emergency mode plan.
    B. redundancy.
    C. a contingency plan.
    D. a business continuity planning.

REFERENCE: Health Information Privacy and Security, p 323
Sayles and Trawick, p 31

50. Richard has asked to view his medical record. Within what timeframe must the facility provide this record to him?
    A. 30 days
    B. 60 days
    C. 14 days
    D. 10 days

REFERENCE: Sayles, p 801

51. The HIPAA security rule impacts which of the following protected health information?
    A. x-ray films stored in radiology
    B. paper medical records
    C. faxed records
    D. clinical data repository

REFERENCE: McWay (2014), p 291

52. To which of the following requesters can a facility release information about a patient without that patient's authorization?
    A. the public health department
    B. the nurse caring for the patient
    C. a court with a court order
    D. a business associate

REFERENCE: Bowie and Green, p 300

53. The data on a hard drive were erased by a corrupted file that had been attached to an e-mail message. Which of the following can be used to prevent this?
    A. messaging standards
    B. acceptance testing
    C. virus checker
    D. encryption

REFERENCE: McWay, p 290

54. Which of the following is the term used to identify who made an entry into a health record?
    A. access control
    B. authentication
    C. authorship
    D. accessibility

REFERENCE: McWay, p 304

55. When logging into a system, you are instructed to enter a string of characters. These characters appear distorted onscreen, however. What kind of access control is this?
    A. CAPTCHA
    B. biometrics
    C. token
    D. two-factor authentication

REFERENCE: Sayles, p 1039

56. Which of the following is an example of two-factor authentication?
    A. username and password
    B. token and smart card
    C. fingerprint and retinal scan
    D. password and token

REFERENCE: Abdelhak, p 287
LaTour, Eichenwald-Maki, and Oachs, p 134
McWay, p 290
Sayles, p 1039
Sayles and Trawick, p 322

57. The three components of a security program are protecting the privacy of data, ensuring the integrity of data, and ensuring the ________.
    A. validity of data
    B. availability of data
    C. security of hardware
    D. security of data

REFERENCE: Sayles, p 1026

The following questions represent advanced competencies.

58. HIPAA states that release to a coroner is allowed. State law says that the coroner must provide a subpoena. Which of the following is a correct statement?
    A. Follow the HIPAA requirement since it is a federal law.
    B. Follow the state law since it is stricter.
    C. You can follow either the state law or the HIPAA rule.
    D. You must request a ruling from a judge.

REFERENCE: McWay (2014), p 70

59. The computer system containing the electronic health record was located in a room that was flooded. As a result, the system is inoperable. Which of the following would be implemented?
    A. SWOT analysis
    B. information systems strategic planning
    C. request for proposal
    D. business continuity processes

REFERENCE: Bowie and Green, p 294
Sayles, p 1044

60. You have been given the responsibility of destroying the PHI contained in the system's old server before it is trashed. What destruction method do you recommend?
    A. crushing
    B. overwriting data
    C. degaussing
    D. incineration

REFERENCE: Sayles and Trawick, p 317

61. A breach has been identified. How quickly must the patient be notified?
    A. As soon as the problem has been resolved
    B. No more than 90 days
    C. No more than 60 days
    D. No more than 30 days

REFERENCE: Rinehart-Thompson, p 150

62. In conducting an environmental risk assessment, which of the following would be considered in the assessment?
    A. placement of water pipes in the facility
    B. verifying that virus checking software is in place
    C. use of single sign-on technology
    D. authentication

REFERENCE: McWay (2014), p 327
Sayles, p 1034

63. Before we can go any further with our risk analysis, we need to determine what systems/information need to be protected. This step is known as
    A. system characterization.
    B. risk determination.
    C. vulnerability.
    D. control analysis.

REFERENCE: Rinehart-Thompson, p 117

64. A hacker recently accessed our database. We are trying to determine how the hacker got through the firewall and exactly what was accessed. The process used to gather this evidence is called
    A. forensics.
    B. mitigation.
    C. security event.
    D. incident.

REFERENCE: Sayles and Trawick, p 310

65. As Chief Privacy Officer, you have been asked why you are conducting a risk assessment. Which reason would you give?
    A. to get rid of problem staff
    B. to change organizational culture
    C. to prevent breach of confidentiality
    D. to learn about the organization

REFERENCE: McWay (2014), p 326

66. Which of the following situations would require authorization before disclosing PHI?
    A. releasing information to the Bureau of Disability Determination
    B. health oversight activity
    C. workers' compensation
    D. public health activities

REFERENCE: Green & Bowie, p 291

67. Which of the following is an example of a security incident?
    A. Temporary employees were not given individual passwords.
    B. An employee took home a laptop with unsecured PHI.
    C. A handheld device was left unattended on the crash cart in the hall for 10 minutes.
    D. A hacker accessed PHI from off site.

REFERENCE: Sayles and Trawick, p 310

68. The HIM director received an e-mail from the technology support services department about her e-mail being full and asking for her password. The director contacted tech support and it was confirmed that their department did not send this e-mail. This is an example of what type of malware?
    A. phishing
    B. spyware
    C. denial of service
    D. virus

REFERENCE: Sayles and Trawick, p 326

69. You have been asked to create a presentation on intentional and unintentional threats. Which of the following should be included in the list of threats you cite?
    A. hard drive failures
    B. data deleted by accident
    C. data loss due to electrical failures
    D. a patient's Social Security number being used for credit card applications

REFERENCE: Sayles and Trawick, p 301

70. The supervisors have decided to give nursing staff access to the EHR. They can add notes, view, and print. This is an example of what?
    A. the termination process
    B. an information system activity review
    C. spoliation
    D. a workforce clearance procedure

REFERENCE: Bowie and Green, p 293

71. The information systems department was performing their routine destruction of data that they do every year. Unfortunately, they accidently deleted a record that is involved in a medical malpractice case. This unintentional destruction of evidence is called
    A. mitigation.
    B. spoliation.
    C. forensics.
    D. a security event.

REFERENCE: Sayles and Trawick, p 310

72. Which of the following examples is an exception to the definition of a breach?
    A. A coder accidently sends PHI to a billing clerk in the same facility.
    B. The wrong patient information was sent to the patient's attorney.
    C. Information was erroneously sent to another healthcare facility.
    D. Information was loaded on the Internet inappropriately.

REFERENCE: Rinehart-Thompson, p 149

73. Which of the following is an example of an administrative safeguard?
    A. access control
    B. physical security of hardware
    C. firewall
    D. training

REFERENCE: Rinehart-Thompson, p 97

74. The physician office you go to has a data integrity issue. What does this mean?
    A. There has been unauthorized alteration of patient information.
    B. Someone in the practice has released information inappropriately.
    C. A break-in attempt has been identified.
    D. The user's access has not been defined.

REFERENCE: Rinehart-Thompson, p 94

75. You have been given some information that includes the patient's account number. Which statement is true?
    A. This is de-identified information because the patient's name and social security are not included in the data.
    B. This is not de-identified information, because it is possible to identify the patient.
    C. These data are individually identified data.
    D. These data are a limited data set.

REFERENCE: McWay (2014), pp 72, 242, 244

76. Which of the following is an example of a trigger that might be used to reduce auditing?
    A. A patient has not signed their notice of privacy practices.
    B. A patient and user have the same last name.
    C. A nurse is caring for a patient and reviews the patient's record.
    D. The patient is a Medicare patient.

REFERENCE: Sayles and Trawick, p 323

77. Bob submitted his resignation from Coastal Hospital. His last day is today. He should no longer have access to the EHR and other systems as of 5:00 PM today. The removal of his privileges is known as
    A. terminating access.
    B. isolating access.
    C. password management.
    D. sanction policy.

REFERENCE: Bowie and Green, p 293

78. The company's policy states that audit logs, access reports, and security incident reports should be reviewed daily. This review is known as
    A. a data criticality analysis.
    B. a workforce clearinghouse.
    C. an information system activity review.
    D. a risk analysis.

REFERENCE: Bowie and Green, p 293

79. If an authorization is missing a Social Security number, can it be valid?
    A. yes
    B. no
    C. only if the patient is a minor
    D. only if the patient is an adult

REFERENCE: McWay (2014), p 75

80. If the patient has agreed to be in the directory, which of the following statements would be true?
    A. The patient has given up the right to privacy.
    B. The patient's condition can be described in detail with family members but not others.
    C. The patient's condition can be described in general terms like "good" and "fair."
    D. The number of visitors is limited to people on the approved visitor list.

REFERENCE: LaTour, Eichenwald-Maki, and Oachs, p 316

81. Intrusion detection systems analyze
    A. authentications.
    B. network traffic.
    C. audit trails.
    D. firewalls.

REFERENCE: Rinehart-Thompson, p 93

82. The purpose of the notice of privacy practices is to
    A. notify the patient of uses of PHI.
    B. notify the patient of audits.
    C. report incidents to the OIG.
    D. notify researchers of allowable data use.

REFERENCE: Bowie and Green, pp 286–287
McWay (2014), pp 72–73
Sayles, p 808

83. You have been asked what should be done with the notice of privacy practice acknowledgment when the patient had been discharged before it was signed. Your response is to
    A. shred it.
    B. try to get it signed, and if not, to document the action taken.
    C. keep trying to get the document signed until you succeed, even if you must go to the patient's home.
    D. File the blank form in the chart.

REFERENCE: LaTour, Eichenwald-Maki, and Oachs, p 314

84. Our Web site was attacked by malware that overloaded it. What type of malware was this?
    A. phishing
    B. virus
    C. denial of service
    D. spyware

REFERENCE: Sayles & Trawick, p 326

85. Which of the following is a true statement about private key encryption?
    A. Public encryption uses a private and public key.
    B. The digital certificate shows that the keys are encrypted.
    C. Public key encryption requires both computers to have the same key.
    D. The sending computer uses the public key.

REFERENCE: Rinehart-Thomas, p 92

86. The facility had a security breach. The breach was identified on October 10, 2015. The investigation was completed on October 15, 2015. What is the deadline that the notification must be completed?
    A. 60 days from October 10
    B. 60 days from October 15
    C. 30 days from October 10
    D. 30 days from October 15

REFERENCE: Sayles, pp 826–827

87. Miles has asked you to explain the rights he has via HIPAA privacy standards. Which of the following is one of his HIPAA-given rights?
    A. He can review his bill.
    B. He can ask to be contacted at an alternative site.
    C. He can discuss financial arrangements with business office staff.
    D. He can ask a patient advocate to sit in on all appointments at the facility.

REFERENCE: LaTour, Eichenwald-Maki, and Oachs, pp 314–315
McWay (2014), p 104
Sayles, p 802

88. The patient calls and has a telephone consultation. Which of the following is true about notice of privacy practices?
    A. The patient must come in within 72 hours to sign the document.
    B. Telephone encounters are not allowed since the patient cannot be handed a notice of privacy practices.
    C. Telephone encounters are exempt from the requirement for providing the patient a notice of privacy practices.
    D. The notice of privacy practices can be mailed to the patient.

REFERENCE: Rinehart-Thompson, p 50

89. Before an employee can be given access to the EHR, someone has to determine what they have access to. What is this known as?
    A. workforce clearance procedure
    B. authentication
    C. health care clearinghouse
    D. authorization

REFERENCE: Rinehart-Thompson, p 101

90. Breach notification is required unless:
    A. the organization is a covered entity.
    B. the organization does not take Medicare patients.
    C. the probability of PHI being compromised is low.
    D. the hacker made an electronic download of the data.

REFERENCE: Rinehart-Thompson, p 150

91. You have to decide which type of firewall you want to use in your facility. Which of the following is one of your options?
   A. packet filter
   B. secure socket layer
   C. CCOW
   D. denial of service

REFERENCE: Abdelhak, p 319

92. You have to determine how likely a threat will occur. What is this assessment known as?
   A. control recommendation
   B. control analysis
   C. risk determination
   D. impact analysis

REFERENCE: Rinehart-Thompson, p 124

93. What type of digital signature uses encryption?
   A. digitized signature
   B. electronic signature
   C. digital signature
   D. encryption is not a part of digital signatures

REFERENCE: Sayles and Trawick, p 253

94. The police came to the HIM Department today and asked that a patient's right to an accounting of disclosure be suspended for two months. What is the proper response to this request?
   A. "I'm sorry officer, but privacy regulations do not allow us to do this."
   B. "I'm sorry officer but we can only do this for one month."
   C. "Certainly officer. We will take care of that right now."
   D. "Certainly officer. We will be glad to do that as soon as we have the request in writing."

REFERENCE: Bowie and Green, p 310

95. Which of the following set(s) is an appropriate use of the emergency access procedure?
   A. A patient is crashing. The attending physician is not in the hospital, so a physician who is available helps the patient.
   B. One of the nurses is at lunch. The nurse covering for her needs patient information.
   C. The coder who usually codes the emergency room charts is out sick and the charts are left on a desk in the ER admitting area.
   D. A and B.

REFERENCE: Bowie and Green, p 295

96. Today is August 30, 2016. When can the training records for the HIPAA privacy training being conducted today be destroyed?
   A. August 30, 2020
   B. August 30, 2021
   C. August 30, 2022
   D. August 30, 2023

REFERENCE: Sayles (2014), p 212

97. Which of the following statements are true?
   A. All patients must be given a notice of privacy practices.
   B. All patients except outpatients must be given a notice of privacy practices.
   C. All patients except inmates must be given a notice of privacy practices.
   D. All patients except home health patients must be given a notice of privacy practices.

REFERENCE: Bowie and Green, p 287

98. Which of the following is allowed by HIPAA?
    A. Releasing patient information to the patient's attorney without an authorization
    B. Letting a business associate use PHI in whatever manner they see fit
    C. Permitting a spouse to pick up medication for the patient
    D. Mandating that a health care facility can amend the health record of a patient at the patient's request

REFERENCE: Bowie and Green, p 287

99. You have been assigned the responsibility of performing an audit to confirm that all of the workforce's access is appropriate for their role in the organization. This process is called
    A. risk assessment.
    B. information system activity review.
    C. workforce clearance procedure.
    D. information access management.

REFERENCE: Sayles and Trawick, p 305

100. A home health care agency employee has contacted the Center for Medicare and Medicaid Services to report health care fraud. Patient information is provided in the report. Which of the following is true?
    A. This is a violation of the patient rights and the employee should be charged with a HIPAA violation.
    B. The disclosure is not a violation of HIPAA even if the employee made up the charges.
    C. The disclosure is not a violation of HIPAA if the information was provided in good faith.
    D. CMS can never access patient information.

REFERENCE: Bowie and Green, p 287

101. You work for an organization that publishes a health information management journal and provides clearinghouse services. What must you do?
    A. Have the same security plan for the entire organization.
    B. Separate the e-PHI from the noncovered entity portion of the organization.
    C. Train the journal staff on HIPAA security awareness.
    D. Follow the same rules in all parts of the organization.

REFERENCE: Sayles and Trawick, p 306

102. Robert Burchfield was recently caught accessing his wife's medical record. The system automatically notified the staff of a potential breach due to the same last name for the user and the patient. This was an example of a
    A. trigger.
    B. biometrics.
    C. telephone callback procedures.
    D. transmission security.

REFERENCE: Sayles and Trawick, p 323

103. John is allowed to delete patients in the EHR. Florence is not. They both have the same role in the organization. What is different?
    A. Their authentication
    B. Their permissions
    C. Their authorization
    D. Their understanding of the system

REFERENCE: McWay (2014), p 290

104. Critique this statement: A business associate has the right to use a health care facility's information beyond the scope of their agreement with the health care facility.
   A. This is a true statement because business associates can use the information for their main source of business as long as the patient's privacy is protected.
   B. This is a true statement as long as they have patient consent.
   C. This is a false statement because the HIPAA privacy rule states that to use it in their own business they must have the health care facility's approval.
   D. This is a false statement because it is prohibited by the HIPAA privacy rule.

REFERENCE: McWay (2016), p 226

105. Researchers can access patient information if it is
   A. protected health information.
   B. a limited data set.
   C. patient specific.
   D. related to identity theft.

REFERENCE: McWay, 223

106. A certification agency validates the use of encryption between two organization's websites. How do they validate it?
   A. portal
   B. hypertext markup language
   C. links
   D. digital certificate

REFERENCE: McWay, p 289

107. The information system has just notified you that someone has attempted to access the system inappropriately. This process is known as
   A. integrity
   B. intrusion protocol
   C. intrusion detection
   D. cryptography

REFERENCE: Sayles, p 1043

Answer Key for Health Information Privacy and Security

ANSWER	EXPLANATION
1. B	
2. C	The release of childbirth information is acceptable because it is related to the reason for admission. The mass mailing of samples violates giving out confidential information to outside agencies.
3. C	
4. A	
5. C	
6. C	
7. B	
8. B	
9. C	The person who recorded the documentation in question should be the one who authorizes the change. While these references may not explicitly state this, it does state that the form should have a place for the provider's signature and comments.
10. A	
11. B	
12. B	
13. D	
14. C	
15. C	
16. C	
17. A	
18. A	
19. C	
20. C	
21. B	
22. D	
23. D	Natural disasters, equipment failure, and human error are usually unintentional threats to security. Data theft is intentional.
24. A	
25. C	
26. B	
27. B	
28. C	
29. B	
30. B	
31. A	
32. D	
33. C	
34. A	
35. B	
36. A	
37. C	
38. C	
39. D	
40. D	
41. B	The request must be acted on within 60 days after receipt; however, the response may be extended once by 30 days, with a written statement with reason and response date.
42. A	
43. B	
44. D	
45. D	
46. C	
47. D	
48. B	
49. B	
50. A	
51. D	
52. C	
53. C	
54. C	
55. A	
56. D	
57. B	
58. B	
59. D	In some facilities, it is referred to as emergency mode operation rather than business continuity planning.
60. C	
61. C	
62. A	
63. A	
64. A	
65. C	
66. A	
67. D	
68. A	
69. D	
70. D	
71. B	
72. A	

Answer Key for Health Information Privacy and Security

ANSWER	EXPLANATION
73. D	
74. A	
75. B	
76. B	
77. A	
78. C	
79. A	
80. C	
81. B	
82. A	
83. B	
84. C	
85. A	
86. A	
87. B	
88. D	The Notice of Privacy must be written in plain English so that it can be understood.
89. A	
90. C	
91. B	
92. C	
93. C	
94. D	
95. D	
96. C	
97. C	
98. C	
99. C	
100. C	
101. B	
102. A	
103. B	
104. D	
105. B	
106. B	
107. C	

REFERENCES

Abdelhak, M., and Hanken, M. A. (2016). *Health information: Management of a strategic resource* (5th ed.). Philadelphia: W. B. Saunders.

Amatayakul, M. (2012). *Electronic health records a practical guide for professionals and organizations* (5th ed.). Chicago: American Health Information Management Association.

Bowie, M. J., and Green, M. A. (2016). *Essentials of health information management* (3rd ed.). Clifton Park, NY: Cengage Learning.

LaTour, K. M., Eichenwald-Maki, S., and Oachs, P. K. (2013). *Health information management: Concepts, principles, and practice* (4th ed.). Chicago: American Health Information Management Association.

McWay, D. C. (2016). *Legal and ethical aspects of health information management* (4th ed.). Clifton Park, NY: Cengage Learning.

McWay, D. C. (2014). *Today's health information management: An integrated approach* (2nd ed.). Clifton Park, NY: Cengage Learning.

Rinehart-Thompson, L. A. (2013). *Introduction to health information privacy and security*. Chicago: AHIMA Press.

Sayles, N. B. (2013). *Health information technology: An applied approach* (4th ed.). Chicago: AHIMA Press.

Sayles, N. B., and Trawick, K. (2014). *Introduction to computer systems for health information technology*. Chicago: AHIMA Press.

U.S. Department of Health and Human Services Office for Civil Rights. *Standards for Privacy of Individually Identifiable Health Information Security Standards for the Protection of Electronic Protected Health Information General Administrative Requirements, Including Civil Money Penalties: Procedures for Investigations, Imposition of Penalties, and Hearings Regulation Text* 45 CFR Parts 160 and 164 (Unofficial version, as amended through March 2013)
The complete suite of HIPAA Administrative Simplification Regulations can be found at 45 CFR Parts 160, 162, and 164, and includes:
Transactions and Code Set Standards
Identifier Standards
Privacy Rule
Security Rule
Enforcement Rule
Breach Notification Rule
http://www.hhs.gov/ocr/privacy/hipaa/administrative/combined/hipaa-simplification-201303.pdf

U.S. Office of Civil Rights. (n.d.). *For consumers.* Retrieved from http://www.hhs.gov/ocr/privacy/hipaa/understanding/consumers/index.html

Health Information Privacy and Security

Chapter Competencies

Question	RHIA Domain	RHIT Domain
1–57	2	2
58–107	2	N/A

XII. Health Law

Barbara W. Mosley, PhD, RHIA
Lon'Tejuana S. Cooper, PhD, RHIA, CPM

CASE STUDY #1

Dr. Roberts, an orthopedic surgeon, and Nurse Parrish, head nurse on the orthopedic surgery unit, have had an acrimonious working relationship for years. While making rounds on the unit, Dr. Roberts discovered that the physical therapy evaluation he had ordered for one of his patients had not been performed and became outraged. Even though he did not have proof, Dr. Roberts placed the blame for the missed evaluation with Nurse Parrish. Dr. Roberts wrote in the patient's medical record that Nurse Parrish failed to properly order the physical therapy evaluation because she was incompetent and could not be trusted to carry out even the simplest order. After having read Dr. Roberts's note, Nurse Parrish countered by making a disparaging remark about Dr. Roberts to the medical personnel at the nurses' station. Nurse Parrish stated that Dr. Roberts was the one who was incompetent and was responsible for the needless suffering of countless patients over the years.

1. Referring to Case Study #1, the written statement by Dr. Roberts about Nurse Parrish's professional competence in the patient's medical record can constitute
   A. libel.
   B. slander.
   C. perjury.
   D. defamation.

REFERENCE: Brodnik, p 99
LaTour, Eichenwald-Maki, and Oachs, p 305
McWay (2016), pp 82, 499
Pozgar, pp 85–87, 560
Roach, p 401

2. Referring to Case Study #1, the oral statement by Nurse Parrish about Dr. Roberts's professional practices at the nurses' station can constitute
   A. libel.
   B. slander.
   C. perjury.
   D. defamation.

REFERENCE: Brodnik, p 99
LaTour, Eichenwald-Maki, and Oachs, p 305
McWay (2016), pp 80, 415
Pozgar, p 600
Roach, p 401

3. Referring to Case Study #1, what should Dr. Roberts be reminded of regarding his notation in the patient's chart about Nurse Parrish?
   A. It is against the law to mention names of persons who are not actively attending to his patient.
   B. His action violates the 1974 Privacy Act.
   C. The medical record must not be used as a battleground against another professional.
   D. He should erase his note about Nurse Parrish because it is malicious.

REFERENCE: Brodnik, pp 6–8
Pozgar, pp 283, 297
Roach, pp 291–292

4. Which type of law is constituted by rules and principles determined by legislative bodies?
   A. statutory law C. common law
   B. administrative law D. case law

REFERENCE: Brodnik, pp 14–15
Bowie and Green, pp 265–267
LaTour, Eichenwald-Maki, and Oachs, pp 301, 950
McWay (2016), pp 8–10
McWay (2014), pp 50, 522
Pozgar, pp 16, 19, 582
Roach, pp 6–7

5. Which of the following elements of negligence must be present in order to recover damages?
   A. duty of care; breach of duty of care; value attached to injury is greater than a certain value (ordinarily $1,000); provisions of the HIPAA privacy rule have been met
   B. duty of care; breach of the duty of care; suffered an injury; value attached to injury is greater than a certain value (ordinarily $1,000)
   C. duty of care; breach of duty of care; suffered an injury; defendant's conduct caused the plaintiff harm
   D. breach of duty of care; suffered an injury; value attached to injury is greater than a certain value (ordinarily $1,000); provision of HIPAA privacy rule have been met

REFERENCE: Brodnik, pp 70–71, 75–76, 79
Bowie and Green, p 267
LaTour, Eichenwald-Maki, and Oachs, p 304
McWay (2016), p 65

6. When the physician failed to give the patient the lips of the famous actress as promised, the physician engaged in which of the following?
   A. slander C. libel
   B. a breach of contract D. invasion of privacy

REFERENCE: LaTour, Eichenwald-Maki, and Oachs, pp 307–308
McWay (2010), p 83
McWay (2014), p 64
Pozgar, p 87

7. Laws that limit the period during which legal action may be brought against another party are known as
   A. case law. C. statutes of limitations.
   B. summons. D. common law.

REFERENCE: Brodnik, pp 81–83
Bowie and Green, pp 94, 267
McWay (2016), pp 84–85, 416
McWay (2014), p 136
Pozgar, pp 90, 130, 582
Roach, pp 43–44

8. The protection of a patient's health information is addressed in each of the following EXCEPT
   A. Health Insurance Portability and Accountability Act.
   B. Privacy Act.
   C. Drug Abuse and Treatment Act.
   D. U.S. Patriot Act.

REFERENCE: Brodnik, pp 238–242, 247–248, 256, 263–264
Bowie and Green, pp 284–285
McWay (2016), pp 47, 285, 292
Pozgar, pp 26–27, 279–280
Roach, pp 104–106

9. In a court of law, Attorney A, the attorney for Sun City Hospital, introduces the medical record from the hospital as evidence. However, Attorney B, the attorney for the defendant, objects on the grounds that the medical record is subject to the hearsay rule, which prohibits its admission as evidence. Attorney B's objection is overridden. Why?
   A. The medical record does not belong to the hospital; therefore, the hospital has no right to release the medical record as evidence.
   B. It would violate physician–patient privilege, even though the patient signed a proper release of information form.
   C. The doctrine of *res ipsa loquitur* prevails; therefore, reference to the medical record is moot.
   D. The medical record may be admitted as business records or as an explicit exception to hearsay rule.

REFERENCE: Brodnik, pp 57–58, 125, 127
Bowie and Green, pp 270–271
McWay (2016), pp 50–51, 409
Pozgar, pp 120–122
Roach, pp 383–384

10. Medical record information may be exempt from the Freedom of Information Act requirements if the request for information meets the test of being an unwarranted invasion of personal privacy. Which of the following is NOT one of the conditions of the test?
   A. The information must be contained in a personal, medical, or similar file.
   B. The information is generated from federally funded research conducted by a private health care organization.
   C. Disclosure of the information constitutes an invasion of personal privacy.
   D. The severity of the invasion must outweigh the public's interest in disclosure.

REFERENCE: Brodnik, pp 154, 254
Bowie and Green, p 284
LaTour and Eichenwald-Maki, pp 310–311
McWay (2016), p 177
Roach, pp 123–127

11. The doctrine that the decisions of the court should stand as precedents for future guidance is
    - A. res ipsa loquitur.
    - B. respondeat superior.
    - C. stare decisis.
    - D. statute of limitations.

REFERENCE: Brodnik, p 17
Bowie and Green, p 257
McWay (2016), pp 12–13, 15, 18, 415
Pozgar, pp 18, 1582
Roach, pp 16–18

12. The body of law founded on custom, natural justice and reason, and sanctioned by usage and judicial decision is known as
    - A. common law.
    - B. lien law.
    - C. constitutional law.
    - D. statutory law.

REFERENCE: Brodnik, pp 17, 20
Bowie and Green, pp 265–267
LaTour and Eichenwald-Maki, pp 300–301, 903
McWay (2016), pp 12, 405
McWay (2014), p 50
Pozgar, pp 16–19, 578
Roach, pp 10, 545

CASE STUDY #2

You are the Director of the Health Information Management Department for Bayshore Hospital. A former patient of the hospital, Barbara Masters, is suing the hospital for negligent care of an infected decubitus ulcer. You are asked by Barbara's attorney to provide sworn verbal testimony and/or written answers to questions.

13. Referring to Case Study #2, Barbara Masters is the ____________ in this case.
    - A. appellant
    - B. appellee
    - C. defendant
    - D. plaintiff

REFERENCE: Brodnik, p 35
Bowie and Green, pp 265, 267
LaTour and Eichenwald-Maki, pp 302–303, 939
McWay (2016), pp 31, 413
McWay (2014), p 60
Pozgar, pp 108, 531, 581

14. Referring to Case Study #2, Bayshore Hospital is the ________________ in this case.
    - A. appellant
    - B. appellee
    - C. defendant
    - D. plaintiff

REFERENCE: Brodnik, p 35
Bowie and Green, pp 265, 337
LaTour and Eichenwald-Maki, pp 302–303, 909
McWay (2016), pp 31, 406
McWay (2014), p 60
Pozgar, pp 108, 578

15. Referring to Case Study #2, the sworn verbal testimony you are asked to provide is called a(n)
    A. interrogatory.
    B. deposition.
    C. physical and mental examination.
    D. court order.

REFERENCE: Brodnik, p 28
Bowie and Green, pp 265, 337
McWay (2016), pp 34, 39, 57, 406
Pozgar, p 578

16. Referring to Case Study #2, the written answers to questions you have been asked to provide are known as a(n)
    A. interrogatory.
    B. deposition.
    C. physical and mental examination.
    D. court order.

REFERENCE: Brodnik, pp 29, 41
Bowie and Green, pp 265, 342
LaTour and Eichenwald-Maki, pp 303, 925
McWay (2016), pp 34, 40, 57, 410
Pozgar, p 580
Roach, p 375

17. Referring to Case Study #2, what phase of the lawsuit are you involved in?
    A. pretrial conference
    B. trial
    C. discovery
    D. appeal

REFERENCE: Brodnik, p 35
Bowie and Green, pp 265, 338
LaTour and Eichenwald-Maki, p 325
McWay (2016), pp 34, 57, 263, 407
McWay (2014), pp 62–63
Pozgar, pp 110–111, 579
Roach, pp 374–375

18. Which of the following claims of negligence fits into the category of *res ipsa loquitur*?
    A. incorrect administration of anesthesia
    B. failure to refer patient to a specialist
    C. leaving a foreign body inside a patient
    D. improper use of x-rays

REFERENCE: Brodnik, pp 71–72
Bowie and Green, pp 267, 350
McWay (2016), pp 75–76, 414
Pozgar, pp 56, 115–117, 582

19. The failure to obtain the written consent of the patient before performing a surgical procedure may constitute
    A. battery.
    B. contempt.
    C. libel.
    D. malpractice.

REFERENCE: Brodnik, pp 115–116
Bowie and Green, p 333
LaTour and Eichenwald-Maki, p 305
McWay (2016), pp 80, 404
McWay (2014), p 64
Pozgar, pp 43–44, 577

20. The fee paid for reimbursement for expenses incurred from providing health information whether for subpoena or reproduction by health care providers is determined by the
    A. American Health Information Management Association.
    B. hospitals and lawyers.
    C. statute or court rules.
    D. plaintiff and defendant lawyers.

REFERENCE: Brodnik, pp 262–263
McWay (2010), p 209

21. Who determines the retention period for health records?
    A. state and federal governments
    B. medical staff
    C. city and state governments
    D. commercial storage vendors

REFERENCE: Brodnik, pp 52, 140–146
Bowie and Green, p 93
LaTour and Eichenwald-Maki, pp 274–275
McWay (2016), pp 159–161, 163, 414
McWay (2014), pp 53, 136, 400, 520
Pozgar, p 282
Roach, pp 40–41

22. The extent to which the HIPAA privacy rule may regulate an individual's rights of access is not meant to preempt other existing federal laws and regulations. This means that if an individual's rights of access
    A. are less under another existing federal law, HIPAA must follow the directions of that law.
    B. are refused by a federal facility, HIPAA must also refuse the individual of the access.
    C. are greater under another applicable federal law, the individual should be afforded the greater access.
    D. are greater under another existing federal law, HIPAA can obstruct freedoms of the other federal law when using electronic health records.

REFERENCE: Brodnik, pp 186, 271
LaTour and Eichenwald-Maki, p 283

CASE STUDY #3

A 73-year-old male was admitted to the Sunset Nursing Facility with senility, cataracts, and S/P cerebrovascular accident with right-side hemiplegia. On his second day at the facility, the resident was discovered to have extensive thermal burns on his buttocks and legs by one of the facility's attendants.

23. Referring to Case Study #3, the resident's family brought legal action against the nursing facility for
    A. medical abandonment.
    B. vicarious liability.
    C. assault and battery.
    D. negligence.

REFERENCE: Brodnik, pp 69–71
Bowie and Green, pp 267, 345
LaTour and Eichenwald-Maki, pp 304–305, 933
McWay (2016), pp 71–72, 412
McWay (2014), p 65
Pozgar, pp 32–40, 150–152, 581

24. Referring to Case Study #3, which of the following can the attorney of the resident's family also use as a basis for the lawsuit and why?
    A. The doctrine of *res ipsa loquitur* because it allows the plaintiff to shift the burden of proof to the defendant because direct evidence is available.
    B. The doctrine of charitable immunity because the nursing facility is a private institution and is shielded from liability for any torts committed on its property.
    C. The Good Samaritan Statutes because they protect the Director of Nursing, an employee of the nursing facility, who was not present when the injury occurred.
    D. The failure to warn theory because the doctor did not inform the resident's family that the resident was in danger at the nursing facility.

REFERENCE: Brodnik, pp 71–72
Bowie and Green, pp 267, 350
McWay (2016), pp 75–76, 414
McWay (2014), p 65
Pozgar, pp 56, 115–117, 582

25. In a negligence or malpractice case, all of the following elements must be present in order to shift the burden of proof onto the defendant EXCEPT the
    A. event would not normally have occurred in the absence of negligence.
    B. health care facility does not have a risk management program.
    C. defendant had exclusive control over the instrumentality that caused the injury.
    D. plaintiff did not contribute to the injury.

REFERENCE: Brodnik, pp 70–71
LaTour and Eichenwald-Maki, pp 304–305
McWay (2016), pp 71–75
McWay (2014), p 65
Pozgar, pp 33–41

26. When a health care facility fails to investigate the qualifications of a physician hired to work as an independent contractor in the emergency room and is accused of negligence, the health care facility can be held liable under
    A. respondeat superior.
    B. corporate negligence.
    C. contributory negligence.
    D. general negligence.

REFERENCE: Brodnik, p 74
LaTour and Eichenwald-Maki, pp 329–330
McWay (2016), pp 77–78
McWay (2013), p 66
Pozgar, pp 150–152

27. What source or document is considered the "supreme law of the land"?
    A. Bill of Rights
    B. Supreme Court decisions
    C. presidential power
    D. Constitution of the United States

REFERENCE: Brodnik, pp 14–15
LaTour and Eichenwald-Maki, p 300
McWay (2014), p 50
Pozgar, p 19

28. Hospitals that destroy their own medical records must have a policy that
    A. ensures records are destroyed and confidentiality is protected.
    B. notifies the physicians when the records of their patients are destroyed.
    C. states that all records are destroyed annually.
    D. ensures that the type of equipment to be used for destruction of records is properly maintained.

REFERENCE: Brodnik, p 147
Bowie and Green, pp 96–97, 349
LaTour and Eichenwald-Maki, p 276
McWay (2016), pp 164–166
McWay (2014), pp 36–139
Roach, pp 49–50

29. A written authorization from the patient releasing copies of his or her medical records is required by all of the following EXCEPT
    A. the patient's attorney.
    B. a physician requesting copies from another physician.
    C. an insurance company.
    D. the hospital attorney for the facility where the patient is treated.

REFERENCE: Brodnik, pp 163–164
Bowie and Green, p 291
LaTour and Eichenwald-Maki, pp 312–324
McWay (2016), pp 207–208

30. Traditionally, the medical record is accepted as being the property of the
    - A. patient's guardian.
    - B. court.
    - C. institution.
    - D. patient.

REFERENCE: Brodnik, pp 239–241
Bowie and Green, pp 72–73
LaTour and Eichenwald-Maki, p 312
McWay (2016), pp 194–196
McWay (2014), pp 73–75
Pozgar, p 279

31. The ownership of the information contained in the physical medical/health record is considered to belong to the
    - A. patient.
    - B. hospital.
    - C. physician.
    - D. insurance company.

REFERENCE: Bowie and Green, pp 72–73
LaTour and Eichenwald-Maki, p 312
McWay (2016), pp 194–196
McWay (2014), pp 73–76
Pozgar, p 279

32. When developing a record retention policy, the HIM professionals should consider all of the following EXCEPT
    - A. current storage space.
    - B. uses of and need for information.
    - C. all applicable statutes and regulations.
    - D. the thickness of the records.

REFERENCE: Brodnik, pp 52, 146–147, 149
Bowie and Green, p 94
LaTour and Eichenwald-Maki, pp 276–280
McWay (2016), pp 160–163
McWay (2014), pp 53, 136, 400, 520
Pozgar, pp 282–283

33. If the patient record is involved in litigation and the physician requests to make a change to that record, what should the HIM professional do?
    - A. Refer request to legal counsel.
    - B. Allow the change to occur.
    - C. Notify the patient.
    - D. Say the record is unavailable.

REFERENCE: Brodnik, pp 138–140
Bowie and Green, pp 84–85
McWay (2016), pp 157–158
Pozgar, pp 287–288

34. One of the greatest threats to the confidentiality of health data is
    A. when medical information is reviewed as a part of quality assurance activities.
    B. disclosure of information for purposes not authorized in writing by the patient.
    C. lack of written authorization by the patient.
    D. when medical information is used for research or education.

REFERENCE: Bowie and Green, p 271
McWay (2016), pp 202–208
McWay (2014), pp 71–72

35. All of the following are areas in which electronically stored information, for example, the electronic health record, differs from paper-based information EXCEPT
    A. volume.
    B. metadata.
    C. variety of sources.
    D. confidentiality.

REFERENCE: Brodnik, p 46
McWay (2016), pp 34–35
McWay (2014), p 62

36. Spoliation is the term that refers to the wrongful destruction of evidence or the failure to preserve property, which addresses which of the following methods of discovery?
    A. interrogatories
    B. deposition
    C. e-discovery
    D. request for admissions

REFERENCE: Brodnik, pp 50–51
LaTour, Eichenwald-Maki, and Oachs, p 325
McWay (2016), pp 34–35

37. What type of testimony is inappropriate for a health information manager serving as custodian of the record when he or she is called to be a witness in court?
    A. whether the record is in the practitioner's possession
    B. title and position held in the health care facility
    C. whether the medical record was made in the usual course of business
    D. interpretation of documentation in the record

REFERENCE: Brodnik, pp 29–31

38. Internal disclosures of patient information for patient care purposes should not be granted
    A. to the facility's legal counsel.
    B. to the attending physician.
    C. on a need to know basis.
    D. to a family member who is a registered nurse at the facility.

REFERENCE: Bowie and Green, pp 271, 275
McWay (2014), pp 69–75

Case Study #4

William is a 16-year-old male who lives at home with his parents and works part-time as a dishwasher at one of the local restaurants. While emptying the dishwasher, William is severely scalded and rendered unconscious. He is taken to the emergency room of the local acute care hospital for emergency treatment.

39. Referring to Case Study #4, given the emergency of the situation, who should the health care provider seek consent from in order to provide treatment to William?
    A. the employer
    B. the parents
    C. the patient
    D. no consent is needed for emergency care

REFERENCE: Brodnik, pp 99–100
LaTour, Eichenwald-Maki, and Oachs, pp 317–319
McWay (2016), pp 187–188
Pozgar, pp 312, 314
Roach, pp 89–91

40. Referring to Case Study #4, in order to release information to his employer, the hospital must receive a
    A. consent signed by the patient.
    B. court order.
    C. consent signed by the doctor.
    D. consent signed by the patient's parent.

REFERENCE: Brodnik, pp 244–245, 255
LaTour, Eichenwald-Maki, and Oachs, p 317
McWay (2016), p 186
Pozgar, p 314

41. A valid authorization for the disclosure of health information should not be
    A. dated prior to discharge of the patient.
    B. in writing.
    C. addressed to the health care provider.
    D. signed by the patient.

REFERENCE: Brodnik, pp 259–260
LaTour, Eichenwald-Maki, and Oachs, p 317

42. Internal disclosures of patient information for patient care purposes should be granted
    A. to legal counsel.
    B. on a need to know basis.
    C. to any physician on staff.
    D. to a family member who is an employee.

REFERENCE: Brodnik, pp 176–177
Bowie and Green, p 275
LaTour, Eichenwald-Maki, and Oachs, p 319
McWay (2016), pp 99, 102, 203–204
McWay (2014), pp 69–75

43. According to AHIMA's Position on Transmission of Health Information, the health information manager should engage in all of the following to ensure that information is properly sent via facsimile transmission EXCEPT
    A. to always follow up by sending the original record by mail.
    B. to preprogram into the machine the number of destination sites.
    C. encrypt the data if public channels are used for electronic transmittal.
    D. ask the sender to contact the recipient prior to and after transmission.

REFERENCE: Brodnik, p 261
Roach, pp 492–495

44. All of the following need a proper authorization to access a patient's health information EXCEPT
    A. local and state law enforcement officers.
    B. IRS agents.
    C. medical examiners or coroners.
    D. FBI agents.

REFERENCE: Bowie and Green, p 289
LaTour, Eichenwald-Maki, and Oachs, pp 312–324
McWay (2016), pp 200–201

45. One best practice to follow in order to establish safeguards for the security and confidentiality of a patient's information when a person makes a request for his or her records in person is to
    A. ask the requester for identification and the request in writing.
    B. refuse the request.
    C. refer the requester to the facility's attorney.
    D. charge an exorbitant fee.

REFERENCE: Brodnik, pp 258–260
Roach, pp 239–241

46. Which of the following acts was passed to stimulate the development of standards to facilitate electronic maintenance and transmission of health information?
    A. Health Insurance for the Aged
    B. Health Insurance Portability and Accountability Act
    C. Conditions of Participation
    D. Hospital Survey and Construction Act

REFERENCE: Brodnik, pp 155–156
Bowie and Green, pp 10, 320
LaTour, Eichenwald-Maki, and Oachs, pp 151–152, 309–310
McWay (2016), p 161
McWay (2014), pp 68–70
Pozgar, pp 27, 282

47. The premise that charitable institutions could be held blameless for their negligent acts is known as
   A. doctrine of respondeat superior.
   B. doctrine of *res ipsa loquitur*.
   C. doctrine of charitable immunity.
   D. negligence factor.

REFERENCE: Brodnik, pp 291–292
McWay (2016), pp 85, 405
Pozgar, pp 151, 578
Roach, pp 10–11

48. Under traditional rules of evidence, a medical/health record is considered ______________ and is ___________________ into evidence.
   A. hearsay; admissible
   B. hearsay; inadmissible
   C. reliable; admissible
   D. reliable; inadmissible

REFERENCE: Brodnik, pp 56–58
Bowie and Green, pp 270–271
LaTour, Eichenwald-Maki, and Oachs, p 324
McWay (2016), pp 50–51, 409
Roach, pp 383–385

49. Substance abuse records cannot be redisclosed by a receiving facility to another health care facility unless the
   A. patient expires at the receiving facility.
   B. charge nurse signs the release form.
   C. physician signs the DNR form.
   D. patient gives written consent.

REFERENCE: McWay (2016), pp 232–233

50. Who is legally responsible for obtaining the patient's informed consent for surgery?
   A. the admissions clerk
   B. the surgeon performing the surgery
   C. the nurse
   D. medical records personnel

REFERENCE: Brodnik, pp 116
Bowie and Green, pp 129, 132
McWay (2016), pp 188–189
McWay (2014), pp 76–77
Pozgar, pp 199–200
Roach, p 74

51. With regard to confidentiality, when HIM functions are outsourced (i.e., record copying, microfilming, or transcription), the HIM professional should confirm that the outside contractor's
    A. costs are not prohibitive, thus compromising confidentiality.
    B. hours of operation permit easy access by all health care providers.
    C. is contractually bound to handle confidential information appropriately by means of a signed business associate agreement.
    D. is located in an easy to find place.

REFERENCE: Brodnik, pp 158–159
McWay (2016), pp 215–216

52. A 21-year-old employee of National Services was treated in an acute care hospital for an illness unrelated to work. A representative from the personnel department of National Services calls to request information regarding the employee's diagnosis. What would be the appropriate course of action?
    A. Request that the personnel office send an authorization for release of information that is signed and dated by the patient.
    B. Require parental consent.
    C. Release the information because the employer is paying the patient's bill.
    D. Call the patient to obtain verbal permission.

REFERENCE: Brodnik, pp 244–245, 255
Bowie and Green, pp 291–292
LaTour, Eichenwald-Maki, and Oachs, pp 316–317

53. *Darling v. Charleston Community Memorial Hospital* is considered one of the benchmark cases in health care because it was with this case that the doctrine of _______________ was eliminated for nonprofit hospitals.
    A. charitable immunity
    B. corporate negligence
    C. professional negligence
    D. contributory negligence

REFERENCE: Brodnik, pp 291–292
Bowie and Green, p 267
McWay (2016), p 77
Pozgar, pp 150–152

54. All of the following are elements of a contract EXCEPT
    A. offer/communication.
    B. duty.
    C. price/consideration.
    D. acceptance.

REFERENCE: Brodnik, p 83
LaTour, Eichenwald-Maki, and Oachs, pp 307–308
McWay (2016), p 5
Pozgar, pp 87–88

55. A valid authorization for release of information contains
    A. the name, agency, or institution to which the information is to be provided.
    B. the name of the hospital or provider who is releasing the medical information.
    C. the date and signature of the patient or the patient's authorized representative.
    D. All of these answers apply.

REFERENCE: Brodnik, pp 259–262
LaTour, Eichenwald-Maki, and Oachs, p 317
McWay (2016), pp 202–203

56. In which of the following circumstances would release of information without the patient's authorization be permissible?
    A. release to an attorney
    B. release to third-party payers
    C. release to state workers' compensation agencies
    D. release to insurance companies

REFERENCE: Brodnik, pp 170–175, 281–282
Bowie and Green, p 291
LaTour, Eichenwald-Maki, and Oachs, p 318
McWay (2016), pp 202–209

57. Who decides whether all or portions of the medical record will be received in evidence in a court of law?
    A. presiding judge/court
    B. subpoenaing attorney
    C. clerk of the court
    D. defendant

REFERENCE: Brodnik, p 44
McWay (2016), p 42

58. Which of the following health care systems have to comply with the requirements of the Freedom of Information Act?
    A. private hospitals
    B. physicians' offices
    C. veterans' hospitals
    D. single-day surgery clinics

REFERENCE: Brodnik, p 157
LaTour, Eichenwald-Maki, and Oachs, p 310
McWay (2016), p 177
Roach, p 123

59. Which of the following measures should a health care facility incorporate into its institution-wide security plan to protect the confidentiality of the patient record?
    A. verification of employee identification
    B. locked access to data processing and record areas
    C. use of unique computer passwords, key cares, or biometric identification
    D. All of these answers apply.

REFERENCE: Brodnik, pp 199–200
Bowie and Green, pp 282–283
LaTour, Eichenwald-Maki, and Oachs, p 188
McWay (2016), pp 289, 291–295
Roach, pp 462–470

60. A signed consent for release of information dated December 1, 2010, is received with a request for the chart from the patient's admission of 12/5/2010. Indicate the appropriate response from the options below.
    A. Request another authorization that is dated closer but prior to the admission date.
    B. Request another authorization dated after the discharge date.
    C. Release the requested information.
    D. Call the patient for a verbal authorization.

REFERENCE: Brodnik, pp 168–171
LaTour, Eichenwald-Maki, and Oachs, p 317
McWay (2016), p 204

61. Willful disregard of a subpoena is considered
    A. breach of contract.
    B. abuse of process.
    C. contributory negligence.
    D. contempt of court.

REFERENCE: Brodnik, p 30
McWay (2016), p 204
McWay (2014), pp 77–78
Pozgar, p 115
Roach, p 322

62. HIM personnel charged with the responsibility of bringing a medical record to court would ordinarily do so in answer to a
    A. personal subpoena.
    B. deposition.
    C. subpoena duces tecum.
    D. judgment.

REFERENCE: Brodnik, p 31
Bowie and Green, p 289
McWay (2016), pp 40–41, 54, 416
McWay (2014), p 77
Pozgar, p 115
Roach, p 317

63. HIPAA requires that certain covered entities provide every patient a Notice of Privacy Practices that sets forth all of the following EXCEPT
    A. covered entities provide every patient with its annual business report.
    B. how covered entities may use and disclose PHI.
    C. patient's rights regarding the covered entities' uses and disclosures.
    D. covered entities' obligations for protecting the patient's PHI.

REFERENCE: Brodnik, pp 165–166
Bowie and Green, p 273
LaTour, Eichenwald-Maki, and Oachs, pp 244, 314
McWay (2016), pp 196–205
McWay (2014), pp 72–73, 274, 441–450
Roach, pp 218–222

64. A record that has been requested by subpoena duces tecum is currently located at an off-site microfilm company. By contacting the microfilm provider, you learn that the microfilm is ready and the original copy of the record still exists. What legal requirement would compel you to produce the original record for the court?
    A. best evidence rule
    B. hearsay rule
    C. motion to quash
    D. subpoena instanter

REFERENCE: Brodnik, pp 56–57
Roach, pp 487–488

65. Under which category of law would Marleana Harrison bring a cause of action against Dr. Billy Ray for disclosing information regarding her previous physical examination to his wife, Jana Ray, who is Ms. Harrison's hairstylist?
    A. administrative law
    B. criminal law
    C. private law
    D. procedural law

REFERENCE: Brodnik, p 14
McWay (2016), pp 45–46
McWay (2014), pp 49–50
Pozgar, pp 15–16
Roach, p 2

66. As a general rule, a person making a report in good faith and under statutory command (e.g., on child abuse, communicable diseases, births, deaths, etc.) is
    A. not protected from liability claims.
    B. subject to penalties imposed by federal law.
    C. subject to penalties imposed by state law.
    D. protected.

REFERENCE: Brodnik, pp 67–68
Bowie and Green, p 288
LaTour, Eichenwald-Maki, and Oachs, p 313
McWay (2016), pp 217–218
Pozgar, pp 323–324
Roach, pp 247–248

67. According to AHIMA and AHA guidelines, which of the following would be an acceptable authorization for release of information from the medical record of an adult, mentally competent patient hospitalized from 4/16/2011 to 5/10/2011? An authorization dated
    A. 7/10/2013 and presented 7/15/2013
    B. 5/09/2013 and presented 1/15/2014
    C. 3/10/2013 and presented 5/15/2013
    D. 2/15/2013 and presented 1/10/2013

REFERENCE: Brodnik, pp 168–170
Bowie and Green, pp 122, 124–125
McWay (2016), pp 96–98, 203
McWay (2014), p 73

68. Which would be the better "best practice" for handling fax transmission of a physician's orders?
    A. Treat faxed orders like verbal orders and require authentication of the orders by appropriate medical staff within the required period.
    B. Faxed orders should be placed on the patient's chart immediately upon receipt after the head nurse signs the orders.
    C. Wait 24 hours before placing faxed orders on the patient's chart to ensure that the orders are legitimate.
    D. Faxed orders should never be accepted.

REFERENCE: Brodnik, pp 131, 386
Bowie and Green, p 81
Roach, p 494

69. The *Darling v. Charleston Community Memorial Hospital* case established the following doctrine for hospitals to observe and changed the way hospitals dealt with liability.
    A. doctrine of respondeat superior
    B. doctrine of continuing wrong
    C. doctrine of *res ipsa loquitur*
    D. doctrine of corporate negligence

REFERENCE: Brodnik, pp 291–292
Bowie and Green, p 257
LaTour, Eichenwald-Maki, and Oachs, pp 329–330
McWay (2016), pp 50–51
Pozgar, p 150

70. HIM professionals have a duty to maintain health information that complies with
    A. state statutes.
    B. federal statutes.
    C. accreditation standards.
    D. All of these answers apply.

REFERENCE: Brodnik, p 128
Bowie and Green, p 273
LaTour, Eichenwald-Maki, and Oachs, p 328
McWay (2016), pp 147, 201
McWay (2014), pp 70–71
Roach, pp 40–41

71. In general, which of the following statements is correct?
    A. When federal and state laws conflict, valid federal laws supersede state laws.
    B. When federal and state laws conflict, valid state laws supersede federal laws.
    C. When federal and state laws conflict, valid local laws supersede federal and state laws.
    D. When federal and state laws conflict, valid corporate policies supersede federal and state laws.

REFERENCE: Brodnik, p 128
LaTour, Eichenwald-Maki, and Oachs, p 300
McWay (2016), p 201
McWay (2014), p 70

72. Which of the following statements is correct regarding HIPAA preemption analysis?
    A. If the state law that recognizes a patient's right to health care information privacy is more stringent than the HIPAA federal rule, then the state law prevails.
    B. State law regarding a patient's right to health care information privacy can never prevail over the HIPAA federal rule.
    C. If a state law that recognizes a patient's right to health care information privacy is more stringent than the HIPAA federal rule, then the courts must decide which shall prevail.
    D. Even if the state law that recognizes a patient's right to health care information privacy is more stringent than the HIPAA federal rule, the HIPAA federal rule will still prevail.

REFERENCE: Brodnik, pp 186, 271
Bowie and Green, p 283
LaTour, Eichenwald-Maki, and Oachs, p 313
McWay (2016), p 201
McWay (2014), p 70
Roach, pp 100–101

73. The minimum record retention period for patients who are minors is
    A. age of majority.
    B. age of majority plus the statute of limitations.
    C. 5 years past treatment.
    D. 2 years past treatment.

REFERENCE: Brodnik, pp 141–146
Bowie and Green, p 94
McWay (2014) pp 53, 136, 400, 520
Roach, pp 43–44

74. In which type of facility does the Privacy Act of 1974 permit patients to request amendments to their medical record?
    A. private proprietary health care facility
    B. mental health and chemical dependency facility
    C. university-based teaching facility
    D. Department of Defense health care facility

REFERENCE: Brodnik, p 157
Bowie and Green, p 285
LaTour, Eichenwald-Maki, and Oachs, p 310
Pozgar, pp 279–280

75. What advice should be given to a physician who has just informed you that she just discovered that a significant portion of a discharge summary she dictated last month was left out?
    A. Squeeze in the information omitted by writing in available spaces such as the top, bottom, and side margins.
    B. Dictate the portion omitted with the heading "Discharge Summary—Addendum" and make a reference to the addendum with a note that is dated and signed on the initial Discharge Summary (e.g., "9/1/11—See Addendum to Discharge Summary"—Signature).
    C. Redictate the discharge summary and replace the old one with the new one.
    D. Inform the physician that nothing can be done about the situation.

REFERENCE: Brodnik, pp 138–140
Bowie and Green, pp 84–85
McWay (2016), p 177
Roach, p 70

76. While performing routine quantitative analysis of a record, a medical record employee finds an incident report in the record. The employee brings this to the attention of her supervisor. Which best practice should the supervisor follow to deal with this situation?
    A. Remove the incident report and send it to the patient.
    B. Tell the employee to leave the report in the record.
    C. Remove the incident report and have nursing personnel transfer all documentation from the report to the medical record.
    D. Refer this record to the Risk Manager for further review and removal of the incident report.

REFERENCE: Brodnik, pp 295–297
Bowie and Green, p 88
LaTour, Eichenwald-Maki, and Oachs, p 335
McWay (2016), pp 262–263
McWay (2014), p 132
Pozgar, pp 329–330
Roach, p 393

77. Which of the following is considered confidential information if the patient is seeking treatment in a substance abuse facility?
    A. patient's name
    B. patient's address
    C. patient's diagnosis
    D. All of these answers apply.

REFERENCE: Brodnik, pp 247–250
Bowie and Green, pp 284–285

78. In electronic health records, authentication may be achieved by
    A. handwritten signature.
    B. digital signature.
    C. verbal statement.
    D. all of the above

REFERENCE: Brodnik, pp 133–135
Bowie and Green, pp 26, 278
LaTour, Eichenwald-Maki, and Oachs, p 87
McWay (2016), p 286
McWay (2014), p 125

79. It is common practice to forgo patient authorization for the release of information when the
    A. patient is an employee.
    B. patient is a physician.
    C. patient has a direct transfer from the hospital to a long-term care facility.
    D. patient is incompetent.

REFERENCE: LaTour, Eichenwald-Maki, and Oachs, p 319

80. Many states have recognized a minor's right to seek treatment without parental consent in all of the following situations EXCEPT a(n)
    A. minor seeking treatment for breast reduction.
    B. minor seeking treatment for a sexually transmitted disease.
    C. minor seeking treatment for alcohol and substance abuse.
    D. emancipated minor seeking treatment for breast enlargement.

REFERENCE: Brodnik, pp 113–115
Pozgar, pp 313–314
Roach, pp 89–90

81. When a health information professional (record custodian) brings the medical record to court in response to a subpoena duces tecum, it is his or her responsibility to
   A. confirm whether or not the record is complete, accurate, and made in the ordinary course of business.
   B. present the case favorably for the patient involved.
   C. leave the original record in the possession of the plaintiff's attorney.
   D. explain details of the medical treatment given to the patient.

REFERENCE: Brodnik, pp 30–31, 54–55
McWay (2016), p 52

82. When substituting a photocopy of the original record in response to legal process, which of the following can be helpful in convincing the court to accept the photocopy as a true and exact copy of the original?
   A. certificate of authentication
   B. consent from the patient
   C. consent from the hospital administrator
   D. correspondence from the attending physician

REFERENCE: Brodnik, pp 33–34, 54–55

83. Which of the following should be required to sign a confidentiality statement before having access to patients' medical information?
   A. nursing students
   B. medical students
   C. HIM students
   D. All of these answers apply.

REFERENCE: Brodnik, pp 158, 215, 442
Bowie and Green, pp 43–48
Pozgar, pp 290–292

84. All of the following have laws and regulations addressing medical records EXCEPT
   A. accrediting agencies.
   B. corporate law.
   C. state laws.
   D. federal laws.

REFERENCE: Brodnik, pp 156–158
Bowie and Green, p 265

85. The proper method for correcting a documentation error in a medical record is for the author to
   A. draw an "X" through the incorrect documentation.
   B. draw a single line through the incorrect information, date and initial the change.
   C. white it out, date and initial the change.
   D. remove the form from the chart and add a revised form.

REFERENCE: Brodnik, pp 138–140
Bowie and Green, pp 84–85
McWay (2016), p 157
Pozgar, p 297
Roach, p 70

86. Dr. Vincent Orangeburg performed a cesarean on Mrs. Greentree, who later returned to the emergency room 5 days after the surgery with abdominal pain. An x-ray performed revealed that a sponge was left in the lower abdominal cavity from the cesarean. Which case law principle can be used in a lawsuit against Dr. Orangeburg?
   A. res gestae
   B. star decis
   C. res ipsa loquitur
   D. res judicata

REFERENCE: Brodnik, pp 71–72
Bowie and Green, p 267
McWay (2016), p 75
McWay (2014), pp 65–66
Pozgar, pp 56, 115–117

87. To be admitted into court as evidence, medical records or health information are introduced as
   A. torts or contracts.
   B. privileged information.
   C. business records or exception to hearsay rule.
   D. product liability.

REFERENCE: Brodnik, pp 44–45
Bowie and Green, pp 270–271
LaTour, Eichenwald-Maki, and Oachs, p 333
McWay (2016), p 51
Roach, pp 383–386

88. A health care organization's compliance plans should not only focus on regulatory compliance, but also have a
   A. strong personnel component that reduces the rapid turnover of nursing personnel.
   B. coding compliance program that prevents fraudulent coding and billing.
   C. component that increases the security of medical records.
   D. substantial program that increases the availability of clinical data.

REFERENCE: Brodnik, pp 316–318
Bowie and Green, p 323
LaTour, Eichenwald-Maki, and Oachs, pp 453–454
McWay (2016), p 318
McWay (2014), pp 81, 158
Pozgar, pp 332–333

89. A written consent from the patient is required from which of the following entities in order to learn a patient's HIV status?
   A. insurance companies
   B. emergency medical personnel
   C. spouse or needle partner
   D. health care workers

REFERENCE: Brodnik, pp 250–251
Bowie and Green, p 292
McWay (2016), pp 181–183
McWay (2014), pp 78, 109
Pozgar, pp 358–559
Roach, pp 352–362

90. Dr. Sam Vineyard improperly performed a knee replacement surgery, which caused the patient to develop an infection that lead to the amputation of the leg and thigh. The best term to describe the action performed is
   A. misfeasance.
   B. malpractice.
   C. nonfeasance.
   D. malfeasance.

REFERENCE: Brodnik, p 70
LaTour, Eichenwald-Maki, and Oachs, p 304
Pozgar, p 33

91. The ideal consent for medical treatment obtained by the physician is
   A. expressed.
   B. informed.
   C. implied.
   D. verbal.

REFERENCE: Brodnik, pp 96–99
Bowie and Green, pp 129, 132, 134
McWay (2016), p 173
McWay (2014), pp 76–77
Pozgar, pp 302–303
Roach, pp 78–81

92. Which of the following is an example of the breach of confidentiality?
   A. a nurse speaking with the physician in the patient's room
   B. staff members discussing patients in the elevator
   C. the admission clerk verifying over the phone that the patient is in-house
   D. the hospital operator paging code blue in room 3 north

REFERENCE: Brodnik, pp 78–79
Pozgar, p 52
Roach, pp 406–408

93. Which of the following would be an inappropriate procedure for the custodian of the medical record to perform prior to taking a medical record from a health care facility to court?
    A. Number each page of the record in ink.
    B. Document in the file folder the total number of pages in the record.
    C. Remove any information that might prove detrimental to the hospital or physician.
    D. Prepare an itemized list of sheets contained in the medical record.

REFERENCE: Brodnik, pp 33–34
Pozgar, pp 284–287

94. Which of the following agencies is empowered to implement the law governing Medicare and Medicaid?
    A. Centers for Medicare and Medicaid Services (CMS) formerly known as Health Care Financing Administration (HCFA)
    B. Joint Commission
    C. Institutes of Health
    D. Department of Health and Human Services

REFERENCE: Brodnik, p 128
Bowie and Green, p 65
LaTour, Eichenwald-Maki, and Oachs, p 37
McWay (2016), p 12
McWay (2014), pp 12, 52, 56–57
Pozgar, pp 25–28

95. Consent forms may be challenged on all the following grounds EXCEPT
    A. wording was too technical.
    B. the treating physician obtained the patient's signature.
    C. it is written in a language that the patient could not understand.
    D. the signature was not voluntary.

REFERENCE: Brodnik, pp 115–118
Bowie and Green, pp 129, 132, 134
Roach, p 97

96. Mandatory reporting requirements for vital statistics generally
    A. do not require authorization by the patient.
    B. require authorization by the physician.
    C. require authorization by the payer.
    D. do not apply to health care facilities.

REFERENCE: Brodnik, pp 172–175
Bowie and Green, p 277
McWay (2016), p 301
McWay (2014), p 202
Pozgar, p 330

97. The responsibility of obtaining an informed consent for a surgical or invasive procedure rests with the
    A. patient.
    B. nurse.
    C. physician.
    D. hospital.

REFERENCE: Brodnik, pp 115–118
Bowie and Green, pp 129, 132, 134
Pozgar, pp 302–303
Roach, pp 91–94

98. Courts have released adoption records based on
    A. the request of the adoptee.
    B. the request of the biological parent(s).
    C. the Freedom of Information Act.
    D. a court order for good cause.

REFERENCE: Brodnik, pp 152–153
McWay (2016), p 218
Roach, p 301

99. The legislation that required all federally funded facilities to inform patients of their rights under state law to accept or refuse medical treatment is known as
    A. advance directives.
    B. living wills.
    C. Patient Self-Determination Act.
    D. durable power of attorney.

REFERENCE: Brodnik, p 105
Bowie and Green, p 129
McWay (2016), pp 114, 142, 186–187
McWay (2014), p 77
Pozgar, pp 316–317, 424, 430
Roach, p 97

100. An improper disclosure of patient information to unauthorized individuals, agencies, or news media may be considered a(n)
    A. invasion of privacy.
    B. libel.
    C. slander.
    D. defamation.

REFERENCE: Bowie and Green, p 271
McWay (2016), p 81
McWay (2014), p 64
Pozgar, p 52
Roach, pp 406–407, 410

Answer Key for Health Law

1. A
2. B
3. C
4. A
5. C
6. B
7. C
8. D
9. D
10. B
11. C
12. A
13. D
14. C
15. B
16. A
17. C
18. C
19. A
20. C
21. A
22. C
23. D
24. A
25. B
26. B
27. D
28. A
29. D
30. C
31. A
32. D
33. A
34. B
35. B
36. C
37. D
38. D
39. D
40. D
41. A
42. B
43. A
44. C
45. A
46. B
47. C
48. B
49. D
50. B
51. C
52. A
53. A
54. B
55. D
56. C
57. A
58. C
59. D
60. B
61. D
62. C
63. A
64. A
65. C
66. D
67. A
68. A
69. D
70. D
71. A
72. A
73. B
74. D
75. B
76. D
77. D
78. B
79. C
80. A
81. A
82. A
83. D
84. B
85. B
86. C
87. C
88. B
89. A
90. A
91. B
92. B
93. C
94. A
95. B
96. A
97. C
98. D
99. C
100. A

REFERENCES

Brodnik, M. S., Rinehart-Thompson, L. A., Reynolds, R. B. et al. (2013). *Fundamentals of law for health informatics and information management* (2nd ed.). Chicago: American Health Information Management Association.

Bowie, M. J. and Green, M. A. (2016). *Essentials of health information management: Principles and practices* (3rd ed.). Clifton Park, NY: Cengage Learning.

LaTour, K., Eichenwald-Maki, S., and Oachs, P. (2013). *Health information management: Concepts, principles, and practice* (4th ed.). Chicago: American Health Information Management Association (AHIMA).

McWay, D. C. (2016). *Legal and ethical aspects of health information management* (4th ed.). Clifton Park, NY: Cengage Learning.

McWay, D. C. (2014). *Today's health information management: An integrated approach* (2nd ed.). Clifton Park, NY: Cengage Learning.

Pozgar, G. D. (2016). *Legal aspects of health care administration* (13th ed.). Sudbury, MA: Jones & Bartlett.

Roach, W. H. (2006). *Medical records and the law* (4th ed.). Sudbury, MA: Jones & Bartlett.

Health Law Competency Domains

Question	RHIA Domain	RHIT Domain
1–100	2	
1–100		6

XIII. Health Statistics and Research

Kathy C. Trawick, EdD, RHIA, FAHIMA

As noted in the main Introduction section, you will be able to access some statistical formulas on the computer to use during the exam. You may not find them in any set location—be prepared to look around for them a little. Of course, there are some formulas (for example: mean, median, and average) you will be responsible for knowing. When preparing for the exam, practice using the calculator located in the program accessories bar on your computer and the formulas that are provided in this text.

Although some questions are included from the Commonly Computed Rates and Percentages for Hospital Inpatients, you will often be asked to interpret everyday data and/or solve questions that have more to do with common sense and good math skills than with memorized formulas. To help you distinguish among the types of questions you might expect, and to make sure you realistically evaluate your skills in this area, this chapter has been divided into four sections:

1. Statistical basics
2. Commonly computed rates
3. Data display and interpretation
4. Research and financial statistics

According to the breakdown of content for both the RHIA and RHIT exams, the health statistics questions have been included in Domain II. This section not only covers statistics and research, but also may include data collection, interpretation, and presentation as well as knowledge of registries, specialized databases, and the Institutional Review Board (IRB). You should also be prepared to analyze and interpret statistical charts and graphs. Some questions will refer to a graphical representation of data when asking for the answer. Refer to the specific details of these items in the domain and subdomain competencies found in the Certification Guide.

You will want to work with statistical formulas from this chapter, from your formal courses, and from previous textbooks until you get your speed up. Sometimes the length of time it takes in calculating formulas and mathematical computations can make or break you on the entire examination as far as your testing time. Thus, increasing your speed by practicing formulas can really help you at exam time.

Most answers in this section should be rounded to the first decimal point. On the national examination, let the answers provided in the test be your guide, or follow the examination instructions in order to round correctly.

Do not let the word problems throw you off. Some of these are quite long; look for the pertinent data.

Do not panic—approach word problems just as you did in your formal classes. You will have the formulas provided for you as appropriately required on the exam. For problems that you may not have a formula for, try the memory device of "what did happen divided by what could have happened." Here, the "what did happen" is always the numerator (top number) and the "what could have happened" is always the denominator (bottom number).

We recommend that you review the textbooks listed at the end of this chapter as you study for this section of your exam.

Health Statistics Definitions and Formulas

There are a number of important things to think about when you tackle census and occupancy statistics. First, remember that when it comes to occupancy, beds and bassinets are counted separately. This means newborn discharges are separated from the discharges of adults and children. Next, remember not to be fooled by beds set up temporarily to meet unusual admission needs; all occupancy statistics should be calculated based on approved, permanent beds only. The common rates used for census and occupancy statistics are as follows:

Census Statistics

Daily Inpatient Census	Total number of patients treated during a 24-hour period
Inpatient Service Day	Services received by one inpatient in one 24-hour period
Total Inpatient	Sum of all inpatient service days for each of the days in the period
Service Days	
FORMULA: Average Daily Census	$\frac{\text{Total inpatient service days for a period (excluding newborns)}}{\text{Total number of days in the period}}$

Length of Stay

Length of Stay (LOS)	Number of calendar days from admission to discharge
Total Length of Stay	Sum of the days' stay of any group of inpatients discharged during a specific period
FORMULA: Average LOS	$\frac{\text{Total length of stay (discharge days)}}{\text{Total number of discharges}}$

Bed Count

Inpatient Bed Count	Number of available hospital beds, both occupied and vacant, on any given day
Inpatient Bed Count Day	Counts the presence of one inpatient bed (occupied or vacant) that is set up and staffed for use in one 24-hour period
Total Inpatient Bed Count Day	Sum of inpatient bed count days for each of the days in a period

Percentage of Occupancy

FORMULA:	$\frac{\text{Total number of inpatient service days for a period} \times 100}{\text{Total inpatient bed count days} \times \text{number of days in the period}}$

Bed Turnover Rate

Direct Formula:

$$\frac{\text{Total number of discharges for a period}}{\text{Average bed count for the same period}}$$

Indirect Formula:

$$\frac{\text{Percentage of occupancy} \times \text{Days in the period} \times 100}{\text{Average length of stay}}$$

NOTE: The indirect formula must be used in cases where the bed count changes during the period in question.

Death (Mortality) Rates

Anesthesia Death Rate

$$\frac{\text{Total number of deaths caused by an anesthetic agent} \times 100}{\text{Total number of anesthetics administered}}$$

Fetal Death Rate (Stillbirth Rate)

$$\frac{\text{Total number of intermediate and late fetal deaths} \times 100}{\text{Total number of births (plus intermediate and late fetal deaths)}}$$

Gross Hospital Death Rate

$$\frac{\text{Total number of inpatient deaths (including newborns)} \times 100}{\text{Total number of discharges (including deaths and newborns)}}$$

Net Hospital Death Rate

$$\frac{\text{Number of inpatient deaths (including NB) minus deaths <48 hours of admission} \times 100}{\text{Total discharges (including deaths and NB, minus deaths <48 hours)}}$$

Maternal Death Rate

$$\frac{\text{Total number of maternal deaths for a period} \times 100}{\text{Total number of obstetrical discharges}}$$

Neonatal Death Rate (Infant Mortality Rate)

$$\frac{\text{Total number of newborn (NB. deaths for a period} \times \text{100)}}{\text{Total number of newborn (NB. Discharges)}}$$

Postoperative Death Rate

$$\frac{\text{Number of deaths within 10 days of surgery} \times 100}{\text{Total number of patients operated on}}$$

Autopsy Rates

Newborn (NB) Autopsy Rate

$$\frac{\text{Number of autopsies on NB deaths} \times 100}{\text{Total number of NB deaths}}$$

Fetal Autopsy Rate

$$\frac{\text{Number of autopsies on intermediate and late fetal deaths} \times 100}{\text{Total number of intermediate and late fetal deaths}}$$

Gross Autopsy Rate

$$\frac{\text{Total inpatient autopsies for a period} \times 100}{\text{Total inpatient deaths for the period}}$$

Net Autopsy Rate

$$\frac{\text{Total inpatient autopsies for a period} \times 100}{\text{Total inpatient deaths minus unautopsied coroner's or medical examiner's cases for the period}}$$

Hospital Autopsy Rate (Adjusted)

$$\frac{\text{Total hospital autopsies} \times 100}{\text{Number of deaths of hospital patients whose bodies are available for hospital autopsy}}$$

The hospital patients whose bodies after death are available for hospital autopsy include inpatients, unless the bodies are removed from the hospital by legal authorities. However, in any such case, if the hospital pathologist or delegated physician of the medical staff performs an autopsy while acting as an agent for the coroner, the autopsy is included in the numerator and the death in the denominator.

In addition, other hospital patients (including hospital home care patients, outpatients, and previous hospital patients who have died elsewhere) whose bodies have been made available for the performance of hospital autopsy, the autopsy is included in the numerator and the death in the denominator.

Infection (Morbidity) Rates

Total Hospital (Morbidity) Infection Rate	Total number of hospital infections × 100 / Total number of discharges
Nosocomial Infection Rate	Number of hospital acquired infections × 100 / Total number of discharges (including deaths)
Community-Acquired Infection Rate	Number of community-acquired infections × 100 / Total number of discharges
Postoperative Infection Rate	Number of postoperative infections for a period (within 10 days postoperatively) × 100 / Total number of operations performed

Other Rates

Cesarean Section Rate	Total number of cesarean sections performed in a period × 100 / Total number of deliveries in the period
Consultation Rate	Total number of consultations for a period × 100 / Total number of discharges for the period
Delinquent Medical Record Rate	Total number of delinquent records × 100 / Average number of discharges during a completion period
Incomplete Medical Record Rate	Total number of incomplete records × 100 / Total number of discharges during the completion period
Percentage of Medicare Patients	Total number of Medicare discharges × 100 / Total number of adult and children discharges
Percentage of Medicare Discharge Days	Total number of Medicare discharge days × 100 / Total number of discharge days for adults and children
Readmission Rate	Number of readmissions for a period × 100 / Number of total admissions (including readmissions)

Generic Formulas

Percentage Rates	Total number of times events actually happened × 100 / Total number of times events could have happened
Mean	Add all the available values and divide the sum by the total number of values involved. Example: Average length of stay or average daily inpatient census.
Median	The midpoint of an ordered series of numbers arranged in numerical order from highest to lowest or vice versa.
Mode	The most frequently recurring value in a set of numbers is the mode.

Section I—Math and Statistical Basics

The basics include mathematical and statistical terminology as well as the measures of central tendency and variations around those measures. It is unlikely that you will get instructions for calculating the measures of central tendency, so they are supplied along with the statistical formulas at the beginning of this chapter.

1. Sandy Beach Hospital reports 1,652 discharges for September. The infection control report documents 21 nosocomial infections and 27 community-acquired infections for the same month. What is the community-acquired infection rate?

   A. 1.3
   B. 1.4
   C. 1.6
   D. 2.9

REFERENCE: Koch, p 189
Sayles, p 497

2. Physicians at South Seas Clinic are expected to see six patients per hour on average. The physicians with the highest productivity each week are exempted from on-call responsibilities for the weekend. Which physician will get the weekend off this week?

SOUTH SEAS CLINIC PHYSICIAN PRODUCTIVITY Week 1 January 2016		
PHYSICIAN NAME	NUMBER OF HOURS WORKED	NUMBER OF PATIENTS SEEN
Robinson	32	185
Beasley	30	161
Hiltz	35	200
Wolf	26	157

   A. Robinson
   B. Beasley
   C. Hiltz
   D. Wolf

REFERENCE: Abdelhak, pp 383–384
Horton, pp 147–148
Koch, pp 70
LaTour, Eichenwald-Maki, and Oachs, p 807
McWay, pp 221–222

3. If there are 150,000 medical records and the Health Information Department receives 3,545 requests for records in a week, what percentage of the records are requested weekly?

   A. 2.4%
   B. 3.5%
   C. 4.6%
   D. 5.1%

REFERENCE: Abdelhak, pp 383–384
Horton, pp 14, 19–20
Koch, p 69
LaTour, Eichenwald-Maki, and Oachs, pp 484–485
McWay, p 204

4. You are conducting a study on the pain associated with a specific illness. For the purpose of your study, you classify pain level as follows:

CODE	PAIN LEVEL (as described by the patient)
01	None
02	Little or Minimal
03	Moderate
04	Heavy
05	Severe

These data are best described as

A. discrete.
B. continuous.
C. nominal.
D. ordinal.

REFERENCE: Abdelhak, pp 393–395
Horton, pp 196–199
Koch, pp 5–6
LaTour, Eichenwald-Maki, and Oachs, pp 482–483
McWay, p 212

5. You are choosing restaurants where you might eat while you are in Chicago at the AHIMA Leadership Conference. You have collected the following information about four possible lunch restaurants that are all located within easy walking distance of the meeting site. The data are displayed below.

RESTAURANT NAME	MEAN LUNCH COST	STANDARD DEVIATION
Bon Appetite	$8.00	0.75
Mario's	$7.50	1
Au Courant	$9.00	1.25
The Windy City Grill	$7.50	1.5

You want to stay within the reimbursement rate allowed by your Component State Association, so it is important to you that you have at least a 95% chance of eating a lunch that costs no more than $10.00. Therefore, when lunchtime comes, you head to

A. Bon Appetite or Mario's.
B. Mario's or Au Courant.
C. Au Courant or The Windy City Grill.
D. The Windy City Grill or Bon Appetite.

REFERENCE: Horton, pp 184–186
Koch, pp 231–241
McWay, p 206

6. Organizations collect statistics to increase their knowledge of a specified population. The knowledge does not come automatically—it is developed in the following sequence:

A. data → facts → information → knowledge.
B. data → information → facts → knowledge.
C. facts → data → information → knowledge.
D. facts → information → data → knowledge.

REFERENCE: Horton, pp 2–3

Questions 7 and 8 are based on the study and data below.

The coding supervisor at Bayside Hospital regularly has the coders recode records from the previous week in an effort to improve and monitor coding consistency. The supervisor has collected the data displayed below on four coders.

Coder	Records Under Review	Same Code on Self-Coding Review	Same Code on Peer Coding Review
Coder A	28	22	20
Coder B	18	16	16
Coder C	45	42	43
Coder D	17	15	16

7. The data in the column on the far right were collected when the coders traded records for recoding. This is a common practice used to check
   A. interrater reliability.
   B. intrarater reliability.
   C. interrater validity.
   D. intrarater validity.

REFERENCE: Abdelhak, pp 421–422
Sayles, pp 574–575

8. The coder with the highest overall accuracy rating will get the day after Thanksgiving off. Which coder will get to spend the day after Thanksgiving off rather than coding?
   A. Coder A
   B. Coder B
   C. Coder C
   D. Coder D

REFERENCE: Abdelhak pp 483–484
Koch, p 69
Horton, pp 14, 19–20
Sayles, pp 475–476

9. Which of the following interactions fits the definition of a patient encounter?

Phyllis saw Dr. Holland during a scheduled office visit. Dr. Holland prescribed a new medication.

Jean called Dr. Holland with a question about her medication. Dr. Holland returned the telephone call and answered Jean's question.

Howard was seen by Dr. Holland in the hospital emergency department after having a reaction to his medication.

The pharmacy received telephone approval from Dr. Horton for a refill on Jackson's prescription.

   A. Phyllis, Jean, Howard, and Jackson
   B. Jackson, Howard, and Jean
   C. Jean, Phyllis, and Howard
   D. Phyllis and Howard

REFERENCE: Abdelhak, p 133
Horton, pp 4, 148
LaTour, Eichenwald-Maki, and Oachs, p 498

10. A small portion of the form you are using for a research study is reproduced below.

Male	1
Female	2

This is an example of

A. ordinal data.
B. ranked data.
C. nominal data.
D. discrete data.

REFERENCE: Abdelhak, pp 393–395
Horton, pp 196–199
Koch, pp 5–6
LaTour, Eichenwald-Maki, and Oachs, pp 482–483
McWay, p 212

11. You have made a list of the advantages and disadvantages of a measure of central tendency.

ADVANTAGES	DISADVANTAGES
Easy to obtain and interpret	May not be descriptive of the distribution
Not sensitive to extreme observations in the frequency distribution	May not be unique
Easy to communicate and explain to others	Does not provide information about the entire distribution

The measure of central tendency you are describing is the

A. mean.
B. median.
C. range.
D. mode.

REFERENCE: Abdelhak, pp 399–401
Horton, pp 175–181
Koch, pp 222–226
LaTour, Eichenwald-Maki, and Oachs, pp 518–520
McWay, pp 205–206
Sayles, pp 538–541

The following data were collected in your physician office practice from one morning's visits. Use the data for questions 12, 13, and 14.

Office Visit ID Number	Minutes with the Physician	Physician
508-123	5	Robinson
508-124	9	Robinson
508-125	8	Beasley
508-126	12	Wolf
508-127	6	Beasley
508-128	7	Beasley
508-129	5	Wolf
508-130	10	Baumstark
508-131	7	Baumstark
508-132	9	Robinson
508-133	11	Wolf

12. The median number of minutes with the physician (considering all physicians) is
    A. 7 minutes.
    B. 8 minutes.
    C. 8.4 minutes.
    D. 9 minutes.

REFERENCE: Abdelhak, pp 399–401
Horton, pp 222–226
Koch, pp 234–237
McWay, pp 205–206
Sayles, pp 538–541

13. The mean number of minutes with the physician (considering all physicians) is
    A. 7 minutes.
    B. 8 minutes.
    C. 8.4 minutes.
    D. 9 minutes.

REFERENCE: Abdelhak, pp 399–401
Horton, pp 175–181
Koch, pp 222–226
McWay, p 194
Sayles, pp 538–541

14. Which physician spent the longest average time with patients on that day?
    A. Beasley
    B. Wolf
    C. Baumstark
    D. Robinson

REFERENCE: Abdelhak, pp 399–401
Koch, pp 222–226
Sayles, pp 538–541

Use this portion of the discharges printout below to answer questions 15 and 16.

Discharge List					
Patient #	Admit Date	Service	Physician ID	Room #	LOS
12-32-21	1/02/15	MED	212	44-A	13
12-32-22	1/02/15	SURG	218	32	13
12-32-85	1/14/15	PEDS	214	23-B	1
11-99-94	1/12/15	MED	212	46-A	3
10-93-23	1/10/15	MED	212	45	5
12-35-94	1/11/15	SURG	218	33	4
10-85-14	1/01/15	PEDS	214	23-A	14

15. Without even performing any complex calculations, you can get a quick, simple measure of dispersion in the LOS for yesterday's discharges by computing the
    A. range of the data set.
    B. mean of the data set.
    C. variance of the data set.
    D. coefficient of variation of the data set.

REFERENCE: Abdelhak, pp 399–401
Horton, pp 175–182
Koch, pp 222–226
Sayles, pp 538–542

16. Looking more closely at the LOS for these patients, when you calculate the standard deviation on the data, you would expect
    A. a large standard deviation because the dispersion is large.
    B. a small standard deviation because the dispersion is small.
    C. a large standard deviation because the dispersion is small.
    D. a small standard deviation because the dispersion is large.

REFERENCE: Abdelhak, pp 399–401
Horton, pp 183–186
Koch, pp 231–241
McWay, pp 206–204
Sayles, p 542

17. Englewood Health Center collected the following data on patients discharged on January 1, 2016. Which measure of central tendency would be most affected by Mallory's extremely long LOS?

Patient Name	Length of Stay
Ben	1
Josh	2
Emma	3
Bryan	4
Mallory	29
Taylor	2
Matthew	3
Aiden	2
Trevor	4
Tyler	2

A. variance
B. median
C. mean
D. mode

REFERENCE: Abdelhak, pp 399–401
Horton, pp 175–181
Koch, pp 222–226
LaTour, Eichenwald-Maki, and Oachs, pp 518–520
McWay, pp 205–206
Sayles, pp 538–541

CASE NUMBER	BRIEF DESCRIPTION
101-43-26	A 32-year-old female was admitted through the ED following an automobile accident. She spontaneously delivered a 720-g fetus that showed no sign of life.
101-44-23	A 22-year-old female was admitted in labor. Following an uneventful course, she delivered a 7-lb 4-oz term male. The child developed sudden and unexpected respiratory distress. All attempts at resuscitation failed; the baby was pronounced dead less than 2 hours after delivery.
101-48-69	A 19-year-old female spontaneously delivered a 475-g fetus following a fall down the stairs at home.
101-56-29	A 28-year-old female was admitted for a late-term therapeutic abortion. The procedure was completed without complication; product of conception weighed 728 g.

18. The OB/GYN Department reported the information in the table shown above to the Quality Management/Statistics Committee. When the committee considers these adverse outcomes from the OB/GYN Department, which of the cases will be included in the numerator of the facility's fetal death rate?

A. 101-43-26
B. 101-43-26 and 101-44-23
C. 101-43-26 and 101-48-69
D. 101-43-26 and 101-56-29

REFERENCE: Abdelhak, pp 383–387
Horton, pp 88–89
Koch, pp 161–162
LaTour, Eichenwald-Maki, and Oachs, p 492

19. Which of the cases listed in the table above will have an impact on the facility's gross death rate?
    A. 101-43-26
    B. 101-44-23
    C. 101-48-69
    D. 101-56-29

REFERENCE: Abdelhak, pp 383–389
Horton, pp 72–74
Koch, p 142
LaTour, Eichenwald-Maki, and Oachs, p 490
Sayles, p 489

20. Patients in the pediatrics ward were studied to determine their favorite color. The survey results are listed below. The results of the favorite color study are reported in a

REPORTED FAVORITE COLOR OF PEDIATRIC PATIENTS AZURE TIDES HOSPITAL JANUARY 18, 2016	
FAVORITE COLOR	NUMBER OF RESPONDENTS
RED	12
GREEN	14
BLUE	22
YELLOW	18
ORANGE	16

A. frequency polygon.
B. line graph.
C. frequency distribution.
D. systematic fashion.

REFERENCE: Abdelhak, pp 395–399
Horton, pp 202–212
Koch, pp 23–40
McWay, pp 212–215
Sayles, pp 522–533

21. All of the following items mean the same thing, EXCEPT
    A. inpatient service day.
    B. daily inpatient census.
    C. daily census.
    D. inpatient census.

REFERENCE: Abdelhak, pp 391–393
Horton, pp 24–27
Koch, pp 88–92
LaTour, Eichenwald-Maki, and Oachs, pp 510–516
McWay, pp 201–216

22. Pasadena Bay Hospital reports an average LOS in January of 3.7 days with a standard deviation of 20. This tells us that
   A. most patients had an LOS of 3 to 4 days.
   B. there was a small variation in the LOS.
   C. patients at Pasadena Bay stay longer than average.
   D. there was a large variation in the LOS.

REFERENCE: Abdelhak, pp 399–401
Horton, pp 184–186
Koch, pp 231–241
LaTour, Eichenwald-Maki, and Oachs, pp 520–521
McWay, pp 206–207
Sayles, pp 542–545

23. Jason collected data on the length of stay (LOS) for 10 patients and then determined the median LOS as follows:

1	
2	
4	
3	
1	← median
3	
2	
4	
2	
8	

What is wrong with Jason's determination of the median?
   A. There is nothing wrong with Jason's determination of the median.
   B. Jason forgot to put the numbers in sequential order before determining the median.
   C. It is not possible to determine the median on such a small number of data points.
   D. It is not possible to determine the median on an even number of data points.

REFERENCE: Abdelhak, pp 399–401
Horton, pp 175–181
Koch, pp 222–226
McWay, pp 204–206
Sayles, pp 538–541

Section II—Commonly Computed Rates and Percentages for Hospital Inpatients

24. All Women's Hospital reports the following statistics:

Single births	
Vaginal	40
C-section	0
Twin births	
Twins—vaginal	12 (6 sets)
Twins—C-section	8 (4 sets)
Other multiple births	0
Intermediate fetal deaths	
Vaginal	5
C-section	0
Late fetal deaths	
Vaginal	2
C-section	0

How many deliveries occurred?

A. 50
B. 57
C. 60
D. 67

REFERENCE: Horton, pp 124–125
Koch, p 154

25. The inpatient census at midnight is 67. Two patients were admitted in the morning; one died 2 hours later; the second patient was transferred to another facility that same afternoon. The inpatient service days for that day will be

A. 65.
B. 67.
C. 68.
D. 69.

REFERENCE: Abdelhak, pp 391–393
Horton, pp 27–32
Koch, pp 91–92
LaTour, Eichenwald-Maki, and Oachs, pp 486–487
Sayles, p 481

26. Bayside Hospital has 275 adult beds, 30 pediatric beds, and 40 bassinets. In a nonleap year, inpatient service days were 75,860 for adults, 7,100 for pediatrics, and 11,800 for newborns. What was the average daily census for the year?

A. 227
B. 208
C. 207
D. 259

REFERENCE: Abdelhak, pp 391–393
Horton, pp 38–42
Koch, pp 97–98
LaTour, Eichenwald-Maki, and Oachs, pp 486–487
Sayles, pp 481–482

27. In order to derive the total inpatient service days for any given day, you would need to
    A. subtract intra-hospital transfers from the inpatient census.
    B. add same-day admits and discharges to the inpatient census.
    C. add intra-hospital transfers to the inpatient census.
    D. subtract same day admits and discharges from the inpatient census.

REFERENCE: Abdelhak, pp 391–393
Horton, pp 91–92
Koch, pp 68–69
LaTour, Eichenwald-Maki, and Oachs, p 487

28. Mr. McDonaldson was admitted to your hospital at 10:45 PM on January 1. He died at 4:22 AM on January 3. How many inpatient service days did Mr. McDonaldson receive?
    A. 1
    B. 2
    C. 3
    D. 4

REFERENCE: Abdelhak, pp 395–399
Horton, pp 27–32
Koch, pp 91–92
LaTour, Eichenwald-Maki, and Oachs, pp 486–487
McWay, p 209
Sayles, p 481

29. A patient admitted to the hospital on January 24 and discharged on February 9 has a length of stay of
    A. 16 days.
    B. 15 days.
    C. 17 days.
    D. 14 days.

REFERENCE: Abdelhak, pp 391–393
Horton, pp 58–61
Koch, pp 124–127
McWay, p 209
Sayles, pp 485–487

Use the data in the table below to answer the next two questions.

Royal Palm Hospital has 500 beds and 55 bassinets. In February of a nonleap year, it reported the following statistics:

Inpatient service days:	
Adult and pediatric	12,345
Newborn	553
Discharges:	
Adult and pediatric	1,351
Newborn	77
Discharge days:	
Adult and pediatric	9,457
Newborn	231

30. What was the percentage of occupancy for adults and pediatrics in February?
    A. 84.8%
    B. 88.2%
    C. 79.6%
    D. 80.5%

REFERENCE: Abdelhak, pp 391–393
Koch, pp 108–109
Horton, pp 46–48
LaTour, Eichenwald-Maki, and Oachs, p 488
Sayles, pp 483–484

31. What was the average length of stay at Royal Palm Hospital in February?
    A. 6.8 days
    B. 7 days
    C. 9 days
    D. 9.1 days

REFERENCE: Abdelhak, pp 391–393
Koch, pp 129–130
Horton, pp 63–65
LaTour, Eichenwald-Maki, and Oachs, p 490
McWay, p 209
Sayles, p 490

32. You are responsible for calculating and reporting average length of stay (ALOS) for your hospital each month. This month, there were 92 discharges, and the total discharge days equal 875. One of the patients discharged this month had a total of 428 discharge days, so the ALOS is distorted by this unusually long stay. In this situation, you should report an ALOS of
    A. 9.51 days—no further information is necessary.
    B. 9.61 days and make a note that the one patient with an unusually long LOS was subtracted prior to making the calculation.
    C. 4.86 days and make a note that one unusually long LOS was subtracted prior to making the calculation.
    D. 4.91 days and make a note that the data on one patient with an unusually long LOS were subtracted prior to making the calculation.

REFERENCE: Abdelhak, pp 391–393
Horton, pp 63–65
Koch, pp 124–127
McWay, p 209
Sayles, pp 489–488, 487–788

33. A hospital reported the following statistics during a nonleap year. Calculate the percentage of occupancy for the entire year.

Time Period	Bed Count	Inpatient Service Days
January 1 to May 31	200	28,690
June 1 to October 15	250	27,400
October 16 to December 31	275	19,250

A. 85.2%
B. 88%
C. 90.0%
D. 91.2%

REFERENCE: Abdelhak, pp 391–393
Horton, pp 46–48
Koch, pp 108–109
LaTour, Eichenwald-Maki, and Oachs, p 488
Sayles, pp 483–484

34. Lake City Health Center has 200 beds and 20 bassinets. In a nonleap year, Styles Hospital admitted 16,437 adults and children; 16,570 adults and children were discharged. There were 1,764 live births and 1,798 newborns discharged. The bed turnover rate for the year was
    A. 82.2.
    B. 82.7.
    C. 82.9.
    D. 93.5.

REFERENCE: Abdelhak, pp 391–393
Horton, pp 52–53
Koch, pp 116–117
LaTour, Eichenwald-Maki, and Oachs, pp 488–489
Sayles, p 484

35. Sea Crest Hospital has 200 beds and 20 bassinets. There was a sudden spurt in the birth rate in the town in November. The hospital set up five additional bassinets for the entire month. Total bed count days for Sea Crest Hospital in a nonleap year would be

A. 73,000.
B. 80,300.
C. 80,450.
D. 80,455.

REFERENCE: Abdelhak, pp 391–393
Horton, p 45
Koch, p 108
LaTour, Eichenwald-Maki, and Oachs, p 488
Sayles, pp 483–484

36. Use the statistics provided in the table to compute the fetal death rate at All Women's Hospital for March.

All Women's Hospital March Statistics	
Live births	225
Intermediate and late fetal deaths	5
Early fetal deaths	4
Newborn discharges	235

A. 4.0%
B. 1.78%
C. 2.2%
D. 1.77%

REFERENCE: Abdelhak, pp 383–387
Horton, pp 88–89
Koch, pp 161–162
LaTour, Eichenwald-Maki, and Oachs, p 492
Sayles, pp 490–491

The following obstetrical statistics were collected for the month of October. Use the data in the table below to answer the next two questions.

DELIVERED		TOTAL	DELIVERED BY C-SECTION
Live			
	Single infant	50	15
	Twins	3 sets	1 set
Dead			
	Early fetal	1	0
	Late fetal	1	1

37. The number of births in the facility in October is

A. 53.
B. 55.
C. 56.
D. 58.

REFERENCE: Horton, pp 124–125
Koch, pp 215–216
Sayles, pp 509–511

38. The number of deliveries in the facility in October is
   A. 53.
   B. 55.
   C. 56.
   D. 58.

REFERENCE: Horton, pp 124–125
Koch, p 154

39. Ocean View Healthcare Center recorded six fetal deaths during the last year; details are listed below.

Fetal Death Information		
ID	WEIGHT	GESTATIONAL AGE
A	526 g	22 weeks
B	405 g	18 weeks
C	817 g	26 weeks
D	1,023 g	30 weeks
E	629 g	24 weeks
F	1,113 g	29 weeks

How should these deaths be counted in the hospital death rates?
   A. All the deaths except B will be included in the gross death rate.
   B. Deaths D and F will be included in the gross death rate.
   C. Deaths C, D, and F will be included in the gross death rate.
   D. None of these deaths will be included in the gross death rate.

REFERENCE: Abdelhak, pp 383–387
Horton, pp 72–74
Koch, p 142
LaTour, Eichenwald-Maki, and Oachs, pp 490–492
Sayles, pp 488–489

40. William Rumple was pronounced dead on arrival (DOA). The hospital pathologist performed an autopsy on Mr. Rumple's body. This statistical event would be counted in the
   A. net death rate.
   B. gross death rate.
   C. net autopsy rate.
   D. hospital autopsy rate.

REFERENCE: Abdelhak, pp 388–389
Horton, pp 72–76, 95–105
Koch, pp 142, 174–177
LaTour, Eichenwald-Maki, and Oachs, pp 490–495
Sayles, pp 488–496

Tampa Bay Health Center discharged 6,069 adults/children and 545 newborns last year. A total of 1,648 adults/children and 1,279 newborns were seen in the emergency department. Information on the deaths at Happy Valley last year is listed below. Use the data to answer the next two questions.

INPATIENT DEATHS		
Adult/child	245 < 48 hr	105 > 48 hr
Newborn	8 < 48 hr	3 > 48 hr

OUTPATIENT (ED) DEATHS		
Adult/child	2	
Newborn	0	

FETAL DEATHS		
Early	1	
Intermediate	3	
Late	2	

41. What was the gross (hospital) death rate at Tampa Bay Health Center last year?
    A. 3.8%
    B. 5.4%
    C. 5.5%
    D. 5.6%

REFERENCE: Abdelhak, pp 383–388
Horton, pp 72–74
Koch, p 142
LaTour, Eichenwald-Maki, and Oachs, p 490
Sayles, p 489

42. What was the net death rate at Tampa Bay Health Center last year?
    A. 1.6%
    B. 1.7%
    C. 1.8%
    D. 1.9%

REFERENCE: Abdelhak, pp 383–388
Horton, pp 75–76
Koch, p 142
LaTour, Eichenwald-Maki, and Oachs, p 492
Sayles, p 489

43. During the month of September, Superior Health Care Center had 1,382 inpatient discharges, including 48 deaths. There were 38 deaths over 48 hours. Statistics also show 4 fetal deaths, 3 DOAs, and 4 inpatient coroner's cases. Which of the following calculations is correct to figure the net death rate?
    A. (48 × 100) / (1,382 – 10)
    B. (48–10 × 100) / (1,382 – 10)
    C. (1,382 × 100) / (48 – 10)
    D. (1,382 – 10) × 100 / (48 – 10)

REFERENCE: Abdelhak, pp 383–388
Horton, pp 75–76
Koch, p 142
LaTour, Eichenwald-Maki, and Oachs, p 492
Sayles, p 489

44. The best form/graph for demonstrating trends over time would be
    A. frequency polygon.
    B. line graph.
    C. pie chart.
    D. histogram.

REFERENCE: Horton, p 212
Koch, pp 247–267
McWay, p 201

45. Joseph Woodley has been on a third-floor nursing unit since October 2014 and was finally discharged to a nursing home in December 2015. When the average length of stay is calculated for the year 2015, this very long length of stay will
    A. have little impact on the average length of stay.
    B. result in a special cause variation in the average length of stay.
    C. result in a small variation in the average length of stay.
    D. result in a common cause variation in the average length of stay.

REFERENCE: Abdelhak, pp 399–401
Horton, pp 62–64
Koch, pp 129–133
Sayles, pp 486–488

46. Still thinking about Mr. Woodley and his long stay, if you were to graph the ALOS for the facility for 2015, which of the following graphs would you expect to see?

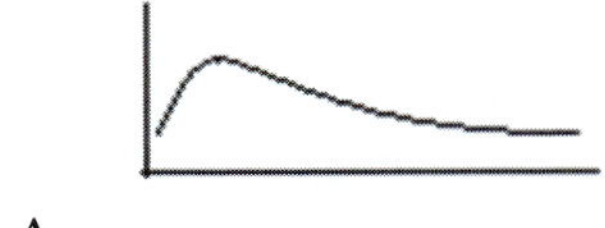

A.

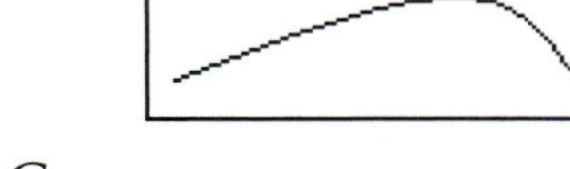

C.

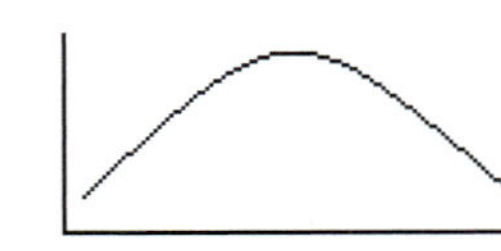

B.

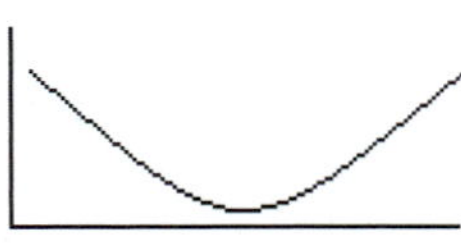

D.

REFERENCE: Abdelhak, pp 399–401
Horton, pp 187–189
Koch, pp 227–230
LaTour, Eichenwald-Maki, and Oachs, pp 510–516

47. The New Beginnings Maternity Center recorded the following statistics in December:

FETAL DEATHS:	
EARLY	240
INTERMEDIATE	40
LATE	32
BIRTHS	980
DELIVERIES	994
NEWBORN DISCHARGES	1,008

What was the fetal death rate at New Beginnings Maternity Center in December?

A. 6.8%
B. 7.3%
C. 7.4%
D. 31.8%

REFERENCE: Abdelhak, pp 383–388
Horton, pp 88–89
Koch, pp 161–162
LaTour, Eichenwald-Maki, and Oachs, p 492
Sayles, pp 490–491

48. The statistics reported for a 300-bed hospital for 1 year were 20,932 discharges with 136,651 discharge days and 3,699 consultations performed. What was the consultation rate for the year?

A. 16.5%
B. 17.0%
C. 17.7%
D. 18.0%

REFERENCE: Horton, pp 126–127
Koch, pp 192–194
Sayles, pp 498–499

Section III—Data Display

You have already practiced reading tables in many of the preceding questions. Data display—the selection, interpretation, and construction of data—is an important part of HIM practice. Therefore, a number of data display questions should be expected. Examples of these kinds of questions follow.

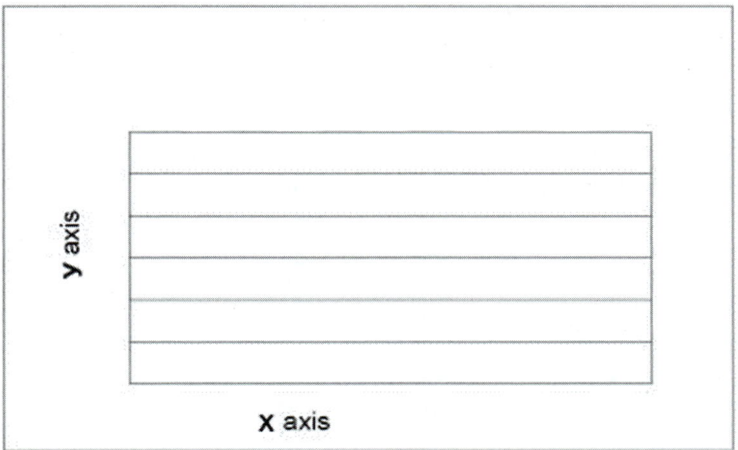

49. Look at the graph grid displayed above. If you want to follow accepted principles for graph construction, you will follow the three-quarter-high rule. That means the
    A. height of the graph should be three-fourths the length of the graph.
    B. length of the graph should be three-fourths the height of the graph.
    C. height of the graph should display three-fourths of the data in the graph.
    D. length of the graph should display three-fourths of the data in the graph.

REFERENCE: Horton, p 207
LaTour, Eichenwald-Maki, and Oachs, p 510
Sayles, p 522

50. You are preparing data from a series of weight loss studies for display. The data collected during the study are as follows:

POUNDS LOST	NUMBER IN GROUP A WITH THIS WEIGHT LOSS	NUMBER IN GROUP B WITH THIS WEIGHT LOSS
7.5–9.4	1	2
9.5–11.4	3	2
11.5–13.4	6	5
13.5–15.4	5	4
15.5–17.4	8	7
17.5–19.4	2	3

If you want to allow the reader to compare the results of Group A with those of Group B on one graphic display, your best choice would be to construct a

A. bar chart.
B. line graph.
C. histogram.
D. frequency polygon.

REFERENCE: Abdelhak, pp 393–395
Horton, pp 207–212
Koch, pp 247–267
LaTour, Eichenwald-Maki, and Oachs, pp 510–513
McWay, pp 213–215
Sayles, pp 522–529

51. A distribution is said to be positively skewed when the mean is

A. bimodal.
B. multimodal.
C. shifted to the left.
D. shifted to the right.

REFERENCE: Horton, pp 187–189
Koch, pp 227–230

52. You want to graph the number of patients admitted to three different medical staff services on each day of the last month. Because you have a large number of observations (one for each day of the month) and you want to be able to compare the observations for each of the three services on one data display, your best choice is a

A. table.
B. bar chart.
C. line graph.
D. histogram.

REFERENCE: Horton, pp 207–212
Koch, pp 264–284
LaTour, Eichenwald-Maki, and Oachs, pp 510–516
McWay, pp 247–267
Sayles, pp 522–533

53. You have just constructed the chart displayed below.

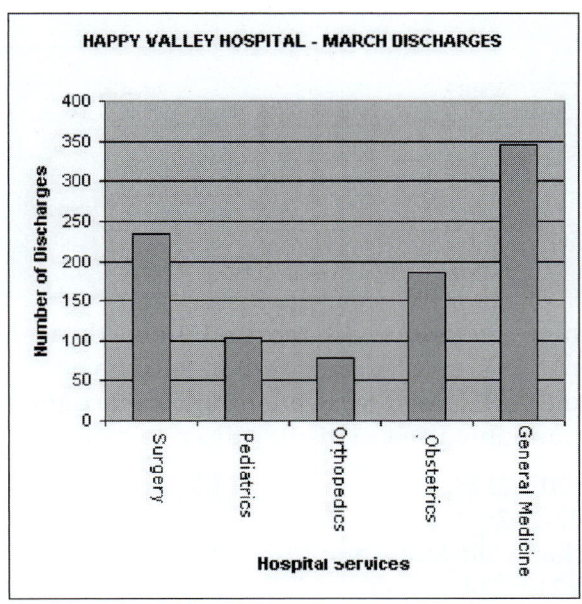

The names of the hospital services are hard to read. The best way to deal with this problem would be to

A. construct a line graph instead of a bar chart.
B. use a column chart instead of a bar chart.
C. plot your primary variable along the x-axis.
D. divide the data into two charts.

REFERENCE: Horton, pp 206–209
Koch, pp 247–267
LaTour, Eichenwald-Maki, and Oachs, pp 508–509
Sayles, pp 520–522

54. The display below is a

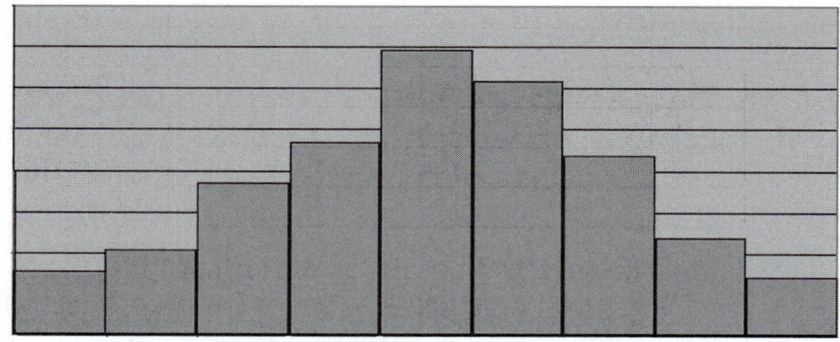

A. bar chart, which is commonly used to display continuous data.
B. bar chart, which is commonly used to display discrete data.
C. histogram, which is commonly used to display continuous data.
D. histogram, which is commonly used to display discrete data.

REFERENCE: Horton, pp 207–212
Koch, pp 247–267
LaTour, Eichenwald-Maki, and Oachs, pp 510–513
McWay, pp 213–214
Sayles, pp 522–528

55. The data display below is a

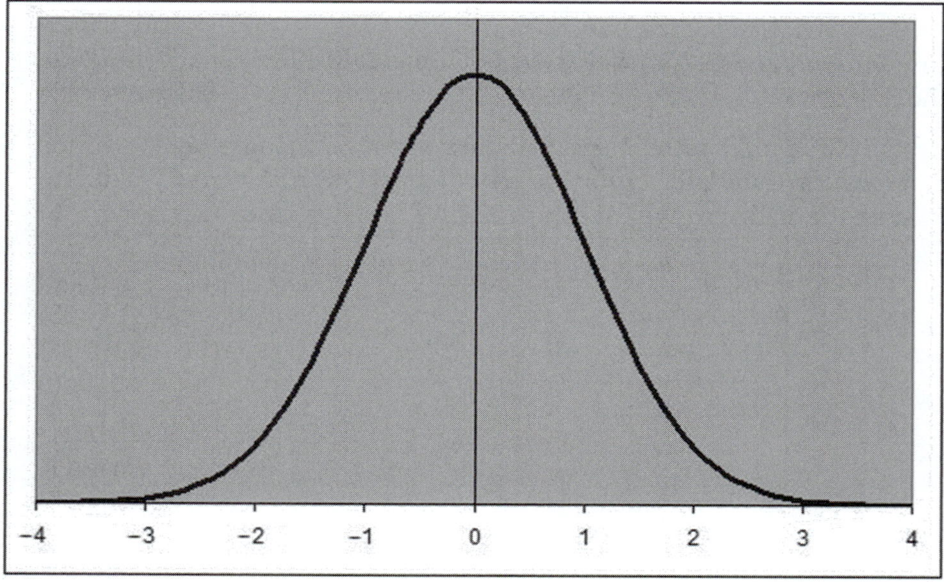

A. normal distribution or curve.
B. positive skewed curve.
C. negative skewed curve.
D. heterogeneous curve.

REFERENCE: Horton, pp 187–189
Koch, pp 227–240
McWay, pp 219–220

56. What conclusion can you make from the pie graph below?

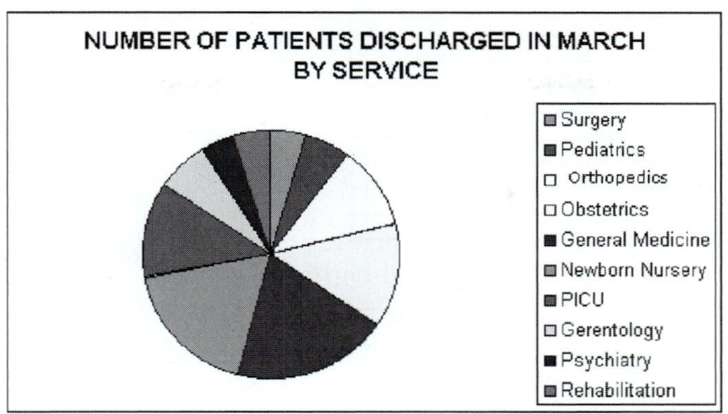

A. A pie graph should not be used, because there are too many categories for effective display.
B. A pie graph should not be used, because the data are representational instead of quantitative.
C. A pie graph should not be used, because the data are qualitative instead of quantitative.
D. A pie graph is a good choice and is often used to display this kind of data.

REFERENCE: Abdelhak, pp 396–397
Horton, pp 210–211
Koch, pp 256–257
LaTour, Eichenwald-Maki, and Oachs, pp 510–511
McWay, pp 213–214
Sayles, p 525

57. You are trying to improve communication with your staff by posting graphs of significant statistics on the employee bulletin board. You recently calculated the percentage of time employees spend on each of six major tasks. Because you would like the employees to appreciate each task as a percentage of their whole day, you will post these figures using a

A. line graph.
B. bar graph.
C. scatter diagram.
D. pie graph.

REFERENCE: Abdelhak, pp 395–395
Horton, pp 207–216
Koch, pp 247–267
LaTour, Eichenwald-Maki, and Oachs, pp 510–514
McWay, pp 213–215
Sayles, pp 522–531

58. The graph below can best be described as

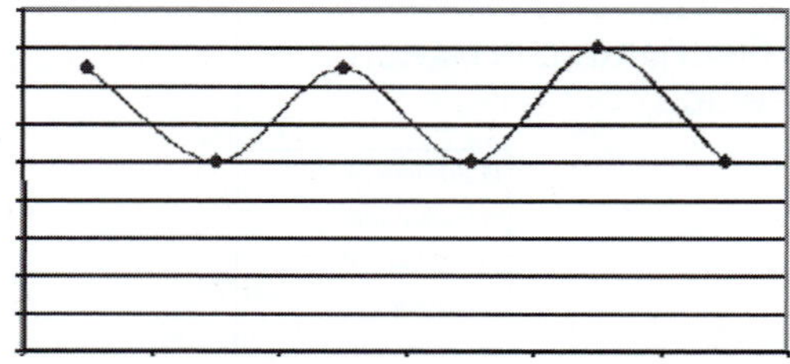

A. sequential.
B. multimodal.
C. substitutional.
D. erratic.

REFERENCE: Koch, pp 227–230
Horton, pp 187–189

59. Looking at the data represented in the scatter diagram below, you would conclude that there is

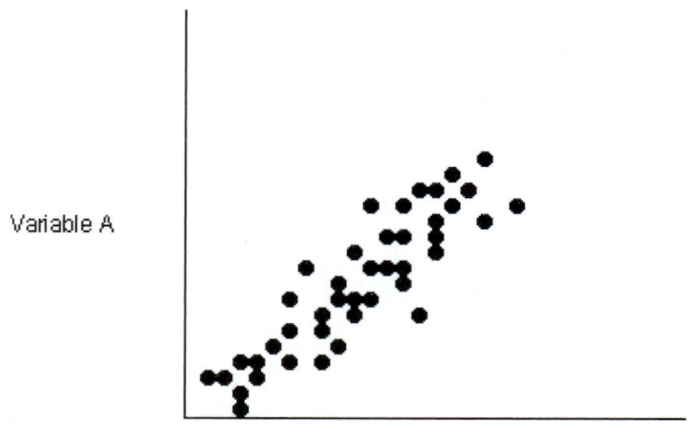

A. no correlation between Variable A and Variable B.
B. a positive correlation between Variable A and Variable B.
C. a negative correlation between Variable A and Variable B.
D. a cause and effect relationship between Variable A and Variable B.

REFERENCE: Horton, pp 216–219
LaTour, Eichenwald-Maki, and Oachs, pp 513–514
McWay, pp 219–220
Sayles, pp 544–545

60. The data displayed in the histogram below could best be described as

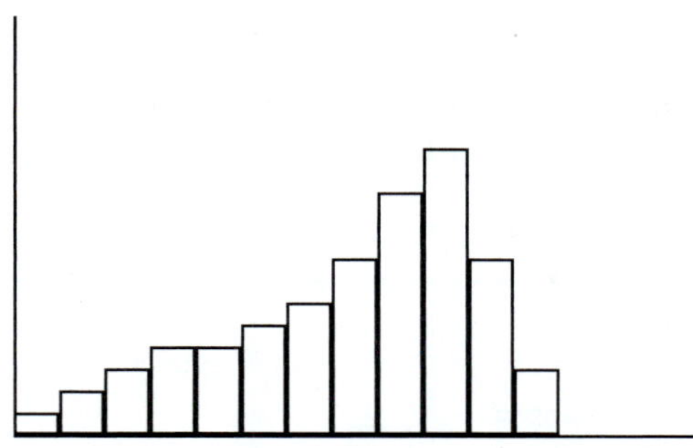

A. negatively skewed.
B. positively skewed.
C. evenly distributed.
D. normally distributed.

REFERENCE: Horton, pp 187–189
Koch, pp 227–230
LaTour, Eichenwald-Maki, and Oachs, pp 513–514
Sayles, pp 544–545

61. You want to construct a data display for a frequency distribution. You will use a
A. frequency polygon or histogram.
B. frequency polygon or bar chart.
C. line graph or histogram.
D. line graph or bar chart.

REFERENCE: Abdelhak, pp 395–399
Horton, pp 207–212
LaTour, Eichenwald-Maki, and Oachs, pp 510–513
McWay, pp 213–215
Sayles, pp 522–529

62. Look at the graph below. It is an example of a

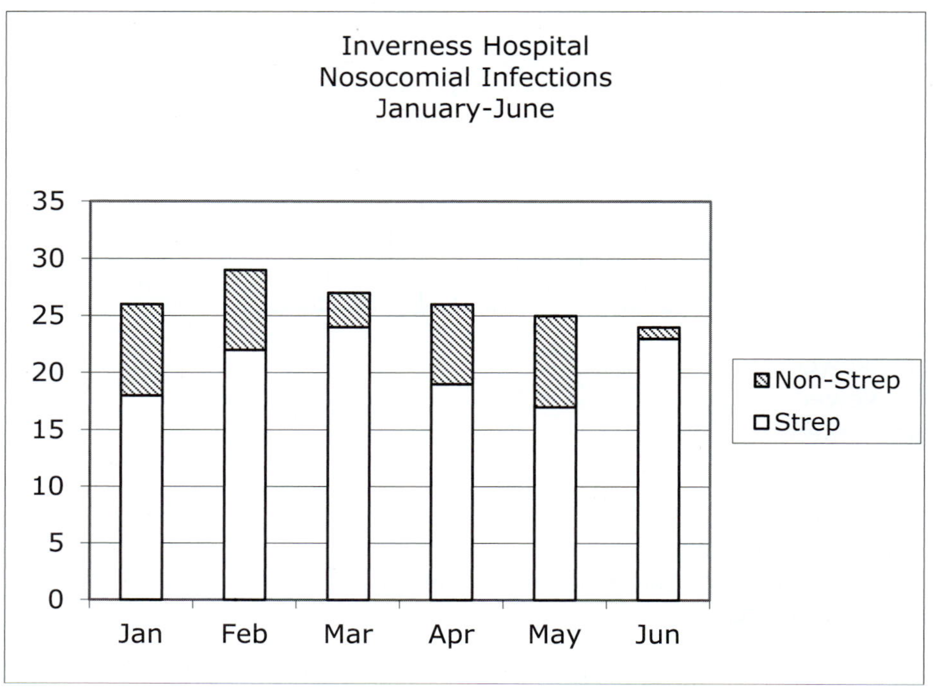

A. stacked bar chart; it is well constructed.
B. histogram; it is well constructed.
C. comparison bar chart; it is not well constructed.
D. frequency polygon; it is not well constructed.

REFERENCE: Abdelhak, pp 395–399
Koch, pp 247–267
McWay, pp 213–215
Sayles, pp 522–529

Use the historical graph below to answer questions 63 and 64.

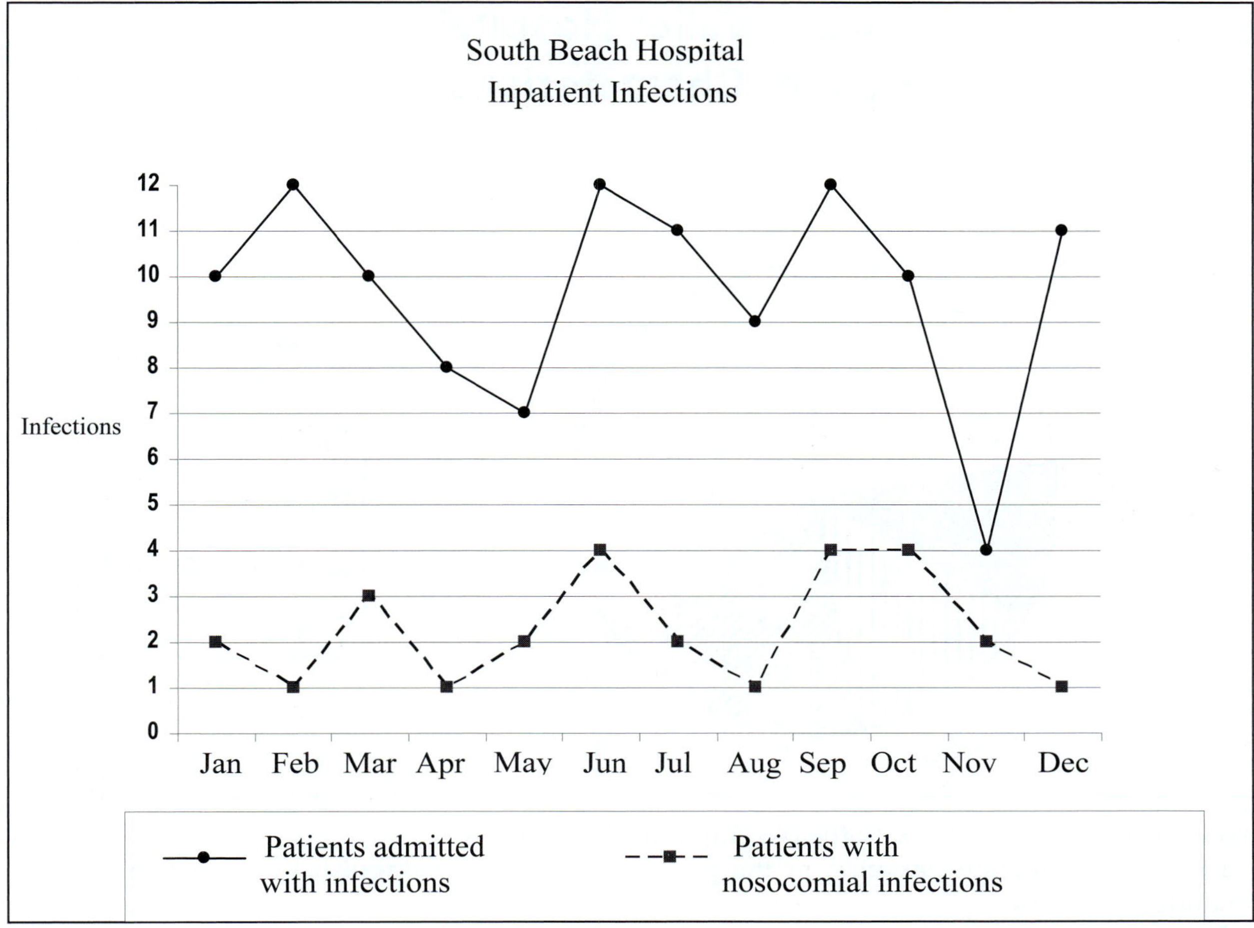

63. The total number of infections at South Beach Hospital during the first quarter (January–March) was
   A. 6.
   B. 12.
   C. 22.
   D. 38.

REFERENCE: Abdelhak, pp 395–399
Horton, pp 212–214
Koch, pp 188–192
LaTour, Eichenwald-Maki, and Oachs, pp 495–496
McWay, pp 210–211
Sayles, pp 497–498

64. Look again at the graph you used for the last question. From this graph, you can assume that more people
   A. were admitted to the facility with infections than without infections.
   B. were admitted to the facility with infections than is typical for U.S. hospitals.
   C. were admitted to the facility with infections than acquired infections in the hospital.
   D. acquired infections in the hospital than were admitted with infections.

REFERENCE: Abdelhak, pp 395–399
Horton, pp 212–214
Koch, pp 247–267
McWay, pp 213–214

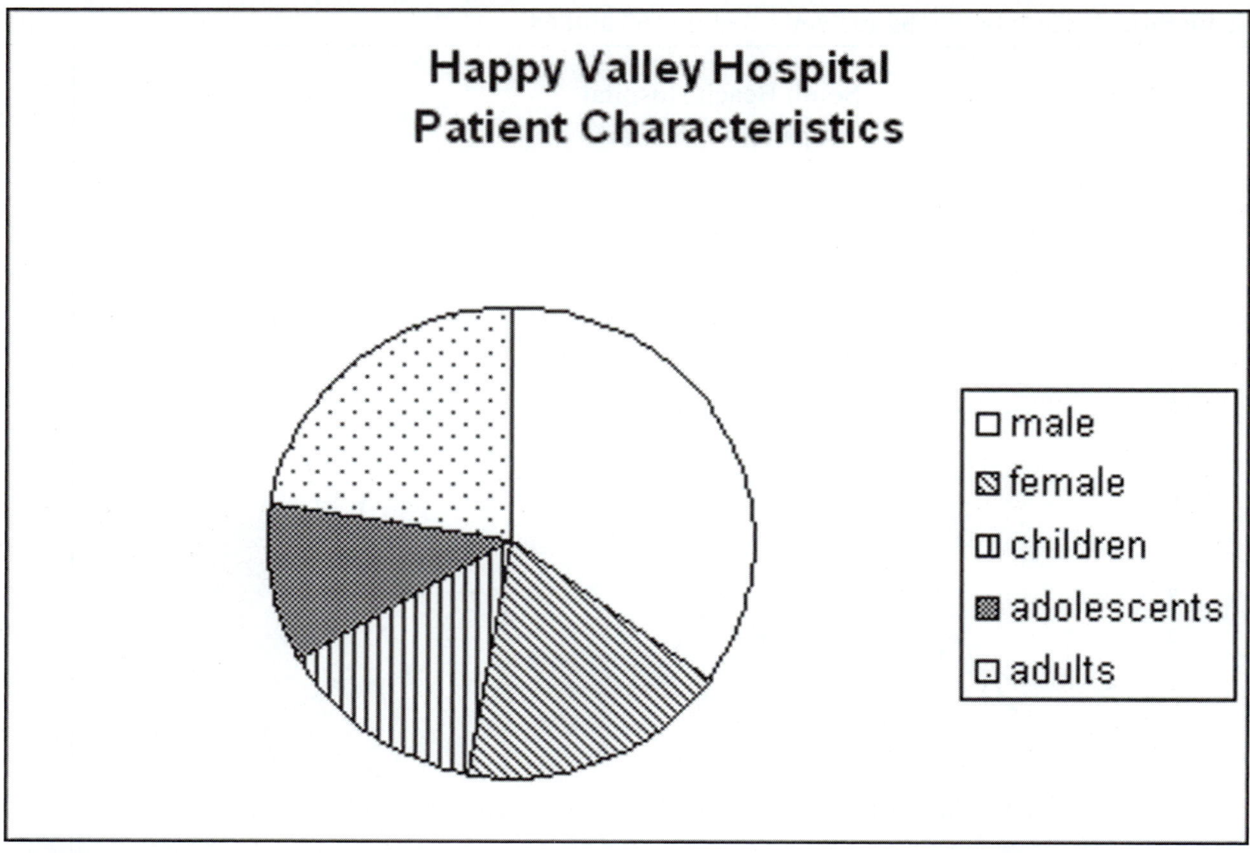

65. What is the biggest problem with the pie graph displayed above?
   A. There is not enough variation in the patterns to clearly distinguish between females and children.
   B. The total males and females do not equal the total children, adolescents, and adults.
   C. There are no definitions for children, adolescents, and adults.
   D. There is more than one variable displayed on the chart.

REFERENCE: Horton, pp 210–211
Koch, pp 256–257
LaTour, Eichenwald-Maki, and Oachs, pp 510–511
McWay, pp 213–214

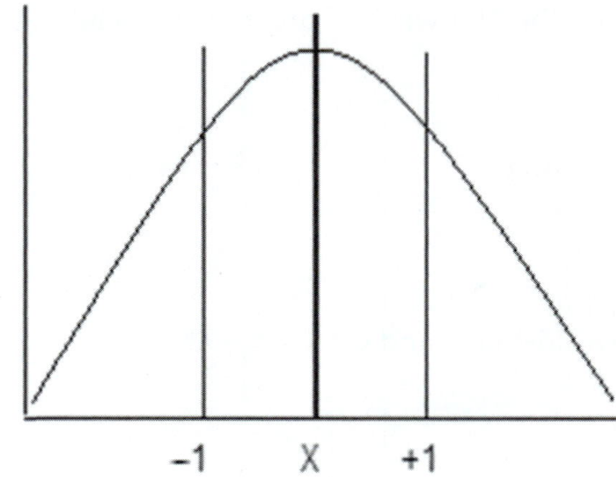

66. The chart above shows a normal distribution. What percentage of the cases fall within the two lines showing the standard distribution between –1 and +1 on either side of the mean?
   A. 68%
   B. 75%
   C. 95%
   D. 99%

REFERENCE: Horton, pp 184–186
Koch, pp 227–240
LaTour, Eichenwald-Maki, and Oachs, pp 520–521

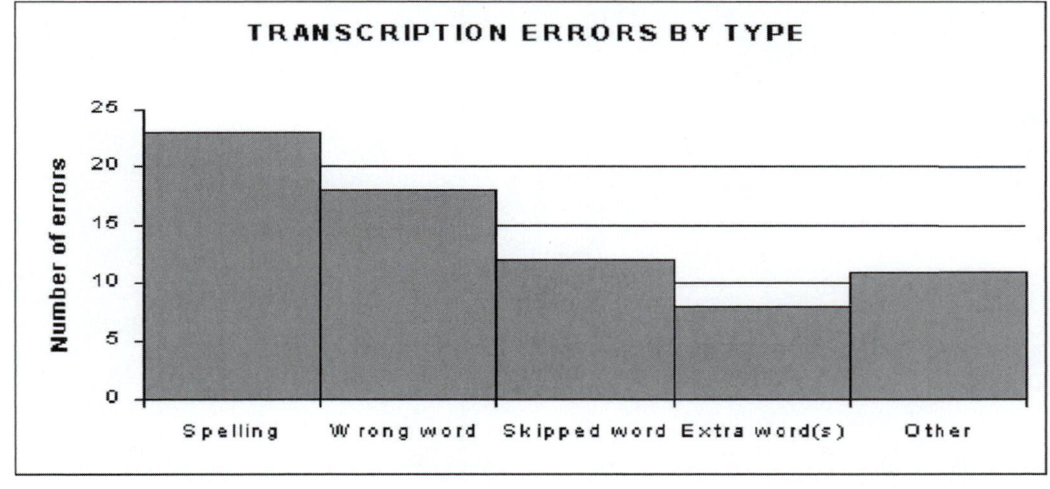

67. A transcription supervisor collected the data displayed above. What kind of data display is it? And how many errors are attributed to skipped words?
   A. This is a Pareto diagram; twelve (12) errors were due to skipped words.
   B. This is a bar chart; eighteen (18) errors were due to skipped words.
   C. This is a Pareto diagram; eighteen (18) errors were due to skipped words.
   D. This is a bar chart; twelve (12) errors were due to skipped words.

REFERENCE: Abdelhak, pp 127, 395–399
LaTour, Eichenwald-Maki, and Oachs, p 510
McWay, p 213

68. A fetal death occurring during the 21st week of pregnancy, weighing 1,000 g is considered to be a(n)
    A. early fetal death.
    B. preterm neonate.
    C. intermediate fetal death.
    D. late fetal death.

REFERENCE: Horton, p 88
Koch, pp 156–158
LaTour, Eichenwald-Maki, and Oachs, p 492
Sayles, pp 490–491

Section IV—Research, Financial Statistics, Etc.

You will use your statistics skills for a number of HIM functions. As usual, you must be prepared for that nebulous category we call "other." For these questions, use your basic problem-solving skills along with the terminology you learned in your statistics class. Many of these questions deal primarily with research and budgeting matters, so they are typically considered more appropriate for the RHIA than the RHIT. The RHIA questions are listed last and are so labeled.

69. Harry H. Potts was admitted to your hospital to receive a second round of chemotherapy for an invasive tumor. Four days after admission, Harry complained of a sore throat and developed a fever. Harry's throat culture was positive for strep. His strep throat will be
    A. added to the denominator of the hospital's nosocomial infection rate.
    B. added to the numerator of the hospital's community-acquired infection rate.
    C. considered separately because Harry H. Potts is immune suppressed from chemotherapy.
    D. added to the numerator of the hospital's nosocomial infection rate.

REFERENCE: Abdelhak, pp 390–391
Horton, pp 116–117
Koch, pp 189–190
LaTour, Eichenwald-Maki, and Oachs, p 495
McWay, pp 201–211
Sayles, p 497

70. Twelve new cases of a certain disease occurred during the month of August. If 4,000 persons were at risk during August, then the
    A. prevalence was 3 per 1,000 persons.
    B. prevalence was 6 per 1,000 persons.
    C. incidence was 3 per 1,000 persons.
    D. incidence was 6 per 1,000 persons.

REFERENCE: Abdelhak, p 391
Koch, pp 210–211
LaTour, Eichenwald-Maki, and Oachs, p 506
McWay, p 210
Sayles, pp 516–517

71. The primary difference between an experimental (randomized) clinical trial and other observational study designs in epidemiology is that in an experimental trial, the
    A. study is prospective.
    B. investigator determines who is and who is not exposed.
    C. study is case controlled.
    D. study and control maps are selected on the basis of exposure to the suspected causal factor.

REFERENCE: Abdelhak, pp 435–436
Horton, pp 232–234
McWay, pp 234–237

72. The ability to obtain the same results from different studies using different methodologies and different populations is

    A. reliability.
    B. validity.
    C. confidence.
    D. specificity.

REFERENCE: Abdelhak, pp 421–422
Horton, pp 232–233
Layman and Watzlaf, pp 221–222
McWay, pp 240–241

73. You have been conducting productivity studies on your coders and find that 20% of their time is devoted to querying physicians about missing or unclear diagnoses. Assuming your coders work a 7-hour day, how many minutes do they spend per day querying physicians?

    A. 21
    B. 56
    C. 84
    D. 140

REFERENCE: Horton, pp 147–148
Koch, pp 77–80

Use these data to calculate answers to questions 74 and 75.

Venice Bay Health Center collected the data displayed below concerning its four highest volume MS-DRGs.

MS-DRG A		MS-DRG B		MS-DRG C		MS-DRG D	
CMS WEIGHT	NUMBER PATIENTS WITH THIS MS-DRG	CMS WEIGHT	NUMBER PATIENTS WITH THIS MS-DRG	CMS WEIGHT	NUMBER PATIENTS WITH THIS MS-DRG	CMS WEIGHT	NUMBER PATIENTS WITH THIS MS-DRG
2.023	323	0.987	489	1.925	402	1.243	386

74. The MS-DRG that generated the most revenue for Venice Bay Health Center is
    A. MS-DRG A.
    B. MS-DRG B.
    C. MS-DRG C.
    D. MS-DRG D.

REFERENCE: Horton, pp 158–159
LaTour, Eichenwald-Maki, and Oachs, pp 496–497
Sayles, p 269

75. CMS has increased the weight for MS-DRG A by 14%, increased the weight for MS-DRG B by 20%, and decreased the weight for MS-DRG D by 10%. Given these new weights, which MS-DRG generated the most revenue for Venice Bay Health Center?
    A. MS-DRG A
    B. MS-DRG B
    C. MS-DRG C
    D. MS-DRG D

REFERENCE: Horton, pp 158–159
Sayles, p 269

Use these data to answer questions 76 and 77.

Sea Side Clinic (SSC) provides episode of care service for four insurance companies. Data on services provided and reimbursement received are provided below.

COMPANY	UNITS OF SERVICE A	REIMBURSEMENT FOR SERVICE A	UNITS OF SERVICE B	REIMBURSEMENT FOR SERVICE B	TOTAL REIMBURSEMENT
Lifecare	259	31,196.55	812	163,577.40	194,773.95
Get Well	786	100,859.52	465	96,929.25	197,788.77
SureHealth	462	54,631.50	509	107,093.60	161,725.10
Be Healthy	219	26,991.75	417	89,425.65	116,417.40

76. It would be most profitable for Sea Side Clinic to increase episode of care service with
    A. Lifecare.
    B. Get Well.
    C. SureHealth.
    D. BeHealthy.

REFERENCE: Horton, pp 175–180
Koch, pp 222–226
LaTour, Eichenwald-Maki, and Oachs, pp 518–520
Sayles, pp 538–541

77. The most profitable insurance company for the units of services Sea Side Clinic performs is
    A. service A with Lifecare.
    B. service B with GetWell.
    C. service A with SureHealth.
    D. service B with BeHealthy.

REFERENCE: Horton, pp 175–180
Koch, pp 222–226
LaTour, Eichenwald-Maki, and Oachs, pp 518–520
Sayles, pp 538–541

Use these statistics to calculate answers to questions 78 and 79.

The physicians at Sunset Shore Clinic reported the following statistics last Tuesday.

PHYSICIAN	SERVICE A	SERVICE B	SERVICE C
Truba	10	18	14
Wooley	14	22	9
Howe	18	5	6
Masters	12	20	7

78. The physician who performed the highest number of services overall last Tuesday was Doctor
    A. Truba.
    B. Wooley.
    C. Howe.
    D. Masters.

REFERENCE: Horton, pp 147–148
Koch, pp 77–80

79. It takes twice as long to perform Service C, so the doctors decided Service C should count as two services for the purpose of calculating workload. If Service C counts twice as much as Service A or Service B, then the physician who provided the most services was Doctor
    A. Truba.
    B. Wooley.
    C. Howe.
    D. Masters.

REFERENCE: Horton, pp 147–148
Koch, pp 77–80

The following questions begin advanced competencies.

80. Your facility conducted a study of patient satisfaction, but you question the reliability of the questionnaire you used. The high degree of patient satisfaction expressed on the questionnaire just does not match the large number of complaints you have been receiving. You decide to try switching to an investigative strategy that will give you an immediate opportunity to review patient responses and correct errors. You have decided to use
    A. samples.
    B. interviews.
    C. observations.
    D. questionnaires.

REFERENCE: Horton, pp 232–233
LaTour, Eichenwald-Maki, and Oachs, pp 562–564

The next five questions are based on this study and the data collected for it.

The American Health Information Management Association conducted a study on job stress and job satisfaction in HIM professionals with more than 5 years of experience. The data they collected are displayed below.

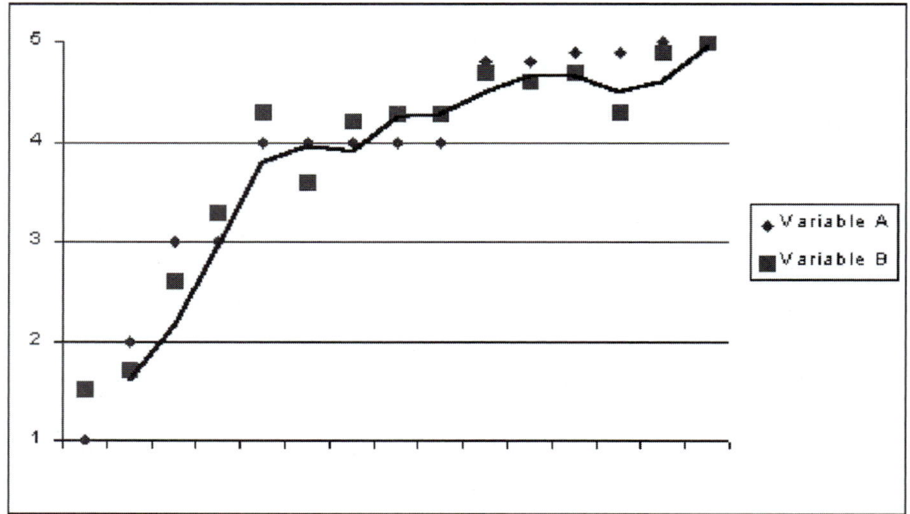

81. The researchers at AHIMA started by assuming there was no relationship between job stress and job satisfaction. This statement is generally called the
    A. study statement.
    B. false assumption.
    C. null hypothesis.
    D. correlation statement.

REFERENCE: Abdelhak, pp 402–404
Horton, pp 231–232
LaTour, Eichenwald-Maki, and Oachs, pp 570–571
McWay, p 239

82. Based on the data displayed in the graph AHIMA created,
    A. you can assume there is a positive relationship between variable A and variable B.
    B. you can assume there is a negative relationship between variable A and variable B.
    C. you can assume there is a causal relationship between variable A and variable B.
    D. you cannot make any assumptions without additional data.

REFERENCE: Horton, pp 216–219
Koch, pp 227–230
LaTour, Eichenwald-Maki, and Oachs, pp 513–514
McWay, pp 219–220
Sayles, pp 544–545

Very Dissatisfied	Somewhat Dissatisfied	Neutral	Somewhat Satisfied	Very Satisfied
1	2	3	4	5

83. The researchers at AHIMA who had professionals with 5 or more years' HIM experience rate their stress on a scale of 1–5, as shown in the chart above. Both job satisfaction and job stress are continuous variables. If the AHIMA researchers want to assess both the direction and the degree of the relationship between these two continuous variables, they may choose to compute the
    A. variable correlation coefficient.
    B. Pearson correlation coefficient.
    C. continuous correlation coefficient.
    D. Danbury correlation coefficient.

REFERENCE: Abdelhak, p 393
McWay, pp 215–216

84. There were some HIM professionals who refused to participate in a job stress/job satisfaction study. This is of great concern to the AHIMA researchers, who worry about the introduction of
    A. recall bias.
    B. selection bias.
    C. interviewer bias.
    D. nonresponse bias.

REFERENCE: Abdelhak, pp 405–406
LaTour, Eichenwald-Maki, and Oachs, p 583

85. A researcher has repeated the same study 10 times. Each time the study is repeated, the p value decreases. As the p value approaches zero, the
    A. size of the sample increases.
    B. value of the study decreases.
    C. chance that the results are due to a sampling error decreases.
    D. chance that the results are due to a sampling error increases.

REFERENCE: Abdelhak, pp 402–404
Horton, pp 250–253
LaTour, Eichenwald-Maki, and Oachs, pp 527–528

86. You and your colleague are designing a study to try to determine the ideal mean cost for a discretionary service. You will market your service to a very large population. Your colleague thinks you will get the best data if you take lots of small samples. You think the data will be more reliable if you take one or two very large samples.
    A. Your colleague is right—the mean of multiple samples will yield more reliable results.
    B. You are right—the means of a few large samples will yield more reliable results.
    C. You are equally correct—there is little difference in the reliability of these sampling methods.
    D. You are equally wrong—unless you use stratified sampling, you cannot expect reliable results.

REFERENCE: Abdelhak, pp 409–411
Horton, pp 241–242
LaTour, Eichenwald-Maki, and Oachs, pp 528–530

87. You are conducting a patient satisfaction survey in your outpatient clinic using interviewers who administer a questionnaire. Because you typically see about 300 people per day in the clinic, you decide to have the interviewers administer the questionnaire on every tenth patient. You are using
    A. systematic sampling.
    B. stratified sampling.
    C. variable sampling.
    D. convenience sampling.

REFERENCE: Abdelhak, pp 409–410
Horton, pp 242–246
LaTour, Eichenwald-Maki, and Oachs, pp 578–580

88. The people of Treasure Island Beach have been struck with a rash that seems to be infecting almost everyone in town. The staff of the hospital is working to design a study of this mysterious disease. They decide to do a cross-sectional study because cross-sectional or prevalence studies are known for
    A. quickly identifying cause and effect relationships that can serve as a basis for treatment.
    B. concurrently describing characteristics and health outcomes at one specific point in time.
    C. providing the information necessary to test for the most effective treatment of an illness or condition.
    D. supplying entire populations with therapeutic interventions on an epidemiologically sound basis.

REFERENCE: Abdelhak, pp 425–426
Koch, pp 210–211
LaTour, Eichenwald-Maki, and Oachs, pp 622–626
McWay, pp 237–238

89. You are planning a prospective study to try to prove a cause and effect relationship between dipping snuff and throat cancer. First, you identify subjects who regularly dip snuff and who are free of any signs of throat cancer. Next, you need to identify subjects who
    A. dip snuff regularly and who currently have throat cancer.
    B. dip snuff regularly and who currently have significant signs of throat cancer.
    C. do not dip snuff and who currently have significant signs of throat cancer.
    D. do not dip snuff and who are free of any signs of throat cancer.

REFERENCE: Abdelhak, pp 430–433
LaTour, Eichenwald-Maki, and Oachs, pp 622–624
McWay, p 237

90. Your administrator is concerned about the snuff study (see question 88). The administrator would like to consider using a case–control study model rather than the prospective one you are planning. One of the biggest reasons the administrator is promoting the case–control model is because case–control is
    A. more likely to be free of design errors than a prospective study.
    B. the best way to analytically test the hypothesis of cause and effect.
    C. more likely to decrease recall bias errors than prospective studies.
    D. less expensive than prospective studies because it uses existing records.

REFERENCE: Abdelhak, pp 430–432
LaTour, Eichenwald-Maki, and Oachs, pp 622–624
McWay, p 237

91. You point out to your administrator that the study model generally accepted to be the best method to determine the magnitude of risk in the population with the characteristic or suspected risk factor is the
    A. descriptive study design.
    B. analytic study design.
    C. prospective study design.
    D. case–control study design.

REFERENCE: Abdelhak, pp 430–436
LaTour, Eichenwald-Maki, and Oachs, pp 622–624
McWay, p 237

92. Investigator A claims that his results are statistically significant at the 10% level. Investigator B argues that significance should be announced only if the results are statistically significant at the 5% level. From this we can conclude that
   A. if investigator A has significant results at the 10% level, they will never be significant at the 5% level.
   B. it will be more difficult for investigator A to reject statistical null hypotheses if he always works at the 10% level compared with investigator B who works at the 5% level.
   C. if investigator A has significant results at the 10% level, they will also be significant at the 5% level.
   D. it will be less difficult for investigator A to reject statistical null hypotheses if he always works at the 10% level compared with investigator B who works at the 5% level.

REFERENCE: Abdelhak, pp 402–404
LaTour, Eichenwald-Maki, and Oachs, pp 571–573
McWay, pp 215–220

93. John Parker surveyed members of AHIMA's student COP regarding the relationship between clinical experiences and job opportunities. All respondents were seniors in HIA programs and each one expected to graduate and take the national exam within the next 6 months. Fifteen of the 18 respondents indicated that at least one clinical rotation had resulted in a job offer. Based on this information, Parker expects to be offered a job during senior clinical rotations. John is basing this expectation on
   A. scientific inquiry.
   B. empiricism.
   C. inductive reasoning.
   D. deductive reasoning.

REFERENCE: LaTour, Eichenwald-Maki, and Oachs, pp 548–549

Use the formula below as a resource to answer questions 94 and 95.

FORMULA FOR CALCULATING SAMPLE SIZE
$n = \dfrac{Np\,(1-p)}{(N-1)\,\dfrac{(B^2)}{4} + (p)\,(1-p)}$

94. If population size (N) = 1,200 and the proportion of subjects needed (p) = 0.5 and the acceptable amount of error (B) = 0.05, then sample size (n) =
   A. 200.
   B. 300.
   C. 400.
   D. 600.

REFERENCE: Abdelhak, pp 409–410
LaTour, Eichenwald-Maki, and Oachs, pp 579–580

95. After the researchers see the number of subjects they will have to interview, they reexamine their criteria. The researchers could decrease the number of subjects while having the least impact on the reliability of the study by
   A. increasing *p* and decreasing B.
   B. increasing *p* or decreasing B.
   C. decreasing *p* and increasing B.
   D. decreasing *p* or increasing B.

REFERENCE: Abdelhak, pp 409–410
LaTour, Eichenwald-Maki, and Oachs, pp 571–573

96. Which statistical analysis would be the best technique to use on the following problem?

> A study compared the effects of retesting on the scores of students who failed a writing test. Students who did not pass on their first attempt were allowed to retest. Results showed that students had higher mean scores at retest whether they attended additional training before retesting or not.

   A. descriptive stats
   B. ANOVA
   C. regression
   D. T test

REFERENCE: Abdelhak, pp 402–407
Horton, pp 250–257
McWay, pp 215–220

97. The name given to the error committed when the null hypothesis is rejected and it is actually true is
   A. type II error.
   B. selection bias.
   C. type I error.
   D. alternative hypothesis.

REFERENCE: Abdelhak, pp 402–404
LaTour, Eichenwald-Maki, and Oachs, pp 571–572
McWay, pp 224, 241

98. The major purpose of random assignment in a clinical trial is to
    A. reduce selection bias in allocation of treatment.
    B. help ensure that study subjects are representative of the general population.
    C. facilitate double-blinding.
    D. ensure that the study groups are comparable on baseline characteristics.

REFERENCE: Abdelhak, pp 432–436
LaTour, Eichenwald-Maki, and Oachs, pp 624–625
McWay, pp 235–237

99. In statistics, the notation "$\sum XY$" means
    A. summed all the values of the X variable and then multiplied this result times the values of the Y variable.
    B. summed all the values of the X variable, all the values of the Y variable, then multiplied all of these results.
    C. multiplied each pair of the X and Y scores, then summed their values.
    D. variation of the X and Y variable is multiplied then squared.

REFERENCE: Horton, p 183
Koch, p 222
LaTour, Eichenwald-Maki, and Oachs, p 518
Sayles, p 538

100. A major disadvantage of cross-sectional studies is that
    A. the time sequence of exposure and disease is usually not known.
    B. they are usually more expensive and can take a long time to complete.
    C. prevalence rates cannot be calculated.
    D. they cannot provide information on both exposure and disease status in the same individual.

REFERENCE: Abdelhak, pp 424–426
LaTour, Eichenwald-Maki, and Oachs, pp 622–623

101. A study found that liver cancer rates per 100,000 males among cigarette smokers and nonsmokers in a major U.S. city were 48.0 and 25.4, respectively. The relative risk of developing liver cancer for male smokers compared to nonsmokers is
   A. 1.89.
   B. 15.6.
   C. 22.6.
   D. 48.0.

REFERENCE: Abdelhak, pp 430–432
LaTour, Eichenwald-Maki, and Oachs, p 625
McWay, p 251

102. The standard deviation of a particular set of measures was found to be 20.00. The sample variance would then be
   A. 20
   B. 5
   C. 400
   D. 10

REFERENCE: Horton, pp 182–185
Koch, pp 231–232
LaTour, Eichenwald-Maki, and Oachs, p 520

103. If a constant is added to all measurements within a sample
   A. the mean remains the same.
   B. the standard deviation remains the same.
   C. the mean remains the same *and* the standard deviation remains the same.
   D. neither the mean nor the standard deviation remains the same.

REFERENCE: Horton, pp 182–185
Koch, pp 231–232
LaTour, Eichenwald-Maki, and Oachs, pp 518–520

104. Measurements within sample A are assumed to be more variable than measurements within sample B when
   A. sample A and sample B have the same mean.
   B. individuals within sample A are more alike than individuals within sample B.
   C. individuals within sample A differ more from one another than individuals within sample B.
   D. sample A and sample B have the same standard deviation.

REFERENCE: Horton, pp 182–185
Koch, pp 231–232
LaTour, Eichenwald-Maki, and Oachs, pp 518–520

105. _______________ refers to the flatness or peakedness of one distribution in relation to another distribution.
   A. Skewness
   B. Correlation
   C. Central tendency
   D. Kurtosis

REFERENCE: Horton, pp 187–189
Koch, pp 227–230
LaTour, Eichenwald-Maki, and Oachs, p 521

106. Given a positively skewed frequency distribution
   A. the frequencies are identical between the mean, median, and mode.
   B. larger frequencies are concentrated at the low end of the variable.
   C. larger frequencies are concentrated at the high end of the variable.
   D. largest frequencies occur at both low and high ends of the variable.

REFERENCE: Horton, pp 187–189
Koch, pp 227–230
LaTour, Eichenwald-Maki, and Oachs, p 521

Answer Key for Health Statistics and Research

ANSWER EXPLANATION

1. C (27 × 100) / 1,652 = 1.6%
2. D Calculate the answer as follows:

PHYSICIAN NAME	NUMBER OF HOURS WORKED	NUMBER OF PATIENTS SEEN	NUMBER OF PATIENTS SEEN PER HOUR WORKED
Robinson	32	185	185/32 = 5.78
Beasley	30	161	161/30 = 5.37
Hiltz	35	200	200/35 = 5.71
Wolf	26	157	157/26 = 6.04

3. A 3,545 requested records × 100 / 150,000 total records = 354,500/150,000 = 2.36 = 2.4%.
4. D
5. A Calculations: 95% of the observations fall within two standard deviations of the mean, so the cost of a lunch at Bon Appetite will be between $6.50 [8 – (2 × 0.75)] and $9.50 [8 + (2 × 0.75)].
   Lunch at Mario's will be between $5.50 [7.5 – (2 × 1)] and $9.50 [7.5 + (2 × 1)].
   Lunch at Au Courant will cost too much [$9 + (2 × 1.25) = $11.50].
   As will the Windy City Grill [$7.50 (2 × 1.5) = $10.50].
6. B
7. A
8. C Calculations:

	Records under Review	Same Code on Self-Coding Review	Intrarater Reliability Percentage	Same Code on Peer-Coding Review	Interrater Reliability Percentage	Mean Reliability Percentage
Coder A	28	22	78.57	20	71.43	75.00
Coder B	18	16	88.89	16	88.89	88.89
Coder C	45	42	93.33	43	95.56	94.44
Coder D	17	15	88.24	16	94.12	91.18

9 D
10. C
11. D
12. B
13. B Calculation: 5 + 9 + 8 + 12 + 6 + 7 + 5 + 10 + 7 + 9 + 11 = 89 / 11 = 8.09
14. B Calculate the mean time each physician spent with patients as follows:

PHYSICIAN	TIMES WITH PATIENTS	AVERAGE (MEAN) TIME WITH PATIENTS
Beasley	8, 6, 7	7
Robinson	5, 9, 9	7.7
Baumstark	10, 7	8.5
Wolf	12, 5, 11	9.3

15. A
16. A

Answer Key for Health Statistics and Research

	ANSWER	EXPLANATION
17.	C	
18.	A	
19.	B	
20	C	
21.	D	
22.	D	
23.	B	
24.	B	40 + 10 + 5 + 2 = 57
25.	D	67 + 2 = 69 admissions/discharges same day (Transfers to other facilities and deaths are forms of discharge.)
26.	A	(75,860 + 7,100) / 365 = 227 (Note: Average daily census includes adult and pediatrics, but NOT newborns.)
27.	B	
28.	B	The day of admission is counted as an inpatient service day, but the day of discharge is not.
29.	A	1/24 – 31 = 8 days + 2/1 through 2/8 = 8 days, so 8 + 8 = 16 (Count the day of admission but not discharge.)
30.	B	(12,345 × 100) / (500 × 28) = 88.2%
31.	B	9,457 discharge days/1,351 discharges = 7 days (Count the day of admission but not discharge.)
32.	D	Only two answers, "9.51 days" and "4.91 days," are correctly calculated. Should you choose to include the unusually long LOS, you should make a note to avoid confusing readers, which makes the answer "9.51 days—no further information is necessary" a poor choice. Should you choose to eliminate the potentially confusing LOS, you must subtract both the patient from the total discharges and the discharge days from the total discharge days.
33.	B	$\frac{(28{,}690 + 27{,}400 + 19{,}250) \times 100}{(151 \times 200) + (137 \times 250) + (77 \times 275)} = 88.0 = 88\%$
34.	C	Use the direct method, bed turnover. 16,570 adult and peds discharges/200 adult and peds beds = 82.85 = 82.9%
35.	A	200 beds × 365 days in a nonleap year = 73,000 (Note: Bassinets are excluded.)
36.	C	$\frac{(5 \times 100)}{(225 + 5)} = 2.2\%$
37.	C	50 + (3 sets of twins × 2 births per set) = 56 births
38.	B	Multiple births are one delivery; fetal deaths are counted as deliveries 50 + 3 + 1 + 1 = 55
39.	D	
40.	D	
41.	C	Calculations: 361 total inpatient deaths × 100/6,614 total discharges = 5.45 = 5.5% Fetal deaths and outpatient deaths are not included in this calculation.

Answer Key for Health Statistics and Research

ANSWER EXPLANATION

42. B Calculations:

$$\frac{(108 \text{ total inpatient deaths} > 48 \text{ hours}) \times 100}{(6{,}614 \text{ total discharges} - 253 \text{ deaths} < 48 \text{ hours})} = \frac{10800}{6{,}361} = 1.697 = 1.7\%$$

43. B 48 – 38 deaths over 48 hours = 10 deaths less than 48 hours. $\frac{(48 - 10)\,(100)}{(1{,}382 - 10)}$

44. B

45. B

46. C LOS would increase through the year and drop when patient is discharged.

47. A

$$\frac{(72 \text{ intermediate and late fetal deaths} \times 100)}{(980 \text{ births} + 72 \text{ intermediate and late fetal deaths})} = \frac{7{,}200}{1{,}052} = 6.8\%$$

48. C (3,699 × 100) / 20,932 = 17.7%

49. A

50. C

51. D

52. C

53. B

54. C

55. A

56. A

57. D

58. B

59. B

60. A

61. A

62. A

63. D

64. C

65. D

66. A

67. A

68. C

69. D

70. C

71. B

72. A

73. C 7 hours per day × 60 minutes per hour = 420 minutes per day. 20% of 420 = 84

Answer Key for Health Statistics and Research

ANSWER EXPLANATION

74. C Calculations:
- MS-DRG A = 2.023 × 323 = 653.43
- MS-DRG B = 0.987 × 489 = 482.64
- MS-DRG C = 1.925 × 402 = 773.85
- MS-DRG D = 1.243 × 386 = 479.80

75. C Calculations:
- MS-DRG A = 2.023 × 0.14 = 0.283; 0.283 + 2.023 = 2.306 × 323 = 744.84
- MS-DRG B = 0.987 × 0.20 = 0.197; 0.987 + 0.197 = 1.184 × 489 = 578.98
- MS-DRG C = 1.925 × 402 = 773.85
- MS-DRG D = 1.243 × 0.10 = 0.124; 1.243 – 0.124 = 1.119 × 386 = 431.93

76. D Arrive at the answer by calculating the reimbursement per unit for each service and averaging those answers, as shown below.

INSURANCE COMPANY	UNITS OF SERVICE A	REIMBURSE-MENT FOR SERVICE A	REIMBURSE-MENT PER UNIT FOR SERVICE A	UNITS OF SERVICE B	REIMBURSE-MENT FOR SERVICE B	REIMBURSE-MENT PER UNIT FOR SERVICE B	TOTAL REIMBURSE MENT	AVERAGE REIMBURSE-MENT PER UNIT OF SERVICE
Lifecare	259	31,196.55	120.45	812	163,577.40	201.45	194,773.95	160.95
Get-Well	786	100,859.52	128.32	465	96,929.25	208.45	197,788.77	168.39
SureHealth	462	54,631.50	118.25	509	107,093.60	210.40	161,725.10	164.33
Be-Healthy	219	26,991.75	123.25	417	89,425.65	214.45	116,417.40	168.85

77. D Refer the table above.

78. B Calculate by adding total services.

PHYSICIAN	SERVICE A	SERVICE B	SERVICE C	TOTAL SERVICES
Truba	10	22	10	42
Wooley	14	22	9	45
Howe	18	5	6	29
Masters	12	20	7	39

79. A Double Service C in the table above.

80. B

81. C

82. A

83. C

84. D

85. C

86. B

87. A

88. B

89. D

90. D

91. C

Answer Key for Health Statistics and Research

ANSWER EXPLANATION

92. B
93. C
94. B

$$n = \frac{(1200)\,(0.5)\,(1-0.5)}{(1200-1)\,\frac{(0.05^2)}{4} + (0.5)\,(1-0.5)}.$$

$$n = \frac{300}{(1199)\,(0.000625) + 0.25}.$$

$$n = \frac{300}{0.749 + 0.25} = \frac{300}{1} = 300$$

95. D
96. D
97. C
98. A
99. C
100. A
101. A RR = risk exposed divided by risk not exposed = 48 divided by 25.4 = 1.89
102. C
103. B
104. C
105. D
106. B

REFERENCES

Abdelhak, M., and Hanken, M. A. (2016). *Health information: Management of a strategic resource* (5th ed.). St. Louis, MO: Saunders Elsevier.

Horton, L. (2012). *Calculating and reporting health care statistics* (4th ed.). Chicago: American Health Information Management Association (AHIMA).

Koch, G. (2015). *Basic allied health statistics and analysis* (4th ed.). Clifton Park, NY: Cengage Learning.

LaTour, K., Eichenwald-Maki, S., and Oachs, P. (2013). *Health information management: Concepts, principles, and practice* (4th ed.). Chicago: American Health Information Management Association (AHIMA).

McWay, D. C. (2014). *Today's health information management: An integrated approach* (2nd ed.). Clifton Park, NY: Cengage Learning.

Sayles, N. B. (2013). *Health information management technology: An applied approach* (4th ed.). Chicago: AHIMA Press.

Health Statistics and Research Competency Domains

COMPETENCIES FOR HEALTH STATISTICS AND RESEARCH					
Question	RHIA Domain Competencies				
	1	2	3	4	5
1-106			X		

COMPETENCIES FOR HEALTH STATISTICS AND RESEARCH							
Question	RHIT Domain Competencies						
	1	2	3	4	5	6	7
1	X						
2	X						
3					X		
4					X		
5					X		
6	X						
7	X						
8	X						
9	X						
10					X		
11					X		
12	X						
13	X						
14	X						
15	X						
16	X						
17	X						
18	X						
19	X						
20	X						
21	X						
22	X						
23	X						
24	X						
25	X						
26	X						
27	X						
28	X						
29	X						
30	X						
31	X						
32	X						
33	X						
34	X						
35	X						
36	X						
37	X						
38	X						
39	X						
40	X						
41	X						
42	X						
43	X						
44					X		
45					X		

Question	RHIT Domain Competencies						
	1	2	3	4	5	6	7
46					X		
47	X						
48	X						
49					X		
50	X						
51					X		
52					X		
53					X		
54					X		
55					X		
56					X		
57					X		
58					X		
59					X		
60					X		
61					X		
62					X		
63					X		
64					X		
65					X		
66					X		
67					X		
68	X						
69					X		
70					X		
71					X		
72					X		
73		X					
74		X					
75		X					
76		X					
77		X					
78		X					
79		X					

XIV. Quality and Performance Improvement

Shelley C. Safian, PhD, CCS-P, CPC-H, CPC-I, CHA

AHIMA-Approved ICD-10-CM/PCS Trainer

1. What process assists a health care facility in continuously looking at the ways that problems develop and seeking ways to prevent problems from happening in the future?
   A. risk management
   B. quality control
   C. utilization management
   D. performance improvement

REFERENCE: Abdelhak, p 470
Davis and LaCour, pp 359–360
LaTour, Eichenwald-Maki, and Oachs, pp 650–652
McWay, pp 172, 187–189
Sayles, pp 595–598
Shaw, p 4

2. The current hospital policy time frame for authenticating verbal orders adheres to the CMS COP that requires the ordering physician, or another health care practitioner responsible for the care of the patient, to write orders according to hospital policy and authenticate
   A. based on the physician's time schedule.
   B. based on the severity of the illness.
   C. within 12 hours.
   D. as per governmental and facility policies.

REFERENCE: CMS CM (1)
AHIMA (2012a)
LaTour, Eichenwald-Maki, and Oachs, p 248

3. The Blood Usage Review Committee has a quality monitor established to review all blood transfusion reaction cases. The HIM Director will be working with the committee to identify and abstract patient outcome information for committee evaluation. What data should be collected?
   A. effects of transfusion reaction (e.g., rash, death, etc.)
   B. type and cross-match accuracy
   C. justification for the transfusion
   D. all relevant data

REFERENCE: LaTour, Eichenwald-Maki, and Oachs, pp 665–666
Shaw, pp 136–137

4. As supervisor of the record completion function of the HIM department, you are asked for record completion statistics for specific physicians who are being evaluated for reappointment to the medical staff. Which of the following information elements would you report for each physician?
   A. physician education and training
   B. number of delinquent records
   C. state licensure expiration date
   D. prior physician malpractice claims history

REFERENCE: Abdelhak, pp 122–123, 476–477
Davis and LaCour, p 130
LaTour, Eichenwald-Maki, and Oachs, p 266
McWay, p 24
Shaw, p 296

5. The Recovery Audit Contractor (RAC) program was developed to identify and reduce improper payments for
   A. Medicaid claims.
   B. Medicare claims.
   C. both Medicare claims and collection of overpayments.
   D. collection of overpayments.

REFERENCE: CMS (2)
Davis and LaCour, pp 208, 354–355
LaTour, Eichenwald-Maki, and Oachs, pp 855–856
McWay, p 71
Sayles, p 310

6. A document requirement of health facilities pursuant to HIPAA legislation, that informs patient how a covered entity intends to use and disclose protected health information is called
   A. Notice of Privacy Practices (NPP).
   B. informed consent.
   C. incident report.
   D. periodic performance review (PPR).

REFERENCE: CMS (4)
CMS (5)
Davis and LaCour, p 389
LaTour, Eichenwald-Maki, and Oachs, pp 244, 314
McWay, pp 72–73
Sayles, pp 102–103
Shaw, p 432

7. Clinical privileges are granted to the physician for an interval specified in the medical staff by laws, but not longer than
   A. 6 months.
   B. 1 year.
   C. 2 years.
   D. 3 years.

REFERENCE: LaTour, Eichenwald-Maki, and Oachs, p 331
Sayles, pp 102–103, 451
Shaw, p 296

8. The hospital implemented an electronic query system to allow more effective communication with physicians and other health practitioners to improve clinical documentation in the patient record. This program is known as
   A. core measure reporting.
   B. clinical documentation improvement (CDI).
   C. tumor registry (TR).
   D. evidence-based medicine.

REFERENCE: AHIMA (3)
Davis and LaCour, pp 191–192
LaTour, Eichenwald-Maki, and Oachs, p 442
Sayles, pp 120–121

9. The person or group who is overall responsible and accountable for maintaining the quality and safety of patient care is the
   A. Chief Nursing Officer (CNO).
   B. Board of Directors (BOD) or governing body.
   C. Chief Executive Officer (CEO).
   D. Quality Improvement Director.

REFERENCE: LaTour, Eichenwald-Maki, and Oachs, p 663
Sayles, pp 597, 674
Shaw, p 318

10. What quality indicator would prove useful in tracking customer satisfaction in the correspondence/release of information function?
   A. the number of medical record personnel required to perform the function
   B. the amount of overtime necessary to stay current
   C. the number of charts pulled for correspondence requests
   D. the turnaround time from the date a request is received to the date the information is provided to the requester

REFERENCE: LaTour, Eichenwald-Maki, and Oachs, pp 653, 815
Shaw, pp 118–119

11. Most acute care facilities use this type of screening criteria for utilization review purposes to determine the need for inpatient services and justification for continued stay.
   A. severity of illness/intensity of service criteria (SI/IS)
   B. critical pathways
   C. Joint Commission defined and developed criteria
   D. Health Plan Employer Data & Information (HEDIS) measures

REFERENCE: Abdelhak, pp 470–474
LaTour, Eichenwald-Maki, and Oachs, p 464
Davis and LaCour, p 377
Sayles, p 610
Shaw, p 119

12. The improvement process of comparing the collection and coding of POA indicators at your facility with those of comparable departments of superior performance of other health care facilities is referred to as
   A. focused review.
   B. benchmarking.
   C. peer review.
   D. occurrence screening.

REFERENCE: Abdelhak, pp 458–459
Davis and LaCour, pp 65, 363
LaTour, Eichenwald-Maki, and Oachs, pp 653, 808
McWay, pp 179, 183
Sayles, pp 594, 625, 1122
Shaw, p 16

13. With the passage of Medicare (Title XVIII of the Social Security Act) in 1965, which of the following functions became mandatory?
    A. quality improvement
    B. risk management
    C. quality assessment
    D. utilization review

REFERENCE: Abdelhak, pp 471–474
CMS 6
LaTour, Eichenwald-Maki, and Oachs, pp 15–16
McWay, pp 192–195
Sayles, pp 654–655
Shaw, p xxv

14. An ophthalmologist has requested permission to perform specialized laser procedures within the hospital. His request is evaluated by the Credentials Committee through a process to determine the specific procedures and services this physician can perform. This is known as
    A. discharge planning.
    B. medical staff evaluation.
    C. delineation of privileges.
    D. reappointment.

REFERENCE: Abdelhak, p 476
LaTour and Eichenwald-Maki, pp 330–331
McWay, pp 23–24
Sayles, p 834
Shaw, p 294

15. Major responsibilities of the Risk Manager generally include
    A. loss prevention and reduction.
    B. vetting physician appointment applicants.
    C. evaluating HIE data.
    D. defining PHI.

REFERENCE: Abdelhak, pp 470–471
LaTour and Eichenwald-Maki, pp 860–863
McWay, pp 189–191
Sayles, pp 613–620
Shaw, pp 189, 196–200

16. Needlesticks, patient or employee falls, medication errors, or any event not consistent with routine patient care activities would require risk reporting documentation in the form of an
    A. operative report.
    B. emergency room report.
    C. incident report.
    D. insurance claim.

REFERENCE: Abdelhak, p 465
Davis and LaCour, pp 378–379
LaTour and Eichenwald-Maki, pp 860–863
McWay, p 189
Sayles, pp 613–620
Shaw, p 189

17. The responsibility for performing quality monitoring and evaluation activities in a departmentalized hospital is delegated to the
    A. director of utilization management.
    B. chairman of the board of trustees.
    C. clinical chairpersons of medical staff committees or ancillary department directors.
    D. chief executive officer.

REFERENCE: LaTour and Eichenwald-Maki, pp 860–863
Sayles, pp 613–620
Shaw, pp 318, 320

18. What criterion is critical in selecting performance indicators for a health information management department?
    A. The indicators must include the most important aspects of performance.
    B. Indicators must correlate with Deming's 14 points.
    C. Identify at least 25 indicators that are reflective of all department functions.
    D. Select only indicators that reflect positively on the department.

REFERENCE: LaTour and Eichenwald-Maki, pp 652–653, 807
Sayles, p 358
Shaw, pp 6–7

19. In the Act phase of the PDSA method (also the PSDA method), what step can assist in implementing change in a department?
    A. analyzing data
    B. distributing new policies and procedures to people affected by the changes and explaining the rationale for the changes
    C. collecting data
    D. preparing for implementation of the new strategy

REFERENCE: Abdelhak, pp 456–457
Davis and LaCour, pp 359–361
LaTour and Eichenwald-Maki, p 820
McWay, pp 173–175
Sayles, pp 613–620

20. What feature distinguishes the Nominal Group Technique (NGT) from brainstorming?
    A. NGT can be accomplished by mail.
    B. NGT uses a visual device like a flip chart to keep track of responses.
    C. NGT draws responses from a large group of people.
    D. NGT determines the importance of responses through a rating system.

REFERENCE: Abdelhak, p 460
LaTour and Eichenwald-Maki, p 822
McWay, p 179
Sayles, pp 593–594
Shaw, pp 20–21

21. When the policy and procedures manual no longer reflect current practices, it creates a situation that becomes a risk management issue because
    A. supervisory time and effort will be wasted to correct the manual.
    B. training of new personnel will not be standardized.
    C. broad and permissive policy statements cannot commit the organization to a course of action.
    D. policy and procedures should represent the normal course of business.

REFERENCE: LaTour and Eichenwald-Maki, pp 560, 804–805
Sayles, p 807
Shaw, p 189

22. The medical malpractice crisis of the 1970s prompted the development of ____________________ in health care facilities.
    A. utilization management
    B. financial analysis programs
    C. quality improvement programs
    D. risk management

REFERENCE: LaTour and Eichenwald-Maki, pp 44, 860–861
McWay, p 189
Shaw, p 426

23. The following legislation requires that patient-identifiable health information remains confidential and protected against unauthorized disclosure, alteration, or destruction.
    A. HIPAA Security Rule
    B. Patient Care Act
    C. Privacy Act of 1974
    D. Workman's Compensation Act

REFERENCE: LaTour and Eichenwald-Maki, pp 208, 310
McWay, pp 11, 69, 291–293
Sayles, pp 170, 833, 1026–1027

24. The hospital Quality Department adopted the Lean Management quality model using JIT, which ensures required process items and resources are
    A. available at the right place and the right time.
    B. for the correct patient, using the correct procedure, at the correct site.
    C. always kept stocked in Central Processing.
    D. automatically restocked to maintain a surplus.

REFERENCE: LaTour, Eichenwald-Maki, and Oachs, pp 742, 829

25. The Utilization Review Coordinator reviews inpatient records at regular intervals to justify necessity and appropriateness of care to warrant further hospitalization. Which of the following utilization review activities is being performed?
    A. admission review
    B. preadmission
    C. retrospective review
    D. continued stay review

REFERENCE: Abdelhak, pp 471–474
LaTour, Eichenwald-Maki, and Oachs, p 464
McWay, pp 191–193
Sayles, p 113
Shaw, p 113

26. The Joint Commission recently surveyed an acute care hospital. The hospital just received the survey report and the accreditation decision. Which of the following categories should the hospital leaders address first?
    A. Requirements for Improvement
    B. Grid Elements
    C. Written Progress Reports
    D. Triennial Exception Rules

REFERENCE: LaTour, Eichenwald-Maki, and Oachs, pp 817–819
Shaw, p 341

27. What feature is a trademark of an effective PI program?
    A. a one-time cure—all for a facility's problems
    B. an unmanageable project that is too expensive
    C. a cost-containment effort
    D. a continuous cycle of improvement projects over time

REFERENCE: Davis and LaCour, p 359
LaTour, Eichenwald-Maki, and Oachs, pp 818–820
McWay, pp 172, 187–189
Sayles, p 595
Shaw, pp 4–5

28. What quality improvement (QI) tool uses criteria to weigh different alternatives? This display would assist in viewing all relevant information at the same time.
    A. the PDSA method
    B. a decision matrix
    C. a flowchart
    D. a customer satisfaction survey

REFERENCE: Abdelhak, p 461
Davis and LaCour, pp 369–370
LaTour, Eichenwald-Maki, and Oachs, p 695

29. The QI plan for your hospital requires each coder maintain a minimum of 94.5% accuracy in coding. You manage the coding department, and the past year's average accuracy rating was 95.3%. The QI plan allows a standard deviation (SD) of ±2 against the minimum of 94.5% accuracy. Did your coding staff's overall average meet within standard deviation range?
    A. Yes, within ±2 below SD
    B. Yes, within ±2 above SD
    C. No, because it is >±2 below SD
    D. No, because it is >±2 above SD

REFERENCE: Abdelhak, pp 400–401
LaTour, Eichenwald-Maki, and Oachs, pp 520–521
Shaw, p 442

30. Surgical case review includes all the following EXCEPT
    A. determination of surgical justification based on clinical indication(s) in cases where no tissue has been removed.
    B. cases with elements missing in the preoperative anesthesia consultation.
    C. cases where there is a significant discrepancy between preoperative, postoperative, and pathological diagnoses.
    D. cases with serious surgical complications or surgical mortalities.

REFERENCE: LaTour, Eichenwald-Maki, and Oachs, p 665

31. What federal legislation passed in 1986 gave immunity from legal action to practitioners regarding some peer review process activities?
    A. Healthcare Quality Improvement Act
    B. Utilization Review Act
    C. Patient Protection and Affordable Care Act (PPACA)
    D. Health Insurance Portability and Accountability Act (HIPAA)

REFERENCE: Davis and LaCour, p 353
LaTour, Eichenwald-Maki, and Oachs, p 16
Sayles, pp 605–606
Shaw, p 430

32. The credentialing process requires healthcare facilities to
    A. query the NPDB to collect and report malpractice judgement and settlements.
    B. review and file the provider's resume.
    C. interview previous patients.
    D. watch the provider perform surgery.

REFERENCE: LaTour, Eichenwald-Maki, and Oachs, p 330
McWay, pp 22–24
Sayles, p 451

33. A plantiff must establish which burden of proof to recover damages for medical negligence or malpractice?
    1. A breach of the duty to care by the defendant.
    2. Damages or injury resulted from the defendant's negligence.
    3. A duty of care relationship between the defendant and patient.
    4. Causation existed for harm to the plantiff from the defendant's conduct.

    A. Only 1
    B. 1 and 3
    C. 1, 2, 3, and 4
    D. 2 and 4

REFERENCE: LaTour, Eichenwald-Maki, and Oachs, p 304
Sayles, p 783
Shaw, p 427

34. Reporting the monthly average turnaround time for the release of information (ROI) over a 6-month period using a run or line chart will reflect
    A. the quality of informed consents.
    B. trends and detect if improvements were made.
    C. the quality of appropriate authorized consents.
    D. the number of denied requests.

REFERENCE: Abdelhak, pp 463–464
LaTour, Eichenwald-Maki, and Oachs, p 824
McWay, pp 180, 213
Sayles, p 581

35. As an HIM coding supervisor, you are asked to compare the current coding process with a proposed concurrent coding process. What visual tool would be the best to identify all the logical steps and sequence of each procedure?
   A. decision matrix
   B. cause and effect diagram
   C. flowchart
   D. checksheet

REFERENCE: Abdelhak, pp 460–461
LaTour, Eichenwald-Maki, and Oachs, pp 804–805
McWay, pp 348–349
Sayles, p 585
Shaw, pp 166–172

36. Physicians who are members of the Surgery Committee meet to review surgical cases referred for quality issues and deviations from standard care norms. This type of review in which a physician's record is reviewed by his or her professional colleagues is known as
   A. concurrent review.
   B. clinical pertinence review.
   C. incident screening.
   D. peer review.

REFERENCE: Abdelhak, p 477
LaTour, Eichenwald-Maki, and Oachs, p 35
Sayles, p 585
Shaw, pp 324–325

37. Patient mortality, infection and complication rates, adherence to living will requirements, adequate pain control, and other documentation that describe end results of care or a measurable change in the patient's health are examples of
   A. outcome measures.
   B. threshold level.
   C. sentinel events.
   D. incident reports.

REFERENCE: Abdelhak, pp 438–439
LaTour, Eichenwald-Maki, and Oachs, pp 627–631
McWay, pp 127–128, 183
Sayles, pp 600, 604
Shaw, pp 14, 16

38. In quality review activities, departments are directed to focus on clinical processes that are
   A. low volume.
   B. expensive.
   C. the most commonplace.
   D. high risk.

REFERENCE: LaTour, Eichenwald-Maki, and Oachs, p 652
Shaw, pp 6, 17

39. The HIM department frequently experiences a backlog in loose report filing. A quality improvement team is assembled to identify the outcome variables and the major or root causes. What visual QI tool is helpful to report the findings?
   A. PDCA method
   B. run chart
   C. fishbone (cause and effect) diagram
   D. scatter diagram

REFERENCE: Abdelhak, p 461
Davis and LaCour, p 356
LaTour, Eichenwald-Maki, and Oachs, pp 822–823
McWay, p 179
Sayles, p 587

40. According to the HIPAA Privacy Rule, the following persons must adhere to the minimum necessary standard when releasing patient-specific information.
    A. physicians
    B. employees
    C. volunteers
    D. all members of the organization: clinicians, staff, and volunteers

REFERENCES: Davis and LaCour, p 391
LaTour, Eichenwald-Maki, and Oachs, p 133
McWay, pp 73, 515
Sayles, p 799

41. As the new Coding Manager, you met with the coding staff to encourage feedback on ways to increase coding accuracy to meet established benchmarks. The coders provided feedback through brainstorming that you compiled on flipcharts and organized into categories. This is known as a(n)
    A. affinity diagram.
    B. cause-and-effect diagram.
    C. flow process chart.
    D. nominal group technique.

REFERENCE: Abdelhak, p 460
LaTour, Eichenwald-Maki, and Oachs, p 822
McWay, pp 347, 349
Sayles, p 593
Shaw, pp 20–21

42. You sit on the quality improvement team for the Nursing department that meets to generate ideas to address verbal order documentation problems about the "Read Back Verbal Order" policy. What QI tool would prove useful in sharing input and various recommendations for solving this problem?
    A. flowchart
    B. scatter diagram
    C. check sheet
    D. brainstorming

REFERENCE: Abdelhak, p 460
Davis and LaCour, p 366
LaTour, Eichenwald-Maki, and Oachs, pp 821–822
McWay, pp 179, 346
Sayles, pp 592–593
Shaw, p 20

43. A histogram is a valuable tool for representing
    A. the solution to a problem.
    B. priorities in problem solving.
    C. a frequency distribution with continuous-interval data.
    D. the root causes of a problem.

REFERENCE: Abdelhak, p 462
Davis and LaCour, pp 309–310
LaTour, Eichenwald-Maki, and Oachs, pp 513, 824
McWay, pp 180–181
Sayles, pp 527–528

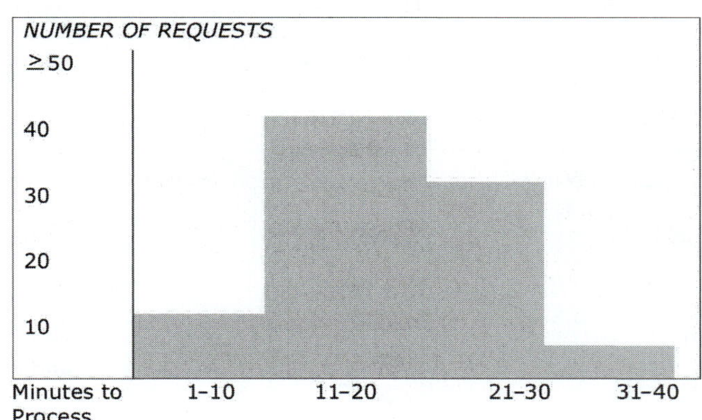

44. Eighty (80) requests for records to be pulled for the emergency room were processed in January. From the histogram provided above, what was the most frequent amount of time taken to process a request?
    A. 1–10 minutes
    B. 11–20 minutes
    C. 21–30 minutes
    D. 31–40 minutes

REFERENCE: Abdelhak, p 462
LaTour, Eichenwald-Maki, and Oachs, pp 513, 824
McWay, pp 180–181
Sayles, pp 527–528
Shaw, pp 57–58

45. Which quality management theorist focused on zero defects as the goal of performance improvement efforts?
    A. Kaizen
    B. Crosby
    C. Peters
    D. Deming

REFERENCE: Davis and LaCour, p 347
LaTour, Echenwald-Maki, and Oachs, p 651
McWay, pp 172–173
Sayles, pp 563, 565
Shaw, p xxvii

46. As Director of the HIM department, you are asked to chair a committee that will review, select, and implement a CPOE system. The information has been collected, and you bring your committee together to prioritize their suggestions. This method of working with information is known as
    A. force field analysis.
    B. Delphi process.
    C. nominal group process.
    D. correlation analysis.

REFERENCE: LaTour, Eichenwald-Maki, and Oachs, p 822
McWay, pp 179, 347
Sayles, pp 593–594
Shaw, pp 20–21

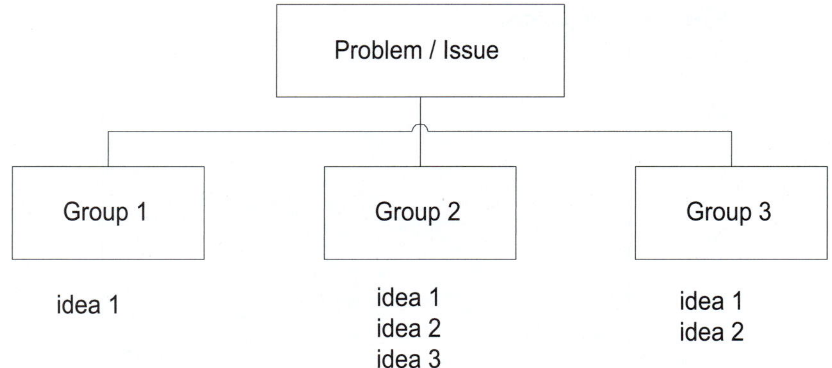

47. The performance tool shown above is used to provide structure by classifying information into smaller groups. What is the name of this chart/diagram?
    A. flowchart
    B. matrix
    C. affinity diagram
    D. arrow diagram

REFERENCE: Abdelhak, p 460
LaTour, Eichenwald-Maki, and Oachs, p 822
McWay, pp 179, 347, 349, 500
Sayles, p 593
Shaw, pp 20–21

48. Which quality management theorist believed that merit raises, formal evaluations, and quotas established through benchmarking hinder worker productivity and growth?
    A. Brian Joiner
    B. Philip Crosby
    C. Joseph Juran
    D. W. Edwards Deming

REFERENCE: Davis and LaCour, p 347
LaTour, Eichenwald-Maki, and Oachs, pp 687–688
Sayles, p 564
Shaw, p xxvii

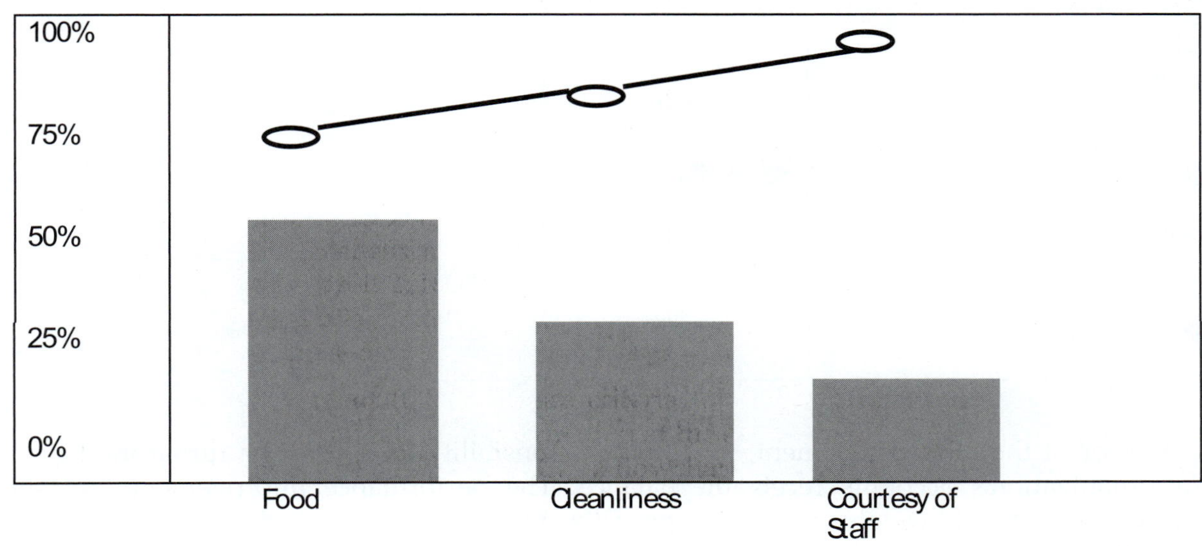

49. As head of the Performance Improvement Department, you are asked to evaluate patient satisfaction and offer recommendations for action. The performance tool shown above is used to graphically display the results. What is the name of this chart?
    A. Pareto chart
    B. line chart
    C. bar chart
    D. run chart

REFERENCE: Abdelhak, p 463
LaTour, Eichenwald-Maki, and Oachs, p 823
McWay, pp 179–180
Sayles, pp 591–592
Shaw, pp 58–59

50. Based on the previous graphic chart, which two areas should you recommend be acted upon first in order to address 80% of the patients' complaints?
    A. food and cleanliness
    B. food and courtesy of staff
    C. cleanliness and courtesy of staff
    D. not enough information to determine

REFERENCE: LaTour, Eichenwald-Maki, and Oachs, p 823
McWay, pp 179–180
Sayles, pp 591–592
Shaw, pp 58–59

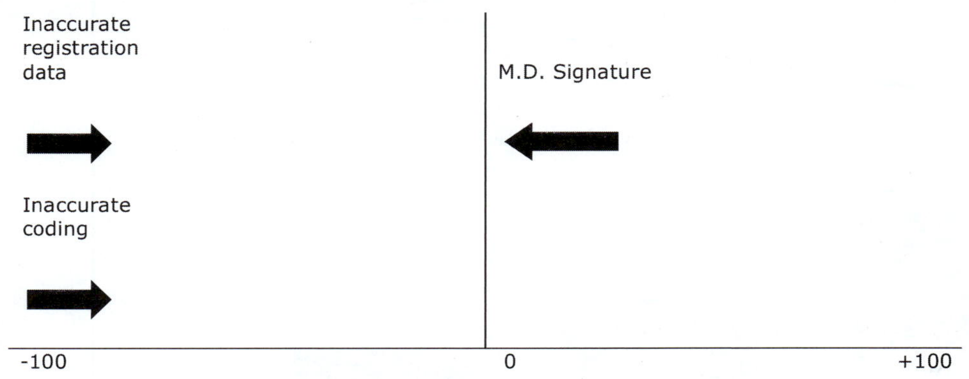

51. As Director of the HIM department, it is your responsibility to reduce the turnaround time for your organization's accounts receivable balance. The performance improvement tool shown above was used to add weights in order to prioritize ideas. What is it called?
    A. fishbone diagram
    B. precision matrix
    C. flowchart
    D. force field analysis

REFERENCE: Abdelhak, p 462
LaTour, Eichenwald-Maki, and Oachs, p 823
McWay, p 347
Sayles, p 588

52. Which of the following processes is mandatory for health care facilities?
    A. accreditation
    B. certification
    C. AHA registration
    D. licensure

REFERENCE: Abdelhak, pp 11–12
Davis and LaCour, p 23
LaTour, Eichenwald-Maki, and Oachs, p 37
McWay, p 17
Shaw, p 330

53. A surgeon left a clamp in a patient, resulting in a return to the operating room. In an integrated organizational quality management model, all of the following entities would receive data about the investigation EXCEPT the
    A. Tissue Committee.
    B. Credentials Committee.
    C. Risk Management Program.
    D. Pharmacy and Therapeutics Committee.

REFERENCE: LaTour, Eichenwald-Maki, and Oachs, pp 672–674, 862
Sayles, pp 27, 435, 451, 612–621
Shaw, p 198

54. The Joint Commission requires health care facilities manage the environment of care by implementing seven (7) various safety plans, which must be evaluated at least
    A. monthly.
    B. quarterly.
    C. biannually.
    D. annually.

REFERENCE: LaTour, Eichenwald-Maki, and Oachs, pp 202–203
Sayles, p 73
Shaw, p 271

55. The type of indicator about the placement and number of fire extinguishers would be a(n)
    A. process.
    B. outcome.
    C. structure.
    D. regulation.

REFERENCE: Sayles, p 568
Shaw, pp xxviii, 14

56. The Joint Commission has a standard stating that a hospital must plan and design information management processes to meet ____________ information needs.
    A. internal
    B. external
    C. both internal and external
    D. patient record

REFERENCE: Abdelhak, pp 100, 127
Shaw, p 366

57. HEDIS gathers data in which of the following areas?
    A. average length of stay
    B. prenatal care
    C. severity of illness indicators
    D. breast cancer screenings

REFERENCE: Abdelhak, p 506
Davis and LaCour, p 241
LaTour, Eichenwald-Maki, and Oachs, pp 200, 426–427
McWay, p 412
Sayles, p 254
Shaw, pp 332–333

58. If administrators of a home health agency wanted to measure the outcomes of adult patients receiving their agency's services, which tool would they use?
   A. OASIS
   B. HEDIS
   C. ORYX
   D. QAI

REFERENCE: Abdelhak, pp 137–138
LaTour, Eichenwald-Maki, and Oachs, pp 199, 438
McWay, pp 10, 186, 270
Sayles, pp 278–279
Shaw, p 151

59. Your hospital is required by the Joint Commission and CMS to participate in national benchmarking on specific disease entities for quality of care measurement. This required collection and reporting of disease-specific data is considered
   A. an environment of care.
   B. a group of sentinel events.
   C. a series of core measures.
   D. risk assessment.

REFERENCE: LaTour, Eichenwald-Maki, and Oachs, pp 201, 382, 670–671
Sayles, pp 156, 968
Shaw, pp 132, 359

60. Continuous quality improvement is best described by the following statements EXCEPT
   A. corrective action targets clinicians more so than processes.
   B. standards are defined, measured, and systematically applied.
   C. monitoring is ongoing with periodic feedback.
   D. all personnel support quality improvement efforts, including top management and the governing body.

REFERENCE: LaTour, Eichenwald-Maki, and Oachs, pp 35, 294, 442, 650, 658–659, 663, 687, 818, 825, 833, 852, 905
McWay, p 142
Sayles, pp 583–584, 565–568, 598, 684
Shaw, pp 4–9

61. Which of the following is a disadvantage of retrospective data collection?
   A. Data are all available.
   B. Fewer data collectors are required.
   C. Deficiencies in documentation can effect reimbursement.
   D. Reviewer bias is reduced.

REFERENCE: Davis and LaCour, pp 336–337
LaTour, Eichenwald-Maki, and Oachs, p 624
McWay, pp 208, 521
Sayles, pp 262, 350, 396

62. According to current theory in the quality management field, should concurrent data collection or retrospective data collection be utilized?
    A. Concurrent and retrospective data collection methods are both necessary in order to effect meaningful interventions and contain costs.
    B. Concurrent data collection methods alone are meaningful because they emulate health practitioner training.
    C. Concurrent data collection methods alone are meaningful because interventions must always be immediate.
    D. Retrospective data collection methods alone are appropriate in the reimbursement realities of this decade.

REFERENCE: Davis and LaCour, pp 336–337
LaTour, Eichenwald-Maki, and Oachs, p 624
McWay, pp 208, 521
Sayles, pp 262, 350, 396

63. You are determining the sample size for a quality study. Which of the following factors should you consider first?
    A. cost
    B. personnel
    C. size of the target population
    D. confidentiality of the record

REFERENCE: Abdelhak, pp 409–410
LaTour, Eichenwald-Maki, and Oachs, p 455
Shaw, p 46

64. The Anesthesia Department is adding a new indicator to its plan. The Chief Anesthesiologist has come to you, the Director of Quality Management, to help her design a data collection methodology. The two of you are now considering who will be doing the data collection. All of the following are factors in your deliberations EXCEPT
    A. quality management organizational model of the institution.
    B. Joint Commission standards and required characteristics.
    C. the location of data.
    D. the expertise of the staff.

REFERENCE: McWay, pp 124–125
Shaw, pp 46–47

65. The manager of the utilization review department wants to monitor and evaluate the prevention of inappropriate admissions. When would the manager need to collect data?
    A. prospective review
    B. concurrent review
    C. retrospective review
    D. long-term care review

REFERENCE: Abdelhak, pp 471–473
Davis and LaCour, pp 173–175, 377
LaTour, Eichenwald-Maki, and Oachs, pp 331, 464
McWay, p 227
Sayles, pp 610–611

66. The manager of the Quality Department is listing various sources of data. Which of the following data sources would be an example of an external source?
    A. emergency room logs
    B. incident reports
    C. patient registration and admission, discharge, transfer (ADT) information
    D. quality improvement organization (QIO) information

REFERENCE: Davis and LaCour, pp 290–292
LaTour, Eichenwald-Maki, and Oachs, pp 189, 368
McWay, pp 142, 160
Sayles, p 433
Shaw, p 46

67. The primary advantage of concurrent quality data collection is that
    A. multiple chart reviews eliminate collector bias.
    B. chart completion issues can be remedied promptly.
    C. practitioners receive immediate feedback about patient processes and outcomes.
    D. staffing is decreased.

REFERENCE: Davis and LaCour, pp 128, 337, 427–428
LaTour, Eichenwald-Maki, and Oachs, p 263
McWay, pp 107–209
Sayles, pp 350, 1188

SUMMARY OF SELECTED BLOOD PRODUCT REVIEW

Monitoring Element	Packed Red Blood Cells		Fresh Frozen Plasma		Platelets	
(*N* = 295)	(*N* = 256)		(*N* = 29)		(*N* = 10)	
	Met *N* (%)	Unmet *N* (%)	Met *N* (%)	Unmet *N* (%)	Met *N* (%)	Unmet *N* (%)
Indications	232 (91%)	24 (9%)	7 (24%)	22 (76%)	10 (100%)	0 (0%)

68. Refer to the Summary of Selected Blood Product Review table shown above. Which blood component or derivative had the most units reviewed?
    A. packed red blood cells
    B. fresh frozen plasma
    C. platelets
    D. unable to determine from the table

REFERENCE: Davis and LaCour, pp 367–368
LaTour, Eichenwald-Maki, and Oachs, pp 508, 523, 589–590
McWay, p 229
Sayles, pp 518, 520, 557
Shaw, pp 53–54

69. Refer to the Summary of Selected Blood Product Review table shown above. Which quality improvement function would prompt the production of the table?
    A. pharmacy and therapeutics function
    B. drug usage evaluation
    C. medical record review
    D. blood usage review

REFERENCE: LaTour, Eichenwald-Maki, and Oachs, pp 665–666

70. Refer to the Summary of Selected Blood Product Review table shown above. What percent of the fresh frozen plasma units met indications?
    A. 7%
    B. 24%
    C. 22%
    D. 76%

REFERENCE: McWay, pp 192–193, 218
Shaw, pp 53–54, 119

71. Refer to the Summary of Selected Blood Product Review table shown above. Based on the results reported in the table, which blood component or derivative should first be the topic of an in-depth study?
    A. packed red blood cells
    B. fresh frozen plasma
    C. platelets
    D. unable to determine from the table

REFERENCE: Davis and LaCour, pp 367–368
LaTour, Eichenwald-Maki, and Oachs, pp 508, 523, 589–590
Sayles, pp 518, 520, 557
Shaw, pp 47–48, 57

CASE STUDY #1

Upon employment at your facility, all new employees read, demonstrate understanding, and sign Confidentiality Statements. Disclosure of confidential information is grounds for immediate dismissal. Each year, during the annual performance evaluation, every employee again reads, demonstrates understanding, and signs the Confidentiality Statement.

You are the Director of the Quality Department. Your department has found that the femoral-popliteal bypass failure rate of one of your vascular surgeons, Dr. Z, is twice that of the national average. Members of the surgery department have reviewed that vascular surgeon's performance both by reading the medical records and by watching videos of her surgery. The Surgery Department and the Executive Committee have decided to deny reappointment for this surgeon.

Lucille X, the mother of one of your quality coordinators, has severe peripheral vascular disease. She was admitted to your facility and had an angiogram. The angiogram shows that she should have a femoral-popliteal bypass. She had told you that she would be in your facility and asked you to visit her. You are now fulfilling that promise and are also bringing her flowers. While pausing to knock on her door, you hear your employee, Mary G, vehemently state to her mother, "Mom, Dr. Z is a quack; half of her bypass surgeries fail. You must have Dr. DoGood!"

72. Referring to Case Study #1, what do you do as Director of the Quality Department?
    A. Seek the advice of the facility's legal counsel.
    B. Immediately dismiss Mary G upon her arrival back in the department.
    C. Walk into Lucille's room and state that Dr. Z is a fine surgeon and also advise Mary G to lower her voice.
    D. Upon Mary G's arrival back in the department, give her a written warning.

REFERENCE: LaTour, Eichenwald-Maki, and Oachs, pp 775–776
McWay, p 378
Sayles, pp 1033, 1103

73. Referring to Case Study #1, are the meeting minutes about the decisions regarding Dr. Z of the Department of Surgery and of the Executive Committee admissible in court?
    A. Yes, federal amendments to the Medicare Act require release of peer review.
    B. Yes, state laws allow discovery of medical review committee records.
    C. No, the federal Freedom of Information Act and state "sunshine laws" protect peer review.
    D. No, under state laws, records of medical review committees are not subject to introduction into evidence.

REFERENCE: LaTour, Eichenwald-Maki, and Oachs, p 665
Shaw, p 429

CASE STUDY #2

You are helping the nursing department to write indicators to determine appropriate formulas for ratios and to determine data collection time frames. One important aspect of care is the documentation of education of patients. More specifically, the nursing department would like to assess its documentation of education on colostomy care for patients with new colostomies.

74. Referring to Case Study #2, what would be the most cost-effective and appropriate data collection time frame?
    A. prospective
    B. concurrent
    C. retrospective
    D. long-term care review

REFERENCE: Davis and LaCour, pp 336–337
LaTour, Eichenwald-Maki, and Oachs, pp 331–332, 470, 624, 658
McWay, pp 237, 531
Sayles, pp 53, 350–361, 968

75. Referring to Case Study #2, which of the following ratios would you recommend?
    A. Number of records with documentation of colostomy-care teaching / Total number of patients on surgery unit
    B. Number of records with documentation of teaching / Total number of discharges
    C. Number of records with documentation of colostomy-care teaching / Total number of patients with new colostomy
    D. Number of records reviewed with documentation of colostomy-care teaching / Total number of records reviewed

REFERENCE: Davis and LaCour, pp 310–311
LaTour, Eichenwald-Maki, and Oachs, pp 540–541
McWay, pp 204, 519
Sayles, pp 472, 474–475, 478
Shaw, p 119

76. A culture and sensitivity report was returned to the inpatient unit of Brian Hospital. The sensitivity showed bacterial resistance to the current antibiotic the patient was receiving. The patient continued on the same antibiotic without improvement. A generic quality screen identified this case for review. At a minimum, which committee should review this case?
    A. Surgical Case Review
    B. Safety Committee
    C. Information Governance Committee
    D. Pharmacy and Therapeutics Committee

REFERENCE: Sayles, p 647
Shaw, p 219

77. The outpatient coding staff has been working to improve coding accuracy. The standard for the number of cases that must be coded has been raised four times in the past year. The staff said, "the more cases that must be coded, the greater the error rate will be for the corresponding time period." The department keeps statistics on both the numbers of cases coded and the corresponding error rate. What is the best QI tool for testing the coding staff's theory?
    A. control chart
    B. Pareto chart
    C. run chart
    D. scatter diagram

REFERENCE: LaTour, Eichenwald-Maki, and Oachs, pp 513–514, 537
McWay, pp 180–181, 184, 210–211
Sayles, pp 589, 591

78. The health information reception desk is experiencing a huge influx of phone calls on Monday, Tuesday, and Wednesday mornings. This is creating a problem in getting requested patient information out within an acceptable time frame. The reception staff work group has agreed to start recording the reason for the phone calls for the next 4 weeks. They want to focus on solving the response-time problem by reducing the turnaround time for the largest category of phone calls. Which QI tool best supports this goal?
    A. control chart
    B. Pareto chart
    C. run chart
    D. scatter diagram

REFERENCE: LaTour, Eichenwald-Maki, and Oachs, p 823
McWay, pp 179–180, 347, 349
Sayles, pp 591–592
Shaw, pp 58–59

79. The board of directors of a 400-bed women's hospital receives a report of key quality indicator results on a periodic basis. The report always includes the quarterly cesarean section rate. This reporting period, they see a rise in the rate and want to know if it is a significant increase. What is the best QI tool for this purpose?
    A. control chart
    B. Pareto chart
    C. run chart
    D. scatter diagram

REFERENCE: LaTour, Eichenwald-Maki, and Oachs, p 825
McWay, pp 148–151
Sayles, pp 581–582
Shaw, pp 62–63

80. What is the best tool for differentiating between common cause variation and special cause variation?
    A. control chart
    B. Pareto chart
    C. run chart
    D. scatter diagram

REFERENCE: LaTour, Eichenwald-Maki, and Oachs, p 825
McWay, pp 211–212
Sayles, pp 581–582
Shaw, pp 62–63

81. Which department will most likely be responsible for taking corrective action regarding the following quality indicator?

> QUALITY INDICATOR:
> Ninety-five percent (95%) of physician appointments/reappointments will be completed within 90 days of receipt of all required materials.

    A. Admissions
    B. Business Office
    C. Health Information Department
    D. Medical Staff Office

REFERENCE: Davis and LaCour, pp 370–372
LaTour, Eichenwald-Maki, and Oachs, p 26
Sayles, p 834
Shaw, p 294

82. Which department will most likely be responsible for taking corrective action regarding the following quality indicator?

> QUALITY INDICATOR:
> The number of DRG validation changes made by the QIO will not exceed 2%.

A. Admissions
B. Business Office
C. Health Information Department
D. Medical Staff Office

REFERENCE: Abdelhak, p 452

83. All of the following are among the Joint Commission's initial core measure sets for hospitals EXCEPT

A. acute myocardial infarction.
B. diabetes.
C. pneumonia.
D. surgical infection prevention.

REFERENCE: LaTour, Eichenwald-Maki, and Oachs, pp 201, 670–671
Sayles, pp 156, 578–579
Shaw, pp 131–132

84. Which department will most likely be responsible for taking corrective action regarding the following quality indicator?

> QUALITY INDICATOR:
> Number of insurance claims requiring resubmission due to errors (not related to coding) will not exceed 3%.

A. Admissions
B. Business Office
C. Health Information Department
D. Medical Staff Office

REFERENCE: Abdelhak, pp 686–687

85. What quality indicator would identify improvement needs in hospital electronic transmission of health care claims and remittances to allow interoperability with ICD-10 codes?

A. an increase in requests for operative reports
B. denied requests for medical record copies for continued care
C. an increase in hospital-acquired infections
D. an increase in 5010 rejections

REFERENCE: CMS (7)
LaTour, Eichenwald-Maki, and Oachs, p 206

86. Historic accomplishments impacting quality in medical care include all EXCEPT

A. ensuring competent practitioners.
B. *Darling v. Charleston Community Hospital.*
C. implementation of OTRA.
D. medical education reform (Flexner report findings).

REFERENCE: LaTour, Eichenwald-Maki, and Oachs, pp 9, 626
McWay, p 238
Sayles, pp 641–642

87. An accreditation agency counterpart to the Joint Commission for managed care organizations is the
    A. AHRQ.
    B. AHCPR.
    C. IOM.
    D. NCQA.

REFERENCE: LaTour, Eichenwald-Maki, and Oachs, p 200
McWay, pp 52–53, 177–178, 247, 271, 412, 439
Sayles, pp 74–75, 254, 952
Shaw, p 145

88. The PQRS is a reporting system established by the federal government for physician practices who participate in Medicare for
    A. monetary incentives.
    B. meaningful use incentives.
    C. quality measure reporting.
    D. credentialing.

REFERENCE: LaTour, Eichenwald-Maki, and Oachs, p 129
Sayles, p 968

89. Which data bank is a result of HIPAA legislation?
    A. Fraud and Abuse Data Bank
    B. Health Care Integrity and Protection Data Bank
    C. National Practitioner Data Bank
    D. Privacy Information Breach Data Bank

REFERENCE: LaTour, Eichenwald-Maki, and Oachs, pp 377–378
McWay, p 71
Sayles, pp 451–452
Shaw, p 295

90. The following "sentinel events" must be available for Joint Commission review EXCEPT
    A. infant abduction.
    B. petechiae due to adverse drug reaction.
    C. rape.
    D. surgery on wrong patient or wrong body part.

REFERENCE: Abdelhak, p 468
Joint Commission (2)
LaTour, Eichenwald-Maki, and Oachs, pp 672–673, 862
McWay, pp 190, 521
Sayles, pp 621–622
Shaw, pp 187–188

Year 2014 Month	Percent Patients with Unacceptable Waiting Time (%)
January	5
February	4
March	3
April	5
May	3
June	10
July	5
August	2
September	1
October	2
November	1
December	3

91. Use the information shown in the table above. Calculate the average percentage of patients for the entire year who waited longer than an acceptable amount of waiting time. (The sample size for each month's data is 100.)
   A. 3.1%
   B. 3.6%
   C. 3.7%
   D. 4.0%

REFERENCE: McWay, p 204
Sayles, p 538

92. Which of the following is incorrect about the use of control charts?
   A. Control charts can be used to measure key processes over time.
   B. The upper and lower control limits are always ±2 standard deviations.
   C. The lower control limits are always ±2 standard deviations.
   D. The upper control limits are always ±1.8 standard deviations.

REFERENCE: LaTour, Eichenwald-Maki, and Oachs, pp 825, 950
McWay, pp 180, 223–224
Sayles, pp 581–582
Shaw, pp 62–63

93. The average percent of patients exceeding acceptable waiting time was 3.7% (see table for question 91). The calculated UCL (upper control limit) is 9.4. When you plot the upper and lower limits, what would you suggest as the reason for the June variation?
   A. common cause variation
   B. root cause variation
   C. special cause variation
   D. unable to determine with the data given

REFERENCE: LaTour, Eichenwald-Maki, and Oachs, pp 825, 950
McWay, pp 180, 223–224
Sayles, pp 581–582
Shaw, p 62

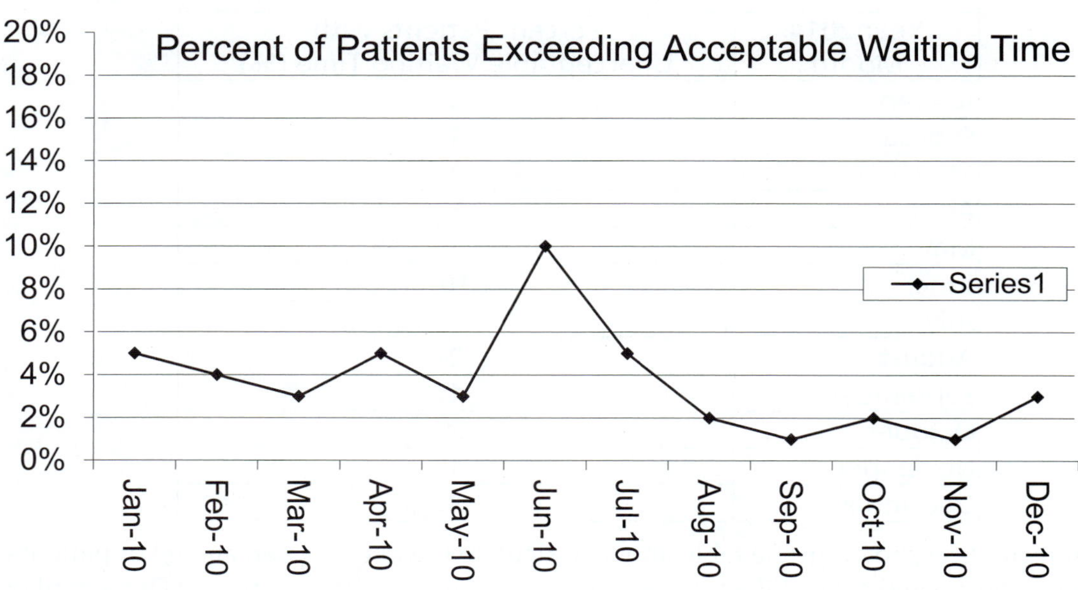

94. Adding the UCL (upper control limit) and LCL (lower control limit) to the chart above (from question 93) creates a
    A. control chart.
    B. frequency distribution.
    C. run chart.
    D. variation graph.

REFERENCE: Abdelhak, pp 463–464
LaTour, Eichenwald-Maki, and Oachs, pp 825, 950
McWay, pp 180, 223–224
Sayles, pp 581–582
Shaw, pp 62–63

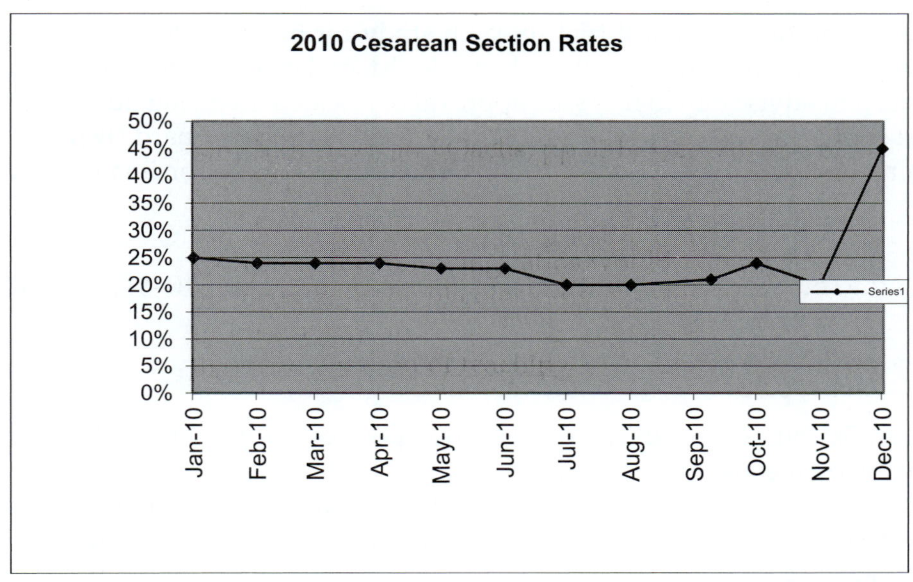

95. You are the Quality Coordinator for the medical staff. Analyze the chart above and determine the steps to be taken next.
   A. Plot the control limits, check the indicator threshold, and take the December charts to the OB/GYN Committee if the threshold is exceeded.
   B. Plot the control limits and take the December charts to the OB/GYN Committee if the December data point exceeds UCL.
   C. Plot the control limits, pull the charts for December, and do a focused review screening.
   D. Plot the control limits and refer to the Medical Executive Committee for variation review.

REFERENCE: Abdelhak, pp 463–464
LaTour, Eichenwald-Maki, and Oachs, pp 825, 950
McWay, pp 130, 223–224
Sayles, pp 581–582
Shaw, pp 62–63

96. The U.S. federal government's CMS substitutes compliance of its Conditions of Participation requirements to hospitals that already have accreditation awarded by various other agencies that include the Joint Commission, CARF, AOA, or AAAHC. This is known as
   A. deemed status.
   B. due process.
   C. contingent statutory.
   D. waiver status.

REFERENCE: Abdelhak, p 10
CMS (3)
LaTour, Eichenwald-Maki, and Oachs, pp 37–38, 309, 909
McWay, p 52
Sayles, pp 72–74, 404, 687–688, 1200
Shaw, p 334

97. Dr. Jeremy is establishing a clinical trial research study for his patients with lung cancer wishing to participate in a chemotherapy clinical trial. As Assistant Director, you are responsible for clinical abstract of data and advise him to first seek approval of research involving human subjects through the
   A. medical staff.
   B. governing board.
   C. institutional review board (IRB).
   D. Office of National Coordinator (ONC).

REFERENCE: Abdelhak, pp 415, 418–419
Davis and LaCour, pp 298–299
LaTour, Eichenwald-Maki, and Oachs, pp 321, 580, 610–611, 620–621, 923
McWay, pp 214–248, 512
Sayles, p 752
Shaw, p 92

98. The Joint Commission on-site survey process incorporates tracer methodology, which emphasizes surveyor review by means of
   A. patient tracers.
   B. system tracers.
   C. both system tracers and patient tracers.
   D. policy and procedure manual reviews.

REFERENCE: Davis and LaCour, p 375
LaTour, Eichenwald-Maki, and Oachs, pp 671, 953
McWay, pp 10–11, 524
Sayles, pp 404, 604–605, 628
Shaw, pp 336–337

99. Storyboards are a method used in health care that
   A. graphically display a performance improvement project conducted.
   B. serve as a documentation format in patient records.
   C. serve as a teaching tool for third-party auditors.
   D. illustrate the marketing plan.

REFERENCE: Shaw, pp 74–75

100. The Six Sigma methodology differs from other quality improvement models by defining improvement opportunities using
   A. scientific management.
   B. critical quality tree.
   C. nonvalue activities/processes.
   D. brainstorming.

REFERENCE: Abdelhak, pp 457–458
Davis and LaCour, pp 362–363
LaTour, Eichenwald-Maki, and Oachs, pp 828–829
McWay, p 175
Sayles, pp 625–626
Shaw, p 443

101. The FOCUS PDCA model used in performance improvement is best known for its change strategy technique of
   A. Business Process Engineering.
   B. Plan, Do, Study, Act.
   C. Input, Through-Put, Output.
   D. Cause and Effect Diagramming.

REFERENCE: Abdelhak, pp 456–457
Davis and LaCour, pp 356–361
LaTour, Eichenwald-Maki, and Oachs, pp 819–820
McWay, pp 173–175, 183, 185, 346
Sayles, p 1237

102. The quality review process of invasive and noninvasive procedures to ensure performance of appropriate procedure, preparation of patient, monitoring and postoperative care, and education of patient describes

A. universal protocol.
B. infection review.
C. surgical review.
D. blood and blood component usage.

REFERENCE: Abdelhak, pp 452–453, 477–478
LaTour, Eichenwald-Maki, and Oachs, p 665

103. The Institute of Medicine (IOM) published report titled *To Err Is Human: Building a Safer Health System*, heightened concern by the U.S. government and accrediting agencies. This led the Joint Commission to place emphasis on improving patient safety and sentinel event occurrences through its safety program, known as

A. ORYX Initiative Set.
B. National Patient Safety Goals (NPSG).
C. Health Care Quality Improvement Program (HCQIP).
D. Health Plan Employer Data & Information (HEDIS).

REFERENCE: Abdelhak, pp 126–127
Davis and LaCour, p 215
LaTour, Eichenwald-Maki, and Oachs, pp 672–674
Sayles, pp 604, 622, 666, 1228
Shaw, pp 138–139, 185–188

104. When a decision is made to restrict or deny clinical privileges during the recredentialing or reappointment process to a medical staff member, a _______________ must be offered.

A. privilege suspension
B. revocation of license
C. due process
D. crisis intervention

REFERENCE: LaTour, Eichenwald-Maki, and Oachs, pp 26, 634
McWay, pp 22–24
Sayles, p 834
Shaw, p 296

105. A patient satisfaction survey conducted after discharge is a method of quality measurement through

A. prospective indicator.
B. structure indicator.
C. process indicator.
D. outcomes indicator.

REFERENCE: Abdelhak, p 439
LaTour, Eichenwald-Maki, and Oachs, pp 653–656
Sayles, p 568
Shaw, pp 14, 95–96

106. The Joint Commission's emphasis on improving quality of patient care for a participating facility is exemplary through the required self-assessment process tool known as
   A. total quality management (TQM).
   B. focused standards asessment.
   C. intracycle monitoring.
   D. real-time analytics.

REFERENCE: Joint Commission (1)

107. During the Utilization Review Committee meeting, a case presented for discussion involved a surgical case resulting in unexpected loss of lower extremity below the knee due to complications requiring extended length of stay. Being a sentinel event, the committee requested that an investigation and reporting was required to identify the cause and prevention of future occurrences. This investigation and required reporting to the Joint Commission is known as
   A. root cause analysis.
   B. potential compensable event.
   C. medication review.
   D. report card.

REFERENCE: Joint Commission (2)
LaTour, Eichenwald-Maki, and Oachs, pp 672–673
McWay, pp 190, 251
Sayles, p 587
Shaw, pp 146, 157, 187–189

108. Traditional management functions, such as ________, must be applied to performance improvement initiatives.
   A. education
   B. planning
   C. accreditation
   D. reimbursement

REFERENCE: LaTour, Eichenwald-Maki, and Oachs, p 662

109. The process of reviewing and validating qualifications, granting professional or medical staff membership, and awarding delineated privileges is called the _____.
   A. licensure
   B. appointment
   C. professional review
   D. credentialing

REFERENCE: LaTour, Eichenwald-Maki, and Oachs, p 664

110. Integration of decision support systems and best practices in medicine is known as the practice of __________.
   A. subjective determination
   B. case management
   C. evidence-based medicine
   D. outcome measures

REFERENCE: LaTour, Eichenwald-Maki, and Oachs, p 669

111. An area identified for needed improvement through benchmarking and continuous quality improvement is known as a ____________.
   A. key attribute
   B. measure hierarchy
   C. knowledge base
   D. key performance indicator

REFERENCE: LaTour, Eichenwald-Maki, and Oachs, pp 473, 926

112. A retrospective review as part of quality improvement activities are conducted after the patient has been ____.
   A. admitted
   B. cleared for surgery
   C. released from the surgical recovery room
   D. discharged

REFERENCE: LaTour, Eichenwald-Maki, and Oachs, p 331

113. To properly implement performance improvement (PI), organizations should ensure that all employees participate in an integrated, continuous PI program. This is known as ______.
   A. shared leadership
   B. organizational PI
   C. quality management liaison group
   D. shared vision

REFERENCE: LaTour, Eichenwald-Maki, and Oachs, p 663

114. To accomplish the Joint Commission's safety goal to eliminate wrong-site, wrong-patient procedures, the organization can use all of these EXCEPT _______.
   A. preoperative verification processes
   B. mark the surgical site
   C. available patient records
   D. using imaging guidance on all procedures

REFERENCE: LaTour, Eichenwald-Maki, and Oachs, p 672

115. The use of metrics to conduct root cause analysis that will facilitate changes throughout the organization can best be presented using a _______.
   A. pie chart
   B. fishbone diagram
   C. scatter diagram
   D. flow chart

REFERENCE: LaTour, Eichenwald-Maki, and Oachs, p 822

Answer Key for Quality and Performance Improvement

1. D
2. D
3. D
4. B
5. B
6. A
7. C
8. B
9. B
10. D
11. A
12. B
13. D
14. C
15. A
16. C
17. C
18. A
19. B
20. D
21. D
22. D
23. A
24. A
25. D
26. A
27. D
28. B
29. A
30. B
31. A
32. D
33. C
34. B
35. C
36. D
37. A
38. D
39. C
40. D
41. A
42. D
43. C
44. B
45. B
46. C
47. C
48. D
49. A
50. A
51. D
52. D
53. D
54. D
55. D
56. C
57. D
58. A
59. C
60. A
61. C
62. A
63. C
64. B
65. A
66. D
67. B
68. A
69. D
70. B
71. B
72. B
73. D
74. C
75. C Number of times an event occurred divided by number of times the event could have occurred
76. D
77. D
78. B
79. A
80. A
81. D
82. C
83. B
84. B
85. D
86. C
87. D
88. C
89. B
90. B

Answer Key for Quality and Performance Improvement

91. C (5 + 4 + 3 + 5 + 3 + 10 + 5 + 2 + 1 + 2 + 1 + 3) ÷ 12 = 3.66 = 3.7
92. D
93. C Data points that lie outside the upper or lower control limits may signal special cause variation.
94. A
95. A
96. A
97. C
98. C
99. A
100. B
101. B
102. C
103. B
104 C
105. D
106. C
107. A
108. B
109. D
110. C
111. D
112. D
113. A
114. D
115. B

REFERENCES

Abdelhak, M. & Hanken, M. A. (2016). *Health information: Management of a strategic resource* (5th ed.). Philadelphia: W. B. Saunders.

AHIMA. (1) (2012a), August 15). *Body of knowledge—Practice brief, verbal/telephone order authentication and time frames (Updated).* Retrieved from http://AHIMA.org

AHIMA. (2012b). "Electronic Documentation Templates Support ICD-10-CM/PCS Implementation (Updated)," *Journal of AHIMA* 86, no. 6 (June 2015): 56–62.

CMS (1). Updated Federal Register, October 1, 2015, pp 582–583. Retrieved from http://www.gpo.gov/fdsys/pkg/CFR-2005-title42-vol3/pdf/CFR-2005-title42-vol3.pdf

CMS (2). Recovery Audit Program. Retrieved from https://www.cms.gov/Research-Statistics-Data-and-Systems/Monitoring-Programs/Medicare-FFS-Compliance-Programs/Recovery-Audit-Program/

CMS (3). Updated Federal Register, October 1, 2015, pp 653–654. Retrieved from http://www.gpo.gov/fdsys/pkg/CFR-2005-title42-vol3/pdf/CFR-2005-title42-vol3.pdf

CMS (4). Notice of Privacy Practices. Retrieved from http://www.hhs.gov/ocr/privacy/hipaa/understanding/summary/privacysummary.pdf

CMS (5). Notice of Privacy Practices. Retrieved from http://www.gpo.gov/fdsys/pkg/CFR-2011-title45-vol1/pdf/CFR-2011-title45-vol1-sec164-520.pdf

CMS (6). Conditions of Participation Utilization Review. Retrieved from http://www.gpo.gov/fdsys/pkg/CFR-2011-title42-vol5/pdf/CFR-2011-title42-vol5-sec482-30.pdf

CMS (7). Important Update Regarding Version 5010/D.0 Implementation. Retrieved from https://www.cms.gov/Regulations-and-Guidance/HIPAA-Administrative-Simplification/Versions5010andD0/downloads/Important_5010_Update_PDF_for_March_2012.pdf

Joint Commission. (n.d.) (1) Facts about the Intracycle Monitoring Process. Retrieved from http://www.jointcommission.org/facts_about_the_intracycle_monitoring_process/

Joint Commission. (n.d.) (2) Sentinel Event Data Root Causes by Event Type 2004–2014. Retrieved from http://www.jointcommission.org/assets/1/18/Root_Causes_by_Event_Type_2004–2014.pdf

LaTour, K., Eichenwald, S., and Oachs, P. (2013). *Health information management: Concepts, principles, and practice* (4th ed.). Chicago: American Health Information Management Association (AHIMA).

McWay, D. (2014). *Today's health information management: An integrated approach* (2nd ed.). Clifton Park, NY: Cengage Learning.

Sayles, N. B. (2013). *Health information management technology: An applied approach* (4th ed.). Chicago: American Health Information Management Association (AHIMA).

Shaw, P. (2010). *Quality and performance improvement in health care: A tool for programmed learning* (4th ed.). Chicago: American Health Information Management Association (AHIMA).

Quality and Performance Improvement Competencies

Question	RHIA Domain	RHIT Domain
1–115	5	5

XV. Organization and Management

Kristy Courville, MHA, RHIA

1. The manager of a Health Information Department has many training and development methods available for the departmental and nondepartmental staff. Consider the following situation. The department's working hours are 8:00 AM to 6:00 PM. After 6:00 PM, if a record is needed in the emergency room for a possible readmission, the ER clerk has access to the facility's electronic health record (EHR) in order to retrieve the record. On the occasions when the ER clerk has retrieved a record, it appears as if the clerk was viewing records unnecessarily within the EHR. What would be the best training or development method for the ER clerk in order to rectify this situation?
   A. receive training by an ER coworker
   B. receive training by an expert in record documentation
   C. attend an outside workshop or seminar
   D. receive training by the supervisor of files

REFERENCE: Abdelhak, pp 630–631
LaTour, Eichenwald-Maki, and Oachs, pp 743, 745–748
McWay, pp 364–365

2. Strong lateral relationships within a facility are most likely when
   A. vertical relationships are less than adequate.
   B. individual departments cooperate together to achieve organizational goals.
   C. individual departments are only interested in their internal goals.
   D. individual departments avoid one another.

REFERENCE: LaTour, Eichenwald-Maki, and Oachs, pp 688–694

3. The Director of the Health Information Services Department has asked that the supervisor of coding institute a method to monitor the accuracy of coding. What method would be the most effective approach?
   A. Perform a 100% review of one of the employees' work each day.
   B. Review a sample of each employee's work annually.
   C. Review a random sample of each employee's work monthly.
   D. Have each employee check each other's work and report any problems to the supervisor.

REFERENCE: Abdelhak, pp 641–642
LaTour, Eichenwald-Maki, and Oachs, pp 806–809
McWay, pp 364–365

4. You are the Coding Supervisor and wish to know the amount of time spent on coding by eight employees this month. You have the following productivity log. What percentage of time was spent on coding?

Productivity Log January			
Number of Employees	Charts Coded	Standard	Hours Worked
8	725	12 minutes per chart	1,280

   A. 14.7%
   B. 6.8%
   C. 8.8%
   D. 11.3%

REFERENCE: Abdelhak, pp 641–642
Davis and LaCour, pp 425, 443
McWay, pp 221–223

5. The Director of Health Information Services has asked the supervisor over imaging to determine productivity standards for the imaging clerks. In initiating this process, the supervisor has determined that the best way to institute work standards is to
   A. determine which employee can work the fastest.
   B. perform time and motion studies.
   C. improve employee morale.
   D. develop standards based on professional standards and industry benchmarks.

REFERENCE: Abdelhak, pp 641–642
Davis and LaCour, pp 441–443
McWay, pp 221–223

6. A new health information management clerk has been on staff for 2 days. She has thus far analyzed charts incorrectly, sent out confidential information improperly, and used the copy machine inappropriately. Evaluate this situation and determine the best resolution.
   A. Review the job description and job procedure with the clerk and follow up with an in-service.
   B. Review the job procedure with the clerk and have the analysis supervisor monitor her progress.
   C. Review the job description and job procedure with the clerk and follow up with a merit evaluation.
   D. Review job procedures with the clerk and follow up with an in-service.

REFERENCE: Abdelhak, p 631
LaTour, Eichenwald-Maki, and Oachs, pp 730–739
McWay, pp 364–365

7. "Qualified employees should be given priority when vacancies within the organization occur" is an example of
   A. a policy of the organization.
   B. an objective for the organization.
   C. a rule for the organization.
   D. a procedure for the organization.

REFERENCE: Abdelhak, p 665
Davis and LaCour, pp 435–436
LaTour, Eichenwald-Maki, and Oachs, pp 724–725
McWay, p 326

8. A rule is helpful to both managers and the employees in the decision-making process. A rule
   A. allows judgments to be made.
   B. requires interpretation.
   C. predecides issues.
   D. provides the necessary details.

REFERENCE: Davis and LaCour, p 49
LaTour, Eichenwald-Maki, and Oachs pp 722–731
McWay, pp 23, 49

9. Which of the following statements describes a method of following a procedure?
   A. Medical records requested by the emergency room will be retrieved and delivered within 30 minutes.
   B. Multiple-page discharge summaries are stapled together in the left-hand corner.
   C. Transcription turnaround time is established as 24 hours following completion of dictation by the physician.
   D. Only HIM personnel have access to the medical record filing area.

REFERENCE: Abdelhak, p 666
Davis and LaCour, pp 435–436
LaTour, Eichenwald-Maki, and Oachs, pp 724–725
McWay, p 240

10. The supervisor over imaging was receiving frequent complaints from the scanning clerks regarding the prepping clerk's job performance. The scanning clerks stated that it was becoming difficult to maintain their productivity levels because the prepping clerk was not processing the discharge charts in a timely manner. In order to get a clearer understanding of the situation, the supervisor asked the scanning clerks and the prepping clerk to complete a task list for a 2-week period. The supervisor is constructing a
    A. flow process chart.
    B. movement diagram.
    C. work distribution chart.
    D. procedure flowchart.

REFERENCE: Abdelhak, pp 637–641
LaTour, Eichenwald-Maki, and Oachs, pp 800–801
McWay, pp 335, 525

11. Choose the system below that is the type of identification system in which the patient is issued a different number for each admission or encounter for care and the records of past episodes of care are brought forward to be filed under the last number issued.
    A. serial unit numbering
    B. unit numbering system
    C. family numbering system
    D. serial-unit number system

REFERENCE: Davis and LaCour, pp 255–256
LaTour, Eichenwald-Maki, and Oachs, p 270

12. The standard for record retrieval is 200 work units per month. Based on the table below, what is the variance from standard for the month of May?

May Productivity Report—Chart Retrieval			
Week 1	Week 2	Week 3	Week 4
30	40	25	35

    A. 75%
    B. 65%
    C. 53%
    D. 15%

REFERENCE: McWay, pp 398–399

13. Ms. Wolf, supervisor of coding and abstracting, would like to determine the coders' accuracy. Which type of management tool would provide her with the information she needs?
    A. a stopwatch study
    B. a coding audit
    C. an employee-reported log
    D. a time log

REFERENCE: Davis and LaCour, pp 441–443
LaTour, Eichenwald-Maki, and Oachs, pp 808–811
McWay, pp 338–339

14. After a work sampling study was completed, it was found that 20% of a coder's time was devoted to creating electronic queries to be sent to the physicians' inboxes. How many minutes of a 7-hour day are taken up with this activity?
    A. 140
    B. 84
    C. 21
    D. 56

REFERENCE: Abdelhak, pp 619–621
LaTour, Eichenwald-Maki, and Oachs, pp 808–811
McWay, pp 339–340

15. Written documents that assist an organization in achieving its objectives and carrying out its mission statement are known as
    A. strategic plans.
    B. game plans.
    C. tactical plans.
    D. operational plans.

REFERENCE: Abdelhak, pp 636–637
Burns, Bradley, and Weiner, pp 460–461
Davis and LaCour, p 429
LaTour, Eichenwald-Maki, and Oachs, pp 866–867
McWay, pp 324–325

16. Anna Kathryn is attending budget training for new supervisors. The representative from Finance explains that _____ costs will vary in direct proportion to changes in the volume of care provided.
    A. fixed
    B. periodic
    C. variable
    D. semivariable

REFERENCE: LaTour, Eichenwald-Maki, and Oachs, pp 781–782

17. The organizing process determines how the work in a particular department will be divided and accomplished. In order to be in the best position to organize the work effectively, the manager must first engage in which management function?
    A. staffing
    B. directing
    C. planning
    D. controlling

REFERENCE: Davis and LaCour, pp 429–430
LaTour, Eichenwald-Maki, and Oachs, p 690
McWay, p 323

18. The director of a Health Information Department has discovered that the department's policy regarding the usage of the copy machine has been consistently abused by the majority of the staff. To put an end to this inappropriate use of the copy machine, the director should institute a department
    A. method.
    B. rule.
    C. objective.
    D. procedure.

REFERENCE: LaTour, Eichenwald-Maki, and Oachs, pp 724–725
McWay, p 49

19. The average number of transcribed lines per month at Bent Tree Hospital is 142,500. The daily production standard is 950 lines per day. With 20 workdays in the month, calculate the minimum number of FTEs needed for this volume.
    A. 13
    B. 8
    C. 6
    D. 7.5

REFERENCE: Davis and LaCour, pp 415–416
LaTour, Eichenwald-Maki, and Oachs, pp 806–807

20. The supervisor of release of information in a Health Information Department is preparing a work distribution chart in the hopes of identifying some problem areas. Although the work distribution chart can provide the supervisor with a great deal of information concerning the work performed by her staff, it will not indicate
    A. if a task is divided among employees disproportionately.
    B. the solution to a specific problem area.
    C. if the skills of each employee are utilized appropriately.
    D. the appropriate method of work division.

REFERENCE: Abdelhak, pp 614–619
LaTour, Eichenwald-Maki, and Oachs, pp 800–801

21. Emma Grace is a transcriptionist. Her productivity level, as determined by line count per day, has dropped significantly over the past 2 weeks. As a result, there is a backlog in transcription of history and physical reports and surgical reports. Several doctors and the operating room supervisor have complained. An appropriate initial course of action for the Supervisor of Transcription is to
    A. counsel the transcriptionist privately.
    B. fire the transcriptionist immediately.
    C. refer the matter to the Human Resources Department.
    D. suspend the transcriptionist without pay for 3 days.

REFERENCE: LaTour, Eichenwald-Maki, and Oachs, pp 815–816
McWay, p 379

22. The Director of the Health Information Services Department has determined that an in-service for department supervisors on improving productivity levels in their respective areas is needed. As an outcome of this in-service, the director would like the supervisors to understand that when setting productivity levels, a supervisor must
    A. tailor any training needs to each individual employee to achieve the productivity levels.
    B. direct training needs to the most efficient employee within the department in order to achieve the productivity levels.
    C. determine the productivity standards for each area and job function.
    D. consider only quantity and not quality.

REFERENCE: Davis and LaCour, pp 466–470
LaTour, Eichenwald-Maki, and Oachs, pp 806–811
McWay, p 365

23. The coding supervisor reviewed the productivity logs of four newly hired coders after their first month. The report below illustrates each coder's output. Based on analysis of this report, which employee will require additional assistance in order to meet the coding standards?

PRODUCTIVITY REPORT Coding Standard: 20 charts per day				
Coder	Week 1	Week 2	Week 3	Week 4
1	90	100	95	100
2	100	105	105	95
3	70	75	90	85
4	85	85	90	100

A. Coder 1
B. Coder 2
C. Coder 3
D. Coder 4

REFERENCE: Davis and LaCour, pp 426–427, 443–445
LaTour, Eichenwald-Maki, and Oachs, pp 811–817
Sayles, pp 546–547

24. Which of the following statements best describes the scalar or chain of command principle?
    A. Effective organization is made up of people who perform the work assigned.
    B. There is a clear flow of authority from superior to subordinate throughout the organization.
    C. The objectives of a business or a group of functions within the business must be clearly defined and understood.
    D. The number of subordinates under the immediate supervision of the supervisor should be limited.

REFERENCE: LaTour, Eichenwald-Maki, and Oachs, pp 686, 690
McWay, pp 417–418

The following questions represent advanced competencies.

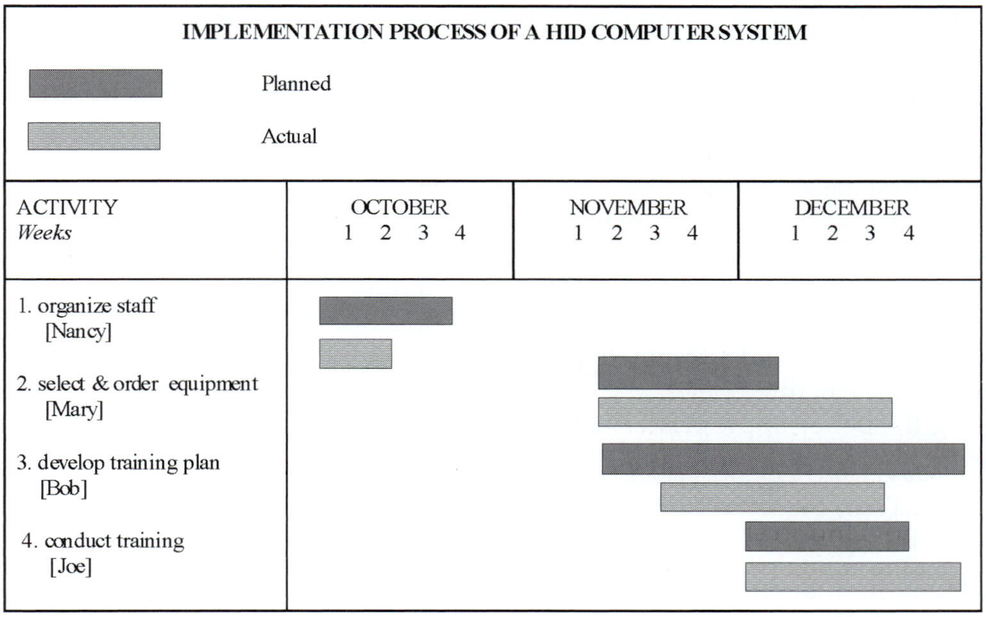

IMPLEMENTATION PROCESS OF A HID COMPUTER SYSTEM

Planned

Actual

ACTIVITY *Weeks*	OCTOBER 1 2 3 4	NOVEMBER 1 2 3 4	DECEMBER 1 2 3 4
1. organize staff [Nancy]			
2. select & order equipment [Mary]			
3. develop training plan [Bob]			
4. conduct training [Joe]			

25. Based on the Gantt chart shown above, which planned activities can be done simultaneously?
    A. activities 1 and 2
    B. activities 3 and 4
    C. activities 1, 3, and 4
    D. activities 2 and 3

REFERENCE: LaTour, Eichenwald-Maki, and Oachs, p 847
McWay, p 179

26. In order to improve efficiency and productivity, which of the following sequence of steps is the most effective?
    A. Break down the work into component activities, assign personnel, and delegate authority.
    B. Delegate authority, assign personnel, and define individual job duties.
    C. Know the objective; assign personnel and group activities into proper organizational units.
    D. Know the objective; break down the work into component activities, and the group activities into proper organizational units.

REFERENCE: LaTour, Eichenwald-Maki, and Oachs, pp 107, 811–813, 847

27. Amelia Claire is a CNA and an RHIA who is a clinical documentation trainer for a large health system. The results of a quality improvement study indicated that an informed consent was not obtained for 25% of the surgical procedures performed. Amelia has discussed the problem with the director of the Health Information Department and they have decided to begin corrective action by providing an in-service. The most important participants who should attend this in-service are
    A. nurses and unit clerks.
    B. medical record and quality improvement personnel.
    C. physicians and residents.
    D. administrators.

REFERENCE: Davis and LaCour, pp 466–467
LaTour, Eichenwald-Maki, and Oachs, p 731
McWay, pp 364–365

28. The Director of Health Information Services has recently received approval to purchase a new high-speed scanner. The director plans to redo the department layout to accommodate the equipment and to ensure that the equipment is placed in the most appropriate area of the department. Which of the following tools will best assist the director with this new layout?
    A. proximity chart
    B. frequency chart
    C. Gantt chart
    D. replacement chart

REFERENCE: Abdelhak, p 647

29. One of your first tasks as the new Manager of Health Information Services is to review the department policy and procedure manual. You have determined that several policy statements are incongruent with appropriate current employee practices. Proper management conventions require
    A. leaving the policy as written in the manual.
    B. contacting the hospital attorney to decide what action to take.
    C. enforcing the existing policy.
    D. revising the policy appropriately and documenting the date of the change.

REFERENCE: Davis and LaCour, pp 436–437
LaTour, Eichenwald-Maki, and Oachs, p 723
McWay, p 326

30. Elizabeth Home is the Chief Executive Officer (CEO) at St. Augustine Medical Center. At the beginning of each fiscal year, she begins a formal planning cycle. Her annual planning process should begin with which of the following?
    A. revising the institutional mission
    B. developing strategic plans
    C. establishing the annual organizational objectives
    D. developing strategic goals

REFERENCE: Davis and LaCour, pp 429–443
LaTour, Eichenwald-Maki, and Oachs, p 690
McWay, pp 323–329

31. Which of the following statements is false in regard to departmental reengineering?
    A. It is mainly done to reduce departmental costs.
    B. It is intended to make small or minor changes in order to improve a function or process.
    C. It is intended to improve departmental productivity.
    D. It is intended to ensure satisfied customers.

REFERENCE: Davis and LaCour, pp 346–348
LaTour, Eichenwald-Maki, and Oachs, pp 695, 825–826
McWay, pp 96, 395

32. In preparing a capital budget request, the first priority will be to document
    A. the specific type of equipment requested.
    B. where the new equipment will be located.
    C. the need for the new equipment.
    D. the cost of the new equipment.

REFERENCE: Davis and LaCour, p 330
McWay, p 398

33. Based on the information displayed in the decision matrix below, which vendor would you recommend for the purchase of a scanner?

		Vendor A	Vendor B	Vendor C	Vendor D
Criteria	Weight	Rating	Rating	Rating	Rating
Quality	5	4	3	3	3
Speed	4	3	1	3	2
Service	2	3	3	5	2

A. Vendor A
B. Vendor B
C. Vendor C
D. Vendor D

REFERENCE: Davis and LaCour, pp 336–338
LaTour, Eichenwald-Maki, and Oachs, p 695
McWay, pp 94, 390

34. As the Director of the Health Information Department, you are preparing a request for approval for the purchase of an encoding system. Because this is considered a capital request, you are required to submit the cost–benefit ratio. The software and license cost $6,000, hardware maintenance is $1,500, and the training of two employees will cost $500. It is expected that the encoding system will increase reimbursement by $10,000. The cost–benefit ratio is
A. 0.8.
B. 1.7.
C. 1.25.
D. 1.33.

REFERENCE: Abdelhak, p 332
McWay, pp 94, 390

35. What two types of budgets are often prepared by managers of health information departments?
A. capital budget and the finance budget
B. capital budget and the operational or revenue and expense budget
C. profit and loss budget and the finance budget
D. finance budget and the revenue and expense budget

REFERENCE: Davis and LaCour, pp 430–431

36. Both Mary and Sue are employed as medical transcriptionists at All Children's Hospital. They are able to set their own work hours provided the department is covered by one of them during regular office hours. This kind of work arrangement is referred to as
A. compressed work week.
B. job sharing.
C. flex time.
D. telecommuting.

REFERENCE: LaTour, Eichenwald-Maki, and Oachs, pp 727–728

37. The most important consideration in planning the office layout for a Health Information Services department is the
A. number of employees.
B. cost.
C. types of furniture to be purchased.
D. workflow.

REFERENCE: Davis and LaCour, p 454
LaTour, Eichenwald-Maki, and Oachs, pp 796–797

38. Allison has conducted a timely performance evaluation for one of her employees and awarded the employee a 4% merit increase. She is currently completing the paperwork to submit to Human Resources. If the employee's hourly salary is presently $7.10, what will the hourly salary be with this increase?
    A. $7.33
    B. $7.38
    C. $7.80
    D. $7.54

REFERENCE: Abdelhak, pp 594–595

39. The span of control in an organization refers to the
    A. number of supervisors for each functional area.
    B. amount of space assigned to one supervisor.
    C. amount of work expected of an employee.
    D. number of people who report to one supervisor.

REFERENCE: Davis and LaCour, p 419
LaTour, Eichenwald-Maki, and Oachs, p 690

40. A work environment that is not ergonomically sound could lead to
    A. injuries.
    B. conflict among departments.
    C. employee arguments.
    D. increases in department equipment budgets.

REFERENCE: Davis and LaCour, pp 454–456
LaTour, Eichenwald-Maki, and Oachs, pp 799–800
McWay, pp 335–336

41. Jessica is the leader of a project team working on the definition of the women's health service line. Several departments are so enthusiastic about the progress that they ask for additions to the project. This is not uncommon, and is known as
    A. add-ons.
    B. scope creep.
    C. effort expansion.
    D. deliverable increase.

REFERENCE: LaTour, Eichenwald-Maki, and Oachs, pp 836–837

42. The transcription production for February was 225,333 lines. The total work hours for all transcriptionists for the same period was 2,000. The average hourly cost was $13.50. Determine the cost per line for operating this service for this month.
    A. $1.20
    B. $0.24
    C. $2.40
    D. $0.12

REFERENCE: Abdelhak, pp 619–621

HEALTH INFORMATION DEPARTMENT MONTHLY BUDGET JANUARY		
Items	Budget	Actual
Supplies	495	675
Travel	300	150
Rental Equipment	1,250	1,250
Service Contracts	900	1,130

43. Based on the budget illustrated above, what is the monthly budget variance percent for supplies?
   A. 13.6%
   B. 36%
   C. 26.6%
   D. 11.9%

REFERENCE: Davis and LaCour, pp 430–443
LaTour, Eichenwald-Maki, and Oachs, pp 785–787
McWay, p 398

44. The most realistic approach that could encourage increased productivity in the tedious prepping area is to
   A. shorten the workday by 1 hour.
   B. vary and rotate the work assigned to each prepper.
   C. have all the preppers work on a part-time basis.
   D. arrange for all the preppers to have flex time.

REFERENCE: McWay, pp 221–223

45. The HIM Department of a local hospital will experience a 20% increase in the number of discharges processed per day as the result of a merger with a smaller facility. This 20% increase is projected as 120 additional records per day. The standard time for coding a record is 15 minutes. Compute the number of FTEs required to process this increased volume in coding based on an 8-hour day.
   A. 3.75
   B. 2.8
   C. 6.5
   D. 5.25

REFERENCE: Davis and LaCour, pp 415–416
LaTour, Eichenwald-Maki, and Oachs, pp 724, 806–807

46. Cheryl is the Director of the Health Information Services Department and Suzanne is the Assistant Director. Cheryl notices one of Suzanne's subordinates leaving the department for an unscheduled break. When the employee returns, Cheryl immediately asks the employee to step into her office and begins discussing the unauthorized break. Which organizational principle is this director violating?
   A. organizational function
   B. grievance procedure
   C. span of control
   D. unity of command

REFERENCE: Davis and LaCour, p 419
LaTour, Eichenwald-Maki, and Oachs, p 690

47. As the Director of Health Information Services, you manage the department with the assistance of four supervisors. One day you observe a coder coding charts from the face sheet without reviewing the record for additional documentation. The most appropriate course of action would be to
    A. discuss your concerns with the supervisor of coding and direct her to address this issue immediately.
    B. discuss the problem with the CFO.
    C. discuss the matter directly with the coder and instruct him to review the entire record for correct assignment of codes.
    D. do nothing because the coding area is extremely productive.

REFERENCE: Davis and LaCour, p 419
LaTour, Eichenwald-Maki, and Oachs, p 690

48. During the month of May, there were 800 discharge abstracts processed at a cost of $0.90 per abstract for a total of $720.00. In June, 732 discharge abstracts were processed for a total cost of $658.80. This type of cost is known as
    A. semivariable.
    B. adjustable rate.
    C. fixed.
    D. variable.

REFERENCE: LaTour, Eichenwald-Maki, and Oachs, p 781

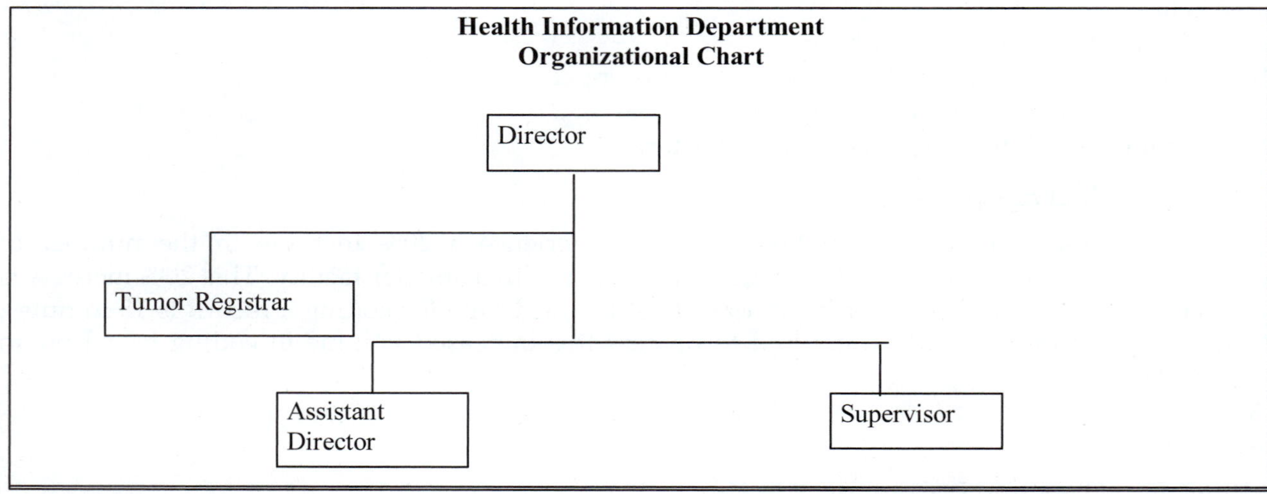

49. Which statement is an inaccurate description of the organization chart shown above?
    A. The director has authority over others in the department.
    B. The director has subordinates.
    C. The assistant director and the supervisor have a lateral relationship.
    D. The tumor registrar has authority over the assistant director.

REFERENCE: Davis and LaCour, pp 417–418
LaTour, Eichenwald-Maki, and Oachs, pp 690–691
McWay, pp 331–333

50. The director of a Health Information Department has received the quarterly variance budget report. The report indicates the "overtime" category is unfavorable. The director is required to justify this overtime expense. Which of the following would be considered an acceptable explanation for this expenditure? Overtime is unfavorable this quarter due to
    A. the annual purging of inactive files.
    B. a chronic backlog in transcription.
    C. a decrease in admissions this quarter.
    D. a lack of supervision in the file area.

REFERENCE: Davis and LaCour, pp 430–431
LaTour, Eichenwald-Maki, and Oachs, pp 786–788
McWay, pp 398–399

51. The director of a Health Information Department has asked the department supervisors to review and revise all job descriptions. Missy Harris, the supervisor over coding and analysis, has determined that the job description for the senior coders must be revised. Ms. Harris' decision to revise the job description is probably due to a change in the
    A. number of coders.
    B. recruitment practices for coders.
    C. scope of coding responsibilities.
    D. method in which the coders' performance is evaluated.

REFERENCE: Davis and LaCour, p 437
LaTour, Eichenwald-Maki, and Oachs, pp 723–724
McWay, p 334

52. Which of the following is false in regard to budget variances?
    A. Variances are often calculated on the monthly budget report.
    B. Permanent budget variances do not resolve during the current fiscal year.
    C. A variance analysis identifies whether the variance is favorable or unfavorable.
    D. Temporary budget variances are expected to continue in subsequent months.

REFERENCE: Davis and LaCour, pp 430–431
LaTour, Eichenwald-Maki, and Oachs, pp 786–788
McWay, pp 389–399

53. The expense budget is also known as the
    A. production budget.
    B. operating budget.
    C. contract budget.
    D. profit and loss budget.

REFERENCE: Davis and LaCour, pp 430–431
LaTour, Eichenwald-Maki, and Oachs, pp 785–786

54. The Supervisor of a Health Information Department has aspirations of becoming the HID director. She works very long hours so that she can address all department issues herself rather than relying on her staff to assist her. Which type of management skills is she in need of improving in order to attain her goal of department director?
    A. delegating skills
    B. leadership skills
    C. motivating skills
    D. political skills

REFERENCE: Davis and LaCour, pp 419–420
LaTour, Eichenwald-Maki, and Oachs, p 754
McWay, pp 334, 392

55. The supervisor over release of information has requested a meeting with her superior, the director of Health Information Services. She begins the meeting by describing how overwhelmed she is feeling. She is extremely behind in her work and she does not know what she can do to change the situation. In advising the supervisor, the director suggests that perhaps she should begin addressing her problem by attending a management workshop. Which of the following workshop topics is more likely to help the supervisor with her problem?
    A. "Leadership Styles for Women Managers and Supervisors"
    B. "The Nature of Delegation"
    C. "Understanding Your Employee"
    D. "Writing Skills for the Release of Information Supervisor"

REFERENCE: Davis and LaCour, pp 419–420
LaTour, Eichenwald-Maki, and Oachs, p 754
McWay, pp 334, 392

56. The director of the Health Information Services Department is developing a plan to convert their existing filing system to an electronic document management system (EDMS). The tool that is most useful to the director in displaying the steps and completion schedule for each phase of the conversion is a
    A. work distribution chart.
    B. Gantt chart.
    C. procedure flowchart.
    D. flow process chart.

REFERENCE: LaTour, Eichenwald-Maki, and Oachs, p 847
McWay, p 329

57. Mr. Beasley determined that the rate of absenteeism with three of his employees was 15%. He felt that this was unacceptable and decided that there were two different ways he could handle this situation. He evaluated these alternatives and thought the best thing to do would be to suspend all three for 2 days. Once he implemented this idea, he analyzed the consequences. How would you label this process?
    A. decision making
    B. planning
    C. crisis management
    D. communicating

REFERENCE: LaTour, Eichenwald-Maki, and Oachs, pp 695–696
McWay, pp 336–337

58. The project manager is responsible for all of the following functions, EXCEPT
    A. approval of the budget for the project.
    B. creation of project plan.
    C. recruitment of project team.
    D. recommending plan revisions.

REFERENCE: LaTour, Eichenwald-Maki, and Oachs, pp 840–842
McWay, pp 345–346

59. A basic concept of office layout and workflow is that the
    A. paper and employee move to a predetermined location.
    B. employee moves to the paper.
    C. office layout and workflow should be revised frequently.
    D. paper moves to the employee.

REFERENCE: Davis and LaCour, p 442
LaTour, Eichenwald-Maki, and Oachs, pp 796–798
McWay, p 335

60. Which of the following tasks is the most appropriate for the Health Information Services Director to delegate to the Supervisor of Record Processing and Statistics?
    A. formulating a record retention policy for the entire facility
    B. reviewing monthly statistical reports to verify accuracy
    C. interviewing applicants for the position of Tumor Registrar
    D. completing a performance rating on the Assistant Director of the department

REFERENCE: Davis and LaCour, pp 419–420
LaTour, Eichenwald-Maki, and Oachs, p 754
McWay, pp 334, 392

61. When interviewing a prospective employee, which question would be inappropriate to ask?
    A. "Can you type?"
    B. "Where may we contact you?"
    C. "What language other than English can you speak or write?"
    D. "Do you own a home?"

REFERENCE: Davis and LaTour, pp 448–451
LaTour, Eichenwald-Maki, and Oachs, pp 720–721

62. If the budgeted payroll expense was $24,300 and the actual payroll expense was $25,800, what is the percentage of cost variance?
    A. 6.0%
    B. 0.58%
    C. 6.17%
    D. 6.7%

REFERENCE: LaTour, Eichenwald-Maki, and Oachs, pp 786–788
McWay, pp 398–399

63. Which of the following actions illustrates the use of a participative management style?
    A. discussing suggested approaches of improving productivity and performance with employees
    B. basing decisions on information found in the manual of operations
    C. providing supervision only when requested by employees
    D. micromanaging all aspects and functions performed in the department

REFERENCE: Davis and LaCour, p 419
LaTour, Eichenwald-Maki, and Oachs, p 687
McWay, pp 344, 380

64. In deciding to purchase or lease a new dictation system, the director of Health Information Services calculated the payback period and rate of return on the investment. The hospital's required payback period is 3 years with a required rate of return of 20%. If the equipment costs $32,000 and generates $8,000 per year in savings, what would the payback period for this equipment be?
    A. 2 years
    B. 5 years
    C. 3 years
    D. 4 years

REFERENCE: LaTour, Eichenwald-Maki, and Oachs, p 791
McWay, p 390

65. The director of a Health Information Department prepared a document in which the following information could be obtained: job title, reporting line, span of control, and routes of promotion. The document she was preparing was a(n)
    A. job description.
    B. organizational chart.
    C. work distribution chart.
    D. job procedure.

REFERENCE: Davis and LaCour, pp 418–422
LaTour, Eichenwald-Maki, and Oachs, pp 690–691
McWay, pp 330–333

66. The director of the Health Information Department had to resign immediately due to a family crisis requiring her to leave the country. Her superior, the Administrator of Support Services, must appoint an Acting Director as soon as possible but is questioning who might be the best individual for this temporary role. What tool would assist the administrator with this decision?
    A. staffing table
    B. replacement chart
    C. proximity chart
    D. frequency chart

REFERENCE: Abdelhak, pp 584–585

67. Which of the following statements best describes information governance?
    A. An initiative that leads an organization toward change for an improved process
    B. An initiative that leads an organization toward completion of a project on time and within cost expectations
    C. An initiative that focuses on the view that data as a strategic asset needs to be protected and accounted for across all levels of the health care enterprise
    D. An initiative that focuses on protection and accuracy of individual data elements within the organization at an operational level

REFERENCE: Abdelhak, p 127

68. Lizzie O'Leary, director of the Health Information Services Department, is writing a memo about a recent problem the department has had with a contracted copy service when she is notified of an emergency, hospital-wide department-head meeting. Because it is necessary that the memo be completed by the end of the day, it is most appropriate for the director to delegate its completion to the supervisor of
    A. storage and retrieval.
    B. transcription.
    C. coding and abstracting.
    D. release of information.

REFERENCE: LaTour, Eichenwald-Maki, and Oachs, p 690
McWay, pp 334, 392

69. Of the following, which is NOT considered justification to approve overtime? Overtime is not justified
    A. for unpredictable fluctuations in volume.
    B. when there is unusually high absenteeism.
    C. when there is a temporary change of work methods.
    D. for employees who want to supplement their wages.

REFERENCE: LaTour, Eichenwald-Maki, and Oachs, pp 786–788

70. A job analysis includes the
    A. summation of the qualifications needed in a worker for a specific job.
    B. collection of data to determine the content of a job.
    C. title of the job and summary of the basic tasks making up a job.
    D. goals to be achieved by a worker over a specified period.

REFERENCE: Abdelhak, pp 586–587
Davis and LaCour, pp 440–441
LaTour, Eichenwald-Maki, and Oachs, p 731
McWay, p 333

71. The Director of Health Information Management has been asked to lead the existing medical record committee toward a new initiative to educate employees within the health care system about viewing data as a strategic asset that must be managed appropriately across the entire enterprise of health care facilities within the system. What initiative has the director been asked to lead?
    - A. Clinical Documentation Improvement
    - B. Strategic Planning
    - C. Data Governance
    - D. Information Governance

REFERENCE: Abdelhak, p 127

72. The manager of a transcription agency is preparing December's staffing schedule. Because this month has several holidays, there are more requests for vacation and personal days than usual. Additionally, it is apparent to the supervisor that she will not be able to approve all requests for time off. It will be best for the supervisor to construct the schedule by
    - A. processing requests based on seniority.
    - B. granting requests on a first-come basis.
    - C. adhering to the hospital and department policy regarding requests for time off.
    - D. not approving any time off, thus eliminating any conflicts.

REFERENCE: LaTour, Eichenwald-Maki, and Oachs, p 802
McWay, p 326

73. The supervisor over the file section has discovered an enormous backlog of loose lab reports. The first step that the supervisor should take in attempting to resolve this matter is to
    - A. analyze possible courses of action.
    - B. gather relevant data regarding the problem.
    - C. identify and clarify the problem.
    - D. choose the best course of action.

REFERENCE: LaTour, Eichenwald-Maki, and Oachs, pp 695–696

74. New equipment has just been purchased for a Health Information Services Department. Prior to its arrival and placement in the department, it is important for the manager to adhere to the rules and regulations governed by
    - A. FDA.
    - B. OSHA.
    - C. CMS.
    - D. SSA.

REFERENCE: Davis and LaCour, pp 216–217
LaTour, Eichenwald-Maki, and Oachs, p 722
McWay, p 368

75. The best source for obtaining data for a job analysis is the
    - A. department director.
    - B. supervisor of the job.
    - C. the person who performs the job.
    - D. procedures manual.

REFERENCE: Abdelhak, pp 586–587
McWay, p 333

76. Mike is an information specialist in the Department of Information Technology. He has been asked to assist with the Joint Commission survey process, which accounts for approximately 75% of his time. He also receives project assignments from the HIM director, his immediate supervisor, as well as the overall project manager. This refers to what type of authority relationship?
    - A. functional
    - B. parallel
    - C. matrix
    - D. divisional

REFERENCE: Burns, Bradley, and Weiner, p 77

77. The department director is responsible for budget costs that are controllable. Which of the following costs would be out of the director's control?
   A. equipment purchases
   B. fringe benefit cost per employee
   C. supply requisitions
   D. overtime authorizations

REFERENCE: Davis and LaCour, pp 730–731
LaTour, Eichenwald-Maki, and Oachs, p 781
McWay, pp 397–398

78. Kim Khoury is planning a luncheon for the team members and stakeholders on the CPOE implementation to celebrate reaching a major milestone. Which of the following is true?
   A. Acknowledging accomplishments and milestones motivates teams.
   B. Budgets rarely permit these extra expenses.
   C. Celebrations are only appropriate at the close of a project.
   D. Professionals are self-motivated, making celebrations unnecessary.

REFERENCE: LaTour, Eichenwald-Maki, and Oachs, p 850
McWay, pp 345–346

79. Beth Huber, director of Health Information, has been selected to participate in a strategic planning retreat for her health system. In preparation, she refreshes her understanding of strategic planning. Which of the following will likely be included in the retreat?
   A. improvement of existing programs and services
   B. opportunities to review internal structures and systems
   C. enhancing customer and patient satisfaction
   D. focus on the organization's fit with the external environment

REFERENCE: LaTour, Eichenwald-Maki, and Oachs, pp 866–867
McWay, pp 323–325

80. The project definition justifies the need for the new project. What would you expect to see in the project justification?
   A. project scope, resources needed, and amount of time required
   B. project scope, resources needed, and developing the solution
   C. resources needed, amount of time required, and preparing supporting documentation for the system chosen
   D. amount of time required, alternative analysis, and implementation review

REFERENCE: LaTour, Eichenwald-Maki, and Oachs, pp 841–842
McWay, pp 345–346

81. Roberta Little Eagle is the new HIM supervisor at a large South Dakota reservation clinic. In order to become familiar with the specific steps currently used in record processing, she uses which graphic tool?
   A. force field analysis
   B. histogram
   C. fishbone analysis
   D. flowchart

REFERENCE: Davis and LaCour, pp 370–371
LaTour, Eichenwald-Maki, and Oachs, p 822
McWay, pp 335–336

82. Megan is the new director of Health Information at Blue Ridge Rehabilitation Associates, a large multispecialty clinic. Her initial assessment of the department's functioning is that there is considerable duplication of effort. To collect information on the systems used in the current functions and to analyze and improve the process, she chose to use a
    A. work process flowchart.
    B. systems diagram.
    C. decision tree.
    D. Pareto chart.

REFERENCE: LaTour, Eichenwald-Maki, and Oachs, p 821
McWay, p 338

83. Which of the following would NOT be a scientific method of establishing standards?
    A. stopwatch studies
    B. work sampling
    C. personal experience
    D. time-log studies

REFERENCE: LaTour, Eichenwald-Maki, and Oachs, pp 806–807
McWay, pp 339–340

84. Lucy Ann manages a claims review unit for an insurance company. Her staff keys a high volume of data daily. She has scheduled a staff physical therapist to do the annual ergonomics presentation to help prevent repetitive strain injuries. All of the following would be included EXCEPT
    A. using a footrest.
    B. wrists should be elevated.
    C. monitor placed directly in front and elevated.
    D. lumbar support provided.

REFERENCE: Davis and LaCour, pp 454–456
LaTour, Eichenwald-Maki, and Oachs, p 799
McWay, p 335

85. South Beach Medical Center is preparing to open as a new 250-bed acute care hospital. This facility is located in a growing area of the city and is projected to have 85% occupancy within 3 years. To determine the number of employees needed in the HIM department, the director must first
    A. determine employee salary ranges.
    B. develop a departmental organizational chart.
    C. collect data from hospitals that are of comparable size.
    D. identify the departmental functions to be performed.

REFERENCE: Davis and LaCour, pp 415–416
LaTour, Eichenwald-Maki, and Oachs, pp 722–723
McWay, pp 339–340

86. A national HIM publication routinely requests that practitioners submit statistics from their facility regarding department functions. These are then summarized and published in graphic form, providing a tool for which of the following activities?
    A. benchmarking
    B. work standards
    C. job evaluation
    D. job redesign

REFERENCE: Davis and LaCour, pp 65, 363–364
LaTour, Eichenwald-Maki, and Oachs, p 808
McWay, pp 179, 188

87. In project management, the series of specific tasks that determine the overall project duration is referred to as
    - A. project network.
    - B. critical path.
    - C. risk analysis.
    - D. project definition.

REFERENCE: LaTour, Eichenwald-Maki, and Oachs, p 844

88. The formalized road map that describes how your institution executes the chosen strategy defines
    - A. operations improvement.
    - B. strategic thinking.
    - C. operational mission.
    - D. strategic planning.

REFERENCE: LaTour, Eichenwald-Maki, and Oachs, p 866

89. Which of the following is a tool for strategic thinking?
    - A. storytelling
    - B. driving force
    - C. innovations
    - D. critical issues

REFERENCE: LaTour, Eichenwald-Maki, and Oachs, pp 866–868

90. Which of the following helps the organization prioritize investment opportunities?
    - A. return on investment
    - B. profitability index
    - C. net present value
    - D. internal rate of return

REFERENCE: LaTour, Eichenwald-Maki, and Oachs, p 792

91. Which of the following emphasizes the work climate in which harmony and cohesion promote good work?
    - A. effectiveness
    - B. chain of command
    - C. scalar chain
    - D. esprit de corps

REFERENCE: LaTour, Eichenwald-Maki, and Oachs, p 686

92. Which of the following is often characterized as a manager's version of a pilot's cockpit as it contains all the critical information for leading the organization?
    - A. balanced scorecard
    - B. revenge effect
    - C. executive dashboard
    - D. groupthink

REFERENCE: LaTour, Eichenwald-Maki, and Oachs, p 692

93. The statement "Managers must understand the informal organization of workers (groups, group sentiments, team work), the need of workers to be listened to and to participate in the design of their work" is characteristic of which of the following schools of management?
    - A. Classical School of Administration
    - B. Human Relations School
    - C. Scientific Management School
    - D. Decision-making School

REFERENCE: Burns, Bradley, and Weiner, pp 16–17
LaTour, Eichenwald-Maki, and Oachs, pp 686–687, 689–690, 712
McWay, pp 343, 386, 389–391, 712

94. Units that provide support services to the organization, such as human resources, finances, and information systems, are referred to as
    - A. line managers.
    - B. integrated delivery systems.
    - C. matrix organization.
    - D. staff departments.

REFERENCE: Burns, Bradley, and Weiner, p 79
LaTour, Eichenwald-Maki, and Oachs, p 690

95. In Maslow's "hierarchy or needs," the term that describes the need for a positive self-image or self-respect, and the need for recognition and respect from others best describes
   A. belonging needs.
   B. security needs.
   C. esteem needs.
   D. self-actualization needs.

REFERENCE: Burns, Bradley, and Weiner, pp 97–98
LaTour, Eichenwald-Maki, and Oachs, pp 687, 712
McWay, pp 340–341

96. The Occupational Safety and Health Act of 1970, the Americans with Disability Act, and the Vocational Rehabilitation Act are all federal legislation designed to
   A. prevent sexual harassment.
   B. ensure equal pay for equal work.
   C. keep the workplace safe and accessible to all employees and customers.
   D. protect child labor.

REFERENCE: Abdelhak, p 577
Davis and LaCour, pp 263–266, 311, 451
LaTour, Eichenwald-Maki, and Oachs, pp 721, 722, 728
McWay, pp 367–373

97. Which of the following methods of performance appraisal requires the supervisor to document exceptional behavior by the employee?
   A. Behaviorally Anchored Rating
   B. Graphic Rating Scales
   C. Goal Setting
   D. Critical Incident Method

REFERENCE: Abdelhak, pp 594–595

98. The HIM employee is consistently late for work. Her supervisor has given her an oral warning. According to the definition of progressive discipline, what would the next step be?
   A. written warning and reprimand
   B. meeting with the supervisor of her supervisor
   C. suspension
   D. termination

REFERENCE: Abdelhak, p 601
LaTour, Eichenwald-Maki, and Oachs, pp 240, 755
McWay, p 378

99. There are several methods used to evaluate jobs. Which of the following is the simplest but the least precise?
   A. factor comparison
   B. job ranking
   C. job grading
   D. point system

REFERENCE: Abdelhak, pp 605–606
LaTour, Eichenwald-Maki, and Oachs, p 755

100. An example of a communication network that is suitable to use when you have to communicate with several people who have no need to communicate directly with each other describes
   A. a wheel.
   B. a chain.
   C. a circle.
   D. a "Y" pattern.

REFERENCE: Burns, Bradley, and Weiner, p 181

101. A type of job evaluation that requires the identification of essential factors or elements common to all jobs and the comparison of jobs on the basis of rating those elements (not the job as a whole), refers to
   A. job ranking.
   B. job grading.
   C. factor comparison.
   D. point system.

REFERENCE: Abdelhak, p 607
LaTour, Eichenwald-Maki, and Oachs, p 755

102. The mechanism that provides a communication and problem-solving tool for employees to express a complaint that management has violated one of its own policies, and caused adverse consequences to the employee, refers to
   A. employee discipline.
   B. the grievance process.
   C. involuntary retirement.
   D. employee counseling.

REFERENCE: Abdelhak, p 601
LaTour, Eichenwald-Maki, and Oachs, p 756
McWay, pp 378–379

103. The National Labor Relations Act (NLRA), which serves as the foundation for U.S. labor laws and collective bargaining, is also known as
   A. the Equal Pay Act.
   B. the Fair Labor Standards Act.
   C. the Family and Medical Leave Act.
   D. the Wagner Act.

REFERENCE: Abdelhak, p 578
LaTour, Eichenwald-Maki, and Oachs, p 722
McWay, p 367

104. Which of the following examples would NOT be considered "reasonable accommodation" under the Americans with Disabilities Act?
   A. completely renovating an entire department to accommodate a disabled employee
   B. providing qualified readers or interpreters
   C. reassigning a current employee to a vacant position
   D. acquiring or modifying equipment

REFERENCE: Abdelhak, p 576
Davis and LaCour, p 451
LaTour, Eichenwald-Maki, and Oachs, p 742
McWay, pp 335, 367, 370

105. An amendment to the Civil Rights Act of 1964 that extends the 180-day statute of limitations previously applied to the filing of an equal-pay lawsuit refers to the
   A. Americans with Disabilities Act.
   B. Lilly Ledbetter Fair Pay Act.
   C. Age Discrimination in Employment Act.
   D. Family and Medical Leave Act.

REFERENCE: Abdelhak, p 573
McWay, pp 367, 374

106. Which of the following is NOT a main objective of reengineering?
   A. to improve quality
   B. to increase revenue
   C. to increase cost
   D. to reduce risk

REFERENCE: Abdelhak, p 645
LaTour, Eichenwald-Maki, and Oachs, pp 35, 688

Answer Key for Organization and Management

ANSWER EXPLANATION

NOTE: Explanations are provided for those questions that require mathematical calculations and questions that are not clearly explained in the references that are cited.

1. D
2. B The reference pages indicated do not answer the question directly. The references relate to discussions of the organizational structure and design. Based on that information, assumptions regarding organizational relationships (vertical, lateral, matrix, etc.) can be made.
3. C
4. D Remember to convert the hours to minutes.
   725×12 minutes = 8,700 minutes
   1,280 hours $\times$ 60 minutes = 76,800 minutes
   8,700 minutes on coding / 76,800 minutes worked = 11.3% spent on coding
5. D
6. B This is clearly a problem of not understanding the procedures of the tasks; therefore, reviewing the job description probably will not be of much help. This rules out "review the job description and job procedure with the clerk and follow up with an in-service" and "review the job description and job procedure with the clerk and follow up with a merit evaluation." This also does not seem to be a problem that would require an in-service, thereby ruling out "review job procedures with the clerk and follow up with an in-service." Therefore, the best solution is to review the procedures with her and have the analysis clerk monitor her progress to ensure that she fully understands the procedures.
7. A
8. C
9. B "Medical records requested by the emergency room will be retrieved and delivered within 30 minutes" and "transcription turnaround time is established as 24 hours following completion of dictation by the physician" describe a standard. "Only HIM personnel have access to the medical record filing area" describes a rule.
10. C
11. D
12. B Formula: Total actual work units $\times$ 100/ Standard work units = variance percent
    $(30 + 40 + 25 + 35) \times 100 = 13{,}000$ $13{,}000/200 = 65\%$
13. B
14. B The hours must first be converted to minutes.
    7 hours $\times$ 60 = 420 minutes
    420 minutes $\times$ 0.20 = 84 minutes
15. A
16. C
17. C
18. B
19. D $950 \times 20 = 19{,}000$; $142{,}500 / 19{,}000 = 7.5$ FTEs
20. B
21. A
22. C
23. C 20 charts × 5 days = 100 per week × 4 weeks = 400
    A standard of 400 charts coded over 4 weeks per coder.
    Coder 3 has coded only 320 charts over the 4 weeks.

Answer Key for Organization and Management

ANSWER	EXPLANATION
24. B	
25. D	
26. D	
27. C	It is the physician's responsibility to ensure that a patient has consented to a surgical procedure.
28. A	
29. D	
30. C	Although a CEO is involved in all of the options given, only the organizational objectives are completed annually. The mission statement is reviewed to ensure that the organizational objectives are consistent with it, but it is not revised annually. Strategic goals and objectives are completed on a long-term basis, not annually.
31. B	
32. C	
33. A	In order to determine which vendor to choose, each vendor's scores are added. The vendor that scores the highest for all three criteria is chosen. Calculations: Multiply the weight for each criterion by the rating. After this is done, each column is totaled. Vendor A scores 38; Vendor B, 25; Vendor C, 37; Vendor D, 27.
34. C	Costs = \$6,000 + \$1,500 + \$500 = \$8,000. Benefits = \$10,000. (That is the increase in reimbursement.) 10,000 / 8,000 = 1.25. Benefits/Costs Ratio = 1.25. (This also known as the cost–benefit figure.) In other words, for every dollar invested in the encoding system, it will have a return of \$1.25 after 1 year.
35. B	
36. C	
37. D	
38. B	\$7.10 × 0.04 = 0.284 + \$7.10 = \$7.384
39. D	
40. A	
41. B	
42. D	2,000 × \$13.50 = \$27,000; \$27,000 / 225,333 = 0.1198, rounded to 0.12
43. B	The formula for budget variance percent is actual minus budget divided by budget. 675 – 495 = 180 (180 × 100) / 495 = 36%
44. B	
45. A	To determine the number of employees needed for a specific job, first determine how much time the work requires. In this case, we know we will have an additional 120 records per day and each record will average about 15 minutes. To figure the amount of total time, multiply 120 × 15 = 1,800 minutes. Compute this to hours by dividing by 60 (60 minutes in an hour): 1,800/60 = 30 hours. Based on the 8-hour day, divide 30 hours by 8 = 3.75 FTEs.
46. D	
47. A	
48. D	
49. D	
50. A	
51. C	
52. D	
53. B	

Answer Key for Organization and Management

	ANSWER	EXPLANATION
54.	A	
55.	B	
56.	B	A Gantt chart is a scheduling tool.
57.	A	
58.	A	
59.	D	
60.	B	
61.	D	One must be familiar with the various labor laws to ensure that an interviewee is not asked questions that could be considered discriminating or illegal.
62.	C	25,800 – 24,300 = 1,500; 1,500/24,300 = 0.0617 × 100 = 6.17%
63.	A	
64.	D	Formula: initial investment/annual cash flow = payback period $32,000/$8,000 = 4 years
65.	B	
66.	B	
67.	C	
68.	D	
69.	D	
70.	B	
71.	D	
72.	C	
73.	C	
74.	B	
75.	C	
76.	C	
77.	B	
78.	A	
79.	D	
80.	A	
81.	D	
82.	A	
83.	C	Personal experience is subjective. The other answer choices rely on objective measurement of job performance.
84.	B	Wrists should be in a neutral position.
85.	D	
86.	A	
87.	B	
88.	D	
89.	A	
90.	B	
91.	D	
92.	C	
93.	B	
94.	D	
95.	C	
96.	C	
97.	D	
98.	A	

Answer Key for Organization and Management

	ANSWER	EXPLANATION
99.	B	
100.	A	
101.	C	
102.	B	
103.	D	
104.	A	
105.	B	
106.	C	

REFERENCES

Abdelhak, M., and Hanken, M. A. (2016). *Health information: Management of a strategic resource* (5th ed.). Philadelphia: W. B. Saunders.

Burns, L., Bradley, E. H., and Weiner, B. J. (2012). *Shortell & Kalunzy's health care management: Organization design and behavior* (6th ed.). Clifton Park, NY: Cengage Learning.

Davis, N., and LaCour, M. (2014). *Health information technology* (3rd ed.). Philadelphia: W. B. Saunders.

LaTour, K., Eichenwald-Maki, S., and Oachs, P. (2013). *Health information management: Concepts, principles, and practice* (4th ed.). Chicago: American Health Information Management Association (AHIMA).

McWay, D. (2014). *Today's health information management: An integrated approach* (2nd ed.). Clifton Park, NY: Cengage Learning.

Competency Domains for Organization and Management

Question	RHIA Domain	RHIT Domain
1–106	4	
1–24		1

XVI. Human Resources

Shelley C. Safian, PhD, CCS-P, CPC-H, CPC-I, CHA

AHIMA-Approved ICD-10-CM/PCS Trainer

Use the following information to answer questions 1–3.

The staff in the Human Resources Department is proposing a cloud training program for 200 employees and needs to prepare a budget for the time and cost of the training.

- The training program will be 30 minutes in length.
- The employees can take the training online at any time.
- There are 200 employees to be trained.
- The rate of pay for 50 of the employees is $15.50 per hour.
- The rate of pay for 50 employees is $12.00 per hour.
- The rate of pay for the other 100 employees is $18.00 per hour.

1. How many employee clock hours will be needed to complete the training?
   A. 200 hours
   B. 150 hours
   C. 100 hours
   D. 50 hours

REFERENCE: Davis and LaCour, pp 466–468
Horton, p 138
Koch, p 77
Liebler and McConnell, pp 243, 385–387

2. How much should the training staff request in the budget for doing the computer-based training program?
   A. $3,175.00
   B. $1,975.00
   C. $1,887.50
   D. $1,587.50

REFERENCE: Davis and LaCour, pp 466–468
Horton, p 138
Koch, p 77
Liebler and McConnell, pp 243, 385–387

3. What would be the average cost for training an individual employee?
   A. $7.94
   B. $9.00
   C. $15.50
   D. $15.87

REFERENCE: Davis and LaCour, pp 466–468
Horton, p 138
Koch, p 77

4. At Great Plains Regional Hospital, record processing takes approximately 18 minutes. If there are 15,620 discharges for the month, how many staff hours are needed for this volume of work?
   A. 2,891
   B. 4,686
   C. 5,496
   D. 3,394

REFERENCE: Abdelhak, p 641
Davis and LaCour, pp 424–426
Horton, pp 148–149
Koch, p 77
LaTour, Eichenwald-Maki, and Oachs, p 724
Liebler and McConnell, pp 243, 385–387
McConnell, pp 350–351

5. The advantages of teams or committees over individuals in complex situations include all of the following EXCEPT:
   A. Decision making is accomplished more quickly.
   B. Complex problems can be better assessed.
   C. Authority can be counterbalanced.
   D. Coordination and cooperation can be increased.

REFERENCE: LaTour, Eichenwald-Maki, and Oachs, p 740
McWay, pp 380–381
Sayles, pp 1082–1083

6. Mallory, data integrity unit supervisor, must determine the number of full-time employees (FTEs) needed to code 600 discharges per week. It takes an average of 20 minutes to code each record and each coder will work 40 hours per week. How many coders are needed?
   A. 6.0
   B. 5.0
   C. 12.0
   D. 4.5

REFERENCE: Abdelhak, p 641
Davis and LaCour, pp 415–416
Horton, p 148
Koch, p 77
LaTour, Eichenwald-Maki, and Oachs, p 806
Liebler and McConnell, p 243
McConnell, pp 350–351

7. Under the Americans with Disabilities Act (ADA), prior to employment, it is illegal to require a
   A. math aptitude test.
   B. typing skill test.
   C. coding proficiency test.
   D. physical exam.

REFERENCE: Abdelhak, pp 597–598
McWay, p 370
Safian, p 236
Sayles, p 836

8. Jason, an HIM educator, plans to lecture on department design and the legislative act or agency that was created to ensure that workers have a safe and healthy work environment. Which of the following legal issues will he describe?
   A. OSHA
   B. Wagner Act
   C. Taft–Hartley Law
   D. Labor Management Relations Act

REFERENCE: Abdelhak, pp 598–599
LaTour, Eichenwald-Maki, and Oachs, p 722
McWay, p 373
Sayles, p 1231

9. Dana has prepared a performance appraisal for one of her employees. As the HIM director reviews the evaluation, he notes that the employee received an overall rating of "needs improvement." After reading the comments, the director asks Dana to document specific performance improvement recommendations. Dana is unable to do so because she is basing her assessment on her memory of incidents that have occurred over the past year. The director suggests that Dana reassess the employee's evaluation because, ideally, performance appraisals should
   A. be signed off by two supervisors.
   B. contain a day-by-day assessment.
   C. document specific performance levels.
   D. praise all staff workers to avoid a lawsuit.

REFERENCE: Abdelhak, pp 616–618
Davis and LaCour, pp 443–445
LaTour, Eichenwald-Maki, and Oachs, p 814
McConnell, p 205
McWay, p 376
Sayles, pp 1101–1102

10. Trevor is a new scanning technician. To fulfill your responsibility as a supervisor and to help him learn and complete his work correctly, the best training resource to use would be a(n)
   A. job description.
   B. service level agreement.
   C. organization policies and procedures manual.
   D. job procedure.

REFERENCE: Abdelhak, p 610
LaTour, Eichenwald-Maki, and Oachs, p 804
Sayles, pp 407–409

11. Gregg is a recent graduate who has applied for a Trauma Registry position at a Chicago hospital while he prepares to apply to graduate school. In making the decision, he considers the offer of $15 per hour for a 40-hour week, benefits of 27.5% of his salary, and tuition waivers of six credits per year at $145. He calculated that his total compensation, rounded to the nearest dollar, would be
   A. $40,650.
   B. $39,563.
   C. $38,599.
   D. $31,030.

REFERENCE: Horton, pp 138–139
Koch, p 77

12. Yanique is a new supervisor at a mental health facility. She discovers that one of her employees has shared her password with a coworker. This action violates policies and procedures and is the first occasion of difficulty with this employee. Disciplinary action should be taken by
   A. waiting for another occurrence to act.
   B. referring the action to Human Resources.
   C. asking for guidance from Human Resources and then acting.
   D. immediately dismissing the employee.

REFERENCE: LaTour, Eichenwald-Maki, and Oachs, pp 755–758
Liebler and McConnell, pp 425–426
McWay, pp 302–303

13. Conflict is inevitable. What is the LEAST effective way to manage conflict?
    A. Do not intervene: creative solutions often come from conflict.
    B. Encourage the parties to compromise by each willing to lose part of their position.
    C. Limit or control interaction when emotions are intense.
    D. Use an objective third party to seek a constructive outcome for both parties.

REFERENCE: LaTour, Eichenwald-Maki, and Oachs, p 756
Liebler and McConnell, p 333
McWay, p 342
Sayles, pp 735, 1103–1105

14. The HIPAA Privacy and Security Rule requires that training be documented. What methods of documenting training efforts need to be used?
    A. retention of training aids and handouts
    B. meeting handouts and minutes
    C. training content, training dates, and attendee names
    D. signed confidentiality statements

REFERENCE: AHIMA (1)
LaTour, Eichenwald-Maki, and Oachs, pp 859–860
Sayles, 829

15. Holly is the day supervisor who works from 7:00 AM to 4:00 PM. Kim is the evening supervisor who works from 2:00 PM to 11:00 PM. Sarah is a transcriptionist who works from 10:00 AM to 7:00 PM, which overlaps the day and evening shifts. Sarah asked Holly, the day supervisor, if she could leave early for personal reasons. Holly said Sarah could leave early if Kim, the evening supervisor, agrees. Which theory of management does this situation violate?
    A. span of control
    B. formal theory of authority
    C. specialization of labor
    D. unity of command

REFERENCE: Davis and LaCour, p 419
LaTour, Eichenwald-Maki, and Oachs, p 686
Liebler and McConnell, p 130
McConnell, pp 56–57
McWay, p 686

16. You are preparing a training program for specific functional areas of the department (e.g., coding, transcription, etc.). Which of the following is the primary factor to consider in developing an effective training program?
    A. credentials of the employees
    B. objectives of each functional area
    C. cost of training the employees
    D. number of employees to be trained

REFERENCE: Abdelhak, p 630
Davis and LaCour, p 466
LaTour, Eichenwald-Maki, and Oachs, pp 733–735
McWay, p 365
Sayles, p 1099

17. Grace Holt, RHIA, is the HIM Department Manager. She is reviewing interviewing techniques with Maria Hernandez, RHIT, as she prepares to interview for a new analyst. Grace recommends that Maria should
    A. ask questions that encourage a "yes" or "no" response.
    B. politely interrupt as necessary to seek clarification.
    C. talk down to the applicant to show authority.
    D. phrase questions so the expected answer is encouraged.

REFERENCE: Abdelhak, pp 614–615
Davis and LaCour, pp 448–449
LaTour, Eichenwald-Maki, and Oachs, p 726
McConnell, pp 139–141
Sayles, pp 1096–1097

18. Your job description states that as Assistant Director of the HIM Department, you will supervise day-to-day operations for the record processing, transcription, and release of information areas. What principle of management is described?
    A. specialization
    B. centralized authority
    C. span of control
    D. delegation

REFERENCE: Davis and LaCour, p 419
LaTour, Eichenwald-Maki, and Oachs, p 690
Liebler and McConnell, pp 131–132
McConnell, p 57

19. Rachel's work performance has diminished over the last 2 weeks. In addition, she has uncharacteristic mood swings and has exhibited difficulty concentrating. She is also having difficulties with tardiness and attendance. As her supervisor, you meet with Rachel to discuss your concerns. She reveals that she is struggling financially. What action should you take?
    A. Assure her that as long as she can perform her job acceptably, her personal life is none of your concern.
    B. Put her on probation.
    C. Refer her to the Employee Assistance Program.
    D. Terminate her.

REFERENCE: Abdelhak, p 624
LaTour, Eichenwald-Maki, and Oachs, pp 690–694
McConnell, pp 244–245
McWay, pp 377–378

20. Hannah arrives for work Monday through Friday any time between 7:00 and 9:00 AM, is on the job until at least 3:00 PM, and then may leave any time between 3:00 and 6:00 PM. Hanna's schedule is an example of
    A. the 8/80 workweek.
    B. the staggered work hours program.
    C. variable work schedule.
    D. flextime.

REFERENCE: LaTour, Eichenwald-Maki, and Oachs, p 727

21. Use the following statistics from Utah Home Health to calculate the absenteeism rate.

Month: January	
Number of employees	20
Number of workdays	22
Total work days lost	25

A. 0.44%
B. 5.68%
C. 5.8%
D. 0.568%

REFERENCE: Horton, pp 14–19
LaTour, Eichenwald-Maki, and Oachs, p 808
McWay, p 221

22. As an HIM supervisor, one of your employees reports that a coworker has returned from lunch on numerous occasions with the smell of alcohol on his breath. What is the best approach in handling this problem?
A. Confront the employee and place him on suspension for 1 week.
B. Terminate the employee immediately.
C. Ignore the report because it is hearsay.
D. Handle the situation as you would any other disease that affects an employee's work.

REFERENCE: Abdelhak, p 624
LaTour, Eichenwald-Maki, and Oachs, pp 755–756
McConnell, pp 243–245
Sayles, pp 546–547

23. Gary's primary concern is job continuity and adequate health insurance for his large family. What level of Maslow's hierarchy of needs does Gary operate from?
A. physiological
B. self-actualization
C. esteem
D. safety

REFERENCE: LaTour, Eichenwald-Maki, and Oachs, p 687
McConnell, pp 180–182
McWay, pp 340–341

24. Employers may be able to demonstrate that age is a reasonable requirement for a position. Such an exception to the Age Discrimination in Employment Act (ADEA) is called a
A. job description essential.
B. bona fide occupational qualification.
C. essential element for employment.
D. there is no such exception to ADEA.

REFERENCE: Abdelhak, p 598
LaTour, Eichenwald-Maki, and Oachs, p 721
McConnell, pp 456–457
McWay, p 370

25. Julian supervises the department's coding section. He notices that the coding technician is working 30 additional minutes each day before clocking in at her scheduled starting time. After discussing her timecard with her, he discovers that she is starting work early in order to check the unbilled account report. Under which act are you required to pay her for all hours worked?
    A. ERISA
    B. Fair Labor Standards Act
    C. National Labor Relations Act
    D. Equal Pay Act

REFERENCE: Abdelhak, pp 599–600
LaTour, Eichenwald-Maki, and Oachs, p 754
McConnell, pp 551–553
McWay, p 374
Sayles, p 1207

26. Puget Sound Health System has set hiring goals and taken steps to guarantee equal employment opportunities for members of protected groups (e.g., American Indians, veterans, etc.). It is complying with
    A. Affirmative Action.
    B. Equal Pay Act.
    C. Minority Hiring Act.
    D. Civil Rights Act.

REFERENCE: Abdelhak, pp 595–596
LaTour, Eichenwald-Maki, and Oachs, p 721
McConnell, pp 453–454
McWay, p 374

27. Southwest Health System has numerous semiretired staff. The Human Resources Department has provided training regarding the Age Discrimination in Employment Act (ADEA). They emphasized that it protects employees and applicants between what ages?
    A. 50 and 75
    B. 45 and 99
    C. 62 and 85
    D. 40 and 70

REFERENCE: Abdelhak, p 598
LaTour, Eichenwald-Maki, and Oachs, p 894
McConnell, pp 456–457
McWay, p 370
Sayles, p 835

28. Which of the following HIPAA components would the general New Employee Orientation training most likely cover?
    A. marketing issues
    B. business associate agreements
    C. physical/workstation security
    D. job-specific training (e.g., patient's right to amend record)

REFERENCE: AHIMA Practice Brief 1
LaTour, Eichenwald-Maki, and Oachs, pp 730–732

29. Krista combined her HIM and legal education and is now a Risk Manager. An employee has a complaint that may be considered a grievance. She should listen to the employee and then
    A. put the complaint aside to see if other employees complain about the same issue.
    B. deal with the issue as if it were a bona fide grievance.
    C. deal with the complaint only if the employee seldom complains.
    D. ignore the complaint until it is in writing.

REFERENCE: Abdelhak, p 624
LaTour, Eichenwald-Maki, and Oachs, p 756
McWay, pp 378–379
Sayles, p 1106

30. Human Resources provide training for new supervisors. It includes discussion of the Equal Pay Act, which was passed to eliminate discrimination based on which of the following?
    A. merit of the employee
    B. seniority of the employee
    C. employee gender
    D. personal productivity, such as in an incentive compensation system

REFERENCE: Abdelhak, pp 599–600
Davis and LaCour, pp 448–450
LaTour, Eichenwald-Maki, and Oachs, p 722
McConnell, p 456
McWay, p 374
Sayles, p 835

31. The transcription area has an opening for a transcriptionist with demonstrated skill in medical and surgical reports. Which of the following types of tests should be administered?
    A. skill
    B. personality
    C. intelligence
    D. stress

REFERENCE: Abdelhak, p 614
Davis and LaCour, pp 449–450
LaTour, Eichenwald-Maki, and Oachs, p 725
McConnell, p 135
McWay, p 363

32. As manager of release of information, you supervise an employee who has been a correspondence clerk for many years. Her performance has gradually diminished and has become substandard. What method would most likely prove to be INEFFECTIVE in assisting this employee in improving her performance?
    A. threatening to fire the employee
    B. asking the employee to cross-train with other employees
    C. delegation of special assignments
    D. creating an action plan with the employee

REFERENCE: Abdelhak, pp 601–602
LaTour, Eichenwald-Maki, and Oachs, p 755
McConnell, pp 224–225
McWay, p 376

33. Rebecca, the revenue cycle manager, has received permission to check references for the candidate she would like to add to her team. Which of the following questions is the candidate's previous employer least likely to answer?
    A. What was her previous position?
    B. What was her previous salary?
    C. What was their personal impressions of her?
    D. What was the reason for her leaving her previous position?

REFERENCE: Abdelhak, pp 633–634
LaTour, Eichenwald-Maki, and Oachs, p 726
McWay, p 363

34. After receiving completed requisitions to fill positions within the HIM Department, Human Resources can be most effective in recruiting qualified applicants with the assistance of a
    A. departmental organizational chart.
    B. current job description.
    C. salary schedule.
    D. employee benefits handbook.

REFERENCE: Abdelhak, p 610
Davis and LaCour, pp 401–402
LaTour, Eichenwald-Maki, and Oachs, pp 723–724
Liebler and McConnell, pp 437–441
McConnell, p 259
McWay, p 376

35. You are interviewing a candidate for a subpoena clerk position in the release of information section. Which of the following is the LEAST appropriate information to ask an interviewee to provide?
    A. Do you have transportation for attendance at depositions and court?
    B. Please share an experience where you had to determine applicable state law.
    C. Please provide a copy of your most recent CE certificate and AHIMA membership.
    D. Do you have family responsibilities that would keep you from remaining at a trial?

REFERENCE: LaTour, Eichenwald-Maki, and Oachs, pp 725–726
McConnell, pp 136–137
Sayles, p 1097

36. Samantha is the evening discharge analysis clerk. As the evening supervisor, you personally trained her regarding the correct job procedures and policies. Within the last 2 months, Samantha has received an oral and written warning for failure to follow job procedures. Your facility utilizes a progressive discipline system. What is the next appropriate step?
    A. demotion
    B. suspension
    C. oral reprimand from the evening supervisor
    D. written warning from the director of the department

REFERENCE: Abdelhak, pp 624–626
LaTour, Eichenwald-Maki, and Oachs, pp 755–756
Liebler and McConnell, pp 415–416
McConnell, pp 215–219
McWay, pp 302–303
Sayles, p 1103

37. Federal legislation has a significant impact on the workplace. Which of the following requires employers to make reasonable accommodations for individuals to perform essential job functions?
    A. Age Discrimination Act
    B. Americans with Disabilities Act
    C. Rehabilitation Act
    D. Equal Opportunity Employment Act

REFERENCE: Abdelhak, pp 597–598
LaTour, Eichenwald-Maki, and Oachs, p 721
Liebler and McConnell, pp 455–456
McConnell, pp 457–458
McWay, p 378

38. Eva Pulaski supervises the electronic document management (EDM) section. She is preparing a report that includes a graphic that displays data over time and provides an excellent visualization of quality and quantity trends. This style of a report is called a
    A. Pareto chart.
    B. correlation analysis.
    C. run or control chart.
    D. scatter diagram.

REFERENCE: Horton, pp 216–218
LaTour, Eichenwald-Maki, and Oachs, pp 824–825
Liebler and McConnell, p 216
McWay, p 223
Sayles, pp 581–582, 1246

39. Selena works 40 hours per week at Rio Grande Radiology, which pays time-and-a-half for overtime and double-time for holidays. During the past week, Selena took 6 hours of unpaid personal leave and worked an 8-hour holiday. How many hours will Selena be paid?
    A. 34
    B. 42
    C. 48
    D. 50

REFERENCE: McConnell, pp 448–451
Koch, p 77

40. Natalie was an orientation counselor in college and knows that a well-designed program can help those new to a setting feel comfortable. As a new manager, she continues her commitment and contributes to new employee orientation. Which of the following statements about orientation programs is NOT true?
    A. A good orientation program can substitute for a job-specific departmental training.
    B. The most meaningful training program includes a peer "show and tell" format.
    C. The orientation assists the employee in learning about the workplace culture.
    D. Proper training can enhance employee satisfaction.

REFERENCE: Abdelhak, pp 630–631
Davis and LaCour, pp 460–465
LaTour, Eichenwald-Maki, and Oachs, pp 730–731
McWay, pp 286–290
Sayles, pp 1096, 1099–1100

41. Gina is the HIPAA Privacy and Security Officer and primary trainer for a regional health system. In determining how a certain department staff position uses health information, she must certainly review the
    A. past performance evaluations of persons in the position.
    B. position or job description.
    C. facility policy on protecting health information.
    D. facility policy and procedure on documenting training.

REFERENCE: AHIMA (1)
LaTour, Eichenwald-Maki, and Oachs, p 723
McWay, p 336
Sayles, pp 1100, 1121

42. Mary Ellen Smith has been an excellent biller for the past 5 years. Lately, you have noticed that she has the highest error rate and the lowest productivity rate of the entire billing section. She also seems to be distracted and unhappy. You have a conversation with her and she confides that she is having many "personal problems" that are causing her enormous stress. As her supervisor, you
    A. accept this explanation and determine that it is probably a temporary situation.
    B. issue a verbal warning to Mary Ellen to shape up.
    C. issue a written warning with a date to review her progress.
    D. refer her to the Employee Assistance Program.

REFERENCE: Abdelhak, pp 605, 624
LaTour, Eichenwald-Maki, and Oachs, pp 755–756
McConnell, pp 244–245
McWay, pp 377–378

43. At orientation a new employee receives the Employee Handbook. All of the following information about the Employee Handbook is true, EXCEPT that
    A. it provides a contractual obligation to continued employment.
    B. it provides policies and procedures developed by management.
    C. a receipt must be documented in writing.
    D. it must be reviewed periodically by legal counsel to avoid legal risk.

REFERENCE: Abdelhak, p 611
Davis and LaCour, p 460
LaTour, Eichenwald-Maki, and Oachs, pp 730–731

44. Fareeda's methods improvement objectives are to use an organized approach to determine how to accomplish a task with less effort in less time or at a lower cost while maintaining or improving the quality of the outcome. Frequently, methods improvement is referred to as
    A. benchmarking.
    B. work distribution.
    C. work simplification.
    D. data quality improvement.

REFERENCE: Abdelhak, pp 645–652
McWay, p 338

45. You work in a unionized organization and have filed a grievance. Which of the following will most likely take place?
   A. You can be terminated for registering a grievance.
   B. The grievance procedure regulations stipulated in the union contract will be followed.
   C. The facility policies and procedures for prompt and fair action on any grievance will be followed.
   D. The time from complaint to resolution should be no longer than 90 days.

REFERENCE: Abdelhak, p 624
LaTour, Eichenwald-Maki, and Oachs, p 756
McWay, p 378
Sayles, p 1106

46. Mission Health Systems has contracted with an agency to conduct recruitment and screening of potential candidates. This approach is called
   A. outsourcing.
   B. partnership.
   C. consulting.
   D. decentralized hiring.

REFERENCE: Abdelhak, p 28
LaTour, Eichenwald-Maki, and Oachs, pp 730, 803
McWay, pp 11, 40

47. When analyzing discipline problems, which of the following should be considered?
   A. the prior performance of the employee in question
   B. the frequency of the problem
   C. the seriousness of the problem
   D. All answers apply.

REFERENCE: Abdelhak, p 622
LaTour, Eichenwald-Maki, and Oachs, p 755
Liebler and McConnell, pp 413–416
McConnell, pp 225–227
McWay, p 378
Sayles, p 1122

48 Chris and Amy, two coders on your team, have come to you complaining that Jane, the discharge clerk, is deliberately holding back charts, causing a coding backlog. You are not sure Jane is really the cause of this problem because Chris and Amy have a history of blaming others for their work-related delays. To determine if Jane is truly a "problem employee" it would be best to first
   A. determine the source of the conflict.
   B. discretely ask other employees if they are having similar problems with Jane.
   C. request assistance from the Human Resources Department.
   D. observe Jane's interaction with others.

REFERENCE: Abdelhak, p 642
LaTour, Eichenwald-Maki, and Oachs, p 755
McWay, p 342
Sayles, pp 1103–1105

49. There is an opening for a coder in a 150-bed acute care hospital. The position requires someone who can code from a wide variety of medical records using both ICD and CPT. Of the following candidates interviewing for this position, which would be the most appropriate to hire?
   A. a high-school graduate who has applied for entry into the 2-year college RHIT program
   B. a recent graduate of a 4-year HIM program, RHIA eligible, who hopes to become a department manager within 1 year
   C. a graduate of a 2-year community college HIT program, RHIT eligible, with 1 year of outpatient coding experience
   D. an RHIA with 5 years of supervisory experience in medical records who recently moved to this city and can find no other available position as a supervisor at this time

REFERENCE: Abdelhak, pp 611–613
LaTour, Eichenwald-Maki, and Oachs, p 725
McWay, p 363
Sayles, pp 1095–1097

50. Employers are required to report the status of employees to the federal government. You plan to hire an ICD-10 trainer for 6 months with the skills to perform the training. This employee would likely be reported as
   A. a project based independent contractor.
   B. a leased employee.
   C. a full-time employee.
   D. a part-time employee.

REFERENCE: Davis and LaCour, pp 416, 450–451
LaTour, Eichenwald-Maki, and Oachs, p 804
Leibler and McConnell, p 181
McWay, p 357

51. One of your new employees has just completed orientation, receiving basic HIPAA training. You are now providing more specific training related to her job. She asks whether the information she provided during the hiring process, as well as benefits claims, are also protected under HIPAA. Which of the following can you assure her that the Human Resources Department protects?
   A. all personal health information (PHI)
   B. benefits enrollment
   C. Employee Assistance Program contacts
   D. OSHA information

REFERENCE: Abdelhak, p 599
LaTour, Eichenwald-Maki, and Oachs, pp 756–757
McConnell, pp 272, 477
McWay, p 375

The following questions represent advanced competencies.

52. The employee selection process increasingly involves a background check. All of the following are true EXCEPT
    A. that it requires the employee's consent.
    B. that the extent depends on the level of the employee's authority.
    C. it may include criminal and credit checks.
    D. it is most useful in selecting the best candidate.

REFERENCE: LaTour, Eichenwald-Maki, and Oachs, p 726
Liebler and McConnell, pp 513–514
McWay, pp 363–364

53. Emma Miller, RHIA, interviewed one applicant for the new position of data analyst and subsequently hired the applicant. During the 20-minute interview, she told the applicant about the department and hospital and what the job entailed. Much to Emma's disappointment, this newly hired employee did not work out. What went wrong?
    A. Emma asked too many questions during the interview.
    B. Emma should not have told the applicant anything about the hospital because that is the responsibility of Human Resources.
    C. Emma failed to interview enough applicants.
    D. Emma did not allow enough time for the interview.

REFERENCE: Abdelhak, pp 614–615
LaTour, Eichenwald-Maki, and Oachs, pp 725–726
McConnell, pp 129–130
Sayles, pp 1095–1097

54. University Health Systems is focusing on fostering a learning environment in the organization. Which of the following characteristics is NOT required?
    A. academic organization
    B. formal and on-the-job training
    C. reflection on learning
    D. intentional career development

REFERENCE: Abdelhak, p 631
LaTour, Eichenwald-Maki, and Oachs, pp 740–742
McWay, p 365

55. One of the most common rater biases that affect an employee's evaluation is the "halo effect," which suggests that the supervisor
    A. rates everyone as average.
    B. is too lenient or too strict in rating employee performance.
    C. rates the employee on the basis of a strong like or dislike of the person.
    D. bases the employee evaluation on behavior in the most recent period rather than the entire evaluation period.

REFERENCE: Abdelhak, pp 621–622
McConnell, p 199

56. In developing a training "to-do list," Susan is reviewing the staff and what general training and specialized training topics would be necessary. What tool would be most helpful in organizing this information?
    A. Gantt chart to show who gets trained when
    B. spreadsheet with grids identifying who needs what type of training
    C. a "train-the-trainers" training manual to help in consistency in training
    D. documentation of previous orientation training to see what has already been covered

REFERENCE: AHIMA (1)
LaTour, Eichenwald-Maki, and Oachs, pp 736–737

57. To ensure consistency of coverage among trainers, you may want to develop
    A. training manuals.
    B. meeting handouts and minutes.
    C. signed confidentiality statements acknowledging receipt and understanding of any training attended.
    D. ongoing training to keep the issues in front of the workforce.

REFERENCE: AHIMA (1)
LaTour, Eichenwald-Maki, and Oachs, pp 737–738

58. Mark Beck is a new graduate preparing for an interview. In school, he had the opportunity to role-play a technique that requires applicants to give specific examples of how they have performed a specific task or handled a specific problem in the past. This technique is becoming more popular and is known as a(n)
    A. audition interview.
    B. behavioral interview.
    C. structured interview.
    D. targeted interview.

REFERENCE: Abdelhak, pp 614–615
LaTour, Eichenwald-Maki, and Oachs, p 726
Sayles, pp 1096–1097

59. Which of the following is NOT an advantage of committee meetings?
    A. Group judgment improves decision making.
    B. Group process stimulates creativity.
    C. Committees enhance acceptance.
    D. Committees are cost effective.

REFERENCE: Liebler and McConnell, pp 290–295
McConnell, p 326

60. All of the following principles are illustrated in an organizational chart EXCEPT
    A. chain of authority.
    B. unity of command.
    C. unity of direction.
    D. span of control.

REFERENCE: Davis and LaCour, pp 417–420
LaTour, Eichenwald-Maki, and Oachs, pp 686, 690
Liebler and McConnell, pp 150–151

61. As the manager of the billing department, Jessica has heard from her employees that rumors have been circulating throughout the hospital concerning centralization and layoffs. At a meeting with the CFO, all departments were asked to cut back 15%. What should Jessica tell her employees?
    A. nothing, because it would only depress them
    B. that no one in the HIM department will be laid off
    C. share with employees the facts because she knows them from the meeting
    D. tell one employee who likes to spread rumors so employees will learn from each other

REFERENCE: Davis and LaCour, pp 474–475
LaTour, Eichenwald-Maki, and Oachs, pp 697–698
McConnell, pp 304–346
McWay, pp 340–343

62. Which appraisal method places the employees into a set of ordered groups (e.g., top 10%, above average 20%, middle 40%) on the basis of a global measure?
    A. critical incident method
    B. behaviorally anchored ranking scales
    C. Management by Objectives
    D. forced ranking

REFERENCE: Abdelhak, pp 618–622
LaTour, Eichenwald-Maki, and Oachs, pp 811–816
McConnell, pp 189–191

63. There are a variety of approaches to career development. Which of the following is NOT one of the recognized strategies?
    A. Supervisors may identify employee potential and set goals, particularly in performance evaluations.
    B. Mentors have a formal relationship with the proteges, providing expert advice based on personal career experience.
    C. Coaches focus on the learning process, guiding the employee in developing knowledge and skills.
    D. HR recruiters refer employees for new opportunities within the organization.

REFERENCE: Abdelhak, pp 630–632
LaTour, Eichenwald-Maki, and Oachs, pp 751–752
McWay, pp 379–380

64. A union is engaged in an organizing campaign in a hospital facility. Which activity should management personnel AVOID during this time?
    A. telling employees that they are free to join or not to join any organization without threat to their status with the facility
    B. telling employees of the disadvantages that may result from belonging to a union
    C. promising employees a pay increase or promotion if they vote against the union
    D. telling employees the benefits they presently enjoy

REFERENCE: Abdelhak, pp 600–602
LaTour, Eichenwald-Maki, and Oachs, p 722
McConnell, pp 505–507

65. Kimberly Wolf wants a Mercedes and the position of Vice President of Information Services. She feels that achieving these goals will provide her with a sense of achievement, prestige, and reputation in the eyes of others. At what level of Maslow's hierarchy of needs is she operating?
    A. esteem
    B. safety
    C. self-actualization
    D. basic physiological

REFERENCE: LaTour, Eichenwald-Maki, and Oachs, p 687
McConnell, pp 180–181
McWay, pp 340–341

66. Research has shown that productivity increases with all of the following actions EXCEPT when
    A. employees are rewarded for extra output.
    B. it becomes the primary goal of management.
    C. it is measured.
    D. the office environment is reengineered.

REFERENCE: Abdelhak, p 643
LaTour, Eichenwald-Maki, and Oachs, p 807

67. Human Resource managers increasingly advise which of the following as the best approach for obtaining a legally sound and reliable reference?
    A. a telephone reference from a personal friend of the applicant
    B. a written reference from a former supervisor of the applicant
    C. a telephone reference from a former supervisor of the applicant
    D. a written reference from the HR department of the applicant's former employer

REFERENCE: Abdelhak, pp 613–614
LaTour, Eichenwald-Maki, and Oachs, p 726
McConnell, p 139
McWay, p 363

68. In your new position as Director of Health Information Services, you have noticed that department supervisors arbitrarily allow employees to make up missed time due to absences. You decide that you need a policy to reinforce the attendance policy and cut down on tardiness and absences. Which policy statement would support your overall departmental goals?
    A. Advance approval is required for changes in work schedules and depend upon departmental operations.
    B. Sick days can be used in lieu of time missed due to tardiness or absences.
    C. No makeup time for absences and tardiness is allowed.
    D. Changes in work schedules must be approved in advance and depend upon departmental operations.

REFERENCE: Davis and LaCour, pp 435–436
LaTour, Eichenwald-Maki, and Oachs, p 724
McConnell, pp 240–243
McWay, p 326
Sayles, pp 407–409

69. As HIM Director, you receive a call from the CEO informing you that she has received a complaint from a patient. The patient reported that one of the coders in your department revealed his diagnosis to his neighbor. What action is recommended?
    A. Gather all the facts prior to meeting with the employee.
    B. Give the employee a written warning.
    C. Terminate the employee immediately for violation of the confidentiality policy.
    D. Immediately call a departmental meeting to discuss the importance of maintaining confidentiality.

REFERENCE: Abdelhak, p 622
LaTour, Eichenwald-Maki, and Oachs, p 756
McConnell, p 226
McWay, p 337

70. Miranda has decided to accept a position as a manager in a large health system. A key factor was the opportunity to work for a transformational leader. She recognizes all but one of the following characteristics observed that the Health Information Director is a transformational leader. Which of the following characteristics would be least likely to support her decision?
    A. risk taking
    B. mentoring
    C. charisma
    D. dependency

REFERENCE: Davis and LaCour, pp 481–482
LaTour, Eichenwald-Maki, and Oachs, p 691
McWay, p 340

71. Human Resources has recently provided training for and implemented a new performance appraisal system that includes input from managers, peers, and staff. This approach is typically known as
    A. 360-degree evaluation.
    B. group appraisal.
    C. holistic appraisal.
    D. multifactor evaluation.

REFERENCE: LaTour, Eichenwald-Maki, and Oachs, p 755
McWay, p 337

72. Employee turnover is expensive and stressful on staff and reflects poorly on managers. The best defense against employee dissatisfaction is
    A. the employee handbook.
    B. open and honest communication.
    C. written policies and procedures.
    D. weekly departmental meetings.

REFERENCE: LaTour, Eichenwald-Maki, and Oachs, p 727
Liebler and McConnell, pp 491–496
McConnell, pp 149–150
McWay, p 365

73. Human Resources use a systematic procedure to determine the relative worth of a position to the organization. When this approach is used, compensation for the position is most likely based on
    A. job evaluation.
    B. job planning.
    C. job survey.
    D. job ranking.

REFERENCE: LaTour, Eichenwald-Maki, and Oachs, p 755
Liebler and McConnell, p 195
McWay, p 334

74. Summer is the document imaging manager. She has had a meeting with the scanning clerks. They are complaining that the pay rate for their position is too low in their facility. What would be the best way to deal with this complaint?
   A. Submit a request for merit raises for all scanning clerks.
   B. Work with HR on a job evaluation and current wage and salary survey.
   C. Explain that health care cost containment means little money for raises.
   D. Listen to the complaint and recommend applying for a higher position.

REFERENCE: Abdelhak, pp 627–630
LaTour, Eichenwald-Maki, and Oachs, pp 722, 752, 754
McConnell, p 256
McWay, p 334

75. The teaching method selected by an instructor influences the student's ability to understand the material. Instructor-led classrooms work best when
   A. in-depth training and interaction are desired.
   B. there are three shifts of employees to train.
   C. you want to minimize the cost for training.
   D. employees from all departments must be trained.

REFERENCE: AHIMA (1)
LaTour, Eichenwald-Maki, and Oachs, p 744

76. Which of the following scenarios best describes job enrichment as a motivational technique?
   A. Anna is an effective data analyst. In addition to her regular job duties, her supervisor has assigned her to special projects and committee assignments.
   B. Becky prefers to work where she can be active and have personal contacts. The supervisor rotates her through all clerical jobs in the department so that she can have variety in her work.
   C. Cheryl's job keeps her fully occupied all day. In fact, she frequently has to rush to get the work completed daily. Cheryl's supervisor decides to remove some responsibility from her job so she has less stress.
   D. Derek has worked in the department for several years. His supervisor decided to combine several jobs and add other tasks to enable Derek to use his knowledge and skills gained in school. With these increased responsibilities he is increasing his chances of being promoted.

REFERENCE: LaTour, Eichenwald-Maki, and Oachs, pp 741, 750–752
McConnell, pp 187–188
McWay, p 341

77. Amanda, an EHR project manager, wants to increase her implementation staff's problem-solving skills. Which of the following approaches is likely to have the best and most long-lasting results?
   A. hiring a consultant to assess the EHR implementation strategies
   B. providing training to develop an EHR implementation work team
   C. taking a field trip to a neighboring facility known for project management
   D. request that Human Resources provide an online module teaching program-solving skills

REFERENCE: LaTour, Eichenwald-Maki, and Oachs, pp 744, 753
Liebler and McConnell, pp 358–360
McWay, pp 380–381

78. According to Frederick Herzberg, challenging work, recognition of workers and their accomplishments, and employee self-improvement are examples of
    A. maintenance factors.
    B. needs.
    C. motivators.
    D. hygienic factors.

REFERENCE: LaTour, Eichenwald-Maki, and Oachs, p 741
Liebler and McConnell, p 370
McConnell, pp 177–179
McWay, p 431

79. Tina, the Coding Supervisor at Highlands Hospital, has heard rumors that her facility is starting a coding training program. Rumor also has it that the HIM Director is trying to recruit the coding supervisor from a neighboring hospital to head up the training position. Tina makes the following statement to the assistant director: "I'm obviously not good enough for the training position. Perhaps I should resign." How should the assistant director respond?
    A. ignore Tina's statement
    B. refer Tina to the Employee Assistance Program
    C. assist Tina in developing her career goals
    D. guarantee Tina that she will be considered for the position

REFERENCE: LaTour, Eichenwald-Maki, and Oachs, pp 750–751
Liebler and McConnell, p 240
McWay, p 365

80. Madison Taylor, RHIA will be attending an AHIMA conference on information governance on Friday from 7:00 PM to 9:00 PM and Saturday from 8:30 AM to 4:30 PM with 90 minutes for lunch. This represents ___ of her hours for her continuing education cycle. (Report a whole number.)
    A. 28%
    B. 32%
    C. 36%
    D. 43%

REFERENCE: AHIMA (2)

81. Your organization's employees consist of a mixture of women and men. The women are of all ages, some are single mothers, others are married women with no children, and still others are women who care for older parents at home. The men also have varying personal lifestyles. Human Resources have designed a new benefit program that allows employees to choose from an array of benefits based on their own needs or lifestyle. The new benefit program is called a(n)
    A. prepaid benefit plan.
    B. cafeteria benefit plan.
    C. flexible benefit plan.
    D. employee-driven benefit plan.

REFERENCE: Abdelhak, pp 589–590

82. As telecommuting becomes more common, HIM supervisors will increasingly need to evaluate employees for these virtual office opportunities. Typical criteria include all the following EXCEPT that the employee
    A. is computer literate.
    B. independently identifies required work products.
    C. successfully plans a work production schedule.
    D. checks in frequently with the supervisor.

REFERENCE: McWay, pp 381–382
LaTour, Eichenwald-Maki, and Oachs, p 728

83. In your department, employee performance is rated using a continuous scale range of unsatisfactory through average to outstanding. Some other departments use a discrete system in which the supervisor assigns "fails to meet standards," "meets standards," and "exceeds standards." Both systems being used are
    A. rating scales.
    B. checklists.
    C. critical incident methods.
    D. ranking methods.

REFERENCE: Abdelhak, p 618
LaTour, Eichenwald-Maki, and Oachs, pp 811–813
McConnell, pp 194–195

84. Virginia is the Record Processing Coordinator, which is a lead position. She has an excellent work record and is able to assist in most work areas of the department. She knows that she could easily get another job within the hospital for the asking. Recently, she has been arriving late and has been uncooperative in dealing with others. As her immediate supervisor, what is the BEST first step in dealing with this situation?
    A. Institute progressive discipline.
    B. Ignore the situation and hope she will return to being a good employee.
    C. Counsel her by encouraging self-analysis and problem-solving processes.
    D. Suggest that she transfer to another department.

REFERENCE: Abdelhak, pp 622, 630
LaTour, Eichenwald-Maki, and Oachs, pp 755–756
McConnell, p 220
McWay, pp 377–378

85. Health care is known for rapid change. Melissa, an RHIA who has just been hired as a systems analyst in Information Technology, understands the importance of being a positive change agent. Which of the following approaches would be LEAST likely to support her approach?
    A. easing up on delegating
    B. holding on to the vision
    C. being available to listen to staff
    D. measuring and celebrating success

REFERENCE: LaTour, Eichenwald-Maki, and Oachs, p 708
Liebler and McConnell, pp 48–49
McWay, pp 344–345
Sayles, pp 583–584, 592

86. HIM professionals increasingly participate on project teams. Tuckman has developed a model describing predictable stages. Which of the following reflects the stage where teams may experience disequilibrium?
   A. forming
   B. storming
   C. norming
   D. performing

REFERENCE: LaTour, Eichenwald-Maki, and Oachs, pp 740, 753
Liebler and McConnell, pp 352–354
Sayles, p 1092
Umiker, pp 119–120

87. Rita Mizner, MBA, RHIA, is Director of Information Services for Mt. Sinai Medical Center. She is well respected for a management style that empowers her staff. All of the following are characteristics of effective delegation, EXCEPT
   A. explaining exactly what needs to be done.
   B. agreeing on performance standards.
   C. providing necessary resources.
   D. retaining authority to make key decisions.

REFERENCE: LaTour, Eichenwald-Maki, and Oachs, pp 690, 750–751
McConnell, p 180
McWay, pp 377–378
Sayles, p 1100

88. Tara is an RHIA who works at a large academic medical center. Her salary of $37,540 is paid 60% from research grants as clinical trial coordinator and 40% by HIM as a database manager. The hospital's fringe benefit rate is 23%. How much must the HIM director include in the budget (rounded to the nearest dollar) to cover Sarah's database management role?
   A. $15,016
   B. $18,470
   C. $22,524
   D. $27,705

REFERENCE: Horton, p 138
Koch, p 77

89. Christina is a pharmacy tech who recently earned her RHIA. She is interviewing to become a representative of an international pharmaceutical firm. She would work from home, log in to the corporate website several times a day, and make calls on various pharmacies in her territory. She would visit headquarters about once a quarter. This proposed work arrangement can best be described as
   A. flextime.
   B. outsourcing.
   C. consulting.
   D. telecommuting.

REFERENCE: LaTour, Eichenwald-Maki, and Oachs, pp 727–728
Liebler and McConnell, pp 147–150
McWay, p 381

90. Which of the following employees is exempt under the Fair Labor Standards Act?
    A. an RHIA who performs record analysis and coding 90% of the time and who supervises three employees
    B. an RHIT who manages the Health Information Services department and is involved with planning and decision-making activities 90% of the time
    C. the department secretary who spends 100% of her time performing clerical duties for the Director of Health Information Services
    D. a file clerk who spends 100% of the time on filing activities

REFERENCE: Abdelhak, p 578
Davis and LaCour, p 422
LaTour, Eichenwald-Maki, and Oachs, p 754
McConnell, pp 446–448
McWay, pp 373–374

91. Charles Jones is employed as a regional coding consultant by a corporate hospital chain. In the organization chart, this position would be
    A. shown as a line position.
    B. shown as a staff position.
    C. not shown, because it is a consulting position.
    D. not shown, because this function is outsourced.

REFERENCE: Liebler and McConnell, pp 134–136
McConnell, pp 51–52

92. Keith is director at a medical center that includes a daycare center and has several employees who have young children. He knows that it is important to be familiar with the provisions of the Family Medical Leave Act (FMLA), which includes all the following provisions EXCEPT
    A. ensuring any job the employee is qualified for upon return.
    B. that both men and women qualify under the FMLA.
    C. that it covers leave to care for a spouse, child, or parent.
    D. that it provides up to 12 weeks of unpaid leave annually.

REFERENCE: Abdelhak, p 600
LaTour, Eichenwald-Maki, and Oachs, pp 722, 915
Liebler and McConnell, p 156
McWay, p 374

93. Ty Ngynn is Assistant Director in Information Services. He has made an appointment with the Director of Human Resources to discuss his recent trip to the state HIM meeting with his Director, Wendy Richards. During the trip, Wendy repeatedly asked Ty to her room, suggesting they work on new plans for the department. When Ty declined, Wendy suggested it might not be worthwhile for him to attend future state meetings. The HR Director should
    A. explain that off-site events are outside the scope of the HR Department.
    B. provide Ty with additional training on resisting unwanted advances.
    C. take the complaint seriously and begin a sexual harassment investigation.
    D. explain that it is the Director's right to select who attends professional meetings.

REFERENCE: Abdelhak, pp 596–597
McWay, p 369
LaTour, Eichenwald-Maki, and Oachs, p 721
Liebler and McConnell, pp 456–457

94. Which of the following types of members is best for a committee?
    A. individuals of equal rank and authority
    B. a diverse group with widely varied rank and authority
    C. a blend of managers and entry-level staff
    D. There is no clear benefit to one form or another.

REFERENCE: Liebler and McConnell, pp 297–298

95. As a new RHIA and coding manager, how likely is it that you will participate on committees?
    A. Infrequently until you are promoted to a higher position.
    B. You should expect committee participation to be a regular part of your job.
    C. Occasionally, mostly with your staff.
    D. It depends on whether your organization chooses to use the committee structure.

REFERENCE: Liebler and McConnell, pp 327–328
Umiker, p 446

96. Niagara Falls Health Center needs occasional help in coding to remain current. Rena, the coding manager, is seeking an individual who is available evenings and weekends and will be responsible for his or her own actions. At a regional HIM meeting, Rena announces that she is looking for a(n)
    A. consultant.
    B. statutory employee.
    C. part-time employee.
    D. independent contractor.

REFERENCE: LaTour, Eichenwald-Maki, and Oachs, p 730
Leibler and McConnell, p 181
McWay, p 358
Umiker, p 446

97. Under the Immigration Reform and Control Act, all of the following apply EXCEPT
    A. undocumented workers may not be hired.
    B. U.S. citizens must be given preference.
    C. noncitizens may not be discriminated against.
    D. applicant must have I-9 documentation.

REFERENCE: Abdelhak, p 598
McConnell, p 462
McWay, p 358
Umiker, p 446

98. Using Donabedian's framework for quality assessment (structure, process, and outcome), which of the following is an appropriate human resource outcome?
    A. turn-over rate
    B. organizational climate
    C. salary and benefit compared with competitors
    D. None, Donabedian is a clinical framework.

REFERENCE: Abdelhak, p 616
LaTour, Eichenwald-Maki, and Oachs, pp 664, 727

99. Nina is participating in Human Resources training for new supervisors and has a question for the presenter. "I have an employee who is at the top of the pay scale for her position. Do I still need to do a performance evaluation?" The presenter most likely answers
   A. "Yes, at this stage, she should be asked to participate in evaluating other staff."
   B. "Yes, every employee deserves to know how he or she is performing and to set goals."
   C. "No, once no salary increase can be provided, an evaluation is not necessary."
   D. "Maybe, it is typically an optional process at this stage of employment."

REFERENCE: Abdelhak, pp 616–618
LaTour, Eichenwald-Maki, and Oachs, p 755
McWay, pp 376–377

100. Postage charges for Health Information Services have increased over the last quarter. As the Director, you have seen mail envelopes that have been meter-stamped that did not appear to be official hospital business. The best course of action is to
   A. remove the postage meter from the department.
   B. keep a watchful eye to see who is using the postage meter improperly.
   C. call a department meeting and issue employee warnings.
   D. put one person in charge of the meter.

REFERENCE: McConnell, pp 58–59
McWay, pp 376–377

101. LaToya Evans has accepted a new position and has given her current manager one month's notice. Human Resources has made an appointment with LaToya to discuss her benefits, investment plan, and an exit interview. The primary value of an exit interview is:
   A. changing the employee's mind.
   B. compliance with labor laws.
   C. improving the organization.
   D. finding out more about the competition.

REFERENCE: LaTour, Eichenwald-Maki, and Oachs, p 727
McWay, p 366

102. Part of the employment application process is completing I-9 documentation. This compliance requirement is related to
   A. HIPAA.
   B. immigration.
   C. criminal background check.
   D. disabilities.

REFERENCE: Abdelhak, p 598
LaTour, Eichenwald-Maki, and Oachs, p 726
McConnell, p 462

103. Members of the clinical documentation improvement (CDI) team have developed an extensive communication "grapevine" throughout the hospital. Which of the following is the LEAST effective approach for a manager to take over this type of informal communication?
   A. be acutely aware of the grapevine
   B. check out any disturbing content or comments
   C. control and limit interaction as best you can
   D. feed in some real, positive facts when possible

REFERENCE: LaTour, Eichenwald-Maki, and Oachs, p 749
Liebler and McConnell, pp 492–493
McConnell, pp 495–496

Answer Key for Human Resources

	ANSWER	EXPLANATION
NOTE:		*Explanations are provided for those questions that require mathematical calculations and questions that are not clearly explained in the references that are cited.*
1.	C	200 × 30/60 = 100 hours total
2.	D	50 employees × \$15.50 per hour × ½ hour = 387.50 50 employees × \$12.00 per hour × ½ hour = 300.00 100 employees × \$18.00 per hour × ½ hour = 900.00 \$387.50 + \$300.00 + \$900.00 = \$1,587.50
3.	A	Calculate by time: \$1,587.50 total cost for training/100 hours needed to train = \$15.88 per hour/2 to get cost for ½ hour of training = 7.938 = \$7.94 OR Calculate by employee: \$1,587.50/200 employees = 7.938 = \$7.94
4.	B	To determine the number of hours needed to perform a volume of work or "service units," in this case discharges (15,620) are multiplied by the "time standard" (18 minutes) and then divided by the number of minutes per hour (60 minutes). (15,620 × 18) = 281,160 divided by 60 = 4,686.
5.	D	
6.	B	To determine the number of employees needed for a specific position, you must first determine how much time is being spent on work currently being done. The "service units," in this case discharges (600), are multiplied by the "time factor," 20 minutes (600 × 20 = 12,000 minutes). Because this problem's time factor is in minutes, you must also compute the number of available minutes per week. The "actual hours" in this case, 40 hours, is multiplied by 60 (60 minutes per hour) (40 × 60 = 2,400). The earned time, 12,000 minutes, is then divided by the actual minutes, 2,400 minutes, to determine the number of employees needed to perform a specific job duty. So, 12,000 divided by 2,400 = 5.
7.	D	
8.	A	
9.	C	Without proper documentation, an evaluation of "needs improvement" will be difficult to justify.
10.	D	
11.	A	Calculation: \$15.00 × 2,080 hours per year = \$31,200 × 27.5% = \$8,580 Tuition waiver = 6 credits at \$145 = \$870 Therefore, \$31,200, + \$8,580 + \$870 = \$40,650
12.	C	
13.	A	
14.	C	You are required to document the training content, dates, and attendees.
15.	D	
16.	B	
17.	B	
18.	C	
19.	C	
20.	D	

Answer Key for Human Resources

	ANSWER	EXPLANATION
21.	B	To calculate the absenteeism rate, use the following formula as suggested by the U.S. Department of Labor: $\frac{\text{Worker-days lost during period} \times 100}{\text{(Avg. number of workers) (Number of days in period)}}$ $\frac{25 \times 100}{20 \times 22} = 5.68\%$
22.	D	
23.	D	
24.	B	
25.	B	
26.	D	
27.	D	
28.	C	Physical/workstation security training would be appropriate for all employees in general orientation training. Answers A and B are higher-level functions that would not be performed by all new employees. Answer D. Job-specific training would be better suited to training in the department in which the employee will work.
29.	B	
30.	C	
31.	A	
32.	A	
33.	C	
34.	B	Job descriptions should be reviewed and updated before beginning the hiring process.
35.	D	
36.	B	
37.	B	
38.	C	
39.	B	Selena took 6 hours unpaid leave (40 – 6 = 34), but worked a holiday at double-time (8 × 2 = 16). Because 8 hours of the holiday are already figured in the work week, add an additional 8 hours for holiday pay. So, 34 + 8 = 42.
40.	A	
41.	B	A well-written job description includes what and how health information is used in a position. The job description would be the document Gina would review for choosing appropriate training levels for staff members in different positions.
42.	D	
43.	A	
44.	C	
45.	B	It is illegal for an organization to fire an employee for filing a grievance. The union contract stipulates the policy and procedures for resolving grievances. You would need to refer to the union contract for any specific time boundaries.
46.	A	
47.	D	
48.	A	
49.	C	
50.	A	

Answer Key for Human Resources

	ANSWER	EXPLANATION
51.	A	
52.	B	
53.	C	
54.	A	
55.	C	
56.	B	A spreadsheet with grids identifying who needs what type of training would help in defining the department privacy and security training plan.
57.	A	Training manuals would help ensure consistency of coverage of the materials among trainers. B and C serve to help in documenting the training that was given. D. In addition to initial training, the security rule requires ongoing training/reminders.
58.	B	
59.	D	Employee salary expense is significant.
60.	C	All three are among Fayol's 14 principles, though unity of direction refers to all workers being aligned toward one single outcome.
61.	C	Managers should not attempt to "water down" information, even if it is bad news. Fueling the grapevine can also lead to additional misinformation. Managers should make every effort to communicate factual information to their employees in a calm and timely manner.
62.	D	
63.	D	
64.	C	
65.	A	
66.	D	
67.	C	Increasing legal challenges have made this an area best left to HR professionals.
68.	D	
69.	A	Even though a serious incident such as this could result in termination of an employee, it is important to gather all the facts prior to meeting with the employee to substantiate any claims.
70.	D	
71.	A	
72.	B	Weekly department meetings, having an employee handbook, and written policies and procedures are all part of the necessary open and honest communication.
73.	A	
74.	B	A common and easy solution to this problem is to ignore the complaint, although this will not solve the problem; it will only prolong it. If the clerks complain that their job rate is too low, a job evaluation seeks to determine the position's relative worth to maintain pay equity within the organization and a wage and salary survey helps in determining the market value of the position.

Answer Key for Human Resources

	ANSWER	EXPLANATION
75.	A	In-depth training and interaction are best obtained in an instructor-led classroom style of training. Answers B, C, and D are disadvantages of instructor-led training. Instructor-led training becomes expensive and time intensive when scheduling and training many shifts of employees from all departments.
76.	A	Job enrichment involves assigning more challenging tasks and responsibilities without combining jobs, which is called job enlargement. Switching job tasks among employees is called job rotation. All of these are attempts to diversify work and motivate employees. Redesigning a job by removing responsibility, however, would probably not be a motivational factor.
77.	B	
78.	C	
79.	C	
80.	A	Madison attended 2 hours on Friday and 8 hours on Saturday minus 1.5 hours lunch for a total of 8.5 hours. She is an RHIA, which requires 30 hours of continuing education every 2-year cycle. 8.5/30 = 28.3. The question asks for a whole number, so the answer is 28%. Tip: You can do a reasonableness check. 8.5 hours is almost one-third of the total, so the percent should be close to, but less than, 33%.
81.	B	
82.	B	
83.	A	
84.	C	
85.	A	
86.	C	
87.	D	To be effective, authority needs to be delegated along with responsibility.
88.	B	Calculations: $37,540 × 123% = $46,174.20 HIM pays 40% or $46,174.20 × 0.40 = $18,469.68, rounded to $18,470
89.	D	
90.	B	
91.	B	Although the person in the position is outsourced, the organizational chart would show this "position" as a "staff" position.
92.	A	
93.	C	
94.	A	
95.	C	
96.	D	
97.	B	
98.	A	
99.	B	
100.	D	Although putting one person in charge of the meter may not stop the abuse of the postage meter, it is the best first course of action to take. Answers A and C are too drastic, and answer B is not efficient use of a manager's time.
101.	C	
102.	B	
103.	C	

REFERENCES

Abdelhak, M., & Hanken, M. A. (2016). *Health information: Management of a strategic resource* (5th ed.). Philadelphia: W. B. Saunders.

AHIMA (1) AHIMA Practice Brief HIPAA Privacy and Security Training. (*Journal of AHIMA* 84, no.10 (October 2013). Chicago: American Health Information Management Association. (Updated.) Retrieved from http://www.ahima.org, August 1, 2015.

AHIMA (2) AHIMA Certification. http://www.ahima.org/certification/Recertification

Davis, N., & LaCour, M. (2014). *Introduction to health information technology* (3rd ed.). Philadelphia: W. B. Saunders.

Horton, L. (2012). *Calculating and reporting health care statistics* (4th ed.). Chicago: American Health Information Management Association (AHIMA).

Koch, P. G. (2015). *Basic allied health statistics and analysis* (4th ed.). Clifton Park, NY: Cengage Learning.

LaTour, K., Elchenwald-Maki, S., & Oachs, P. K. (2013). *Health information management: Concepts, principles and practice* (4th ed.). Chicago: American Health Information Management Association (AHIMA).

Liebler, J. G., & McConnell, C. R. (2012). *Management principles for health professionals* (6th ed.). Sudbury, MA: Jones & Bartlett.

McConnell, C. (2012). *The effective health care supervisor* (7th ed.). Sudbury, MA: Jones & Bartlett.

McWay, D. C. (2014). *Today's health information management, an integrated approach* (2nd ed.). Clifton Park, NY: Cengage Learning.

Safian, S. (2014). *Fundamentals of health care administration*. Upper Saddle River, NJ: Pearson Education, Inc.

Sayles, N. B. (2013). *Health information technology: An applied approach* (4th ed.). Chicago: American Health Information Management Association (AHIMA).

Human Resources Competencies

Question	RHIA Domain Competencies					
	1	2	3	4	5	6
1–103				X		

Question	RHIT Domain Competencies						
	1	2	3	4	5	6	7
1	X						
2	X						
3	X						
4	X						
5	X						
6	X						
7						X	
8						X	
9	X						
10	X						
11	X						
12						X	
13	X						
14						X	
15	X						
16	X						
17	X						
18	X						
19	X						
20	X						
21	X						
22						X	
23	X						
24						X	
25		X					
26						X	
27						X	
28						X	
29						X	
30						X	
31	X						
32	X						
33	X						
34	X						
35						X	
36	X						
37						X	
38					X		
39					X		
40	X						
41						X	
42						X	
43	X						
44					X		
45						X	
46						X	
47	X						
48	X						
49		X					
50	X						
51						X	

XVII. Mock Examination

Patricia J. Schnering, RHIA, CCS

Debra W. Cook, MAEd, RHIA

Sheila Carlon, PhD, RHIA, FAHIMA

NOTE:
If you are taking the mock for the RHIT examination, you may choose to complete the first 150 questions. The mock for the RHIA examination has 180 questions to complete. In timing your speed at answering questions, allow about 1.35 minutes per question. For example, if you are taking the entire mock exam in one sitting, you should allow about 4 hours and 3 minutes (180 questions × 1.35 minutes for a total of 243 minutes = 4 hours and 3 minutes).

GULFSIDE HEALTHCARE CENTER AVERAGE CLINIC WAITING TIME BY TIME BLOCK DECEMBER 2015				
TIME BLOCK	PEDIATRICS	OBSTETRICS	CARDIOLOGY	ORTHOPEDICS
8:00–11:00	12	18	10	9
11:01–2:00	8	10	8	14
2:01–5:00	10	7	7	12

1. Each month, the staff of the clinic with the lowest overall waiting time is awarded a free dessert in the Gulfside Healthcare Center cafeteria. Take a look at the information listed above. The winner will be selected based on
   A. demonstrative clinical data.
   B. comparative aggregate data.
   C. objective individual data.
   D. duplicate thematic data.

REFERENCE: Abdelhak, p 451
LaTour, Eichenwald-Maki, and Oachs, pp 138, 242
McWay (2014), p 208

2. A union campaign is being conducted at your facility. As a department manager, it is appropriate for you to tell employees that
   A. a strike is inevitable if the union wins.
   B. wages will increase if the union is defeated.
   C. you need the names of those involved in union activities.
   D. you are opposed to the union.

REFERENCE: Abdelhak, pp 600–601
Sayles, p 835

3. As the Coding Supervisor, your job description includes working with agents who have been charged with detecting and correcting overpayments made to your hospital in the Medicare Fee for Service program. You will need to develop a professional relationship with
   A. the OIG.
   B. MEDPAR representatives.
   C. QIO physicians.
   D. recovery audit contractors.

REFERENCE: Bowie and Green, p 341
McWay (2016), pp 332-334
Sayles, p 309

4. Employing the SOAP style of progress notes, choose the "assessment" statement from the following:
   A. Patient states low back pain with sciatica is as severe as it was on admission.
   B. Patient moving about very cautiously appears to be in pain.
   C. Adjust pain medication; begin physical therapy tomorrow.
   D. Sciatica unimproved with hot pack therapy.

REFERENCE: Abdelhak, p 119
Bowie and Green, p 99
LaTour, Eichenwald-Maki, and Oachs, pp 256–257
Sayles, p 126

5. In preparation for an EHR, you are conducting a total facility inventory of all forms currently used. You must name each form for bar coding and indexing. The unnamed document in front of you includes a checklist for assessing an obstetric patient's lochia, fundus, and perineum. The document type you give to this form is
   A. prenatal record.
   B. labor record.
   C. delivery room record.
   D. postpartum record.

REFERENCE: Abdelhak, p 113
Bowie and Green, p 191

SAMPLE MS-DRG REPORT		
MS-DRG IDENTIFIER	RELATIVE WEIGHT	NUMBER OF PATIENTS WITH THIS MS-DRG
A	1.234	12
B	3.122	10
C	2.165	19
D	5.118	16

6. Based on the MS-DRG report above, what is the case-mix index for this facility?
   A. 0.204193
   B. 2.965807
   C. 11.639
   D. 57

REFERENCE: Bowie and Green, pp 331–332
LaTour, Eichenwald-Maki, and Oachs, pp 470, 496–498
McWay (2014), p 165
Sayles, p 499

7. The special form or view that plays the central role in planning and providing care at skilled nursing, psychiatric, and rehabilitation facilities is the
   A. interdisciplinary patient care plan.
   B. medical history and review of systems.
   C. interval summary.
   D. problem list.

REFERENCE: Abdelhak, pp 136–137
LaTour, Eichenwald-Maki, and Oachs, p 254
Sayles, pp 111–112, 114

8. Four patients were discharged from Crestview Hospital yesterday. A final progress note is an appropriate discharge summary for
   A. Howard, who died within 24 hours after his admission for a second heart attack in 2 weeks.
   B. Jackson, who had no comorbidities or complications during his admission for replacement of a pacemaker battery.
   C. Fieldstone, who was admitted just 15 days following a heart attack for the acute onset of chest pain.
   D. Babson, who delivered a healthy 8-pound boy without complications for either mother or child, and was discharged within 36 hours of admission.

REFERENCE: Abdelhak, p 106
Bowie and Green, p 154
LaTour, Eichenwald-Maki, and Oachs, p 251

Use the information in the tables below to answer the next two questions.

Make Me Better Clinic (MMBC) provides well child visits and childhood immunizations for four insurance companies. Data on the services they provided and the reimbursement they received from the four companies are listed in the two tables below.

Table 1 Well Child Visits

INSURANCE COMPANY	NUMBER OF WELL CHILD VISITS	REIMBURSEMENT FROM PAYER
Lifecare	259	$ 31,196.55
Getwell	786	$100,859.52
SureHealth	462	$ 54,631.50
BeHealthy	219	$ 26,991.75

Table 2 Immunizations

INSURANCE COMPANY	NUMBER OF IMMUNIZATIONS	TOTAL REIMBURSEMENT FROM PAYER
Lifecare	412	2,175.36
Getwell	1,465	9,053.70
SureHealth	609	3,580.92
BeHealthy	417	2,118.36

9. MMBC receives the best reimbursement for well child visits from
   A. Lifecare.
   B. Getwell.
   C. SureHealth.
   D. BeHealthy.

REFERENCE: Math Calculation

10. Most of the children who are seen at MMBC will have a well child visit and two immunizations. If you add the reimbursement for two immunizations to the reimbursement for each well child visit, which insurance company benefits MMBC most?
   A. Lifecare
   B. Getwell
   C. SureHealth
   D. BeHealthy

REFERENCE: Math Calculation

11. You are calculating the fee schedule payment amount for physician services covered under Medicare Part B. You already have the relative value unit figure. The only other information you need is

A. the facility's case-mix index.
B. a national conversion factor.
C. the facility's base rate.
D. MS-DRG relative weights.

REFERENCE: Green, p 1011
LaTour, Eichenwald-Maki, and Oachs, p 434
Sayles, p 272

KEY WEST HOSPITAL FOUR HIGHEST MS-DRGs							
MS-DRG A		MS-DRG B		MS-DRG C		MS-DRG D	
CMS WEIGHT	NUMBER OF PATIENTS WITH MS-DRG A	CMS WEIGHT	NUMBER OF PATIENTS WITH MS-DRG B	CMS WEIGHT	NUMBER OF PATIENTS WITH MS-DRG C	CMS WEIGHT	NUMBER OF PATIENTS WITH MS-DRG D
2.023	323	0.987	489	1.925	402	1.243	386

12. Key West Hospital collected the data displayed above concerning its four highest volume MS-DRGs. Which MS-DRG generated the most revenue for the hospital?

A. MS-DRG A
B. MS-DRG B
C. MS-DRG C
D. MS-DRG D

REFERENCE: Abdelhak, pp 283–284
LaTour, Eichenwald-Maki, and Oachs, pp 433, 496–497
Sayles, pp 266, 270

13. In reviewing a health record for coding purposes, the coder notes that the patient was put on Keflex post-surgery. There is no mention of a postoperative complication in the attending physician's discharge summary. Before querying the doctor, the coder will seek to confirm the infection by reviewing the

A. lab report.
B. nurses' notes.
C. operative report.
D. pathology report.

REFERENCE: Green, p 186
LaTour, Eichenwald-Maki, and Oachs, p 442
Sayles, p 85

14. Stan works in an acute care general hospital, Fran works for a skilled nursing facility, Ann is employed at an assisted living facility, and Dan works for a home care provider. Which people are employed in facilities that may seek Joint Commission accreditation?

A. only Stan and Fran
B. only Stan and Dan
C. only Fran and Dan
D. Dan, Stan, and Fran

REFERENCE: Abdelhak, p 13
LaTour, Eichenwald-Maki, and Oachs, pp 11, 76
McWay (2014), pp 52–53
Sayles, pp 645–646

15. Sunset Beach Clinic allows patients to communicate by e-mail to ask questions regarding their treatment and request appointment changes. E-mails and text messages are
    A. considered health care business records and are subject to the same regulations as records created in face-to-face patient encounters.
    B. considered proof of patient contact and should be summarized in a progress note in the patient record.
    C. generally maintained in a facility's electronic mail system until the next face-to-face patient encounter.
    D. not typically maintained or documented as patient encounters.

REFERENCE: McWay (2016), pp 315-318

16. Down syndrome, Edwards' syndrome, and Patau's syndrome are all examples of __________defects.
    A. musculoskeletal
    B. chromosomal
    C. genitourinary tract
    D. digestive system

REFERENCE: Green, pp 306–307
Bowie (2014), pp 252–253

17. The facility's policy for physician's verbal orders in accordance with state law and regulations needs updating. The first area of investigation is the qualifications of those individuals who have been authorized to record verbal orders. For this information you will consult the
    A. policy and procedure manual.
    B. hospital's Quality Management Plan.
    C. data dictionary.
    D. hospital bylaws, rules, and regulations.

REFERENCE: Bowie and Green, p 21
LaTour, Eichenwald-Maki, and Oachs, pp 247–248
McWay (2014), p 23
Sayles, p 676

18. Parker has type 1 diabetes with hypertension that is currently controlled with medication. Parker was admitted through the ED for an emergency appendectomy. Following surgery, the patient developed an infection at the wound site that was treated with antibiotics. When making decisions about sequencing the codes for this case, the coder should rely on definitions found in the
    A. UHDDS.
    B. Coding Clinic.
    C. CMS Coding Guidelines.
    D. Federal Register.

REFERENCE: Bowie (2014), p 53

19. Parker has type 1 diabetes with hypertension that is currently controlled with medication. Parker was admitted through the ED for an emergency appendectomy. Following surgery, the patient developed an infection at the wound site that was treated with antibiotics. Parker's principal diagnosis is the
    A. complications of hypertension.
    B. comorbidity of the wound infection.
    C. comorbidity of type 1 diabetes.
    D. acute appendicitis.

REFERENCE: Bowie (2014), p 53
Eichenwald-Maki and Oachs, pp 196, 932

20. Dr. Reed tried to explain wound care to Mr. Baker prior to discharge, but Baker (who is 104 and moderately senile) just could not seem to understand or remember what the doctor said. Mr. Baker's daughter was with him, so Dr. Reed explained Mr. Baker's aftercare to his daughter. Dr. Reed should document discharge instructions
    A. in the discharge summary.
    B. on a patient instructions form signed by Dr. Reed and Mr. Baker and filed in Mr. Baker's medical record.
    C. in the discharge summary and on a patient instructions form signed by Dr. Reed and Mr. Baker and filed in Baker's medical record.
    D. in the discharge summary and on a patient instructions form signed by Dr. Reed and Mr. Baker's daughter and filed in Mr. Baker's medical record.

REFERENCE: Abdelhak, p 106
Bowie and Green, pp 155, 158
LaTour, Eichenwald-Maki, and Oachs, pp 251–253
Sayles, pp 93–94

21. The physician has documented the final diagnoses as acute myocardial infarction, COPD, CHF, hypertension, atrial fibrillation, and status-post cholecystectomy. The following conditions should be reported:

I10	Essential hypertension, benign
I10	Essential hypertension, unspecified
I11	Hypertension, heart disease, unspecified as to malignant or benign, with heart failure
I21.3	Acute myocardial infarction, unspecified site, initial episode of care
I48.91	Atrial fibrillation
I50.9	Congestive heart failure, unspecified
J44.9	Chronic obstructive pulmonary disease
Z90.89	Acquired absence of gallbladder

A. I21.3, J44.9, I21.3, I48.91, Z90.89

B. I11, J44.9, I50.9, I10, I48.91

C. I11, J44.9, I50.9, I10, I48.91, Z90.89

D. I11, J44.9, I50.9, I10, I48.91

REFERENCE: AHA, pp 30–36, 229–231, 251, 386–387, 394–395, 404, 429

22. Mary is 6 weeks postmastectomy for carcinoma of the breast. She is admitted for chemotherapy. What is the correct sequencing of the codes?

C50.911	Malignant neoplasm of the breast
Z85.3	Personal history of malignant neoplasm of breast
Z51.11	Encounter for antineoplastic chemotherapy
Z08	Follow-up exam after surgery

A. Z51.11, C50.911
B. Z51.11, Z85.3
C. Z08, Z51.11
D. Z85.3

REFERENCE: AHA, p 127
Bowie (2014), pp 427–428, 438–439

23. Which of the following is coded as an adverse effect in ICD-10-CM?
    A. tinnitus due to allergic reaction after administration of eardrops
    B. mental retardation due to intracranial abscess
    C. rejection of transplanted kidney
    D. nonfunctioning pacemaker due to defective soldering

REFERENCE: AHA, pp 516–517
Bowie (2014), pp 395–396

24. Which of the following scenarios identifies a pathologic fracture?
    A. greenstick fracture secondary to fall from a bed
    B. compression fracture of the skull after being hit with a baseball bat
    C. vertebral fracture with cord compression following a car accident
    D. compression fracture of the vertebrae as a result of bone metastasis

REFERENCE: AHA, p 491
Bowie (2014), p 295

25. If the same condition is described as both acute and chronic and separate subentries exist in the ICD-10-CM alphabetic index at the same indentation level,
    A. they should both be coded, acute sequenced first.
    B. they should both be coded, chronic sequenced first.
    C. only the acute condition should be coded.
    D. only the chronic condition should be coded.

REFERENCE: AHA, pp 58–59
Bowie (2014), p 49

26. Which of the following statements is true?
    A. A surgical procedure may include one or more surgical operations.
    B. The terms *surgical operation* and *surgical procedure* are synonymous.
    C. A surgical operation may include one or more surgical procedures.
    D. The term *surgical procedure* is an incorrect term and should not be used.

REFERENCE: Koch, p 10
LaTour, Eichenwald-Maki, and Oachs, p 496
Sayles, p 498

27. Which of the following would be coded as a poisoning?
    A. Coumadin intoxication due to a cumulative effect
    B. idiosyncratic reaction to Artane
    C. interaction between Aldomet and a vasodilating agent
    D. reaction between Coumadin and an over-the-counter medication

REFERENCE: AHA, pp 516-518
Bowie (2014), pp 395–396

28. Which of the following diagnoses or procedures would prevent the normal delivery code, O80, from being assigned?
    A. occiput presentation
    B. single liveborn
    C. episiotomy
    D. low forceps

REFERENCE: AHA, p 319
Bowie (2014), p 331

29. Which of the following are considered a late effect regardless of time?
    A. congenital defect
    B. nonunion
    C. nonhealing fracture
    D. poisoning

REFERENCE: AHA, pp 60–61
Bowie (2014), p 50

30. Four people were seen in your emergency department yesterday. Which one will be coded as a poisoning?

- Josh was diagnosed with digitalis intoxication.
- Ben had an allergic reaction to a dye administered for a pyelogram.
- Bryan developed syncope after taking Contac pills with a double scotch.
- Matthew had an idiosyncratic reaction between two properly administered prescription drugs.

    A. Josh
    B. Ben
    C. Bryan
    D. Matthew

REFERENCE: AHA, pp 516-518
Bowie (2014), pp 395–396

31. Patient is admitted for elective cholecystectomy for treatment of chronic cholecystitis with cholelithiasis. Prior to administration of general anesthesia, patient suffers cerebral thrombosis. Surgery is subsequently canceled. Code and sequence the coding from the following codes.

I66.9	Cerebral thrombosis without cerebral infarction
K80.10	Chronic cholecystitis with cholelithiasis
Z53.09	Surgery canceled, contraindication
I97.821	Iatrogenic cerebrovascular infarction or hemorrhage
0FT40ZZ	Cholecystectomy, total

    A. I97.821, K80.10, 0FT40ZZ
    B. K80.10, I66.9, Z53.09
    C. I97.821, I66.9, Z53.09
    D. I66.9, Z53.09

REFERENCE: AHA, pp 125–127, 249–250, 400

32. The discharge diagnosis for this inpatient encounter is rule out myocardial infarction. The coder would assign
    A. a code for a myocardial infarction.
    B. a code for the patient's symptoms.
    C. a code for an impending myocardial infarction.
    D. no code for this condition.

REFERENCE: AHA, pp 57–58
Bowie (2014), p 57

33. Staging
    A. refers to the monitoring of incidence and trends associated with a disease.
    B. is continued medical surveillance of a case.
    C. is a system for documenting the extent or spread of cancer.
    D. designates the degree of differentiation of cells.

REFERENCE: Abdelhak, pp 491–492
LaTour, Eichenwald-Maki, and Oates, pp 371, 949
Sayles, p 439

34. Which of these conditions are always considered "present on admission" (POA)?
   A. congenital conditions
   B. E codes
   C. acute conditions
   D. possible, probable, or suspected conditions

REFERENCE: LaTour, Eichenwald-Maki, and Oachs, pp 443, 921, 940
Sayles, p 439

35. In your state, it is legal for minors to seek medical treatment for a sexually transmitted disease without parental consent. When this occurs, who would be expected to authorize the release of the medical information documented in this episode of care to the patient's insurers?
   A. the patient
   B. a court-appointed guardian on behalf of the patient
   C. the custodial parent of the patient
   D. the patient's doctor on behalf of the patient

REFERENCE: Eichenwald-Maki and Oachs, p 317
McWay (2016), p 193

36. A patient is admitted through the emergency department. Three days after admission, the physician documents uncontrolled diabetes mellitus. What is the "present on admission" (POA) indicator for uncontrolled diabetes mellitus?
   A. "Y"
   B. "U"
   C. "W"
   D. "N"

REFERENCE: Sayles, pp 270, 1238

37. The patient had a thrombectomy, without catheter, of the peroneal artery, by leg incision.

34203	Embolectomy or thrombectomy, with or without catheter; popliteal-tibioperoneal artery, by leg incision
35226	Repair blood vessel, direct; lower extremity
35302	Thromboendarterectomy, including patch graft if performed; superficial femoral artery
37799	Unlisted procedure, vascular surgery

   A. 34203
   B. 37799
   C. 35302
   D. 35226

REFERENCE: Bowie (2015), pp 211–212
Green, p 776

38. Patient was seen for excision of two interdigital neuromas from the left foot.

28080	Excision, interdigital (Morton) neuroma, single, each
64774	Excision of neuroma; cutaneous nerve, surgically identifiable
64776	Excision of neuroma; digital nerve, one or both, same digit

   A. 64774
   B. 64776
   C. 28080
   D. 28080, 28080

REFERENCE: AMA CPT

39. Patient was seen in the Emergency Department with lacerations on the left arm. Two lacerations, one 7 cm and one 9 cm, were closed with layered sutures.

12002	Simple repair of superficial wounds of scalp, neck, axillae, external genitalia, trunk, and/or extremities (including hands and feet); 2.6–7.5 cm
12004	Simple repair of superficial wounds of scalp, neck, axillae, external genitalia, trunk, and/or extremities (including hands and feet); 7.6–12.5 cm
12035	Layer closure of wounds of scalp, axillae, trunk, and/or extremities (excluding hands and feet); 12.6–20.0 cm
12045	Layer closure of wounds of neck, hands, feet, and/or external genitalia; 12.6–20.0 cm

A. 12045
B. 12035
C. 12002, 12004
D. 12004

REFERENCE: Bowie (2015), pp 119–120
Green, pp 658–660

40. Office visit for 43-year-old male, new patient, with no complaints. Patient is applying for life insurance and requests a physical examination. A detailed health and family history was obtained and a basic physical was done. Physician completed life insurance physical form at patient's request. Blood and urine were collected.

99381	Initial comprehensive preventive medicine evaluation and management of an individual including an age and gender appropriate history, examination, counseling/anticipatory guidance/risk factor reduction interventions, and the ordering of appropriate immunization(s), laboratory/diagnostic procedures, new patient; infant (age under 1 year)
99386	Initial comprehensive preventive medicine evaluation and management of an individual including a comprehensive history, a comprehensive examination, counseling/anticipatory guidance/risk factor reduction interventions, and the ordering of appropriate immunization(s), laboratory/diagnostic procedures, new patient; 40–64 years
99396	Periodic comprehensive preventive medicine reevaluation and management of an individual including an age and gender appropriate history, examination, counseling/anticipatory guidance/risk factor reduction interventions, and the ordering of appropriate immunization(s), laboratory/diagnostic procedures, established patient; 40–64 years
99450	Basic life and/or disability examination that includes completion of a medical history following a life insurance pro forma

A. 99450
B. 99386
C. 99396
D. 99381

REFERENCE: AMA CPT
Bowie (2015), p 79
Green, p 582

41. Patient was seen today for regular hemodialysis. No problems reported, tolerated procedure well.

90935	Hemodialysis procedure with single physician evaluation
90937	Hemodialysis procedure requiring repeated evaluations(s) with or without substantial revision of dialysis prescription
90945	Dialysis procedure other than hemodialysis (e.g., peritoneal dialysis, hemofiltration, or other continuous renal replacement therapies), with single physician evaluation
+99354	Prolonged physician service in the office or other outpatient setting requiring direct (face-to-face) contact beyond the usual service; first hour (list separately in addition to code for office or other outpatient Evaluation and Management service)

A. 90937
B. 99354
C. 90945
D. 90935

REFERENCE: Bowie (2015), p 432
Green, pp 952–953

42. An established patient was seen by the physician in the office for DTaP vaccine and Hib.

90471	Immunization administration (includes percutaneous, intradermal, subcutaneous, intramuscular injections); one vaccine (single or combination vaccine/toxoid)
90700	Diphtheria, tetanus toxoids, and acellular pertussis vaccine (DTaP), when administered to individuals younger than 7 years, for intramuscular use
90720	Diphtheria, tetanus toxoids, and whole cell pertussis vaccine and Hemophilus influenza B vaccine (DTP-Hib), for intramuscular use
90721	Diphtheria, tetanus toxoids, and acellular pertussis vaccine and Hemophilus influenza B vaccine (DTaP-Hib), for intramuscular use
90748	Hepatitis B and Hemophilus influenza b vaccine (HepB-Hib), for intramuscular use
99211	Office or other outpatient visit for the evaluation and management of an established patient, which may not require the presence of a physician. Usually, the presenting problem(s) are minimal. Typically, 5 minutes are spent performing or supervising these services.

A. 90721
B. 90720, 90471
C. 90700, 90748, 99211
D. 90471, 90721

REFERENCE: AMA CPT
Green, pp 948–950

43. A patient with lung cancer and bone metastasis is seen for complex treatment planning by a radiation oncologist.

77263	Therapeutic radiology treatment planning; complex
77290	Therapeutic radiology simulation-aided field setting; complex
77315	Teletherapy, isodose plan (whether hand or computer calculated); complex (mantle or inverted Y, tangential ports, the use of wedges, compensators, complex blocking, rotational beam, or special beam considerations)
77334	Treatment devices, design and construction; complex (irregular blocks, special shields, compensators, wedges, molds, or casts)

A. 77315
B. 77263
C. 77290
D. 77334

REFERENCE: AMA CPT
Bowie (2015), pp 408–409
Green, pp 898–900

44. A 4-year-old had a repair of an incarcerated inguinal hernia. This is the first time this child had been treated for this condition.

49496	Repair initial inguinal hernia full-term infant, under age 6 months, or preterm infant over 50 weeks' post conception age and under 6 months at the time of surgery, with or without hydrocelectomy; incarcerated or strangulated
49501	Repair initial inguinal hernia, age 6 months to under 5 years, with or without hydrocelectomy; incarcerated or strangulated
49521	Repair recurrent inguinal hernia, any age; incarcerated or strangulated
49553	Repair initial femoral hernia, any age; incarcerated or strangulated

A. 49553
B. 49496
C. 49521
D. 49501

REFERENCE: Bowie (2015), pp 272–273
Green, pp 796–798

45. A quantitative drug assay was performed for a patient to determine digoxin level.

80050	General health panel
80101	Drug screen, qualitative; single drug class method (e.g., immunoassay, enzyme assay), each drug class
80162	Digoxin (therapeutic drug assay, quantitative examination)
80166	Doxepin (therapeutic drug assay, quantitative examination)

A. 80101
B. 80050
C. 80166
D. 80162

REFERENCE: Bowie (2015), p 222
Green, pp 924–925

46. Provide the CPT code for anesthesia services for the transvenous insertion of a pacemaker.

00530	Anesthesia for permanent transvenous pacemaker insertion
00560	Anesthesia for procedures on heart, pericardial sac, and great vessels of chest; without pump oxygenator
33202	Insertion of epicardial electrode(s); open incision
33206	Insertion or replacement of permanent pacemaker with transvenous electrode(s); atrial

A. 00560
B. 33202, 00530
C. 00530
D. 33206, 00560

REFERENCE: Bowie (2015), pp 90–92
Green, pp 599–600

47. The transcriptionists have collected data on the number and types of problems with the dictation equipment. The best tool to display the data they collected is a
A. flowchart.
B. Pareto chart.
C. Gantt chart.
D. PERT chart.

REFERENCE: LaTour, Eichenwald-Maki, and Oachs, p 823
McWay (2014), pp 212–215
Sayles, pp 591–592, 1233

48. Based on the information below, what was the net death rate at Seaside Hospital in January?

SEASIDE HOSPITAL SELECTED STATISTICS JANUARY				
Admissions	Discharged to Home	Discharge Transfers	Deaths <48 hours	Deaths >48 hours
280	212	28	8	6

A. 2.4%
B. 2.8%
C. 3.8%
D. 5.8%

REFERENCE: Horton, pp 75–76
Koch, pp 142–143
LaTour, Eichenwald-Maki, and Oachs, p 393
Sayles, pp 489–490, 1229

49. The formula used to calculate the percentage of ambulatory care visits made with same day appointments is
    A. $\frac{\text{number of patients seen with same day appointments for a period} \times 100}{\text{number of patients seen with advance appointments for the same period}}$
    B. $\frac{\text{number of patients seen with advance appointments for a period} \times 100}{\text{number of patients seen with same day appointments for the same period}}$
    C. $\frac{\text{number of patients seen with same day appointments for a period} \times 100}{\text{number of patients seen in the same period}}$
    D. $\frac{\text{number of patients seen with advance appointments for a period} \times 100}{\text{number of patients seen in the same period}}$

REFERENCE: Horton, pp 14–18
Koch, p 108
LaTour, Eichenwald-Maki, and Oachs, pp 493, 881
McWay (2014), pp 210–211
Sayles, 1242

50. An HIM Department Budget Report for May shows a payroll budget of $25,000 and an actual payroll expense of $22,345. The percentage of budget variance for the month is
    A. $2,655.
    B. 11%.
    C. $265.
    D. 0.9%.

REFERENCE: LaTour, Eichenwald-Maki, and Oachs, pp 787–788

51. Generally, CMS requires the submission of a claim (CMS 1450) for inpatient services provided to a Medicare beneficiary for inpatient services. An exception to this requirement would be when
    A. the beneficiary refuses to authorize the submission of a bill to Medicare.
    B. the physician furnishes a covered service to the beneficiary.
    C. attempts are made to charge a beneficiary for a service that is covered by Medicare.
    D. an ABN was given to the beneficiary for services unlikely to be covered by Medicare.

REFERENCE: AHIMA (1)

52. Your facility is engaged in a research project concerning patients newly diagnosed with type 2 diabetes. The researchers notice older patients have a longer length of stay than younger patients. They have seen a
    A. positive correlation between age and length of stay.
    B. negative correlation between age and length of stay.
    C. causal relationship between age and length of stay.
    D. homologous relationship between age and length of stay.

REFERENCE: Koch, p 276
LaTour, Eichenwald-Maki, and Oachs, p 536
McWay (2014), pp 215–216
Sayles, p 529

53. Johnston City was set upon by a swarm of killer bees. All 5,000 residents are at risk of a bee attack. If 25 residents were attacked by the bees, the incidence of bee attacks
   A. is 5 in 1,000.
   B. is 5 in 5,000.
   C. is 25 in 1,000.
   D. cannot be determined at this time.

REFERENCE: Abdelhak, p 391
Koch, p 211
LaTour, Eichenwald-Maki, and Oachs, p 506
Sayles, p 516

54. A 335-bed hospital opened a new wing on June 1 of a nonleap year, increasing its bed count to 350 beds. The total bed count days for the year at the hospital was
   A. 122,275.
   B. 125,485.
   C. 127,750.
   D. The answer cannot be calculated with the information provided.

REFERENCE: Koch, pp 114–116
LaTour, Eichenwald-Maki, and Oachs, p 488
Sayles, p 483

55. A patient who was admitted to the hospital on January 14 and discharged on March 2 in a nonleap year has a length of stay of
   A. 45 days.
   B. 46 days.
   C. 47 days.
   D. 48 days.

REFERENCE: Koch, pp 126–127
LaTour, Eichenwald-Maki, and Oachs, p 489
Sayles, p 485

56. Release of information has increased its use of part-time prn clerical support in order to respond to increased requests for release of information. The budget variance report will reflect
   A. the increase in the cost of part-time clerical support for ROI but not the increase in revenue from this area.
   B. the increase in revenue from increased volume in ROI but not the increased costs of part-time clerical support.
   C. both the increases in revenue and increased costs for clerical support in ROI.
   D. neither the increased costs nor increased revenue, as temporary changes are rarely reflected on variance reports.

REFERENCE: Abdelhak, p 695
LaTour, Eichenwald-Maki, and Oachs, p 787

57. Improving clinical outcomes and optimal continuity of care for patients are common goals of clinical documentation improvement programs in acute care hospitals. Additionally, CDI programs may work together with UM programs to
    A. reduce clinical denials for medical necessity.
    B. decrease medication errors through CPOE systems.
    C. increase patient engagement through patient portals.
    D. report sentinel events to the Joint Commission.

REFERENCE: AHIMA (2)

58. Your HMO manager has requested a report on the number of patient visits per year for preschool children. Which of the age groupings below will you use for your report?

A.	B.	C.	D.
0–1 year	<12 months	>12 months	0–2 years
1–2 years	12–24 months	12–24 months	3–4 years
2–3 years	25–37 months	25–37 months	5 years
3–4 years	38–50 months	38–50 months	
4–5 years	51–63 months	<51 months	

REFERENCE: Koch, p 6
LaTour, Eichenwald-Maki, and Oachs, p 508
Sayles, p 520

59. Collins Family Hospital had a bed count of 150 for the first 6 months of the year. On June 1, it added 15 beds when it opened a new wing. If you are given the average length of stay for the year, can you calculate the annual bed turnover rate? How?
    A. Yes, using the direct method.
    B. Yes, using the indirect method.
    C. Yes, using the Joint Commission method.
    D. No, there is insufficient data to complete the calculation.

REFERENCE: Abdelhak, p 393
Horton, pp 52–53
Koch, pp 116–118
LaTour, Eichenwald-Maki, and Oachs, p 488
Sayles, p 484

60. In a research study that includes a patient questionnaire, five of the questions will be answered using the following scale:

1	Strongly disagree
2	Disagree
3	No opinion
4	Agree
5	Strongly agree

The data collected using this scale are called
A. cardinal data.
B. ordinal data.
C. nominal data.
D. continuous data.

REFERENCE: Abdelhak, p 393
Horton, p 197
Koch, p 6
LaTour, Eichenwald-Maki, and Oachs, pp 482–483, 522
McWay (2014), p 212
Sui, p 293

61. Gail Smith has presented to the ER in a coma with injuries sustained in a motor vehicle accident. According to her sister, Gail has had a recent medical history taken at the public health department. The physician on call is grateful that she can access this patient information using the area's
A. EDMS system.
B. CPOE.
C. expert system.
D. RHIO.

REFERENCE: Bowie and Green, pp 121–122
Sayles, p 326

62. The patient's family asked the attending physician to keep the patient in the hospital for a few days more until they could make arrangements for the patient's home care. Because the patient no longer meets criteria for continued stay, if the physician complies with the family's request, this would be considered
A. the best utilization of the hospital's resources.
B. an inappropriate use of the hospital's resources.
C. a compassionate use of the hospital's resources.
D. appropriate provided it is limited to a few days.

REFERENCE: Abdelhak, p 472
LaTour, Eichenwald-Maki, and Oachs, pp 15–16, 430
Sayles, pp 609–611

63. The state is considering the closure of the Arcadia Hospital. In reviewing the hospital statistics, which indicator will best help state officials determine whether closure is warranted?
A. daily census
B. percentage of occupancy
C. inpatient service days
D. average length of stay

REFERENCE: Koch, p 106
LaTour, Eichenwald-Maki, and Oachs, pp 486–488
Sayles, p 480

64. The census taken at midnight on January 1 showed 99 patients remaining in the hospital. On January 2, four patients were admitted, there was one fetal death, one DOA, and seven patients were discharged. One of these patients was admitted in the morning and remained only 8 hours. How many inpatient service days were rendered on January 2?
    A. 94
    B. 95
    C. 96
    D. 97

REFERENCE: Abdelhak, p 392
Koch, p 91
LaTour, Eichenwald-Maki, and Oachs, pp 486–488
Sayles, p 480

65. You are implementing a quality improvement plan that utilizes the PDSA cycle. If you correctly implement PDSA, which phase of the project will take the most of your time?
    A. P
    B. D
    C. S
    D. A

REFERENCE: LaTour, Eichenwald-Maki, and Oachs, pp 419–420
McWay (2014), pp 184–185

66. A run or line chart would be most useful for collecting data on
    A. waiting time in the Pediatrics Clinic.
    B. patient satisfaction with the food.
    C. delays in scheduling elective surgical procedures.
    D. medication errors and their causes.

REFERENCE: Koch, pp 257–260
LaTour, Eichenwald-Maki, and Oachs, p 824
McWay (2014), pp 213–214
Sayles, p 582

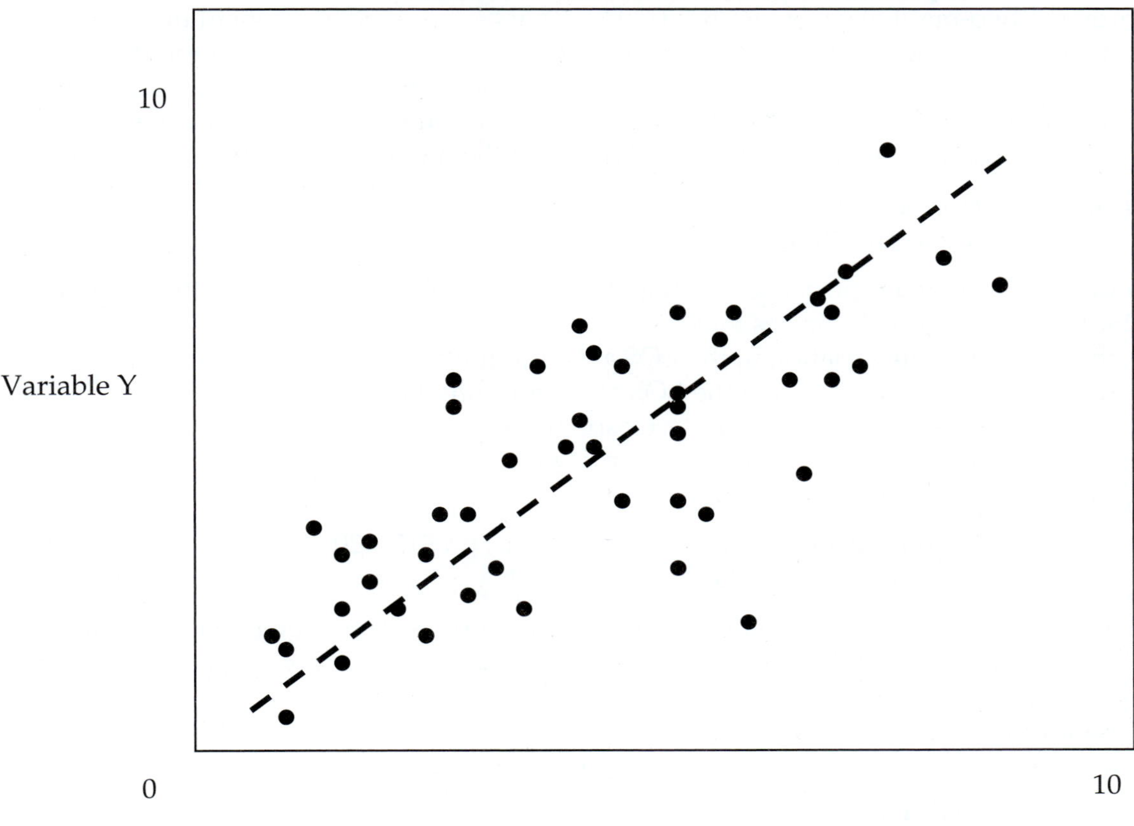

67. The ER staff has collected the data on the number of visits and corresponding wait times in the ER. The data are displayed on the chart shown above. Based on this information, what kind of correlation do you see between the number of visits (Variable X) and the wait times (Variable Y)?
    A. a positive correlation between Variable X and Variable Y
    B. a negative correlation between Variable X and Variable Y
    C. a conjunctive correlation between Variable X and Variable Y
    D. a causative correlation between Variable X and Variable Y

REFERENCE: Koch, p 283
LaTour, Eichenwald-Maki, and Oachs, p 536
McWay (2014), pp 215–217
Sayles, pp 591, 529

68. Fred is recovering nicely, so he asks Dr. Jones if he can go home for the weekend. Dr. Jones approves a two-night leave of absence (LOA). Chances are Fred is a patient in
    A. an acute care facility; his LOA will decrease the month's average daily inpatient census.
    B. a long-term care facility; his LOA will increase the month's percentage of occupancy.
    C. an acute care facility; his LOA will increase the month's total discharge days.
    D. a long-term care facility; his LOA will decrease the month's total inpatient service days.

REFERENCE: Horton, p 27
Koch, pp 125–126

69. Community Hospital reported an average LOS in December of 3.7 days with a standard deviation of 23. This information indicates that
    A. there was a small variation in the LOS at Community Hospital.
    B. there was a large variation in the LOS at Community Hospital.
    C. most of the patients at Community Hospital stay 3 to 4 days.
    D. patients stay longer at Community than at most hospitals.

REFERENCE: Koch, pp 231–241
LaTour, Eichenwald-Maki, and Oachs, pp 517–520
McWay (2014), p 206

70. A Clinical Documentation Specialist performs many duties. These include reviewing the data, and looking for trends or patterns over time, as well as noting any variances that require further investigation. In this role, the CDS professional is acting as a(n)
    A. reviewer.
    B. analyst.
    C. educator.
    D. ambassador.

REFERENCE: AHIMA (2)

71. Sun City reported 12 cases of chronic heart disease in a population of 8,000 in 2008. In 2011, Sun City reported there were still 12 cases of chronic heart disease, but its population had decreased to 6,000. This represents an increase in the
    A. prevalence of chronic heart disease in Sun City.
    B. incidence of chronic heart disease in Sun City.
    C. reliability of reporting chronic heart disease in Sun City.
    D. occurrence of chronic heart disease in Sun City.

REFERENCE: Koch, pp 201–211
LaTour, Eichenwald-Maki, and Oachs, p 506
McWay (2014), pp 210
Sayles, pp 516–517

72. Community Hospital Administration decided to change the number of adult and children beds from 300 to 375 effective July 1. The total number of inpatient service days for adults and children for the year was 111,963. What was the percentage of occupancy rate for adults and children for the entire year?
   A. 0.9%
   B. 45.4%
   C. 90.8%
   D. 91.0%

REFERENCE: Horton, pp 49–50
Koch, p 109
LaTour, Eichenwald-Maki, and Oachs, p 488
Sayles, pp 483–484

73. When checking the census data at South Beach Women's Center, you see that just yesterday, there were four sets of triplets, five sets of twins, and eight single births. Yesterday, South Beach Women's Center had
   A. 17 deliveries.
   B. 25 deliveries.
   C. 30 deliveries.
   D. 39 deliveries.

REFERENCE: Horton, p 124
Koch, p 154

74. In preparing the retention schedule for health records, the most concrete guidance in determining when records may be destroyed will be
   A. the average readmission rate for the facility.
   B. the available options for inactive records.
   C. the statute of limitations in your state.
   D. Joint Commission and AOA standards regarding minimum retention periods.

REFERENCE: LaTour, Eichenwald-Maki, and Oachs, pp 274–275
Sayles, p 346

The Credentialing Committee reviewed Dr. Hernandez's application for renewal of his medical staff privileges. They noted that Dr. Hernandez had a high incidence of nosocomial infections after hip replacement surgery. The committee recommended renewal of Dr. Hernandez's general medical staff privileges but suspended his permission to perform hip replacement surgery until he completed an AMA-approved course on infection control and successfully demonstrated improved technique to the department chair.

75. The 2014 AHIMA Foundation's "Clinical Documentation Improvement Job Description Summative Report" identified that most Clinical Documentation Improvement Specialists report directly to the
   A. HIM Department.
   B. CEO.
   C. Quality Management Department.
   D. CFO.

REFERENCE: AHIMA (2)

76. You are starting your new job as the sole HIM professional at a small psychiatric practice. The practice uses DSM for billing purposes. You find this "theoretically" reasonable because DSM
    A. is a widely used and accepted classification system.
    B. codes are also valid ICD-10-CM codes.
    C. codes are also valid CPT codes.
    D. is the industry standard for psychiatric billing systems.

REFERENCE: Bowie and Green, p 321
LaTour, Eichenwald-Maki, and Oachs, pp 388–389
Sayles, pp 208–210, 395

77. As the Information Security Officer at your facility, you have been asked to provide examples of the physical safeguards used to manage data security measures throughout the organization. Which of the following would you provide?
    A. audit controls
    B. entity authentication
    C. chain-of-trust partner agreements
    D. workstation use and location

REFERENCE: Bowie and Green, p 294
LaTour, Eichenwald-Maki, and Oachs, pp 330, 947
Sayles, pp 1055–1056

78. The MS-DRG weight in a particular case is 2.0671 and the hospital's payment rate is $3,027. How much would the hospital receive as reimbursement in this case?
    A. $3,027.00
    B. $5,094.10
    C. $6,257.11
    D. $960.00

REFERENCE: Abdelhak, pp 283–284
LaTour, Eichenwald-Maki, and Oachs, pp 432–433
Sayles, pp 449–450

79. A patient's husband slipped and fell in your HIM reception area and now he is suing the facility. You have to prepare detailed written answers to a long list of questions and send them to your hospital attorney. You will spend the afternoon working on
    A. affidavits.
    B. allocutions.
    C. interrogatories.
    D. depositions.

REFERENCE: Abdelhak, p 544
LaTour, Eichenwald-Maki, and Oachs, p 925
McWay (2016), pp 35, 41, 58

Use the information on errors in indexing of scanned material that you have collected and presented in the table below to answer the next two questions.

TYPE OF MATERIAL	NUMBER SCANNED	NUMBER INDEXING ERRORS
CONSULTATION REPORTS	2,879	431
LAB SLIPS	15,242	458
CORRESPONDENCE	1,426	114
OTHER	6,271	313

80. If you want to begin with the type of material that has the highest error rate, you will start by working on problems with
    A. consultation reports.
    B. lab slips.
    C. correspondence.
    D. other.

REFERENCE: Abdelhak, p 524
Koch, pp 107–108

81. Referring again to the data collected on scanning errors, if you want to work on the type of material with the highest volume, you will work on problems with
    A. consultation reports.
    B. lab slips.
    C. correspondence.
    D. other.

REFERENCE: Abdelhak, p 452
Koch, pp 107–108

82. You are providing an educational session to new hires at your hospital. You tell the new employees that hospital records may be used as evidence in court even though hearsay laws bar the use of most evidence that does not represent personal knowledge of the witness. That is because the hospital record
    A. is written rather than spoken.
    B. was kept in the regular course of business.
    C. has not been tampered with in any way.
    D. is accurate and complete.

REFERENCE: Abdelhak, pp 548–549
LaTour, Eichenwald-Maki, and Oachs, pp 86–87, 142–143, 241, 264, 282
McWay (2016), pp 51–52
McWay (2014), pp 58–59, 68, 126
Sayles, pp 35, 42, 131, 391, 733, 787–788

83. Which of the following responsibilities would you expect to find on the job description of a facility's Information Security Officer but NOT on the job description of Chief Privacy Officer?
    A. Cooperate with the Office of Civil Rights in compliance investigations.
    B. Conduct audit trails to monitor inappropriate access to system information.
    C. Oversee the patient's right to inspect, amend, and restrict access to protected health information.
    D. Monitor the facility's business associate agreements.

REFERENCE: Bowie and Green, p 51
LaTour, Eichenwald-Maki, and Oachs, pp 99–101, 134, 208, 360
McWay (2014), p 40
Sayles, pp 1041, 1043, 1056–1057

84. One of the patients at your physician group practice has asked for an electronic copy of her medical record. Your electronic computer system will not allow you to accommodate this request. Chances are, you are NOT in compliance with
    A. Joint Commission standards.
    B. the HIPAA privacy rule.
    C. Conditions of Coverage rules.
    D. meaningful use requirements.

REFERENCE: cms.gov

85. An 11-year-old female is brought to the emergency room with a compound, comminuted fracture of the right tibia and fibula. Her mother was very seriously injured in the same accident and is unconscious. What should be done?
    A. Nothing, until consent can be obtained from the nearest relative.
    B. The mother can be treated under implied consent but not the child.
    C. The hospital should quickly seek a court-appointed guardian for the child.
    D. Both patients can be treated under implied consent.

REFERENCE: Sayles, p 102

86. A pharmacist at your facility was caught running a drug ring. The pharmacist filled orders of valuable medications with cheap outdated ones purchased on the Internet and then sold the good drugs for profit. Patients have been injured and the lawsuits are starting. Unfortunately, your facility is going to be held responsible for the pharmacist's negligent acts under the doctrine of
    A. adjudicus res.
    B. res ipsa loquitur.
    C. respondeat superior.
    D. stare decisis.

REFERENCE: LaTour, Eichenwald-Maki, and Oachs, p 331
McWay (2016), pp 77-78, 88

87. A patient was treated for meningitis at age 3 (15 years ago). The patient is now 18. The patient's attorney is requesting information on the admission. You tell the clerk the information is
    A. no longer available because your facility retains information for 10 years after the last patient visit.
    B. available, but the attorney will have to obtain a court order before you will release it.
    C. available, but the patient's parents will have to sign a consent for you to release it.
    D. available, and the patient may sign consent to release the information in the record.

REFERENCE: Abdelhak, pp 164–165
LaTour, Eichenwald-Maki, and Oachs, p 317

88. A patient has written to request a copy of his own record. When the clerk checked the record, it was noted that the patient was last admitted to the psychiatric unit of the facility. You advise the clerk to
    A. comply with the request immediately.
    B. contact the patient's attending physician before complying.
    C. ignore the request and advise you if it is repeated.
    D. ask the patient to send the required fee prior to the release.

REFERENCE: Abdelhak, pp 538–539
LaTour, Eichenwald-Maki, and Oachs, pp 314, 319
Sayles, p 800

89. Your HIS Department receives an authorization for Sara May's medical history to be sent to her attorney, but the expiration date noted on the authorization has passed. What action is appropriate according to HIPAA privacy rules?
    A. Do not honor because the authorization is invalid.
    B. Contact the patient to get permission to respond.
    C. Contact the attending physician for permission to respond.
    D. Honor the authorization since the patient obviously approves of the release.

REFERENCE: LaTour, Eichenwald-Maki, and Oachs, pp 618–619
Sayles, pp 788, 810–812

90. The hospital's strategic plan calls for having the entire health record content recorded in discrete form within the next 10 years. Which system will the HIM Director most likely recommend in the early stages of the project as a transition strategy?
    A. electronic document management system
    B. clinical data repository system
    C. CPOE system
    D. speech recognition system

REFERENCE: Abdelhak, p 224
McWay (2014), pp 302–303

91. As the Information Security Officer at your facility, you have been asked to provide examples of technical security safeguards adopted as a result of HIPAA legislation. Which of the following would you provide?
    A. audit controls
    B. evidence of security awareness training
    C. surge protectors
    D. workstation use and location

REFERENCE: Bowie and Green, p 295
LaTour, Eichnewald-Maki, and Oachs, pp 133–134, 332
McWay (2014), p 292
Sayles, p 1057

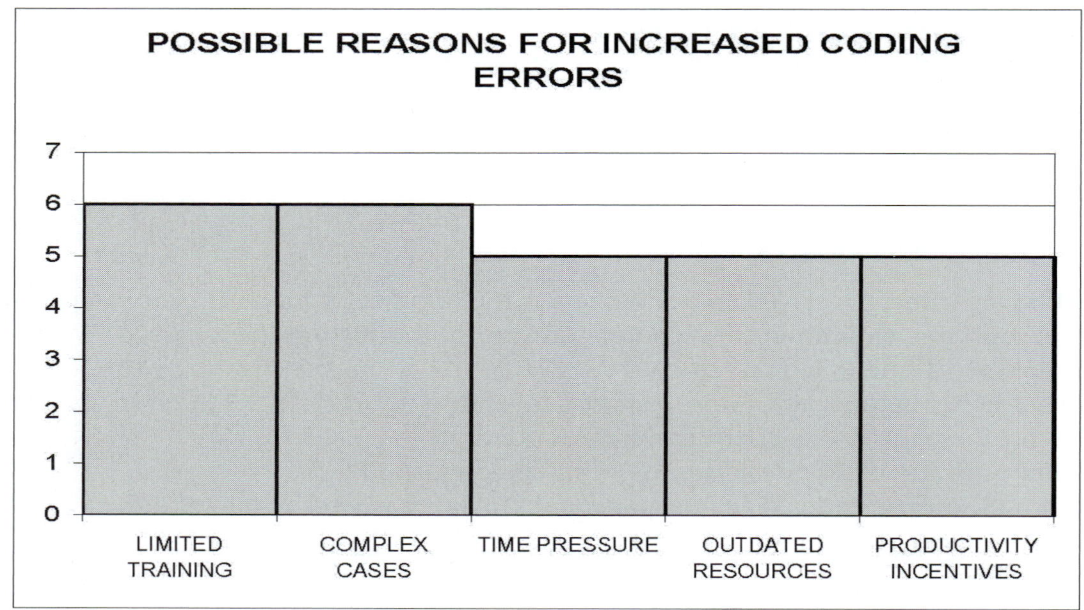

92. After your coders helped you rank the reasons for coding errors in the order of their importance, you then plotted the results on the chart above. The results of your work surprise you because
    A. you expected the coders to put more emphasis on time pressure.
    B. you thought limited training was the primary reason for the errors.
    C. the rankings show surprising disagreement on the issue.
    D. the results appear to violate the Pareto principle.

REFERENCE: LaTour, Eichenwald-Maki, and Oachs, p 823
McWay (2014), pp 148–149, 274
Sayles, pp 591–592

93. Joanie Howell presents to Dr. Franklin requesting rhinoplasty. Because Howell is covered by Medicare, Dr. Franklin must provide Howell with
   A. a Notice of Exclusion, because rhinoplasty is not a Medicare covered service.
   B. an Advance Beneficiary Notice, because rhinoplasty is not a Medicare covered service.
   C. a Notice of Exclusion, because Howell's rhinoplasty may not be medically necessary.
   D. an Advance Beneficiary Notice, because Howell's rhinoplasty may not be medically necessary.

REFERENCE: Green and Rowell, pp 463–465
LaTour, Eichenwald-Maki, and Oachs, pp 449, 894
Sayles, p 295

94. A 19-year-old former patient faxes a request to your facility requesting the release of his medical records of all episodes of care to the Army. The release of information clerk should
   A. send the records as requested.
   B. inform the young man that specific reports must be identified in his request.
   C. send a letter informing him that faxed requests are not accepted.
   D. deny the request.

REFERENCE: Abdelhak, pp 555–558
LaTour, Eichenwald-Maki, and Oachs, pp 285, 316–317
Sayles, p 102

95. A 16-year-old male was treated at your facility for a closed head injury. The patient's 18-year-old wife accompanied him to the hospital and signed the consent for admission and treatment because of the patient's incapacity at the time. The patient has requested that copies of his medical records be sent to his attorney. Who should sign the authorization to release the records?
   A. the patient
   B. either of the patient's parents
   C. the patient's parent or legal guardian
   D. the patient's wife

REFERENCE: Abdelhak, p 555
LaTour, Eichenwald-Maki, and Oachs, pp 243, 316–317
Sayles, p 102

96. When a patient is admitted because of a primary neoplasm with metastasis and treatment is directed toward the secondary neoplasm only,
   A. code only the primary neoplasm as the principal diagnosis.
   B. the primary neoplasm is coded as the principal diagnosis, and the secondary neoplasm is coded as an additional diagnosis.
   C. the secondary neoplasm is coded as the principal diagnosis, and the primary neoplasm is coded as an additional diagnosis.
   D. code only the secondary neoplasm as the principal diagnosis.

REFERENCE: Bowie (2014), p 106

97. A patient initially consulted with Dr. Vasseur at the request of Dr. Meche, the patient's primary care physician. Dr. Vasseur examined the patient, prescribed medication, and ordered tests. Additional visits to Dr. Vasseur's office for continuing care would be assigned from which E/M section?
    A. office and other outpatient services, new patient
    B. office and other outpatient services, established patient
    C. office or other outpatient consultations, new or established patient
    D. confirmatory consultations, new or established patient

REFERENCE: Bowie (2015), p 63
Green, p 570

98. A transcription unit has been asked to tally the number of times they have to leave sections of a report blank for various reasons (poor dictation technique, background noise, etc.). The quality improvement tool most likely to help collect these data would be
    A. force field analysis.
    B. decision matrix.
    C. flowchart.
    D. check sheet.

REFERENCE: LaTour, Eichenwald-Maki, and Oachs, p 823
Sayles, p 578

99. As the Director of a Health Information Technology Program, you are reviewing the workforce development forecast for electronic health record specialists as outlined by ARRA and HITECH. In order to keep abreast of changes in this program, you will need to regularly access the Web site of which governmental agency?
    A. ONC
    B. CMS
    C. OSHA
    D. CDC

REFERENCE: LaTour, Eichenwald-Maki, and Oachs, pp 17, 35, 83, 195
Sayles, p 25

100. The Chief of Staff, Chief of Medicine, President of the Governing Body, and most departmental managers have already completed CQI training. Unfortunately, the hospital administrator has not been to training, refuses to get involved with CQI, and refuses to let the administrative departmental staff get training.
    A. This level of involvement is enough to meet Joint Commission standards.
    B. The Joint Commission only expects involvement from clinical staff.
    C. This will not do because it violates Joint Commission standards and CQI philosophy.
    D. If you can talk him into training his staff, you can let him skip the training.

REFERENCE: LaTour, Eichenwald-Maki, and Oachs, pp 658, 819
McWay (2014), pp 52–53
Sayles, pp 567, 572

RECORD COMPLETION INFORMATION FOR DECEMBER				
INCOMPLETE RECORDS	DELINQUENT RECORDS	AVERAGE MONTHLY DISCHARGES	AVERAGE MONTHLY OPERATIVE PROCEDURES	DELINQUENT OPERATIVE REPORTS
604	304	845	526	14

101. Use the information provided in the table above to calculate the delinquent rate. The delinquent rate
   A. cannot be determined.
   B. is 36%.
   C. is 50%.
   D. is 71%.

REFERENCE: Abdelhak, pp 122–123
Bowie and Green, p 84
LaTour, Eichenwald-Maki, and Oachs, p 652
Sayles, p 567

102. The percentage of records delinquent due to the absence of an operative report
   A. is 1.7%.
   B. is 2.7%.
   C. is 4.6%.
   D. cannot be determined from the information given.

REFERENCE: Abdelhak, p 128
Bowie and Green, p 109
LaTour, Eichenwald-Maki, and Oachs, p 652

103. The purpose of the Correct Coding Initiative is to
   A. increase fines and penalties for bundling services into comprehensive CPT codes.
   B. restrict Medicare reimbursement to hospitals for ancillary services.
   C. teach coders how to unbundle codes.
   D. detect and prevent payment for improperly coded services.

REFERENCE: LaTour, Eichenwald-Maki, and Oachs, pp 447–448
Sayles, p 289

104. Access to radiologic images has been improved through the use of which of the following?
   A. LOINC
   B. PACS
   C. EDMS
   D. CPOE

REFERENCE: Abdelhak, pp 202–205
LaTour, Eichenwald, and Oachs, pp 124, 249
Sayles, p 914

105. The difference between an Institutional Review Board (IRB) and a hospital's Ethics Committee is that
   A. the IRB focuses on patient care only, and the Ethics Committee addresses both patient care and business practices.
   B. the Ethics Committee reviews ethics complaints, and the IRB focuses on developing policies and procedures.
   C. the IRB deals with the ethical treatment of human research subjects, and the Ethics Committee covers a wide range of issues.
   D. the IRB is made up entirely of patient care providers, and the Ethics Committee is multidisciplinary.

REFERENCE: LaTour, Eichenwald-Maki, and Oachs, pp 558, 580, 608, 913
McWay (2014), pp 241–248
Sayles, p 752

106. A common goal of the Office of the National Coordinator for Health Information Technology, RHIOs, and a national infrastructure for information is
   A. translating images into a digital format.
   B. sharing information among providers.
   C. transferring health information within a hospital system.
   D. promoting telemedicine.

REFERENCE: LaTour, Eichenwald-Maki, and Oachs, pp 17, 83, 117, 137, 204, 212
Sayles, pp 34, 162

107. According to CPT, a biopsy of the breast that involves removal of only a portion of the lesion for pathologic examination is
   A. percutaneous.
   B. incisional.
   C. excisional.
   D. punch.

REFERENCE: AMA CPT, pp 89–91
Bowie, p 115

108. Your facility would like to improve physician documentation in order to allow improved coding. As coding supervisor, you have found it very effective to provide the physicians with
   A. a copy of the facility coding guidelines, along with written information on improved documentation.
   B. the UHDDS and information on where each data element is collected and/or verified in your facility.
   C. regular in-service presentations on documentation, including its importance and tips for improvement.
   D. feedback on specific instances when improved documentation would improve coding.

REFERENCE: Abdelhak, p 219
LaTour, Eichenwald-Maki, and Oachs, pp 243, 442, 470
Sales, pp 121, 292–293, 306–307

109. A piece of objective data collected upon initial assessment of the patient is the
   A. review of systems.
   B. history of present illness.
   C. chief complaint.
   D. vital signs.

REFERENCE: Abdelhak, pp 103–106
Bowie and Green, pp 145–148
LaTour, Eichenwald-Maki, and Oachs, pp 245–246

110. You are the Director of Coding and Billing at a large group practice. The Practice Manager stops by your office on his way to a planning meeting to ask about the timeline for complying with HITECH requirements to adopt meaningful use EHR technology. You reply that the incentives began in 2011 and end in 2014. You remind him that by 2015, sanctions for noncompliance will appear in the form of

A. downward adjustments to Medicare reimbursement.
B. withdrawal of permission to treat Medicare and Medicaid patients.
C. a mandatory action plan for implementing a meaningful use EHR.
D. monetary fines up to $100,000.

REFERENCE: LaTour, Eichenwald, and Maki, pp 264–265
McWay (2014), p 305
Sayles, pp 954, 987

111. A number of key elements for your facility's computerized patient record are still input by clerical staff from handwritten data entry sheets. You are concerned about the transfer of data. If the vital signs stored in the database are not what were originally recorded, the impact on patient care could be severe. You are concerned about the

A. stability of the data.
B. validity of the data.
C. legitimacy of the data.
D. reliability of the data.

REFERENCE: Bowie and Green, p 272
LaTour, Eichenwald-Maki, and Oachs, pp 90, 129, 205–206, 382, 385, 956
McWay (2014), p 143
Sayles, p 462

112. ORYX is a program that was developed by

A. CMS to track Medicare costs.
B. Joint Commission to link patient outcomes to accreditation.
C. NIH to track communicable diseases.
D. AMA to allow for rapid CPT updates.

REFERENCE: Bowie and Green, p 36
LaTour, Eichenwald-Maki, and Oachs, pp 21, 201, 906, 936
McWay (2014), p 188
Sayles, pp 155–156

113. In preparation for conversion to a computerized patient record, a committee at your facility is defining each of the data elements in a patient record to determine which elements should be required and to set parameters for each element. The committee is working on the data

A. edits.
B. reasonableness.
C. dictionary.
D. feasibility.

REFERENCE: Abdelhak, pp 501–505
Eichenwald-Maki and Peterson, pp 37–38
Bowie and Green, p 266
LaTour, Eichenwald-Maki, and Oachs, pp 202, 368, 383, 907
McWay (2014), p 262
Sayles, pp 882, 954, 987

114. An effective means of protecting the security of computerized health information would be to
   A. require all facility employees to change their passwords at least once a month.
   B. write detailed procedures for the entry of data into the computerized information system.
   C. install a system that would require fingerprint scanning and recognition for data access.
   D. develop clear policies on data security that are supported by the top management of the facility.

REFERENCE: Abdelhak, pp 317–319
LaTour, Eichenwald-Maki, and Oachs, pp 129, 134, 160, 172, 204, 316, 318, 319, 328, 336, 343–344
McWay (2014), pp 291–293
Sayles, pp 12, 131, 415, 794, 829–830

115. In reviewing the policies on release of information in respect to the privacy rules, you note that it is still acceptable to allow release of protected health information without patient permission to
   A. the patient's spouse.
   B. a health care provider interested in the case.
   C. the quality assurance committee for review purposes.
   D. a third-party payer with a direct interest in the case.

REFERENCE: LaTour, Eichenwald-Maki, and Oachs, pp 314, 318–319
Sayles, p 799

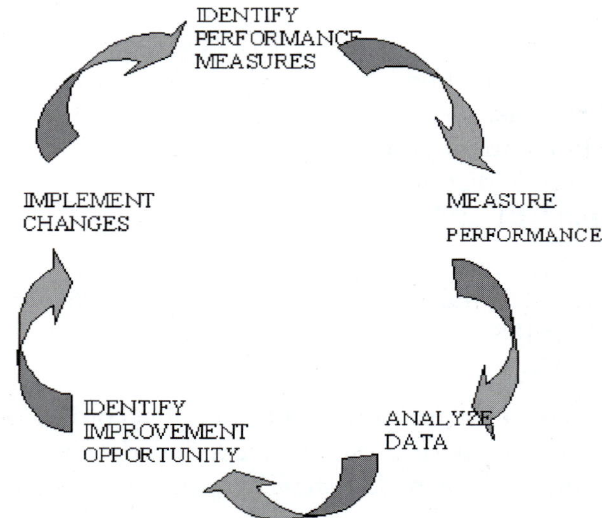

116. Your facility has a team that has been working to develop a strong performance improvement model, and they have come up with the model shown above. The team asks if you see anything missing from the model. You tell them they
   A. are missing a step requiring regular employee input into the process.
   B. are missing a step requiring reporting to the board of directors.
   C. are missing a step requiring ongoing monitoring and reassessment.
   D. are not missing any steps; the model is a good one.

REFERENCE: LaTour, Eichenwald-Maki, and Oachs, pp 659–660
McWay (2014), p 185
Sayles, p 799

117. The new electronic system recently purchased at your physician practice allows for e-prescribing and the exchange of data to a centralized immunization registry, and lets your physicians report on key clinical quality measures. In all likelihood, your practice has succeeded in choosing

A. a Joint Commission-approved system.
B. a certified EHR.
C. a functional EMR.
D. an AMA-approved product.

REFERENCE: Sayles, p 959

118. Your hospital has purchased a number of outpatient facilities. You have been assigned to chair an interdisciplinary committee that will write record retention policies for the new corporation. You begin by telling the committee their primary consideration when making retention decisions must be

A. space considerations.
B. statutory requirements.
C. provider preferences.
D. professional standards.

REFERENCE: Abdelhak, pp 164–168
LaTour, Eichenwald-Maki, and Oachs, pp 284–285, 288, 311–312
McWay (2014), pp 136–138
Sayles, pp 788–789

119. A major drug company wants to promote a fundraiser targeting patients with congestive heart failure. The drug company representative has requested a list of patients treated at your facility. As privacy and security officer, you tell them that

A. they just need to send a written request for the list.
B. a prior authorization is required before any PHI can be released.
C. you will need to confer with the medical director.
D. if the fundraising was conducted by a business associate without authorization, and the funds were to benefit your facility (the covered entity), that you could disclose the information.

REFERENCE: LaTour, Eichenwald-Maki, and Oachs, p 318
Sayles, pp 827–828, 836, 1050, 1160

120. Your facility is storing scanned records for long-term storage on optical disk. The Risk Management Committee's Disaster Task Force has recommended that copies of the disks be stored at a facility across town. The administrator is concerned that records may be altered on the disks stored off-site. You tell the administrator

A. this is a legitimate concern; it should be addressed in the contract written with the storage facility.
B. this is not a concern because WORM technology makes it impossible to alter the documents.
C. this is a legitimate concern; perhaps the committee should consider storing duplicates in two locations in this facility.
D. this is not a concern; there is really no need to make and store duplicate disks as they are difficult to damage.

REFERENCE: Abdelhak, p 239
LaTour, Eichenwald-Maki, and Oachs, pp 87, 278
Sayles, pp 346, 1032

121. The Pharmacy and Therapeutics Committee has asked you to find out more about a computerized order entry system that calculates drug dosages based on patient parameters (weight, age, etc.) and even suggests the best drug given the patient's diagnosis and current treatment. The committee is asking for information on a(n)

A. application system.
B. clinical decision support system.
C. ordering system.
D. practice parameters system.

REFERENCE: Abdelhak, pp 207–208
LaTour, Eichenwald-Maki, and Oachs, pp 94–95, 115, 118, 125–127
Sayles, pp 915, 964–965

122. A portion of a deficiency slip is reproduced below. This patient was discharged yesterday. Your greatest concern regarding deficiencies on this record would be the missing

Physician: Hunter, J. T.				
Missing Signatures			Missing Reports	
X	History			Diagnoses/Procedure
	Physical			History
	Consultative Report			Physical
X	Operative Report			Consultation Report
	Discharge Summary		X	Operative Report
	X-ray Report			Discharge Summary
	Other			X-ray Report
				Others

A. signature on the physical exam.
B. signature on the discharge summary.
C. diagnoses and procedures.
D. operative report.

REFERENCE: Abdelhak, pp 107, 124
Bowie and Green, p 182

123. In the past, Joint Commission standards have focused on promoting the use of a facility approved abbreviation list to be used by hospital care providers. With the advent of the Commission's national patient safety goals, the focus has shifted to the

A. prohibited use of any abbreviations.
B. flagrant use of specialty-specific abbreviations.
C. use of prohibited or "dangerous" abbreviations.
D. use of abbreviations used in the final diagnoses.

REFERENCE: Abdelhak, p 111
Sayles, pp 72–74, 406, 786

124. Annual costs for the only Release of Information Clerk at Jacksonville Beach Healthcare Center (salary and benefits) are $36,429. The monthly cost for the copier used solely for ROI is $89 (supplies and repairs). It costs the department $0.95 on average for ROI mailings (envelopes and postage). There were 687 requests filled for ROI last month. The cost per request for release of information last month was

A. $4.42.
B. $4.55.
C. $4.63.
D. $5.50.

REFERENCE: Horton, p 140

125. The decision makers in the HIM department have decided to use the decision analysis matrix method to select coding software. Use of this method will help ensure

A. all alternatives/vendors are evaluated subjectively.
B. the personalities of individual vendors will not influence the decision.
C. consistent criteria are used to evaluate the alternatives/vendors.
D. the level of software support will be considered in the decision.

REFERENCE: Abdelhak, p 461
LaTour, Eichenwald-Maki, and Oachs, pp 601–602
Sayles, p 759

126. Many of the departments in your facility create and modify forms often. A major key to forms control in this setting is

A. consistent formatting of each page of each form.
B. capturing every data item required by UHDDS.
C. giving each form or view an identifiable name, number, and revision date.
D. providing instructions when necessary for appropriate data fields.

REFERENCE: Abdelhak, pp 100–101
Bowie and Green, pp 216–217
LaTour, Eichenwald-Maki, and Oachs, pp 335, 337
McWay (2014), pp 131–132
Sayles, p 357

Record #	Patient Last Name	Date of Birth	Date of Service
32-15-65	Smith	02/03/76	03/20/2015
02-45-77	Cook	09/12/86	10/21/2015
10-88-48	Baker	01/23/24	11/14/2015

127. Which means of data modeling is illustrated in the table shown above?

A. entity-relationship model
B. object-oriented model
C. data management model
D. relational data model

REFERENCE: Abdelhak, pp 298–299
LaTour, Eichenwald-Maki, and Oachs, pp 128–129
Sayles, pp 879–881, 900, 992–993

128. Which of the following is the unique identifier in the database illustrated in the table for question 127?

A. record number
B. patient's last name
C. date of birth
D. date of service

REFERENCE: Abdelhak, pp 298–299
LaTour, Eichenwald-Maki, and Oachs, p 129
Sayles, pp 880–881

129. Stage I of meaningful use focuses on data capture and sharing. Which of the following is included in the menu set of objectives for eligible hospitals in this stage?
   A. Use CPOE for medication orders
   B. Smoking cessation counseling for MI patients
   C. Appropriate use of HL-7 standards
   D. Establish critical pathways for complex, high-dollar cases

REFERENCE: HealthIT.hhs.gov
LaTour, Eichenwald-Maki, and Oachs, pp 204–212, 219–221, 856–857
Sayles, p 144

130. As supervisor of the cancer registry, you report the registry's annual caseload to administration. The most efficient way to retrieve this information would be to use
   A. patient abstracts.
   B. patient index.
   C. accession register.
   D. follow-up files.

REFERENCE: LaTour, Eichenwald-Maki, and Oachs, p 371
Sayles, p 439

131. A supervisor reviews a job to determine the required content, skills, knowledge, abilities, and responsibilities for the position. The tasks are grouped and lines of responsibility and authority are defined. The supervisor is writing a job
   A. description.
   B. analysis.
   C. process.
   D. detail.

REFERENCE: Abdelhak, pp 586–587
LaTour, Eichenwald-Maki, and Oachs, p 723
McWay (2014), p 334
Sayles, p 1121

132. The final HITECH Omnibus Rule expanded some of HIPAA's original requirements, including changes in immunization disclosures. As a result, where states require immunization records of a minor prior to admitting a student to a school, a covered entity is permitted to
   A. require written authorization from a custodial parent before disclosing proof of the child's immunization to the school.
   B. allow the minor to authorize the disclosure of the proof of immunization to the school.
   C. simply document a written or oral agreement from a parent or guardian before releasing the immunization record to the school.
   D. allow school officials to authorize immunization disclosures on behalf of a child attending their school.

REFERENCE: AHIMA (1)

133. As your meeting with the clerical staff on the stat report continues, one clerk suggests a possible reason for the delays is a lack of training concerning the nature of stat reports. On the cause and effect diagram, this would most appropriately be listed under

A. personnel.
B. equipment.
C. materials.
D. methods.

REFERENCE: Abdelhak, p 461
LaTour, Eichenwald-Maki, and Oachs, pp 822–823
McWay (2014), p 179
Sayles, p 528

	Rule 1	Rule 2	Rule 3	Rule 4
Condition 1				
Condition 2				
Condition 3				
Condition 4				
Action 1				
Action 2				
Action 3				
Action 4				

134. You stop by the office to meet a friend for lunch. Looking on her desk, you see the grid above. Your friend is trying to

A. plan a conversion.
B. design a system.
C. analyze a workflow.
D. make a decision.

REFERENCE: Abdelhak, p 651
LaTour, Eichenwald-Maki, and Oachs, p 695

SAINT JOSEPH HOSPITAL CODING PRODUCTIVITY WEEK ENDING JANUARY 2, 2016			
EMPLOYEE NUMBER	INPATIENT	OUTPATIENT PROCEDURE	EMERGENCY OR OBSERVATION
425	120	35	16
426	48	89	95
427	80	92	4
428	65	109	16

135. The performance standard for coders is 28–33 workload units per day. Workload units are calculated as follows:

Inpatient record = 1 workload unit

Outpatient surgical procedure records = 0.75 workload units

Outpatient observation/emergency records = 0.50 workload units

One week's productivity information is shown in the table above. What percentage of the coders is meeting the productivity standards?

A. 100%
B. 75%
C. 50%
D. 25%

REFERENCE: Abdelhak, p 461
McWay (2014), p 221

136. The coding supervisor tends to deal with issues as they come up, prioritizing only when problems are pressing or appear to be important to upper management. This crisis manager is particularly weak in which management function?

A. planning
B. organizing
C. controlling
D. budgeting

REFERENCE: LaTour, Eichenwald-Maki, and Oachs, pp 686, 690
McWay (2014), p 338

137. As a new HIM manager, you recognize that employee development is a necessary investment for the long-term survival and growth of the organization. Your goal is to design and implement a staff development program for your employees, so one of your first steps is to

A. implement training programs that emphasize teamwork.
B. establish a budget for all hospital employee training.
C. survey the HIM employees to assess their need for new skills or knowledge.
D. establish HIPAA training programs hospital-wide.

REFERENCE: Abdelhak, pp 630–631
LaTour, Eichenwald-Maki, and Oachs, pp 736, 739
McWay (2014), pp 290, 303–304
Sayles, pp 1106–1111

138. Now that the EHR has been fully implemented, you are ready to move old records to basement storage. You are ordering shelving for those old paper files. You have 18,000 records. The files average is three files per filing inch. The shelf units you have selected have six shelves that will hold 34 inches per shelf. You will have to plan for a 20% expansion rate to accommodate miscellaneous paper records over the next 10 years. How many shelving units should you order?

A. 30
B. 31
C. 35
D. 36

REFERENCE: Bowie and Green, p 235
LaTour, Eichenwald-Maki, and Oachs, p 274
Sayles, pp 338–339

139. Postage charges in the Health Information Department have increased during the last quarter. The department director has seen metered envelopes in the mail bin that do not appear to be those used for departmental business. The best course of action for the director would be to
   A. remove the postage meter from the department.
   B. keep a watchful eye on the meter and who uses it.
   C. issue employee warnings at the next departmental meeting.
   D. assign responsibility for the postage meter to one employee.

REFERENCE: LaTour, Eichenwald-Maki, and Oachs, p 750
McWay (2014), p 335

140. A clerk's work performance has diminished dramatically during the past 2 weeks. The supervisor initiates a discussion with the clerk, during which the clerk reveals that he recently accepted that he has an alcohol addiction. The clerk states an intention to quit drinking completely. The supervisor should
   A. terminate the clerk if it can be proved that alcohol was used on the job.
   B. suspend the clerk if alcohol has diminished the clerk's job performance.
   C. give the clerk a leave of absence until these problems can be resolved.
   D. refer the clerk to the facility's Employee Assistance Program.

REFERENCE: Abdelhak, p 624
McWay (2014), pp 376–377

141. Everyone in the Health Information Department has been working overtime to complete a major record conversion. The supervisor will have to plan for overtime pay for all personnel who are not
   A. hourly employees.
   B. salaried exempt employees.
   C. salaried nonexempt employees.
   D. temporary employees.

REFERENCE: Abdelhak, pp 599–600
LaTour, Eichenwald-Maki, and Oachs, p 728
McWay (2014), pp 364–365

142. The coder works 7.5 hours per day. If a time standard is determined from sample observations to be 2.50 minutes per record for coding emergency room records, what is the daily standard for the number of records coded when a 15% fatigue factor is allowed?
   A. 153 records per day
   B. 180 records per day
   C. 192 records per day
   D. 200 records per day

REFERENCE: Horton, pp 135–140
McWay (2014), pp 221–226

143. The correspondence section of your department receives an average of 50 requests per day for release of information. It takes an average of 30 minutes to fulfill each request. Using 6.5 productive hours per day as your standard, calculate the staffing needs for the correspondence section.
   A. 3.8 FTE
   B. 2.5 FTE
   C. 3 FTE
   D. 4 FTE

REFERENCE: Horton, pp 14, 18
Koch, p 55

144. Your hospital takes advantage of the 8/80 exemption for health care facilities. Assuming that no employee worked more than 8 hours in a day, which of the employees listed in the table below will be paid overtime this pay period?

EMPLOYEE NUMBER	SCHEDULED HOURS PER WEEK	ACTUAL HOURS THIS WEEK	ACTUAL HOURS LAST WEEK
101	40	42	40
102	40	38	42
103	30	40	40
104	20	22	24
105	40	40	48

A. Employees 101 and 105
B. Employees 101, 102, and 105
C. Employees 101, 104, and 105
D. Employees 101, 103, 104, and 105

REFERENCE: Abdelhak, pp 599–600

145. During the work sampling of a file clerk's activity, it is noted that the employee is speaking on the telephone during 76 of 300 observations. How much of the employee's time is spent on the phone if the employee works 7 hours a day?

A. 1.77 hours
B. 3.28%
C. 3.94 hours
D. 9.2%

REFERENCE: Horton, p 14
Koch, p 59

146. You are conducting an educational session on benchmarking. You tell your audience that the key to benchmarking is to use the comparison to

A. implement your QI process.
B. make recommendations for improvement.
C. improve your department's processes.
D. compare your department with another.

REFERENCE: Abdelhak, p 452
LaTour, Eichenwald-Maki, and Oachs, p 708
McWay (2014), p 179
Sayles, pp 449, 1222

147. In conducting an educational session for your staff about implementing a benchmarking program, you tell your staff that when an organization uses benchmarking, it is important to compare your facility's outcomes to

A. nationally known facilities.
B. larger facilities.
C. facilities within your corporation.
D. facilities with superior performance.

REFERENCE: Abdelhak, pp 458–459
LaTour, Eichenwald-Maki, and Oachs, p 708
McWay (2014), p 179
Sayles, pp 449, 1222

148. You supervise five clerical employees who will be moving when a new wing of your facility is completed. When you meet with the architect to plan their space, you will ask for

A. 200 square feet of space for your clerical staff.
B. 250 square feet of space for your clerical staff.
C. 300 square feet of space for your clerical staff.
D. 350 square feet of space for your clerical staff.

REFERENCE: Abdelhak, p 673

149. How long will it take to complete the project described below?

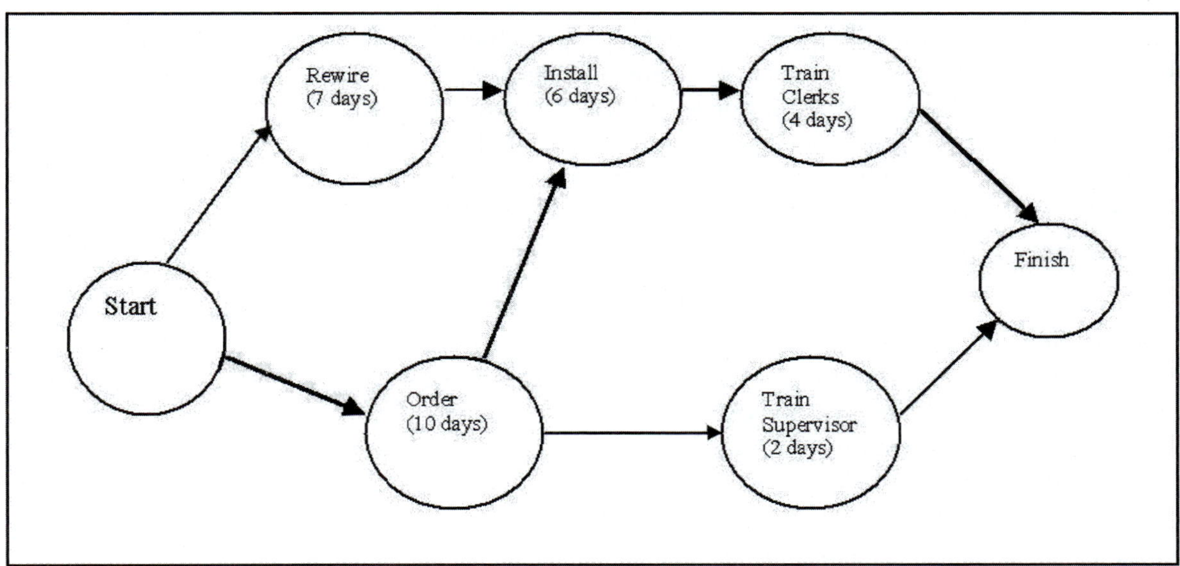

A. 12 days
B. 17 days
C. 20 days
D. 29 days

REFERENCE: Abdelhak, p 662
McWay (2014), pp 345–346

150. The file clerks in your department's main file area report that they are able to locate 400 out of 450 requested records during the past month. There are a total of 4,500 records in the main file. What is the area's accuracy rate?

A. 1.1%
B. 8.9%
C. 10.0%
D. 88.9%

REFERENCE: Calculation

END OF THE RHIT MOCK EXAMINATION

FOR THE RHIA MOCK EXAMINATION CONTINUE TESTING AND COMPLETE THE REMAINING 30 QUESTIONS.

151. The protocol that allows a browser to connect to a server and authenticate identities for data transfer is known as a(n) ____________ connection.

A. packet filter
B. public key
C. secure socket layer
D. application gateway

REFERENCE: Abdelhak, p 319
Sayles, p 1043

152. A clerical-level employee reports an incident in which the clerk felt the first-line supervisor discriminated on the basis of the clerk's gender. The best action for you to take at this time is to

A. thoroughly investigate the matter and document your findings.
B. talk with the first-line supervisor to determine what happened.
C. ask the other clerical level staff if they have had similar experiences.
D. ask the clerk to provide objective evidence of the discrimination.

REFERENCE: Abdelhak, pp 596–597
LaTour, Eichenwald-Maki, and Oachs, p 756

153. A section of a job description states that the incumbent will handle day-to-day operations in the transcription and release of information areas. This section defines the

A. skills required to perform the job.
B. time required for each function.
C. authority associated with the job.
D. scope of responsibility in the job.

REFERENCE: Abdelhak, pp 610–611
LaTour, Eichenwald-Maki, and Oachs, p 723
McWay (2014), p 334

154. There are 15 employees in your department. There were 21 working days last month. There were a total of 12 lost workdays last month due to absenteeism of all types. The absenteeism rate for your department last month was

A. 21%.
B. 57%.
C. 4%.
D. 5%.

REFERENCE: Calculation

155. As part of a team responsible for revenue analysis at your facility, you recommend a yearly review of which of the following?

A. JCAHO requirements
B. the OIG Workplan
C. the CMS Scope of Work
D. Blue Cross-Blue Shield beneficiary notices

REFERENCE: oig.hhs.gov

156. You are a new supervisor in the HIM department and find it difficult to deal with performance issues. Laney, an employee in the Release of Information section, has been late several times this month. She has already been given a verbal warning. She was late again today. According to the progressive discipline process, your next step will be to

A. reinforce the institution's policies.
B. reissue the verbal warning.
C. suspend the employee.
D. issue a written warning.

REFERENCE: Abdelhak, pp 623–624
LaTour, Eichenwald-Maki, and Oachs, pp 755–756
McWay (2014), p 378
Sayles, p 1103

157. The CFO of your facility asks you to prepare a budget for the fiscal year based on the past volume and expected capacity for the coming year. This process is an example of using the "____________" budgeting method.

A. rolling budget
B. fixed budget
C. flexible or statistics budget
D. zero-based budget

REFERENCE: Abdelhak, pp 693–694
LaTour, Eichenwald-Maki, and Oachs, p 785

158. The committee that is preparing your acute care hospital for an electronic health record is planning for an imaging system for record archiving in the immediate future. They are looking for a solution for data interfacing or integration of the imaging system into other computer systems. You recommend

A. data dictionary guidelines.
B. Health Level 7 standards.
C. Regional Health Information Organization guidelines.
D. Joint Commission standards.

REFERENCE: Abdelhak, p 189
LaTour, Eichenwald-Maki, and Oachs, p 206

159. Your facility has decided to purchase an integrated patient information system. Your part in the initial work plan is to develop system specifications that will ultimately be sent out to vendors who will potentially submit a bid on your system. You are working on the systems specs that will become part of the

A. CPR.
B. IRB.
C. RFP.
D. CRS.

REFERENCE: Abdelhak, p 373
LaTour, Eichenwald-Maki, and Oachs, pp 105–106
McWay (2014), p 401
Sayles, pp 862, 1117

160. Reference checks are conducted on potential employees to help assess the applicant's fit with the position and also to

A. confirm the accuracy of information provided on the application.
B. uncover skills the applicant may have neglected to report.
C. get another opinion on the applicant's emotional stability.
D. alert the past employer that the applicant is job hunting.

REFERENCE: Abdelhak, pp 313–314
LaTour, Eichenwald-Maki, and Oachs, p 720
McWay (2014), p 363
Sayles, p 1097

161. In order to perform their jobs, facility employees should have full and timely access only to the information they need to complete the task at hand. This is similar to HIPAA's provision for

A. a Notice of Privacy Practices (NOPP).
B. amending a record.
C. accessing need to know information only.
D. an informed consent.

REFERENCE: Abdelhak, p 562
LaTour, Eichenwald-Maki, and Oachs, p 273
Sayles, pp 54, 756, 1037, 1062

162. Authentication is one of the components necessary to produce a legal document in an EHR. This means

A. tracking changes in the EHR system.
B. establishing access controls for individual employees.
C. creating audit trails.
D. identifying who created a document and when.

REFERENCE: Abdelhak, p 138
LaTour, Eichenwald-Maki, and Oachs, pp 264, 334
Sayles, pp 366, 974, 1184

163. The Hospital Value-Based Purchasing (Hospital VBP) Program adjusts a hospital's payments based on their performance in all of these domains except
 A. the Outcomes Domain.
 B. the Patient Experience of Care Domain.
 C. the Patient Safety Domain.
 D. the Clinical Process of Care Domain.

REFERENCE: medicare.gov

164. The purpose of a Health Information Exchange (HIE) is to
 A. improve the interoperability of health care systems.
 B. link patient data to government agencies.
 C. build connectivity in rural areas.
 D. improve health care delivery and information gathering.

REFERENCE: Abdelhak, p 523

165. You have been asked to reduce your department's operating budget by 20%. In order to do so, you will have to effect reductions in your largest budget line. You will have to make cuts in
 A. equipment.
 B. personnel.
 C. supplies.
 D. contracts.

REFERENCE: Abdelhak, p 694
LaTour, Eichenwald-Maki, and Oachs, p 786
Sayles, p 1090

166. Take a look at the comparison of the two life cycles below.

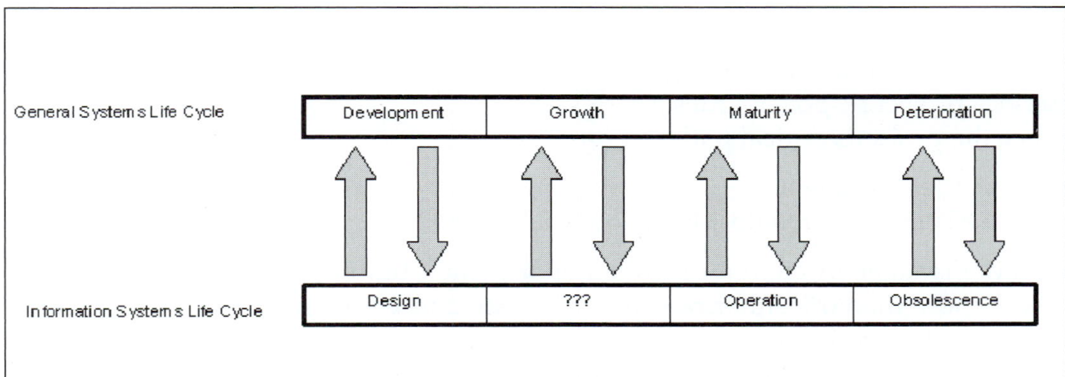

Look at the cell in the Information Systems Life Cycle that is filled with question marks. Which of the following should replace those question marks to make a complete, correct comparison?
 A. Growth
 B. Installation
 C. Implementation
 D. Reevaluation

REFERENCE: Abdelhak, p 341
LaTour, Eichenwald-Maki, and Oachs, p 105
McWay (2014), pp 286–288
Sayles, pp 857, 900

167. The use of "public" and "private" keys is part of what type of data protection?
   A. Firewalls
   B. Biometrics
   C. Encryption
   D. Phishing

REFERENCE: Abdelhak, p 319
LaTour, Eichenwald-Maki, and Oachs, p 100
Sayles, pp 1042–1043

168. In your job as Chief Security Officer, you are evaluating software programs that will support your policy on sound terminal controls within your facility. One of the features you include in your request for information to vendors is
   A. auto log off.
   B. encryption.
   C. voice recognition feature.
   D. unique identifier for log-on.

REFERENCE: Sayles, p 1021

169. The most sophisticated level of interoperability of an EHR and other such systems is the ______________ level.
   A. basic
   B. functional
   C. semantic
   D. exchange

REFERENCE: Abdelhak, p 249
LaTour, Eichenwald-Maki, and Oachs, p 397

170. As the Project Manager for the upcoming EHR implementation, you ask your assistant to develop a work breakdown structure (WBS). Critical to implementations and project success, the WBS
   A. lists steps needed to complete the project.
   B. determines dependencies among project tasks.
   C. describes project responsibilities.
   D. defines the project's critical path.

REFERENCE: Abdelhak, p 660
LaTour, Eichenwald-Maki, and Oachs, p 842

171. As the HIM manager in charge of your department's budget, you are mandated to report on variances of more than 6% either positive or negative to your Chief Financial Officer and include the reasons for the variance and any action plans necessary. Based on the table below for the December variance report, what category would you be required to report on to the CFO?

Variance Report for December			
Description	December Budget	December Actual	Variance
Office Supplies	5,120	5,550	(430)
Contract Services	8,500	8,340	160
Travel	3,500	3,700	(200)
Education	2,500	2,400	100

   A. office supplies
   B. contract services
   C. travel
   D. education

REFERENCE: Abdelhak, p 695
LaTour, Eichenwald-Maki, and Oachs, pp 786–788
McWay (2014), p 398

172. Evidence-based management and decision making is an emerging model now used to make more informed decisions. The premise of this model is
   A. using intuition based on previous experience.
   B. using a decision tree with branches that show the alternatives.
   C. using the best clinical and research practices available.
   D. using an alternative that meets minimum requirements.

REFERENCE: Abdelhak, pp 444, 451
LaTour, Eichenwald-Maki, and Oachs, p 128
Sayles, pp 685, 962

Document Imaging Implementation						
Beginning Date:	**December 2015**		**Planning Date:**	**October 2015**		
Activity	**Assigned:**	**October 2015**	**November 2015**	**December 2015**	**January 9, 2016**	**February 9, 2016**
Kickoff	Team	•				
RFP	PM	•				
System Anal	PM	•				
Design	ITS		•			
RFP Eval	Team			•		
Select Vendor	Team			•		
Purchase	CFO/ITS				•	
Build System	ITS				•	
Implement	Team					•

173. As a member of the project team for document imaging implementation, you were asked to provide the information in the grid above. This is an example of a
   A. PERT diagram.
   B. Gantt chart.
   C. PMBOK chart.
   D. work flow diagram.

REFERENCE: Abdelhak, p 663
LaTour, Eichenwald-Maki, and Oachs, p 107

174. Identification of threats and vulnerabilities, security measures, and implementation priorities are part of a health care organization's
   A. intrusion detection plan.
   B. identity management plan.
   C. security plan.
   D. risk management plan.

REFERENCE: Sayles, pp 612–613

175. A _________uses a private tunnel through the Internet as a transport medium between locations for secure access and transmission.
   A. TCPIP protocol
   B. firewall
   C. hub
   D. VPN

REFERENCE: Abdelhak, p 313
LaTour, Eichenwald-Maki, and Oachs, p 33
Sayles, p 219

176. A technique that uncovers new information from existing information by probing data sets is known as

A. data mining.
B. systems query language (SQL).
C. neural network analysis.
D. data warehousing.

REFERENCE: Abdelhak, p 321
LaTour, Eichenwald-Maki, and Oachs, pp 86, 539, 569, 908
Sayles, pp 381, 887, 925

177. Your HIM department is moving to a new location and in order to arrange your employees and functions for optimal work flow efficiency and to decide which employees need to be placed close to each other, the tool you decide to use is a

A. data flow diagram.
B. PERT chart.
C. proximity chart or movement diagram.
D. flow process chart.

REFERENCE: LaTour, Eichenwald-Maki, and Oachs, p 821

178. A p value of less than 0.05 is what researchers commonly use to reject the null hypothesis. A smaller p value may place interpretation of the results of the study at risk for a

A. sampling error.
B. stratification error.
C. type 1 (a) error.
D. type 2 (b) error.

REFERENCE: Abdelhak, p 402
LaTour, Eichenwald-Maki, and Oachs, pp 579–580

179. Which of the following employees would be considered exempt under the Fair Labor Standards Act?

A. the head of the Department of Health Information Services who is involved in decision making and planning 90% of the time
B. the coding supervisor who has responsibility for three employees and performs analysis and coding 80% of the time
C. the departmental secretary who is responsible for performing a variety of clerical and administrative tasks
D. the sole employee in the physician's workroom who has responsibility for maintaining and tracking medical record deficiencies

REFERENCE: Abdelhak, p 599
McWay (2014), p 367

180. In order to prevent the accidental introduction of a virus into your facility's local area network, your facility has a policy that strictly prohibits

A. doing personal work on the computer system, even during personal time.
B. sharing disks from one workstation to another within the facility.
C. downloading executable files from electronic bulletin boards.
D. sending or receiving e-mail from addresses that have not been authorized.

REFERENCE: LaTour, Eichenwald-Maki, and Oachs, pp 383–384
Sayles, pp 577, 934–935, 1037, 1256

END OF RHIA MOCK EXAMINATION

Answer Key for the Mock Examination

ANSWER EXPLANATION

1. B
2. D
3. D
4. D Progress note elements written in the acronym "SOAP" style are:
   S-subjective; records what the patient states is the problem
   O-objective; records what the practitioner identifies through history, physical examination, and diagnostic tests
   A-assessment; combines the subjective and objective into a conclusion
   P-plan; what approach is going to be taken to resolve the problem
5. D
6. B Calculation: $\frac{\text{169.051 total relative weight}}{\text{57 total patients seen}} = 2.965807$
7. A The interdisciplinary care plan is the foundation around which patient care is organized. It contains input from the unique perspective of each discipline involved. It includes an assessment, statement of goals, identification of specific activities, or strategies to achieve those goals and periodic assessment of goal attainment.
8. D
9. B Calculations: Reimbursement from payor for one well child visit equals total reimbursement divided by number of visits to the clinic.

INSURANCE COMPANY	NUMBER OF WELL CHILD VISITS	REIMBURSEMENT FROM PAYER FOR WELL CHILD VISITS	REIMBURSEMENT FROM PAYER FOR ONE WELL CHILD VISIT (TOTAL REIMBURSEMENT/ NUMBER OF VISITS)
Lifecare	259	$31,196.55	$120.45
Getwell	786	$100,859.52	$128.32
SureHealth	462	$54,631.50	$118.25
BeHealthy	219	$26,991.75	$123.25

Answer Key for the Mock Examination

ANSWER EXPLANATION

10. B Calculations

Reimbursement for one well child visit = total reimbursement divided by number of visits.

Reimbursements for two immunizations = total reimbursement divided by number of immunizations × 2.

Total reimbursement for one average visit = reimbursement for one well child visit + reimbursement for two immunizations.

INSURANCE COMPANY	REIMBURSEMENT FOR ONE WELL CHILD VISIT	REIMBURSEMENT FOR TWO IMMUNIZATIONS [(TOTAL REIMBURSEMENT/NUMBER OF IMMUNIZATIONS) × 2]	TOTAL REIMBURSEMENT FOR ONE AVERAGE VISIT (REIMBURSEMENT FOR ONE WELL CHILD VISIT + REIMBURSEMENT FOR TWO IMMUNIZATIONS)
Lifecare	$120.45	$10.56	$131.01
Getwell	$128.32	$12.36	$140.68
SureHealth	$118.25	$11.76	$130.01
BeHealthy	$123.25	$10.16	$133.41

11. B
12. C Calculations:

MS-DRG A	2.023 × 323 = 653.43
MS-DRG B	0.987 × 489 = 485.65
MS-DRG C	**1.925 × 402 = 773.85**
MS-DRG D	1.243 × 386 = 479.80

13. A
14. D
15. A
16. B
17. D
18. A
19. D
20. D
21. B
22. A The cancer is coded as a current condition as long as the patient is receiving adjunct therapy.
23. A
24. D
25. A
26. C A surgical operation is one or more surgical procedures performed at one time for one patient using a common approach or for a common purpose.
27. D
28. D
29. B

Answer Key for the Mock Examination

ANSWER	EXPLANATION
30. C	The condition should be coded as a poisoning when there is an interaction of an over-the-counter drug and alcohol. Answers A, B, and D are adverse effects of a correctly administered prescription drug.
31. B	
32. A	When a diagnosis is preceded by the phrase "rule out" in the inpatient setting, the condition is coded as though it is confirmed.
33. C	*Staging* is a term used to refer to the progression of cancer. In accessing most types of cancer, a method (staging) is used to determine how far the cancer has progressed. The cancer is described in terms of how large the main tumor is, the degree to which it has invaded surrounding tissue, and the extent to which it has spread to lymph glands or other areas of the body. Staging not only helps to assess outlook but also the most appropriate treatment.
34. A	
35. A	
36. D	Not all of the components of the combination code were POA. "Y" = yes, present on admission. "U"= no information in the record. "W"= clinically undetermined. "N" = no, not present on admission.
37. A	
38. D	Look up in CPT codebook index under foot, neuroma.
39. B	The sizes of the layered wound repairs of the same body area are added together in order to select the correct CPT code.
40. A	The codes in this subsection are used to report evaluations for life or disability insurance baseline information.
41. D	*Dialysis* is the main term to be referenced in the CPT manual index.
42. D	If the immunization is the only service that the patient receives, then two codes are used to report the service. The immunization administration code is first and then the code for the vaccine/toxoid.
43. B	
44. D	
45. D	
46. C	
47. B	
48. A	Calculation: $\frac{(6 \times 100)}{(212 + 28 + 6)} = 2.4\%$
49. C	
50. B	Calculation: $2,655 × 100 divided by $25,000 = 10.6 = 11%
51. A	When a beneficiary refuses to authorize the submission of a bill to Medicare, the Medicare provider is not required to submit a claim to Medicare.
52. A	
53. A	
54. B	Calculation: $(335 \times 151) + (350 \times 214) = 125{,}485$
55. C	Calculation: $31 - 14 + 28 + 2 = 47$ days
56. A	

Answer Key for the Mock Examination

ANSWER	EXPLANATION
57. A	"Decrease medication errors through CPOE systems" and "Report sentinel events to the Joint Commission" are more closely associated with patient safety programs than CDI programs, and answer "Increase patient engagement through patient portals" relates to HITECH goals for physician practices.
58. B	
59. D	
60. B	
61. D	
62. B	
63. B	
64. D	Calculation: Remaining at midnight 8/1 99 Admissions +4 Discharges –7 In and Out Same Day +1 Inpatient Service Days 8/2 97 Fetal Deaths and DOA have no impact on inpatient service days.
65. A	
66. A	
67. A	
68. D	
69. B	
70. B	The CDS professional may act as a "reviewer" and "educator," but the duties described are most representative of his/her role as an "analyst." "Ambassador" is a distractor.
71. A	
72. C	Calculation: $\frac{(111{,}963 \times 100)}{(300 \times 181) + (375 \times 184)} = 90.8\%$
73. A	Multiple births are still considered one delivery for statistical purposes.
74. C	
75. A	Although CDI programs differ in hierarchy, MOST CDS professionals report to the HIM Department, according to the Foundation report.
76. B	
77. D	
78. C	Calculation: $3,027 × 2.0671 = $6,257.11
79. C	
80. A	Calculation: (431 × 100) / 2,879 = 14.97% (458 × 100) / 15,242 = 3% (114 × 100) / 1,426 = 8% (313 × 100) / 6,271 = 5% The highest percentage of error is in consultation reports.
81. B	The highest volume (number) of errors is in lab slips.
82. B	
83. B	
84. D	
85. D	
86. C	
87. D	
88. B	
89. A	

Answer Key for the Mock Examination

ANSWER	EXPLANATION
90. A	Many hospitals use the EDMS as a transition strategy to support their EHR effort.
91. A	
92. D	
93. D	
94. A	
95. A	
96. C	
97. B	Consultation codes can no longer be coded when the physician has taken an active part in the continued care of the patient.
98. D	
99. A	
100. C	It is the responsibility of organizational leaders to participate in the QI process.
101. B	Calculation: (304 × 100) / 845 = 36%
102. B	Calculation: (14 × 100) / 526 = 2.66% or 2.7%
103. D	
104. B	Picture archiving and communication systems provide a means to store and rapidly access digitized file images.
105. C	
106. B	Health information exchange is a term used to refer to a "plan in which health information is shared among providers."
107. B	
108. D	
109. D	
110. A	
111. B	
112. B	
113. C	
114. D	
115. C	
116. C	
117. B	
118. B	
119. B	
120. B	
121. B	
122. D	
123. C	The Joint Commission requires hospitals to prohibit abbreviations that have caused confusion or problems in their handwritten form (e.g., "U" for unit, which can be mistaken for "0" (zero) or "4"). Spelling out "unit" is preferred.
124. D	Calculations: • $36,429 annual labor costs / 12 = $3,035.75 cost per month • $3,035.75 + $89 copier cost = $3,124.75 monthly costs/687 • ROI last month = 4.548 or $4.55 unit cost (not counting mailing) • $4.55 + 0.95 average mailing cost = $5.50 per ROI
125. C	
126. C	
127. D	
128. A	

Answer Key for the Mock Examination

ANSWER	EXPLANATION
129. C	
130. C	
131. A	
132. C	The "Disclosure of Student Immunizations to Schools" provision of the final rule permits a covered entity to disclose proof of immunization to a school (where state law requires it prior to admitting a student) without written authorization of the parent. An agreement must still be obtained and documented, but no signature by the parent is required.
133. A	
134. D	
135. A	employee # 425: 120 + (35 × 0.75) + (16 × 0.5) = 154.25 154.25/5 = 30.85 average work units per day employee # 426: 48 + (89 × 0.75) + (95 × 0.5) = 162.25 162.25/5 = 32.45 average work units per day employee # 427: 80 + (92 × 0.75) + (4 × 0.5) = 151 151/5 = 30.2 average work units per day employee # 428: 65 + (109 × 0.75) + (16 × 0.5) = 154.75 154.75 = 30.95 average work units per day
136. A	
137. C	
138. D	Calculation: (You can only purchase whole shelf units.) 34 × 3 = 102 records per shelf 102 × 6 = 612 records per filing unit 18,000 × 0.20 = 3,600 records for projected expansion 18,000 + 3,600 = 21,600 total records 21,600/612 = 35.29 = 36 total filing units needed
139. D	
140. D	
141. B	
142. A	Calculation: 7.5 hours × 60 minutes per hour = 450 minutes per day 450 × 15% = 67.5 450 – 67.5 = 382.5 382.5/2.5 = 153
143. A	Calculation: 50 × 30 = 1,500 1,500/60 = 25 25/6.5 = 3.8
144. A	Although employees 103 and 104 worked more hours than scheduled, they still did not work overtime using the 8/80 rules.
145. A	Calculation: 76/300 = 0.253 0.253 × 7 hours = 1.77 hours
146. C	Benchmarking involves comparing your department to other departments or organizations known to be excellent in one or more areas. The success of benchmarking involves finding out how the other department functions and then incorporating their ideas into your department.
147. D	
148. C	Generally, allow 60 sq ft per employee. However, as time progresses, less area is being allotted for personal space.
149. C	
150. D	Calculation: (400 × 100) / 450 = 88.9%
151. C	
152. A	
153. D	
154. C	Calculation: (12 × 100) / (15 × 21) = 3.80 = 4%

Answer Key for the Mock Examination

ANSWER	EXPLANATION
155. B	
156. D	
157. B	
158. B	
159. C	
160. A	
161. C	
162. D	
163. C	
164. D	
165. B	
166. C	
167. C	
168. A	
169. C	
170. A	
171. A	
172. C	
173. B	
174. D	
175. D	
176. A	
177. D	
178. A	
179. A	
180. C	

REFERENCES

Abdelhak, M., & Hanken, M. A. (2015). *Health information: Management of a strategic resource* (5th ed.). Philadelphia: Elsevier.

AHIMA (1). Rose, Angela Dinh and Greene, Adam H., "HITECH Frequently Asked Privacy, Security Questions: Part 3," *Journal of AHIMA* 88, no. 3 (March 2014): 42–44.

AHIMA (2). "Best Practices in the Art and Science of Clinical Documentation Improvement," *Journal of AHIMA* 86, no. 7 (July 2015): 46–50.

American Medical Association (AMA) (2015). *Physicians' current procedural terminology: CPT 2016, professional edition.* Chicago: Author.

Bowie, M. J. (2015). *Understanding procedural coding: A worktext.* Clifton Park, NY: Cengage Learning.

Bowie, M. J. (2014). *Understanding ICD-10-CM and ICD-10-PCS coding: A worktext.* Clifton Park, NY: Cengage Learning.

Bowie, M. J., & Green, M. A. (2016). *Essentials of health information management: Principles and practice* (3rd ed.). Clifton Park, NY: Cengage Learning.

cms.gov: http://www.cms.gov/eHealth/ListServ_Stage2_EngagingPatients.html (retrieved 9/27/2015).

Green, M. A. (2016). *3-2-1 code it!* (5th ed.) Clifton Park, NY: Cengage Learning.

Horton, L. (2011). *Calculating and reporting health care statistics* (4th ed.). Chicago: American Health Information Management Association (AHIMA).

Koch, G. (2015). *Basic allied health statistics and analysis* (4th ed.). Clifton Park, NY: Cengage Learning.

LaTour, S., Eichenwald-Maki, S., & Oachs, P. (2013). *Health information management: Concepts, principles and practice* (4th ed.). Chicago: American Health Information Management Association (AHIMA).

McWay, D. C. (2016). *Legal and ethical aspects of health information management* (4th ed.). Clifton Park, NY: Cengage Learning.

McWay, D. C. (2014). *Today's health information management: An integrated approach* (2nd ed.). Clifton Park, NY: Cengage Learning.

medicare.gov (updated: July 16, 2015) https://www.medicare.gov/hospitalcompare/search.html

oig.hhs.gov Office of Inspector General http://www.oig.hhs.gov/about-oig/about-us/index.asp

Sayles, N. B. (2013). *Health information technology: An applied approach* (4th ed.). Chicago: American Health Information Management Association (AHIMA).

RHIA AND RHIT COMPETENCIES BY QUESTION FOR MOCK EXAMINATION												
Question	RHIA Domain Competencies					RHIT Domain Competencies						
	1	2	3	4	5	1	2	3	4	5	6	7
1			X			X						
2					X						X	
3				X							X	
4	X					X						
5	X								X			
6			X									X
7	X					X						
8					X			X				
9				X								X
10				X								X
11				X								X
12				X			X					
13	X						X					
14					X			X				
15		X									X	
16	X					X						
17					X			X				
18					X			X				
19	X						X					
20	X					X						
21	X						X					
22	X						X					
23	X						X					
24	X						X					
25	X						X					
26		X						X				
27	X					X						
28	X						X					
29	X						X					
30	X						X					
31	X						X					
32	X						X					
33	X					X						
34	X						X					
35		X									X	
36	X						X					
37	X						X					
38	X						X					
39	X						X					
40	X						X					

RHIA AND RHIT COMPETENCIES BY QUESTION FOR MOCK EXAMINATION												
Question	RHIA Domain Competencies					RHIT Domain Competencies						
	1	2	3	4	5	1	2	3	4	5	6	7
41	X						X					
42	X						X					
43	X						X					
44	X						X					
45	X						X					
46	X						X					
47			X							X		
48			X							X		
49			X							X		
50					X					X		
51				X								X
52			X							X		
53			X							X		
54		X				X						
55		X				X						
56					X	X						
57	X							X				
58				X						X		
59			X					X				
60			X							X		
61			X						X			
62					X			X				
63			X							X		
64			X				X					
65					X					X		
66		X								X		
67		X								X		
68			X			X						
69			X			X						
70	X							X				
71			X							X		
72		X				X						
73		X				X						
74		X										X
75					X						X	
76	X						X					
77			X						X			
78				X								
79		X									X	

RHIA AND RHIT COMPETENCIES BY QUESTION FOR MOCK EXAMINATION												
Question	RHIA Domain Competencies					RHIT Domain Competencies						
	1	2	3	4	5	1	2	3	4	5	6	7
80					X		X					
81					X		X					
82		X									X	
83		X							X			
84			X								X	
85		X					X					
86		X									X	
87		X									X	
88		X									X	
89		X									X	
90			X						X			
91			X						X			
92			X							X		
93				X								X
94				X								X
95		X					X					
96	X						X					
97	X						X					
98		X								X		
99	X							X				
100					X			X				
101	X							X				
102	X							X				
103	X						X					
104			X						X			
105					X			X				
106		X							X			
107	X						X					
108	X						X					
109	X					X						
110					X			X				
111			X						X			
112	X							X				
113		X							X			
114			X						X			
115		X									X	
116			X							X		
117			X						X			

RHIA AND RHIT COMPETENCIES BY QUESTION FOR MOCK EXAMINATION												
Question	RHIA Domain Competencies					RHIT Domain Competencies						
	1	2	3	4	5	1	2	3	4	5	6	7
118		X						X				
119		X									X	
120		X							X			
121			X						X			
122	X							X				
123	X							X				
124					X	X						
125			X			X						
126			X			X						
127			X			X						
128			X			X						
129			X			X						
130					X				X			
131					X	X						
132		X							X			
133			X						X			
134			X						X			
135					X				X			
136					X	X						
137					X	X						
138					X	X						
139					X					X		
140					X						X	
141					X	X						
142					X	X						
143					X	X						
144					X					X		
145					X	X						
146					X					X		
147					X					X		
148					X					X		
149					X					X		
150					X	X						
						END OF RHIT EXAMINATION						

Continue on for RHIA Mock Examination

RHIA COMPETENCIES BY QUESTION FOR MOCK EXAMINATION					
Question	RHIA Domain Competencies				
	1	2	3	4	5
151		X			
152					X
153					X
154					X
155				X	
156					X
157					X
158			X		
159			X		
160					X
161	X				
162	X				
163				X	
164	X				
165					X
166			X		
167	X				
168	X				
169			X		
170					X
171					X
172					X
173					X
174		X			
175		X			
176			X		
177			X		
178			X		X
179				X	
180	X				

EVALUATION FORM FOR THE BOOK

As we have learned through quality improvement concepts, there is always the opportunity to do something better. Therefore, if you have suggestions for improving the book, please let us know. We invite your input and feedback.

Please rate each of the following aspects of this book on a scale of 1 to 5, where: **5 is excellent, 4 is above average, 3 is average, 2 is below average, and 1 is poor.**

Depth/completeness of coverage	5	4	3	2	1
Organization of material	5	4	3	2	1
Study tips	5	4	3	2	1
Appropriate level of writing	5	4	3	2	1
Cover design and attractiveness	5	4	3	2	1
Overall design and layout of book	5	4	3	2	1
Overall satisfaction with book	5	4	3	2	1

Would you recommend this book to future graduates studying for the RHIA-RHIT examination?

What can we do to make these products better for you to use? ______________________________

____

____

____

____

____

____

Please attach additional comments if you have further suggestions. Thank you!

Attention: Patricia J. Schnering
c/o Cengage Learning
Executive Woods
5 Maxwell Drive
Clifton Park, NY 12065

Email your comments and questions to the author at: *PJSPRG@AOL.COM*